CLARKSTON INDEPENDENCE DISTRICT LIBRARY
6495 Clarkston Road
Clarkston, MI 48346
(248) 625-2212

WITHDRAWN

Library of America, a nonprofit organization,
champions our nation's cultural heritage
by publishing America's greatest writing in
authoritative new editions and providing resources
for readers to explore this rich, living legacy.

RACHEL CARSON

RACHEL CARSON
THE SEA TRILOGY

Under the Sea-Wind
The Sea Around Us
The Edge of the Sea

Sandra Steingraber, *editor*

THE LIBRARY OF AMERICA

RACHEL CARSON: THE SEA TRILOGY
Introduction, volume compilation, notes, and
chronology copyright © 2021 by
Literary Classics of the United States, Inc., New York, N.Y.
All rights reserved.
No part of this book may be reproduced in any manner whatsoever without
the permission of the publisher, except in the case of brief
quotations embodied in critical articles and reviews.

Published in the United States by Library of America.
Visit our website at www.loa.org.

Under the Sea-Wind copyright © 1941 by Rachel L. Carson, renewed 1969
by Roger Christie. Reprinted by arrangement with Dutton, an imprint of
Penguin Publishing Group, a division of Penguin Random House LLC.

The Sea Around Us copyright © 1950, 1951, 1961 by Rachel L. Carson,
renewed 1979 by Roger Christie. Reprinted by arrangement with
Frances Collin, Trustee under-the-will-of Rachel Carson.

The Edge of the Sea copyright © 1955 by Rachel L. Carson,
renewed 1983 by Roger Christie. Illustrations copyright © 1955,
renewed 1983 by Robert W. Hines. All reprinted by arrangement
with Houghton Mifflin Harcourt Publishing Company.

Other writings reprinted by arrangement with Frances
Collin, Trustee under-the-will-of Rachel Carson.

Great care has been taken to locate and acknowledge all
owners of copyrighted material included in this book.
If any such owner has inadvertently been omitted,
acknowledgment will gladly be made in future printings.

This paper exceeds the requirements of
ANSI/NISO Z39.48–1992 (Permanence of Paper).

Distributed to the trade in the United States
by Penguin Random House Inc.
and in Canada by Penguin Random House Canada Ltd.

Library of Congress Control Number: 2021934740
ISBN 978–1–59853–705–5

First Printing
The Library of America—352

Manufactured in the United States of America

3 4633 00362 9746

Contents

Introduction by Sandra Steingraber xi

UNDER THE SEA-WIND 1

BOOK I   EDGE OF THE SEA
  1   Flood Tide 7
  2   Spring Flight 18
  3   Arctic Rendezvous 28
  4   Summer's End 45
  5   Winds Blowing Seaward 53

BOOK II   THE GULL'S WAY
  6   Migrants of the Spring Sea 63
  7   Birth of a Mackerel 67
  8   Hunters of the Plankton 74
  9   The Harbor 80
  10 Seaways 90
  11 Indian Summer of the Sea 99
  12 Seine Haul 109

BOOK III   RIVER AND SEA
  13 Journey to the Sea 119
  14 Winter Haven 130
  15 Return 142
      Glossary 153

THE SEA AROUND US 183
  Preface to the Revised Edition 187

PART I   MOTHER SEA
  The Gray Beginnings 201
  The Pattern of the Surface 214
  The Changing Year 225
  The Sunless Sea 233
  Hidden Lands 249
  The Long Snowfall 264
  The Birth of an Island 271
  The Shape of Ancient Seas 285

PART II   THE RESTLESS SEA
  Wind and Water 297

Wind, Sun, and the Spinning of the Earth 316
The Moving Tides 332

PART III   MAN AND THE SEA ABOUT HIM

The Global Thermostat 349
Wealth from the Salt Seas 367
The Encircling Sea 379
Appendix 393
Suggestions for Further Reading 404

THE EDGE OF THE SEA 408

    Acknowledgments 413
    Preface 415
I.   The Marginal World 421
II. Patterns of Shore Life 429
III. The Rocky Shores 457
IV. The Rim of Sand 537
V. The Coral Coast 599
VI. The Enduring Sea 653
    Appendix: Classification 655

OTHER WRITINGS

Shad Going Way of the Buffalo 679
Undersea 686
Memo to Mrs. Eales on *Under the Sea-Wind* 693

Chronology 703
Note on the Texts 716
Notes 721
Index 727

Introduction

BY SANDRA STEINGRABER

On a blustery morning in October 1945, Rachel Carson, a marine biologist and government science writer, climbed to the summit of Hawk Mountain. She was accompanied by other birdwatchers, including her companion, artist and illustrator Shirley Briggs, who worked with her in the U.S. Fish and Wildlife Service and was known as a very fine amateur ornithologist.[1]

Briggs memorialized the moment in a photograph that offers a more ecstatic presentation of Carson than the prim, resolute figure we have come to know from later publicity photos and media appearances. After the National Book Award. After the meeting with the President's science advisors and the testimony before the Government Operations Subcommittee of the U.S. Senate.

After her findings on the harms of pesticides kicked off a massive campaign by the chemical industry to discredit her.

After the cancer diagnosis.

In the Hawk Mountain photo of 1945, Rachel Carson is both beautiful and at ease. Balanced on a rocky outcrop, black leather jacket open to the wind, she scans the horizon with a pair of leather-strapped binoculars, the whole of Berks County, Pennsylvania, unfurling before her—forest and valley, field and mountain—like a verse from a Pete Seeger song.

An officially designated sanctuary for raptors along the Appalachian flyway, Hawk Mountain had become, by the mid-1930s, *the* spot in Pennsylvania to witness the annual fall migration of hawks and eagles. By the time Briggs and Carson ascended to the north overlook in fall 1945—mere weeks after the dropping of two atomic bombs ended World War II—Carson had already read classified papers documenting harm to wildlife from exposure to DDT and other untested wartime chemicals that were now receiving a hero's welcome in American society. She was already piecing together the first inklings of what would become her final legacy as both scientist and author: public documentation of widespread ecological damage from pesticide-spraying programs that broadcast inherently toxic substances across the landscape, sabotaging, among other things, the ability of predators atop the food chain to reproduce.

Indeed, the declining numbers of juvenile bald eagles migrating along the ridge of Hawk Mountain in the decade following 1945 are cited in her landmark 1962 book, *Silent Spring*, as a critical piece of evidence for the unintended but "ever-widening wave of death" set in motion when persistent poisons are released into the environment.[2]

But her field notes from that particular day on the mountain reveal that she was not up there solely to tabulate the number of raptors flying by:

> And always in these Appalachian highlands there are reminders of those ancient seas that more than once lay over all this land. . . . these whitened limestone rocks on which I am sitting—these, too, were formed under that Paleozoic ocean, of the myriad tiny skeletons of creatures that drifted in its waters. Now I lie back with half closed eyes and try to realize that I am at the bottom of another ocean—an ocean of air on which the hawks are sailing.[3]

Rachel Carson sat astride a mountaintop and imagined herself at the bottom of the sea that made the mountain.

Rachel Carson was born on May 27, 1907, and grew up on the outskirts of Springdale, sixteen miles from Pittsburgh. Her lifelong devotion to the sea began as a small child when she discovered, on a rocky hillside near her family's farm, a fossilized fish,[4] a sea creature in Allegheny County, Pennsylvania. As she would later report in an author questionnaire to her publisher's marketing department (See "Memo to Mrs. Eales" on page 693–700 in this volume):

> As long as I can remember [the sea] has fascinated me. Even as a child—long before I had ever seen it—I used to imagine what it would look like, and what the surf sounded like. Since I grew up in an inland community, where we hadn't even a migrating seagull, I had to wait a long time to have

my curiosity satisfied. As a matter of fact, it wasn't until I had graduated from college and gone on to the famous Marine Biological Laboratory at Woods Hole, Massachusetts, that I saw the ocean.

By the time she turned her attention, in the late 1950s, to the problem of chemical pollution, which became the topic of *Silent Spring*, Carson was already the celebrity author of three books about ocean ecology. It is this trilogy—*Under the Sea-Wind* (1941), *The Sea Around Us* (1951), and *The Edge of the Sea* (1955)—that is collected here. Altogether these three titles reveal the complex, hitherto unseen majesties of a world in which the human race scarcely appears. If readers could visualize the watery world below the mirrored surface of the sea—teeming with communities of interacting creatures, each possessed with emotions and personality—if we could travel back through geological time and witness the birth of an oceanic island, if we understood the physics of waves, if we could look down at the surf through the eyes of a storm-tossed shorebird, or up at the moon from the stony bottom of a tide pool, we might, the author believed, experience wonder and humility. And wonder and humility, said Carson, "do not exist side by side with a lust for destruction."[5]

What emerges, then, are not just popular accounts of marine biology or guides for beachcombers (although you can use these books for those purposes, too), but what amounts to an ocean-centric planetary ethic and philosophy of life.[6]

And yet, as intentional as the writing is, Carson's sea trilogy began almost by happenstance. In 1936, the chief of the Division of Scientific Inquiry in what was at that time called the Bureau of Fisheries asked Carson to write an introduction to a forthcoming publication—and then deemed the eleven pages she submitted too literary for a government brochure. He was, nevertheless, sufficiently captivated by the rhythms and imagery of Carson's draft to urge her to submit the original as an essay for *The Atlantic*. Desperate for additional income, she finally did.[7] And its publication there in 1937 caught the attention of an editor at Simon & Schuster who solicited from her a book proposal and so launched her career as a literary writer.[8] "I had never seriously considered writing a book," she would say later (in her "Memo to Mrs. Eales"). "But naturally that letter put ideas in my head." Thus, four years after the publication of her much revised and carefully tooled essay "Undersea" came the first book in the trilogy, *Under the Sea-Wind*. As Carson later said, "everything else followed."[9]

The seductive power of "Undersea" surely arises from Carson's descriptive voice, which beseeches the reader to suspend terrestrial ways of understanding and simply, in an act of negative capability, enter, behold, and wonder at the alien world of the deep sea:

> To sense this world of waters known to the creatures of the sea we must shed our human perceptions of length and breadth and time and place, and enter vicariously into a universe of all-pervading water. For to the sea's children nothing is so important as the fluidity of their world. It is water that they breathe; water that brings them food; water through which they see, by filtered sunlight from which first the red rays, then the greens, and finally the purples have been strained; water through which they sense vibrations equivalent to sound.

The dreamlike, cinematic quality of "Undersea" is extended in *Under the Sea-Wind*. To it is added Carson's specific expertise as a fisheries biologist and naturalist. This knowledge base allows her to structure the book as a series of narratives with shifting points of view, each told from the perspective of a different marine or ocean-dependent animal. In a daring choice, Carson gives her animal narrators individual names. They have agency—consciousness, even. And memories. ("Before the moon had come to the full, Rynchops had remembered the island.") They investigate, assess situations, and make decisions—sometimes catastrophic ones. They stalk and are stalked. ("Down along the cliff raced the two fishes—the mackerel a slim, tapered creature flashing iridescent in the sun; the eel as long as a man is tall and thick and drab as a piece of fire hose.") They are harassed beyond endurance. They are disquieted, become confused, panic. They narrowly escape and need to calm down. (". . . so today he only listened, perhaps to reassure himself that the weasels had not raided the lemming colony since his last visit.")

And yet, the thirteen animal characters that sequentially reveal to us the mysteries of ocean ecosystems in *Under the Sea-Wind* are not sentimentally personified. Their narratives are not fables. Instead, the book compels continued acts of de-personification on the part of readers. For example, as revealed in her author questionnaire ("Memo to Mrs. Eales"), Carson chose an eel and a sanderling to serve as two of *Under the Sea-Wind*'s narrators—both are long-range migrants—so that she could use their journeys to showcase a multitude of marine habitats, from arctic ice to the dark abyss. The long odysseys of these protagonists are often narrated in the passive voice (in contrast to the active voice of the many chase scenes) as they are seized by elemental forces beyond themselves and joined, each to each, in the fluidic circulation of life. The recurring theme of *Under the Sea-Wind* is that the power of the ocean itself directs the movements of migratory species. These are not Homeric-style heroic voyages. Again, from "Memo to Mrs. Eales":

> I very soon realized that the central character of the book was the ocean itself. The smell of the sea's edge, the feeling of vast movements of water, the sound of waves, crept into every page, and over all was the ocean as the force dominating all its creatures.

The task required of us as readers of *Under the Sea-Wind* is to begin to unlearn our necessarily anthropomorphic perspectives:

> I decided that the author as a person or a human observer should never enter the story, but that it should be told as a simple narrative of the lives of certain animals of the sea. As far as possible, I wanted my readers to feel that they were, for a time, actually living the lives of sea creatures. To bring this about I had first, of course, to think myself into the role of an animal that lives in the sea. I had to forget a lot of human conception.

Given the attention attracted by her essay "Undersea," Rachel Carson had every reason to hope that the publication of *Under the Sea-Wind* would receive notice. But that's not what happened. Within weeks of her book launch, the U.S. naval base in Pearl Harbor was attacked and the United States suddenly at war. *Under the Sea-Wind* became a commercial failure, selling just two-thousand copies before going out of print.

In July 1951, a full decade and many, many U.S. Fish and Wildlife reports later, Carson released a second sea book in a different historical moment—and enjoyed the opposite kind of publishing experience. *The Sea Around Us* won the National Book Award for nonfiction. Almost half of the book was serialized in *The New Yorker*. The title stayed on *The New York Times* best-seller list for eighty-six weeks, and the reviews poured in, full of praise and admiration. Riding on the coattails of this success, *Under the Sea-Wind* was reissued—and it too, the second time around, swiftly became a best seller. By 1952, royalties from both books provided her enough financial independence that Carson could resign from government service and write full-time. *The Sea Around Us* was a life-changing book for its author.

As in *Under the Sea-Wind*, the ocean in *The Sea Around Us* serves not as the setting but as the main character of the story. The sea is the driver of the plot, the inhuman, magisterial Overmind. Vast. Fecund. Ruthless. Indifferent. Indomitable. Its plungings and risings provide rhythm and dictate the order of events.

Indeed, the ocean emerges as an even more formidable and awesome force in the second book of the trilogy as the narrative is directed not by the life histories of its individual inhabitants but by the recent findings of oceanography itself. In *The Sea Around Us*, presentation of science, rather than empathic identification with other species, allows readers to extend their senses and plunge into the alien depths of the open ocean.

In contrast to *Under the Sea-Wind*, which travels across vast distances of geological space by tracing migratory patterns of individual birds and fishes and other creatures but is confined by their life spans, the scenes in *The Sea Around Us* transport us across deep time, as only science can do. Beginning with the story of the ocean's creation, Carson explicates the physical, geological, and chemical processes that allowed the ocean to become the creator and sustainer of all life on the planet, including human life, and to serve as the final repository of its constituent parts. Here is the ocean as Earth's cradle and grave. The chapter "The Birth of an Island," begins this way:

> Millions of years ago, a volcano built a mountain on the floor of the Atlantic. In eruption after eruption, it pushed up a great pile of volcanic rock, until it had accumulated a mass a hundred miles across at its base, reaching upward toward the surface of the sea. Finally its cone emerged as an island with an area of about 200 square miles. Thousands of years passed, and thousands and thousands. Eventually the waves of the Atlantic cut down the cone and reduced it to a shoal—all of it, that is, but a small fragment which remained above water. This fragment we know as Bermuda.

The Sea Around Us appeared at a time when public interest in the watery realm below the ocean's waves was high—piqued by developments in radar, echolocation, and submarine operations during World War II—but before observational equipment, fiber optics, and low-light cameras brought moving images of this world into our living rooms. The manned bathyscaphe christened *Trieste* would not reach the bottom of the Mariana Trench in the western Pacific Ocean until 1960. The research submersible named *Alvin*—operated by the Woods Hole Oceanographic Institution and, as of 2021, still in service—did not begin its own operations until 1964.[10]

Hence, during the postwar, science-ascendant 1950s, *The Sea Around Us* filled a curiosity void. Combining evocative metaphor and vivid, lyrical imagery with the latest oceanographic findings, Carson created a language for the book that functioned like an underwater documentary film at a time when there were none.

As she drafted the various chapters of her second book, Carson was working in a moving stream of oceanographic data. Indeed, even before the book was published, she started a file of new findings in marine science for inclusion in a possible second edition. A revised and updated version of *The Sea Around Us* did appear ten years later, in 1961, for which she also wrote a new preface. It is this second edition that is included in this collection.

The Sea Around Us, in both its editions, alternates timeless truths about the sea—which lend certain passages an almost biblical tone—with emerging findings from areas of oceanic science not yet settled, even while acknowledging that this new evidence is subject to further revision. Full of the "sense of wonder" she learned at her mother's side in the woods of Pennsylvania, and the lyrical gifts that broke through in her early essay "Undersea," the book is also a tour de force of hard-nosed, fact-based reporting and data synthesis.

Throughout the 1930s and '40s, especially as family members suffered health problems and increasingly relied on her for financial support, Carson had picked up extra income by filing freelance stories in daily and weekly news outlets on breaking developments in the fishing industry or the latest findings of federal fisheries research, to which she had access. (See, for example, "Shad Going Way of the Buffalo" on pages 679–685 of this volume.) These news and feature stories gave her the chance to make the case for conservation but also showcased her facility with placing new findings in the context of the old, identifying emerging trends in the data, offering commentary, and upending previously held suppositions and conclusions when newer data provided a corrective.

This reportorial training and discipline is evident also in the preface to the second edition of *The Sea Around Us* when Carson corrects a previously held supposition of her own. She had earlier claimed (in *Under the Sea-Wind*) that the ocean "is too big and vast and its forces are too mighty to be much affected by human activity." Now, living in the Atomic Age, she needed to retract that statement in light of new information about leaking barrels of radioactive waste in deep-sea basins— plankton siphoning radioactivity up the marine food chain— and patterns of fallout from aboveground nuclear testing.[11]

Carson had once believed the ocean was impervious to desecration. Deep-sea dumping of nuclear waste by the Atomic Energy Commission stripped her of this belief. From the preface of *The Sea Around Us*, second edition:

> Although man's record as a steward of the natural resources of the earth has been a discouraging one, there has long been a certain comfort in the belief that the sea, at least, was inviolate, beyond man's ability to change and to despoil.

But this belief, unfortunately, has proved to be naïve. In unlocking the secrets of the atom, modern man has found himself confronted with a frightening problem—what to do with the most dangerous materials that have ever existed in all the earth's history, the by-products of atomic fission. The stark problem that faces him is whether he can dispose of these lethal substances without rendering the earth uninhabitable.

No account of the sea today is complete unless it takes note of this ominous problem. . . . The whole practice, despite protestations of safety by the regulatory agency, rests on the most insecure basis of fact.

The third book of the triptych, *The Edge of the Sea*, explores the liminal zone between the tide lines where ocean meets land, "the place of our dim, ancestral beginnings." Of the three books, it is the most intimate and requires no imaginative time travel or descents into the abyss.

Here are tide pools, sandy beaches, and rocky shores. These landscapes exist on a human scale and, when the tide goes out far enough, can be gazed upon with human eyes—like those of any casual beachcomber. If *The Sea Around Us* provides a macrocosmic view of a complex, generative planetary system, *The Edge of the Sea* is about the microcosm found within, say, the body of a single loggerhead sponge tucked among the corals of a Florida reef. (Living sponges provide housing for amphipods, worms, isopods, and, most notably, snapping shrimp. "Wandering through its dark halls, they scrape food from the walls of the sponge . . . filling the water world with a continuous sizzling, crackling sound.")

Book three, then, represents a return to the biological world of book one, but with a key difference: *The Edge of the Sea* is an exploration of marine communities—and the forces of mutuality and interdependence that bind their inhabitants together—rather than portraits of individual organisms as in *Under the Sea-Wind*. The wonderment of book three is in illuminating the powers of adaptability ("compromise, conflict, and eternal change") and cooperation among the organisms who reside in places that are continuously shifting between landscape and seascape. Its ethical message is to go forth into the natural world—even on an ordinary beach—in a spirit of discovery, with an open, inquiring mind, and your attention will be sustaining. In leading these explorations, *The Edge of the Sea* follows a three-part structure as it heads south along the U.S. Atlantic coast with Carson serving as interpretive guide. First, we investigate a shoreline north of Cape Cod. Here the controlling, shaping element of the living shoreline is the power of the tides. Further south, we walk with her along a sandy beach where the governing force is the action of waves. Finally, we reach the Florida Keys where coasts of coral reefs and mangrove forests are created and nourished by ocean currents.[12]

Perhaps the most breathtaking passages in this third book are those narrated in the first person. These carefully wrought set pieces show Carson as a working naturalist—observing and identifying the living organisms she discovers, thinking and posing questions about them, forming relationships with them, and, in some cases, extending acts of kindness toward them. In these passages, the author is finally speaking directly to us, and she shares not only the secrets of her discoveries but her feelings of thrall and reverence to be alive and in the presence of such beauty. And so we encounter Rachel Carson in conversation for the first time, addressing us in her own voice and encouraging us to see new worlds in what might otherwise just be overlooked flotsam or wave-battered rocks.

These autobiographical passages are particularly reverent and sensual. In the opening chapter, titled "The Marginal World," Carson takes us with her into an "enchanted place on the threshold of the sea," a pool-filled cave that is accessible only at the lowest of the year's low tides:

> And so I knelt on the wet carpet of sea moss and looked back into the dark cavern that held the pool in a shallow basin. The floor of the cave was only a few inches below the roof, and a mirror had been created in which all that grew on the ceiling was reflected in the still water below.
>
> Under water that was clear as glass the pool was carpeted with green sponge. Gray patches of sea squirts glistened on the ceiling and colonies of soft coral were a pale apricot color. In the moment when I looked into the cave a little elfin starfish hung down, suspended by the merest

thread.... The beauty of the reflected images and of the limpid pool itself was the poignant beauty of things that are ephemeral, existing only until the sea should return to fill the little cave.

Whenever I go down into this magical zone of the low water of the spring's tides, I look for the most delicately beautiful of all the shore's inhabitants—flowers that are not plant but animal, blooming out on the threshold of the deeper sea.... I knew that they were merely waiting, in that moment of the tide's ebbing, for the return of the sea. Then in the rush of water, in the surge of the surf and the pressure of the incoming tide, the delicate flower heads would stir with life. They would sway on their slender stalks, and their long tentacles would sweep the returning water, finding in it all that they needed for life.

And so in that enchanted place on the threshold of the sea the realities that possessed my mind were far from those of the land world I had left an hour before.

So profound and systemic is the ongoing global climate crisis that it is hardly possible to overstate the level of peril now confronting the world's oceans or to exaggerate the magnitude of harms, present and to come, afflicting or soon to afflict every creature living within them—from diatoms to angler fish, coral reefs to whales—and those who depend upon them.[13] Which includes, of course, all of us. Photosynthesizing plankton drifting on the sunlit surface of the sea provide more than half the oxygen in Earth's atmosphere, which is to say, more than half the oxygen in the air that we breathe. These plankton stocks are now in decline. Oxygen levels in the surface waters of the open ocean are also falling. (Warm water holds less oxygen than cold water.)

Forty percent of Americans live in counties that touch the sea. Communities in these counties, along with the magical shoreline habitats described by Carson in *The Edge of the Sea*, are now endangered by increasingly violent coastal storms. (Warm water evaporates more rapidly than cold water.) And, if they have not been dashed apart or flooded out already, they are also menaced by sea level rise, which is caused primarily by increased rates of ice loss from the Greenland and Antarctic ice sheets and secondarily by thermal expansion. (Warm water takes up more room than cold water.)

Also, because the sea gathers carbon dioxide from the atmosphere and transforms it into carbonic acid, the ocean's acidity rises in tandem with atmospheric carbon emissions from fossil fuel operations. Accordingly, seawater is now 20–30 percent more acidic than it was at the beginning of the twentieth century, with acidification now affecting 95 percent of the ocean's surface area. This drop in pH matters because acidity pulls calcium carbonate into solution. As a result, shelled animals at the base of the marine food chain—barnacles, oysters, mussels, crabs, corals—are currently experiencing difficulty secreting and maintaining their calcified exoskeletons. Rising ocean acidity is also, according to a recent study, corroding the teeth and skin of sharks. Plainly put: our dependency on burning oil, coal, and gas has, within the span of a human life, altered the chemistry of the world's oceans in ways that are dissolving their inhabitants.[14]

It would be wrong to fault Carson, so masterful at following where science led, for failing to foresee and predict these outcomes. In her three books that serve as love letters to the sea, she neither denies nor turns away from the evidence for an imminent, oceanwide ecological unraveling caused by heat-trapping emissions from fossil fuel combustion. Rather, that evidence was simply was not yet available to her. Hawaii's Mauna Loa Observatory, with the longest record of direct measurements of carbon dioxide in the atmosphere, only started collecting data in 1958. The first subtle evidence for rising sea surface temperatures came in 1970. (It's less subtle now: the rate of ocean warming and heat uptake has doubled since 1993.) The dataset documenting loss of oxygen in the world's oceans also began in 1970. The phenomenon of marine heat waves—triggered by high-pressure systems that stall over the open ocean and act like a magnifying glass to the sun's rays—was first recognized in 2011 when superheated water devastated a kelp forest off the coast of western Australia and collapsed the fishing industry. (A few years later, another marine heat wave, nicknamed The Blob, killed phytoplankton stocks across a swath of the Northwest Pacific, and in its wake, chinook salmon disappeared, and a million seabirds died in the Gulf of Alaska.)

We now understand, in ways that Carson could not have, that coral is exceedingly vulnerable to both ocean acidification and marine heat waves. Acid water brings frailty to the reefs, thinning and fracturing their architecture. Absent rapid decarbonization of our energy systems, current models predict that ocean pH could, by midcentury, fall low enough to prevent corals from excreting a calcium skeleton at all. Meanwhile, superheated currents of water cause corals to expel the symbiotic algae that live inside their polyps and provide them food (and also brilliant colors). These so-called bleaching events further weaken the coral and cause it to wither and starve. Climate change is thus a double crisis for coral, which, although it fills only 0.1 percent of the planet's ocean floor, offers food and shelter for fully one-third of all marine life in the ocean—including four-thousand species of fish.[15]

And yet, even without a working understanding of the myriad ways in which an accumulation of heat-trapping gases can damage marine ecosystems, Carson comes very close to a theory of climate change in *The Sea Around Us*. From the chapter titled "The Global Thermostat," which documents how ocean currents circulate energy and water and so regulate Earth's climate:

> But for the present, the evidence that the top of the world is growing warmer is to be found on every hand. The recession of the northern glaciers is going on at such a rate that many smaller ones have already disappeared. If the present rate of melting continues others will soon follow.

One utilitarian way of approaching Carson's sea trilogy in the present day is with the idea that it depicts a disappearing natural baseline: this is how the all-creating ocean functioned, how its creatures lived and interacted, before the catastrophe of climate change began to tear it all apart in an ongoing act of de-creation. And the writing does do that. Just as importantly, in a world full of indifference and avoidance and disinformation and denial, Carson's sea books inspire curiosity and care about what we are in the process of losing. She did not live to see industrial overfishing, or news of the potential collapse of the Gulf Stream, or massive floating garbage patches, or icebergs the size of states breaking off Antarctica, or microplastics replacing plankton in the water column, or plans for deep-sea mining—but her words fortify us for battles she had only begun to imagine.[16] After the publication of *The Edge of the Sea* in 1955, when she discovered what chlorinated pesticides were doing to the eggshells of eagles, she found the courage to confront the chemical industry—sparking the modern environmental movement along the way. By her example and her words, she would urge us now to take notice of what the fossil fuel industry is doing to the corals—and to all the fish in the sea and to the sea itself. Her writing about shorebirds and tide pools emboldens us to confront hard truths about our continued existence on the planet.

On April 14, 1964, following intense radiation treatments for metastatic breast cancer, Rachel Carson died at the Cleveland Clinic. She was fifty-six.

The following year, Shirley Briggs founded the Rachel Carson Council, a national environmental organization envisioned by Carson to carry on her work and promote "an ecological ethic that combines scientific concern for the environment and human health and reverence for all forms of life."[17] Briggs, who became the Council's first director, also went on to publish a personal reflection on Carson's legacy in a Quaker magazine, *Friends Journal*, that issues two still-timely critiques.

First, she excoriates those seeking to address the "urgent environmental matters" (which Carson had brought to the world's attention) by offering narrow technological solutions while yet remaining "reluctant to plunge into the natural world to see for themselves—into storm and swamp as well as sunlit beach." Making clear that she and Rachel had no such hesitation, Briggs recounts an exploration of the Everglades and a dive into the coral reefs near Miami Beach that the two of them had undertaken together, years before. Dressed in men's work clothes and lugging cameras and other field gear onto a city bus, they had attracted the attention of fellow passengers. After prolonged staring, one man finally commented:

"You girls look as though you're off to discover a new world." Briggs writes:

> We were indeed. The worlds I explored with her will always seem richer and more vivid than others, however I may hope that the keenness of perception found with such a companion persists in new scenes. Her ability to transmute these experiences with the natural world into prose that imparts not just the objective facts of the sea, or shore, or forest, but their flavor and vitality as well, seems sometimes to have confused critics trying to define the impact of her books.[18]

Next, Briggs takes aim at the other kind of nature writer—the kind not in possession of science or objective facts but who head into the surf and the tide pools with an inward focus, making "careful notes of their own feelings, not the reality that brought them there." These authors, too, says Briggs, are lesser lights than Carson, who possessed both music and precision. The words of these emotive authors, lacking the power to transform readers to action, are pleasant but forgettable.

Finally, Briggs identifies what she believes to have been Carson's true aim as a writer. In her sentences, Rachel Carson strove, says Briggs,

> to recreate the circumstances that had led her to new insights so that the reader would experience much the same sequence and final seizing upon meaning that she had known. The shock of recognition and the emotions that accompany such understanding are then the reader's own.[19]

On this point, I think Briggs is exactly right, and there may be no more apt introduction to this collection. Reader, may you be shocked by the words that follow. And moved to understanding. And to action.

---

1. For more on this field trip, see Linda Lear, *Rachel Carson: Witness for Nature* (Henry Holt, 1997), 126–27. For more on the extended relationship of Briggs and Carson, see Robert K. Musil, *Rachel Carson and Her Sisters* (Rutgers University Press, 2015), 101–3.

2. Carson also belonged to the Hawk Mountain Sanctuary Association. Rachel Carson, *Silent Spring & Other Writings on the Environment* (Library of America, 2018), 106–7, 318.

3. Rachel Carson, "Road of the Hawks," in Linda Lear, ed., *Lost Woods: The Discovered Writings of Rachel Carson* (Beacon Press, 1998), 30–32.

4. Lear, *Rachel Carson: Witness for Nature*, 44.

5. Rachel Carson, "Speech Accepting the John Burroughs Medal, April 1952," in Linda Lear, ed., *Lost Woods*, 94.

6. See, for example, Gary Kroll, "Rachel Carson's *The Sea Around Us*, Ocean-Centrism, and a Nascent Ocean Ethic," and Kathleen Dean Moore, "The Truth of the Barnacles: Rachel Carson and the Moral Significance of Wonder," in L. H. Sideris and K. D. Moore, eds., *Rachel Carson: Legacy and Challenge* (State University of New York Press, 2008), 118–33, 267–80.

7. Carson served as the sole breadwinner for several extended family members. After the death of her sister in 1937, Carson also took on financial responsibility for the care of her two nieces.

8. Lear, ed., *Rachel Carson: Witness for Nature*, 81–91.

9. Lear, *Lost Woods*, 3.

10. William Beebe, U.S. naturalist and marine biologist, made his first deep-sea dive in the bathysphere—a cylindrical submersible research vessel that was unpowered and lowered by cable into the ocean—in summer 1930 and reached a depth of 803 feet. Carson corresponded with Beebe about his undersea observations while drafting *The Sea Around Us*. See Kroll, "Rachel Carson's *The Sea Around Us*," 118–33.

11. From 1946 to 1958, the United States detonated twenty-three nuclear bombs at the Marshall Islands' Bikini Atoll—some in the air, some in the ocean. For a history of this project and the displacement of the atoll inhabitants, see Jonathan M. Weisgall, *Operation Crossroads: The Atomic Tests at Bikini Atoll* (Naval Institute Press, 1994).

12. For more on the literary structure of *The Edge of the Sea* and Carson's concerns about it, see Paul Brooks, *The House of Life: Rachel Carson at Work* (Houghton Mifflin, 1989), 159.

13. Benjamin S. Halpern et al., 2019, "Recent Pace of Change in Human Impact on the World's Ocean's," *Scientific Reports* 9 (11,609).

14. Philip J. Landrigan et al., 2020, Human Health and Ocean Pollution," *Annals of Global Health* 86(1): 151; Intergovernmental Panel on Climate Change, *Special Report on the Ocean and Cryosphere in a Changing Climate*. Geneva, Switzerland (IPCC, 2019); Giuliana Viglione, 2021. "How Heat Waves Ravage the Seas," *Nature* 593: 26–28; Nina Bednarsek et al., 2020, "Exoskeleton Dissolution with Mechanoreceptor Damage in Larval Dungeness Crab Related to Severity of Present-Day Ocean Acidification Vertical Gradients." *Science of the*

Total Environment 716: 136,610; Jacqueline Dziergwa et al., 2019, "Acid-Base Adjustments and First Evidence of Denticle Corrosion Caused by Ocean Acidification Conditions in a Demersal Shark Species," *Scientific Reports* 9(1).

15. Richard Stone, 2007, "A World Without Corals?" *Science* 316: 678–81.

16. Marine biologist Ayana Elizabeth Johnson, co-creator of the policy initiative The Blue New Deal, makes the case for including the ocean in climate policy, noting that the world's oceans are not just casualties of climate change but also allies, offering many climate solutions, such as the potential for harnessing power from both wave energy and offshore wind, which blows more steadily than onshore wind and could provide four times the present capacity of our electrical grid. Ayana Elizabeth Johnson, "To Save the Climate, Look to the Oceans," *Scientific American*, June 8, 2020. Eight million metric tons of plastic enter the ocean each year, where it is broken into microscopic bits by the action of waves and sun exposure but does not disappear. Evidence shows that consumption of microplastics by zooplankton is now contributing to oxygen loss in the global ocean. See Karin Kvale et al., 2021, "Zooplankton Grazing of Microplastic Can Accelerate Global Loss of Ocean Oxygen," *Nature Communications* 12 (2358). For more on the ecological fragility of the deep sea and current threats posed by deep-sea mining operations, see Elizabeth Kolbert, "The Deep Sea Is Filled with Treasure, but It Comes at a Price," *The New Yorker*, June 14, 2021.

17. The Rachel Carson Council was originally incorporated as the Rachel Carson Living Trust for the Environment. Its current president and CEO is Robert K. Musil, author of *Rachel Carson and Her Sisters*, 2015.

18. Shirley A. Briggs, "A Decade After *Silent Spring*," *Friends Journal*, March 1, 1972.

19. Ibid.

UNDER THE SEA-WIND

A NATURALIST'S PICTURE OF OCEAN LIFE

While the sun and the rain live, these shall be;
Till a last wind's breath upon all these blowing
Roll the sea.

SWINBURNE

CONTENTS

BOOK I EDGE OF THE SEA

1	*Flood Tide*	7
2	*Spring Flight*	18
3	*Arctic Rendezvous*	28
4	*Summer's End*	45
5	*Winds Blowing Seaward*	53

BOOK II THE GULL'S WAY

6	*Migrants of the Spring Sea*	63
7	*Birth of a Mackerel*	67
8	*Hunters of the Plankton*	74
9	*The Harbor*	80
10	*Seaways*	90
11	*Indian Summer of the Sea*	99
12	*Seine Haul*	109

BOOK III RIVER AND SEA

13	*Journey to the Sea*	119
14	*Winter Haven*	130
15	*Return*	142
	Glossary	153

To my mother

BOOK I
EDGE OF THE SEA

I
Flood Tide

THE ISLAND LAY in shadows only a little deeper than those that were swiftly stealing across the sound from the east. On its western shore the wet sand of the narrow beach caught the same reflection of palely gleaming sky that laid a bright path across the water from island beach to horizon. Both water and sand were the color of steel overlaid with the sheen of silver, so that it was hard to say where water ended and land began.

Although it was a small island, so small that a gull might have flown across it with a score of wing beats, night had already come to its northern and eastern end. Here the marsh grasses waded boldly out into dark water, and shadows lay thick among the low-growing cedars and yaupons.

With the dusk a strange bird came to the island from its nesting grounds on the outer banks. Its wings were pure black, and from tip to tip their spread was more than the length of a man's arm. It flew steadily and without haste across the sound, its progress as measured and as meaningful as that of the shadows which little by little were dulling the bright water path. The bird was called Rynchops, the black skimmer.

As he neared the shore of the island the skimmer drifted closer to the water, bringing his dark form into strong silhouette against the gray sheet, like the shadow of a great bird that passed unseen above. Yet so quietly did he approach that the sound of his wings, if sound there were, was lost in the whisper song of the water turning over the shells on the wet sand.

At the last spring tide, when the thin shell of the new moon brought the water lapping among the sea oats that fringed the dunes of the banks, Rynchops and his kin had arrived on the outer barrier strip of sand between sound and sea. They had journeyed northward from the coast of Yucatan where they had wintered. Under the warm June sun they would lay their eggs and hatch their buff-colored chicks on the sandy islands of the sound and on the outer beaches. But at first they were weary after the long flight and they rested by day on sand bars when the tide was out or roamed over the sound and its bordering marshes by night.

Before the moon had come to the full, Rynchops had remembered the island. It lay across a quiet sound from which the banks shouldered away the South Atlantic rollers. To the north the island was separated from the mainland by a deep gutter where the ebbing tides raced strongly. On the south side the beach sloped gently, so that at slack water the fishermen could wade out half a mile before the water came above their armpits as they raked scallops or hauled their long seines. In these shallows young fishes swarmed, feeding on the small game of the waters, and shrimp swam with backward flipping of their tails. The rich life of the shallows brought the skimmers nightly from their nesting grounds on the banks, to take their food from the water as they moved with winnowing flight above it.

About sunset the tide had been out. Now it was rising, covering the afternoon resting places of the skimmers, moving through the inlet, and flowing up into the marshes. Through most of the night the skimmers would feed, gliding on slender wings above the water in search of the small fishes that had moved in with the tide to the shelter of grassy shallows. Because they fed on the rising tide, the skimmers were called flood gulls.

On the south beach of the island, where water no deeper than a man's hand ran over gently ribbed bottom, Rynchops began to wheel and quarter over the shallows. He flew with a curious, lilting motion, lifting his wings high after the downstroke. His head was bent sharply so that the long lower bill, shaped like a scissor blade, might cut the water.

The blade or cutwater plowed a miniature furrow over the placid sheet of the sound, setting up wavelets of its own and sending vibrations thudding down through the water to rebound from the sandy bottom. The wave messages were received by the blennies and killifish that were roving the shallows on the alert for food. In the fish world many things are told by sound waves. Sometimes the vibrations tell of food animals like small shrimps or oar-footed crustaceans moving in swarms overhead. And so at the passing of the skimmer the small fishes came nosing at the surface, curious and hungry. Rynchops, wheeling about, returned along the way he had come and snapped up three of the fishes by the rapid opening and closing of his short upper bill.

Ah-h-h-h, called the black skimmer. *Ha-a-a-a! Ha-a-a-a! Ha-a-a-a!* His voice was harsh and barking. It carried far across the water, and from the marshes there came back, like echoes, the answering cries of other skimmers.

While the water was reclaiming inch after inch of sandy shore, Rynchops moved back and forth over the south beach of the island, luring the fishes to rise along his path and seizing them on his return. After he had taken enough minnows to appease his hunger he wheeled up from the water with half a dozen flapping wing beats and circled the island. As he soared above the marshy eastern end schools of killifish moved beneath him through the forests of sea hay, but they were safe from the skimmer, whose wingspread was too great to allow him to fly among the clumps of grass.

Rynchops swerved out around the dock that had been built by the fisherman who lived on the island, crossed the gutter, and swept far over the salt marshes, taking joy in flight and soaring motion. There he joined a flock of other skimmers and together they moved over the marshes in long lines and columns, sometimes appearing as dark shadows on the night sky; sometimes as spectral birds when, wheeling swallowlike in air, they showed white breasts and gleaming underparts. As they flew they raised their voices in the weird night chorus of the skimmers, a strange medley of notes high-pitched and low, now soft as the cooing of a mourning dove, and again harsh as the cawing of a crow; the whole chorus rising and falling, swelling and throbbing, dying away in the still air like the far-off baying of a pack of hounds.

The flood gulls circled the island and crossed and recrossed the flats to the southward. All through the hours of the rising tide, they would hunt in flocks over the quiet waters of the sound. The skimmers loved nights of darkness and tonight thick clouds lay between the water and the moon's light.

On the beach the water was moving with soft tinkling sounds among the windrows of jingle shells and young scallop shells. It ran swiftly under heaps of sea lettuce to rouse sand fleas that had taken refuge there when the tide ebbed that afternoon. The beach hoppers floated out on the backwash of each wavelet and moved in the returning water, swimming on their backs, legs uppermost. In the water they were comparatively safe from their enemies the ghost crabs, who roamed the night beaches on swift and silent feet.

In the waters bordering the island many creatures besides the skimmers were abroad that night, foraging in the shallows. As the darkness grew and the incoming tide lapped higher and higher among the marsh grasses, two diamondback terrapins slipped into the water to join the moving forms of others of their kind. These were females, who had just finished laying their eggs above the high-tide line. They had dug nests in the soft sand, working with hind feet until they scooped out jug-shaped holes not quite so deep as their own bodies were long. Then they had deposited their eggs, one five, the other eight. These they had carefully covered with sand, crawling back and forth to conceal the location of the nest. There were other nests in the sand, but none more than two weeks old, for May is the beginning of the nesting season among the diamondbacks.

As Rynchops followed the killifish in toward the shelter of the marsh he saw the terrapins swimming in the shallow water where the tide was moving swiftly. The terrapins nibbled at the marsh grasses and picked off small coiled snails that had crept up the flat blades. Sometimes they swam down to take crabs off the bottom. One of the two terrapins passed between two slender uprights like stakes thrust into the sand. They were the legs of the solitary great blue heron who flew every night from his rookery three miles away to fish from the island.

The heron stood motionless, his neck curved back on his shoulders, his bill poised to spear fish as they darted past his legs. As the terrapin moved out into deeper water she startled a young mullet and sent it racing toward the beach in confusion and panic. The sharp-eyed heron saw the movement and with a quick dart seized the fish crosswise in his bill. He tossed it into the air, caught it head first, and swallowed it. It was the first fish other than small fry that he had caught that night.

The tide was almost halfway to the confused litter of sea wrack, bits of sticks, dried claws of crabs, and broken shell fragments that marked high-water level. Above the tide line there were faint stirrings in the sand where the terrapins had lately begun to lay their eggs. The season's young would not hatch until August, but many young of the year before still were buried in the sand, not yet roused from the torpor of hibernation. During the winter the young terrapins had lived on the remnant of yolk left from embryonic life. Many had died, for the winter had been long and the frosts had bitten deep into the sands. Those that survived were weak and emaciated, their bodies so shrunken within the shells that they were smaller than when they had hatched. Now they were moving feebly in the sands where the old terrapins were laying the eggs of a new generation of young.

About the time the tide was midway to the flood, a wave of motion stroked the tops of the grasses above the terrapin egg bed, as though a breeze passed, but there was little wind that night. The grasses above the sand bed parted. A rat, crafty with the cunning of years and filled with the lust for blood, had come down to the water along a path which his feet and his thick tail had worn to a smooth track through the grass. The rat lived with his mate and others of his kind under an old shed where the fisherman kept his nets, faring well on the eggs of the many birds that nested on the island, and on the young birds.

As the rat looked out from the fringe of grass bordering the terrapin nests the heron sprang from the water a stone's throw away with a strong flapping of his wings and flew across the island to the north shore. He had seen two fishermen in a small boat coming around the western tip of the island. The fishermen had been gigging flounders, spearing them on the bottom in shallow water by the light of a torch which flared at the bow. A yellow splotch of light moved over the dark water in advance of the boat and sent trembling streamers across the wavelets that rippled shoreward from the boat's passing. Twin points of green fire glowed in the grass above the sand bed. They remained stationary until the boat had passed on around the south shore and had headed toward the town docks. Only then did the rat glide down from the path onto the sand.

The scent of terrapin and of terrapin eggs, fresh laid, was heavy in the air. Snuffling and squeaking in excitement, the rat began to dig and in a few minutes had uncovered an egg, had pierced the shell, and sucked out the yolk. He then uncovered two other eggs and might have eaten them if he had not heard a movement in a near-by clump of marsh grass—the scrambling of a young terrapin struggling to escape the water that was seeping up around its tussock of tangled roots and mud. A dark form moved across the sand and through the rivulet of water. The rat seized the baby terrapin and carried it in his teeth through the marsh grasses to a hummock of higher ground. Engrossed in gnawing away the thin shell of the terrapin, he did not notice how the tide was creeping up about him and running deeper around the hummock. It was thus that the blue heron, wading back around the shore of the island, came upon the rat and speared him.

There were few sounds that night except those of the water and the water birds. The wind was asleep. From the direction of the inlet there came the sound of breakers on the barrier beach, but the distant voice of the sea was hushed almost to a sigh, a sort of rhythmic exhalation as though the sea, too, were asleep outside the gates of the sound.

It would have taken the sharpest of ears to catch the sound of a hermit crab dragging his shell house along the beach just above the water line: the elfin shuffle of his feet on the sand, the sharp grit as he dragged his own shell across another; or to have discerned the spattering tinkle of the tiny droplets that fell when a shrimp, being pursued by a school of fish, leaped clear of the water. But these were the unheard voices of the island night, of the water and the water's edge.

The sounds of the land were few. There was a thin insect tremolo, the spring prelude to the incessant chitin fiddles that later in the season would salute the night. There was the murmur of sleeping birds in the cedars—jackdaws and mockingbirds—who now and again roused enough to twitter drowsily one to another. About midnight a mockingbird sang for almost a quarter of an hour, imitating all the bird songs he had heard that day and adding trills, chuckles, and whistles all his own. Then he, too, subsided and left the night again to the water and its sounds.

There were many fish moving in through the deep water of the channel that night. They were full-bellied fish, soft-finned and covered with large silvery scales. It was a run of spawning shad, fresh from the sea. For days the shad had lain outside the line of breakers beyond the inlet. Tonight with the rising tide they had moved in past the clanging buoy that guided fishermen returning from the outer grounds, had passed through the inlet, and were crossing the sound by way of the channel.

As the night grew darker and the tides pressed farther into the marshes and moved higher into the estuary of the river, the silvery fish quickened their movements, feeling their way along the streams of less saline water that served them as paths to the river. The estuary was broad and sluggish, little more than an arm of the sound. Its shores were ragged with salt marsh, and far up along the winding course of the river the pulsating tides and the bitter tang of the water spoke of the sea.

Some of the migrating shad were three years old and were returning to spawn for the first time. A few were a year older and were making their second trip to the spawning grounds up the river. These were wise in the ways of the river and of the strange crisscross shadows it sometimes contained.

By the younger shad the river was only dimly remembered, if by the word "memory" we may call the heightened response of the senses as the delicate gills and the sensitive lateral lines perceived the lessening saltiness of the water and the changing rhythms and vibrations of the inshore waters. Three years before they had left the river, dropping downstream to the estuary as young fish scarcely as long as a man's finger, moving out to sea with the coming of autumn's chill. The river forgotten, they roamed widely in the sea, feeding on shrimps and amphipods. So far and so deviously did they travel that no man could trace their movements. Perhaps they wintered in deep, warm water far below the surface, resting in the dim twilight of the continent's edge, making an occasional timid journey out over the rim beyond which lay only the blackness and stillness of the deep sea. Perhaps in summer they roved the open ocean, feeding on the rich life of the surface, packing layers of white muscle and sweet fat beneath their shining armor of scales.

The shad roamed the sea paths known and followed only by fish while the earth moved three times through the cycle of the zodiac. In the third year, as the waters of the sea warmed slowly to the southward-moving sun, the shad yielded to the promptings of race instinct and returned to their birthplaces to spawn.

Most of the fish coming in now were females, heavy with unshed roe. It was late in the season and the largest runs had gone before. The bucks, who came into the river first, were already on the spawning grounds, as were many of the roe shad. Some of the early-run fish had pressed upstream as far as a hundred miles to where the river had its formless beginnings in dark cypress swamps.

Each of the roe fish would shed in a season more than a hundred thousand eggs. From these perhaps only one or two young would survive the perils of river and sea and return in time to spawn, for by such ruthless selection the species are kept in check.

The fisherman who lived on the island had gone out about nightfall to set the gill nets that he owned with another fisherman from the town. They had anchored a large net almost at right angles to the west shore of the river and extending well out into the stream. All the local fishermen knew from their fathers, who had it from their fathers, that shad coming in from the channel of the sound usually struck in toward the west bank of the river when they entered the shallow estuary, where no channel was kept open. For this reason the west bank was crowded with fixed fishing gear, like pound nets, and the fishermen who operated movable gear competed bitterly for the few remaining places to set their nets.

Just above the place where the gill net had been set tonight was the long leader of a pound net fixed to posts driven into the soft bottom. The year before there had been a fight when the fishermen who owned the pound had discovered the gill netters taking a good catch of shad from their own net, which they had set directly downstream from the pound, heading off most of the fish. The gill-net fishermen were outnumbered, and for the rest of the season had fished in another part of the estuary, making poor catches and cursing the pound netters. This year they had tried setting the nets at dusk and returning to fish them by daybreak. The rival fishermen did not tend the pound till about sunrise, and by that time the gill netters were always downstream again, nets in their boat, nothing to prove where they had been fishing.

About midnight, as the tide neared the full, the cork line bobbed as the first of the migrating shad struck the gill net. The line vibrated and several of the cork floats disappeared under the water. The shad, a four-pound roe, had thrust her head through one of the meshes of the net and was struggling to free herself. The taut circle of twine that had slipped under the gill covers cut deeper into the delicate gill filaments as the fish lunged against the net; lunged again to free herself from something that was like a burning, choking collar; something that held her in an invisible vise and would neither let her go on upstream nor turn and seek sanctuary in the sea she had left.

The cork line bobbed many times that night and many fish were gilled. Most of them died slowly of suffocation, for the twine interfered with the rhythmic respiratory movements of the gill covers by which fish draw streams of water in through the mouth and pass them over the gills. Once the line bobbed very hard and for ten minutes was pulled below the surface. That was when a grebe, swimming fast five feet under water after a fish, went through the net to its shoulders and in its violent struggles with wings and lobed feet became hopelessly entangled. The grebe soon drowned. Its body hung limply from the net, along with a score of silvery fish bodies with heads pointing upstream in the direction of the spawning grounds where the early-run shad awaited their coming.

By the time the first half-dozen shad had been caught in the net, the eels that lived in the estuary had become aware that a feast was in the offing. Since dusk they had glided with sinuating motion along the banks, thrusting their snouts into crabholes and seizing whatever they could catch in the way of small water creatures. The eels lived partly by their own industry but were also robbers who plundered the fishermen's gill nets when they could.

Almost without exception the eels of the estuary were males. When the young eels come in from the sea, where they are born, the females press far up into rivers and streams, but the males wait about the river mouths until their mates-to-be, grown sleek and fat, rejoin them for the return journey to the sea.

As the eels poked their heads out of the holes under the roots of the marsh grasses and swayed gently back and forth, savoring eagerly the water that they drew into their mouths, their keen senses caught the taste of fish blood which was diffusing slowly through the water as the gilled shad struggled to escape. One by one they slipped out of their holes and followed the taste trail through the water to the net.

The eels feasted royally that night, since most of the fish caught by the net were roe shad. The eels bit into the abdomens with sharp teeth and ate out the roe. Sometimes they ate out all the flesh as well, so that nothing remained but a bag of skin, with an eel or two inside. The marauders could not catch a live shad free in the river, so their only chance for such a meal was to rob the gill nets.

As the night wore on and the tide passed the flood, fewer shad came upstream and no more were caught by the gill net. A few of those that had been caught and insecurely gilled just before the tide turned were released by the return flow of water to the sea. Of those that escaped the gill net, some had been diverted by the leader of the pound net and had followed along the walls of small-meshed netting into the heart of the pound and thence into the pocket, where they were trapped; but most had gone on upstream for several miles and were resting now until the next tide.

The posts of the wharf on the north shore of the island showed two inches of wet water-mark when the fisherman came down with a lantern and a pair of oars. The silence of the waiting night was broken by the thud of his boots on the wharf; the grating of oars fitting into oarlocks; the splash of water from the oars as he pulled out into the gutter and headed toward the town docks to pick up his partner. Then the island settled to silence again and to waiting.

Although there was as yet no light in the east, the blackness of water and air was perceptibly lessening, as though the darkness that remained were something less solid and impenetrable than that of midnight. A freshening air moved across the sound from the east and, blowing across the receding water, sent little wavelets splashing on the beach.

Most of the black skimmers had already left the sound and returned by way of the inlet to the outer banks. Only Rynchops remained. Seemingly he would never tire of circling the island, of making wide sorties out over the marshes or up the estuary of the river where the shad nets were set. As he crossed the gutter and started up the estuary once more, there was enough light to see the two fishermen maneuvering their boat into position beside the cork line of the gill net. White mist was moving over the water and swirling around the fishermen, who were standing in their boat and straining to raise the anchor line at the end of the net. The anchor came up, dragging with it a clump of widgeon grass, and was dropped in the bottom of the boat.

The skimmer passed upstream about a mile, flying low to the water, then turned by circling widely over the marshes and came down to the estuary again. There was a strong smell of fish and of water weeds in the air which came to him through the morning mists, and the voices of the fishermen were borne clearly over the water. The men were cursing as they worked to raise the gill net, disentangling the fish before they piled the dripping net on the flat bottom of the skiff.

As Rynchops passed about half a dozen wing beats from the boat, one of the fishermen flung something violently over his shoulder—a fish head with what looked like a stout white cord attached. It was the skeleton of a fine roe shad, all that remained, save the head, after the feast of the eels.

The next time Rynchops flew up the estuary he met the fishermen coming downstream on the ebbing tide, net piled in the boat over some half-dozen shad. All the others had been gutted or reduced to skeletons by the eels. Already gulls were gathering on the water where the gill net had been set, screaming their pleasure over the refuse which the fishermen had thrown overboard.

The tide was ebbing fast, surging through the gutter and running out to sea. As the sun's rays broke through the clouds in the east and sped across the sound, Rynchops turned to follow the racing water seaward.

2
Spring Flight

THE NIGHT WHEN the great run of shad was passing through the inlet and into the river estuary was a night, too, of vast movements of birds into the sound country.

At daybreak and the half tide two small sanderlings ran beside the dark water on the ocean beach of the barrier island, keeping in the thin film at the edge of the ebbing surf. They were trim little birds in rust and gray plumage, and they ran with a twinkle of black feet over the hard-packed sand, where puffs of blown spume or sea froth rolled like thistledown. They belonged to a flock of several hundred shore birds that had arrived from the south during the night. The migrants had rested in the lee of the great dunes while darkness remained; now growing light and ebbing water were drawing them to the sea's edge.

As the two sanderlings probed the wet sand for small, thin-shelled crustaceans, they forgot the long flight of the night before in the excitement of the hunt. For the moment they forgot, too, that faraway place which they must reach before many days had passed—a place of vast tundras, of snow-fed lakes, and midnight sun. Blackfoot, leader of the migrant flock, was making his fourth journey from the southernmost tip of South America to the Arctic nesting grounds of his kind. In his short lifetime he had traveled more than sixty thousand miles, following the sun north and south across the globe, some eight thousand miles spring and fall. The little hen sanderling that ran beside him on the beach was a yearling, returning for the first time to the Arctic she had left as a fledgling nine months before. Like the older sanderlings, Silverbar had changed her winter plumage of pearly gray for a mantle heavily splashed with cinnamon and rust, the colors worn by all sanderlings on their return to their first home.

In the fringe of the surf, Blackfoot and Silverbar sought the sand bugs or Hippa crabs that honeycombed the ocean beach with their burrowings. Of all the food of the tide zone they loved best these small, egg-shaped crabs. After the retreat of each wave the wet sand bubbled with the air released from the shallow crab burrows, and a sanderling could, if he were quick and sure of foot, insert his bill and draw out the crab before the next wave came tumbling in. Many of the crabs were washed out by the swift rushes of the waves and left kicking in liquefying sand. Often the sanderlings seized these crabs in the moment of their confusion, before they could bury themselves by furious scrambling.

Pressing close to the backwash, Silverbar saw two shining air bubbles pushing away the sand grains and she knew that a crab was beneath. Even as she watched the bubbles her bright eyes saw that a wave was taking form in the tumbling confusion of the surf. She gauged the speed of the mound of water as it ran, toppling, up the beach. Above the deeper undertones of moving water she heard the lighter hiss that came as the crest began to spill. Almost in the same instant the feathered antennae of the crab appeared above the sand. Running under the very crest of the green water hill, Silverbar probed vigorously in the wet sand with opened bill and drew out the crab. Before the water could so much as wet her legs she turned and fled up the beach.

While the sun still came in level rays across the water, others of the sanderling flock joined Blackfoot and Silverbar and the beach was soon dotted with small shore birds.

A tern came flying along the surf line, his black-capped head bent and his eyes alert for the movement of fish in the water. He watched the sanderlings closely, for sometimes a small beach bird could be frightened into giving up its catch. When the tern saw Blackfoot run swiftly into the path of a wave and seize a crab he slanted down menacingly, screaming threats in a shrill, grating voice.

Tee-ar-r-r! Tee-ar-r-r! rattled the tern.

The swoop of the white-winged bird, which was twice as large as the sanderling, took Blackfoot by surprise, for his senses had been occupied with eluding the onrush of water and preventing the escape of the large crab held in his bill. He sprang into the air with a sharp *Keet! Keet!* and circled out over the surf. The tern whirled after him in pursuit, crying loudly.

In his ability to bank and pivot in the air Blackfoot was fully the equal of the tern. The two birds, darting and twisting and turning, coming up sharply together and falling away again into the wave troughs, passed out beyond the breakers and the sound of their voices was lost to the sanderling flock on the beach.

As he rose steeply into the air in pursuit of Blackfoot, the tern caught sight of a glint of silver in the water below. He bent his head to mark the new prey more certainly and saw the green water spangled with silver streaks as the sun struck the flanks of a school of feeding silversides. Instantly the tern tipped his body steeply into a plane perpendicular to the water. He fell like a stone, although his body could not have weighed more than a few ounces, struck the water with a splash and a shower of spray, and in a matter of seconds emerged with a fish curling in his bill. By this time Blackfoot, forgotten by the tern in the excitement engendered by the bright flashes in the water, had reached the shore and dropped down among the feeding sanderlings, where he was running and probing busily as before.

After the tide turned, the water pressed stronger from the sea. The waves came in with a deeper swell and a heavier crash, warning the sanderlings that feeding on the ocean beach was no longer safe. The flock wheeled out over the sea, with a flashing of the white wing bars that distinguished them from other sandpipers. They flew low over the crests of the waves as they traveled up the beach. So they came to the point of land called Ship's Shoal, where the sea had broken through the barrier island to the sound years before.

At the point the inlet beach lay level as a floor from the sea on the south side to the sound on the north. The wide sand flat was a favorite resting place for sandpipers, plovers, and other shore birds; and it was loved, too, by the terns, the skimmers, and the gulls, who make their living from the sea, but gather to rest on shores and sandspits.

That morning the inlet beach was thronged with birds, resting and waiting for the tide turn that they might feed again, fueling small bodies for the northward journey. It was the month of May, and the great spring migration of the shore birds was at its height. Weeks before, the waterfowl had left the sounds. Two spring tides and two neap tides had passed since the last skein of snow geese had drifted to the north, like wisps of cloud in the sky. The mergansers had gone in February, looking for the first breaking up of the ice in the northern lakes, and soon after them the canvasbacks had left the wild celery beds of the estuary and followed the retreating winter to the north. So, too, the brant, eaters of the eel grass that carpeted the shallows of the sound, the swift blue-winged teal, and the whistling swans, filling the skies with their soft trumpetings.

Then the bell notes of the plovers had begun to ring among the sand hills and the liquid whistle of the curlew throbbed in the salt marshes. Shadowy forms moved through the night skies and pipings so soft as barely to be audible drifted down to fishing villages sleeping below, as the birds of shore and marsh poured northward along ancestral air lanes, seeking their nesting places.

Now while the shore birds slept on the inlet beach the sands belonged to other hunters. After the last bird had settled to rest, a ghost crab came out of his burrow in the loose white sand above the high-water mark. He sped along the beach, running swiftly on the tips of his eight legs. He paused at a mass of sea wrack left by the night tide not a dozen paces from the spot where Silverbar stood on the edge of the sanderling flock. The crab was a creamy tan, matching the sand so closely that he was all but invisible when he stood still. Only his eyes, like two black shoe buttons on stalks, showed color. Silverbar saw the crab crouch behind the litter of sea-oats stubble, leaves of beach grass, and pieces of sea lettuce. He was waiting for a sand hopper or beach flea to show itself by an unwary movement. As the ghost crabs knew, the beach fleas hid in the seaweeds when the tide was out, browsing on them and picking up bits of decaying refuse.

Before the tide had risen another hand's breadth, a beach flea crept out from under a green frond of sea lettuce and leaped with an agile flexing of its legs across a stem of sea oats, as large to it as a fallen pine. The ghost crab sprang like a pouncing cat and seized the flea in his large crushing claw, or chela, and devoured it. During the next hour he caught and ate many of the beach hoppers, stealing on silent feet from one vantage point to another as he stalked his prey.

After an hour the wind changed and blew in across the inlet channel, obliquely from the sea. One by one the birds shifted their position so that they faced the wind. Above the surf at the point they saw a flock of several hundred terns fishing. A shoal of small silvery fish was passing seaward around the point, and the air was filled with the white wing flashes of diving terns.

At intervals the birds on the beach at Ship's Shoal heard the flight music of hurrying flocks of black-bellied plovers, high in the sky; and twice they saw long lines of dowitchers passing northward.

At noon white wings sailed over the sand dunes and a snowy egret swung down long black legs. The bird alighted at the margin of a pond that lay, half encircled by marsh, between the eastern end of the dunes and the inlet beach. The pond was called Mullet Pond, a name given to it years before when it had been larger and mullet had sometimes come into it from the sea. Every day the small white heron came to fish the pond, seeking the killifish and other minnows that darted in its shallows. Sometimes, too, he found the young of larger fishes, for the highest tides of each month cut through the beach on the ocean side and brought in fish from the sea.

The pond slept in noonday quiet. Against the green of the marsh grass the heron was a snow-white figure on slim black stilts, tense and motionless. Not a ripple nor the shadow of a ripple passed beneath his sharp eyes. Then eight pale minnows swam single file above the muddy bottom, and eight black shadows moved beneath them.

With a snakelike contortion of its neck, the heron jabbed violently, but missed the leader of the solemn little parade of fish. The minnows scattered in sudden panic as the clear water was churned to muddy chaos by the feet of the heron, who darted one way and another, skipping and flapping his wings in excitement. In spite of his efforts, he captured only one of the minnows.

The heron had been fishing for an hour and the sanderlings, sandpipers, and plovers had been sleeping for three hours when a boat's bottom grated on the sound beach near the point.

Two men jumped out into the water and made ready to drag a haul seine through the shallows on the rising tide. The heron lifted his head and listened. Through the fringe of sea oats on the sound side of the pond he saw a man walking down the beach toward the inlet. Alarmed, he thrust his feet hard against the mud and with a flapping of wings took off over the dunes toward the heron rookery in the cedar thickets a mile away. Some of the shore birds ran twittering across the beach toward the sea. Already the terns were milling about overhead in a noisy cloud, like hundreds of scraps of paper flung to the wind. The sanderlings took flight and crossed the point, wheeling and turning almost as one bird, and passed down the ocean beach about a mile.

The ghost crab, still at his hunting of beach fleas, was alarmed by the turmoil of birds overhead, by the many racing shadows that sped over the sand. By now he was far from his own burrow. When he saw the fisherman walking across the beach he dashed into the surf, preferring this refuge to flight. But a large channel bass was lurking near by, and in a twinkling the crab was seized and eaten. Later in the same day, the bass was attacked by sharks and what was left of it was cast up by the tide onto the sand. There the beach fleas, scavengers of the shore, swarmed over it and devoured it.

Twilight found the sanderlings resting again at the point of land called Ship's Shoal, listening to the soft roar of wings in the air about them as the curlews came in from the salt marshes to roost for the night on the inlet beach. Silverbar crouched close to some of the older sanderlings because of the strange sounds and the movements of so many large birds. There must have been thousands of curlews. For an hour after dark they were arriving, in long V formations and dense flocks. Every year the big brown birds with the sickle-shaped bills stopped on their northward migration to feed on the fiddler crabs of the mud flats and marshes.

A stone's throw away several crabs, no larger than a man's thumbnail, moved across the beach, but the sound of their feet was like the sound of sand grains disturbed by the wind, and so not even Silverbar, who was resting near the edge of the sanderling flock, heard them passing. They waded into the shallows and let the cool water bathe their bodies. This had been a day of distress and terror for the fiddlers, with all the marshes filled with curlews. Many times each hour the shadow of a bird soaring down to alight in the marsh or the sight of one of the curlews walking down along the water's edge had sent the small crabs scattering like a herd of stampeding cattle. Then the hundreds of feet on the sand had made a sound like the rattling of stiff sheets of paper. As many as could had darted into burrows—their own burrows—any burrows they could reach. But the long, oblique tunnels in the sand had been poor sanctuary, for the curving bills of the curlews could probe them deeply.

Now with the grateful twilight the fiddler herds had moved down to the water line to search for food among the sand windrows left by the receding tide. With their little spoon claws the crabs felt busily among the sand grains, sorting out the microscopic cells of algae.

The crabs that had waded into the water were females carrying eggs on the broad aprons of their abdomens. Because of the egg masses they moved awkwardly and were unable to run from their enemies, and so all day they had remained hidden deep in the burrows. Now they swayed to and fro in the water, seeking to rid themselves of their burdens. This was an instinct that served to aerate the eggs adhering to the mother's body like bunches of miniature purple grapes. Although the season was early, some of the fiddlers carried gray egg masses, signifying that the young were ready for life. For these crabs the evening ritual of washing brought on the hatching of the eggs. With each movement of the mothers' bodies, many eggshells burst and clouds of larvae were hurled into the water. Even the killifish that were nibbling algae from the shells in the quiet shallows of the sound scarcely noticed the throngs of newborn creatures that drifted by, for any of the baby crabs thus abruptly released from the confining sphere of the egg could have passed through the eye of a needle.

The clouds of larvae were carried away on the still-ebbing tide and swept out through the inlet. When the first light should steal across the water they would find themselves in the strange world of the open sea, amid many perils which they must surmount, alone and unaided save for the self-protective instincts with which each was endowed at birth. Many would fail. The others, after long weeks of adventurous living, would put in to some distant shore, where the tides spread abundant feasts for fiddler crabs and marsh grasses offered home and shelter.

The night was noisy with the barking cries of the black skimmers who chased each other in play over the inlet, where the moon struck a white path across the water. The sanderlings had often seen the skimmers in South America, for many of them wintered as far south as Venezuela and Colombia. The skimmers, compared with the sanderlings, were birds of the tropics and knew nothing of the white world to which the shore birds were bound.

At intervals throughout the night the calls of Hudsonian curlews, migrating at a great height, came down from the sky. The curlews sleeping on the beach stirred uneasily and sometimes answered the cries with plaintive whistles.

It was the night of the full moon, the moon of the spring tides when the water presses far into the marshes and laps at the floor boards of fishermen's wharfs and makes boats strain at their anchors.

The sea, that gleamed with the moon's lambent silver, drew to its surface many squids, dazed and fascinated by the light. The squids drifted on the sea, their eyes fixed on the moon. Gently they drew in water and expelled it in jets, propelling themselves backward away from the light at which they gazed. Moon-bewildered, their senses did not warn them that they were drifting into dangerous shoals until the harsh grate of sand brought sharp awakening. As they stranded, the hapless squids pumped water all the harder, driving themselves out of even the thinnest film, onto sand from which all water had ebbed away.

In the morning the sanderlings, moving down to the surf line to feed in the first light, found the inlet beach littered with dead squids. The sanderlings did not linger on this part of the beach, for although it was very early in the morning many large birds had gathered and were quarreling over the squids. They were herring gulls, bound from the Gulf Coast to Nova Scotia. They had been long delayed by stormy weather and they were ravenous. A dozen black-headed laughing gulls came and hovered, mewing, over the beach, dangling their feet as though to alight, but the herring gulls drove them away with fierce screaming and jabs of their bills.

By midday, with the rising tide, a strong wind was blowing in from the sea and storm clouds ran before it. The green ranks of the marsh grasses swayed and their tips bent to touch the rising water. After the first quarter of the tide rise all the marshes stood deep in water. The scattered sand shoals of the sound, favorite resting places of the gulls, were covered as the spring tide ran with the wind's weight behind it.

The sanderlings, along with flocks of other shore birds, took refuge close beneath the landward slopes of the dunes. There the forests of beach grass sheltered them. From their haven they saw the flock of herring gulls sweeping like a gray cloud over the vivid green of the marshes. The flock constantly changed shape and direction as it rolled, the leaders hesitating over a possible resting place, the laggards surging forward. Now they settled on a sand shoal, shrunk to a tenth the size it had been that morning. The water was rising. On they moved, to hover, fluttering and screaming, above a reef of oyster shell, where the water streamed neck-deep to a gull. At last the whole flock veered around and fought its way back into the face of the gale, coming to rest near the sanderlings in the shelter of the dunes.

Stormbound, all the migrants waited, unable to feed because of the heavy surf. At sea, out beyond the sheltering capes, a violent storm was raging. On the ocean beach two small birds, dazed and sick with buffeting, staggered over the sand, fell, and staggered on again. Land was to them a strange realm. Except for a short period each year when they visited small islands in the Antarctic Sea to rear their young, their world was of sky and rolling water. They were Wilson's petrels or Mother Carey's chickens, blown in by the storm from miles at sea. And once during the afternoon a dark-brown bird with slender wings and hawklike bill came beating its way over the dunes and across the sound. Blackfoot the sanderling and many of the other shore birds crouched in terror, recognizing an ancestral enemy, the scourge of the northern breeding grounds. Like the petrels, the jaeger had ridden in on the gale from the open sea.

Before sunset, the skies lightened and the wind abated. While it was yet light the sanderlings left the barrier island and set out across the sound. Beneath them as they wheeled over the inlet was the deep green ribbon of the channel that wound, with many curvings, across the lighter shallows of the sound. They followed the channel, passing between the leaning red spar buoys, past the tide rips where the water streamed, broken into swirls and eddies, over a sunken reef of oyster shell, and came at last to the island. There they joined a company of several hundred white-rumped sandpipers, least sandpipers, and ring-necked plovers that were resting on the sand.

While the tide was still ebbing, the sanderlings fed on the island beach, but settled to rest before the arrival, at dusk, of Rynchops the black skimmer. As they slept, and as the earth rolled from darkness toward light, birds from many feeding places along the coast were hurrying along the flyways that lead to the north. For with the passing of the storm the air currents came fresh again and the wind blew clean and steady from the southwest. All through the night the cries of curlews and plovers and knots, of sandpipers and turnstones and yellowlegs, drifted down from the sky. The mockingbirds who lived on the island listened to the cries. The next day they would have many new notes in their rippling, chuckling songs to charm their mates and delight themselves.

About an hour before dawn the sanderling flock gathered together on the island beach, where the gentle tide was shifting the windrows of shells. The little band of brown-mottled birds mounted into the darkness and, as the island grew small beneath them, set out toward the north.

3
Arctic Rendezvous

WINTER STILL GRIPPED the northland when the sanderlings arrived on the shores of a bay shaped like a leaping porpoise, on the edge of the frozen tundras of the barren grounds. They were among the first to arrive of all the migrant shore birds. Snow lay on the hills and drifted deep in the stream valleys. The ice was yet unbroken in the bay, and on the ocean shore it was piled in green and jagged heaps that moved, straining and groaning, with the tides.

But the lengthening days filled with sun had already begun to melt the snow on the south slopes of the hills, and on the ridges the wind had helped wear the snow blanket thin. There the brown of earth and the silver gray of reindeer moss showed through, and now for the first time that season the sharp-hoofed caribou could feed without pawing away the snow. At noon the white owls beating across the tundra beheld their own reflections in many small pools among the rocks, but by midafternoon the water mirrors were clouded with frost.

Already the rusty feathers were showing about the necks of the willow ptarmigans and brown hairs had appeared on the white coats of the foxes and weasels. Snow buntings hopped about in flocks that grew day by day, and the buds on the willows swelled and showed the first awakening of color under the sunshine.

There was little food for the migrant birds—lovers of warm sun and green, tossing surf. The sanderlings gathered miserably under a few dwarf willows that were sheltered from the northwest winds by a glacial moraine. There they lived on the first green buds of the saxifrage and awaited the coming of thaws to release the rich animal food of the Arctic spring.

But winter was yet to die. The second sun after the sanderlings' return to the Arctic burned dimly in the murky air. The clouds thickened and rolled between the tundra and the sun, and by midday the sky was heavy with unfallen snow. Wind came in over the open sea and over the ice packs, carrying a bitter air that turned to mist as it moved, swirling, over the warmer plains.

Uhvinguk, the lemming mouse who yesterday had sunned himself with many of his fellows on the bare rocks, ran into the burrows, winding tunnels in the deep, hard drifts, and to the grass-lined chambers where the lemmings dwelt in warmth even in midwinter. In the twilight of that day a white fox paused above the lemming burrow and stood with lifted paw. In the silence his sharp ears caught the sound of small feet along the runways below. Many times that spring the fox had dug down through the snow into these burrows and seized as many lemmings as he could eat. Now he whined sharply and pawed a little at the snow. He was not hungry, having killed and eaten a ptarmigan an hour before when he had come upon it, in a willow thicket, snipping off twigs; so today he only listened, perhaps to reassure himself that the weasels had not raided the lemming colony since his last visit. Then he turned and ran on silent feet along the path made by many foxes, not even pausing to glance at the sanderlings huddled in the lee of the moraine, and passed over the hill to the distant ridge where a colony of thirty small white foxes had their burrows.

Late that night, about the time the sun must have been setting somewhere behind the thick cloud banks, the first snow fell. Soon the wind rose and poured across the tundra like a flood of icy water that penetrated the thickest feathers and the warmest fur. As the wind came down shrieking from the sea, the mists fled before it across the barrens, but the snow clouds were thicker and whiter than the mists had been.

Silverbar, the young hen sanderling, had not seen snow since she had left the Arctic nearly ten months before to follow the sun southward toward the limit of its orbit, to the grasslands of the Argentine and the shores of Patagonia. Almost her whole existence had been of sun and wide white beaches and rippling green pampas. Now, crouched under the dwarf willows, she could not see Blackfoot through the swirling whiteness, although she could have reached his side with a quick run of twenty paces. The sanderlings faced into the blizzard, as shore birds everywhere face into the wind. They huddled close together, wing to wing, and the warmth of their bodies kept the tender feet from freezing as they crouched on them.

If the snow had not drifted so, that night and all the next day, the loss of life would have been less. But the stream valleys filled up, inch by inch, throughout the night, and against the ridges the white softness piled deeper. Little by little, from the ice-strewn sea edge across miles of tundra, even far south to the fringe of the forests, the undulating hills and the ice-scoured valleys were flattening out, and a strange world, terrifying in its level whiteness, was building up. In the purple twilight of the second day the fall slackened, and the night was loud with the crying of the wind, but with no other voice, for no wild thing dared show itself.

The snow death had taken many lives. It had visited the nest of two snowy owls in a ravine that cut a deep scar in the hillside, near the willow copse that sheltered the sanderlings. The hen had been brooding the six eggs for more than a week. During the first night of wild storm the snow had drifted deep about her, leaving a round depression like a stream-bed pothole in which she sat. All through the night the owl remained on the nest, warming the eggs with her great body that was almost furry in its plumage. By morning the snow was filling in around the feather-shod talons and creeping up around her sides. The cold was numbing, even through the feathers. At noon, with flakes like cotton shreds still flying in the sky, only the owl's head and shoulders were free of the snow. Several times that day a great form, white and silent as the snowflakes, had drifted over the ridge and hovered above the place where the nest was. Now Ookpik, the cock owl, called to his mate with low, throaty cries. Numb and heavy-winged with cold, the hen roused and shook herself. It took many minutes to free herself from the snow and to climb, half fluttering, half stumbling, out of the nest, deep-walled with white. Ookpik clucked to her and made the sounds of a cock owl bringing a lemming or a baby ptarmigan to the nest, but neither owl had had food since the blizzard began. The hen tried to fly but her heavy body flopped awkwardly in the snow for stiffness. When at last the slow circulation had crept back into her muscles, she rose into the air and the two owls floated over the place where the sanderlings crouched and out across the tundra.

As the snow fell on the still-warm eggs and the hard, bitter cold of the night gripped them, the life fires of the tiny embryos burned low. The crimson streams ran slower in the vessels that carried the racing blood from the food yolks to the embryos. After a time there slackened and finally ceased the furious activity of cells that grew and divided, grew again and divided to make owl bone and muscle and sinew. The pulsating red sacs under the great oversized heads hesitated, beat spasmodically, and were stilled. The six little owls-to-be were dead in the snow, and by their death, perhaps, hundreds of unborn lemmings and ptarmigans and Arctic hares had the greater chance of escaping death from the feathered ones that strike from the sky.

Farther up the ravine, several willow ptarmigans had been buried in a drift, where they had bedded for the night. The ptarmigans had flown over the ridge on the evening of the storm, dropping into the soft drifts so that never a print of their feet—clad in feathered snowshoes—was left to guide the foxes to their resting place. This was a rule of the game of life and death which the weak play with the strong. But tonight there was no need to observe the rules, for the snow would have obliterated all footprints and would have outwitted the keenest enemy—even as it drifted, by slow degrees, so deeply over the sleeping ptarmigans that they could not dig themselves out.

Five of the sanderling flock had died of the cold, and snow buntings by the score were stumbling and fluttering over the snow crust, too weak to stand when they tried to alight.

Now, with the passing of the storm, hunger was abroad on the great barrens. Most of the willows, food of the ptarmigans, were buried under snow. The dried heads of last year's weeds, which released their seeds to the snow buntings and the longspurs, wore glittering sheaths of ice. The lemmings, food of the foxes and the owls, were safe in their runways, and nowhere in this silent world was there food for shore birds that live on the shellfish and insects and other creatures of the water's edge. Now many hunters, both furred and feathered, were abroad during the night, the short, gray night of the Arctic spring. And when night wore into day the hunters still padded over the snow or beat on strong wings across the tundra, for the night's kill had not satisfied their hunger.

Among the hunters was Ookpik, the snowy owl. The coldest months of every winter, the icebound months, Ookpik spent hundreds of miles south of the barren grounds, where it was easier to find the little gray lemming mice that were his favorite food. During the storm nothing living had showed itself to Ookpik as he sailed over the plains and along the ridges that overlooked the sea, but today many small creatures moved over the tundra.

Along the east bank of the stream a flock of ptarmigans had found a few twigs of willow showing above the snow, part of a shrubby growth that had been as high as the antlers of a barren-grounds caribou until the snow had covered it. Now the ptarmigans could easily reach the topmost branches, and they nipped off the twigs in their bills, content with this food until the tender new buds of spring should be put forth. The flock still wore the white plumage of winter except for one or two of the cocks whose few brown feathers told of approaching summer and the mating season. When a ptarmigan in winter dress feeds on the snow fields, all of color about him is the black of bill and roving eye, and of the under tail feathers when he flies. Even his ancient enemies, the foxes and the owls, are deceived from a distance; but they, too, wear the Arctic's protective colorings.

Now Ookpik, as he came up the stream valley, saw among the willows the moving balls of shining black that were the ptarmigans' eyes. The white foe moved nearer, blending into the pale sky; the white prey moved, unfrightened, over the snow. There was a soft *whoosh* of wings—a scattering of feathers—and on the snow a red stain spread, red as a new-laid ptarmigan egg before the shell pigments have dried. Ookpik bore the ptarmigan in his talons over the ridge to the higher ground that was his lookout, where his mate awaited him. The two owls tore apart the warm flesh with their beaks, swallowing also the bones and feathers as was their custom, to cast them up later in neat pellets.

The gnawing pang of hunger was a sensation new to Silverbar. A week before, with the others of the sanderling flock, she had filled her stomach with shellfish gathered on the wide tidal flats of Hudson Bay. Days before that they had gorged on beach fleas on the coasts of New England, and on Hippa crabs on the sunny beaches of the south. In all the eight-thousand-mile journey northward from Patagonia there had been no lack of food.

The older sanderlings, patient in the acceptance of hardship, waited until the ebb tide, when they led Silverbar and the other year-old birds of the flock to the edge of the harbor ice. The beach was piled with irregular masses of ice and frozen spray, but the last tide had shifted the broken floe and on retreating had left a bare patch of mud flat. Already several hundred shore birds had gathered—all the early migrants from miles around who had escaped death in the snow. They were clustered so thickly that there was scarcely space for the sanderlings to alight, and every square inch of surface had been probed or dug by the bills of the waders. By deep probing in the stiff mud Silverbar found several shells coiled like snails, but they were empty. With Blackfoot and two of the yearling sanderlings, she flew up the beach for a mile, but snow carpeted the ground and the harbor ice and there was no food.

As the sanderlings hunted fruitlessly among the ice chunks, Tullugak the raven flew overhead and passed up the shore on deliberate wings.

Cr-r-r-uck! Cr-r-r-uck! he croaked hoarsely.

Tullugak had been patrolling the beach and the near-by tundra for miles, on the lookout for food. All the known carcasses which the ravens had resorted to for months had been covered by snow or carried away by the shifting of the bay ice. Now he had located the remains of a caribou which the wolves had run down and killed that morning, and he was calling the other ravens to the feast. Three jet-black birds, among them Tullugak's mate, were walking briskly about over the bay ice hunting a whale carcass. The whale had come ashore months before, providing almost a winter's supply of food for Tullugak and his kin, who lived the year round in the vicinity of the bay. Now the storm had opened a channel into which the shifting ice masses had pushed the dead whale and closed over it. At the welcome food cry of Tullugak, the three ravens sprang into the air and followed him across the tundra to pick off the few shreds of meat that remained on the bones of the caribou.

*

The next night the wind shifted and the thaw began.

Day by day the blanket of snow grew thinner. Irregular holes rent the white covering—brown holes where the naked earth showed through, green holes where ponds that still held their hearts of ice were uncovered. Hillside trickles grew to rivulets and rivulets to rushing torrents as the Arctic sent its melted snows to the sea, to eat jagged cuts and gullies through the salt ice, to accumulate in pools along the shore. Lakes brimmed with the clear cold water and teemed with new life as the young of crane flies and May flies stirred in the bottom muds and the larvae of the northland's myriad mosquitoes squirmed in the water.

As the drifts melted away and the low-lying grasslands became flooded, the lemming burrows, which honeycombed the Arctic underworld with hundreds of miles of tunnels, became uninhabitable. The quiet runways, the peaceful grass-lined burrows that had been secure from even the fiercest blizzards of winter, now knew the terrors of rushing waters, of swirling floods. As many of the lemmings as could escape took refuge on high rocks and gravel ridges and sunned their plump gray bodies, quickly forgetting the dark horror from which they had lately fled.

Now hundreds of migrants arrived from the south each day and the tundra heard other noises besides the booming cries of the cock owls and the bark of the foxes. There were the voices of curlews and plovers and knots, of terns and gulls and ducks from the south. There were the braying cries of the stilt sandpipers and the tinkling song of the redbacks; there was the shrill bubbling of the Baird sandpiper, akin to the sleigh-bell chorus of spring peepers in the smoky twilight of a New England spring.

As the patches of earth spread over the snow fields, the sanderlings, plovers, and turnstones gathered in the cleared spots, finding abundant food. Only the knots resorted to the unthawed marshes and the protected hollows of the plains, where sedges and weeds lifted dry seed heads above the snow and rattled when the wind blew and dropped their seed for the birds.

Most of the sanderlings and the knots passed on to the distant islands scattered far over the Arctic sea, where they made their nests and brought forth their young. But Silverbar and Blackfoot and others of the sanderlings remained near the bay shaped like a leaping porpoise, along with turnstones, plovers, and many other shore birds. Hundreds of terns were preparing to nest on near-by islands, where they would be safe from the foxes; while most of the gulls retired inland to the shores of the small lakes which dotted the Arctic plains in summer.

In time Silverbar accepted Blackfoot as her mate and the pair withdrew to a stony plateau overlooking the sea. The rocks were clothed with mosses and soft gray lichens, first of all plants to cover the open and wind-swept places of the earth. There was a sparse growth of dwarf willow, with bursting leaf buds and ripe catkins. From scattered clumps of green the flowers of the wild betony lifted white faces to the sun, and over the south slope of the hill was a pool fed by melting snow and draining to the sea by way of an old stream bed.

Now Blackfoot grew more aggressive and fought bitterly with every cock who infringed upon his chosen territory. After such a combat he paraded before Silverbar, ruffling his feathers. While she watched in silence he leaped into the air and hovered on fluttering wings, uttering neighing cries. This he did most often in the evening as the shadows lay purple on the eastern slopes of the hills.

On the edge of a clump of betony Silverbar prepared the nest, a shallow depression which she molded to her body by turning round and round. She lined the bottom with last year's dried leaves from a willow that grew prostrate along the ground, bringing the leaves one at a time and arranging them in the nest along with some bits of lichen. Soon four eggs lay on the willow leaves, and now Silverbar began the long vigil during which she must keep all wild things of the tundra from discovering the place of her nest.

During her first night alone with the four eggs Silverbar heard a sound new to the tundra that year, a harsh scream that came again and again out of the shadows. At early dawn light she saw two birds, dark of body and wing, flying low over the tundra. The newcomers were jaegers, birds of the gull tribe turned hawk to rob and kill. From that time on, the cries, like weird laughter, rang every night on the barrens.

More and more jaegers arrived each day, some from the fishing grounds of the North Atlantic, where they had lived by stealing fish from the gulls and shearwaters, others from the warm oceans of half the globe. Now the jaegers became the scourge of all the tundra. Singly or in twos and threes they beat back and forth over the open places, on the watch for a solitary sandpiper or plover or phalarope who, being defenseless, would provide easy game. They whirled down in sudden attack on the flocks of shore birds feeding on the broad, weed-strewn mud flats, hoping to separate a single bird from its fellows for the swift pursuit that ends in death. They harried the gulls on the bay, tormenting them until they disgorged the fish they had caught. They hunted among the rock crevices and little mounds of stones, where they often surprised a lemming sunning himself at the mouth of his burrow or came upon a snow bunting brooding her eggs. They perched on rocky elevations or ridges from which they watched the pattern of the rolling tundra, mottled dark and light with moss and gravel, with lichen and shale. Even the fierce eyes of a jaeger could not distinguish at a distance the speckled eggs of the many birds that lay unconcealed on the open plain. So skillful was the camouflage of the tundra that only by sudden movement did a nesting bird or a foraging lemming betray its presence.

Now for twenty hours out of the twenty-four the tundra lay in sun and for four hours it slept in soft twilight. Arctic willow and saxifrage, wild betony and crowberry hastened to put forth new leaves to draw to themselves the strength of the sun. Into a few brief and sun-filled weeks the plants of the Arctic must crowd a lifetime of living. Only the kernel of life, fortified and protected, endures the months of darkness and cold.

Soon the cloak of the tundra was embroidered with many flowers: first, the white cups of the mountain avens; then the purple of saxifrage; then the yellow of the buttercup glades, loud with the drone of bees trampling the shiny golden petals and jostling the laden anthers, so that each bore away its load of pollen on the bristles of its body. The tundra was gay, too, with moving bits of color, for the midday sun coaxed out butterflies from the willow thickets where they drooped and hid when the colder airs blew or when clouds stole between earth and sun.

In temperate lands the birds sing their sweetest songs in the dim light that falls after sundown and comes before dawn. But in the Arctic barrens the June sun dips so briefly below the horizon that each of the night hours is an hour of twilight or song light, filled with the bubbling song of the longspur and the calls of the horned lark.

On a day in June a pair of phalaropes drifted, light as corks, on the glazed sheet of the sanderlings' pool. Now and then they spun in a circle by rapid thrusts of their lobed feet, then jabbed again and again with needlelike bills to capture the insects stirred up by their movements. The phalaropes had spent the winter on the open sea far to the southward, following the whales and the ever-drifting clouds of whale food. On their migration they had come northward by an ocean route as far as possible before striking inland. The phalaropes prepared a nest on the south slope of the ridge not far from the sanderling nest and lined it, as most of the tundra nests are lined, with willow leaves and catkins. Then the cock phalarope took charge of the nest, to sit for eighteen days, warming the eggs to life.

By day the soft *coo-a-hee, coo-a-hee,* of the knots came down flutelike from the hills, where on the plateaus the nests lay hidden amid the curling brown tufts of Arctic sedges and the leaves of the mountain avens. Every evening Silverbar watched a solitary knot tumbling and soaring in the still air over the low mounds of the hills. The song of Canutus, the knot, was heard by other knots along miles of hilltop and by the turnstones and sandpipers on the tide flats of the bay. But another heard and responded to it most of all, his small dappled mate who was brooding their four eggs in the nest far below.

Then for a season many of the voices of the tundra were hushed, as all over the barrens eggs were hatching and there were young to be fed and concealed from enemies.

When Silverbar had begun to brood her eggs, the moon had been at the full. Since then it had dwindled to a thin white rim in the sky and now had grown again to the quarter, so that once more the tides in the bay were slacker and milder. One morning when the shore birds gathered over the flats to feed on the ebb tide, Silverbar did not join them. Throughout the night there had been sounds in the eggs under her breast feathers, now worn and frayed. They were the peckings of the sanderling chicks, after twenty-three days made ready for life. Silverbar inclined her head and listened to the sounds; sometimes she withdrew a little from the eggs and watched them intently.

On the near-by ridge a Lapland longspur was singing his tinkling, many-syllabled song, mounting high into the air again and again and spilling out his song as he lowered himself on widespread wings to the grass. The little bird had a feather-lined nest on the edge of the phalarope pool, where his mate was brooding their six eggs. The longspur was glad of the brightness and warmth of noonday and unmindful of the shadow that dropped between him and the sun as Kigavik, the gyrfalcon, fell from the sky. Silverbar neither heard the song of the longspur nor was conscious of its sudden ceasing; nor did she notice when a single breast feather fluttered downward almost at her side. She was watching a hole that had appeared in one of the eggs. The only sound she heard was a thin, mouse-like squeak, the first cry of her young. By the time the gyrfalcon had reached his eyrie on a crag of rock facing northward to the sea and had fed the longspur to his nestlings, the first sanderling chick had emerged from its shell and two more of the eggs were cracked.

Now for the first time an abiding fear entered the heart of Silverbar—the fear of all wild things for the safety of their helpless young. With quickened senses she perceived the life of the tundra—with ears sharpened to hear the screams of the jaegers harrying the shore birds on the tide flats—with eyes quickened to note the white flicker of a gyrfalcon's wing.

After the fourth chick had hatched, Silverbar began to carry the shells, piece by piece, away from the nest. So countless generations of sanderlings had done before her, by their cunning outwitting the ravens and foxes. Not even the sharp-eyed falcon from his rock perch nor the jaegers watching for lemmings to come out of their holes saw the movement of the little brown-mottled bird as she worked her way, with infinite stealth, among the clumps of betony or pressed her body closely to the wiry tundra grass. Only the eyes of the lemmings who ran in and out among the sedges or sunned themselves on flat rocks near their burrows saw the mother sanderling until she reached the bottom of the ravine on the far side of the ridge. But the lemmings were gentle creatures who neither feared nor were feared by the sanderling.

All through the brief night that followed the hatching of the fourth chick Silverbar worked, and when the sun had come around to the east again she was hiding the last shell in the gravel of the ravine. A polar fox passed near her, making no sound as he trotted with sure foot over the shales. His eye gleamed as he watched the mother bird, and he sniffed the air, believing she had young near by. Silverbar flew to the willows farther up the ravine and watched the fox uncover the shells and nose them. As he started up the slope of the ravine the sanderling fluttered toward him, tumbling to the ground as though hurt, flapping her wings, creeping over the gravel. All the while she uttered a high-pitched note like the cry of her own young. The fox rushed at her. Silverbar rose rapidly into the air and flew over the crest of the ridge, only to reappear from another quarter, tantalizing the fox into following her. So by degrees she led him over the ridge and southward into a marshy bottom fed by the overflow of upland streams.

As the fox trotted up the slope, the cock phalarope on the nest heard a low *Plip! Plip! Chiss-ick! Chiss-ick!* from the hen, who was on guard near by and had seen the fox coming up the slope. The cock crept silently from the nest, through the grassy tunnels he had fashioned as runways of escape, until he came to the waterside where his mate was awaiting him. The two birds sailed into the middle of the pool and swam anxiously in circles, preening their feathers, jabbing long bills into the water in a pretense of feeding until the air came clean again, untainted by the musky smell of fox. The cock's breast showed a worn spot where the feathers had frayed away, for the phalarope chicks were soon to hatch.

When Silverbar had led the fox far enough from her young she circled around by the bay flats, pausing to feed nervously for a few minutes at the edge of the salty tide. Then she flew swiftly to the betony clump and the four chicks on which the down was yet dark with the dampness of the egg, although soon it would dry to tones of buff and sand and chestnut.

Now the sanderling mother knew by instinct that the depression in the tundra, lined with dry leaves and lichens and molded to the shape of her breast, was no longer a safe place for her young. The gleaming eyes of the fox—the soft pad, pad of his feet on the shales—the twitch of his nostrils testing the air for scent of her chicks—became for her the symbols of a thousand dangers, formless and without name.

When the sun had rolled so low on the horizon that only the high cliff with the eyrie of the gyrfalcon caught and reflected its gleam, Silverbar led the four chicks away into the vast grayness of the tundra.

Throughout the long days the sanderling with her chicks wandered over the stony plains, gathering the young ones under her during the short chill nights or when sudden gusts of rain drove across the barrens. She led them by the shores of brimming fresh-water lakes into which loons dropped on whistling wings to feed their young. Strange new food was to be found on the shores of the lakes and in the swelling turbulence of feeder streams. The young sanderlings learned to catch insects or to find their larvae in the streams. They learned, too, to press themselves flat against the ground when they heard their mother's danger cry and to lie quite still among the stones until her signal brought them crowding about her with fine, high-pitched squeakings. So they escaped the jaegers, the owls, and the foxes.

By the seventh day after hatching, the chicks had quill feathers a third grown on their wings, although their bodies were still covered with down. After four more suns the wings and shoulders were fully clothed in feathers, and when they were two weeks old the fledgling sanderlings could fly with their mother from lake to lake.

Now the sun dipped farther below the horizon; the grayness of the nights deepened; the hours of twilight lengthened. The rains that came more often and lashed with sharper violence were matched by a gentler rain as the flowers of the tundra dropped their petals. The foodstuffs—the starches and the fats—had been stored away in the seeds to nourish the precious embryos, into which had passed the immortal substance of the parent plants. The summer's work was done. No more need of bright petals to lure the pollen-carrying bees; so cast them off.

No more need of leaves spread to catch the sunshine and harness it to chlorophyll and air and water. Let the green pigments fade. Put on the reds and yellows, then let the leaves fall, too, and the stalks wither away. Summer is dying.

Soon the first white hairs appeared in the coats of the weasels, and the hair of the caribou began to lengthen. Many of the cock sanderlings, who had been gathering in flocks about the fresh-water lakes almost from the time the chicks had begun to hatch, had already left for the south. Among them was Blackfoot. On the mud flats of the bay young sandpipers gathered by the thousand and in the new-found joy of flight their flocks soared and swooped over a calm sea. The knots had brought their young down from the hills to the seacoast, and day by day more of the adults were leaving. On the pool near the place where Silverbar had brooded her eggs, a family of three young phalaropes now spun with lobed feet and jabbed for insects along the shore. The cock and the hen phalarope were already hundreds of miles to the east, setting a course southward over open ocean.

There came a day in August when Silverbar, who had been feeding with her grown young on the shores of the bay in company with other sanderlings, suddenly rose into the air with some twoscore of the older birds. The little flock wheeled out over the bay in a wide circle, flashing white wing bars; they returned, crying loudly as they passed over the flats where the young were still running and probing at the edge of the curling wavelets; they turned their heads to the south and were gone.

There was no need for the parent birds to remain longer in the Arctic. The nesting was done; the eggs had been faithfully brooded; the young had been taught to find food, to hide from enemies, to know the rules of the game of life and death. Later, when they were strong for the journey down the coast lines of two continents, the young birds would follow, finding the way by inherited memory. Meanwhile the older sanderlings felt the call of the warm south; they would follow the sun.

That evening about sunset Silverbar's four young, now wandering with a score of other fledgling sanderlings, came to an inland plain cut off from the sea by a coastwise ridge and rimmed to the south by higher hills. The floor of the plain was grassy and patched in many places with the softer, intense green of marsh. The sanderlings came into the plain along a meandering stream and settled on its banks for the night.

To the sanderlings' ears all the plain was alive with a kind of rustling—a soft murmur—a persistent stirring. It was like the sound of the wind when it moves through pine trees; but on the great barrens there are no trees. It was like the soft spilling of a stream over its bed, water striking stone, pebble rubbing against pebble. But tonight the stream was locked beneath the first thin ice of the summer's end.

The sound was the stirring of many wings, the passage of many feathered bodies through the low vegetation of the plain, the murmur of myriad bird voices. The flocks of the golden plover were gathering. From the wide beaches of the sea, from the shores of the bay shaped like a leaping porpoise, from all the tundras and uplands for miles around, the black-bellied birds with the golden-speckled backs were assembling on the plain.

The plovers were in a state of excitement that mounted as evening shadows cloaked the tundra and darkness spread over the Arctic world, save for a fiery glow on the horizon, as though the wind stirred the ashes of the sun's fires. The sound of the bird voices, constantly augmented by new arrivals and increasing in volume as the mass excitement grew, swept over the plain like a wind. Above the general murmur there arose at intervals the high, quavering cries of the leaders of the flock.

About midnight the flight began. The first flock of some threescore birds rose into the air, circled over the plain, and straightening out into flight formation headed south and east. Another and another flock found its wings and hurtled after the leaders, flying low over the tundra that rolled like a deep purple sea beneath them. There was strength and grace and beauty in every stroke of the pointed wings; there was power without end for the journey.

Que-e-e-e-ah! Que-e-e-e-ah!

High-pitched and quavering, the calls of the migrants came down clear from the sky.

Que-e-e-e-ah! Que-e-e-e-ah!

Every bird of the tundra heard the call and stirred in vague unrest at its urgency.

Among those who heard there must have been the young plovers, the birds of the year, scattered in little wandering groups over the tundra. But none among them joined the flight of the older birds. Not until weeks later, alone and with none to guide them, would they undertake the journey.

From the end of the first hour onward the flight was no longer divided into flocks but became continuous. Now a mighty river of birds poured through the sky, lengthening as it flowed south and east across the barrens, across the head of the northland bay, and on and on through skies that lightened to the coming of another day.

People said of it that it was the greatest golden plover flight of many years. Father Nicollet, the old priest in his mission on the west shore of Hudson Bay, declared it reminded him of the great flights he had seen in his youth, before the gunners had thinned the plover flocks to a remnant of their former size. Eskimos and trappers and traders along the Bay raised their eyes to the morning sky to watch the last of the flight crossing the Bay and fading into the east.

Somewhere in the mists beyond them lay the rocky shores of Labrador, carpeted with the bushes of the crowberry hung with purple fruit; beyond lay the tide flats of Nova Scotia. From Labrador to Nova Scotia the birds would slowly work their way, feeding on the ripening crowberries, on beetles and caterpillars and shellfish, growing fat and storing away energy to be burned by active muscles.

But soon there would come a day when again the flocks would spring into the air, this time to head southward into the misty horizon where sky met sea. Southward they would lay their course across more than two thousand miles of ocean from Nova Scotia to South America. They would be seen by men in boats far at sea, flying a swift, straight course low to the water, like those who know their destination and suffer nothing to deter them.

Some, perhaps, would fall by the way. Some, old or sick, would drop out of the caravan and creep away into a solitary place to die; others would be picked off by gunners, defying the law for the fancied pleasure of stopping in full flight a brave and fiercely burning life; still others, perhaps, would fall in exhaustion into the sea. But no awareness of possible failure or disaster dwelt in the moving host, flying with sweet pipings through the northern sky. In them burned once more the fever of migration, consuming with its fires all other desires and passions.

4
Summer's End

It was September before the sanderlings, now in whitening plumage, ran again on the island beach or hunted Hippa crabs in the ebbing tide at the point of land called Ship's Shoal. Their flight from the northern tundras had been broken by many feeding stops on the wide mud flats of Hudson Bay and James Bay and on the ocean beaches from New England southward. In their fall migration the birds were unhurried, the racial urge that drove them northward in the spring having been satisfied. As the winds and the sun dictated, they drifted southward, their flocks now growing as more birds from the north joined them, now dwindling as more and more of the migrants found their customary winter home and dropped behind. Only the fringe of the great southward wave of shore birds would push on and on to the southernmost part of South America.

As the cries of the returning shore birds rose once more from the frothy edge of the surf and the whistle of the curlews sounded again in the salt marshes, there were other signs of the summer's end. By September the eels of the sound country had begun to drop downstream to the sea. The eels came down from the hills and the upland grasslands. They came from cypress swamps where black-watered rivers had their beginnings; they moved across the tidal plain that dropped in six giant steps to the sea. In the river estuaries and in the sounds they joined their mates-to-be. Soon, in silvery wedding dress, they would follow the ebbing tides to the sea, to find—and lose—themselves in the black abysses of mid-ocean.

By September, the young shad, come from the eggs shed in river and stream by the spawning runs of spring, were moving with the river water to the sea. At first they moved slowly in the vaster currents as the sluggish rivers broadened toward their estuaries. Soon, however, the speed of the little fish, no longer than a man's finger, would quicken, when the fall rains came and the wind changed, chilling the water and driving the fish to the warmer sea.

By September the last of the season's hatch of young shrimp were coming into the sounds through the inlets from the open sea. The coming of the young was symbolic of another journey which no man had seen and no man could describe —a journey taken weeks before by the elder generation of shrimp. All through the spring and summer more and more of the grown shrimp, come to maturity at the age of a year, had been slipping away from the coastal waters, journeying out across the continental shelf, descending the blue slopes of undersea valleys. From this journey they never returned, but their young, after several weeks of ocean life, were brought by the sea into the protected inside waters. All through the summer and fall the baby shrimp were brought into the sounds and river mouths—seeking warm shallows where brackish water lay over muddy bottoms. Here they fed eagerly on the abundant food and found shelter from hungry fish in the carpeting eel grass. And as they grew rapidly, the young turned once more to the sea, seeking its bitter waters and its deeper rhythms. Even as the youngest shrimp from the last spawning of the season came through the inlets on each flood tide of September, the larger young were moving out through the sounds to the sea.

By September the panicles of the sea oats in the dunes had turned a golden brown. As the marshes lay under the sun, they glowed with the soft greens and browns of the salt meadow grass, the warm purples of the rushes, and the scarlet of the marsh samphire. Already the gum trees were like red flares set in the swamps of the river banks. The tang of autumn was in the night air, and as it rolled over the warmer marshes it turned to mist, hiding the herons who stood among the grasses at dawn; hiding from the eyes of the hawks the meadow mice who ran along the paths they had made through the marshes by the patient felling of thousands of marsh-grass stems; hiding the schools of silversides in the sound from the terns who fluttered above the rolling white sea, and caught no fish until the sun had cleared away the mists.

The chill night air brought a restlessness to many fish scattered widely throughout the sound. They were steely gray fish with large scales and a low, four-spined fin set on the back like a spread sail. The fish were mullet who had lived throughout the summer in the sound and estuary, roving solitary among the eel grass and widgeon grass, feeding on the litter of animal and vegetable fragments of the bottom mud. But every fall the mullet left the sounds and made a far sea journey, in the course of which they brought forth the next generation. And so the first chill of fall stirred in the fish the feeling of the sea's rhythm and awakened the instinct of migration.

The chilling waters and the tidal cycles of the summer's end brought to many of the young fish of the sound country, also, a summons to return to the sea. Among these were the young pompano and mullet, silversides and killifish, who lived in the pond called Mullet Pond, where the dunes of the barrier island fell away to the flat sands of the Ship's Shoal. These young fish had been spawned in the sea, but had found their way to the pond through a temporary cut earlier that year.

On a day when the full harvest moon sailed like a white balloon in the sky, the tides, which had grown in strength as the moon swelled to roundness, began to wash out a gully across the inlet beach. Only on the highest tides did the torpid pond receive water from the ocean. Now the beat of the waves and the strong backwash that sucked away the loose sand had found the weak place in the beach, where a cut had been made before, and in less time than it took a fishing launch to cross from the mainland docks to the banks a narrow gully or slough had been cut through to the pond. Not more than a dozen feet across, it made a bottleneck into which the surf rolled as the waves broke on the beach. The water surged and seethed as in a mill race, hissing and foaming. Wave after wave poured through the slough and into the pond. They dug out an uneven, corrugated bottom over which the water leaped and tobogganed. They spread out into the marshes that backed the pond, seeping silently and stealthily among the grass stems and the reddening stalks of the marsh samphire. Into the marshes they carried the frothy brown scud thrown off by the waves. The sandy foam filled the spaces between the grass stalks so closely that the marsh looked like a beach thickly grown with short grass; in reality the grass stood a foot in water and only the upper third of the stalks showed above the froth.

Leaping and racing, foaming and swirling, the incoming flood brought release to the myriads of small fishes that had been imprisoned in the pond. Now in thousands they poured out of the pond and out of the marshes. They raced in mad confusion to meet the clean, cold water. In their excitement they let the flood take them, toss them, turn them over and over. Reaching mid-channel of the slough they leaped high in the air again and again, sparkling bits of animate silver, like a swarm of glittering insects that rose and fell, rose again and fell. There the water seized them and held them back in their wild dash to the sea, so that many of them were caught on the slopes of the waves and held, tails uppermost, struggling helplessly against the might of the water. When finally the waves released them they raced down the slough to the ocean, where they knew once more the rolling breakers, the clean sandy bottoms, the cool green waters.

How did the pond and the marshes hold them all? On they came, in school after school, flashing bright among the marsh grasses, leaping and bounding out of the pond. For more than an hour the exodus continued, with scarcely a break in the hurrying schools. Perhaps they had come in, many of them, on the last spring tide when the moon was a pencil stroke of silver in the sky. And now the moon had grown fat and round and another spring tide, a rollicking, roistering, rough-and-ready tide, called them back to the sea again.

On they went, passing through the surf line where the white-capped waves were tumbling. On they went, most of them, past the smoother green swells to the second line of surf, where shoals tripped the waves coming in from the open sea and sent them sprawling in white confusion. But there were terns fishing above the surf, and thousands of the small migrants went no farther than the portals of the sea.

Now there came days when the sky was gray as a mullet's back, with clouds like the flung spray of waves. The wind, that throughout most of the summer had blown from the southwest, began to veer toward the north. On such mornings large mullet could be seen jumping in the estuary and over the shoals of the sound. On the ocean beaches fishermen's boats were drawn up on the sand. Gray piles of netting lay in the boats. Men stood on the beach, with eyes on the water, patiently waiting. The fishermen knew that mullet were gathering in schools throughout the sound because of the change in the weather. They knew that soon the schools would run out through the inlet before the wind and then would pass down along the coast, keeping, as the fishermen had told it from one generation to the next, "their right eyes to the beach." Other mullet would come down from the sounds that lay to the north and still others would come by the outside passage, following down along the chain of barrier islands. So the fishermen waited, confident in their generations of tested lore; and the boats waited with the nets that were empty of fish.

Other fishers besides the men awaited the runs of mullet. Among them was Pandion, the fish hawk, whom the mullet fishermen watched every day as he floated, a small dark cloud, in wide circles in the sky. To pass the hours as they stood watch on the sound beach or among the dunes, the fishermen wagered among themselves when the osprey would dive.

Pandion had a nest in a clump of loblolly pines on the shore of the river three miles away. There he and his mate had hatched and reared a brood of three young that season. At first the young had been clothed in down that was the color of old, decaying tree stumps; now they had grown their pinions and had gone away to fish for themselves, but Pandion and his mate, who had been faithful to each other throughout life, continued to live in the nest which they had used year after year.

The nest was six feet across at its base and more than half as wide at the top. Its bulk would have overflowed any of the farm carts that were drawn by mules along the dirt roads of the sound country. The two ospreys had repaired the nest and added to it during the years anything they could find washed up on the beaches by the tides. Now practically the whole top of a forty-foot pine served as support for the nest, and the great weight of sticks, branches, and pieces of sod had killed all but a few of the lower branches. In the course of years the ospreys had woven or worked into the nest a twenty-foot piece of haul seine with ropes attached that they had picked up on the shore of the sound, perhaps a dozen cork floats from fishing gear, many cockle and oyster shells, part of the skeleton of an eagle, parchmentlike strings of the egg cases of conchs, a broken oar, part of a fisherman's boot, tangled mats of seaweed.

In the lower layers of the huge, decaying mass many small birds had found nesting places. That summer there had been three families of sparrows, four of starlings, and one of the Carolina wren. In the spring an owl had taken up quarters in the osprey nest, and once there had been a green heron. All these lodgers Pandion had suffered good-naturedly.

After the third day of grayness and chill, the sun broke through the clouds. Watched by the mullet fishermen, Pandion sailed on set wings, riding the mounting columns of warm air that shimmered upward from the water. Far below him the water was like green silk rippling in a breeze. The terns and skimmers resting on the shoals of the sound were the size of robins. The black, glistening backs of a school of dolphins, diving and rolling, moved, a dark serpent, over the face of the sound. The amber eyes of Pandion flickered as a whipper ray leaped three times from the water, coming down with a sharp spat that was carried away on the wind and lost.

A shadow took form on the green screen beneath the osprey and the surface dimpled as a fish nosed at the film. In the sound two hundred feet below the fish hawk, Mugil, the mullet—the leaper—gathered his strength and flung himself in exhilaration into the air. As he was flexing his muscles for the third leap a dark form fell out of the sky and viselike talons seized him. The mullet weighed more than a pound, but Pandion carried him easily in his taloned feet, bearing the fish across the sound and to the nest three miles away.

Flying up the river from the estuary the osprey carried the mullet head first in his talons. As he neared the nest he relaxed his grip with the left foot and, checking flight, alighted on the outer branches of the nest with the fish still gripped in his right foot. Pandion lingered over his meal of fish for more than an hour, and when his mate came near he crouched low over the mullet and hissed at her. Now that the nesting was done, every bird must fish for itself.

Later in the day, as he returned down the river to fish, Pandion swooped low to the water and for the space of a dozen wing beats dragged his feet in the river, cleansing them of the adhering fish slime.

On his return Pandion was watched by the sharp eyes of a large brown bird perched in one of the pines on the west bank of the river, overlooking the marshes of the estuary. White Tip, the bald eagle, lived as a pirate, never fishing for himself when he could steal from the ospreys of the surrounding country. When Pandion moved out over the sound the eagle followed, mounting into the air and taking up a position far above the fish hawk.

For an hour two dark forms circled in the sky. Then from his high station White Tip saw the body of the osprey suddenly dwindle to sparrow size as he fell in a straight drop, saw the white spray mount from the water as the fish hawk disappeared. After the passing of thirty seconds Pandion emerged from the water, mounting straight for fifty feet with short, heavy wing beats and then leveling out into straight flight toward the river's mouth.

Watching him, White Tip knew that the osprey had caught a fish and was taking it home to the nest in the pines. With a shrill scream that fell down through the sky to the ears of the osprey, the eagle whirled in pursuit, keeping his elevation of a thousand feet above the fish hawk.

Pandion cried out in annoyance and alarm, redoubling the force of his wing beats in an effort to reach the cover of the pines before his tormentor should attack. The speed of the hawk was retarded by the weight of the catfish that he carried and by the convulsive struggles of the fish, held firmly in the strong talons.

Between the island and the mainland and several minutes' flight from the mouth of the river the eagle gained a position directly over the hawk. On half-closed wings he dropped with terrific speed. The wind whined through his feathers. As he passed the osprey he whirled in air, back to the water, presenting his talons to the attack. Pandion dodged and twisted, eluding the eight curved scimitars. Before White Tip could recover himself Pandion had shot aloft two hundred, five hundred feet. The eagle hurtled after him, mounted above him. But even as he began the stoop, the fish hawk, in another upward soaring, surmounted the position of his enemy.

Meanwhile the fish, drained of life by separation from the water, grew limp as all its struggles ceased. Like a mist gathering on a clear glass surface, a film clouded its eyes. Soon the iridescent greens and golds that made its body, in life, a thing of beauty had faded to dullness.

By turns rising and swooping, hawk and eagle rose to a great height, into the empty places of the air, of which the sound and its shoals and white sands had no part.

Cheep! Cheep! Chezeek! Chezeek! screamed Pandion in a frenzy of excitement.

A dozen white feathers, ripped from his breast as he barely evaded White Tip's talons on the last stoop, fluttered earthward. Of a sudden the osprey bent his wings sharply and dropped like a stone toward the water. The wind roared in his ears, half blinded him, plucked at his feathers as the sound rushed up to meet him. It was his final effort to outwit a stronger and more enduring enemy. But from above, the relentless dark form fell even faster than Pandion, gained on him, passed him as the fishing boats on the sound grew big as gulls afloat, whirled and tore the fish from his grasp.

The eagle carried the fish to his pine-tree perch to rend it, muscle from bone. By the time he reached the perch Pandion was beating out heavily over the inlet to new fishing grounds at sea.

5
Winds Blowing Seaward

THE NEXT MORNING the north wind was tearing the crests off the waves as they came over the inlet bar, so that each was trailing a heavy smoke of spray. Mullet were jumping in the channel, excited by the change in the wind. In the shallow river estuary and over the many shoals of the sound, the fish sensed the sudden chill that passed to the water from the air moving over it. The mullet began to seek the deeper waters which held the stored warmth of the sun. Now from all parts of the sound they were assembling in large schools that moved toward the channels of the sound. The channels led to the inlet, and the inlet was the gateway to the open sea.

The wind blew from the north. It blew down the river, and the fish moved before it to the estuary. It blew across the sound to the inlet, and the fish ran before it to the sea.

The ebbing tide carried the mullet through the deeper green glooms and over the white sandy bottom of the channel, scoured clean of living things by the strong currents that raced through it each day, twice running seaward, twice landward. Above them, as they moved, the surface of the water was broken into a thousand glittering facets that shone with the sun's gold. One after another the mullet rose to the shimmering ceiling of the sound. One after another they flexed their bodies in a quickening rhythm, gathering their strength and leaping into the air.

Going out with the tide the mullet passed a long, narrow sandspit called Herring Gull Shoal, where a wall of massive stone was built along the channel to prevent the washing in of the loose sand. Green, turgid fronds of seaweed were anchored by their holdfasts to the stones, which were crusted whitely with barnacles and oysters. From the shadow of one of the stones of the breakwater a pair of small, malignant eyes watched the mullet as they passed seaward. The eyes belonged to the fifteen-pound conger eel who lived among the rocks. The thick-bodied conger preyed on the schools of fish that roved down along the dark wall of the breakwater, hurling itself out of its gloomy cavern to seize them in its jaws.

In the upper layer of water, a dozen feet above the swimming mullet, schools of silversides quivered in formation, each fishlet a gleaming mote reflecting the sunlight. From time to time scores of them leaped out of the water, bursting through the surface film of the fish's world and falling back again like raindrops—first denting, then piercing the tough skin between air and water.

Past a dozen sandspits of the sound, each with its little colony of resting gulls, the tide took the mullet. On an old shell rock which the sea was in process of turning into an island by dropping silt and sand among the shells and by bringing, on its ebb tides, the seeds of marsh grasses to bind the soil, two gulls were hunting busily for sunray clams, which lay half buried in the wet sand. Finding them, the gulls chipped away at the heavy, vitreous shells, rayed with bands of fawn color and lilac. After much work with their strong bills the gulls were able to crack the shells and eat the soft clam bodies within.

On the mullet went, past the big inlet buoy that was leaning toward the sea with the press of the tide. Its iron bulk rose and fell with the water, even as the music of its iron throat changed pitch and tempo with the changing rhythms of the sea. The inlet buoy was a cosmos unto itself, rolling in the waters of the sound. Ebb tide and flood tide were of its own making, coming alternately as the buoy lifted to the passing of a wave and rolled in its trough.

The buoy had not been taken in for scraping and repainting since the previous spring, and it was thickly crusted with the shells of barnacles and mussels and with saclike sea squirts and the soft moss patches of the bryozoa. Deposits of sand and silt and green threads of algae had lodged in the many crevices between the shells and among the rootlike attachments of the dense mat of animals. Over and among this thick, living growth, slender-bodied animals called amphipods, in jointed armor, clambered in and out in endless search of food; starfish crept over the oysters and mussels and preyed upon them, gripping the shells with the sucking discs of their strong arms and forcing them open. Among the shells the flowerlets of the sea anemones opened and closed, spreading fleshy tentacles to seize food from the water. Most of the twenty or more kinds of sea animals that lived on the buoy had come to it months before, during the season when the waters of the sound and inlet swarmed with larvae. Many of these myriad beings, as transparent as glass and more fragile, were doomed to die in infancy unless they found a solid place of attachment. Those that chanced upon the great bulk of the buoy in the sound attached themselves by cementing fluids from their own bodies or by byssus thread or holdfast. There they would remain throughout life, a part of the swaying world, rolling in watery space.

Within the inlet the channel widened and the pale-green water grew murky with the wave scourings of loose sand. On the mullet went. The mutter and rumble of the surf grew. With their sensitive flanks the fish perceived the heavy jar and thud of sea vibrations. The changing pulse of the sea was caused by the long inlet bar, where the water foamed to a white froth as the waves spilled over it. Now the mullet passed out through the channel and felt the longer rhythms of the sea—the rise, the sudden lift and fall of waves come from the deep Atlantic. Just outside the first surf line the mullet leaped in these larger swells of ocean. One after another swam upward to the surface and jumped into the air, falling back with a white splash to resume its place in the moving school.

The lookout who stood on a high dune above the inlet saw the first of the mullet running out of the sound. With practiced eye, he estimated the size and speed of the school from the spurts of spray when the mullet jumped. Although three boats with their crews were waiting farther down the ocean beach, he gave no signal at the passing of the first mullet. The tide was still on the ebb; the pull of the water was seaward and the nets could not be drawn against it.

The dunes are a place of high winds and driven sand, of salt spray and sun. Now the wind is from the north. In the hollows of the dunes the beach grasses lean in the wind and with their pointed tips write endless circles in the sand. From the barrier beach the wind is picking up the loose sand and carrying it seaward in a haze of white. From a distance the air above the banks looks murky, as though a light mist is rising from the ground.

The fishermen on the banks do not see the sand haze; they feel its sting in eyes and face; they feel it as it sifts into their hair and through their clothing. They take out their handkerchiefs and tie them across their faces, and they pull long-visored caps low on their heads. A wind from the north means sand in your face and rough seas under your boat keel, but it means mullet, too.

The sun is hot as it beats down on the men standing on the beach. Some of the women and children are there, too, to help their men with the ropes. The children are bare-footed, wading in the pools left in the scoured-out depressions of the beach, ribbed with sand waves.

The tide has turned, and now one of the boats is shot out between the breakers to be ready for the fish when they come. It's not easy, launching a boat in this surf. The men leap to their places like parts of a machine. The boat rights itself, wallows into the green swells. Just outside the surf line the men wait at the oars. The captain stands in the bow, arms folded, leg muscles flexing to the rise and fall of the boat, his eyes on the water, looking toward the inlet.

Somewhere in that green water there are fish—hundreds of fish—thousands of fish. Soon they will come within reach of the nets. The north wind's blowing, and the mullet are running before it out of the sound, running down along the coast, as mullet have done for thousands upon thousands of years.

Half a dozen gulls are mewing above the water. That means the mullet are coming. The gulls don't want the mullet; they want the minnows that are milling about in alarm as the larger fish move through the shallows. The mullet are coming down just outside the breakers, traveling about as fast as a man could walk on the beach. The lookout has marked the school. He walks toward the boat, keeping opposite the fish, signaling their course to the crew by waving his arms.

The men brace their feet against the thwarts of the boat and strain to the oars, pulling the boat in a wide semicircle to the shore. The net of heavy twine spills silently and steadily into the water over the stern and cork floats bob in the water in the wake of the boat. Ropes from one end of the net are held by half a dozen men on shore.

There are mullet in the water all around the boat. They cut the surface with their back fins; they leap and fall. The men lean harder to the oars, pulling for the shore to close the net before the school can escape. Once in the last line of surf and in water not more than waist-deep, the men jump into the water. The boat is seized by willing hands and is dragged out on the beach.

The shallow water in which the mullet are swimming is a pale, translucent green, murky with the loose sand which the waves are stirring up. The mullet are excited by their return to the sea with its bitter salt waters. Under the powerful drive of instinct they move together in the first lap of a journey that will take them far from the coastal shallows, into the blue haze of the sea's beginnings.

A shadow looms in the green, sun-filled water in the path of the mullet. From a dim, gray curtain the shadow resolves itself into a web of slender, crisscross bars. The first of the mullet strike the net, back water with their fins, hesitate. Other fish are crowding up from behind, nosing at the net. As the first waves of panic pass from fish to fish they dash shoreward, seeking a way of escape. The ropes held by fishermen on the shore have been drawn in so that the netting wall extends into water too shallow for a fish to swim. They run seaward, but meet the circle of the net that is growing smaller, foot by foot, as the men on shore and in water up to their knees brace themselves in the sliding sand and pull on the ropes—pull against the weight of water—against the strength of the fish.

As the net is closed and gradually drawn in to shore, the press of fish in the seine becomes greater. Milling in frantic efforts to find a way of escape, the mullet drive with all their combined strength of thousands of pounds against the seaward arc of the net. Their weight and the outward thrust of their bodies lift the net clear of the bottom, and the mullet scrape bellies on the sand as they slip under the net and race into deep water. The fishermen, sensitive to every movement of the net, feel the lift and know they are losing fish. They strain the harder, till muscles crack and backs ache. Half a dozen men plunge out into water chin-deep, fighting the surf to tread the lead line and hold the net on the bottom. But the outer circle of cork floats is still half a dozen boat lengths away.

Of a sudden the whole school surges upward. In a turmoil of flying spray and splashing water mullet by the hundred leap over the cork line. They pelt against the fishermen, who turn their backs to the fish raining about them. The men strive desperately to lift the cork line above the water so that the fish will fall back into the circle when they strike the net.

Two piles of slack netting are growing on the beach, the heads of many small fishes no longer than a man's hand caught in the meshes. Now the ropes attached to the lead lines are drawn in faster and the net takes on the shape of a huge, elongated bag, bulging with fish. As the bag is drawn at last into the shallow fringe of the surf the air crackles with a sound like the clapping of hands as a thousand head of mullet, with all the fury of their last strength, flap on the wet sand.

The fishermen work quickly to take the mullet from the net and toss them into the waiting boats. By a dexterous shake of the net, they toss on the beach the small fish that are gilled in the seine. There are young sea trout and pompano, mullet of the last year's spawning, young ceros and sheepshead and sea bass.

Soon the bodies of the young fish—too small to sell, too small to eat—litter the beach above the water line, the life oozing from them for want of means to cross a few yards of dry sand and return to the sea. Some of the small bodies the sea would take away later; others it would lay up carefully beyond reach of the tides among the litter of sticks and seaweeds, of shells and sea-oats stubble. Thus the sea unfailingly provides for the hunters of the tide lines.

After the fishermen had made two more hauls and then, as the tide neared the full, had gone away with laden boats, a flock of gulls came in from the outer shoals, white against the graying sea, and feasted on the fish. As the gulls bickered among themselves over the food, two smaller birds in sleek, black plumage walked warily among them, dragging fish up on the higher beach to devour them. They were fish crows, who took their living from the edge of the water, where they found dead crabs and shrimps and other sea refuse. After sundown the ghost crabs would come in legions out of their holes to swarm over the tide litter, clearing away the last traces of the fish. Already the sand hoppers had gathered and were busy at their work of reclaiming to life in their own beings the materials of the fishes' bodies. For in the sea, nothing is lost. One dies, another lives, as the precious elements of life are passed on and on in endless chains.

All through the night, as the lights in the fishing village went out one by one and fishermen gathered around their stoves because of the chill north wind, mullet were passing unmolested through the inlet and running westward and southward along the coast, through black water on which the wave crests were like giant fish's wakes, silver in the light of the moon.

BOOK II
THE GULL'S WAY

6
Migrants of the Spring Sea

BETWEEN THE CHESAPEAKE Capes and the elbow of Cape Cod the place where the continent ends and the true sea begins lies from fifty to one hundred miles from the tide lines. It is not the distance from shore, but the depth, that marks the transition to the true sea; for wherever the gently sloping sea bottom feels the weight of a hundred fathoms of water above it, suddenly it begins to fall away in escarpments and steep palisades, descending abruptly from twilight into darkness.

In the blue haze of the continent's edge the mackerel tribes lie in torpor during the four coldest months of winter, resting from the eight months of strenuous life in the upper waters. On the threshold of the deep sea they live on the fat stored up from a summer's rich feeding, and toward the end of their winter's sleep their bodies begin to grow heavy with spawn.

In the month of April the mackerel are roused from their sleep as they lie at the edge of the continental shelf, off the Capes of Virginia. Perhaps the currents that drift down to bathe the resting places of the mackerel stir in the fish some dim perception of the progress of the ocean's seasons—the old, unchanging cycle of the sea. For weeks now the cold, heavy surface water—the winter water—has been sinking, slipping under and displacing the warmer bottom water. The warm water is rising, carrying into the surface rich loads of phosphates and nitrates from the bottom. Spring sun and fertile water are wakening the dormant plants to a burst of activity, of growth and multiplication. Spring comes to the land with pale, green shoots and swelling buds; it brings to the sea a great increase in the number of simple, one-celled plants of microscopic size, the diatoms. Perhaps the currents bring down to the mackerel some awareness of the flourishing vegetation of the upper waters, of the rich pasturage for hordes of crustaceans that browse in the diatom meadows and in their turn fill the water with clouds of their goblin-headed young.

Soon fishes of many kinds will be moving through the spring sea, to feed on the teeming life of the surface and to bring forth their own young.

Perhaps, also, the currents moving over the place where the mackerel lie carry a message of the inpouring of fresh water as ice and snow dissolve in floods to rush down the coastal rivers to the sea, diminishing ever so slightly its bitter saltiness and attracting the spawn-laden fishes by the lesser density. But however the feeling of awakening spring comes to the dormant fishes, the mackerel stir in swift response. Their caravans begin to form and to move through the dim-lit water, and by thousands and hundreds of thousands they set out for the upper sea.

About a hundred miles beyond the place where the mackerel winter, the sea rises out of the deep, dark bed of the open Atlantic and begins its own climb up over the muddy sides of the continental slope. In utter blackness and stillness the sea climbs those hundred miles, rising from depths of a mile or more until black begins to fade to purple, and purple to deep blue, and blue to azure.

At one hundred fathoms the sea rolls over a sharp edge—the rim of the bowl formed by the foundations of the continent—and starts up the gentler acclivity of the continental shelf. Over the shelving edge of the continent, the sea contains for the first time roving herds of fishes that browse over the fertile undersea plains, for in the deep abyss there are only small, lean fishes hunting singly or in small bands for the sparse food. But here the fishes have rich pasturage—meadows of plantlike hydroids and moss animals, clams and cockles that lie passive in the sand; prawns and crabs that start up and dart away before the rooting snout of a fish, like a rabbit before a hound.

Now small, gasoline-engined fishing boats move over the sea and here and there the water pours through the meshes of miles of gill-net webbing suspended from floats or resists the drag of otter trawls over the sandy floor beneath. And now for the first time the gulls' white wings are patterned in numbers on the sky above, for the gulls—except the kittiwakes—hug the fringes of the sea, feeling uneasy on the open ocean.

As the sea comes in over the continental shelf it meets a series of shoals that run parallel to the coast. In the fifty to one hundred miles to tidewater the sea must hurdle each of these shoals or chains of shoals, climbing up the sides of the hills from the surrounding valleys to shelly plateaus a mile or so wide, then on the shoreward side descending again into the deeper shadows of another valley. The plateaus are more fertile than the valleys in the thousand-odd kinds of backboneless animals that fishes live on, and so more and larger fish herds browse on them. Often the water above the shoals is especially rich in the moving clouds of small plants and animals of many different kinds that drift with the currents or swim feebly about in search of food—the wanderers or plankton of the sea.

The mackerel do not follow the road over the hills and valleys of the sea's floor as they leave their wintering grounds and turn shoreward. Instead, as though in eagerness to reach at once the sun-lit upper water, they climb steeply the hundred-fathom ascent to the surface. After four months in the gloom of deep water the mackerel move in excitement through the bright waters of the surface layers. They thrust their snouts out of the water as they swim and behold once more the gray expanse of sea cupped in the paleness of arching sky.

Where the mackerel come to the surface there is no sign by which to distinguish the great sea out of which the sun rises from the lesser sea into which it sets; but without hesitation the schools turn from the deep-blue saline water of the open sea and move toward the coastal waters, paled to greenness by the fresh inpouring of the rivers and bays. The place they seek is a great, irregular patch of water that runs from south by west to north by east, from the Chesapeake Capes to southward of Nantucket. In some places it is only twenty miles from shore, in others fifty or more—the spawning grounds in which, from ancient times, the Atlantic mackerel have shed their eggs.

Throughout all the latter part of April mackerel are rising from off the Virginia Capes and hurrying shoreward. There is a stir of excitement in the sea as the spring migration begins. Some of the schools are small; some are as much as a mile wide and several miles long. By day the sea birds watch them rolling landward like dark clouds across the green of the sea; but at night they pour through the water like molten metal, as by their movements they disturb the myriad luminescent animals of the plankton.

The mackerel are voiceless and they make no sound; yet their passage creates a heavy disturbance in the water, so that schools of launce and anchovies must feel the vibrations of an approaching school a long way off and hurry in apprehension through the green distances of the sea; and it may be that the stir of their passage is felt on the shoals below—by the prawns and crabs that pick their way among the corals, by the starfish creeping over the rocks, by the sly hermit crabs, and by the pale flowers of the sea anemone.

As the mackerel hurry shoreward they swim in tier above tier. Throughout those weeks when the fish are rolling in from the open sea the scattered shoals between the edge of the continent and the shore are often darkened as the earth was once dimmed by the passing of another living cloud—the flights of the passenger pigeons.

In time the shoreward-running mackerel reach the inshore waters, where they ease their bodies of their burden of eggs and milt. They leave in their wake a cloud of transparent spheres of infinitesimal size, a vast, sprawling river of life, the sea's counterpart of the river of stars that flows through the sky as the Milky Way. There are known to be hundreds of millions of eggs to the square mile, billions in an area a fishing vessel could cruise over in an hour, hundreds of trillions in the whole spawning area.

After spawning, the mackerel turn toward the rich feeding grounds that lie to seaward of New England. Now the fish are bent only on reaching the waters they knew of old, where the small crustaceans called Calanus move in red clouds through the water. The sea will care for their young, as it cares for the young of all other fishes, and of oysters and crabs and starfish, of worms and jellyfish and barnacles.

7
Birth of a Mackerel

So it came about that Scomber, the mackerel, was born in the surface waters of the open sea, seventy miles south by east from the western tip of Long Island. He came into being as a tiny globule no larger than a poppy seed, drifting in the surface layers of pale-green water. The globule carried an amber droplet of oil that served to keep it afloat and it carried also a gray particle of living matter so small that it could have been picked up on the point of a needle. In time this particle was to become Scomber, the mackerel, a powerful fish, streamlined after the manner of his kind, and a rover of the seas.

The parents of Scomber were fish of the last big wave of mackerel migration that came in from the edge of the continental shelf in May, heavy with spawn and driving rapidly shoreward. On the fourth evening of their journey, in a flooding current straining to landward, the eggs and milt had begun to flow from their bodies into the sea. Somewhere among the forty or fifty thousand eggs that were shed by one of the female fish was the egg that was to become Scomber.

There could be scarcely a stranger place in the world in which to begin life than this universe of sky and water, peopled by strange creatures and governed by wind and sun and ocean currents. It was a place of silence, except when the wind went whispering or blustering over the vast sheet of water, or when sea gulls came down the wind with their high, wild mewing, or when whales broke the surface, expelled the long-held breath, and rolled again into the sea.

The mackerel schools hurried on into the north and east, their journey scarcely interrupted by the act of spawning. As the sea birds were finding their resting places for the night on the dark water plains, swarms of small and curiously formed animals stole into the surface waters from hills and valleys lying in darkness far below. The night sea belonged to the plankton, to the diminutive worms and the baby crabs, the glassy, big-eyed shrimp, the young barnacles and mussels, the throbbing bells of the jellyfish, and all the other small fry of the sea that shun the light.

It was indeed a strange world in which to set adrift anything so fragile as a mackerel egg. It was filled with small hunters, each of which must live at the expense of its neighbors, plant and animal. The eggs of the mackerel were jostled by the newly hatched young of earlier spawning fishes and of shellfish, crustaceans, and worms. The larvae, some of them only a few hours old, were swimming alone in the sea, busily seeking their food. Some snatched out of the water with pincered claws anything small enough to be overpowered and swallowed; others seized any prey less swift and agile than themselves in biting jaws or sucked into cilium-studded mouths the drifting green or golden cells of the diatoms.

The sea was filled, too, with larger hunters than the microscopic larvae. Within an hour after the parent mackerel had gone away, a horde of comb jellies rose to the surface of the sea. The comb jellies, or ctenophores, looked like large gooseberries, and they swam by the beating of plates of fused hairs or cilia, set in eight bands down the sides of the transparent bodies. Their substance was scarcely more than that of sea water, yet each of them ate many times its own bulk of solid food in a day. Now they were rising slowly toward the surface, where the millions of new-spawned mackerel eggs drifted free in the upper layers of the sea. They twirled slowly back and forth on the long axes of their bodies as they came, flashing a cold, phosphorescent fire. Throughout the night the ctenophores flicked the waters with their deadly tentacles, each a slim, elastic thread twenty times the length of the body when extended. And as they turned and twirled and flashed frosty green lights in the black water, jostling one another in their greed, the drifting mackerel eggs were swept up in the silken meshes of the tentacles and carried by swift contraction to the waiting mouths.

Often during this first night of Scomber's existence the cold, smooth body of a ctenophore collided with him or a searching tentacle missed by a fraction of an inch the floating sphere in which the speck of protoplasm had already divided into eight parts, thus beginning the development by which a single fertile cell would swiftly be transformed into an embryo fish.

BIRTH OF A MACKEREL

Of the millions of mackerel eggs drifting alongside the one that was to produce Scomber, thousands went no farther than the first stages of the journey into life until they were seized and eaten by the comb jellies, to be speedily converted into the watery tissue of their foe and in this reincarnation to roam the sea, preying on their own kind.

Throughout the night, while the sea lay under a windless sky, the decimation of the mackerel eggs continued. Shortly before dawn the water began to stir to a breeze from the east and in an hour was rolling heavily under a wind that blew steadily to the south and west. At the first ruffling of the surface calm the comb jellies began to sink into deep water. Even in these simple creatures, which consist of little more than two layers of cells, one inside the other, there exists the counterpart of an instinct of self-preservation, causing them in some way to sense the threat of destruction which rough water holds for so fragile a body.

In the first night of their existence more than ten out of every hundred mackerel eggs either had been eaten by the comb jellies or, from some inherent weakness, had died after the first few divisions of the cell.

Now, the rising up of a strong wind blowing to southward brought fresh dangers to the mackerel eggs, left for the time being with few enemies in the surface waters about them. The upper layers of the sea streamed in the direction urged upon them by the wind. The drifting spheres moved south and west with the current, for the eggs of all sea creatures are carried helplessly wherever the sea takes them. It happened that the southwest drift of the water was carrying the mackerel eggs away from the normal nursery grounds of their kind into waters where food for young fish was scarce and hungry predators abundant. As a result of this mischance fewer than one egg in every thousand was to complete its development.

On the second day, as the cells within the golden globules of the eggs multiplied by countless divisions, and the shield-like forms of embryo fish began to take shape above the yolk spheres, hordes of a new enemy came roving through the drifting plankton. The glassworms were transparent and slender creatures that cleaved the water like arrows, darting in all directions to seize fish eggs, copepods, and even others of their own kind. With their fierce heads and toothed jaws they were terrible as dragons to the smaller beings of the plankton, although as men measure they were less than a quarter of an inch long.

The floating mackerel eggs were scattered and buffeted by the dartings and rushes of the glassworms, and when the driftings of current and tide carried them away to other waters a heavy toll of the mackerel had been taken as food.

Again the egg that contained the embryonic Scomber had drifted unscathed while all about him other eggs had been seized and eaten. Under the warm May sun the new young cells of the egg were stirred to furious activity—growing, dividing, differentiating into cell layers and tissues and organs. After two nights and two days of life, the threadlike body of a fish was taking form within the egg, curled halfway around the globe of yolk that gave it food. Already a thin ridge down the midline showed where a stiffening rod of cartilage—forerunner of a backbone—was forming; a large bulge at the forward end showed the place of the head, and on it two smaller outpushings marked the future eyes of Scomber. On the third day a dozen V-shaped plates of muscle were marked out on either side of the backbone; the lobes of the brain showed through the still-transparent tissues of the head; the ear sacs appeared; the eyes neared completion and showed dark through the egg wall, peering sightlessly into the surrounding world of the sea. As the sky lightened preparatory to the fifth rising of the sun a thin-walled sac beneath the head—crimson tinted from the fluid it contained—quivered, throbbed, and began the steady pulsation that would continue as long as there was life within the body of Scomber.

Throughout that day development proceeded at a furious pace, as though in haste to make ready for the hatching that was soon to come. On the lengthening tail a thin flange of tissue appeared—the fin ridge from which a series of tail finlets, like a row of flags stiff in the wind, was later to be formed. The sides of an open groove that traversed the belly of the little fish, beneath and protected by the plate of more than seventy muscle segments, grew steadily downward and in midafternoon closed to form the alimentary canal. Above the pulsating heart the mouth cavity deepened, but it was still far short of reaching the canal.

Throughout all this time the surface currents of the sea were pouring steadily to the southwest, driven by the wind and carrying with them the clouds of plankton. During the six days since the spawning of the mackerel the toll of the ocean's predators had continued without abatement, so that already more than half of the eggs had been eaten or had died in development.

It was the nights that had seen the greatest destruction. They had been dark nights with the sea lying calm under a wide sky. On those nights the little stars of the plankton had rivaled in number and brilliance the constellations of the sky. From underlying depths the hordes of comb jellies and glassworms, copepods and shrimps, medusae of jellyfish, and translucent winged snails had risen into the upper layers to glitter in the dark water.

When the first dilution of blackness came in the east, warning of the dawn into which the revolving earth was carrying them, strange processions began to hurry down through the water as the animals of the plankton fled from the sun that had not yet risen. Only a few of these small creatures could endure the surface waters by day except when clouds deflected the fierce lances of the sun.

In time Scomber and the other baby mackerel would join the hurrying caravans that moved down into deep green water by day and pressed upward again as the earth swung once more into darkness. Now, while still confined within the egg, the embryonic mackerel had no power of independent motion, for the eggs remained in water of a density equal to their own and were carried horizontally in their own stratum of the sea.

On the sixth day the currents took the mackerel eggs over a large shoal thickly populated with crabs. It was the spawning season of the crabs—the time when the eggs, that had been carried throughout the winter by the females, burst their shells and released the small, goblinlike larvae. Without delay the crab larvae set out for the upper waters, where through successive moltings of their infant shells and transformations of appearance they would take on the form of their race. Only after a period of life in the plankton would they be admitted to the colony of crabs that lived on that pleasant undersea plateau.

Now they hastened upward, each newborn crab swimming steadily with its wandlike appendages, each ready to discern with large black eyes and to seize with sharp-beaked mouth such food as the sea might offer. For the rest of that day the crab larvae were carried along with the mackerel eggs, on which they fed heavily. In the evening the struggle of two currents—the tidal current and the wind-driven current—carried many of the crab larvae to landward while the mackerel eggs continued to the south.

There were many signs in the sea of the approach to more southern latitudes. The night before the appearance of the crab larvae the sea had been set aglitter over an area of many miles with the intense green lights of the southern comb jelly Mnemiopsis, whose ciliated combs gleam with the colors of the rainbow by day and sparkle like emeralds in the night sea. And now for the first time there throbbed in the warm surface waters the pale southern form of the jellyfish Cyanea, trailing its several hundred tentacles through the water for fish or whatever else it might entangle. For hours at a time the ocean seethed with great shoals of salpae—thimble-sized, transparent barrels hooped in strands of muscle.

On the sixth night after the spawning of the mackerel the tough little skins of the eggs began to burst. One by one the tiny fishlets, so small that the combined length of twenty of them, head to tail, would have been scarcely an inch, slipped out of the confining spheres and knew for the first time the touch of the sea. Among these hatching fish was Scomber.

He was obviously an unfinished little fish. It seemed almost that he had burst prematurely from the egg, so unready was he to care for himself. The gill slits were marked out but were not cut through to the throat, so were useless for breathing. His mouth was only a blind sac. Fortunately for the newly hatched fishlet, a supply of food remained in the yolk sac still attached to him, and on this he would live until his mouth was open and functioning. Because of the bulky sac, however, the baby mackerel drifted upside down in the water, helpless to control his movements.

The next three days of life brought startling transformations. As the processes of development forged onward, the mouth and gill structures were completed and the finlets sprouting from back and sides and underparts grew and found strength and certainty of movement. The eyes became deep blue with pigment, and now it may be that they sent to the tiny brain the first messages of things seen. Steadily the yolk mass shrank, and with its loss Scomber found it possible to right himself and by undulation of the still-rotund body and movement of the fins to swim through the water.

Of the steady drift, the southward pouring of the water day after day, he was unconscious, but the feeble strength of his fins was no match for the currents. He floated where the sea carried him, now a rightful member of the drifting community of the plankton.

8
Hunters of the Plankton

THE SPRING SEA was filled with hurrying fishes. Scup were migrating northward from their wintering grounds off the Capes of Virginia, bound for the coastal waters of southern New England where they would spawn. Shoals of young herring moved swiftly just under the surface, rippling the water no more than the passing of a breeze, and schools of menhaden, moving in closely packed formation with bodies flashing bronze and silver in the sun, appeared to the watching sea birds like dark clouds ruffling to a deep blue the smooth sheet of the sea. Mingled with the wandering menhaden and herring were late-running shad, following in along the sea lanes that led to the rivers of their birth, and across the silvery warp of this living fabric the last of the mackerel wove threads of flashing blue and green.

Now, above the water where these hurrying fishes jostled the new-hatched mackerel, there fluttered for the first time that season the little flocks of Oceanites, the petrel, come back to the sea from the far south. The birds moved lightly from place to place on the level plains or the gentle hills of the sea, settling down daintily over some surface-drifting bit of plankton, hovering like butterflies come to sip the nectar from a flower. The little petrels know nothing of the northern winter, for then, in the southern summer, they have gone home from the sea to the far South Atlantic and Antarctic islands where they rear their young.

Sometimes for hours on end the surface of the sea was white with spurting spray as the last of the spring flights of gannets, bound for the rocky ledges of the Gulf of St. Lawrence, plunged from high in the air, pursuing their fish prey far beneath the surface with strong strokes of wings and webbed feet. As the southward drift of the water continued, the gray forms of sharks appeared more often in pursuit of the menhaden schools; the backs of porpoises flashed in the sun; and old, barnacled sea turtles swam at the surface.

As yet Scomber knew little of the world in which he lived. His first food had been the minute, one-celled plants in the water which he drew into his mouth and strained through his gill rakers. Later he had learned to seize the flea-sized crustaceans of the plankton and to dart into their drifting clouds, snapping up the new food with quick snatches. Along with the other young mackerel he spent most of his days many fathoms below the surface and at night rose again to move through dark water that sparkled with the phosphorescent plankton. These movements were made involuntarily as the young fish followed his food, for as yet Scomber knew little of the difference between day and night or the sea's surface and its depths. But sometimes when he climbed with his fins he came into water that was a shining golden green, where moving forms burst upon his vision with swift and terrible vividness.

In the surface waters Scomber first knew the fear of the hunted. On the tenth morning of his life he had lingered in the upper fathoms of water instead of following down into the soft gloom below. Out of the clear green water a dozen gleaming silver fishes suddenly loomed up. They were anchovies, small and herringlike. The foremost anchovy caught sight of Scomber. Swerving from his path, he came whirling through the yard of water that separated them, open-mouthed, ready to seize the small mackerel. Scomber veered away in sudden alarm, but his powers of motion were new-found and he rolled clumsily in the water. In a fraction of a second he would have been seized and eaten, but a second anchovy, darting in from the opposite side, collided with the first and in the confusion Scomber dashed beneath them.

Now he found himself in the midst of the main school of several thousand anchovies. Their silver scales flashed on all sides of him. They bumped and jostled him as he sought in vain to escape. The shoal surged over and beneath and around Scomber, driving furiously onward just under the shining ceiling of the sea. None of the anchovies was now aware of the little mackerel, for the shoal itself was in full flight. A pack of young bluefish had picked up the scent of the anchovies and swung into swift pursuit. In a twinkling they were upon their prey, fierce and ravening as a pack of wolves. The leader of the bluefish lunged. With a snap of razor-toothed jaws he seized two of the anchovies. Two clean-severed heads and two tails floated away. The taste of blood was in the water. As though maddened by it, the bluefish slashed to right and left. They drove through the center of the anchovy school, scattering the ranks of the smaller fish so that they darted in panic and confusion in every direction. Many dashed to the surface and leaped through into the strange element beyond. There they were seized by the hovering gulls, companion fishers of the bluefish.

As the carnage spread, the clear green of the water was slowly clouded with a spreading stain. A strange new taste came with the rusty color and was drawn in by Scomber with the water he passed through mouth and gills. The taste was disquieting to a small fish that had never tasted blood or experienced the lust of the hunter.

When at last pursued and pursuers had passed, the thudding vibrations of the last carnage-mad bluefish were stilled and Scomber's sense cells received once more only the messages of the strong, steady rhythms of the sea. The little mackerel's senses were numbed by the encounter with the swirling, slashing, buffeting monsters. It was in the bright waters of the surface that he had looked upon the racing apparitions, and now they had passed he made his way down from brightness into green dusk, led down fathom by fathom by the reassuring quality of the gloom which concealed whatever terrors might lurk near by.

With the descent Scomber came into a cloud of feed, the transparent, big-headed larvae of a crustacean that had spawned in these waters the week before. The larvae moved jerkily through the water, waving the plumelike legs that sprang in two rows from the slender bodies. Scores of young mackerel were feeding on the crustaceans and Scomber joined them. He seized one of the larvae and crushed its transparent body against the roof of his mouth before he swallowed it. Excited and eager for more of the new food he darted among the drifting larvae; and now the sense of hunger possessed him, and the fear of the great fishes was as though it had never been.

As Scomber pursued the larvae in emerald haze five fathoms under the surface he saw a bright flash sweep in a blinding arc across his sphere of vision. Almost instantly the flash was followed by a second blaze of iridescent glitter that curved sharply upward and seemed to thicken as it moved toward a shimmering oval globe above. Once more the thread of the tentacle crept down, all its cilia ablaze in the sunlight. Scomber's instincts warned him of danger, although never before in his larval life had he encountered one of the race of Pleurobrachia, the comb jelly, the foe of all young fishes.

Of a sudden, like a rope swiftly uncoiling from a hand above, one of the tentacles was dropped more than two feet below the inch-long body of the ctenophore, and thus swiftly extended it looped around the tail of Scomber. The tentacle was set with a lateral row of hairlike threads, as barbs grow from the shaft of a bird's feather, but the threads were filmy and tenuous as the strands of a spider's web. All the lateral hairs of the tentacle poured out a gluelike secretion, causing Scomber to become hopelessly entangled in the many threads. He strove to escape, beating the water with his fins and flexing his body violently. The tentacle, contracting and enlarging steadily from the thickness of a hair to that of a thread and then to that of a fishing line, drew him closer and closer to the mouth of the comb jelly. Now he was within an inch of the cold, smooth-surfaced blob of jelly that spun gently in the water. The creature, like a gooseberry in shape, lay in the water with the mouth uppermost, keeping its position by an easy, monotonous beating of the eight rows of ciliated plates or combs. The sun that found its way down from above set the cilia aglow with a radiance that half blinded Scomber as he was drawn up along the slippery body of his foe.

In another instant he would have been seized by the lobelike lips of the creature's mouth and passed into the central sac of its body, there to be digested; but for the moment he was saved by the fact that the ctenophore had caught him while it was still in the midst of digesting another meal. From its mouth there protruded the tail and hinder third of a young herring it had caught half an hour before. The comb jelly was greatly distended, for the herring was much too large to be swallowed whole. Although it had tried by violent contractions to force all of the herring past its lips it was unable to do so and had perforce to wait until enough of the fish was digested to make room for the tail. Scomber was held in further reserve, to be eaten after the herring.

In spite of his spasmodic struggles, Scomber was unable to break away from the entangling net of the tentacle hairs, and moment by moment his efforts grew feebler. Steadily and inexorably the contortions of the comb jelly's body were drawing the herring farther into the deadly sac, where digestive ferments worked with marvelous speed to convert the fish tissues, by subtle alchemy, into food for the ctenophore.

Now a dark shadow came between Scomber and the sun. A great, torpedo-shaped body loomed in the water and a cavernous mouth opened and engulfed the ctenophore, the herring, and the entrapped mackerel. A two-year-old sea trout mouthed the watery body of the comb jelly, crushed it experimentally against the roof of its mouth, and spat it out in disgust. With it went Scomber, half dead with pain and exhaustion, but freed from the grip of the dead ctenophore.

When a mass of seaweed that had been torn by the tides from some underlying bed or distant shore floated into Scomber's field of vision, he crept among the fronds and drifted with the weed for a day and a night.

That night as the schools of young mackerel swam near the surface they passed over a sea of death, for ten fathoms below them lay millions of the comb jellies in layer after layer, their bodies almost touching one another, twirling, quivering, tentacles extended and sweeping the water as far as they could reach, sweeping the water clean of every small living thing. Those few young mackerel that strayed down in the night to the level of this solid floor of comb jellies never returned, and when the paling of the water to grayness sent clouds of plankton and many young fishes hurrying down from above, they quickly met their death.

The hordes of the ctenophore Pleurobrachia extended for miles, but fortunately they lay at a deep level and few rose into the upper waters, for in this fashion the sea's creatures are often assorted in layers, one above another. But on the second night the large, lobed ctenophore Mnemiopsis roved through the upper fathoms, and wherever their green lights gleamed in the darkness some small unfortunate of the sea was in peril of its life.

Late that night came the legions of Beroë, the cannibal ctenophore, a sac of pinkish jelly large as a man's fist. The tribe of Beroë was moving out into the coastal waters on a tide of less saline water from a great bay. The sea brought them to the place where the hordes of Pleurobrachia lay twirling and quivering. The big ctenophores fell upon the small ones; they ate them by hundreds and thousands. The loose sacs of their bodies were capable of enormous distension, and scarcely had they been filled when the rapid processes of digestion made space for more.

When morning came once more over the sea, the tribes of Pleurobrachia were reduced to a scattered remnant of their former numbers, but a strange stillness lay over the sea where they had been, for in these waters scarcely any living thing remained.

9
The Harbor

AS THE SUN entered the sign of the crab, Scomber arrived in the mackerel waters of New England, and with the first spring tides of the month of July he was carried into a small harbor protected from the sea by an outthrust arm of land. From many miles to the southward where the winds and the currents had carried him as a helpless larva, he had returned to the rightful home of young mackerel.

In his third month of life Scomber was more than three inches long. On the journey up the coast the heavy, unmolded lines of a larval fish had been sculptured to a torpedo-shaped body with a hint of power in the shoulders and of speed in the tapering flanks. Now he had put on the sea coat of the adult mackerel. He was clothed in scales, but they were so fine and small that he was soft as velvet to the touch. His back was a deep blue green—the color of the deep places of the sea that Scomber had not yet seen—and over the blue-green background irregular inky stripes ran from the back fin halfway down his flanks. His underparts gleamed of silver, and when the sun found him as he moved just under the surface of the sea he glittered with the colors of the rainbow.

Many young fishes lived in the harbor—cod and herring, mackerel and pollock, cunner and silverside—for the water was rich in food. Twice in every twenty-four hours the flood tide surged in from the open sea through the narrow entrance, flanked on one side by a long sea wall and on the other by a rocky point. The tides came in swiftly, with the push of a great weight of water being forced through a narrow passage, and as they swirled through the cove they carried a wealth of plankton animals mingled with the other small creatures that had been swept off the bottom or plucked from the rocks with the passage of the tide. Twice in every twenty-four hours when the clean, sharp salt water came into the harbor the young fish moved out in excitement to seize the food which the sea had brought them by way of the tide.

Among the young fish in the harbor were several thousand mackerel, who had spent their first weeks of life in many different parts of the coastal waters, but had been brought at last into the harbor by the interplay of currents and by their own wanderings. With the instinct of gregariousness already strong within them, the young mackerel quickly became one school. After the long migrations which each of them had made they were content to live day after day in the waters of the harbor, to rove up and down along the weed-grown sea wall, to feel the spreading of the water over the warm shallows of the cove, and to move out to meet the incoming flood, eager for the swarming copepods and small shrimps it never failed to bring.

The sea coming in through the narrow inlet sucked and swirled over holes scoured out of the bottom and raced in whirlpools and eddies and broke over the rocks in white rips. The tides here moved violently but uncertainly, for the time when the flood turned to the ebb or the ebb to the flood was different within and without the harbor, and what with the push and pull and shifting weight of tides from two sides the water in the inlet race was never still. The rocks of the inlet were matted with creatures that love the swiftly moving current and the ceaseless eddy, and from dark bulges and weed-grown ledges of rock they thrust out eager tentacles and jaws to seize the food animals that swarmed in the water.

Once through the inlet, the sea spread out fanwise into the cove, running swiftly along the old sea wall that formed the eastward rim of the harbor to slap against the wharf pilings and tug at the fishing boats that lay at anchor. Spreading into the western half of the harbor, the water caught the reflection of overhanging scrub oak and cedar and stirred the stones of the shore line to a soft chatter. Toward the northern rim of the cove the water spread out thinly to a sandy beach, wind-rippled above the water line and wave-rippled below.

Over the floor of much of the cove the sea poured through patches of seaweed that grew waist-high to a man. Wherever a rock lay on the bottom one of these underwater gardens grew, and as the floor of the cove was very rocky its pattern as seen from above by the gulls and the terns was mottled darkly with many weed patches. Over the sand-bottomed clearings between the seaweed thickets, the little fishes of the cove poured in restless shoals. The shining green and silver caravans wound in and out, swerving, diverging, and merging again, or at a sudden fright darting away like a shower of silver meteors.

By the same path followed by the sea Scomber came into the harbor, bumped and jostled in the tide rip, whirled and tumbled through the inlet until, seeking quiet water, he found and followed the sandy paths between the rockweed thickets. So he came to the old sea wall, on which the weeds grew in a thick-piled tapestry of browns and reds and greens. As he swam into the swift current that was sweeping the wall a small fish, dark and squat of form, darted out fiercely from the tangle of weeds, causing him to veer away in alarm. The fish was a cunner, like all of its kind a lover of wharfs and harbors. The cunner had lived its whole life in the cove and much of it in the shelter of the sea wall and the fishing wharfs, biting off the barnacles and small mussels that grew on the wharf pilings and finding amphipods and moss animals and scores of other creatures among the seaweeds of pilings and wall. Only the smallest of fish fell prey to the cunner, but by its savage rushes it frightened larger fish away from its feeding places.

Now as Scomber moved up along the wall and came to a dark, quiet place where the deep shadow of a fishing wharf fell across the water, a vast shoal of herring fry burst upon him out of the gloom. The sun struck from their bodies flashes of emerald and silver and bronze. The herring were fleeing from a young pollock that lived in the harbor, terrorizing and preying upon all the smaller fish. As they swirled around Scomber, a new instinct stirred swiftly to life in the young mackerel. He swerved, banked steeply, and seized a young herring athwart its body. His sharp teeth bit deeply into the tender tissues. He carried the herring down into deeper water, just above the swaying ribbons of the weed beds, where he worried it and tore from it several mouthfuls.

As Scomber turned away from his victim, the pollock swung back to look for any herring that might still be lingering in the shadow of the wharf. Seeing Scomber, he swerved down menacingly, but the young mackerel was now too large and swift for him to attack successfully.

The pollock was in his second summer of life, having been born in the winter seas off the Maine coast. As an inch-long fry he had been swept southward in the ocean currents and out to sea, far from his birthplace. Later, as a young fish, pitting the new-found strength of fin and muscle against the sea, he had returned to the coastal shallows, in which he had wandered far to the south of his native waters, preying in season upon the young of other fishes as they schooled close inshore. The pollock was a fierce and ravenous little fish. He could put to rout a school of several thousand cod fry, causing them to scatter in panic and to creep, half paralyzed with fear, into the shelter of seaweeds and rocks.

That morning the pollock killed and ate sixty young herring and in the afternoon, as the launce were coming out of the sand to feed in the flood tide, he played back and forth in the shallows of the cove, slashing at the sharp-nosed, silvery little fish as they emerged. The summer before, when the pollock had been a yearling, the launce had appeared to him the most fearful fish in the sea as they followed and harried the pollock fry, singling out their victims and falling upon them with the ferocity of a pike.

At sunset, Scomber and several score of other small mackerel lay in school formation in blue-gray water a fathom under the surface. For them it was one of the best feeding times of the day, with myriads of the plankton animals streaming by.

The water of the cove lay very still. It was the hour when fishes rise and push their snouts against the surface film, peering out into a strange world of arching sky; when the slow tolling of bells buoyed on distant reefs or shoals comes clear across the water; when the hosts of bottom-living things creep out of burrows and mud tubes and crawl from under stones and loose their grip on wharf pilings to rise into the upper waters.

Before the last shimmer of gold had faded from the surface, Scomber's flanks began to tingle with quick, light vibrations as the water filled with a shoal of clamworms. Nereis, the six-inch clamworm, the bronze water sprite with a scarlet girdle about his middle, rose by the hundred from holes in the sand and under shells of the cove's shallows. By day they lurked in dark recesses under rocks or among the protecting tangles of eel-grass roots, to the end that when a bottom-roving worm or a creeping amphipod moved near they might thrust out their fierce heads armed with amber beaks and seize it. No small bottom dweller could stray near the hole of a nereid and escape death in the waiting jaws.

Although by day the nereids were fierce little beasts of prey in their own domains, with the evening the males among them came forth and swam upward with their fellows to the silver ceiling of the sea. The females remained in their burrows as the night fell fast among the eel-grass roots and the shadows of the overhanging rocks lengthened and grew black. The female nereids wore no scarlet doublets, and the appendages that sprang in a double row from the sides of their bodies were thin and weak, not flattened into swimming paddles as were those of their mates.

A shoal of the big-eyed shrimp had come into the harbor before sunset, followed by more young pollock and, until darkness fell, by a large flock of herring gulls. Although the bodies of the shrimp were transparent they appeared to the gulls like a cloud of moving red dots, for each had a row of brightly colored spots along its sides. Now in the darkness these spots glowed with a strong phosphorescence as the shrimp darted about in the waters of the cove, mingling their fires with the steely green flashes of the ctenophores—creatures that held no further terrors for the young Scomber.

But during that night many strange shapes moved into the water near the fishing wharfs, where the school of young mackerel lay in formation in the black, quiet water. A band of squid, ancestral enemies of all young fishes, had come into the cove. The squid had moved in during the spring from the high seas, their winter home, that they might feed on the hosts of schooling fishes that swarmed over the continental shelf in summer. And as the fishes spawned and their young came to shelter in the protected harbors, the squid, rapacious in their hunger, pressed in more closely to the land.

Moving against the ebbing tide the squid approached the cove where Scomber and his kind rested. They gave few signs of their coming. They moved more silently than the water that slapped about the wharf pilings. They darted, swift as arrows, through the moving tide, tracing gleaming wakes in the water.

In the chill light of early morning the squids attacked. With the speed of a living bullet the first squid darted into the midst of the school of mackerel, swerved obliquely to the right, and dealt one of the fish an unerring blow just behind the head. The little fish was killed instantly, without ever knowing or having time to fear its foe, for the beak of the squid cut out a clean triangular bite, deep into the spinal cord.

Almost in the same moment half a dozen other squid darted into the mackerel school, but the rush of the first attacker had sent the young fish scattering in all directions. Now the pursuit began, the squid darting among the milling fish, the mackerel dashing and banking and twisting and turning—eluding only by the utmost skill and effort the bottle shapes of the squids that loomed up at terrific speed in the water, tentacles outstretched and grasping.

After the first mad melee Scomber had dashed into the shadow of the wharf and, racing up along the sea wall, had taken shelter under the weeds that grew there. Many other mackerel had done likewise or had darted out into the open water of the cove, scattering widely. Finding that the mackerel had dispersed, the squid dropped to the bottom of the harbor, where their body pigments underwent a subtle change, causing them to match the color of the underlying sand. Soon even the sharpest-eyed fish could not have detected an enemy anywhere about.

The mackerel began to forget their fears and to wander back singly and in little groups to the wharfs where they had been lying, waiting for the turn of the tide. As one by one they swam over the place where a squid lay in motionless invisibility, what had appeared a water-mounded ridge of sand suddenly whirled up from the bottom and seized them.

By these tactics the squid harassed the mackerel all the morning, and only those that remained hidden in the seaweeds of the stone wall were safe from the threat of sudden death.

At the full of the tide the waters of the cove seethed with movement as droves of sand eels or launce raced shoreward. The launce were pursued by a small band of whiting—slender but muscular fish about as long as a man's forearm—with flashing silver underparts and teeth sharp as lancets. The whiting had fallen upon the launce as they emerged from the sand of a shoal two miles to seaward of the cove, to feed on the copepods that the tide was bringing in from farther at sea. The launce fled in terror, not seaward against the tide where they might have found safety by scattering, but with the tide into the cove and into shoaling waters.

As the launce fled, the whiting harried them, driving back and forth across the thousands of slim, finger-long fish. Scomber, lying a foot under water with fins aquiver, felt with suddenly taut nerves the thin staccato vibrations of the racing launce and the heavier roll of the pursuing whiting. The waters about him filled with hurrying shadows. Scomber darted into the shadow of the wharf and hid in the weeds of one of the pilings. Once he would have feared the launce. Now he was as large as they, but the waters were filled with warnings of a hunt and of danger.

As the launce drove deeper into the cove the water began to thin away beneath them, but in their overmastering terror of the whiting they failed to heed the warnings of shoaling water and stranded by hundreds and thousands. The gulls that had followed in expectantly from outside the inlet, sensing what was happening in the seething water below, mewed and squealed and laughed their excitement when they saw the sandy flats beneath them turn to silver. Black-headed laughing gulls and gray-mantled herring gulls came down with flapping wings, plunging shoulder-deep into the water and seizing the launce, screaming threats to the newcomers that dropped down to the feast, although there was an abundance for all.

As the launce piled up inches deep on the shelving beach, the whiting, whirling after in reckless pursuit, drove up on the beach by the dozen, and as the water had now turned to the ebb there was no means of escape. When the tide withdrew the beach was silvered for half a mile with the bodies of the launce, and among them were scattered the larger forms of their pursuers. The squid had followed into the shallow water, attracted by the slaughter, and many of them had stranded while feeding on the hapless launce. Now gulls and fish crows gathered from miles around and, with the crabs and beach fleas, ate of the fish. During that night, wind and tide combined to sweep the beach clean.

The next morning a small bird in bold black and white and ruddy plumage alighted on one of the rocks of the harbor inlet and sat, dozing and dreaming, through fully a quarter of the tide rise before it could rouse itself to pick off and eat some of the small black snails that clung to the rock. The bird was exhausted from fighting the west winds that had threatened to blow it out to sea as it came down the coast from far to the north. It was a ruddy turnstone—one of the first of the great fall flights.

And now as July gave way to August the warm air moving in on the west wind met the cool sea air, and the harbor lay under a dense, dripping fog. From the point a mile down the coast the reedy voice of the foghorn cut through the mist day and night, and bells rang on all the reefs and shoals. For seven days no throb of boat engines came down through the water to the fish in the harbor, for nothing moved over the sea except the gulls, who knew their way in the fog, and the herons, who came to perch on the wharf pilings, guided by the scent of fish in the bait compartments of the boats.

Then the fog passed, and days of blue sky and bluer water followed swiftly one upon another. On these days the flocks of shore birds hurried over the harbor like gusts of autumn leaves, and like wind-blown leaves their passing betokened the end of summer.

But if knowledge of approaching fall came early to the creatures of shore and marsh, it was slow to awaken in the water world of the cove. When it came it was brought by the southwest wind. Toward the end of August an onshore blow brought rain out of a sky that was grayer than the leaden surface of the harbor. For two days and nights the southwest storm continued, with slanting sheets of water piercing the surface film of the sea with an endless barrage of drops. The rain beat down the incoming and the outgoing tides, so that they rose and lapsed in a waveless surge of water. The flood tides brimmed to the top of the sea wall and swamped many of the fishing boats, so that they wallowed to the bottom, attracting the fishes who nosed curiously at the strange shapes. All the fish lay deeper under water, and the terns huddled, drenched and disconsolate, on the rocks of the harbor inlet, for with the rain pelting down into the gray opacity of the water they could not see to fish. Unlike the terns, the gulls feasted, for the high storm tides had brought into the harbor much food in the form of injured sea animals and refuse.

After the first day of storm many weeds with narrow, toothed leaves and air vessels like clusters of berries began to appear in the cove, and on the following day the water was filled with floating sargassum weed, which the wind had blown in from the Gulf Stream. Among the fronds of the weed were small and brightly colored fishes that had been carried by the Stream from far to the southward, beginning their long journey as larvae in tropical waters. They had been sheltered by the gulfweed, during the many days and nights of the northward journey, and when the wind blew the weed out of the blue river of warm tropical water the fish accompanied it to the coastal shallows. There most of them would remain, until the coming of unaccustomed cold should abruptly end their lives.

After the storm the waters of the flood tides came in laden with the moon jelly, Aurelia. It was a fateful journey for the beautiful white jellyfish. For a season the ocean had carried them, raised from the algae-grown rocks and shells of the shore line, where they had begun life as small, plantlike things clinging to stones throughout the winter. In the spring there had budded off from these small creatures a series of flattened discs. These had been quickly transformed into tiny swimming bells, and these to the adult stages. They had lived at the surface when the sun shone and the wind held its breath, often gathering in winding columns miles in length at the meeting places of two currents, where their forms were seen by the gulls, the terns, and the gannets, shimmering in opalescent splendor.

After a time the jellyfish had matured their eggs and then they carried the young in the folds and margins of the tissues that hung like empty sleeves from the under side of the disc. Perhaps the spawning effort had left them weakened, for with bloated tissues and air-inflated egg sacs many of them capsized and floated helplessly in the seas of the late summer. These were set upon by swarms of small crustaceans with hungry jaws and further weakened or destroyed.

Now the southwest storm, kneading the waters deeply, had found the moon jellies. Rough waters seized them and hurried them shoreward. In the jostling and tumbling many tentacles were lost and delicate tissues torn. Every flood tide brought more of the pale discs of the jellyfish into the harbor and cast them up on the rocks of the shore line. Here their battered bodies became once more a part of the sea, but not until the larvae held within their arms had been liberated into the shallow waters. Thus the cycle came to the full, for even as the substance of the moon jellies was reclaimed for other uses by the sea, the young larvae were settling down for the winter on the stones and shells, so that in the spring a new swarm of tiny bells might rise and float away.

10
Seaways

Now the hours of darkness were as many as the hours of daylight; the sun passed through the constellation of the scales; and September's moon waned to a thin ghost of itself. And as the tides poured through the inlet race into the harbor, creaming with white ripplings over the rocks, and lapsed again to the sea from which they came, they carried away day after day more of the small fish of the harbor. So there came a night when the flood tide stirred in the young mackerel Scomber a strange uneasiness, and on that night the ebb tide, running to the sea, drew him with it. With him went many of the young mackerel who had spent the late summer in the harbor, a school of several hundred cleanly molded young fish each longer than a man's hand. Now they had left behind the pleasant life of the harbor; until death should claim them their world would be open sea.

In the inlet race the mackerel yielded to the eddies and were carried in a swift rush of water past the rocks of the harbor mouth. The water was sharply salt and clean and cold; in its scramble over rocks and shoals it had burst so many rents and tatters in its surface film that it was heavily charged with oxygen. Through this water the mackerel darted in exhilaration, aquiver from their snouts to their last tail finlets—ready and eager for the new life that awaited them. In the inlet the mackerel passed the dark forms of sea bass ranged in the tide, waiting to snap up small crustaceans and sandworms that the water plucked from the rocks or washed out of the holes in the bottom of the channel. The mackerel fled the dark shapes, streaking in swift silver flashes beyond the surging channel where the bass lay, heads into the tide.

Outside the harbor the tide moved with a steadier but heavier pulse, carrying the mackerel out into deeper water. Here the sea came in over shallowing ledges that raised its floor in giant steps from the open basin beyond. Now and again the mackerel felt the drag of current beneath them as they moved above a sandy shoal or weed-grown rocky reef, but ever the undertones of water moving over sand or shells or rock grew more remote as the bottom fell away beneath them, and most of the rhythms and the sound vibrations that came to the hurrying fish were of water and water alone.

The young mackerel moved in a school almost as one fish. None was leader, yet each had a keen awareness of the presence and the movements of all the others, and as those on the margins of the school swung to right or left, or quickened or slackened their pace, so likewise did all the fish of the school.

Now and again the mackerel veered away in sudden alarm from the black shapes of fishing boats that crossed their path, and more than once they darted in momentary panic through the meshes of nets set athwart the tides, being yet too small to become entangled in the twine. Sometimes dark forms lunged at them out of the black water; and once a large squid loomed up and gave them chase, the fish and mollusk darting in and out among a frightened shoal of two-year-old herring, or sperling, on which the squid had been feeding.

Some three miles to seaward of the harbor the mackerel sensed the water shallowing again beneath them as they approached a small island. The island belonged to the sea birds. In season the terns nested on its sands, and the herring gulls brought forth their young under the bushes of beach plum and bayberry and on the flat rocks overlooking the sea. Running out into the sea from the island was a long underwater reef—called by the fishermen The Ripplings—and over it the water was broken into white surges and frothy eddies. As the mackerel passed, scores of pollock were leaping in play in the tide rip, and their bodies gleamed white as the wave froth in the thin light of the risen moon.

When the island and its reef had been left a mile behind, the mackerel school was thrown into sudden panic by the appearance among them of a herd of some half-dozen porpoises which had risen to the surface to blow. The porpoises had been feeding on an underlying sandy shoal, where they were rooting out the launce who had buried themselves there. When the porpoises found themselves among schooling mackerel they slashed at the little fish with their narrow, grinning jaws, killing a few mackerel in sport. But when the school fled in swift alarm through the sea they did not follow, for they had already gorged on the launce to the point of sluggishness.

At early dawn light, the young mackerel, now many miles at sea, came for the first time upon older fish of their own kind. A school of adult mackerel was moving swiftly at the surface of the sea, over which they swept with a heavy rippling. Their snouts were breaking water and their eyes, eager and staring, looked out with water-dimmed sight into the world of air and sky. The two schools—the old fish and the young—merged for a moment of milling confusion as their paths crossed and then continued their separate ways in the sea.

The gulls had come early from their resting places on coastal islands and now they patrolled the sea, their eyes missing nothing that happened in the upper layers and seeing farther down into the water as the sun rose and the shimmer of the level rays faded from the surface. The gulls saw the school of young mackerel swimming a foot under water. Across half a dozen wave hills to the eastward they saw two dark fins, like sickle blades, cutting the water. Because of their elevation the gulls could see that the fins were part of a large fish who drifted just under water, with only the long back fin and the upper blade of the tail fin protruding. The swordfish, who measured eleven feet from the tip of his sword to his tail, often lay idly just beneath the surface, perhaps testing the thrust of the surface ripples with his dorsal fin and so directing his course into the wind. In this way he was certain to meet the shoals of plankton, often accompanied by predatory fish, that drifted with the moving surface water before the wind.

The gulls, who watched the swordfish and the school of young mackerel, now saw a great disturbance approaching from the southeast. An enormous shoal of the big-eyed shrimp was being borne along on the flooding tidal current, which was strengthened by a wind blowing landward. But the shrimp were not browsing on smaller plankton, as the gulls sometimes saw them do, nor drifting peacefully at the surface of the sea. Instead they were fleeing from something that surged through the water with them—open-mouthed and terrible. It was a school of herring, feeding on the shrimp with swift, short rushes. The shrimp were propelling themselves at frantic speed, using all the force of their swimming legs that were flattened into paddlelike blades. And as the space between pursued and pursuers lessened steadily, a shrimp, finding in its transparent body some unused remnant of strength, would fling itself clear of the water just as the jaws of a herring yawned open behind it. But the herring followed relentlessly in pursuit and, though a shrimp might leap half a dozen times into the air, rarely did it escape once a herring had marked it as its victim.

The wind- and current-borne shoal of plankton and the following fish were carried landward; toward them the mackerel swam from the northeast and the swordfish drifted from the northwest. When the fringes of the streaming cloud of plankton reached the mackerel the young fish began to snap eagerly at the shrimp, which were larger food than most of their harbor fare. In a moment, however, they found themselves in the midst of the herring shoal, and the rushes of the larger fishes frightened them and sent them hurrying into deeper water.

The gulls saw the two black fins sink beneath the surface; saw the outlines of the swordfish blur as the large fish dropped deeper into the water and moved beneath the herring. What happened next was partly hidden from the gulls by the seething water and spurting spray; but as they dropped closer and hovered with short wing beats—drawn by awareness of a kill— they could see a great dark shadow that whirled and darted and lunged in a frenzy of attack in the midst of the closely packed ranks of herring. And when the water that foamed to whiteness had grown calmer, more than a score of herring floated at the surface with broken backs and many others swam feebly and listed dizzily, as though they had been injured by glancing blows from the sword. These the great fish now captured easily in its weak-jawed mouth, but many of the dead herring it lost to the gulls, who dropped down to feast on what the swordfish had killed.

When the large fish had killed and eaten to repletion it drifted at the surface of the sea, where the sun-warmed water lulled it to drowsiness. The herring shoals sank into deeper water and the gulls ranged farther to sea, waiting and watching for what might be driven up from below.

Five fathoms down, the school of young mackerel had come upon a crimson cloud made up of millions of the small copepod, called Calanus, that were drifting in the tidal current.

The mackerel fed on these red crustaceans, which were their favorite food. When the flooding current slackened, hesitated, and grew too weak to carry the plankton with it, the red feed sank into deeper water, followed by the fish. At a depth of only a hundred feet the mackerel came to a gravelly bottom. It was the flat top or plateau of a long undersea hill that curved away to the southward and met another hill coming in from the west, so that the two formed a semicircular ridge with a gully of deep water between. Because of its shape the shoal was known as the Horseshoe to the fishermen, who set their trawl lines over it for haddock, cod, and cusk, and sometimes dragged over it their cone-shaped nets or otter trawls.

As the mackerel moved across the shoal they found the bottom beginning to slope away steadily beneath them, and about fifty feet below the highest part of the shoal they came to the edge of the central gully. Three hundred feet below them lay a deep gully floored with soft, sticky mud instead of gravel and broken shell. Many fish called hake lived in the gully, hunting their food in darkness by moving just above the bottom and dragging their long, sensitive fins in the mud. In instinctive fear of deep water, the mackerel school turned and ascended the slope of the shoal. There they moved just above the bottom, in a world that was new and strange to young surface-living fish.

As the mackerel swam over the shoal they were watched by many eyes that looked up from the sand, seeing everything that passed close overhead. They were the eyes of dabs or flounders lying with a thin film of sand over their flat, grayish bodies, so that they were well concealed both from the large predatory fish who would have eaten them and from the shrimps and crabs who scurried over the bottom and were easy prey. The large mouths of the flounders were rimmed with sharp teeth and gaped open as far as the level of the eyes, marking them as occasional fish eaters, but the mackerel were too active and quick-moving to tempt them to rise from their places of concealment and give chase.

Often, as the young mackerel moved over the shoal, a large, heavily built fish with high and pointed back fins would loom up alarmingly close in the water as a haddock swept past and was enveloped again in the gloom. The haddock were very numerous on the Horseshoe, for it was rich in the shelled animals and the spiny-skinned creatures and the tube-dwelling worms that haddock eat. Many times the mackerel came upon small herds of a dozen or more haddock rooting like pigs in the bottom. They were digging out the burrowing worms that had their tunnels deep in the soft sand. As they pushed and dug with their snouts, the black shoulder patches, or "devil's marks," and the black lateral lines stood out vividly in the dim light. The haddock continued their digging, heedless of the young mackerel that darted past with frightened flirts of their tails, for they seldom ate fish when the bottom animals were plentiful.

Once a large, batlike creature fully nine feet across rose from the sand and with a flapping of its thin body passed just above the bottom. So evil and so menacing was its appearance that the school of young mackerel went hurrying upward several fathoms, until the screen of underlying water shut out the sight of the sting ray.

Before a steep ledge of rock they came upon an unfamiliar object dangling in the water. It swayed with the movement of the tide, which ran with great force over the shoal, but it had no motion of its own, although the taste which diffused into the water from it was fishlike. Scomber nosed at the piece of split herring that was bound to a large steel hook and, as he did so, frightened away several small sculpins that had been nibbling at the bait, which was too large for so small a fish to take. Above the hook a thin, dark streak of line stretched away toward a longer line that ran horizontally through the water for a mile over the shoal. As Scomber and his companions ranged over the plateau they saw many of the baited hooks, attached by short lines to the main trawl line. On some of them large fish like haddock were caught, turning and twisting slowly on the hooks that they had swallowed. On one of the hooks was a large cusk, a powerful and heavily built fish some three feet long. The cusk had lived on the shoal, a solitary fish of its kind, spending much of its time hiding among the weeds that grew on the shelving rocks on the outer rim. The scent of the herring bait had drawn it from its hiding place and it had taken the hook. In its struggles the cusk had coiled its powerful body several times about the line.

As the little mackerel fled from the strange sight, the cusk was drawn slowly upward through the water, toward a dim shadow like that of a monster fish on the surface above. The fishermen were running their trawls, rowing from one to another of the lines. If there was a fish on the hook they dispatched it by a blow from a short club, tossing the marketable fish into the bottom of the dory and throwing the other fish back to the sea. It was now an hour after the turn of the tide to the flood, and although the lines had been down only two hours the fishermen had to take them up. On the Horseshoe the currents were very strong, and the line trawls could be set and run only on the slack of the tides.

Now the mackerel came to the seaward rim of the shoal, where the rocky wall fell away in a sheer cliff to the sea bottom some five hundred feet below. All of this outer part of the shoal was solid rock and so it withstood the press of water from the open ocean. Scomber, passing over the rim and above the intense blue water that lay below, found a narrow ledge some twenty feet below the crest of the cliff. Brown, leathery oarweed grew in the crevices and rock layers above the ledge and sent its ribbons streaming out twenty feet or more into the stronger currents that poured by the wall of rock. Scomber nosed his way in among the flat, swaying fronds of the weed and startled a lobster who was resting on the ledge, hidden from the sight of passing fish by the seaweeds. On the under side of her body the lobster carried several thousand eggs attached to the hairs of her swimming legs. The eggs would not hatch until the following spring; meanwhile the lobster was in constant danger of being found by some hungry and inquisitive eel or cunner and stripped of the eggs.

Moving along above the ledge, Scomber suddenly came upon a six-foot rock cod, a two-hundred-pound monster of his kind, who lived on the ledge among the rockweeds. The cod had grown old and very large because of his cunning. He had found the rock ledge above the deep pit of the sea years before and, knowing it instinctively for a good hunting place, he had adopted the ledge for his own, fiercely driving away the other cod. He spent much of his time lying on the ledge, which was in deep purple shadow after the sun had passed the zenith. From this lair he could move out suddenly to seize fishes as they roved along the rock wall. Many fishes met their death in his jaws, among them cunners and hook-eared sculpins, sea ravens with ragged fins, flounders and sea robins, blennies and skates.

Sight of the young mackerel roused the cod from the semitorpor in which he had lain since the last feeding time and kindled his hunger. He swung his heavy body out from the ledge and climbed steeply to the shoal. Scomber fled before him. As the young mackerel rejoined his fellows who had been lying in an updraught of current from the face of the cliff, the whole school quickened to a sense of alarm and fled away across the shoal as the dark form of the cod loomed into sight at the brink of the rock wall.

The cod roved over the Horseshoe. He fed on all the small creatures—shelled or shell-less—that lived on the bottom or moved above it. He started flounders from where they lay on the sand and sent them darting away before him; he captured small haddock, swinging through the water in swift pursuit of them; he took young fish of his own kind who had recently completed their period of surface life and dropped down to live as true cod on the bottom. He ate dozens of large sea clams, swallowing them whole. After the meats were digested he would expel the shells, although often he carried as many as a dozen of the large shells in his stomach for days, stacked in a neat pile. When he could find no more sea clams he foraged among the Irish moss that carpeted a flat ledge with a thick, spongy mat, searching for crabs hidden deep within its curling fronds.

A mile away, across the Horseshoe, the mackerel school became aware of a strange disturbance in the water. It was like nothing they had experienced in their life in the harbor, nor during that earlier period, now only the dimmest of memories, when they had drifted with the other plankton at the surface of the sea. It came to them as a heavy, thudding vibration felt with the lateral-line canals along their sensitive flanks. It was not the feel of water vibrations over a rocky reef, nor of waves on a tide rip—yet these sensations were perhaps nearest akin to it of anything the young mackerel had known.

The disturbance grew in strength, and now a group of small cod hurried by, swimming steadily toward the sea rim of the shoal. One by one, and then in groups and small schools, other fish streamed through the water: the great, batlike form of the sting ray, haddock, cod, flounders, a small halibut. All were hurrying toward the edge of the cliff and away from the disturbance that grew until it filled the water with its trembling vibration.

Something vast and dark, like a fish of monstrous and incredible size, its whole forward end a vast, gaping mouth, loomed in the water. At the sight of the cone-shaped net the school of mackerel, which had been confused and irresolute in the presence of the strange vibration and the hurrying fish, suddenly moved as one individual and whirled up and up through water that grew clearer and paler, leaving behind the gloom of the strange world of the shoal, and returning to the surface waters to which they belonged.

As for the fish of the shoal, no such instinct led them up to sun-filled waters and escape. The trawl net had been dragged the length of the Horseshoe and had already scooped up in its cavernous bag thousands of pounds of food fish, as well as quantities of basket starfish, prawns, crabs, clams, cockles, sea cucumbers, and white worm tubes.

The old cod—the cod of the ledge on the cliff side—moved just ahead of the trawl. It was not the first trawl net the monster cod had seen, nor the hundredth. Close behind him the ironbound doors that served to spread the mouth of the net were straining at the long towing cables that stretched away obliquely through the water, stretched up and up toward the vessel steaming a thousand feet in advance of the net.

And now, as the cod swam easily if ponderously above the bottom, he saw that the water before him was changing. It was deepening to the color of water that lies over a great depth. So the cod was accustomed to tell when he was nearing the ledge where he lived above the deep chasm of the sea. The doors of the otter trawl grazed his tail fin. Summoning the great strength dormant in the muscles of his body, he put on a sudden burst of speed, shot out over the blue void, and dropped with precision to his ledge twenty feet below.

Only an instant after the cod passed through the swaying brown thongs of the oarweeds and felt the smooth rock of the ledge beneath his body, the trawl pitched over the edge of the cliff and went tumbling end over end into the deep water below.

II
Indian Summer of the Sea

THE SPIRIT OF the autumn sea was heard in the voices of the kittiwakes, or frost gulls, who began to arrive in flocks by mid-October. They whirled in thousands over the water, dropping down on arched wings to seize small fish that darted through translucent green. The kittiwakes had come southward from nesting grounds on the cliffs of the Arctic coast and the Greenland ice packs, and with them the first chill breath of winter moved over the graying sea.

There were other signs that autumn had come to the sea. Every day the flights of ocean birds, that in September had poured in thin aerial streams over the coastal waters from Greenland, Labrador, Keewatin, and Baffin Land, swelled in volume as the birds hastened to return to the sea. There were gannets and fulmars, jaegers and skuas, dovekies and phalaropes. Their flocks spread out over all the waters above the continental shelf, where the shoals of surface fishes moved and the plankton herds browsed in the sea.

The gannets were fish eaters that patterned the sky with the white crosses of their bodies as they scanned the sea for prey. Sighting it, they plunged from a hundred feet in the air, and the shock of the heavy body striking the water was broken by a cushion of air sacs under the skin. The fulmars fed on small schooling fish, squids, crustaceans, offal from fishing boats, or any other food that they could seize from the surface, being unable to dive like the gannets. The small dovekies and the phalaropes were eaters of plankton; the jaegers and the skuas lived chiefly on what they could steal from other birds, seldom fishing for themselves.

Few of these birds would see land again until spring. Now they belonged once more to the winter sea, sharing its daylight and darkness, its storms and calms, its sleet and snow and sun and fog.

The yearling mackerel who had left the harbor in late September had at first lived timidly in the open sea, lost in its vastness after the familiar conformations of the harbor. During the three months in the protected cove they had attuned their movements to the rhythms of the tides, feeding on the flood, resting on the ebb. Now the tidal sweep of the surface waters, which here in the open sea, no less than along the coast, yielded to the pull of sun and moon, was almost imperceptible to the young mackerel. For them the tides were lost in the vaster roll of waters. As they roamed the ocean, as yet unfamiliar with its paths of current and varying saltiness, they sought in vain the safe refuges of the harbor, the shadow of the fishing wharfs, the forests of rockweed. Always they must move on into green space.

Scomber and the other yearlings had grown rapidly since they left the harbor, thriving on the rich food of the open ocean. Now in the sixth month of their lives the young fish were from eight to ten inches long—the size fishermen call "tacks." During their first weeks at sea the yearlings moved steadily north and east. In these colder waters the red copepods, their favorite food, tinged miles of ocean with the crimson of their tiny bodies. As the yearlings swung farther offshore and the days of October were marked off by the sun, they found themselves more often among large mackerel, fish of the past dozen years' spawnings. The fall was a time of vast movements of mackerel. The swing of the summer migration, which had carried many of the fish north to the Gulf of St. Lawrence and the coast of Nova Scotia, had passed its climax; flood tide had turned to ebb; and once more the fish moved south.

Slowly the summer warmth was drained from the water. The young crabs, mussels, barnacles, worms, starfish, and crustaceans of scores of species had disappeared from the plankton, for in the ocean spring and summer are the seasons of birth and youth. Only to some of the simplest creatures did the Indian summer of the sea bring a brief and flaring renewal of life, so that they multiplied a millionfold. Among these were the one-celled animals, or protozoa, small as pinpricks, which are among the chief light producers of the sea. Ceratium, the horned one—a blob of protoplasm with three grotesque prongs—sprinkled the night seas of October with silver points of light and so filled the surface waters that over vast areas the sea lay thickened and moved sluggishly under the wind. The little globes of Noctiluca—just visible to the human eye—were each aglitter with submicroscopic grains of light within themselves. During this autumnal period of their great abundance, every fish that moved where the swarms of protozoa were most dense was bathed in light; the waves that broke on reef or shoal spilled liquid fire; and every dip of a fisherman's oar was a flash of a torch in darkness.

On one such night the mackerel came upon an abandoned gill net swaying in the water. The net was buoyed at the surface by floats, and from the cork line it hung down perpendicularly, like a giant tennis net. Its meshes were large enough to allow the yearling mackerel to slip through, although larger fish would have been gilled in the twine. Tonight no fish would have tried to pass through the net, for all its meshes were hung with tiny warning lamps. Luminous protozoa and water fleas and amphipods clung to the wet twine in the dark sea, and the pulse of the ocean stirred from their bodies countless sparks of light. It was as though all the myriad lesser fry of the sea—the plants small as dust motes and the animals tinier than a sand grain—drifting from birth to death in an ocean of infinite size and endless fluidity, seized upon the meshes of the gill net as the one firm reality in their uneasy world and clung to it with protoplasmic hair and cilia, with tentacle and claw. The gill net glowed as though it had life of itself; its radiance shone out into the black sea and down into the darkness below. The light lured many small creatures to rise from deep water and gather on the meshes of the gill net, where they rested all that night in the dark, wide sea.

The mackerel nosed at the net in curiosity and as they bumped the twine all the plankton lamps flared brighter. They followed along its length for more than a mile, for it was set in sections attached one to the other. Other fish were bumping the net. Some were picking off the small sea creatures that clung to it, but none of the fish became gilled.

On moonlight nights the gleam of the moon's radiance would have dimmed the lights of the plankton animals and then many fish, failing to see the net, would have been caught in it. Knowing this, the gill netters fished only in the bright of the moon. This net had been set two weeks before, when the moon was just past the full. For several days two fishermen had tended it from their gasoline-motored launch. Then there had been a night of heavy seas with wind and rain squalls swirling across the water. Since that night the launch had not returned, for it had been wrecked on a shoal about a mile away, and the currents had brought one of its freshly splintered spars and lodged it in the net.

Left to itself, the gill net fished on night after night, and while the moon's light lasted many fish were taken. Dogfish had found them and had torn great holes in the twine as they swarmed in and took the fish. But as the moon's light waned, the plankton lamps burned brighter and no more fish were caught.

Early one morning as the mackerel school swam into the east, Scomber saw above him a long, narrow patch of shadow made by a log that was being carried in the current. He saw the glint of silvery scales from the bodies of several small fish that were moving in the edge of the shadow and swam up to investigate. The log had been part of the cargo of a lumber freighter southward bound from Nova Scotia until it was caught in a northeast gale off the coast of Cape Cod. The freighter, driven onto a shoal, had gone down with all hands, and much of the lumber had been swept ashore in the wind-driven seas. Some, as the storm abated, had been carried offshore and caught in the vast system of ocean currents that swirled clockwise around the fishing banks. The bulk of the drifting log was shelter of the only sort the open sea afforded, and so Scomber joined the little group of fishes, for a period becoming indifferent to the movements of the mackerel school and harking back in his responses to that earlier period of his life when the shadows of fishing wharfs and of anchored boats in the harbor had represented safety from the raids of gulls and squids and large, marauding fishes.

Not long after Scomber had joined the fishes under the log, half a dozen migrating terns settled on it, alighting with a sharp flapping of wings and a scramble of slender toes as they sought a foothold on the surface of the log, already slippery with algae. This was the first time the terns had paused since they had left a beach far to the north the day before. They feared to alight on the water, for although terns take their living from the sea, they are not truly of it. To them the sea was a strange element to which they must often abandon themselves for a brief and frightening instant of contact as they dived for a fish, but not a place on which they would willingly rest their fragile bodies.

The moving wave hills slid under the forward end of the log, tipped it gently skyward, and running swiftly along its length let it slide into the hollows between. As the log lurched and rolled through the sea, seven small fishes followed beneath it, and the terns rode on it like seamen on a raft. As they rested in the midst of the sea, content to let the log carry them out of their course if it would, the terns preened their feathers; they stretched their wings high above their heads, flexing tired muscles; and presently some of them fell asleep.

A little flock of petrels, or Mother Carey's chickens, came down to the water near the log, carrying themselves daintily just above the surface by a pattering of their feet and a fluttering of their wings. Their voices were the thinnest wisps of sound as they whispered over and over their names, *pitterel, pitterel*. The petrels had come down to investigate a dense mass of very small crustaceans who were feeding on the floating body of a dead squid. No sooner had the petrels assembled than a large shearwater came in a great swoop from his patrol in the sky half a mile away and with loud cries plunged in among the small birds. His excited screams brought scores of his kind hurrying to the spot, although a moment before both sky and sea had seemed almost empty of birds. The shearwaters plunged down heavily to the water, striking it with their breasts and flapping their wings. They scattered the petrels as they searched greedily for the food which had attracted the smaller birds to the spot. The first shearwater had already seized the squid, squealing defiance of his companions. Although the squid was too large to swallow whole, the shearwater struggled to gulp it down, for he feared with good reason to relax his grip for an instant.

Suddenly a harsh chattering came down the wind. A darkbrown bird swept through the upper fringes of the cloud of shearwaters. The jaeger whirled past the bird who had possession of the squid, rose into the wind, looped backward, and dropped on the bird. The shearwater plunged and thrashed air and water with his wings, trying to throw off the jaeger and swallow the squid. Suddenly a large piece of the squid fell away and was seized by the jaeger before it could strike the water. After swallowing the prize, the pirate bird sailed off across the water, while all the shearwaters milled about in angry frustration.

By late afternoon a thick mist had closed down over the sea in a blanket spread at about the ordinary cruising height of a shearwater. From golden green the surface waters paled to a gray in which there was neither warmth nor color. The absence of the sun brought the usual rise to the surface of small animals from the lower layers of the sea, and with the lesser fry of the sea came the squids and the fishes that feed on them.

The fog heralded a week of heavy weather, in which the mackerel lived far below the surface, repelled by rough seas. Though swimming deeper than usual, they were still in the upper layers of the sea, for they were passing over a deep basin hollowed out in the continental shelf. Toward the end of the week they approached the outer rim of the basin, where a chain of undersea mountains lay between the coastal waters and the deep Atlantic.

The fall storms had abated, the sun shone again, and the mackerel came up out of the deep gloom to feed once more at the surface. So they passed over a high ridge of the submarine mountain chain. The seas swept over it with a great surge and roll, although they did not break. The movement was unpleasant to the young mackerel, who turned downward to find deeper and quieter water.

A score of the yearling mackerel followed along a dark cliff, where a deep gorge had been hollowed out eons ago. Between the two walls of the undersea valley the sea poured in a green flood. The sun came down through the clear water, leaving the sheer west wall of the cliff in deep-blue shadow. Here and there it lit up a forest of bright-green weed on a shelving ledge and in the dim haze below struck a blaze of color from a spire of jagged rock.

A conger eel lived on one of the ledges of the cliff. The ledge communicated with a deep fissure in the rocks, into which the eel retreated when occasionally it was hard pressed by some enemy. Sometimes a blue shark, roving through the valley, swerved in to the ledge to attack the thick-bodied conger; or a porpoise came roving along the rock wall, hunting over all the ledges and prying into caves in the cliff for prey. But none of these enemies had been able to capture the conger.

The eel's small eyes saw the mackerel bodies glittering as the little school of fish approached the ledge. The conger gripped the wall of the cave with a muscular tail and drew back its thick body. As the mackerel came abreast of the cave, Scomber swerved out toward the wall of the cliff to investigate a small swarm of amphipods hovering over a fragment of food on a narrow ledge. Instantly the eel loosed its hold on the rock and darted into the open water with a lithe uncoiling of its body. In alarm at the sudden apparition, the mackerel school darted away with a quick acceleration, but Scomber, intent on the amphipods, failed to notice the eel until it was almost upon him.

Down along the cliff raced the two fishes—the mackerel a slim, tapered creature flashing iridescent in the sun; the eel as long as a man is tall and thick and drab as a piece of fire hose. All along the cliff small animals darted back into thickets of weeds or into small holes in the rocks at the passing of the conger, whom they recognized as an enemy. Scomber led the chase up and down along the wall and between spires of projecting rock. At last he dropped down on a weedy ledge. He startled two cunners who had been lying with fins aquiver in a sunlit patch of water just over the margin of the ledge and sent them darting in fear into shelter among the weeds.

Scomber lay very still, his gill covers moving rapidly. Then the currents moving along the rocky wall brought him the taint of conger as the big eel worked its way around the cliff, prying into all the crevices that might shelter a small fish. The scent of his enemy sent Scomber whirling out once more into open water, climbing for the surface. The eel saw the glinting streak of his passage. It turned and gathered speed for the chase, but already it had lost some twenty feet. The conger usually avoided the open water, being a creature of rock ledges and dark, undersea caverns. It hesitated and slackened speed. At this moment its small, deep-set eyes beheld a score of gray fish darting toward it. The eel turned instinctively to race for shelter in its own rock crevice, now left far behind. The school of dogfish bore down upon it. Always ravenous and ever ready to taste blood, the small sharks set upon the eel and in a twinkling had slashed its thick body in a hundred places.

For two days bands of dogfish swarmed in these waters, preying on mackerel, herring, pollock, menhaden, cod, haddock, and every other fish they encountered. On the second day the school to which Scomber belonged, harassed beyond endurance, traveled far to the south and west, above many undersea hills and valleys, and so left behind the shark-infested waters.

That night the mackerel moved through water that was filled with swimming starlets of light. The lights were luminous spots on the bodies of inch-long shrimps, each of which had a pair of light organs under the eyes and twin rows down the sides of their jointed abdomens or tails. When the shrimp flexed their tails in swimming, they could bring the hinder lights to bear on the water beyond and below them and so perhaps were better able to see the small copepods, split-footed shrimps, swimming snails, and one-celled plants and animals which they hunted. Most of the shrimps clutched in their arms, or foremost, bristle-set appendages, a matted pack of the food animals they had already caught by seizing them out of the current set up by the movements of their tails. Following the little darting lights of the shrimps, the mackerel easily found and captured as many of them as they could eat.

At dawn the little sea lamps went out as the first light diluted the water blackness. As they swam toward the sunrise, the mackerel soon found themselves in water that teemed with an enormous shoal of pteropods, or winged snails. As long as the early light lay in level rays across the water, the swarms of pteropods were a hazy, bluish cloud that dimmed the mackerels' vision; but when the sun had been an hour in the sky and its rays came slanting into the sea, the water was filled with a dazzling sparkle and glitter, for the bodies of the pteropods were as transparent and as exquisitely fashioned as the finest glass.

Over miles of sea that morning the mackerel swam through the pteropod shoals, and often they met whales driving open-mouthed through the swarms of mollusks. The mackerel, whom the whales did not seek, fled from the huge, dark forms of the whales; while the winged snails, who were being captured in millions, knew nothing of the monsters who hunted them. Eternally occupied with the quest for food, they browsed peacefully in the sea, unaware of the terrible hunter until the great jaws closed over them and the water rushed away in a torrent through the plates of whalebone.

Swimming down through the school of pteropods, Scomber saw the gleam of a very large fish moving in the water beneath him and felt the heavy roll of displaced water from its wake. But the fish passed from sight as quickly as it had come, and once more Scomber was aware only of feeding mackerel and of the small and glass-clear forms of swimming snails. Then suddenly he felt the great disturbance that troubled the water a few fathoms below him and sensed that mackerel were racing upward from somewhere near the lower fringes of the school. A dozen large tuna had attacked the school of feeding mackerel, having first dropped below the smaller fish to force them to the surface.

As the tuna drove through the milling fish, panic and confusion spread. There was no escape before or behind, nor to right or left. There was none below, where the tuna were. Along with most of his fellows, Scomber climbed up and up. The water was paling as it thinned away above them. Scomber could feel the thudding water vibration of an enormous fish climbing behind him, faster than a small mackerel could climb. He felt the five-hundred-pound tuna graze his flank as it seized the fish swimming beside him. Then he was at the surface, and the tuna were still pursuing. He leaped into the air, fell back, leaped again and again. In the air, birds stabbed at him with their beaks, for the spurting spray was a sign of feeding tuna that brought the gulls hurrying to the spot, to mingle their croaks and screams with the sound of splashing water and of fish bodies falling into the sea.

Now Scomber's leaps were shorter and more labored, and he was falling back with the heaviness of exhaustion. Twice he had barely escaped the jaws of a tuna and many times he had seen one of his companions seized by the attacking fish.

Unseen by mackerel or tuna, a high, black fin was moving over the water from the east. A hundred yards to southeast of the first fin, two other blades, each as high as a tall man, skimmed rapidly over the sea. Three orcas, or killer whales, were approaching, drawn by the scent of blood.

Then for a space Scomber found the water filled with even more terrifying forms and lashed to a greater confusion as the twenty-foot whales attacked the largest of the tunas, falling upon it like a pack of wolves. Scomber fled from the place where the great fish was plunging and rolling in a vain attempt to escape its enemies. And suddenly he was in water where there were no more tunas to pursue and harry small mackerel, for all of the big fish except the one that was attacked had sped away at sight of the orcas. As he swam down into deeper water, the sea grew calm and still and green again, and now once more he was in the midst of feeding mackerel and saw about him the crystal bodies of swimming snails.

12
Seine Haul

That night the sea burned with unusual phosphorescence. Many fish were near the surface, feeding. The chill of November quickened their movements, and as their schools rolled through the water they disturbed the millions of luminous plankton animals, causing them to glow with a fierce luster. So the darkness of the moonless night was broken in many places by flickering patches of light that came and went, flared to brilliance, and died away.

Wandering with half a hundred other yearlings, Scomber saw before him, in darkness pinpricked with silver light, a diffuse glare made by an enormous school of large mackerel, feeding on shrimps, who were pursuing copepods. Thousands of mackerel were drifting slowly with the tide. The whole area covered by the mackerel gleamed mistily, for at every movement of the fish they collided with the myriads of light-producing animals that filled the water.

The yearlings drew closer to the large fish and soon mingled with them. This was a larger school than Scomber had ever known before. All about him were fish—layer upon layer in the water above—layer upon layer below; fish to right and left —fish before him and behind him.

Ordinarily the "tacks," or eight-to-ten-inch mackerel of the year, would have schooled separately, the division of small fish from large being accomplished by the slower swimming speed of the younger fish. But now that even the larger mackerel —the heavy fish six or eight years old—were moving no faster than the great, sprawling cloud of plankton on which they were preying, the tacks easily kept pace with them, and large and small mackerel schooled together.

The movements of the many fish in the water, the sight of the large mackerel darting, wheeling, turning in darkness, their bodies gleaming with a borrowed light, filled the yearlings with tension and excitement. But so engrossed were the mackerel in feeding that none of them, large or small, was at first aware of the passage through the sea overhead of a luminous streak, like the wake of a giant fish swimming at the surface.

The birds resting on the sea heard the night silence broken by a dull throbbing; some of them that slept more deeply than the others got up from the water only just in time to avoid being struck by the cruising vessel. But neither the startled cry of a fulmar nor the sharp flap of a shearwater's wing could send a message of warning to the fish below.

"Mackerel!" called the lookout at the masthead.

The throb of the engine died away to a scarcely audible heartbeat of sound. A dozen men leaned over the rail of the mackerel seiner, peering into darkness. The seiner carried no light. To do so might frighten the fish. Everywhere was blackness—a thick and velvet blackness in which sky was indistinguishable from water.

But wait! Was there a flicker of light—a pale ghost of flame playing over the water there off the port bow? If there had been such a light it faded away into darkness again and the sea lay in black anonymity—a blank negation of life. But there it came again, and, like a nascent flame in a breeze, or a match cupped in the hands, it kindled to a brilliant glow; it spread into the surrounding darkness; it moved, a gleaming, amorphous cloud, through the water.

"Mackerel," echoed the captain after he had watched the light for several minutes. "Listen!"

At first there was no sound but the soft slap of water against the boat. A sea bird, flying out of darkness into darkness, struck the mast, fell to the deck with a frightened cry, and fluttered off.

Silence again.

Then came a faint but unmistakable patter like a squall of rain on the sea—the sound of mackerel, the sound of a big school of mackerel feeding at the surface.

The captain gave the order to attempt a set. He himself ascended to the masthead to direct the operations. The crew fell into their places: ten into the seine boat attached to a boom on the starboard side of the vessel; two into the dory that was towed behind the seine boat. The throb of the engine swelled. The vessel began to move in a wide circle, swinging around the glowing patch of sea. That was to quiet the fish; to round them up in a smaller circle. Three times the seiner circled the school. The second circle was smaller than the first and the third was smaller than the second. The glow in the water was brighter now and the patch of light more concentrated.

After the third circling of the school, the fisherman in the stern of the seine boat passed to the fisherman in the dory one end of the 1200-foot net that lay piled in the bottom of the seine boat. The seine was dry, having caught no fish that night. The dory cast off and the men at the oars backed water. Again the vessel began to move, towing the seine boat. Now, as the space between the seine boat and dory lengthened, the net slid steadily over the side of the larger boat. A line buoyed by cork floats stretched across the water between them. From the cork line the net hung down in a vertical curtain of webbing a hundred feet deep, held down in the water by leads in the lower border. The line marked out by corks grew from an arc to a semicircle; from a semicircle it swung to the full circle to round up the mackerel in a space four hundred feet across.

The mackerel were nervous and uneasy. Those on the outside of the school were aware of a heavy movement, as of some large sea creature in the water near them. They felt the wash of its passage through the sea—the heavy wake of displaced water. Some of them saw above them a moving, silver shape, long and oval. Beside it moved two smaller forms, one before the other. The shapes might have been those of a she-whale with two calves following at her side. Fearing the strange monsters, the mackerel feeding at the edge of the school turned in toward the center. So, all around the great body of feeding fish, mackerel were wheeling about and plunging in through the school where they could not see the great, luminous shapes and where the wake of the passage of monstrous bodies was lost in the lesser vibrations of thousands of swimming mackerel.

As once more the sea monsters began to circle their prey, only one of the small forms followed the large shape. The other drifted overhead, splashing in the water as with long fins or flippers. Now as the seine boat traced its lesser streak of flame in the water beside the wider gleaming path of the vessel, the netting spilled into the water in its wake. The netting kindled a confused glitter of showering sparks as it slid into the water and hung like a thin, swaying curtain that glimmered palely, for the plankton animals were already gathering on it. The fish were afraid of the netting wall. As the arc enclosed by the twine swung wide and then little by little closed in a great circle, the mackerel at first drew even more compactly together, each part of the school shrinking away from the netting.

Somewhere near the center of the school, Scomber was confusedly aware of the increasing press of fish about him and of the blinding glare of their bodies, clothed in sea light. For him the net did not exist, for he had not seen its plankton-spangled meshes nor brushed its twine with snout or flanks. Uneasiness filled the water and passed with electric swiftness from fish to fish. All about the circle they began to bunt against the net and to veer off and dash back through the school, spreading panic.

One of the fishermen in the seine boat had been only two years at sea. Not long enough to forget, if he ever would, the wonder, the unslakable curiosity he had brought to his job —curiosity about what lay under the surface. He sometimes thought about fish as he looked at them on deck or being iced down in the hold. What had the eyes of the mackerel seen? Things he'd never see; places he'd never go. He seldom put it into words, but it seemed to him incongruous that a creature that had made a go of life in the sea, that had run the gauntlet of all the relentless enemies that he knew roved through that dimness his eyes could not penetrate, should at last come to death on the deck of a mackerel seiner, slimy with fish gurry and slippery with scales. But after all, he was a fisherman and seldom had time to think such thoughts.

Tonight, as he fed the seine into the water and watched the scintillating light as it sank, he thought of the thousands of fish that were milling about down there. He could not see them; even those in the upper water looked only like streaks of light curveting in darkness—fireworks lost in a black, inverted sky, he thought a little dizzily. His mind's eye saw the mackerel running up to the net, bunting it with their snouts, backing off. They would be big mackerel, he thought, for the fiery streaks in the water gave a hint of their size. By the way the phosphorescent light, like a mass of molten metal, was becoming concentrated in the water, he knew that the bumping into the net and the backing off in alarm must be going on all around the circle, for now the ends of the net were closed. The seine boat had overlapped the dory and the two ends of netting had been brought together.

He helped lift the big leaden weight, fit the three-hundred-pound tom over the pursing lines, and start it sliding down the rope to close the open circle in the bottom of the net. The men were beginning to haul in the long purse lines. He thought of the mackerel down there, entrapped only by their own inability to see the way of escape through the bottom of the net. He thought of the tom sliding down, down, into the sea; of the big brass rings that hung from the lead line coming closer together as the purse line was drawn through them; of the dwindling circle at the bottom. But the way of escape must still be open.

The fish were nervous, he could tell. The streaks in the upper water were like hundreds of darting comets. The glow of the whole mass alternately dulled and kindled again to flame. It made him think of the light from steel furnaces in the sky. He seemed to see far down below the surface where the tom was shoving the rings along ahead of it, and the straining ropes were taking up the slack, and the fish were milling in the water—the fish that still had a way of escape. He could imagine that the big mackerel were getting wild. It was too large a school to have set about; but a skipper always hated to split a school. That was almost sure to send them off into deep water. Surely the big fellows would sound yet—would dive down through that shrinking circle straight toward the bottom of the sea, carrying the whole school with them.

He turned away from the water and with his hand felt the pile of wet rope in the bottom of the seine boat, trying to feel —for he could not see—the amount of rope piled up there and trying to guess how much was still to come in before the seine would be pursed.

A shout from the man at his elbow. He turned back to the water. The light within the circle of net was fading, flickering, dying away to an ashy afterglow, to darkness. The fish had sounded.

He leaned over the gunwales, peering down into dark water, watching the glow fade, seeing in imagination what he could not see in fact—the race and rush and downward whirl of thousands of mackerel. He suddenly wished he could be down there, a hundred feet down, on the lead line of the net. What a splendid sight to see those fish streaking by at top speed in a blaze of meteoric flashes! It was only later, when they had finished the long, wet task of repiling the 1200-foot length of seine in the boat, their hour's heavy work wasted, that he realized what it meant that the mackerel had sounded.

After their mad rush through the bottom of the seine, the mackerel scattered widely in the sea, and only when the night was nearly spent did any of the fish that had known the terror of the circling net feed quietly again in schools.

Before dawn, most of the seiners that had fished these waters during the night had vanished in darkness toward the west. One remained, having had bad luck all night, for out of six sets of the seine her crew had lost the fish five times by sounding. The solitary vessel was the only moving thing on the sea that morning when the east turned gray and the black water came ashimmer with silver light. Her crew was hoping for one more set—waiting for the mackerel whom the night's fishing had sent into deep water to show themselves at the surface at daybreak.

Moment by moment the light grew in the east. It picked out the tall mast and the deckhouse of the seiner; it spilled over the gunwales of the following seine boat and lost itself in the pile of netting, black with sea water. It shone on the mounds of the low wave hills and left their valleys in darkness.

Two kittiwakes came flying out of the dimness and perched on the mast, waiting for fish to be caught and sorted.

A quarter of a mile to the southwest, a dark, irregular patch appeared on the water—schooling mackerel, moving slowly into the east.

Quickly the seiner's course was changed to cross in front of the drifting school. With swift maneuvering of the boats, the net was dropped around it. Working with furious haste, the crew sent the tom plunging down the purse line, hauled in the ropes, closed the bottom of the net. Little by little, the men took in the slack of the seine, working the fish into the bunt or central part of the net where the twine was heaviest. Now the vessel came alongside the seine boat and received and made fast the mass of slack netting.

In the water beside the boat lay the bag of the seine, buoyed by corks fastened to the cork line in groups of three or four. In the net were several thousand pounds of mackerel. Most of the fish were large, but among them were a hundred or more tacks or yearlings that had summered in a New England harbor and were only recently of the open sea. One of them was Scomber.

The bailing net, like a ladle of twine on a long wooden handle, was brought into position over the seine, dipped down into the churning mass of fish, raised by pulleys, and emptied out on deck. Several score of lithe and muscular mackerel flapped on the floor boards and sent a rainbow mist of fine scales into the air.

Something was wrong about the fish in the net. Something was wrong about the way they boiled up from below, almost leaping to meet the bailing net. Fish pursed in a seine usually tried to drive the net down, to sink it by sounding. But these fish were terrorized by something in the water—something they feared more than the great boat monster in the water alongside.

There was a heavy disturbance in the water outside the seine. A small triangular fin and the long lobe of a tail cut the surface. Suddenly there were dozens of fins all about the net. A four-foot fish, slim and gray, with a mouth set well back under the tip of his snout, lunged across the cork line and drove his body among the mackerel, slashing and biting.

Now all the dogfish of the pack tore at the seine in ravenous fury, eager to seize the mackerel inside. Their razor-sharp teeth ripped the stout twine as if it had been gauze, and great holes appeared in the net. There was a moment of indescribable confusion, in which the space circumscribed by the cork line became a seething vortex of life—a maelstrom of leaping fish, of biting teeth, of flashing green and silver.

Then, almost as suddenly as it had whirled up, the vortex subsided. In a swift draining away of the turmoil and confusion, the mackerel poured through the holes in the seine, fleet as darting shadows, and lost themselves in the sea.

*

Among the mackerel who escaped both the seine and the raiding dogfish was the yearling Scomber. By evening of the same day, following older fish and directed by overmastering instinct, he had migrated many miles to seaward of the waters frequented by gill netters and seiners. He was traveling far below the surface, the pale waters of the summer sea forgotten, and was swimming down through deepening green along sea roads new and strange to him. Always he moved south and west. He was going to a place he himself had never known— the deep, quiet waters along the edge of the continental shelf, off the Capes of Virginia.

There, in time, the winter sea received him.

BOOK III
RIVER AND SEA

13
Journey to the Sea

There is a pond that lies under a hill, where the threading roots of many trees—mountain ash, hickory, chestnut oak, and hemlock—hold the rains in a deep sponge of humus. The pond is fed by two streams that carry the runoff of higher ground to the west, coming down over rocky beds grooved in the hill. Cattails, bur reeds, spike rushes, and pickerel weeds stand rooted in the soft mud around its shores and, on the side under the hill, wade out halfway into its waters. Willows grow in the wet ground along the eastern shore of the pond, where the overflow seeps down a grass-lined spillway, seeking its passage to the sea.

The smooth surface of the pond is often ringed by spreading ripples made when shiners, dace, or other minnows push against the tough sheet between air and water, and the film is dimpled, too, by the hurrying feet of small water insects that live among the reeds and rushes. The pond is called Bittern Pond, because never a spring passes without a few of these shy herons nesting in its bordering reeds, and the strange, pumping cries of the birds that stand and sway in the cattails, hidden in the blend of lights and shadows, are thought by some who hear them to be the voice of an unseen spirit of the pond.

From Bittern Pond to the sea is two hundred miles as a fish swims. Thirty miles of the way is by narrow hill streams, seventy miles by a sluggish river crawling over the coastal plain, and a hundred miles through the brackish water of a shallow bay where the sea came in, millions of years ago, and drowned the estuary of a river.

Every spring a number of small creatures come up the grassy spillway and enter Bittern Pond, having made the two-hundred-mile journey from the sea. They are curiously formed, like pieces of slender glass rods shorter than a man's finger. They are young eels, or elvers, that were born in the deep sea. Some of the eels go higher into the hills, but a few remain in the pond, where they live on crayfish and water beetles and catch frogs and small fishes and grow to adulthood.

Now it was autumn and the end of the year. From the moon's quarter to its half, rains had fallen, and all the hill streams ran in flood. The water of the two feeder streams of the pond was deep and swift and jostled the rocks of the stream beds as it hurried to the sea. The pond was deeply stirred by the inrush of water, which swept through its weed forests and swirled through its crayfish holes and crept up six inches on the trunks of its bordering willows.

The wind had sprung up at dusk. At first it had been a gentle breeze, stroking the surface of the pond to velvet smoothness. At midnight it had grown to a half gale that set all the rushes to swaying wildly and rattled the dead seed heads of the weeds and plowed deep furrows in the surface waters of the pond. The wind roared down from the hills, over forests of oak and beech and hickory and pine. It blew toward the east, toward the sea two hundred miles away.

Anguilla, the eel, nosed into the swift water that raced toward the overflow from the pond. With her keen senses she savored the strange tastes and smells in the water. They were the bitter tastes and smells of dead and rain-soaked autumn leaves, the tastes of forest moss and lichen and root-held humus. Such was the water that hurried past the eel, on its way to the sea.

Anguilla had entered Bittern Pond as a finger-long elver ten years before. She had lived in the pond through its summers and autumns and winters and springs, hiding in its weed beds by day and prowling through its waters by night, for like all eels she was a lover of darkness. She knew every crayfish burrow that ran in honeycombing furrows through the mudbank under the hill. She knew her way among the swaying, rubbery stems of spatterdock, where frogs sat on the thick leaves; and she knew where to find the spring peepers clinging to grass blades, bubbling shrilly, where in spring the pond overflowed its grassy northern shore. She could find the banks where the water rats ran and squeaked in play or tusseled in anger, so that sometimes they fell with a splash into the water—easy prey for a lurking eel. She knew the soft mud beds deep in the bottom of the pond, where in winter she could lie buried, secure against the cold—for like all eels she was a lover of warmth.

Now it was autumn again, and the water was chilling to the cold rains shed off the hard backbones of the hills. A strange restiveness was growing in Anguilla the eel. For the first time in her adult life, the food hunger was forgotten. In its place was a strange, new hunger, formless and ill-defined. Its dimly perceived object was a place of warmth and darkness—darker than the blackest night over Bittern Pond. She had known such a place once—in the dim beginnings of life, before memory began. She could not know that the way to it lay beyond the pond outlet over which she had clambered ten years before. But many times that night, as the wind and the rain tore at the surface film of the pond, Anguilla was drawn irresistibly toward the outlet over which the water was spilling on its journey to the sea. When the cocks were crowing in the farmyard over the hill, saluting the third hour of the new day, Anguilla slipped into the channel spilling down to the stream below and followed the moving water.

Even in flood, the hill stream was shallow, and its voice was the noisy voice of a young stream, full of gurglings and tricklings and the sound of water striking stone and of stone rubbing against stone. Anguilla followed the stream, feeling her way by the changing pressure of the swift water currents. She was a creature of night and darkness, and so the black water path neither confused nor frightened her.

In five miles the stream dropped a hundred feet over a rough and boulder-strewn bed. At the end of the fifth mile it slipped between two hills, following along a deep gap made by another and larger stream years before. The hills were clothed with oak and beech and hickory, and the stream ran under their interlacing branches.

At daybreak Anguilla came to a bright, shallow riffle where the stream chattered sharply over gravel and small rubble. The water moved with a sudden acceleration, draining swiftly toward the brink of a ten-foot fall where it spilled over a sheer rock face into a basin below. The rush of water carried Anguilla with it, down the steep, thin slant of white water and into the pool. The basin was deep and still and cool, having been rounded out of the rock by centuries of falling water. Dark water mosses grew on its sides and stoneworts were rooted in its silt, thriving on the lime which they took from the stones and incorporated in their round, brittle stems. Anguilla hid among the stoneworts of the pool, seeking a shelter from light and sun, for now the bright shallows of the stream repelled her.

Before she had lain in the pool for an hour another eel came over the falls and sought the darkness of the deep leaf beds. The second eel had come from higher up in the hills, and her body was lacerated in many places from the rocks of the thin upland streams she had descended. The newcomer was a larger and more powerful eel than Anguilla, for she had spent two more years in fresh water before coming to maturity.

Anguilla, who had been the largest eel in Bittern Pond for more than a year, dived down through the stoneworts at sight of the strange eel. Her passage swayed the stiff, limy stems of the chara and disturbed three water boatmen that were clinging to the chara stems, each holding its position by the grip of a jointed leg, set with rows of bristles. The insects were browsing on the film of desmids and diatoms that coated the stems of the stoneworts. The boatmen were clothed in glistening blankets of air which they had carried down with them when they dived through the surface film, and when the passing of the eel dislodged them from their quiet anchorage they rose like air bubbles, for they were lighter than water.

An insect with a body like a fragment of twig supported by six jointed legs was walking over the floating leaves and skating on the surface of the water, on which it moved as on strong silk. Its feet depressed the film into six dimples, but did not break it, so light was its body. The insect's name meant "a marsh treader," for its kind often lived in the deep sphagnum moss of bogs. The marsh treader was foraging, watching for creatures like mosquito larvae or small crustaceans to move up to the surface from the pool below. When one of the water boatmen suddenly broke through the film at the feet of the marsh treader, the twiglike insect speared it with the sharp stilettos projecting beyond its mouth and sucked the little body dry.

When Anguilla felt the strange eel pushing into the thick mat of dead leaves on the floor of the pool, she moved back into the dark recess behind the waterfall. Above her the steep face of the rock was green with the soft fronds of mosses that grew where their leaves escaped the flow of water, yet were always wet with fine spray from the falls. In spring the midges came there to lay their eggs, spinning them in thin, white skeins on the wet rocks. Later when the eggs hatched and the gauzy-winged insects began to emerge from the falls in swarms, they were watched for by bright-eyed little birds who sat on overhanging branches and darted open-mouthed into the clouds of midges. Now the midges were gone, but other small animals lived in the green, water-soaked thickets of the moss. They were the larvae of beetles and soldier flies and crane flies. They were smooth-bodied creatures, lacking the grappling hooks and suckers and the flattened, stream-molded bodies that enabled their relatives to live in the swift currents draining to the brink of the falls overhead or a dozen feet away where the pool spilled its water into the stream bed. Although they lived only a few inches from the veil of water that dropped sheer to the pool, they knew nothing of swift water and its dangers; their peaceful world was of water seeping slow through green forests of moss.

The beginning of the great leaf fall had come with the rains of the past fortnight. Throughout the day, from the roof of the forest to its floor, there was a continuous downdrift of leaves. The leaves fell so silently that the rustle of their settling to the ground was no louder than the thin scratching of the feet of mice and moles moving through their passages in the leaf mold.

All day flights of broad-winged hawks passed down along the ridges of the hills, going south. They moved with scarcely a beat of their outspread wings, for they were riding on the updrafts of air made as the west wind struck the hills and leaped upward to pass over them. The hawks were fall migrants from Canada that had followed down along the Appalachians for the sake of the air currents that made the flight easier.

At dusk, as the owls began to hoot in the woods, Anguilla left the pool and traveled downstream alone. Soon the stream flowed through rolling farm country. Twice during the night it dropped over small milldams that were white in the thin moonlight. In the stretch below the second dam, Anguilla lay for a time under an overhanging bank, where the swift currents were undercutting the heavy, grassy turf. The sharp hiss of the water over the slanting boards of the dam had frightened her. As she lay under the bank the eel that had rested with her in the pool of the waterfall came over the milldam and passed on downstream. Anguilla followed, letting the current take her bumping and jolting over the shallow riffles and gliding swiftly through the deeper stretches. Often she was aware of dark forms moving in the water near her. They were other eels, come from many of the upland feeder creeks of the main stream. Like Anguilla, the other long, slender fishes yielded to the hurrying water and let the currents speed their passage. All of the migrants were roe eels, for only the females ascend far into the fresh-water streams, beyond all reminders of the sea.

The eels were almost the only creatures that were moving in the stream that night. Once, in a copse of beech, the stream made a sharp bend and scoured out a deeper bed. As Anguilla swam into this rounded basin, several frogs dived down from the soft mud bank where they had been sitting half out of water and hid on the bottom close to the bole of a fallen tree. The frogs had been startled by the approach of a furred animal that left prints like those of human feet in the soft mud and whose small black mask and black-ringed tail showed in the faint moonlight. The raccoon lived in a hole high up in one of the beeches near by and often caught frogs and crayfish in the stream. He was not disconcerted by the series of splashes that greeted his approach, for he knew where the foolish frogs would hide. He walked out on the fallen tree and lay down flat on its trunk. He took a firm grip on its bark with the claws of his hind feet and left forepaw. The right paw he dipped into the water, reaching down as far as he could and exploring with busy, sensitive fingers the leaves and mud under the trunk. The frogs tried to burrow deeper into the litter of leaves and sticks and other stream debris. The patient fingers felt into every hole and crevice, pushed away leaves and probed the mud. Soon the coon felt a small, firm body beneath his fingers—felt the sudden movement as the frog tried to escape. The coon's grip tightened and he drew the frog quickly up onto the log. There he killed it, washed it carefully by dipping it into the stream, and ate it. As he was finishing his meal, three small black masks moved into a patch of moonlight at the edge of the stream. They belonged to the coon's mate and their two cubs, who had come down the tree to prowl for their night's food.

From force of habit, the eel thrust her snout inquisitively into the leaf litter under the log, adding to the terror of the frogs, but she did not molest them as she would have done in the pond, for hunger was forgotten in the stronger instinct that made her a part of the moving stream. When Anguilla slipped into the central current of water that swept past the end of the log, the two young coons and their mother had walked out onto the trunk and four black-masked faces were peering into the water, preparing to fish the pool for frogs.

By morning the stream had broadened and deepened. Now it fell silent and mirrored an open woods of sycamore, oak, and dogwood. Passing through the woods, it carried a freight of brightly colored leaves—bright-red, crackling leaves from the oaks, mottled green and yellow leaves from the sycamores, dull-red, leathery leaves from the dogwoods. In the great wind the dogwoods had lost their leaves, but they held their scarlet berries. Yesterday robins had gathered in flocks in the dogwoods, eating the berries; today the robins were gone south and in their place flurries of starlings swept from tree to tree, chattering and rattling and whistling to one another as they stripped the branches of berries. The starlings were in bright new fall plumage, with every breast feather spear-tipped with white.

Anguilla came to a shallow pool formed when an oak had been uprooted in a great autumn storm ten years before and had fallen across the stream. Oak dam and pool were new in the stream since Anguilla had ascended it as an elver in the spring of that year. Now a great mat of weeds, silt, sticks, dead branches, and other debris was packed around the massive trunk, plastering all the crevices, so that the water was backed up into a pool two feet deep. During the period of the full moon the eels lay in the oak-dam pool, fearing to travel in the moon-white water of the stream almost as much as they feared the sunlight.

In the mud of the pool were many burrowing, wormlike larvae—the young of lamprey eels. They were not true eels, but fishlike creatures whose skeleton was gristle instead of bone, with round, tooth-studded mouths that were always open because there were no jaws. Some of the young lampreys had hatched from eggs spawned in the pool as much as four years before and had spent most of their life buried in the mud flats of the shallow stream, blind and toothless. These older larvae, grown nearly twice the length of a man's finger, had this fall been transformed into the adult shape, and for the first time they had eyes to see the water world in which they lived. Now, like the true eels, they felt in the gentle flow of water to the sea something that urged them to follow, to descend to salt water for an interval of sea life. There they would prey semiparasitically on cod, haddock, mackerel, salmon, and many other fishes and in time would return to the river, like their parents, to spawn and die. A few of the young lampreys slipped away over the log dam every day, and on a cloudy night, when rain had fallen and white mist lay in the stream valley, the eels followed.

The next night the eels came to a place where the stream diverged around an island grown thickly with willows. The eels followed the south channel around the island, where there were broad mud flats. The island had been formed over centuries of time as the stream had dropped part of its silt load before it joined the main river. Grass seeds had taken root; seeds of trees had been brought by the water and by birds; willow shoots had sprung from broken twigs and branches carried down in flood waters; an island had been born.

The water of the main river was gray with approaching day when the eels entered it. The river channel was twelve feet deep and its water was turbid because of the inpouring of many tributary streams swollen with autumn rains. The eels did not fear the gloomy channel water by day as they had feared the bright shallows of the hill streams, and so this day they did not rest but pushed on downstream. There were many other eels in the river—migrants from other tributaries. With the increase in their numbers the excitement of the eels grew, and as the days passed they rested less often, pressing on downstream with fevered haste.

As the river widened and deepened, a strange taste came into the water. It was a slightly bitter taste, and at certain hours of the day and night it grew stronger in the water that the eels drew into their mouths and passed over their gills. With the bitter taste came unfamiliar movements of the water—a period of pressure against the downflow of the river currents followed by slow release and then swift acceleration of the current.

Now groups of slender posts stood at intervals in the river, marking out funnel shapes from which straight rows of posts ran slanting toward the shore. Blackened netting, coated with slimy algae, was run from post to post and showed several feet above the water. Gulls were often sitting on the pound nets, waiting for men to come and fish the nets so that they could pick up any fish that might be thrown away or lost. The posts were coated with barnacles and with small oysters, for now there was enough salt in the water for these shellfish to grow.

Sometimes the sandspits of the river were dotted with small shore birds standing at rest or probing at the water's edge for snails, small shrimps, worms, or other food. The shore birds were of the sea's edge, and their presence in numbers hinted of the nearness of the sea.

The strange, bitter taste grew in the water and the pulse of the tides beat stronger. On one of the ebb tides a group of small eels—none more than two feet long—came out of a brackish-water marsh and joined the migrants from the hill streams. They were males, who had never ascended the rivers but had remained within the zone of tides and brackish water.

In all of the migrants striking changes in appearance were taking place. Gradually the river garb of olive brown was changing to a glistening black, with underparts of silver. These were the colors worn only by mature eels about to undertake a far sea journey. Their bodies were firm and rounded with fat— stored energy that would be needed before the journey's end. Already in many of the migrants the snouts were becoming higher and more compressed, as though from some sharpening of the sense of smell. Their eyes were enlarged to twice their normal size, perhaps in preparation for a descent along darkening sea lanes.

Where the river broadened out to its estuary, it flowed past a high clay cliff on its southern bank. Buried in the cliff were thousands of teeth of ancient sharks, vertebrae of whales, and shells of mollusks that had been dead when the first eels had come in from the sea, eons ago. The teeth, bones, and shells were relics of the time when a warm sea had overlain all the coastal plain and the hard remains of its creatures had settled down into its bottom oozes. Buried millions of years in darkness, they were washed out of the clay by every storm to lie exposed, warmed by sunshine and bathed by rain.

The eels spent a week descending the bay, hurrying through water of increasing saltiness. The currents moved with a rhythm that was of neither river nor sea, being governed by eddies at the mouths of the many rivers that emptied into the bay and by holes in the muddy bottom thirty or forty feet beneath. The ebb tides ran stronger than the floods, because the strong outflow of the rivers resisted the press of water from the sea.

At last Anguilla neared the mouth of the bay. With her were thousands of eels, come down, like the water that brought them, from all the hills and uplands of thousands of square miles, from every stream and river that drained away to the sea by the bay. The eels followed a deep channel that hugged the eastern shore of the bay and came to where the land passed into a great salt marsh. Beyond the marsh, and between it and the sea, was a vast shallow arm of the bay, studded with islands of green marsh grass. The eels gathered in the marsh, waiting for the moment when they should pass to the sea.

The next night a strong southeast wind blew in from the sea, and when the tide began to rise the wind was behind the water, pushing it into the bay and out into the marshes. That night the bitterness of brine was tasted by fish, birds, crabs, shellfish, and all the other water creatures of the marsh. The eels lay deep under water, savoring the salt that grew stronger hour by hour as the wind-driven wall of sea water advanced into the bay. The salt was of the sea. The eels were ready for the sea—for the deep sea and all it held for them. Their years of river life were ended.

The wind was stronger than the forces of moon and sun, and, when the tide turned an hour after midnight, the salt water continued to pile up in the marsh, being blown upstream in a deep surface layer while the underlying water ebbed to the sea.

Soon after the tide turn, the seaward movement of the eels began. In the large and strange rhythms of a great water which each had known in the beginning of life, but each had long since forgotten, the eels at first moved hesitantly in the ebbing tide. The water carried them through an inlet between two islands. It took them under a fleet of oyster boats riding at anchor, waiting for daybreak. When morning came, the eels would be far away. It carried them past leaning spar buoys that marked the inlet channel and past several whistle and bell buoys anchored on shoals of sand or rock. The tide took them close under the lee shore of the larger island, from which a lighthouse flashed a long beam of light toward the sea.

From a sandy spit of the island came the cries of shore birds that were feeding in darkness on the ebb tide. Cry of shore bird and crash of surf were the sounds of the edge of the land —the edge of the sea.

The eels struggled through the line of breakers, where foam seething over black water caught the gleam of the lighthouse beacon and frothed whitely. Once beyond the wind-driven breakers they found the sea gentler, and as they followed out over the shelving sand they sank into deeper water, unrocked by violence of wind and wave.

As long as the tide ebbed, eels were leaving the marshes and running out to sea. Thousands passed the lighthouse that night, on the first lap of a far sea journey—all the silver eels, in fact, that the marsh contained. And as they passed through the surf and out to sea, so also they passed from human sight and almost from human knowledge.

14

Winter Haven

THE NIGHT OF the next full-moon tide, snow came down the bay on a northwest wind. Mile by mile the blanketing whiteness advanced, covering the hills and valleys and marsh flats of the rivers winding toward the sea. Whirling snow clouds swept across the bay, and all through the night the wind screamed over the water, where the flakes were dropping to instant destruction in the blackness of the bay.

The temperature dropped forty degrees in twenty-four hours, and when the tide went out through the mouth of the bay in the morning it left swiftly congealing pools over all the mud flats where it had spread out thinly, and the last of the ebb did not return to the sea.

The cries of the shore birds—twitter of sandpiper and bell note of plover—were silenced, and only the wind's voice was heard, whining over the levels of salt marsh and tide flat. On the last ebb tide the birds had run at the bay's edge, probing the sand; today they were gone before the blizzard.

In the morning, with the snow still whirling out of the sky, a flock of long-tailed ducks, called old squaws, came out of the northwest before the wind. The long-tails were familiars of ice and snow and wintry wind, and they made merry at the blizzard. They cried noisily to one another as they sighted, through the snowflakes, the tall white shaft of the lighthouse that marked the mouth of the bay and saw beyond it a vast gray sheet that was the sea. The old squaws loved the sea. They would live on it throughout the winter, feeding on the shellfish bars of its shallower waters and resting each night on the open ocean, beyond the surf lines. Now they pitched down out of the blizzard—darker flakes among the snow—into the shallows just outside the great salt marsh at the mouth of the bay. Throughout the morning they fed eagerly on the shellfish beds twenty feet below the surface, diving for the small black mussels.

A few of the bay's shore fish still remained in its deeper holes, off the mouths of its lower rivers. They were sea trout, croakers, spots, sea bass, and flukes. These were the fishes that had summered in the bay and spawned, some of them, over its flats or in its river estuaries or its deep holes; the fish that had escaped gilling in the drift nets that came gliding along the bottom on the ebbing tides—the fish that had missed entrapment in the netting mazes that were called pound nets.

Now the bay's waters were in the grip of winter; ice was sealing all its shallows; and its rivers brought down water from the winter hills. So the fishes turned to the sea, remembering with their whole bodies the gently sloping plain that rolled away from the mouth of the bay; remembering the place of warmth, and quiet water, and blue twilight that lay at the edge of the plain.

On the first night of the blizzard a school of sea trout had been trapped by the cold far up in the shallow bay that lay to seaward of the marsh. The thin water chilled so quickly that the warmth-loving trout were paralyzed by cold and lay on the bottom, half dead. When the tide ebbed to the sea, they were unable to follow, but remained in the thinning water. The next morning ice had formed over all the head of the shallow cove or bay and the trout perished by the hundred.

Another school of trout that had lain in deeper water off the salt marsh escaped death by the cold. Two spring tides before, these trout had come down from their feeding grounds higher in the bay and had lain just inside the channel to the sea. There the strong ebb tides brought them the feeling of icy water come down the rivers and drawn off the shallows and mud flats.

The trout moved into a deeper channel that was one of a chain of three valleys shaped like the imprint of a monstrous gull's foot deep in the soft sand of the bay mouth. The floor of the channel led them down, fathom by fathom, into quieter and warmer water, over dense beds of weed that swayed to the tide movements. Here the press of the tides was less than over the slopes of the shoals, with the strongest movement of the flood tides confined to the upper layers of water. The ebbs were the scouring tides that poured down along the floor of the valleys, stirring up the sand and carrying empty cockleshells bumping and rolling down the gentle slopes into the deep valleys.

As the sea trout entered the channel, blue crabs from the upper bay passed beneath them, sidling down the slopes from the shallows, seeking the deep, warm holes to spend the winter. The crabs crept into the thick carpet of seaweeds that grew on the channel floor and sheltered other crabs, shrimps, and small fishes.

The trout entered the channel just before nightfall, at the beginning of the ebb. During the early hours of the night other fish moved into the tide flow through the channel and pressed toward the sea. They swam close to the bottom, advancing through the thickets of weed which swayed to the passage of the myriad fish bodies. The fish were croakers that were coming down from all the surrounding shoals, driven by the cold. They lay in tiers, three or four fish deep, beneath the trout, enjoying the channel water which was many degrees warmer than the water over the shoals.

In the morning, the light in the channel was like a dense green mist, murky with sand and silt. Ten fathoms overhead the last of the flood tide was pushing to westward the red cone of the nun buoy that marked the beginning of the channel as boats came in from the sea. The buoy strained at its anchor chain and tipped and rolled to the surge of water. The trout had come to the junction of the three channels—the heel or spur of the gull's foot that pointed to the sea.

On the next ebb tide the croakers went out through the channel to the sea, seeking waters that were warmer than the bay. The sea trout lingered.

Near the last of the ebb a flurry of young shad passed through the channel, hurrying seaward. They were finger-long fish with scales like white gold. They were among the last of their kind to leave the bay, in the tributaries of which they had hatched from eggs deposited that spring. Thousands of other young of that year had already passed from the shallow, semifresh waters of the bay into the vastness of the sea, which was unknown to them and strange. The young shad moved quickly in the briny water of the bay mouth, excited by the strange taste of salt and by the rhythms of the sea.

WINTER HAVEN

Snow had ceased to fall, but the wind still blew out of the northwest, piling up the snow into deep drifts and picking up the unpacked surface flakes to whirl them in fantastic wind shapes. The cold was hard and bitter. All the narrower rivers froze from bank to bank, and the oyster boats were locked in their harbors. The bay lay in a hard rim of ice and snow. With every ebb tide, bringing down new water from the rivers, the cold increased in the channel where the sea trout lay.

On the fourth night after the blizzard, the moonglow was strong on the surface of the water. The wind broke the glow into myriad facets of reflected light, and all the ceiling of the bay was aglow with dancing flakes and shaking streamers of light. That night the trout saw hundreds of fish moving into the deep channel above them and passing seaward as dark shadows beneath the silver screen. The fish were other sea trout that had been lying in a ninety-foot hole ten miles up the bay, part of the channel of an ancient river that once had been drowned by the sea to form the bay. The fish that had been lying in the channel like a gull's foot joined the migrants from the deep hole, and together they passed to the sea.

Outside the channel, the trout came to a place of rolling sand hills. The underwater hills were even less stable than the dunes on a windy coast, for they had no roots of sea oats or dune grass to stay them against the thrust of waves that climbed the slope from the deep Atlantic. Some of the hills lay only a few fathoms under water. At every storm they shifted, tons of sand piling up or washing away during a time as short as a single rising of the tide.

After a day of wandering in the sea dunes, the trout rose to a high and tide-swept plateau that marked the seaward end of the sand-hill region. The plateau was half a mile wide and two miles long and overlooked a steeper slope that rolled down steadily into green depths. The shoal itself lay only thirty feet under the surface. Once a strong tide driven in by a southwest wind had shifted the sand and wrecked a fishing schooner bound for port with a ton of fish in its hold. The wreck of the *Mary B.* still lay on the sands, which had sunk away beneath it. Weeds grew from her spars and her masthead, and their long green tapes streamed into the water, pointing landward on the flood tides and seaward on the ebb.

The *Mary B.* lay partly buried in the sand, listing at a forty-five-degree angle to landward. A thick bed of weeds grew under her sheltered or starboard side. The hatch that had covered her fishhold had been carried away in the breaking up of the vessel when she was wrecked, and now the hold was like a dark cave in the sloping floor of the deck—a sea cave for creatures who loved to hide in darkness. The hold was half-full of the crab-cleaned skeletons of the fish that had not washed out of the hold when the vessel sank. The windows of the deckhouse had been smashed by the waves that drove the *Mary B.* aground. Now the windows were used as passageways by all the small fishes that lived about the wreck, nibbling off its encrusting growths. Silvery look-down fish, spadefish, and triggerfish moved in endless little processions in and out of the windows.

The *Mary B.* was like an oasis of life in miles of sea desert, a place where myriads of the sea's lesser fry—the small, backboneless animals—found a place of attachment; and the small fish foragers found living food encrusting all the planks and spars; and larger predators and prowlers of the sea found a hiding place.

The sea trout drew near to the dark hulk of the wreck as the last green light was fading to gray. They took some of the small fishes and crabs which they found about the vessel, satisfying the hunger born of the long, swift flight from the cold of the bay. Then they settled for the night near the weedy timbers of the *Mary B.*

The trout school lay in the water over the wreck in the lethargy that passed for sleep. They moved their fins gently to keep their position with relation to the wreck and to each other as the water pressed steadily over the shoal, moving up the slope from the sea.

At dusk the winding processions of small fishes that moved in and out of the deckhouse windows and through holes in the rotting planks dispersed and their members found resting places about the wreck. With the twilight which came early through the winter sea, the larger hunters who lived in and about the *Mary B.* stirred swiftly to life.

A long, snakelike arm was thrust out of the dark cavern of the fishhold, gripping the deck with double rows of suction cups. One after another, arms to the number of eight appeared, gripping the deck as a dark form clambered out of the hold. The creature was a large octopus who lived in the fishhold of the *Mary B.* It glided across the deck and slid into the recess above the lower wall of the deckhouse, where it concealed itself to begin the night's hunting. As it lay on the old, weed-grown planks its arms were never still, but reached out busily in all directions, exploring every familiar crack and crevice for unwary prey.

The octopus had not long to wait before a small cunner, intent on the mossy hydroids which it was nibbling off the planks of the vessel, came grazing along the wall of the deckhouse. The cunner, unsuspicious of danger, drew nearer. The octopus waited, its eyes fixed on the moving form, its groping arms stilled. The small fish came to the corner of the deckhouse, jutting out at a forty-five-degree angle to the sea bottom. A long tentacle whipped around the corner and encircled the cunner with its sensitive tip. The cunner struggled with all its strength to escape the clasp of the suckers that adhered to scales, fins, and gill covers, but it was drawn down swiftly to the waiting mouth and torn apart by the cruel beak, shaped like a parrot's.

Many times that night the waiting octopus seized unwary fish or crabs that strayed within reach of its tentacles, or launched itself out into the water to capture a fish passing at a greater distance. Then it moved by a pumping of its flaccid, saclike body, propelling itself by jets of liquid squirted from its siphons. Rarely did the encircling arms and gripping suction cups miss their mark, and gradually the gnawing hunger in the maw of the creature was assuaged.

When the weeds under the prow of the *Mary B.* were swaying confusedly to the turn of the tide, a large lobster emerged from its hiding place in the weed bed and moved off in a general shoreward direction. On land the lobster's unwieldy body would have weighed thirty pounds, but on the sea bottom it was supported by the water so that the creature moved nimbly on the tips of its four pairs of slender walking legs. The lobster carried the large crushing claws, or chelae, extended before its body, ready to seize its prey or attack an enemy.

Moving up along the vessel, the lobster paused to pick off a large starfish that was creeping over the mat of barnacles that covered the stern of the wreck with a white crust. The writhing starfish was conveyed by the pincer claws of the foremost walking legs to the mouth, where other appendages, composed of many joints and moving busily, held the spiny-skinned creature against the grinding jaws.

After eating part of the starfish, the lobster abandoned it to the scavenger crabs and moved on across the sand. Once it paused to dig for clams, turning over the sand busily. All the while its long, sensitive antennae were whipping the water for food scents. Finding no clams, the lobster moved into the shadows for its night's foraging.

Just before dusk, one of the younger sea trout had discovered the third of the large, predatory creatures that lived in the wreck. The third hunter was Lophius, the angler fish, a squat, misshapen creature formed like a bellows, with a wide gash of a mouth set with rows of sharp teeth. A curious wand grew above the mouth, like a supple fishing rod at the end of which dangled a lure, or leaflike flap of flesh. Over most of the angler's body ragged tatters of skin streamed out into the water, giving the fish the appearance of a rock grown with seaweeds. Two thickened, fleshy fins—more like the flippers of a water mammal than the fins of a fish—grew from the sides of its body, and when the angler fish moved on the bottom it drew itself forward by its fins.

Lophius was lying under the prow of the *Mary B.* when the young trout came upon him. The angler fish lay motionless, his two small, evil eyes directed upward from the top of his flat head. He was partly concealed by seaweed and his outline was largely obliterated by the rags and tatters of loose skin. To all but the most wary of the fish that moved about the wreck Lophius was invisible. Cynoscion, the sea trout, did not notice the angler fish, but saw instead a small and brightly colored object that dangled in the water about a foot and a half above the sand. The object moved; it rose and fell. So small shrimps or worms or other food animals had moved in the trout's experience, and Cynoscion swam down to investigate. When he was twice his own body's length away, a small spadefish whirled in from the open water and nibbled at the lure. Instantly there was a flash of twin rows of sharp, white teeth where a moment before harmless seaweed had swayed to the tides, and the spadefish disappeared into the mouth of the angler.

Cynoscion darted away in momentary panic at the sudden motion and lay under a rotting deck timber, gill covers moving rapidly to his increased inspiration of water. So perfect was the camouflage of the angler that the trout had not seen his outlines; the only warnings of danger were the flash of teeth and the sudden disappearance of the spadefish. Three times more as he watched the dangling, jerking lure, Cynoscion saw fishes swim up to investigate it. Two were cunners; one was a lookdown fish, high and compressed of body and silvery of color. Each of the three touched the lure and each disappeared into the maw of the angler.

Then twilight passed into darkness, and Cynoscion saw no more as he lay under the rotting deck timbers. But at intervals as the night wore on he felt the sudden movement of a large body in the water beneath him. After about the middle of the night there was no more movement in the weed bed under the prow of the *Mary B.*, for the angler fish had gone out to forage for bigger game than the few small fishes that came to investigate its lure.

A flock of eiders had come down to rest for the night on the water over the shoal. They had alighted first two miles to landward, but the sea ran in broken swells over the rough terrain beneath them and after the tide turn it foamed on the dark water around the ducks. The wind was blowing onshore, and it fought the tide. The ducks were disturbed in their sleep and flew to the outer edge of the shoal, where the water was quieter, and settled down once more on the seaward side of the breakers. The ducks rode low in the water, like laden fishing schooners. Although they slept, some with their heads under the feathers of their shoulders, they often had to paddle with their webbed feet to keep their positions in the swift-running tide.

As the sky began to lighten in the east and the water above the edge of the shoal grew gray instead of black, the forms of the floating ducks looked from below like dark oval shadows encased in a silvery sheen of air imprisoned between their feathers and the surface film. The eiders were watched from below by a pair of small, malignant eyes that belonged to a creature swimming slowly and with awkward motion through the water—a creature like a great, misshapen bellows.

Lophius was well aware that birds were somewhere near, for the scent and taste of duck were strong in the water that passed over the taste buds covering his tongue and the sensitive skin within his mouth. Even before the growing light had brought the surface shadows within his cone-shaped field of vision, he had seen phosphorescent flashes as the feet of the ducks stirred the water. Lophius had seen such flashes before, and often they had meant that birds were resting on the surface. His night's prowling had brought him only a few moderate-sized fishes, which was far from enough to fill a stomach that could hold two dozen large flounders or threescore herring or could pouch a single fish as large as the angler itself.

Lophius moved closer to the surface, climbing with his fins. He swam under an eider that was separated a little from its fellows. The duck was asleep, bill tucked in its feathers, one foot dangling below its body. Before it could waken to knowledge of its danger it was seized in a sharp-toothed mouth with a spread of nearly a foot. In sudden terror the duck beat the water with its wings and paddled with its free foot, seeking to take off from the surface. By a great exertion of strength it began to rise from the water, but the full weight of the angler hung from its body and dragged it back.

The honking of the doomed eider and the thrashing of its wings alarmed its companions, and with a wild churning of the water the remainder of the flock took off in flight, quickly disappearing into the thin mist that lay over the sea. The duck was bleeding spurts of bright-red blood from a severed leg artery. As its life ebbed away in the bright stream, its struggles grew feeble, and the strength of the great fish prevailed. Lophius pulled the duck under, sinking away from the cloud of reddened water just as a shark appeared in the dim light, attracted by the scent of blood. The angler took the duck to the floor of the shoal and swallowed it whole, for his stomach was capable of enormous distension.

Half an hour later Cynoscion, the sea trout, hunting about the wreck for small fishes, saw the angler returning to his hole under the prow of the *Mary B.*, pulling himself over the bottom by his handlike pectoral fins. He saw Lophius creep into the shadow of the vessel and saw the weeds that waved under the prow part to receive him. There the angler would lie in torpor for several days, digesting his meal.

During the day the water chilled by almost imperceptible degrees, and in the afternoon the ebb tide brought a great flood of cold water from the bay. That evening the sea trout, driven by the cold, left the wreck and ran seaward during the entire night, passing down the plain that sloped steadily away beneath them. They moved over smooth, sandy bottoms, sometimes rising to pass over a mound or shoal of broken shell. They hurried on, resting seldom because of the creeping cold. Hour by hour the water above them deepened.

The eels must have passed this way, through the country of underwater sand hills and down the sloping meadowlands and prairies of the sea.

Often during the next few days the trout were overtaken by other schools of fishes when they paused for rest or food and often they met browsing fish herds of many different kinds. The fish had come from all the bays and rivers of many miles of coast line, fleeing the winter cold. Some had come from far to the north, from the coasts of Rhode Island and Connecticut and the shores of Long Island. These were scup, thin-bodied fish with high, arched backs and spiny fins, covered with plate-like scales. Every winter the scup came from New England to the waters off the Capes of Virginia and then returned in spring to spawn in the northern waters and be caught in traps and swiftly encircling seines. The farther the sea trout traveled across the continental shelf, the more often they saw the scup herds in the green haze before them, the large bronze fish rising and sinking as they grubbed on the bottom for worms, sand dollars, and crabs and drifted up a fathom or more to munch their food.

And sometimes there were cod schools, come from Nantucket Shoals to winter in the warmer southern waters. Some of the cod would spawn in this place that seemed alien to their kind, leaving their young to the ocean currents, which might never return them to the northern home of the cod.

The cold increased. It was like a wall moving through the sea across the coastal plain. It was nothing that could be seen or touched; yet it was so real a barrier that no fish would have run back through it any more than if it had been solid as stone. In milder winters the fish would have scattered widely over the continental shelf—the croakers well inshore; the flukes or flounders on all the sandy patches; scup in all the sloping valleys, rich in bottom food; and sea bass over every piece of rocky ground. But this year the cold drove them on, mile after mile, to the edge of the continental shelf—to the edge of the deep sea. There in the quiet water, warmed by the Gulf Stream, they found a winter haven.

Even as the fish were running out across the continental shelf from all the bays and rivers, boats were moving south and out to sea. The boats were squat and ungraceful of line and they pitched and rolled in the winter sea. They were trawlers, come from many northern ports to find the fish in their winter refuge.

Only a decade before, the sea trout, the fluke, the scup, and the croakers had been safe from the fishermen's nets once they had left the bays and sounds. Then, one year, boats had come, dragging nets like long bags. The boats had moved down from the north and out from the coast, towing their nets along the bottom. At first they had taken nothing. Mile by mile, they moved farther out, and finally their nets came up filled with food fishes. The wintering grounds of the shore fish—the summer fish of the bays and river estuaries—had been discovered.

From that time on, the trawlers came every season and took millions of pounds of fishes each year. Now they were on their way, coming down from the northern fishing ports. There were haddock trawlers from Boston and flounder draggers from New Bedford; there were redfish boats from Gloucester and cod boats from Portland. Winter fishing in southern waters is easier than winter fishing on the Scotian Banks or the Grand Banks; easier even than on Georges, or Browns, or the Channel.

But this winter was cold; the bays were icebound, and the sea was gale-ridden. The fish were far out; seventy miles out, a hundred miles out. The fish were deep down in warm water, a hundred fathoms down.

The trawls went over the side, from decks that were slippery with freezing spray. The meshes of the trawl nets were stiff with ice, and all the ropes and the cables groaned and creaked with the frost. The trawls went down through the hundred fathoms of water; down from ice and sleet and heaving sea and screaming wind to a place of warmth and quiet, where fish herds browsed in the blue twilight, on the edge of the deep sea.

15
Return

THE RECORD OF the eels' journey to their spawning place is hidden in the deep sea. No one can trace the path of the eels that left the salt marsh at the mouth of the bay on that November night when wind and tide brought them the feeling of warm ocean water—how they passed from the bay to the deep Atlantic basin that lies south of Bermuda and east of Florida half a thousand miles. Nor is there a clearer record of the journey of those other eel hordes that in autumn passed to the sea from almost every river and stream of the whole Atlantic Coast from Greenland to Central America.

No one knows how the eels traveled to their common destination. Probably they shunned the pale-green surface waters, chilled by wintry winds and bright as the hill streams they had feared to descend by day. Perhaps they traveled instead at middepths or followed the contours of the gently sloping continental shelf, descending the drowned valleys of their native rivers that had cut channels across the coastal plain in sunshine millions of years ago. But somehow they came to the continent's edge, where the muddy slopes of the sea's wall fell away steeply, and so they passed to the deepest abyss of the Atlantic. There the young were to be born of the darkness of the deep sea and the old eels were to die and become sea again.

In early February billions of specks of protoplasm floated in darkness, suspended far below the surface of the sea. They were the newly hatched larvae—the only testament that remained of the parent eels. The young eels first knew life in the transition zone between the surface sea and the abyss. A thousand feet of water lay above them, straining out the rays of the sun. Only the longest and strongest of the rays filtered down to the level where the eels drifted in the sea—a cold and sterile residue of blue and ultraviolet, shorn of all its warmth of reds and yellows and greens. For a twentieth part of the day the blackness was displaced by a strange light of a vivid and unearthly blue that came stealing down from above. But only the straight, long rays of the sun when it passed the zenith had power to dispel the blackness, and the deep sea's hour of dawn light was merged in its hour of twilight. Quickly the blue light faded away, and the eels lived again in the long night that was only less black than the abyss, where the night had no end.

At first the young eels knew little of the strange world into which they had come, but lived passively in its waters. They sought no food, sustaining their flattened, leaf-shaped bodies on the residue of embryonic tissue, and so they were the foes of none of their neighbors. They drifted without effort, buoyed by their leafy form and by the balance between the density of their own tissues and that of the sea water. Their small bodies were colorless as crystal. Even the blood that ran in its channels, pumped by hearts of infinitesimal size, was unpigmented; only the eyes, small as black pinpricks, showed color. By their transparency the young eels were better fitted to live in this twilight zone of the sea, where safety from hungry foragers was to be found only in blending with the surroundings.

Billions of young eels—billions of pairs of black, pinprick eyes peering into the strange sea world that overlay the abyss. Before the eyes of the eels, clouds of copepods vibrated in their ceaseless dance of life, their crystal bodies catching the light like dust motes when the blue gleam came down from above. Clear bells pulsated in the water, fragile jellyfish adjusted to life where five hundred pounds of water pressed on every square inch of surface. Fleeing before the descending light, shoals of pteropods, or winged snails, swept down from above before the eyes of the watching eels, their forms glistening with reflected light like a rain of strangely shaped hailstones—daggers and spirals and cones of glassy clearness. Shrimps loomed up —pale ghosts in the dim light. Sometimes the shrimps were pursued by pale fishes, round of mouth and flabby of flesh, with rows of light organs set like jewels on their gray flanks. Then the shrimps often expelled jets of luminous fluid that turned to a fiery cloud to blind and confuse their enemies. Most of the fishes seen by the eels wore silver armor, for silver is the prevailing color or badge of those waters that lie at the end of the sun's rays. Such were the small dragonfish, long and slender of form, with fangs glistening in their opened mouths as they roamed through the water in an endless pursuit of prey.

Strangest of all were the fishes, half as long as a man's finger and clothed in a leathery skin, that shone with turquoise and amethyst lights and gleamed like quicksilver over their flanks. Their bodies were thin from side to side and tapered to sharp edges. When enemies looked down from above, they saw nothing, for the backs of the hatchetfish were a bluish black that was invisible in the black sea. When sea hunters looked up from below, they were confused and could not distinguish their prey with certainty, for the mirrorlike flanks of the hatchetfish reflected the blueness of the water and their outlines were lost in a shimmer of light.

The young eels lived in one layer or tier of a whole series of horizontal communities that lay one below the other, from the nereid worms that spun their strands of silk from frond to frond of the brown sargassum weed floating on the surface to the sea spiders and prawns that crawled precariously over the deep and yielding oozes of the floor of the abyss.

Above the eels was the sunlight world where plants grew, and small fishes shone green and azure in the sun, and blue and crystal jellyfish moved at the surface.

Then came the twilight zone where fishes were opalescent or silver, and red prawns shed eggs of a bright orange color, and round-mouthed fishes were pale, and the first light organs twinkled in the gloom.

Then came the first black layer, where none wore silvery sheen or opalescent luster, but all were as drab as the water in which they lived, wearing monotones of reds and browns and blacks whereby they might fade into the surrounding obscurity and defer the moment of death in the jaws of an enemy. Here the red prawns shed deep-red eggs, and the round-mouthed fishes were black, and many creatures wore luminous torches or a multitude of small lights arranged in rows or patterns that they might recognize friend or enemy.

Below them lay the abyss, the primeval bed of the sea, the deepest of all the Atlantic. The abyss is a place where change comes slow, where the passing of the years has no meaning, nor the swift succession of the seasons. The sun has no power in those depths, and so their blackness is a blackness without end, or beginning, or degree. No beating of tropical sun on the surface miles above can lessen the bleak iciness of those abyssal waters that varies little through summer or winter, through the years that melt into centuries, and the centuries into ages of geologic time. Along the floor of the ocean basins, the currents are a slow creep of frigid water, deliberate and inexorable as the flow of time itself.

Down beneath mile after mile of water—more than four miles in all—lay the sea bottom, covered with a soft, deep ooze that had been accumulating there through eons upon eons of time. These greatest depths of the Atlantic are carpeted with red clay, a pumicelike deposit hurled out of the earth from time to time by submarine volcanoes. Mingled with the pumice are spherules of iron and nickel that had their origin on some far-off sun and once rushed millions of miles through interstellar space, to perish in the earth's atmosphere and find their grave in the deep sea. Far up on the sides of the great bowl of the Atlantic the bottom oozes are thick with the skeletal remains of minute sea creatures of the surface waters—the shells of starry Foraminifera and the limy remains of algae and corals, the flintlike skeletons of Radiolaria and the frustules of diatoms. But long before such delicate structures reach this deepest bed of the abyss, they are dissolved and made one with the sea. Almost the only organic remains that have not passed into solution before they reach these cold and silent deeps are the ear bones of whales and the teeth of sharks. Here in the red clay, in the darkness and stillness, lies all that remains of ancient races of sharks that lived, perhaps, before there were whales in the sea; before the giant ferns flourished on the earth or ever the coal measures were laid down. All of the living flesh of these sharks was returned to the sea millions of years before, to be used over and over again in the fashioning of other creatures, but here and there a tooth still lies in the red-clay ooze of the deep sea, coated with a deposit of iron from a distant sun.

The abyss south of Bermuda is a meeting place for the eels of the western and eastern Atlantic. There are other great deeps in the ocean between Europe and America—chasms sunk between the mountain ranges of the sea's floor—but only this one is both deep enough and warm enough to provide the conditions which the eels need for the act of spawning. So once a year the mature eels of Europe set out across the ocean on a journey of three to four thousand miles; and once a year the mature eels of eastern America go out as though to meet them. In the westernmost part of the drifting sea of sargassum weed some of them meet and intermingle—those that travel farthest west from Europe and farthest east from America. So in the central part of the vast spawning grounds of the eels, the eggs and young of two species float side by side in the water. They are so alike in appearance that only by counting with infinite care the vertebrae that make up their backbones and the plates of muscle that flank their spines can they be distinguished. Yet some, toward the end of their period of larval life, seek the coast of America and others the coast of Europe, and none ever stray to the wrong continent.

As the months of the year passed, one by one, the young eels grew, lengthening and broadening. As they grew and the tissues of their bodies changed in density, they drifted into light. Upward passage through space in the sea was like passage through time in the Arctic world in spring, with the hours of sunlight increasing day by day. Little by little the blue haze of midday lengthened and the long nights grew shorter. Soon the eels came to the level where the first green rays, filtering down from above, warmed the blue light. So they passed into the zone of vegetation and found their first food.

The plants that received enough energy for their life processes from the sea-strained residue of sunlight were microscopic, floating spheres. On the cells of ancient brown algae the young eels first nourished their glass-clear bodies—plants of a race that had lived for untold millions of years before the first eel, or the first backboned animal of any kind, moved in the earth's seas. Through all the intervening eons of time, while group after group of living things had risen up and died away, these lime-bearing algae had continued to live in the sea, forming their small protective shields of lime that were unchanged in shape and form from those of their earliest ancestors.

Not only the eels browsed on the algae. In this blue-green zone, the sea was clouded with copepods and other plankton foraging on the drifting plants, and dotted with the swarms of shrimplike animals that fed on the copepods, and lit by the twinkling silver flashes of small fishes that pursued the shrimps. The young eels themselves were preyed upon by hungry crustaceans, squids, jellyfish, and biting worms, and by many fishes who roved open-mouthed through the water, straining food through mouth and gill raker.

By midsummer the young eels were an inch long. They were the shape of willow leaves—a perfect shape for drifters in the currents. Now they had risen to the surface layers of the sea, where the black dots of their eyes could be seen by enemies in the bright-green water. They felt the lift and roll of waves; they knew the dazzling brightness of the midday sun in the pure waters of the open ocean. Sometimes they moved in the midst of floating forests of sargassum weed, perhaps taking shelter beneath the nests of flying fishes or, in the open spaces, hiding in the shadow of the blue sail or float of a Portuguese man-of-war.

In these surface waters were moving currents, and where the currents flowed the young eels were carried. All alike were swept into the moving vortex of the north Atlantic drift—the young of the eels from Europe and the young of the eels from America. Their caravans flowed through the sea like a great river, fed from the waters south of Bermuda and composed of young eels in numbers beyond enumeration. In at least a part of this living river, the two kinds or species of eels traveled side by side, but now they could be distinguished with ease, for the young of the American eels were nearly twice as large as their companions.

The ocean currents swept in their great circle, moving from south through west and north. Summer drew to its end. All the sea's crops had been sown and harvested, one by one—the spring crop of diatoms, the swarms of plankton animals that grew and multiplied on the abundant plants, the young of myriad fishes that fed on the plankton herds. Now the lull of autumn was upon the sea.

The young eels were far from their first home. Gradually the caravan began to diverge into two columns, one swinging to the west, one to the east. Before this time there must have been some subtle change in the responses of the faster-growing group of eels—something that led them more and more to the west of the broad river of moving surface water. As the time approached for them to lose the leaflike form of the larva and become rounded and sinuous like their parents, the impulse to seek fresher, shallowing waters grew. Now they found the latent power of unused muscles, and against the urging of wind and current they moved shoreward. Under the blind but powerful drive of instinct, every activity of their small and glassy bodies was directed unconsciously toward the attainment of a goal unknown in their own experience—something stamped so deeply upon the memory of their race that each of them turned without hesitation toward the coast from which their parents had come.

A few eastern-Atlantic eels still drifted in the midst of the western-Atlantic larvae, but none among them felt the impulse to leave the deep sea. All their body processes of growth and development were geared to a slower rate. Not for two more years would they be ready for the change to the eel-like form and the transition to fresh water. So they drifted passively in the currents.

To the east, midway across the Atlantic, was another little band of leaflike travelers—eels spawned a year before. Farther to the east, in the latitude of the coastal banks of Europe, was still another host of drifting eel larvae, these yet a year older and grown to their full length. And that very season a fourth group of young eels had reached the end of their stupendous journey and was entering the bays and inlets and ascending the rivers of Europe.

For the American eels the journey was shorter. By midwinter their hordes were moving in across the continental shelf, approaching the coast. Although the sea was chilled by the icy winds that moved over it, and by the remoteness of the sun, the migrating eels remained in the surface waters, no longer needing the tropical warmth of the sea in which they had been born.

As the young moved shoreward, there passed beneath them another host of eels, another generation come to maturity and clothed in the black and silver splendor of eels returning to their first home. They must have passed without recognition —these two generations of eels—one on the threshold of a new life; the other about to lose itself in the darkness of the deep sea.

The water grew shallower beneath them as they neared the shore. The young eels took on their new form, in which they would ascend the rivers. Their leafy bodies became more compact by a shrinkage in length as well as in depth, so that the flattened leaf became a thickened cylinder. The large teeth of larval life were shed, and the heads became more rounded. A scattering of small pigment-carrying cells appeared along the backbone, but for the most part the young eels were still as transparent as glass. In this stage they were called "glass eels," or elvers.

Now they waited in the gray March sea, creatures of the deep sea, ready to invade the land. They waited off the sloughs and bayous and the wild-rice fields of the Gulf Coast, off the South Atlantic inlets, ready to run into the sounds and the green marshes that edged the river estuaries. They waited off the ice-choked northern rivers that came down with a surge and a rush of spring floods and thrust long arms of fresh water into the sea, so that the eels tasted the strange water taste and moved in excitement toward it. By the hundreds of thousands they waited off the mouth of the bay from which, little more than a year before, Anguilla and her companions had set out for the deep sea, blindly obeying a racial purpose which was now fulfilled in the return of the young.

The eels were nearing a point of land marked by the slim white shaft of a lighthouse. The sea ducks could see it—the piebald old-squaw ducks—when they circled high above the sea on their return every afternoon from inshore feeding grounds, coming down at dusk to the dark water with a great rush and a roar of wings. The whistling swans saw it, too, painted by the sunrise on the green sea beneath them as their flocks swept northward in the spring migration. The leader swans blew a triple note at the sight, for the point of land marked the nearness of the first stop on the swans' long flight from the Carolina Sounds to the great barrens of the Arctic.

The tides were running high with the fullness of the moon. On the ebb tides the taste of fresh water came strongly to the fish that lay at sea, off the mouth of the bay, for all the rivers were in flood.

In the moon's light the young eels saw the water fill with many fish, large and full-bellied and silvery of scale. The fish were shad returned from their feeding grounds in the sea, waiting for the ice to come out of the bay that they might ascend its rivers to spawn. Schools of croakers lay on the bottom, and the roll of their drums vibrated in the water. The croakers, with sea trout and spots, had moved in from their offshore wintering place, seeking the feeding grounds of the bay. Other fish came up into the tide flow and lay with heads to the currents, waiting to snap up the small sea animals that the swiftly moving water had dislodged, but these were bass who were of the sea and would not ascend the rivers.

As the moon waned and the surge of the tides grew less, the elvers pressed forward toward the mouth of the bay. Soon a night would come, after most of the snow had melted and run as water to the sea, when the moon's light and the tide's press would be feeble and a warm rain would fall, mist-laden and bittersweet with the scent of opening buds. Then the elvers would pour into the bay and, traveling up its shores, would find its rivers.

Some would linger in the river estuaries, brackish with the taste of the sea. These were the young male eels, who were repelled by the strangeness of fresh water. But the females would press on, swimming up against the currents of the rivers. They would move swiftly and by night as their mothers had come down the rivers. Their columns, miles in length, would wind up along the shallows of river and stream, each elver pressing close to the tail of the next before it, the whole like a serpent of monstrous length. No hardship and no obstacle would deter them. They would be preyed upon by hungry fishes—trout, bass, pickerel, and even by older eels; by rats hunting the edge of the water; and by gulls, herons, kingfishers, crows, grebes, and loons. They would swarm up waterfalls and clamber over moss-grown rocks, wet with spray; they would squirm up the spillways of dams. Some would go on for hundreds of miles—creatures of the deep sea spreading over all the land where the sea itself had lain many times before.

And as the eels lay offshore in the March sea, waiting for the time when they should enter the waters of the land, the sea, too, lay restless, awaiting the time when once more it should encroach upon the coastal plain, and creep up the sides of the foothills, and lap at the bases of the mountain ranges. As the waiting of the eels off the mouth of the bay was only an interlude in a long life filled with constant change, so the relation of sea and coast and mountain ranges was that of a moment in geologic time. For once more the mountains would be worn away by the endless erosion of water and carried in silt to the sea, and once more all the coast would be water again, and the places of its cities and towns would belong to the sea.

GLOSSARY

ABYSS. *The central deeps of the ocean, enclosed by the steep walls of the continental slope. The floor of the abyss is a vast and desolate plain, lying, on the average, about three miles deep, with occasional valleys or canyons dropping off to depths of five or six miles. The bottom is covered with a deep, soft deposit composed of inorganic clays and of the insoluble remains of minute sea creatures. The abyss is wholly without light and is uniformly cold.*

ALGA *(ăl'-gȧ; pl. algae [-jē]). The algae belong to the first of the four major divisions of the plant kingdom and are the simplest and probably the oldest plants. They do not have true roots, stems, or leaves, but usually consist of a simple, leaflike frond. They range in size from microscopic spheres to giant seaweeds several hundred feet long. (See oarweed.)*

AMPHIPOD *(ăm'-fĭ-pŏd). Belonging to the same large group as crabs, lobsters, and shrimps, the amphipods comprise a large group of crustaceans whose bodies are flattened from side to side and covered with a polished and flexible cuticle that is divided into sections, allowing them to jump or swim with surprising agility. There are about three thousand species of amphipods, most of which live in the sea or about its edge. Perhaps the most familiar of these are the sand fleas. Caprella, the species shown, often attaches itself by the hinder legs to a bit of seaweed and extends its body stiffly, so that it may easily be mistaken for a branch of the weed. It is about half an inch long.*

AMPHIPOD

ANCHOVY *(ăn-chō'-vĭ). Anchovies are small, silvery fish of herringlike appearance. They usually travel in schools which are the prey of many larger fishes. The common anchovy or whitebait is from two to four inches long.*

ANGLER FISH. *The angler is notorious as perhaps the ugliest, most repulsive, and most voracious of fishes. Half of the angler is head, and a good portion of the head is mouth, hence one of its local names: "all-mouth." The angler is found on both sides of the Atlantic and may be as much as four feet long.*

ANGUILLA *(ăng-gwĭl'-à). The scientific name of the common eel.*

AURELIA *(ô-rē'-lĭ-à). A flat, saucer-shaped jellyfish of a white or bluish-white color that may be up to a foot in diameter. Its appearance while swimming has suggested the common name "moon jelly." Unlike many other jellyfishes, it has small and inconspicuous tentacles. The moon jelly is found on both Atlantic and Pacific coasts.*

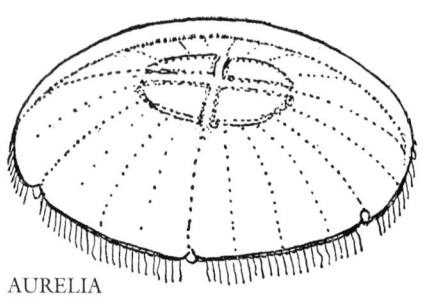
AURELIA

AVENS, MOUNTAIN. *A dwarf, hardy shrub of the rose family, called also "wild betony," found in Arctic and north temperate regions. The flowers are large and white, and the leaves are said to be one of the chief foods of the ptarmigan in winter.*

BARNACLE. *In spite of the hard shells that enclose it, the barnacle is not related to oysters and clams, as many people suppose, but is a crustacean and so related to crabs, lobsters, and water fleas.*

BARNACLE

The shells remain open while they are covered by water, and the legs, as delicately feathered as an ostrich plume, are thrust out rhythmically to aerate the blood contained in the filaments and to kick small food animals into the mouth. When the tide ebbs, barnacles that grow between the tide lines close their shells with an audible click.

BASKET STARFISH. *A species of starfish with intricately branched arms, on the tips of which it walks. It preys on fishes which are so unfortunate as to venture within the brushlike mass of arms; and is found from eastern Long Island northward, in offshore waters.*

BEACH FLEA. *(See sand flea.)*

BEROË *(bĕr'-ŏ-ē). One of the larger ctenophores (about four inches long) which feeds largely on its own relatives, often swallowing prey as large as itself. These ctenophores are abundant in New England waters in July and August, appearing at the surface during the warmest part of the day, and dropping to greater depths when the water is cold or rough.*

BETONY. *(See Avens.)*

BIG-EYED SHRIMP. *So called because of the large eyes which are very conspicuous in the nearly transparent bodies of these shrimplike crustaceans. Especially interesting are the phosphorescent spots which vary in number and arrangement with the species. These shrimps occur at the surface in swarms, usually accompanied by schools of fish and sometimes by immense flocks of gulls. They are often to be seen in tide rips.*

BLENNY. *This small fish lives among seaweeds and stones from the tide lines down to depths of thirty to fifty fathoms or sometimes a little deeper. Its body is elongated and somewhat eel-like, with a fin running almost the entire length of the back.*

BRANT. *Shallow coastal bays are ideal feeding grounds for these black and gray geese, who obtain their favorite food—the roots and lower stems of eel grass—by "tipping up" where the water is shallow enough and pulling up the grass. Their migration routes take them from Virginia and North Carolina to Greenland and the extreme northern Arctic Islands, via Cape Cod, the Gulf of St. Lawrence, and Hudson Bay.*

BROWN ALGAE. *Among the brown algae is a group (called "round lime bearers") whose members wear shields of lime united into a remarkable defensive armor. Remains of these shields are found in very ancient geological deposits, at least as remote as Cambrian time. Present-day forms are practically identical in structure with their prehistoric ancestors.*

BRYOZOA *(brī-ŏ-zō'-à)*. *Marine and fresh-water animals usually of a delicately branched and mosslike form. Early naturalists considered them plants. Some types form limy crusts of lacelike appearance on stones and seaweeds. The group is a very ancient one.*

BYSSUS THREAD *(bĭs'-ŭs)*. *Certain shellfish, such as clams, mussels, and the like, possess (especially during infancy) a gland capable of secreting a fluid that hardens into a tough thread or cord on contact with seawater. This thread, called the byssus, serves to anchor its owner against the pull of surf or tidal flow.*

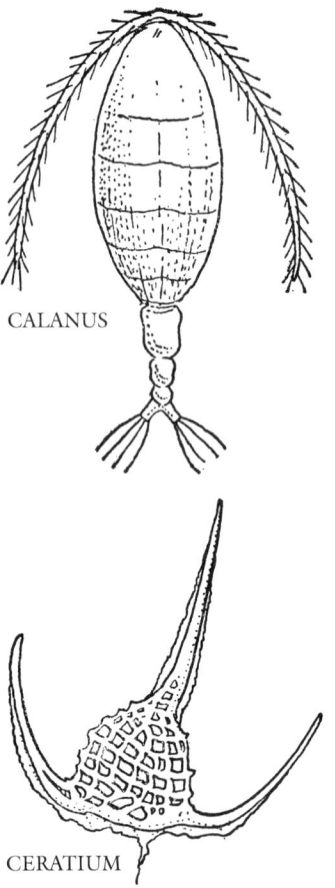

CALANUS

CERATIUM

CALANUS *(căl'-à-nŭs)*. *A small copepod crustacean (about an eighth of an inch long) that is extremely abundant at certain seasons of the year off the New England coast. Its economic importance is considerable, because it is one of the principal foods of the herring and mackerel, also of the Greenland whale. (See copepod and crustacean.)*

CERATIUM *(sĕ-rā'-shĭ-ŭm)*. *A single-celled creature about 1/100 of an inch in diameter, claimed by botanists as well as zoologists, but usually considered an animal. It is extremely phosphorescent, and during the periods of its greatest abundance the sea blazes with light when disturbed.*

CERO *(sē'-rō)*. *A large, silvery fish of the mackerel tribe, found chiefly in southern waters. Another common name is "kingfish." It is a strong and active predator, and often is found among schools of menhaden.*

CHARA *(kā'-rà).* *This fresh-water alga forms underwater meadows in ponds or lakes receiving water from lime-containing soils. The plant is characteristically rough and brittle to the touch because of the carbonate of lime deposited in its tissues and on its surface. In some waters it forms large deposits of marl, a crumbling, limy substance used as a fertilizer for soils deficient in lime. The leaflets grow from the central stem in candelabralike clusters, and the fruiting bodies remind one of translucent Japanese lanterns of pinhead size, some orange and some green.*

CHELA *(kē'-là).* *The large, pincerlike claw of a lobster, the muscles of which are considered the choicest part of the animal for eating. It is an effective weapon for defense or attack.*

CHITIN *(kī'-tĭn).* *A horny substance that forms the harder part of the outer covering of insects, lobsters, crabs, and the like.*

CHLOROPHYLL *(klō'-rō-fĭl).* *The green coloring matter of plants, which plays an essential part in the manufacture of starches and sugars by the leaves.*

CILIUM *(sĭl'-ĭ-ŭm).* *A minute, hairlike projection from a cell. Usually occurring in numbers wherever present, cilia set up a current by rhythmic lashing movements. Some one-celled animals and plants and some larvae of higher forms move by cilia.*

COCKLE. *A mollusk with a heart-shaped shell usually sculptured into radiating ridges and handsomely marked both inside and out. The cockle is a much more active shellfish than the related clams, and progresses along the bottom by surprising leaps and tumbles. These are effected by thrusting out a muscular "foot," bending it under the shell, and suddenly straightening it.*

CONGER EEL *(kŏng'-gēr).* *Conger eels are exclusively marine, reach a weight of fifteen pounds or more in American waters and up to one hundred and twenty-five pounds in European, and are exceedingly voracious.*

CONTINENTAL SHELF. *The gently sloping bottom of the sea from the tide lines down to depths of approximately one hundred fathoms is known as the continental shelf. In places the continental shelf of the United States is about a hundred miles wide; in others, as off the Florida coast, it is only a few miles wide. Many* parts of the present shelf were land in comparatively recent geological times. Most marine commercial fisheries are confined to waters over the shelf. The steeper descent from the edge of the shelf to the oceanic abyss is known as the continental slope.

COPEPOD (kō'-pĕ-pŏd). A large subclass of crustaceans (q.v.) all less than two-fifths of an inch long and most of them much smaller. Many are free-swimming members of the plankton; some use the bodies of living animals as homes from which they come and go without detriment to their host; others are parasites on the gills, skin, or flesh of fish. They are one of the most important links in the marine food chain, making plant foods available to the many young fishes and other creatures that feed on them. (See Calanus, for example.)

CRAB LARVA. Newly hatched crabs are transparent, big-headed creatures that bear no resemblance to their parents. As they grow they must shed the hard cuticle that covers them with an unyielding armor, and so they pass through a series of molts, each of which brings them a little closer to a crablike physique. Their early life is spent near the surface, swimming about actively and snapping up smaller creatures from the surrounding water.

CRANE FLY. An adult crane fly is a long-legged, mosquitolike insect often seen about streams at dusk, or flying about lights after dark. Their larvae live in the water or in moist places.

CROAKER. An abundant fish of the Atlantic Coast south of New England, which owes its common name to its ability to make a grunting or croaking sound by drumming with a pair of specialized muscles on its air bladder (a balloonlike sac under the *backbone). This drumming may be heard a considerable distance under water. Another common name, used especially in the Chesapeake Bay area, is "hardhead."*

CROWBERRY. *A low-growing evergreen shrub of Arctic regions from Alaska to Greenland, found also as far south as northern United States. Its berries are a favorite food of Arctic birds.*

CRUSTACEAN. *Animals that wear a segmented shell and have segmented legs are arthropods; arthropods that live in the water and breathe by gills are crustaceans. Familiar examples are lobsters, barnacles, shrimps, and crabs.*

CTENOPHORE *(tĕn'-ō-fōr). A marine animal much like a jellyfish. Most ctenophores are cylindrical or pear-shaped and swim by the beating of hairlike cilia arranged in eight longitudinal bands or combs, hence the common name "comb jelly." They are beautifully iridescent in sunlight and usually phosphorescent in darkness. They are important economically because they destroy large numbers of young fish.*

CUNNER. *A rather deep-bodied fish with a long, spiny back fin, found especially about wharf piles and sea walls and sometimes offshore, from Labrador to New Jersey.*

CURLEW. *A large, long-billed bird belonging to the same general group as sandpipers. It ranges in winter to the Pacific Coast of South America, from which it migrates, either by way of the Pacific Coast or by Central America, Florida, and the Atlantic Coast, to the shores of the Arctic Ocean, where it breeds. The long-billed and Eskimo curlews were virtually exterminated during the past century, but fair numbers of the Hudsonian curlew remain.*

CURLEW

CYANEA *(sī-ā'-nē-à).* *This is the largest of the Atlantic Coast jellyfishes. In cold northern waters the bell-shaped body may be seven and one half feet across, with tentacles more than a hundred feet long. About ninety-five per cent of this great bulk is water. Common sizes are three to four feet across, with thirty- to forty-foot tentacles. Contact with the tentacles produces a severe burning sensation, because of the discharge of hundreds of minute "darts" from the stinging cells. In northern waters Cyanea is red, but the southern form may be a pale bluish or milky white.*

DESMID *(dĕs'-mĭd).* *A minute, one-celled, fresh-water alga, often beautifully shaped like a crescent, star, or triangle, and bright green in color.*

DIATOMS *(dī'-à-tŏm).* *One-celled algae in which the usual green coloring matter is masked by a yellow-brown pigment. The cell walls are impregnated with silica, and after death accumulate in bottom deposits, forming the basis of diatomaceous earth used in polishing powders. Beds of such earth, three hundred feet deep, have been discovered in the Rocky Mountains. Diatoms are the indispensable first links in aquatic food chains, making the nutrient minerals of the water available to the animals that eat them.*

DOVEKIE *(dŭv'-kĭ).* *A maritime bird a little smaller than a robin, belonging to the same family as the auks and puffins. They go ashore only to nest. At sea they are expert divers, and swim under water with their wings, instead of using their feet as the distantly related loons do.*

DOWITCHER *(dou'-ĭch-ēr).* *A medium-sized, long-billed shore bird of the sandpiper tribe, seen on the Atlantic Coast during migrations. It winters in Florida, the West Indies, and Brazil, and is believed to nest in northern Canada, east of Hudson Bay.*

DRAGONFISH. *In spite of its fierce appearance, only the small inhabitants of the deep sea need fear the dragonfish (called also*

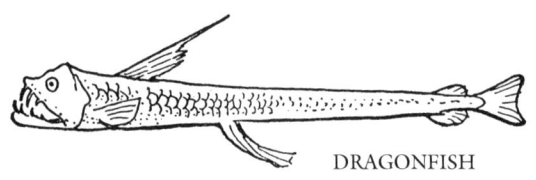

DRAGONFISH

"viperfish"), *for it is only a foot long. Probably it spends its entire life in the dark regions that lie more than a thousand feet deep.*

EGRET, SNOWY *(ē'-grĕt). Often described as the "most dainty and graceful of the herons," the snowy egret once was nearly exterminated because of unrestrained killing for the sake of the beautiful plumes it wears during the breeding season. This bird looks much like a young little-blue heron, but may be distinguished by its yellow feet.*

EIDER. *The eider is a true sea duck, and during its winter migration to the New England and Middle Atlantic Coast spends most of its time offshore, usually over the mussel beds from which it obtains its food by diving. This duck is the principal source of American eider down.*

FATHOM. *A nautical unit of measure equal to six feet.*

FIDDLER CRAB. *A small, gregarious crab of the beaches and salt marshes. In the male, one of the claws is greatly enlarged into a weapon for defense and attack. Possession of this "fiddle" is in one sense a disadvantage to the male, for it leaves him with only one claw to pick up food, while the female has two. Fiddlers usually live in enormous colonies between the tide lines, each crab in its own small burrow.*

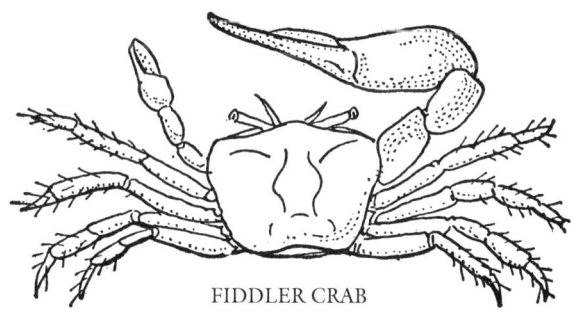

FIDDLER CRAB

FLUKE. *A name often applied to the summer flounder (Paralichthys dentatus) in the Middle Atlantic and Chesapeake Bay area. This is one of the more active and predacious flounders, sometimes pursuing schools of fish to the surface. It has a chameleonlike ability to match the color of its background. Average-sized flukes are two feet long.*

FORAMINIFERA *(fō-răm'-ĭ-nĭf'-ēr-à). A group of one-celled animals usually having limy shells with numerous pores or openings through which long processes of the living substance or protoplasm stream out. The effect is extremely beautiful. After death the shells of these minute creatures sink to the bottom and form chalk beds or deposits of limestone which may be a thousand feet thick. The pyramids of Egypt are built of enormous blocks of limestone formed by fossil Foraminifera.*

FRUSTULE. *The shell of a diatom, which is in two overlapping parts, like a box and its lid. Being almost pure silica, it is nearly indestructible. The shells are varied in shape and are delicately marked in a great diversity of patterns. These markings are sometimes used to test the power of microscope lenses.*

FULMAR *(fōol'-màr). A bird of the open ocean, belonging to the same family as the petrels and shearwaters. It is a little smaller than a herring gull, spends much of its time on the wing, and is especially active in stormy weather. Its summer range includes Greenland, Davis Strait, and Baffin Bay, while its principal winter resort is off the American coast, especially on the Grand Banks and Georges Bank.*

GANNET. *On this side of the Atlantic, gannets nest only on rocky cliffs of the Gulf of St. Lawrence, and winter from North Carolina to the Gulf of Mexico. They are large, white birds of the open sea and obtain their food by*

GANNET

diving with great force, often from a height of more than a hundred feet. Sometimes a flock of several hundred will attack a school of herring or mackerel.

GHOST CRAB. *A large crab, so pale as to be nearly invisible against the sandy beaches where it lives. It is found from New Jersey to Brazil, and is a common inhabitant of our southern beaches. It is very wary and can outdistance a swift runner. Although it does not hesitate to enter the water when necessary, it lives above the tide line in burrows about three feet deep.*

GILL NET. *A gill net may be anchored on the bottom or buoyed at the top or at almost any intermediate depth, but in any event its position in the water is much like that of a tennis net. Fish are caught in gill nets by thrusting their heads through the meshes and becoming caught by the gill covers, which project slightly, like flaps. A drift gill net is weighted so that it sinks to the bottom and drifts along with the tide.*

GILL RAKER. *In breathing, a fish takes in water through the mouth and expels it through the gill openings, which are flanked by the delicate gill filaments that absorb oxygen. The gill rakers are bony projections at the inner entrances to the gill openings. Their function is to strain the food organisms out of the water and also to protect the gill filaments from injury. They have been compared to the human epiglottis, which keeps food from getting into the windpipe.*

GLASSWORM, *also called* ARROWWORM *or* SAGITTA *(sà-jĭt'-à). These are small, elongated, and transparent worms that live only in the sea and are found from the surface to great depths. They are fierce and active predators, and eat large numbers of young fish.*

GREBE. *Grebes on the water bear a general resemblance to ducks, but if startled will dive rather than fly. They are able to swim considerable distances under water and not uncommonly are caught in fishermen's nets. Usually found in lakes, ponds, bays, and sounds, some grebes venture out to sea for fifty miles or more.*

GYRFALCON *(jûr'-fôl-kŭn). A large, predominantly white Arctic falcon that lives chiefly on small birds and lemmings.*

Occasionally it may wander south in winter to New England, New York, and northern Pennsylvania.

HADDOCK. *A fish of the cod family which lives almost exclusively on the bottom at practically all depths over the continental shelf. The largest haddock on record was thirty-seven inches long and weighed twenty-four and one half pounds.*

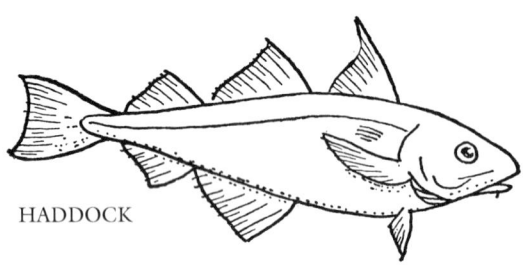
HADDOCK

HAKE. *Like the haddock, the hakes are members of the cod family, although not at all codlike in appearance, being more slender and tapering fishes. A characteristic feature is the long and feelerlike ventral fin, with which the fish is believed to detect the presence of prey on the bottom.*

HATCHETFISH. *A compressed, silvery, deep-sea fish with highly developed light organs.*

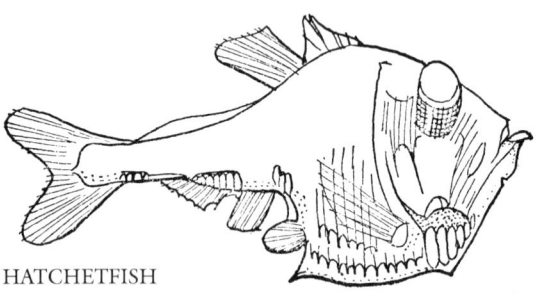
HATCHETFISH

HERMIT CRAB. *These curious crabs live within the shells of snail-like mollusks, dragging this "house" about with them as protection for their delicate abdomens, which are covered only by a thin skin. When a hermit crab grows too large for its house it must seek a new one, and the inspection of possible quarters is made*

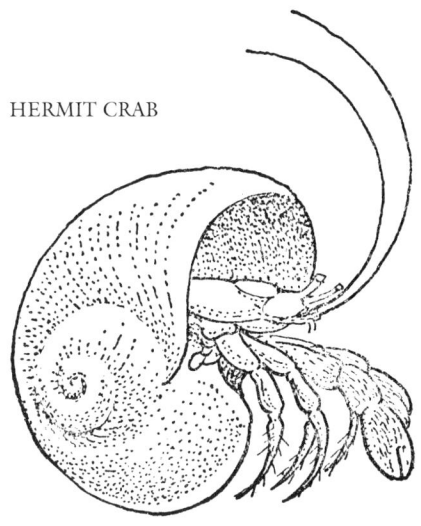

HERMIT CRAB

with great care. Once the selection has been made, the crab whips out of the old shell and into the new with remarkable celerity. Allegedly, it does not confine itself to empty shells, but may forcibly remove the rightful owner.

HOLDFAST. *A rootlike structure, as of algae and other simple plants, for attachment to the substratum.*

HOOK-EARED SCULPIN. *A curious fish with fanlike pectoral fins and conspicuous hooks on the cheeks. It is a cold-water fish, found from Labrador south to Cape Cod and Georges Bank.*

HYDROID *(hī'-droid). A plantlike animal of the jellyfish group, that is attached at one end and usually has a mouth surrounded by tentacles at the other. The resemblance to a many-branched plant is especially strong when hydroid forms occur in colonies, with a central stalk serving to transport food to the various members.*

JAEGER *(yā'-gẽr). The jaegers belong to the same order of birds as gulls and terns, but in their habits they resemble falcons and other birds of prey. On the high seas, where they winter, they play the part of pirates, forcing gulls, shearwaters, and other birds to give up their booty. During their nesting season on the Arctic tundras, they prey on small birds and lemmings.*

JINGLE SHELL. *A small mollusk with a very thin shell, usually of a lustrous golden, lemon, or peach color. The empty shells accumulate in windrows on the beach and are said to produce a ringing or jingling sound when disturbed by wind or tide. Jingles are found from the West Indies to Cape Cod.*

KILLIFISH. *Small minnows of schooling habit, found in droves of thousands of individuals in shallow bays, coves, and marshy places along the coast.*

KITTIWAKE. *The kittiwake is a small gull, one of the hardiest of the tribe, for it is truly an oceanic bird and seldom is seen inland except during migrations. This is the gull that follows transatlantic liners for long distances.*

KNOT. *A somewhat robinlike bird of the shore, arriving in the United States from South America in early April. Its nesting grounds were long unknown, but have now been found in the wildest and most remote parts of Grinnell Land, Greenland, and Victoria Land.*

LATERAL LINE. *The lateral line may be seen in most fishes as a row of pores extending along the flanks from the gill covers to the tail. Internally, these pores communicate with a long, mucous-filled tube which, in turn, is connected with many sensory nerves. The lateral-line organ is believed to allow the fish to detect sound vibrations of a frequency so low that they would scarcely be audible to the human ear. In practice, this means that a fish can sense at a distance the approach of another fish; or can tell that it is coming near to an obstacle, as a wall of rock. According to recent experiments, the lateral line may also help the fish to detect changes in the temperature of the water.*

LAUNCE. *A slender, round-bodied fish, in appearance something like a small eel. Between the tide lines, it buries itself in the sand while the tide is out. It is a plentiful fish along sandy beaches from Cape Hatteras to Labrador and is abundant over the shoaler parts of the offshore banks. Like most other small, schooling fishes, it forms the food of many ocean predators, including finback whales.*

LEMMING *(lĕm'-ing). A small, mouselike rodent chiefly of Arctic regions, with very short tail, small ears, and furry feet. The*

Lapland lemmings are remarkable for the mass migrations which they periodically undertake. At such times they advance in great bands in the chosen direction, heedless of obstacles in their path. When they come to the sea they rush into it and are drowned.

LINE TRAWL. *Line trawling is an old-fashioned method of fishing for groundfish which has not been wholly superseded by the modern diesel-engined otter trawler. In line trawling, each vessel carries dories, from which the gear is set. A trawl line consists of a long ground line to which short baited lines are attached at intervals of about five feet. Each end of the long line is anchored and marked with a buoy. At intervals, the fishermen take up the lines and remove the fish. Sometimes (in "underrunning" the trawl) the line is merely passed across the dory, the fish removed, the hooks rebaited, and returned at once to the water.*

LONGSPUR, LAPLAND. *A bird of the finch and sparrow tribe, about the size of a song sparrow. In winter, longspurs are occasionally to be seen in northern United States and southern Canada, but summer finds them on nesting grounds beyond the tree line in northern Canada and in Greenland and scattered Arctic islands. On the western plains they are described as occurring in "long straggling flocks, all singing together."*

LOOK-DOWN FISH. *A very curious fish common from Chesapeake Bay southward. Its body is high and compressed from side to side, and is a beautiful silvery color with opalescent lights. The*

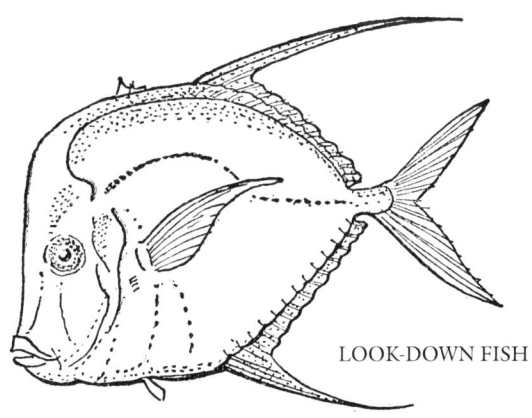

LOOK-DOWN FISH

long, straight profile and high "forehead" give a distinct impression that the fish is looking down its nose.

MARSH SAMPHIRE *(săm'-fīr). The marsh samphire or glasswort is a plant of the salt marshes that turns a vivid red in autumn, forming patches of brilliant color.*

MARSH TREADER. *A long and slender-bodied water insect that walks about deliberately over the leaves of water lilies or on the surface film, watching for the mosquito larvae, water boatmen, and small crustaceans on which it preys.*

MAY FLY. *The greater part of the life of a May fly is spent in the immature stage which lives in clean, fresh water as long as three years, burrowing into banks and under stones or running about over the bottom. At maturity it emerges, mates, lays its eggs, and dies, all within one or two days. The life of the adult May fly has become a symbol of a brief and ephemeral existence.*

MEDUSA. *The familiar jellyfish in the shape of a bell, umbrella, or disc is known as a medusa. Some jellyfishes have alternating medusa and hydroid stages in their life history. (See hydroid.)*

MENHADEN *(měn-hā'-d'n). A schooling fish closely related to shad and herring, found from Nova Scotia to Brazil. It is caught in large quantities for the preparation of oil, meals for stock feeding, and fertilizer, but is not a food fish. It has been described as the prey of every larger predacious animal that swims, including whales, porpoises, tuna, swordfish, pollock, and cod.*

MERGANSER *(mēr-găn'-sēr). Mergansers are fish-eating ducks that are expert divers and underwater swimmers. The bills are equipped with sharp, toothlike points which are excellently adapted for catching and holding slippery prey.*

MNEMIOPSIS *(nē-mĭ-ŏp'-sĭs). This ctenophore reaches a length of four inches and occurs in swarms from Long Island to the Carolinas. It is glitteringly transparent and very phosphorescent.*

MOON JELLY. *(See Aurelia.)*

NEREIS *(nēr'-ē-ĭs). An active and graceful creature to watch, Nereis is a marine worm that may be from two or three to twelve inches long, depending on the species. It is found under stones and among seaweed in shallow water, and at times swims at*

NEREIS

the surface. The usual color is bronze, with a beautiful iridescent sheen. Its strong, horny jaws equip it for its life as an active predator.

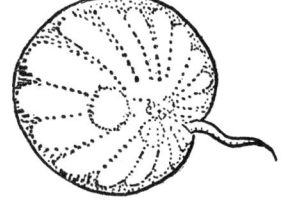
NOCTILUCA

NOCTILUCA *(nŏk'-tĭ-lū'-kà). This single-celled animal (about 3/100 of an inch in diameter) is one of the principal light producers of the sea, at times making large areas glow with an intense phosphorescent light. By day, floating swarms of Noctiluca may tinge the sea with red.*

OARWEED. *A brown seaweed of the genus Laminaria, all of which are large, with broad, leathery fronds. The larger specimens grow in deep water but often are torn up and washed ashore. Other common names for members of the group are "devil's apron," "sole leather," and "kelp." These algae are among the largest plants known. A related Pacific Coast species may be several hundred feet long.*

OLD SQUAW. *A sea duck noted for its restless and lively disposition, its noisiness, and its disregard of stormy winter weather. It breeds on the Arctic Coast and winters south to the Chesapeake Bay and the coast of North Carolina. The long tail feathers of the male distinguish it at once from any other duck.*

ORCA *(ôr'-kà). The orca, or killer whale, is a member of the dolphin family, but is easily distinguished from its relatives by the very high fin on its back. Packs of orcas travel rapidly at the surface of the sea, attacking whales, dolphins, seals, walruses, and large fishes. They are exceedingly strong and bold. Even large whales appear to be paralyzed with fear at their approach.*

OTTER TRAWL. *An otter trawl is a large, cone-shaped bag of netting which is towed along the bottom. The average net is about 120 feet long, and 100 feet wide at the mouth. During the towing, the mouth opens to a height of about fifteen feet, being held open by two heavy oak doors, so adjusted that their resistance to the water makes them pull away from each other. The doors, in turn, are attached by long towing lines to the vessel.*

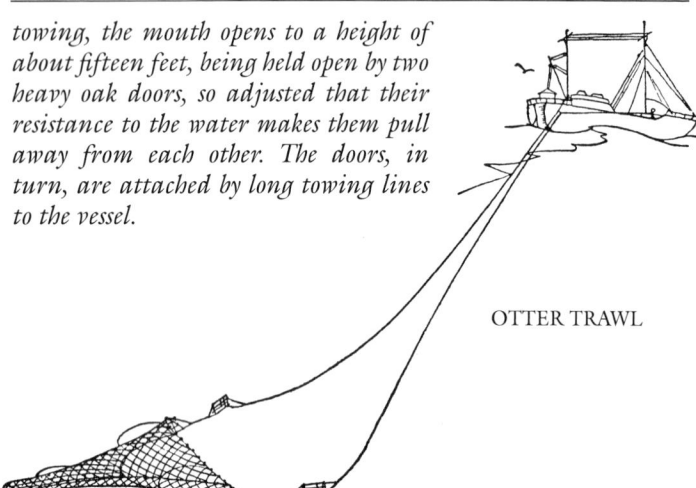

OTTER TRAWL

PANDION *(păn-dī'-ŏn). The scientific name of the osprey.*

PETREL, WILSON'S *(pĕt'-rĕl). These little birds, often called Mother Carey's chickens, visit the coast of the United States during the summer, and in winter return to their nesting grounds on islands off the tip of South America, some within the Antarctic Circle. They are familiar to many as the swallow-like birds that follow in the wake of vessels, apparently dancing on the surface of the water.*

WILSON'S PETREL

PHALAROPE *(făl'-à-rōp). A small bird, between a sparrow and a robin in size. Although it belongs to the shore-bird tribe, its winter range makes it a bird of the open ocean. During migration phalaropes are to be found off our coast in great numbers, but they continue southward, probably well beyond the Equator. They are expert swimmers and feed on plankton when they are at sea. They are said sometimes to alight on the backs of whales to pick off attached sea lice.*

GLOSSARY 171

PLANKTON. *Derived from a Greek word that means "wanderers," the term plankton is applied collectively to all the minute plants and animals that live at or near the surface of oceans or lakes. Some members of the plankton are wholly passive and drift to and fro with the currents; others are able to swim about actively in search of food. All, however, are subject to the stronger movements of the surface waters. Many sea creatures are temporary members of the plankton during infancy. This is true of most fishes and of bottom-living clams, starfish, crabs, and many other animals.*

PLEUROBRACHIA *(plōōr'-ō-brā'-kĭ-à). This is a small ctenophore— about half an inch to an inch long —with very long tentacles which may be white or rose-colored. It destroys large numbers of young fish wherever it is abundant.*

PLOVER *(plŭ'vẽr). Plovers are shore birds that do not, as a rule, run at the edge of the surf as sandpipers do, but remain higher up on the beach. Among the most familiar kinds are the killdeer and ringneck plovers. As further distinguished from sandpipers, they run about with heads up, then probe suddenly as robins do, instead of constantly probing and dabbing. Plovers nest in Canada and the Arctic (a few species in the United States) and winter as far south as Chile and Argentina.*

PLEUROBRACHIA

PORTUGUESE MAN-OF-WAR. *Many people have seen the beautiful blue float of this creature drifting at the surface, especially in tropical waters or in the Gulf Stream. This float acts as an air vessel or sail, and has hanging tentacles that may stretch to a length of forty to fifty feet for anchorage. The Portuguese man-of-war belongs to the same general group as jellyfish and is considered perhaps the most dangerous member of the group, for its sting can cause serious illness or even death. (See top of next page.)*

PORTUGUESE MAN-OF-WAR

POUND NET. *A sort of underwater maze formed of netting attached to stakes driven into the bottom. The opening is so placed that the usual paths of the fish take them into it, and after they have passed through several compartments of the pound it is very difficult to find their way out again. In the last compartment— the "pot" or "crib"—there is also a floor of netting.*

PRAWN. *A shrimp. The two names often are used interchangeably, or "prawn" may be applied to larger specimens, and "shrimp" to smaller.*

PTARMIGAN *(tär'-mĭ-găn). The ptarmigan is a grouselike bird of the Arctic tundras of both the eastern and western hemispheres. In winter, when snow covers the tundra's food supplies, it migrates in immense flocks into protected river valleys of the interior. Occasional specimens have been seen in winter in Maine, New York, and other northern states.*

PTEROPOD *(tĕr'-ṓ-pŏd). A kind of mollusk closely related to the common snail, but bearing little resemblance in appearance or habit to that prosaic creature. Pteropods live in the open waters of the sea, where they swim gracefully through the upper layers. Some have shells of paper thinness; others are without shells and beautifully colored. Sometimes they occur locally in enormous numbers, and are eaten in large quantities by whales.*

PURSE SEINE. *A purse seine is a net of the encircling type, used in deep water to capture fish that school at the surface. Fish must be visible to be caught in a purse seine—either as dark patches on the water in daylight, or by the phosphorescent glow they stir up on dark nights. The net is dropped into the water in such a way that it hangs in a vertical wall in the shape of a circle, in the center of which is the school of fish. The net is then "pursed" or shirred together by drawing in the lines run through its lower border. The next operation is to take in the slack of the net, concentrate the fish in the "bunt," or section where the twine is strongest, and bail them out with a kind of dip net.*

RADIOLARIA *(rā'-dĭ-ṓ-lā'-rĭ-à). Radiolaria are one-celled animals that live only in the sea and are sometimes large enough to be seen with the unaided eye. Usually they are encased in a skeleton of silica which is exquisitely constructed like a star or a snowflake, with the living substance streaming out through perforations in the skeleton in long, raylike strands. Like the Foraminifera (q.v.) their skeletons sink to the bottom and occur in enormous numbers in marine deposits.*

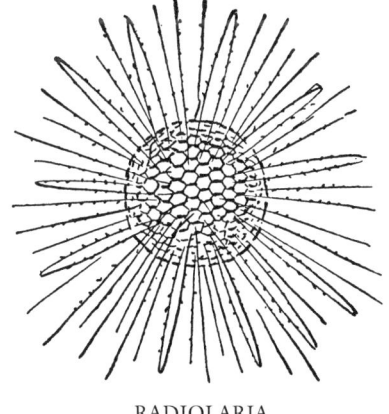

RADIOLARIA

RED CLAY. *A bottom deposit characteristic of the great depths of the ocean (over three miles deep), which carpets a larger area than any other type of deposit. Its basis is hydrated silicate of alumina, and it contains very few organic remains because of the depth at which it lies.*

ROUND-MOUTHED FISH. *An oceanic fish that lives at mid-depths and possesses rows of phosphorescent organs with black rims and silver centers. The fish itself may be pale gray to black, depending on the depth at which it lives. (The deeper and darker the water, the darker the fish.) The mouth is extremely large and round when opened; hence the common name.*

RYNCHOPS *(rĭng'-kŏps). The scientific name of the black skimmer.*

SALPA. *Salpae or salps are transparent, barrel-shaped animals found in the sea. A single individual is an inch or more long, and many individuals may live together in colonies or chains. This is one of the creatures that show the beginnings of the stiffening rod that is perfected as the backbone in the vertebrates; but it is probably a side branch in the evolutionary tree, which did not lead directly to the development of vertebrates.*

SAND BUG. *Sand bugs are common on beaches from Cape Cod to Florida, where they live in great colonies between the tide lines. When the sand looks strongly pitted after a wave has washed over it, investigation will usually show that there are sand bugs scrambling in the film of water. They are covered with an oval shell, under which the tail or abdomen is bent forward for protection. They are distant cousins of the hermit crab, which resorts to a different device to protect its thin-skinned abdomen (see hermit crab), and are sometimes called "hippa crabs" from their scientific name, Hippa talpoida.*

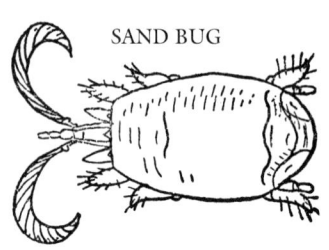

SAND BUG

SAND DOLLAR. *If all marine animals were as conveniently fashioned as the sand dollar, their identification would be a simple matter. The round, flattened shape of the test or shell accounts at once for its common name, and the star-shaped figure beautifully etched on the shell proclaims its relationship to the starfish. Usually the sand dollar lives on bottoms a little distance from the shore, but it is often washed up on beaches, where its shells are reasonably common objects. In life, the shell is covered by soft, silky spines.*

SAND EEL. *(See launce.)*

SANDERLING. *Sanderlings are fairly large sandpipers and are among the characteristic birds of the shore line. They make one of the longest of bird migrations, nesting within the Arctic Circle and wintering as far south as Patagonia.*

SAND FLEA. *These small crustaceans are important scavengers of the beaches, promptly devouring dead fishes and all kinds of organic refuse. Turn over a heap of damp seaweed and dozens of beach fleas, usually less than half an inch long, will spring out with great agility. Some forms live in shallow water; others in wet sand or seaweed.*

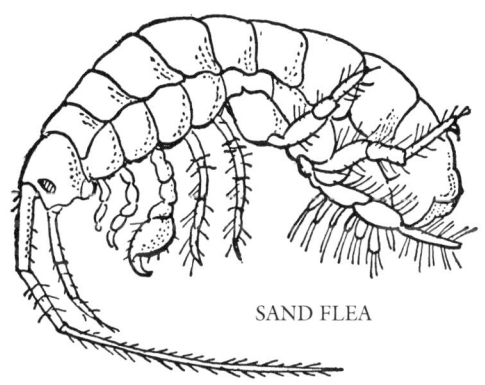

SAND FLEA

SCALLOP. *The empty shells of scallops are common objects on both east and west coasts. The shells are fan-shaped, with strong radial ridges running from the base of the fan, which also sends out laterally projecting wings in many species. The scallop is an edible mollusk like the oyster and the clam, but only the large, strong muscle that opens and closes the shells is eaten. Only this part of the scallop is seen in markets. Scallops are by no means sedentary shellfish, but swim through the water with an erratic, darting motion, achieved by rapidly opening and closing the shells.*

SCOMBER *(skŏm'-bēr). The scientific name of the mackerel.*

SCUP or PORGY. *This bronze and silvery fish is abundant in the coastal waters from Massachusetts to South Carolina. Some scup make regular migrations from wintering grounds off the Virginia Coast to New England, spawning off the coasts of Rhode Island and Massachusetts. Usually they live on the bottom, but sometimes they school at the surface like mackerel.*

SEA ANEMONE. *A peacefully feeding sea anemone strongly resembles a chrysanthemum, but as soon as it is disturbed, this illusion of flowerlike beauty is dispelled and we see a rather unattractive animal, barrel-shaped and flabby. The "flower petals" are the numerous tentacles which the creature expands in feeding to capture small animals by shooting stinging darts into them. Sea anemones are related to jellyfish and coral animals. They are often delicately and beautifully colored, and range in size from a sixteenth of an inch to several feet across. A few specimens are often to be seen in tide pools, or growing attached to wharf pilings.*

SEA CUCUMBER. *Sea cucumbers bear scarcely any family resemblance to their relatives, the starfish and sea urchins. They are somewhat wormlike in appearance, with a tough, muscular skin. They move sluggishly over the sea bottom, swallowing sand or mud from which they extract small bits of organic food. They have a strange method of defense when harassed by enemies: they expel their internal organs en masse, later to regenerate them at leisure. Dried sea cucumbers are the "trepang" or bêche-de-mer from which the Chinese make soup, and sea urchins containing eggs are eaten in Europe.*

SEA LETTUCE. *A bright green seaweed of flattened, leafy appearance. Although the fronds are tissue-paper thin, this species often grows on rocks exposed to heavy pounding by waves.*

SEA RAVEN. *This fish is perhaps the most bizarre member of the sculpin tribe, with its large spiny head, ragged fins, and prickly skin. Found in coastal waters from Labrador to the Chesapeake Bay, it is most abundant north of Cape Cod. When lifted from*

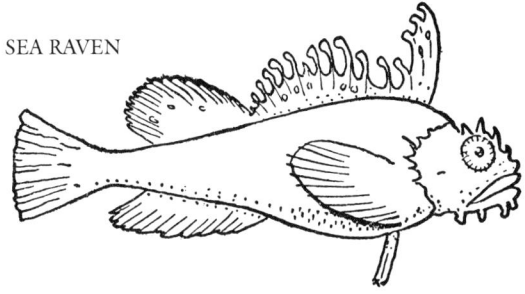

SEA RAVEN

the water it may inflate its body like a balloon, and if thrown back into the water will float helplessly on its back. It is not a market fish, but shore fishermen often save their catches of "ravens" to use for lobster bait.

SEA ROBIN. *The sea robin is a fish found chiefly from South Carolina to Cape Cod, with a few living as far north as the Bay of Fundy. In appearance it suggests the sea raven and other sculpins, having a broad head and large pectoral fins (the fins just behind the gills). Often it lies on the bottom with these fanlike fins outspread and will bury itself in the sand up to the eyes if disturbed. The sea robin eats everything from shrimps, squids, and shellfish to small flounders and herring.*

SEA SQUIRT. *Sea squirts have leathery, saclike bodies, and when touched eject spurts of water from two openings like short teakettle spouts. They grow attached to stones, seaweeds, wharf piles, and the like, straining food animals out of the water by passing it through an elaborate system of internal structures. Sea squirts belong to a group midway between the invertebrates and the true backboned animals. They are eaten in Japan, some South American countries, and in certain Mediterranean ports.*

SHEARWATER. *An oceanic bird seen in American coastal waters only when storms occasionally drive it in. One species—the greater shearwater—performs a remarkable migration. Apparently all the members of this species breed on the isolated Tristan da Cunha islands in the South Atlantic ocean. There they nest in deep, grass-lined tunnels in the ground. Every spring they set out on a long northward migration that brings them to the offshore waters of New England, where they remain from mid-May to the middle or end of October. Then they cross the North Atlantic and continue southward off the coasts of Europe and Africa, returning to their island home. It is believed that this circuit of the oceans may take an individual bird two years, and that the breeding cycle may be a biennial one.*

SHEEPSHEAD. *A food fish taken in coastal waters from Massachusetts to Texas. It is nearly always found around old wrecks, breakwaters, and wharfs. The name probably refers to the peculiar shape of the head and more particularly to the large, sheeplike teeth.*

SHRIMP. *A shrimp in life is much like a miniature lobster. Only the jointed and flexible "tail" of the animal is brought into the fish markets, the heads being removed in the packing plants because they contain very little muscle.*

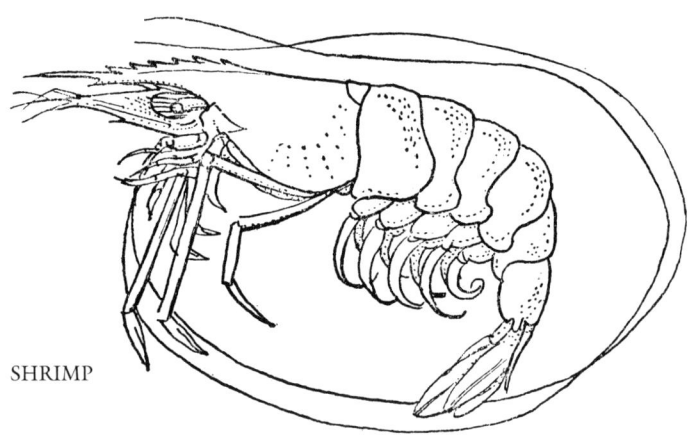

SHRIMP

SILVER EEL. *An eel in migrating condition is sometimes called a "silver eel" in allusion to the lustrous, silvery color of its underparts.*

SILVERSIDE. *A long, slender little fish with a silvery stripe on its sides, found in either fresh or salt water. Schools of this fish are often abundant off sandy coastlines.*

SKUA *(skū'-à). Skuas are the avian pirates of the high seas. In winter they are fairly numerous on the New England fishing banks, where they terrorize the less belligerent gulls, fulmars, shearwaters, and other birds into giving up the fish, squid, or other food they have caught. The skua nests in Greenland, Iceland, and far northern islands.*

SNOW BUNTING. *Sometimes called "snowflake," this small bird of the sparrow tribe nests within the Arctic Zone and in winter wanders south as far as southern Canada and northern United States.*

SOLDIER FLY. *An insect that gets its name from the gay stripes of the adult. The larvae of some species live in the water as spindle-shaped, dead-looking objects, getting air through a long tube which they push through the surface of the water.*

SPADEFISH. *This fish has a body that is almost round and very flat from side to side, and so it is aptly called "moonfish" in some localities. It may be from one to three feet long, and habitually forages about wrecks, pilings, and rocks for encrusting animals. It is found from Massachusetts to South America.*

SPOT. *The fish called spot is so named from a single, round, bronze or yellow spot on each shoulder. It lives in coastal waters from Massachusetts to Texas and is a common food fish. Male spots make a drumming sound like that produced by the croaker, but of less volume.*

SQUID. *The common squid of the Atlantic Coast is about a foot long, and often is to be found in great numbers in coastal waters. Squids are used extensively as bait in the fisheries. These animals are noted for their rapid, darting motions and for their ability to change color to match their surroundings. Squids, like oysters*

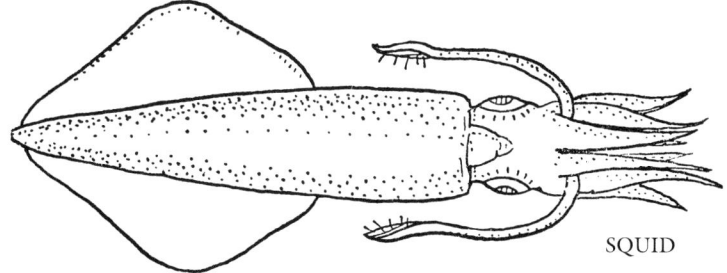

SQUID

and snails, are mollusks, but their shell is reduced to a slender, horny, internal structure called the "pen." These small squids differ in little except size from the almost legendary giant squid, the largest known example of which was fifty feet long, including the extended tentacles.

STING RAY. *The flat, roughly quadrangular body of the sting ray and the long, whiplike tail, set with sharp spines, serve to identify it at once. The tail is capable of inflicting an exceedingly painful wound. Sting rays are found along the coast from Cape Cod to Brazil, and occasionally on the shoaler offshore fishing banks. They are closely related to skates and sharks.*

TEAL. *Although small, the blue-winged teal is one of the swiftest of the ducks. Its migratory range extends from Newfoundland and northern Canada as far south as Brazil and Chile, although many of these birds winter in the latitude of the Middle Atlantic States.*

TERN. *Terns are characteristically birds of the sea coasts. They may be recognized at a glance by their habit of flying about with heads bent to scan the water for signs of fish, which they capture by diving. They nest in enormous colonies on isolated sandy beaches or islands offshore. One species—the Arctic tern—makes one of the longest migrations on record, from the North American Arctic to the Antarctic regions, via Europe and Africa.*

TURNSTONE. *A turnstone, once seen, is never forgotten, so startling is the spectacle of this brightly colored black and white*

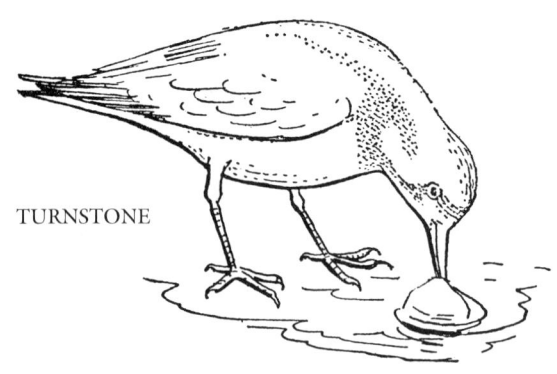

TURNSTONE

and ruddy brown bird of the shore. Its common name refers to its habit of using its short bill to turn over stones, shells, and bits of seaweed in search of sand fleas or other tidbits beneath. It is also called "calico bird."

WATER BOATMAN. *Almost everyone who has ever stood beside a quiet stream or pond has seen this little insect ferryman sculling across the surface film. The oval boat body is only about a quarter of an inch long; the oars are the hindmost pair of legs, much flattened and fringed with hairs. Surprisingly, some water boatmen fly well, indulging this talent at night, and some produce a kind of music by rubbing the forelegs together.*

WHITING. *The whiting is a strong and vigorous fish that roves the water from bottom to surface in search of its prey, which consists chiefly of all the smaller schooling fishes. The whiting, sometimes called "silver hake," is closely related to the cod, but is a much more active and slender fish. It is found from the Bahamas to the Grand Banks, and from tidewater down to depths of nearly two thousand feet.*

WIDGEON GRASS *(wĭj'-ŭn). An aquatic plant which is extensively used as food by waterfowl. Both the small, black seeds and the plant itself are eaten. Widgeon grass grows in brackish water (and sometimes in salt) along the coast, and is found also in interior alkaline waters.*

WINGED SNAIL. *(See pteropod.)*

YELLOWLEGS. *Both the greater and lesser yellowlegs are sometimes called "telltale" or "tattler" from their habit of warning less watchful birds, with loud cries, of approaching danger. The lesser yellowlegs is seldom seen on the Atlantic Coast in spring, for its migration path takes it up the Mississippi flyway to breeding grounds in central Canada. Both species are to be seen on eastern beaches in the fall—large shore birds with rather conspicuous yellow legs. They winter south to Argentina, Chile, and Peru.*

THE SEA AROUND US

To HENRY BRYANT BIGELOW
WHO BY PRECEPT AND EXAMPLE HAS GUIDED ALL
OTHERS IN THE EXPLORATION OF THE SEA

PREFACE TO THE REVISED EDITION

The sea has always challenged the minds and imagination of men and even today it remains the last great frontier of Earth. It is a realm so vast and so difficult of access that with all our efforts we have explored only a small fraction of its area. Not even the mighty technological developments of this, the Atomic Age, have greatly changed this situation. The awakening of active interest in the exploration of the sea came during the Second World War, when it became clear that our knowledge of the ocean was dangerously inadequate. We had only the most rudimentary notions of the geography of that undersea world over which our ships sailed and through which submarines moved. We knew even less about the dynamics of the sea in motion, although the ability to predict the actions of tides and currents and waves might easily determine the success or failure of military undertakings. The practical need having been so clearly established, the governments of the United States and of other leading sea powers began to devote increasing effort to the scientific study of the sea. Instruments and equipment, most of which had been born of urgent necessity, gave oceanographers the means of tracing the contours of the ocean bottom, of studying the movements of deep waters, and even of sampling the sea floor itself.

These vastly accelerated studies soon began to show that many of the old conceptions of the sea were faulty, and by the mid-point of the century a new picture had begun to emerge. But it was still like a huge canvas on which the artist has indicated the general scheme of his grand design but on which large blank areas await the clarifying touch of his brush.

This was the state of our knowledge of the ocean world when *The Sea Around Us* was written in 1951. Since that time the filling in of many of the blank areas has proceeded and new discoveries have been made. In this second edition of the book I have described the most important of the new findings in a series of notes which will be found in the Appendix. These notes are keyed to appropriate passages in the original text by reference numbers. For example, after the discussion of the Arctic ocean ending on page 257, the reader may go on to learn of recent discoveries in this area by turning to note 10 in the Appendix.

The 1950's have comprised an exciting decade in the science of the sea. During this period a manned vehicle has descended to the deepest hole in the ocean floor. During the 'fifties, also, the crossing of the entire Arctic basin was accomplished by submarines traveling under the ice. Many new features of the unseen floor of the sea have been described, including new mountain ranges that now appear to be linked with others to form the longest and mightiest mountains of the earth—a continuous chain encircling the globe. Deep, hidden rivers in the sea, subsurface currents with the volume of a thousand Mississippis, have been found. During the International Geophysical Year, 60 ships from 40 nations, as well as hundreds of stations on islands and seacoasts, co-operated in an enormously fruitful study of the sea.

Yet the present achievements, exciting though they are, must be considered only a beginning to what is yet to be achieved by probing the vast depths of water that cover most of the surface of the earth. In 1959 a group of distinguished scientists comprising the Committee on Oceanography of the National Academy of Sciences declared that "Man's knowledge of the oceans is meager indeed compared with their importance to him." The Committee recommended at least a doubling of basic research on the sea by the United States in the 1960's; anything less would, in its opinion, "jeopardize the position of oceanography in the United States" compared with other nations and "place us at a disadvantage in the future use of the resources of the sea."

One of the most fascinating of the projects now planned for the future is an attempt to explore the interior of the earth by drilling a hole three or four miles deep in the bottom of the sea. This project, which is sponsored by the National Academy of Sciences, is designed to penetrate farther than instruments have ever before reached, to the boundary between the earth's crust and its mantle. This boundary is known to geologists as the Mohorovicic discontinuity (or more familiarly as the Moho) because it was discovered by a Yugoslavian of that name in 1912. The Moho is the point at which earthquake waves show a marked change in velocity, indicating a transition from one kind of material to something quite different. It lies much deeper under the continents than under the oceans, so, in spite of the obvious difficulties of drilling in deep water, an ocean site offers most promise. Above the Moho lies the crust of the earth, composed of relatively light rocks, below it the mantle, a layer some 1800 miles thick enclosing the hot core of the earth. The composition of the crust is not fully known and the nature of the mantle can be deduced only by the most indirect methods. To penetrate these regions and bring back actual samples would therefore be an enormous step forward in understanding the nature of our earth, and would even advance our knowledge of the universe, since the deep structure of the earth may be assumed to be like that of other planets.

As we learn more about the sea through the combined studies of many specialists a new concept that is gradually taking form will almost certainly be strengthened. Even a decade or so ago it was the fashion to speak of the abyss as a place of eternal calm, its black recesses undisturbed by any movement of water more active than a slowly creeping current, a place isolated from the surface and from the very different world of the shallow sea. This picture is rapidly being replaced by one that shows the deep sea as a place of movement and change, an idea that is far more exciting and that possesses deep significance for some of the most pressing problems of our time.

In the new and more dynamic concept, the floor of the deep sea is shaped by racing turbidity currents or mud flows that pour down the slopes of the ocean basins at high speed; it is visited by submarine landslides and stirred by internal tides. The crests and ridges of some of the undersea mountains are swept bare of sediments by currents whose action, in the words of geologist Bruce Heezen, is comparable to "snow avalanches in the Alps (which) sweep down and smother the relief of the lower slopes."

Far from being isolated from the continents and the shallow seas that surround them, the abyssal plains are now known to receive sediments from the margins of the continents. The effect of the turbidity currents, over the vast stretches of geologic time, is to fill the trenches and the hollows of the abyssal floor with sediment. This concept helps us understand certain hitherto puzzling occurrences. Why, for example, have deposits of sand—surely a product of coastal erosion and the grinding of surf—appeared on the mid-ocean floor? Why have sediments at the mouths of submarine canyons, where they communicate with the abyss, been found to contain such reminders of the land as bits of wood and leaves, and why are there sands containing nuts, twigs, and the bark of trees even farther out on the plains of the abyss? In the powerful downrush of sediment-laden currents, triggered by storms or floods or earthquakes, we now have a mechanism that accounts for these once mysterious facts.

Although the beginnings of our present concept of a dynamic sea go back perhaps several decades, it is only the superb instruments of the past ten years that have allowed us to glimpse the hidden movements of ocean waters. Now we suspect that all those dark regions between the surface and the bottom are stirred by currents. Even such mighty surface currents as the Gulf Stream are not quite what we supposed them to be. Instead of a broad and steadily flowing river of water, the Gulf Stream is now found to consist of narrow, racing tongues of warm water that curl back in swirls and eddies. And below the surface currents are others unlike them, running at their own speeds, in their own direction, with their own volume. And below these are still others. Photographs of the sea bottom taken at great depths formerly supposed to be eternally still show ripple marks, a sign that moving waters are sorting over sediments and carrying away the finer particles. Strong currents have denuded the crest of much of the vast range of undersea mountains known as the Atlantic Ridge, and every one of the sea mounts that has been photographed reveals the work of deep currents in ripple marks and scour marks.

Other photographs give fresh evidence of life at great depths. Tracks and trails cross the sea floor and the bottom is studded with small cones built by unknown forms of life or with holes inhabited by small burrowers. The Danish research vessel *Galathea* brought up living animals in dredges operated at great depths, where only recently it was supposed life would be too scanty to permit such sampling.

These findings of the dynamic nature of the sea are not academic; they are not merely dramatic details of a story that has interest but no application. They have a direct and immediate bearing on what has become a major problem of our time.

Although man's record as a steward of the natural resources of the earth has been a discouraging one, there has long been a certain comfort in the belief that the sea, at least, was inviolate, beyond man's ability to change and to despoil. But this belief, unfortunately, has proved to be naïve. In unlocking the secrets of the atom, modern man has found himself confronted with a frightening problem—what to do with the most dangerous materials that have ever existed in all the earth's history, the by-products of atomic fission. The stark problem that faces him is whether he can dispose of these lethal substances without rendering the earth uninhabitable.

No account of the sea today is complete unless it takes note of this ominous problem. By its very vastness and its seeming remoteness, the sea has invited the attention of those who have the problem of disposal, and with very little discussion and almost no public notice, at least until the late 'fifties, the sea has been selected as a "natural" burying place for the contaminated rubbish and other "low-level wastes" of the Atomic Age. These wastes are placed in barrels lined with concrete and hauled out to sea, where they are dumped overboard at previously designated sites. Some have been taken out 100 miles or more; recently sites only 20 miles offshore have been suggested. In theory the containers are deposited at depths of about 1000 fathoms, but in practice they have at times been placed in much shallower waters. Supposedly the containers have a life of at least 10 years, after which whatever radioactive materials remain will be released to the sea. But again this is only in theory, and a representative of the Atomic Energy Commission, which either dumps the wastes or licenses others to do so, has publicly conceded that the containers are unlikely to maintain "their integrity" while sinking to the bottom. Indeed, in tests conducted in California, some have been found to rupture under pressure at only a few hundred fathoms.

But it is only a matter of time until the contents of all such containers already deposited at sea will be free in the ocean waters, along with those yet to come as the applications of atomic science expand. To the packaged wastes so deposited there is now added the contaminated run-off from rivers that are serving as dumping grounds for atomic wastes, and the fallout from the testing of bombs, the greater part of which comes to rest on the vast surface of the sea.

The whole practice, despite protestations of safety by the regulatory agency, rests on the most insecure basis of fact. Oceanographers say they can make "only vague estimates" of the fate of radioactive elements introduced into the deep ocean. They declare that years of intensive study will be needed to provide understanding of what happens when such wastes are deposited in estuaries and coastal waters. As we have seen, all recent knowledge points to far greater activity at all levels of the sea than had ever been guessed at. The deep turbulence, the horizontal movements of vast rivers of ocean water streaming one above another in varying directions, the upwelling of water from the depths carrying with it minerals from the bottom, and the opposite downward sinking of great masses of surface water, all result in a gigantic mixing process that in time will bring about universal distribution of the radioactive contaminants.

And yet the actual transport of radioactive elements by the sea itself is only part of the problem. The concentration and distribution of radioisotopes by marine life may possibly have even greater importance from the standpoint of human hazard. It is known that plants and animals of the sea pick up and concentrate radiochemicals, but only vague information now exists as to details of the process. The minute life of the sea depends for its existence on the minerals in the water. If the normal supply of these is low, the organisms will utilize instead the radioisotope of the needed element if it is present, sometimes concentrating it as much as a million times beyond its abundance in sea water. What happens then to the careful calculation of a "maximum permissible level"? For the tiny organisms are eaten by larger ones and so on up the food chain to man. By such a process tuna over an area of a million square miles surrounding the Bikini bomb test developed a degree of radioactivity enormously higher than that of the sea water.

By their movements and migrations, marine creatures further upset the convenient theory that radioactive wastes remain in the area where they are deposited. The smaller organisms regularly make extensive vertical movements upward toward the surface of the sea at night, downward to great depths by day. And with them goes whatever radioactivity may be adhering to them or may have become incorporated into their bodies. The larger fauna, like fishes, seals, and whales, may migrate over enormous distances, again aiding in spreading and distributing the radioactive elements deposited at sea.

The problem, then, is far more complex and far more hazardous than has been admitted. Even in the comparatively short time since disposal began, research has shown that some of the assumptions on which it was based were dangerously inaccurate. The truth is that disposal has proceeded far more rapidly than our knowledge justifies. To dispose first and investigate later is an invitation to disaster, for once radioactive elements have been deposited at sea they are irretrievable. The mistakes that are made now are made for all time.

It is a curious situation that the sea, from which life first arose, should now be threatened by the activities of one form of that life. But the sea, though changed in a sinister way, will continue to exist; the threat is rather to life itself.

RACHEL CARSON

Silver Spring, Maryland
October 1960

ACKNOWLEDGMENTS

To cope alone and unaided with a subject so vast, so complex, and so infinitely mysterious as the sea would be a task not only cheerless but impossible, and I have not attempted it. Instead, on every hand I have been given the most friendly and generous help by those whose work is the foundation and substance of our present knowledge of the sea. Specialists on many problems of the ocean have read chapters dealing with their fields of study and have made comments and suggestions based on their broad understanding. For such constructive help I am indebted to Henry B. Bigelow, Charles F. Brooks, and Henry C. Stetson of Harvard University; Martin W. Johnson, Walter H. Munk, and Francis P. Shepard of the Scripps Institution of Oceanography; Robert Cushman Murphy and Albert Eide Parr of the American Museum of Natural History; Carl O. Dunbar of Yale University; H. A. Marmer of the U.S. Coast and Geodetic Survey; R. C. Hussey of the University of Michigan; George Cohee of the U.S. Geological Survey; and Hilary B. Moore of the University of Miami.

Many others have cheerfully gone to great trouble to help locate elusive documents, have sent me unpublished information and comments, and in many other ways have lightened my task. Among these are H. U. Sverdrup of the Norsk Polarinstitutt in Oslo; L. H. W. Cooper of the Laboratory at Plymouth; Thor Heyerdahl of Oslo; J. W. Christensen, Jens Eggvin, and Gunnar Rollefsen of the Fiskeridirektoratets Havforskingsinstitutt in Bergen; H. Blegvad, Secretary General of the International Council for the Exploration of the Sea; Hans Pettersson of the Oceanografiska Institutet in Göteborg; and, in the United States, John Putnam Marble of the National Research Council; Richard Fleming of the Hydrographic Office; Daniel Merriman of the Bingham Oceanographic Laboratory; Edward H. Smith of the Woods Hole Oceanographic

Institution; W. N. Bradley and H. S. Ladd of the U.S. Geological Survey; Maurice Ewing of Columbia University; and F. R. Fosberg of George Washington University.

The front end paper is reproduced from a portion of the map, *Il Mare di Amazones*, by permission of the New York Public Library. H. A. Marmer kindly provided a copy of the old Franklin chart of the Gulf Stream, which is here reproduced as the back end paper. The fathograms (illustrations 8 and 9) were furnished by the U.S. Fish and Wildlife Service and the U.S. Coast and Geodetic Survey, respectively. The drawings were prepared by Katherine L. Howe.

The library resources of many Government and private institutions have been placed freely at my disposal, and my especial thanks are due Ida K. Johnson, Reference Librarian of the Interior Department Library, whose tireless researches and thorough knowledge of the available literature have been unfailingly helpful.

My absorption in the mystery and meaning of the sea has been stimulated and the writing of this book aided by the friendship and encouragement of William Beebe.

The leisure to write the book and the means of carrying on some of the studies that contributed to it were in large part made possible by the award of the Eugene F. Saxton Memorial Fellowship.

R. L. C.

Silver Spring, Maryland
January 1951

CONTENTS

PART I. MOTHER SEA

The Gray Beginnings 201
The Pattern of the Surface 214
The Changing Year 225
The Sunless Sea 233
Hidden Lands 249
The Long Snowfall............................ 264
The Birth of an Island 271
The Shape of Ancient Seas 285

PART II. THE RESTLESS SEA

Wind and Water.............................. 297
Wind, Sun, and the Spinning of the Earth 316
The Moving Tides 332

PART III. MAN AND THE SEA ABOUT HIM

The Global Thermostat 349
Wealth from the Salt Seas...................... 367
The Encircling Sea............................ 379

Appendix..................................... 393

Suggestions for Further Reading 404

ILLUSTRATIONS

Page 208–11
  Chart of the History of the Earth and Its Life

Pages 322–23
  Current Systems of the Atlantic and Pacific Oceans

Following Page 372
  Trilobite
  Sargassum Fish
  Noctiluca
  Bottom Organisms
  Bathyscaphe
  Coring Tube
  Fathograms
  Volcanic Island

  Chalk Cliffs
  Surf
  Minot's Light
  Chimney Stack
  Tidal Waves during Hurricane
  Coral Coast
  Seismic Sea Waves
  Clouds

I
MOTHER SEA

The Gray Beginnings

And the earth was without form, and void; and darkness was upon the face of the deep.

—GENESIS

BEGINNINGS ARE APT to be shadowy, and so it is with the beginnings of that great mother of life, the sea. Many people have debated how and when the earth got its ocean, and it is not surprising that their explanations do not always agree. For the plain and inescapable truth is that no one was there to see, and in the absence of eyewitness accounts there is bound to be a certain amount of disagreement. So if I tell here the story of how the young planet Earth acquired an ocean, it must be a story pieced together from many sources and containing whole chapters the details of which we can only imagine. The story is founded on the testimony of the earth's most ancient rocks, which were young when the earth was young; on other evidence written on the face of the earth's satellite, the moon; and on hints contained in the history of the sun and the whole universe of star-filled space. For although no man was there to witness this cosmic birth, the stars and the moon and the rocks were there, and, indeed, had much to do with the fact that there is an ocean.

The events of which I write must have occurred somewhat more than 2 billion years ago. As nearly as science can tell, that is the approximate age of the earth, and the ocean must be very nearly as old. It is possible now to discover the age of the rocks that compose the crust of the earth by measuring the rate of decay of the radioactive materials they contain. The oldest rocks found anywhere on earth—in Manitoba—are about 2.3 billion years old. Allowing 100 million years or so for the cooling of the earth's materials to form a rocky crust, we arrive at the supposition that the tempestuous and violent events connected with our planet's birth occurred nearly 2½ billion years ago. But this is only a minimum estimate, for rocks indicating an even greater age may be found at any time.[1]

The new earth, freshly torn from its parent sun, was a ball of whirling gases, intensely hot, rushing through the black spaces of the universe on a path and at a speed controlled by immense forces. Gradually the ball of flaming gases cooled. The gases began to liquefy, and Earth became a molten mass. The materials of this mass eventually became sorted out in a definite pattern: the heaviest in the center, the less heavy surrounding them, and the least heavy forming the outer rim. This is the pattern which persists today—a central sphere of molten iron, very nearly as hot as it was 2 billion years ago, an intermediate sphere of semiplastic basalt, and a hard outer shell, relatively quite thin and composed of solid basalt and granite.

The outer shell of the young earth must have been a good many millions of years changing from the liquid to the solid state, and it is believed that, before this change was completed, an event of the greatest importance took place—the formation of the moon. The next time you stand on a beach at night, watching the moon's bright path across the water, and conscious of the moon-drawn tides, remember that the moon itself may have been born of a great tidal wave of earthly substance, torn off into space. And remember that if the moon was formed in this fashion, the event may have had much to do with shaping the ocean basins and the continents as we know them.

There were tides in the new earth, long before there was an ocean. In response to the pull of the sun the molten liquids of the earth's whole surface rose in tides that rolled unhindered around the globe and only gradually slackened and diminished as the earthly shell cooled, congealed, and hardened. Those who believe that the moon is a child of Earth say that during an early stage of the earth's development something happened that caused this rolling, viscid tide to gather speed and momentum and to rise to unimaginable heights. Apparently the force that created these greatest tides the earth has ever known was the force of resonance, for at this time the period of the solar tides had come to approach, then equal, the period of the free oscillation of the liquid earth. And so every sun tide was given increased momentum by the push of the earth's oscillation, and each of the twice-daily tides was larger than the one before it. Physicists have calculated that, after 500 years of such monstrous, steadily increasing tides, those on the side toward the sun became too high for stability, and a great wave was torn away and hurled into space. But immediately, of course, the newly created satellite became subject to physical laws that sent it spinning in an orbit of its own about the earth. This is what we call the moon.

There are reasons for believing that this event took place after the earth's crust had become slightly hardened, instead of during its partly liquid state. There is to this day a great scar on the surface of the globe. This scar or depression holds the Pacific Ocean. According to some geophysicists, the floor of the Pacific is composed of basalt, the substance of the earth's middle layer, while all other oceans are floored with a thin layer of granite, which makes up most of the earth's outer layer. We immediately wonder what became of the Pacific's granite covering and the most convenient assumption is that it was torn away when the moon was formed. There is supporting evidence. The mean density of the moon is much less than that of the earth (3.3 compared with 5.5), suggesting that the moon took away none of the earth's heavy iron core, but that it is composed only of the granite and some of the basalt of the outer layers.

The birth of the moon probably helped shape other regions of the world ocean besides the Pacific. When part of the crust was torn away, strains must have been set up in the remaining granite envelope. Perhaps the granite mass cracked open on the side opposite the moon scar. Perhaps, as the earth spun on its axis and rushed on its orbit through space, the cracks widened and the masses of granite began to drift apart, moving over a tarry, slowly hardening layer of basalt. Gradually the outer portions of the basalt layer became solid and the wandering continents came to rest, frozen into place with oceans between them. In spite of theories to the contrary, the weight of geologic evidence seems to be that the locations of the major ocean basins and the major continental land masses are today much the same as they have been since a very early period of the earth's history.

But this is to anticipate the story, for when the moon was born there was no ocean. The gradually cooling earth was enveloped in heavy layers of cloud, which contained much of the water of the new planet. For a long time its surface was so hot that no moisture could fall without immediately being reconverted to steam. This dense, perpetually renewed cloud covering must have been thick enough that no rays of sunlight could penetrate it. And so the rough outlines of the continents and the empty ocean basins were sculptured out of the surface of the earth in darkness, in a Stygian world of heated rock and swirling clouds and gloom.

As soon as the earth's crust cooled enough, the rains began to fall. Never have there been such rains since that time. They fell continuously, day and night, days passing into months, into years, into centuries. They poured into the waiting ocean basins, or, falling upon the continental masses, drained away to become sea.

That primeval ocean, growing in bulk as the rains slowly filled its basins, must have been only faintly salt. But the falling rains were the symbol of the dissolution of the continents. From the moment the rains began to fall, the lands began to be worn away and carried to the sea. It is an endless, inexorable process that has never stopped—the dissolving of the rocks, the leaching out of their contained minerals, the carrying of the rock fragments and dissolved minerals to the ocean. And over the eons of time, the sea has grown ever more bitter with the salt of the continents.

In what manner the sea produced the mysterious and wonderful stuff called protoplasm we cannot say. In its warm, dimly lit waters the unknown conditions of temperature and pressure and saltiness must have been the critical ones for the creation of life from non-life. At any rate they produced the result that neither the alchemists with their crucibles nor modern scientists in their laboratories have been able to achieve.

Before the first living cell was created, there may have been many trials and failures. It seems probable that, within the warm saltiness of the primeval sea, certain organic substances were fashioned from carbon dioxide, sulphur, nitrogen, phosphorus, potassium, and calcium. Perhaps these were transition steps from which the complex molecules of protoplasm arose —molecules that somehow acquired the ability to reproduce themselves and begin the endless stream of life. But at present no one is wise enough to be sure.

Those first living things may have been simple microorganisms rather like some of the bacteria we know today

—mysterious borderline forms that were not quite plants, not quite animals, barely over the intangible line that separates the non-living from the living. It is doubtful that this first life possessed the substance chlorophyll, with which plants in sunlight transform lifeless chemicals into the living stuff of their tissues. Little sunshine could enter their dim world, penetrating the cloud banks from which fell the endless rains. Probably the sea's first children lived on the organic substances then present in the ocean waters, or, like the iron and sulphur bacteria that exist today, lived directly on inorganic food.

All the while the cloud cover was thinning, the darkness of the nights alternated with palely illumined days, and finally the sun for the first time shone through upon the sea. By this time some of the living things that floated in the sea must have developed the magic of chlorophyll. Now they were able to take the carbon dioxide of the air and the water of the sea and of these elements, in sunlight, build the organic substances they needed. So the first true plants came into being.

Another group of organisms, lacking the chlorophyll but needing organic food, found they could make a way of life for themselves by devouring the plants. So the first animals arose, and from that day to this, every animal in the world has followed the habit it learned in the ancient seas and depends, directly or through complex food chains, on the plants for food and life.

As the years passed, and the centuries, and the millions of years, the stream of life grew more and more complex. From simple, one-celled creatures, others that were aggregations of specialized cells arose, and then creatures with organs for feeding, digesting, breathing, reproducing. Sponges grew on the rocky bottom of the sea's edge and coral animals built their habitations in warm, clear waters. Jellyfish swam and drifted in the sea. Worms evolved, and starfish, and hard-shelled creatures with many-jointed legs, the arthropods. The plants, too, progressed, from the microscopic algae to branched and curiously fruiting seaweeds that swayed with the tides and were plucked from the coastal rocks by the surf and cast adrift.

During all this time the continents had no life. There was little to induce living things to come ashore, forsaking their all-providing, all-embracing mother sea. The lands must have been bleak and hostile beyond the power of words to describe. Imagine a whole continent of naked rock, across which no covering mantle of green had been drawn—a continent without soil, for there were no land plants to aid in its formation and bind it to the rocks with their roots. Imagine a land of stone, a silent land, except for the sound of the rains and winds that swept across it. For there was no living voice, and no living thing moved over the surface of the rocks.

Meanwhile, the gradual cooling of the planet, which had first given the earth its hard granite crust, was progressing into its deeper layers; and as the interior slowly cooled and contracted, it drew away from the outer shell. This shell, accommodating itself to the shrinking sphere within it, fell into folds and wrinkles—the earth's first mountain ranges.

Geologists tell us that there must have been at least two periods of mountain building (often called "revolutions") in that dim period, so long ago that the rocks have no record of it, so long ago that the mountains themselves have long since been worn away. Then there came a third great period of upheaval and readjustment of the earth's crust, about a billion years ago, but of all its majestic mountains the only reminders today are the Laurentian hills of eastern Canada, and a great shield of granite over the flat country around Hudson Bay.

The epochs of mountain building only served to speed up the processes of erosion by which the continents were worn down and their crumbling rock and contained minerals returned to the sea. The uplifted masses of the mountains were prey to the bitter cold of the upper atmosphere and under the attacks of frost and snow and ice the rocks cracked and crumbled away. The rains beat with greater violence upon the slopes of the hills and carried away the substance of the mountains in torrential streams. There was still no plant covering to modify and resist the power of the rains.

And in the sea, life continued to evolve. The earliest forms have left no fossils by which we can identify them. Probably they were soft-bodied, with no hard parts that could be preserved. Then, too, the rock layers formed in those early days have since been so altered by enormous heat and pressure, under the foldings of the earth's crust, that any fossils they might have contained would have been destroyed.

For the past 500 million years, however, the rocks have preserved the fossil record. By the dawn of the Cambrian period, when the history of living things was first inscribed on rock pages, life in the sea had progressed so far that all the main groups of backboneless or invertebrate animals had been developed. But there were no animals with backbones, no insects or spiders, and still no plant or animal had been evolved that was capable of venturing onto the forbidding land. So for more than three-fourths of geologic time the continents were desolate and uninhabited, while the sea prepared the life that was later to invade them and make them habitable. Meanwhile, with violent tremblings of the earth and with the fire and smoke of roaring volcanoes, mountains rose and wore away, glaciers moved to and fro over the earth, and the sea crept over the continents and again receded.

It was not until Silurian time, some 350 million years ago, that the first pioneer of land life crept out on the shore. It was an arthropod, one of the great tribe that later produced crabs and lobsters and insects. It must have been something like a modern scorpion, but, unlike some of its descendants, it never wholly severed the ties that united it to the sea. It lived a strange life, half-terrestrial, half-aquatic, something like that of the ghost crabs that speed along the beaches today, now and then dashing into the surf to moisten their gills.

Fish, tapered of body and stream-molded by the press of running waters, were evolving in Silurian rivers. In times of drought, in the drying pools and lagoons, the shortage of oxygen forced them to develop swim bladders for the storage of air. One form that possessed an air-breathing lung was able to survive the dry periods by burying itself in mud, leaving a passage to the surface through which it breathed.

It is very doubtful that the animals alone would have succeeded in colonizing the land, for only the plants had the power to bring about the first amelioration of its harsh conditions. They helped make soil of the crumbling rocks, they held back the soil from the rains that would have swept it away, and little by little they softened and subdued the bare rock, the lifeless desert. We know very little about the first land plants, but they must have been closely related to some of the larger seaweeds that had learned to live in the coastal shallows, developing

Chart of the History of the Earth and Its Life

| ERAS | PERIODS
c. millions years ago
Holmes Scale
(Revised 1959) | Mountains | Volcanoes |
|---|---|---|---|
| CENOZOIC | Pleistocene
0–1 | Coast ranges, western United States: this disturbance probably still in progress | |
| CENOZOIC | Tertiary
1–70 | Alps, Himalayas, Apennines, Pyrenees, Caucasus | Great vulcanism in western United States formed Columbia Plateau (200,000 square miles of lava)
Vesuvius and Etna began to erupt |
| MESOZOIC | Cretaceous
70–135 | Rocky Mountains, Andes
Rising of Panama Ridge: indirect result—Gulf Stream | |
| MESOZOIC | Jurassic
135–180 | Sierra Nevadas | |
| MESOZOIC | Triassic
180–225 | | Many volcanoes in western North America, also in New England |
| PALEOZOIC | Permian
225–270 | Appalachians south of New England | Volcanic outpourings produced Deccan Plateau of India |
| PALEOZOIC | Carboniferous
270–350 | | |
| PALEOZOIC | Devonian
350–400 | Northern Appalachians (this area never again covered by sea) | |
| PALEOZOIC | Silurian
400–440 | Caledonian Mountains (Great Britain, Scandinavia, Greenland—only their roots remain) | Volcanoes in Maine and New Brunswick |

Glaciers	*Seas*	DEVELOPMENT OF LIFE
Pleistocene glaciation—ice sheets over vast areas of North America and northern Europe	Sea level fluctuating because of glaciers	Rise of man Modern plants and animals
	Great submergence of lands Nummulitic limestone formed—later used in Pyramids	Higher mammals, except man Highest plants
	Much of Europe and about half of North America submerged. Chalk cliffs of England formed	Last of dinosaurs and flying reptiles Reptiles dominant on land
	Last invasion of sea into eastern California and Oregon	First birds
		First dinosaurs Some reptiles return to sea Small, primitive mammals
Glaciers in broad equatorial belt: India, Africa, Australia, South America	Extensive seas over western United States; world's largest salt deposits formed in Germany	Primitive reptiles Amphibians declining Earliest cycads and conifers
	Central United States covered by sea for last time. Great coal beds formed	Amphibians developing rapidly First insects Coal-making plants
		Fishes dominate seas First amphibian fossil
	Repeated invasions by sea. Salt beds formed in eastern United States	First life appears on continents

(continued)

209

Chart of the History of the Earth and Its Life (continued)

ERAS	PERIODS c. millions years ago Holmes Scale (Revised 1959)	Mountains	Volcanoes
PALEOZOIC	Ordovician 440–500		
PALEOZOIC	Cambrian 500–600		
PROTEROZOIC	600–3000± (see p. 393, note 1)	Grenville Mountains of eastern North America (only their roots remain)—age 1000 million Penokean Mountains (Minnesota, Ontario) formerly Killarney—age 1700 million	
ARCHEOZOIC	3000± (see p. 393, note 1)	Earliest known mountains (Laurentian of Minnesota and Ontario—only traces remain)—age 2600 million Earliest known sedimentary and volcanic rocks, much altered by heat and pressure, their history obscure	

strengthened stems and grasping, rootlike holdfasts to resist the drag and pull of the waves. Perhaps it was in some coastal lowlands, periodically drained and flooded, that some such plants found it possible to survive, though separated from the sea. This also seems to have taken place in the Silurian period.

The mountains that had been thrown up by the Laurentian revolution gradually wore away, and as the sediments were washed from their summits and deposited on the lowlands, great areas of the continents sank under the load. The seas crept out of their basins and spread over the lands. Life fared well and was exceedingly abundant in those shallow, sunlit seas. But with the later retreat of the ocean water into the deeper basins, many creatures must have been left stranded in shallow, landlocked bays. Some of these animals found means to survive on land. The lakes, the shores of the rivers, and the coastal swamps of those days were the testing grounds in which plants

Glaciers	Seas	DEVELOPMENT OF LIFE
	Greatest known submergence of North America—more than half of continent covered	Earliest known vertebrates Cephalopods common in seas
	Seas advance and withdraw, at one time covering most of United States	First clear fossil record dates from this period; all major groups of invertebrates established
Earliest known ice age		Rise of invertebrates (inferred)
		Earliest life (inferred)

and animals either became adapted to the new conditions or perished.

As the lands rose and the seas receded, a strange fishlike creature emerged on the land, and over the thousands of years its fins became legs, and instead of gills it developed lungs. In the Devonian sandstone this first amphibian left its footprint.

On land and sea the stream of life poured on. New forms evolved; some old ones declined and disappeared. On land the mosses and the ferns and the seed plants developed. The reptiles for a time dominated the earth, gigantic, grotesque, and terrifying. Birds learned to live and move in the ocean of air. The first small mammals lurked inconspicuously in hidden crannies of the earth as though in fear of the reptiles.

When they went ashore the animals that took up a land life carried with them a part of the sea in their bodies, a heritage which they passed on to their children and which even today links each land animal with its origin in the ancient sea. Fish, amphibian, and reptile, warm-blooded bird and mammal—each of us carries in our veins a salty stream in which the elements sodium, potassium, and calcium are combined in almost the same proportions as in sea water. This is our inheritance from the day, untold millions of years ago, when a remote ancestor, having progressed from the one-celled to the many-celled stage, first developed a circulatory system in which the fluid was merely the water of the sea. In the same way, our lime-hardened skeletons are a heritage from the calcium-rich ocean of Cambrian time. Even the protoplasm that streams within each cell of our bodies has the chemical structure impressed upon all living matter when the first simple creatures were brought forth in the ancient sea. And as life itself began in the sea, so each of us begins his individual life in a miniature ocean within his mother's womb, and in the stages of his embryonic development repeats the steps by which his race evolved, from gill-breathing inhabitants of a water world to creatures able to live on land.

Some of the land animals later returned to the ocean. After perhaps 50 million years of land life, a number of reptiles entered the sea about 170 million years ago, in the Triassic period. They were huge and formidable creatures. Some had oarlike limbs by which they rowed through the water; some were web-footed, with long, serpentine necks. These grotesque monsters disappeared millions of years ago, but we remember them when we come upon a large sea turtle swimming many miles at sea, its barnacle-encrusted shell eloquent of its marine life. Much later, perhaps no more than 50 million years ago, some of the mammals, too, abandoned a land life for the ocean. Their descendants are the sea lions, seals, sea elephants, and whales of today.

Among the land mammals there was a race of creatures that took to an arboreal existence. Their hands underwent remarkable development, becoming skilled in manipulating and examining objects, and along with this skill came a superior brain power that compensated for what these comparatively small mammals lacked in strength. At last, perhaps somewhere in the vast interior of Asia, they descended from the trees and became again terrestrial. The past million years have seen their transformation into beings with the body and brain and spirit of man.

Eventually man, too, found his way back to the sea. Standing on its shores, he must have looked out upon it with wonder and curiosity, compounded with an unconscious recognition of his lineage. He could not physically re-enter the ocean as the seals and whales had done. But over the centuries, with all the skill and ingenuity and reasoning powers of his mind, he has sought to explore and investigate even its most remote parts, so that he might re-enter it mentally and imaginatively.

He built boats to venture out on its surface. Later he found ways to descend to the shallow parts of its floor, carrying with him the air that, as a land mammal long unaccustomed to aquatic life, he needed to breathe. Moving in fascination over the deep sea he could not enter, he found ways to probe its depths, he let down nets to capture its life, he invented mechanical eyes and ears that could re-create for his senses a world long lost, but a world that, in the deepest part of his subconscious mind, he had never wholly forgotten.

And yet he has returned to his mother sea only on her own terms. He cannot control or change the ocean as, in his brief tenancy of earth, he has subdued and plundered the continents. In the artificial world of his cities and towns, he often forgets the true nature of his planet and the long vistas of its history, in which the existence of the race of men has occupied a mere moment of time. The sense of all these things comes to him most clearly in the course of a long ocean voyage, when he watches day after day the receding rim of the horizon, ridged and furrowed by waves; when at night he becomes aware of the earth's rotation as the stars pass overhead; or when, alone in this world of water and sky, he feels the loneliness of his earth in space. And then, as never on land, he knows the truth that his world is a water world, a planet dominated by its covering mantle of ocean, in which the continents are but transient intrusions of land above the surface of the all-encircling sea.

The Pattern of the Surface

> There is, one knows not what sweet mystery about this sea, whose gently awful stirrings seem to speak of some hidden soul beneath.
>
> —HERMAN MELVILLE

NOWHERE IN ALL the sea does life exist in such bewildering abundance as in the surface waters. From the deck of a vessel you may look down, hour after hour, on the shimmering discs of jellyfish, their gently pulsating bells dotting the surface as far as you can see. Or one day you may notice early in the morning that you are passing through a sea that has taken on a brick-red color from billions upon billions of microscopic creatures, each of which contains an orange pigment granule. At noon you are still moving through red seas, and when darkness falls the waters shine with an eerie glow from the phosphorescent fires of yet more billions and trillions of these same creatures.

And again you may glimpse not only the abundance but something of the fierce uncompromisingness of sea life when, as you look over the rail and down, down into water of a clear, deep green, suddenly there passes a silver shower of finger-long fishlets. The sun strikes a metallic gleam from their flanks as they streak by, driving deeper into the green depths with the desperate speed of the hunted. Perhaps you never see the hunters, but you sense their presence as you see the gulls hovering, with eager, mewing cries, waiting for the little fish to be driven to the surface.

Or again, perhaps, you may sail for days on end without seeing anything you could recognize as life or the indications of life, day after day of empty water and empty sky, and so you may reasonably conclude that there is no spot on earth so barren of life as the open ocean. But if you had the opportunity to tow a fine-meshed net through the seemingly lifeless water and then to examine the washings of the net, you would find that life is scattered almost everywhere through the surface waters like a fine dust. A cupful of water may contain millions upon millions of diatoms, tiny plant cells, each of them far too small to be seen by the human eye; or it may swarm with an infinitude of animal creatures, none larger than a dust mote, which live on plant cells still smaller than themselves.

If you could be close to the surface waters of the ocean at night, you would realize that then they are alive with myriads of strange creatures never seen by day. They are alive with the moving lamps of small shrimplike beings that spend the daylight hours in the gloom of deep water, and with the shadowy forms of hungry fish and the dark shapes of squid. These things were seen, as few men have seen them, by the Norwegian ethnologist Thor Heyerdahl in the course of one of the most unusual journeys of modern times. In the summer of 1947 Heyerdahl and five companions drifted 4300 miles across the Pacific on a raft of balsa logs, to test a theory that the original inhabitants of Polynesia might have come from South America by raft. For 101 days and nights these men lived practically on the surface of the sea, driven by the trade wind, carried on the strong drift of the Equatorial Current, as much a part of the inexorable westward movement of wind and water as the creatures of the sea. Because of his enviable opportunity to observe the life of the surface while living as an actual part of it for so many weeks, I asked Mr. Heyerdahl about some of his impressions, especially of the sea at night, and he has written me as follows:

> Chiefly at night, but occasionally in broad daylight, a shoal of small squids shot out of the water precisely like flying fish, gliding through the air as much as up to six feet above the surface, until they lost the speed accumulated below water, and fell down helplessly. In their gliding flight with flaps out they were so much like small flying fish at a distance, that we had no idea we saw anything unusual until a live squid flew right into one of the crew and fell down on deck. Almost every night we found one or two on the deck or on the roof of the bamboo hut.
>
> It was my own definite impression that the marine life in general went deeper down in the daytime than during the nights, and that the darker the night was, the more life we had around us. At two different occasions, a snake-mackerel, Gempylus, never before seen by man except as skeletal remains washed ashore on South America and the Galapagos, came jumping clear out of the water and right up on the raft (once right into the hut). To judge from the huge eyes and the fact that the fish

has never before been observed, I am inclined to suspect that it is a deep-sea fish that comes to the surface only at night.

On dark nights we could see much marine life which we were unable to identify. They seemed to be deep-sea fishes approaching the surface at night. Generally we saw it as vaguely phosphorescent bodies, often the size and shape of a dinner plate, but at least one night in the shape of three immense bodies of irregular and changing shape and dimensions which appeared to exceed those of the raft (KON-TIKI measured about 45 by 18 feet). Apart from these greater bodies, we observed occasionally great quantities of phosphorescent plankton, often containing illuminating copepods up to the size of a millimeter or more.

With these surface waters, through a series of delicately adjusted, interlocking relationships, the life of all parts of the sea is linked. What happens to a diatom in the upper, sunlit strata of the sea may well determine what happens to a cod lying on a ledge of some rocky canyon a hundred fathoms below, or to a bed of multicolored, gorgeously plumed seaworms carpeting an underlying shoal, or to a prawn creeping over the soft oozes of the sea floor in the blackness of mile-deep water.

The activities of the microscopic vegetables of the sea, of which the diatoms are most important, make the mineral wealth of the water available to the animals. Feeding directly on the diatoms and other groups of minute unicellular algae are the marine protozoa, many crustaceans, the young of crabs, barnacles, sea worms, and fishes. Hordes of the small carnivores, the first link in the chain of flesh eaters, move among these peaceful grazers. There are fierce little dragons half an inch long, the sharp-jawed arrowworms. There are gooseberrylike comb jellies, armed with grasping tentacles, and there are the shrimplike euphausiids that strain food from the water with their bristly appendages. Since they drift where the currents carry them, with no power or will to oppose that of the sea, this strange community of creatures and the marine plants that sustain them are called "plankton," a word derived from the Greek, meaning "wandering."

From the plankton the food chains lead on, to the schools of plankton-feeding fishes like the herring, menhaden, and mackerel; to the fish-eating fishes like the bluefish and tuna and sharks; to the pelagic squids that prey on fishes; to the great whales who, according to their species but not according to their size, may live on fishes, on shrimps, or on some of the smallest of the plankton creatures.

Unmarked and trackless though it may seem to us, the surface of the ocean is divided into definite zones, and the pattern of the surface water controls the distribution of its life. Fishes and plankton, whales and squids, birds and sea turtles, all are linked by unbreakable ties to certain kinds of water—to warm water or cold water, to clear or turbid water, to water rich in phosphates or in silicates. For the animals higher in the food chains the ties are less direct; they are bound to water where their food is plentiful, and the food animals are there because the water conditions are right.

The change from zone to zone may be abrupt. It may come upon us unseen, as our ship at night crosses an invisible boundary line. So Charles Darwin on H.M.S. *Beagle* one dark night off the coast of South America crossed from tropical water into that of the cool south. Instantly the vessel was surrounded by numerous seals and penguins, which made such a bedlam of strange noises that the officer on watch was deceived into thinking the ship had, by some miscalculation, run close inshore, and that the sounds he heard were the bellowing of cattle.

To the human senses, the most obvious patterning of the surface waters is indicated by color. The deep blue water of the open sea far from land is the color of emptiness and barrenness; the green water of the coastal areas, with all its varying hues, is the color of life. The sea is blue because the sunlight is reflected back to our eyes from the water molecules or from very minute particles suspended in the sea. In the journey of the light rays into deep water all the red rays and most of the yellow rays of the spectrum have been absorbed, so when the light returns to our eyes it is chiefly the cool blue rays that we see. Where the water is rich in plankton, it loses the glassy transparency that permits this deep penetration of the light rays. The yellow and brown and green hues of the coastal waters are derived from the minute algae and other microorganisms so abundant there. Seasonal abundance of certain forms containing reddish or brown pigments may cause the "red water" known from ancient times in many parts of the world, and so common in this condition in some enclosed seas that they owe their names to it—the Red Sea and the Vermilion Sea are examples.

The colors of the sea are only the indirect signs of the presence or absence of conditions needed to support the surface life; other zones, invisible to the eye, are the ones that largely determine where marine creatures may live. For the sea is by no means a uniform solution of water; parts of it are more salty than others, and parts are warmer or colder.

The saltiest ocean water in the world is that of the Red Sea, where the burning sun and the fierce heat of the atmosphere produce such rapid evaporation that the salt content is 40 parts per thousand. The Sargasso Sea, an area of high air temperatures, receiving no inflow of river water or melting ice because of its remoteness from land, is the saltiest part of the Atlantic, which in turn is the saltiest of the oceans. The polar seas, as one would expect, are the least salty, because they are constantly being diluted by rain, snow, and melting ice. Along the Atlantic coast of the United States, the salinity range from about 33 parts per thousand off Cape Cod to about 36 off Florida is a difference easily perceptible to the senses of human bathers.

Ocean temperatures vary from about 28° F. in polar seas to 96° in the Persian Gulf, which contains the hottest ocean water in the world. To creatures of the sea, which with few exceptions must match in their own bodies the temperature of the surrounding water, this range is tremendous, and change of temperature is probably the most important single condition that controls the distribution of marine animals.

The beautiful reef corals are a perfect example of the way the inhabitable areas for any particular class of creatures may be established by temperatures. If you took a map of the world and drew a line 30° north of the equator and another 30° south of it, you would have outlined in general the waters where reef corals are found at the present time. It is true that the remains of ancient coral reefs have been discovered in arctic waters, but this means that in some past ages the climate of these northern seas was tropical. The calcareous structure of the coral reef can be fashioned only in water at least as warm as 70° Fahrenheit. We would have to make one northward extension of our map, where the Gulf Stream carries water warm enough for corals to

Bermuda, at 32° north latitude. On the other hand, within our tropical belt, we would have to erase large areas on the west coasts of South America and Africa, where upwelling of cold water from lower ocean levels prevents the growth of corals. Most of the east coast of Florida has no coral reefs because of a cool inshore current, running southward between the coast and the Gulf Stream.

As between tropical and polar regions, the differences in the kinds and abundance of life are tremendous. The warm temperatures of the tropics speed up the processes of reproduction and growth, so that many generations are produced in the time required to bring one to maturity in cold seas. There is more opportunity for genetic mutations to be produced within a given time; hence the bewildering variety of tropical life. Yet in any species there are far fewer individuals than in the colder zones, where the mineral content of the water is richer, and there are no dense swarms of surface plankton, like the copepods of the Arctic. The pelagic, or free-swimming, forms of the tropics live deeper than those of the colder regions, and so there is less food for large surface-feeders. In the tropics, therefore, the sea birds do not compare in abundance with the clouds of shearwaters, fulmars, auks, whalebirds, albatrosses, and other birds seen over far northern or far southern fishing grounds.

In the cold-water communities of the polar seas, fewer of the animals have swimming larvae. Generation after generation settle down near the parents, so that large areas of bottom may be covered with the descendants of a very few animals. In the Barents Sea a research vessel once brought up more than a ton of one of the siliceous sponges at a single haul, and enormous patches of a single species of annelid worm carpet the east coast of Spitsbergen. Copepods and swimming snails fill the surface waters of the cold seas, and lure the herring and the mackerel, the flocks of sea birds, the whales, and the seals.

In the tropics, then, sea life is intense, vivid, and infinitely varied. In cold seas it proceeds at a pace slowed by the icy water in which it exists, but the mineral richness of these waters (largely a result of seasonal overturn and consequent mixing) makes possible the enormous abundance of the forms that inhabit them. For a good many years it has been said categorically that the total productivity of the colder temperate and polar seas is far greater than the tropical. Now it is becoming plain that there are important exceptions to this statement. In certain tropical and subtropical waters, there are areas where the sheer abundance of life rivals the Grand Banks or the Barents Sea or any antarctic whaling ground. Perhaps the best examples are the Humboldt Current, off the west coast of South America, and the Benguela Current, off the west coast of Africa. In both currents, upwelling of cold, mineral-laden water from deeper layers of the sea provides the fertilizing elements to sustain the great food chains.

And wherever two currents meet, especially if they differ sharply in temperature or salinity, there are zones of great turbulence and unrest, with water sinking or rising up from the depths and with shifting eddies and foam lines at the surface. At such places the richness and abundance of marine life reveals itself most strikingly. This changing life, seen as his ship cut across the pathways of the great currents of the Pacific and the Atlantic, was described with vivid detail by S. C. Brooks:

> Within a few degrees of the equator, the scattered cumulus clouds become thicker and grayer, a confused swell makes up, rain squalls come and go, and birds appear. At first there is only a greater abundance of storm petrels, with here and there petrels of other kinds hunting along utterly indifferent to the ship, or small groups of tropic birds flying along with the ship, off to one side or high overhead. Then scattered groups of various petrels appear, and finally for an hour or two there are birds on every hand. If one is not too far from land, a few hundred miles perhaps, as in the case of the south equatorial drift north of the Marquesas, one may also see multitudes of sooty or crested terns. Occasionally one sees the grayish blue form of a shark gliding along, or a big purplish-brown hammerhead lazily twisting around as though trying to get a better view of the ship. Flying fish, while not so closely localized as the birds, are breaking the water every few seconds, and bewitch the beholder by their myriad sizes, shapes, and antics, and their bewildering patterns and shades of deep brown, opal blue, yellow and purple. Then the sun comes out again, the sea takes on its deep tropical blue, the birds become more and more scarce, and gradually, as the ship moves on, the ocean resumes its desert aspect.

If it were daylight all the time, this same sequence might be seen in a more or less striking fashion twice or perhaps even three or four times. Inquiry soon reveals that this sequence marks the time of passing the edge of one of the great currents . . .

In the North Atlantic ship lanes the same play is staged with different actors. Instead of the equatorial currents there are the Gulf Stream and its continuation, the North Atlantic Drift, and the Arctic Current; instead of confused swell and squalls of rain there are slicks and fogs. Tropic-birds are replaced by jaegers and skuas; and different species of the petrel group, usually here spoken of as shearwaters and fulmars, are flying or swimming about, often in great flocks . . . Here, too, perhaps, one sees less of sharks and more of porpoise racing with the cut-water or doggedly hurrying, school after school, toward some unguessable objective. The flashing black and white of the young orcas, or the distant sudden spurt and lazy drift of a whale's spouting, lend life to the water, as do the antics of flying fish, distant though they be from their traditional home in the tropics . . . One may pass from the blue water of the Stream, with floating gulf weed (Sargassum), and perhaps here and there the iridescent float of a Portuguese man-of-war, into the gray-green water of the Arctic Current with its thousands of jelly fish, and in a few hours back again into the Stream. Each time, at the margin, one is likely to see the surface display of that abundance of life which has made the Grand Banks one of the great fisheries of the world.*

The mid-ocean regions, bounded by the currents that sweep around the ocean basins, are in general the deserts of the sea. There are few birds and few surface-feeding fishes, and indeed there is little surface plankton to attract them. The life of these regions is largely confined to deep water. The Sargasso Sea is an exception, not matched in the anticyclonic centers of other ocean basins. It is so different from any other place on earth that it may well be considered a definite geographic region. A line drawn from the mouth of Chesapeake Bay to Gibraltar would skirt its northern border; another from Haiti to Dakar would mark its southern boundary. It lies all about Bermuda and extends more than halfway across the Atlantic, its entire

---

*From *The Condor*, vol. 36, no. 5, Sept.–Oct. 1934, pp. 186–7.

area being roughly as large as the United States. The Sargasso, with all its legendary terrors for sailing ships, is a creation of the great currents of the North Atlantic that encircle it and bring into it the millions of tons of floating sargassum weed from which the place derives its name, and all the weird assemblage of animals that live in the weed.

The Sargasso is a place forgotten by the winds, undisturbed by the strong flow of waters that girdle it as with a river. Under the seldom-clouded skies, its waters are warm and heavy with salt. Separated widely from coastal rivers and from polar ice, there is no inflow of fresh water to dilute its saltiness; the only influx is of saline water from the adjacent currents, especially from the Gulf Stream or North Atlantic Current as it crosses from America to Europe. And with the little, inflowing streams of surface water come the plants and animals that for months or years have drifted in the Gulf Stream.

The sargassum weeds are brown algae belonging to several species. Quantities of the weeds live attached to reefs or rocky outcroppings off the coasts of the West Indies and Florida. Many of the plants are torn away by storms, especially during the hurricane season. They are picked up by the Gulf Stream and are drifted northward. With the weeds go, as involuntary passengers, many small fishes, crabs, shrimps, and innumerable larvae of assorted species of marine creatures, whose home had been the coastal banks of sargassum weed.

Curious things happen to the animals that have ridden on the sargassum weed into a new home. Once they lived near the sea's edge, a few feet or a few fathoms below the surface, but never far above a firm bottom. They knew the rhythmic movements of waves and tides. They could leave the shelter of the weeds at will and creep or swim about over the bottom in search of food. Now, in the middle of the ocean, they are in a new world. The bottom lies two or three miles below them. Those who are poor swimmers must cling to the weed, which now represents a life raft, supporting them above the abyss. Over the ages since their ancestors came here, some species have developed special organs of attachment, either for themselves or for their eggs, so that they may not sink into the cold, dark water far below. The flying fish make nests of the weed to contain their eggs, which bear an amazing resemblance to the sargassum floats or "berries."

Indeed, many of the little marine beasts of the weedy jungle seem to be playing an elaborate game of disguise in which each is camouflaged to hide it from the others. The Sargasso sea slug—a snail without a shell—has a soft, shapeless brown body spotted with dark-edged circles and fringed with flaps and folds of skin, so that as it creeps over the weed in search of prey it can scarcely be distinguished from the vegetation. One of the fiercest carnivores of the place, the sargassum fish Pterophryne, has copied with utmost fidelity the branching fronds of the weed, its golden berries, its rich brown color, and even the white dots of encrusting worm tubes. All these elaborate bits of mimicry are indications of the fierce internecine wars of the Sargasso jungles, which go on without quarter and without mercy for the weak or the unwary.

In the science of the sea there has been a long-standing controversy about the origin of the drifting weeds of the Sargasso Sea. Some have held that the supply is maintained by weeds recently torn away from coastal beds; others say that the rather limited sargassum fields of the West Indies and Florida cannot possibly supply the immense area of the Sargasso. They believe that we find here a self-perpetuating community of plants that have become adapted to life in the open sea, needing no roots or holdfasts for attachment, and able to propagate vegetatively. Probably there is truth in both ideas. New plants do come in each year in small numbers, and now cover an immense area because of their very long life once they have reached this quiet central region of the Atlantic.

It takes about half a year for the plants torn from West Indian shores to reach the northern border of the Sargasso, perhaps several years for them to be carried into the inner parts of this area. Meanwhile, some have been swept onto the shores of North America by storms, others have been killed by cold during the passage from offshore New England across the Atlantic, where the Gulf Stream comes into contact with waters from the Arctic. For the plants that reach the calm of the Sargasso, there is virtual immortality. A. E. Parr of the American Museum has recently suggested that the individual plants may live, some for decades, others for centuries, according to their species. It might well be that some of the very weeds you would see if you visited the place today were seen by Columbus and his men. Here, in the heart of the Atlantic, the weed drifts endlessly, growing, reproducing vegetatively by a process of fragmentation. Apparently almost the only plants that die are the ones that drift into unfavorable conditions around the edges of the Sargasso or are picked up by outward-moving currents.

Such losses are balanced, or possibly a little more than balanced, by the annual addition of weeds from distant coasts. It must have taken eons of time to accumulate the present enormous quantities of weed, which Parr estimates as about 10 million tons. But this, of course, is distributed over so large an area that most of the Sargasso is open water. The dense fields of weeds waiting to entrap a vessel never existed except in the imaginations of sailors, and the gloomy hulks of vessels doomed to endless drifting in the clinging weed are only the ghosts of things that never were.

The Changing Year

Thus with the year seasons return.

—MILTON

For the sea as a whole, the alternation of day and night, the passage of the seasons, the procession of the years, are lost in its vastness, obliterated in its own changeless eternity. But the surface waters are different. The face of the sea is always changing. Crossed by colors, lights, and moving shadows, sparkling in the sun, mysterious in the twilight, its aspects and its moods vary hour by hour. The surface waters move with the tides, stir to the breath of the winds, and rise and fall to the endless, hurrying forms of the waves. Most of all, they change with the advance of the seasons. Spring moves over the temperate lands of our Northern Hemisphere in a tide of new life, of pushing green shoots and unfolding buds, all its mysteries and meanings symbolized in the northward migration of the birds, the awakening of sluggish amphibian life as the chorus of frogs rises again from the wet lands, the different sound of the wind which stirs the young leaves where a month ago it rattled the bare branches. These things we associate with the land, and it is easy to suppose that at sea there could be no such feeling of advancing spring. But the signs are there, and seen with understanding eye, they bring the same magical sense of awakening.

In the sea, as on land, spring is a time for the renewal of life. During the long months of winter in the temperate zones the surface waters have been absorbing the cold. Now the heavy water begins to sink, slipping down and displacing the warmer layers below. Rich stores of minerals have been accumulating on the floor of the continental shelf—some freighted down the rivers from the lands; some derived from sea creatures that have died and whose remains have drifted down to the bottom; some from the shells that once encased a diatom, the streaming protoplasm of a radiolarian, or the transparent tissues of a pteropod. Nothing is wasted in the sea; every particle of material is used over and over again, first by one creature, then by another. And when in spring the waters are deeply stirred, the warm bottom water brings to the surface a rich supply of minerals, ready for use by new forms of life.

Just as land plants depend on minerals in the soil for their growth, every marine plant, even the smallest, is dependent upon the nutrient salts or minerals in the sea water. Diatoms must have silica, the element of which their fragile shells are fashioned. For these and all other microplants, phosphorus is an indispensable mineral. Some of these elements are in short supply and in winter may be reduced below the minimum necessary for growth. The diatom population must tide itself over this season as best it can. It faces a stark problem of survival, with no opportunity to increase, a problem of keeping alive the spark of life by forming tough protective spores against the stringency of winter, a matter of existing in a dormant state in which no demands shall be made on an environment that already withholds all but the most meager necessities of life. So the diatoms hold their place in the winter sea, like seeds of wheat in a field under snow and ice, the seeds from which the spring growth will come.

These, then, are the elements of the vernal blooming of the sea: the "seeds" of the dormant plants, the fertilizing chemicals, the warmth of the spring sun.

In a sudden awakening, incredible in its swiftness, the simplest plants of the sea begin to multiply. Their increase is of astronomical proportions. The spring sea belongs at first to the diatoms and to all the other microscopic plant life of the plankton. In the fierce intensity of their growth they cover vast areas of ocean with a living blanket of their cells. Mile after mile of water may appear red or brown or green, the whole surface taking on the color of the infinitesimal grains of pigment contained in each of the plant cells.

The plants have undisputed sway in the sea for only a short time. Almost at once their own burst of multiplication is matched by a similar increase in the small animals of the plankton. It is the spawning time of the copepod and the glassworm, the pelagic shrimp and the winged snail. Hungry swarms of these little beasts of the plankton roam through the waters, feeding on the abundant plants and themselves falling prey to larger creatures. Now in the spring the surface waters become a vast nursery. From the hills and valleys of the continent's edge lying far below, and from the scattered shoals and banks, the eggs or young of many of the bottom animals rise to the surface of the sea. Even those which, in their maturity, will sink down to a sedentary life on the bottom, spend the first weeks of life as freely swimming hunters of the plankton. So as spring progresses new batches of larvae rise into the surface each day, the young of fishes and crabs and mussels and tube worms, mingling for a time with the regular members of the plankton.

Under the steady and voracious grazing, the grasslands of the surface are soon depleted. The diatoms become more and more scarce, and with them the other simple plants. Still there are brief explosions of one or another form, when in a sudden orgy of cell division it comes to claim whole areas of the sea for its own. So, for a time each spring, the waters may become blotched with brown, jellylike masses, and the fishermen's nets come up dripping a brown slime and containing no fish, for the herring have turned away from these waters as though in loathing of the viscid, foul-smelling algae. But in less time than passes between the full moon and the new, the spring flowering of Phaeocystis is past and the waters have cleared again.

In the spring the sea is filled with migrating fishes, some of them bound for the mouths of great rivers, which they will ascend to deposit their spawn. Such are the spring-run chinooks coming in from the deep Pacific feeding grounds to breast the rolling flood of the Columbia, the shad moving in to the Chesapeake and the Hudson and the Connecticut, the alewives seeking a hundred coastal streams of New England, the salmon feeling their way to the Penobscot and the Kennebec. For months or years these fish have known only the vast spaces of the ocean. Now the spring sea and the maturing of their own bodies lead them back to the rivers of their birth.

Other mysterious comings and goings are linked with the advance of the year. Capelin gather in the deep, cold water of the Barents Sea, their shoals followed and preyed upon by flocks of auks, fulmars, and kittiwakes. Cod approach the banks of Lofoten, and gather off the shores of Iceland. Birds whose winter feeding territory may have encompassed the whole Atlantic or the whole Pacific converge upon some small island, the entire breeding population arriving within the space of a few days. Whales suddenly appear off the slopes of the coastal banks where the swarms of shrimplike krill are spawning, the whales having come from no one knows where, by no one knows what route.

With the subsiding of the diatoms and the completed spawning of many of the plankton animals and most of the fish, life in the surface waters slackens to the slower pace of midsummer. Along the meeting places of the currents the pale moon jelly Aurelia gathers in thousands, forming sinuous lines or windrows across miles of sea, and the birds see their pale forms shimmering deep down in the green water. By midsummer the large red jellyfish Cyanea may have grown from the size of a thimble to that of an umbrella. The great jellyfish moves through the sea with rhythmic pulsations, trailing long tentacles and as likely as not shepherding a little group of young cod or haddock, which find shelter under its bell and travel with it.

A hard, brilliant, coruscating phosphorescence often illuminates the summer sea. In waters where the protozoa Noctiluca is abundant it is the chief source of this summer luminescence, causing fishes, squids, or dolphins to fill the water with racing flames and to clothe themselves in a ghostly radiance. Or again the summer sea may glitter with a thousand thousand moving pinpricks of light, like an immense swarm of fireflies moving through a dark wood. Such an effect is produced by a shoal of the brilliantly phosphorescent shrimp Meganyctiphanes, a creature of cold and darkness and of the places where icy water rolls upward from the depths and bubbles with white ripplings at the surface.

Out over the plankton meadows of the North Atlantic the dry twitter of the phalaropes, small brown birds, wheeling and turning, dipping and rising, is heard for the first time since early spring. The phalaropes have nested on the arctic tundras, reared their young, and now the first of them are returning to the sea. Most of them will continue south over the open water far from land, crossing the equator into the South Atlantic. Here they will follow where the great whales lead, for where the whales are, there also are the swarms of plankton on which these strange little birds grow fat.

As the fall advances, there are other movements, some in the surface, some hidden in the green depths, that betoken the end of summer. In the fog-covered waters of Bering Sea, down through the treacherous passes between the islands of the Aleutian chain and southward into the open Pacific, the herds of fur seals are moving. Left behind are two small islands, treeless bits of volcanic soil thrust up into the waters of Bering Sea. The islands are silent now, but for the several months of summer they resounded with the roar of millions of seals come ashore to bear and rear their young—all the fur seals of the eastern Pacific crowded into a few square miles of bare rock and crumbling soil. Now once more the seals turn south, to roam down along the sheer underwater cliffs of the continent's edge, where the rocky foundations fall away steeply into the deep sea. Here, in a blackness more absolute than that of arctic winter, the seals will find rich feeding as they swim down to prey on the fishes of this region of darkness.

Autumn comes to the sea with a fresh blaze of phosphorescence, when every wave crest is aflame. Here and there the whole surface may glow with sheets of cold fire, while below schools of fish pour through the water like molten metal. Often the autumnal phosphorescence is caused by a fall flowering of the dinoflagellates, multiplying furiously in a short-lived repetition of their vernal blooming.

Sometimes the meaning of the glowing water is ominous. Off the Pacific coast of North America, it may mean that the sea is filled with the dinoflagellate Gonyaulax, a minute plant that contains a poison of strange and terrible virulence. About four days after Gonyaulax comes to dominate the coastal plankton, some of the fishes and shellfish in the vicinity become toxic. This is because, in their normal feeding, they have strained the poisonous plankton out of the water. Mussels accumulate the Gonyaulax toxins in their livers, and the toxins react on the human nervous system with an effect similar to that of strychnine. Because of these facts, it is generally understood along the Pacific coast that it is unwise to eat shellfish taken from coasts exposed to the open sea where Gonyaulax may be abundant, in summer or early fall. For generations before the white men came, the Indians knew this. As soon as the red streaks appeared in the sea and the waves began to flicker at night with the mysterious blue-green fires, the tribal leaders forbade the taking of mussels until these warning signals should have passed. They even set guards at intervals along the beaches to warn inlanders who might come down for shellfish and be unable to read the language of the sea.

But usually the blaze and glitter of the sea, whatever its meaning for those who produce it, implies no menace to man. Seen from the deck of a vessel in open ocean, a tiny, man-made observation point in the vast world of sea and sky, it has an eerie and unearthly quality. Man, in his vanity, subconsciously attributes a human origin to any light not of moon or stars or sun. Lights on the shore, lights moving over the water, mean lights kindled and controlled by other men, serving purposes understandable to the human mind. Yet here are lights that flash and fade away, lights that come and go for reasons meaningless to man, lights that have been doing this very thing over the eons of time in which there were no men to stir in vague disquiet.

On such a night of phosphorescent display Charles Darwin stood on the deck of the *Beagle* as she plowed southward through the Atlantic off the coast of Brazil.

> The sea from its extreme luminousness presented a wonderful and most beautiful appearance [he wrote in his diary]. Every part of the water which by day is seen as foam, glowed with a pale light. The vessel drove before her bows two billows of liquid phosphorus, and in her wake was a milky train. As far as the eye reached the crest of every wave was bright; and from the reflected light, the sky just above the horizon was not so utterly dark as the rest of the Heavens. It was impossible to behold this plain of matter, as it were melted and consuming by heat, without being reminded of Milton's description of the regions of Chaos and Anarchy.*

Like the blazing colors of the autumn leaves before they wither and fall, the autumnal phosphorescence betokens the approach of winter. After their brief renewal of life the flagellates and the other minute algae dwindle away to a scattered few; so do the shrimps and the copepods, the glassworms and the comb jellies. The larvae of the bottom fauna have long since completed their development and drifted away to take

---

*From *Charles Darwin's Diary of the Voyage of H.M.S. Beagle*, edited by Nora Barlow, 1934 edition, Cambridge University Press, p. 107.

up whatever existence is their lot. Even the roving fish schools have deserted the surface waters and have migrated into warmer latitudes or have found equivalent warmth in the deep, quiet waters along the edge of the continental shelf. There the torpor of semi-hibernation descends upon them and will possess them during the months of winter.

The surface waters now become the plaything of the winter gales. As the winds build up the giant storm waves and roar along their crests, lashing the water into foam and flying spray, it seems that life must forever have deserted this place.

For the mood of the winter sea, read Joseph Conrad's description:

> The greyness of the whole immense surface, the wind furrows upon the faces of the waves, the great masses of foam, tossed about and waving, like matted white locks, give to the sea in a gale an appearance of hoary age, lustreless, dull, without gleams, as though it had been created before light itself.*

But the symbols of hope are not lacking even in the grayness and bleakness of the winter sea. On land we know that the apparent lifelessness of winter is an illusion. Look closely at the bare branches of a tree, on which not the palest gleam of green can be discerned. Yet, spaced along each branch are the leaf buds, all the spring's magic of swelling green concealed and safely preserved under the insulating, overlapping layers. Pick off a piece of the rough bark of the trunk; there you will find hibernating insects. Dig down through the snow into the earth. There are the eggs of next summer's grasshoppers; there are the dormant seeds from which will come the grass, the herb, the oak tree.

So, too, the lifelessness, the hopelessness, the despair of the winter sea are an illusion. Everywhere are the assurances that the cycle has come to the full, containing the means of its own renewal. There is the promise of a new spring in the very iciness of the winter sea, in the chilling of the water, which must, before many weeks, become so heavy that it will plunge downward, precipitating the overturn that is the first act in

---

*From *The Mirror of the Sea*, Kent edition, 1925, Doubleday-Page, p. 71.

the drama of spring. There is the promise of new life in the small plantlike things that cling to the rocks of the underlying bottom, the almost formless polyps from which, in spring, a new generation of jellyfish will bud off and rise into the surface waters. There is unconscious purpose in the sluggish forms of the copepods hibernating on the bottom, safe from the surface storms, life sustained in their tiny bodies by the extra store of fat with which they went into this winter sleep.

Already, from the gray shapes of cod that have moved, unseen by man, through the cold sea to their spawning places, the glassy globules of eggs are rising into the surface waters. Even in the harsh world of the winter sea, these eggs will begin the swift divisions by which a granule of protoplasm becomes a living fishlet.

Most of all, perhaps, there is assurance in the fine dust of life that remains in the surface waters, the invisible spores of the diatoms, needing only the touch of warming sun and fertilizing chemicals to repeat the magic of spring.

The Sunless Sea

> Where great whales come sailing by,
> sail and sail, with unshut eye.
>
> —MATTHEW ARNOLD

BETWEEN THE SUNLIT surface waters of the open sea and the hidden hills and valleys of the ocean floor lies the least-known region of the sea. These deep, dark waters, with all their mysteries and their unsolved problems, cover a very considerable part of the earth. The whole world ocean extends over about three-fourths of the surface of the globe. If we subtract the shallow areas of the continental shelves and the scattered banks and shoals, where at least the pale ghost of sunlight moves over the underlying bottom, there still remains about half the earth that is covered by miles-deep, lightless water, that has been dark since the world began.

This region has withheld its secrets more obstinately than any other. Man, with all his ingenuity, has been able to venture only to its threshold. Wearing a diving helmet, he can walk on the ocean floor about 10 fathoms down. He can descend to an extreme limit of about 500 feet in a complete diving suit, so heavily armored that movement is almost impossible, carrying with him a constant supply of oxygen. Only two men in all the history of the world have had the experience of descending, alive, beyond the range of visible light. These men are William Beebe and Otis Barton. In the bathysphere, they reached a depth of 3028 feet in the open ocean off Bermuda, in the year 1934. Barton alone, in a steel sphere known as the benthoscope, descended to the great depth of 4500 feet off California, in the summer of 1949.[2]

Although only a fortunate few can ever visit the deep sea, the precise instruments of the oceanographer, recording light penetration, pressure, salinity, and temperature, have given us the materials with which to reconstruct in imagination these eerie, forbidding regions. Unlike the surface waters, which are sensitive to every gust of wind, which know day and night, respond to the pull of sun and moon, and change as the seasons change, the deep waters are a place where change comes slowly, if at all. Down beyond the reach of the sun's rays, there is no alternation of light and darkness. There is rather an endless night, as old as the sea itself. For most of its creatures, groping their way endlessly through its black waters, it must be a place of hunger, where food is scarce and hard to find, a shelterless place where there is no sanctuary from ever-present enemies, where one can only move on and on, from birth to death, through the darkness, confined as in a prison to his own particular layer of the sea.

They used to say that nothing could live in the deep sea. It was a belief that must have been easy to accept, for without proof to the contrary, how could anyone conceive of life in such a place?

A century ago the British biologist Edward Forbes wrote: "As we descend deeper and deeper into this region, the inhabitants become more and more modified, and fewer and fewer, indicating our approach to an abyss where life is either extinguished, or exhibits but a few sparks to mark its lingering presence." Yet Forbes urged further exploration of "this vast deep-sea region" to settle forever the question of the existence of life at great depths.

Even then, the evidence was accumulating. Sir John Ross, during his exploration of the arctic seas in 1818, had brought up from a depth of 1000 fathoms mud in which there were worms, "thus proving there was animal life in the bed of the ocean notwithstanding the darkness, stillness, silence, and immense pressure produced by more than a mile of superincumbent water."

Then from the surveying ship *Bulldog*, examining a proposed northern route for a cable from Faroe to Labrador in 1860, came another report. The *Bulldog*'s sounding line, which at one place had been allowed to lie for some time on the bottom at a depth of 1260 fathoms, came up with 13 starfish clinging to it. Through these starfish, the ship's naturalist wrote, "the deep has sent forth the long coveted message." But not all the zoologists of the day were prepared to accept the message. Some doubters asserted that the starfish had "convulsively embraced" the line somewhere on the way back to the surface.

In the same year, 1860, a cable in the Mediterranean was

raised for repairs from a depth of 1200 fathoms. It was found to be heavily encrusted with corals and other sessile animals that had attached themselves at an early stage of development and grown to maturity over a period of months or years. There was not the slightest chance that they had become entangled in the cable as it was being raised to the surface.

Then the *Challenger*, the first ship ever equipped for oceanographic exploration, set out from England in the year 1872 and traced a course around the globe. From bottoms lying under miles of water, from silent deeps carpeted with red clay ooze, and from all the lightless intermediate depths, net-haul after net-haul of strange and fantastic creatures came up and were spilled out on the decks. Poring over the weird beings thus brought up for the first time into the light of day, beings no man had ever seen before, the *Challenger* scientists realized that life existed even on the deepest floor of the abyss.

The recent discovery that a living cloud of some unknown creatures is spread over much of the ocean at a depth of several hundred fathoms below the surface is the most exciting thing that has been learned about the ocean for many years.

When, during the first quarter of the twentieth century, echo sounding was developed to allow ships while under way to record the depth of the bottom, probably no one suspected that it would also provide a means of learning something about deep-sea life. But operators of the new instruments soon discovered that the sound waves, directed downward from the ship like a beam of light, were reflected back from any solid object they met. Answering echoes were returned from intermediate depths, presumably from schools of fish, whales, or submarines; then a second echo was received from the bottom.

These facts were so well established by the late 1930's that fishermen had begun to talk about using their fathometers to search for schools of herring. Then the war brought the whole subject under strict security regulations, and little more was heard about it. In 1946, however, the United States Navy issued a significant bulletin. It was reported that several scientists, working with sonic equipment in deep water off the California coast, had discovered a widespread "layer" of some sort, which gave back an answering echo to the sound waves.

This reflecting layer, seemingly suspended between the surface and the floor of the Pacific, was found over an area 300 miles wide. It lay from 1000 to 1500 feet below the surface. The discovery was made by three scientists, C. F. Eyring, R. J. Christensen, and R. W. Raitt, aboard the U.S.S. *Jasper* in 1942, and for a time this mysterious phenomenon, of wholly unknown nature, was called the ECR layer. Then in 1945 Martin W. Johnson, marine biologist of the Scripps Institution of Oceanography, made a further discovery which gave the first clue to the nature of the layer. Working aboard the vessel *E. W. Scripps*, Johnson found that whatever sent back the echoes moved upward and downward in rhythmic fashion, being found near the surface at night, in deep water during the day. This discovery disposed of speculations that the reflections came from something inanimate, perhaps a mere physical discontinuity in the water, and showed that the layer is composed of living creatures capable of controlled movement.

From this time on, discoveries about the sea's "phantom bottom" came rapidly. With widespread use of echo-sounding instruments, it has become clear that the phenomenon is not something peculiar to the coast of California alone. It occurs almost universally in the deep ocean basins—drifting by day at a depth of several hundred fathoms, at night rising to the surface, and again, before sunrise, sinking into the depths.

On the passage of the U.S.S. *Henderson* from San Diego to the Antarctic in 1947, the reflecting layer was detected during the greater part of each day, at depths varying from 150 to 450 fathoms, and on a later run from San Diego to Yokosuka, Japan, the *Henderson*'s fathometer again recorded the layer every day, suggesting that it exists almost continuously across the Pacific.

During July and August 1947, the U.S.S. *Nereus* made a continuous fathogram from Pearl Harbor to the Arctic and found the scattering layer over all deep waters along this course. It did not develop, however, in the shallow Bering and Chuckchee seas. Sometimes in the morning, the *Nereus* fathogram showed two layers, responding in different ways to the growing illumination of the water; both descended into deep water, but there was an interval of twenty minutes between the two descents.

Despite attempts to sample it or photograph it, no one is

sure what the layer is, although the discovery may be made any day. There are three principal theories, each of which has its group of supporters. According to these theories, the sea's phantom bottom may consist of small planktonic shrimps, of fishes, or of squids.

As for the plankton theory, one of the most convincing arguments is the well-known fact that many plankton creatures make regular vertical migrations of hundreds of feet, rising toward the surface at night, sinking down below the zone of light penetration very early in the morning. This is, of course, exactly the behavior of the scattering layer. Whatever composes it is apparently strongly repelled by sunlight. The creatures of the layer seem almost to be held prisoner at the end—or beyond the end—of the sun's rays throughout the hours of daylight, waiting only for the welcome return of darkness to hurry upward into the surface waters. But what is the power that repels; and what the attraction that draws them surfaceward once the inhibiting force is removed? Is it comparative safety from enemies that makes them seek darkness? Is it more abundant food near the surface that lures them back under cover of night?

Those who say that fish are the reflectors of the sound waves usually account for the vertical migrations of the layer by suggesting that the fish are feeding on planktonic shrimp and are following their food. They believe that the air bladder of a fish is, of all structures concerned, most likely from its construction to return a strong echo. There is one outstanding difficulty in the way of accepting this theory: we have no other evidence that concentrations of fish are universally present in the oceans. In fact, almost everything else we know suggests that the really dense populations of fish live over the continental shelves or in certain very definitely determined zones of the open ocean where food is particularly abundant. If the reflecting layer is eventually proved to be composed of fish, the prevailing views of fish distribution will have to be radically revised.

The most startling theory (and the one that seems to have the fewest supporters) is that the layer consists of concentrations of squid, "hovering below the illuminated zone of the sea and awaiting the arrival of darkness in which to resume their raids into the plankton-rich surface waters." Proponents of this theory argue that squid are abundant enough, and of wide enough distribution, to give the echoes that have been picked up almost everywhere from the equator to the two poles. Squid are known to be the sole food of the sperm whale, found in the open oceans in all temperate and tropical waters. They also form the exclusive diet of the bottlenosed whale and are eaten extensively by most other toothed whales, by seals, and by many sea birds. All these facts argue that they must be prodigiously abundant.

It is true that men who have worked close to the sea surface at night have received vivid impressions of the abundance and activity of squids in the surface waters in darkness. Long ago Johan Hjort wrote:

> One night we were hauling long lines on the Faroe slope, working with an electric lamp hanging over the side in order to see the line, when like lightning flashes one squid after another shot towards the light . . . In October 1902 we were one night steaming outside the slopes of the coast banks of Norway, and for many miles we could see the squids moving in the surface waters like luminous bubbles, resembling large milky white electric lamps being constantly lit and extinguished.*

Thor Heyerdahl reports that at night his raft was literally bombarded by squids; and Richard Fleming says that in his oceanographic work off the coast of Panama it was common to see immense schools of squid gathering at the surface at night and leaping upward toward the lights that were used by the men to operate their instruments. But equally spectacular surface displays of shrimp have been seen, and most people find it difficult to believe in the ocean-wide abundance of squid.

Deep-water photography holds much promise for the solution of the mystery of the phantom bottom. There are technical difficulties, such as the problem of holding a camera still as it swings at the end of a long cable, twisting and turning, suspended from a ship which itself moves with the sea. Some of the pictures so taken look as though the photographer has pointed his camera at a starry sky and swung it in an arc as he exposed

---

*From *The Depths of the Ocean*, by Sir John Murray and Johan Hjort, 1912 edition, Macmillan & Co., p. 649.

the film. Yet the Norwegian biologist Gunnar Rollefson had an encouraging experience in correlating photography with echograms. On the research ship *Johan Hjort* off the Lofoten Islands, he persistently got reflection of sound from schools of fish in 20 to 30 fathoms. A specially constructed camera was lowered to the depth indicated by the echogram. When developed, the film showed moving shapes of fish at a distance, and a large and clearly recognizable cod appeared in the beam of light and hovered in front of the lens.

Direct sampling of the layer is the logical means of discovering its identity, but the problem is to develop large nets that can be operated rapidly enough to capture swift-moving animals. Scientists at Woods Hole, Massachusetts, have towed ordinary plankton nets in the layer and have found that euphausiid shrimps, glassworms, and other deep-water plankton are concentrated there; but there is still a possibility that the layer itself may actually be made up of larger forms feeding on the shrimps—too large or swift to be taken in the presently used nets. New nets may give the answer. Television is another possibility.[3]

Shadowy and indefinite though they be, these recent indications of an abundant life at mid-depths agree with the reports of the only observers who have actually visited comparable depths and brought back eyewitness accounts of what they saw. William Beebe's impressions from the bathysphere were of a life far more abundant and varied than he had been prepared to find, although, over a period of six years, he had made many hundreds of net-hauls in the same area. More than a quarter of a mile down, he reported aggregations of living things "as thick as I have ever seen them." At half a mile—the deepest descent of the bathysphere—Dr. Beebe recalled that "there was no instant when a mist of plankton . . . was not swirling in the path of the beam."

The existence of an abundant deep-sea fauna was discovered, probably millions of years ago, by certain whales and also, it now appears, by seals. The ancestors of all whales, we know by fossil remains, were land mammals. They must have been predatory beasts, if we are to judge by their powerful jaws and teeth. Perhaps in their foragings about the deltas of great rivers or around the edges of shallow seas, they discovered the abundance of fish and other marine life and over the centuries formed the habit of following them farther and farther into the sea. Little by little their bodies took on a form more suitable for aquatic life; their hind limbs were reduced to rudiments, which may be discovered in a modern whale by dissection, and the forelimbs were modified into organs for steering and balancing.

Eventually the whales, as though to divide the sea's food resources among them, became separated into three groups: the plankton-eaters, the fish-eaters, and the squid-eaters. The plankton-eating whales can exist only where there are dense masses of small shrimp or copepods to supply their enormous food requirements. This limits them, except for scattered areas, to arctic and antarctic waters and the high temperate latitudes. Fish-eating whales may find food over a somewhat wider range of ocean, but they are restricted to places where there are enormous populations of schooling fish. The blue water of the tropics and of the open ocean basins offers little to either of these groups. But that immense, square-headed, formidably toothed whale known as the cachalot or sperm whale discovered long ago what men have known for only a short time—that hundreds of fathoms below the almost untenanted surface waters of these regions there is an abundant animal life. The sperm whale has taken these deep waters for his hunting grounds; his quarry is the deep-water population of squids, including the giant squid Architeuthis, which lives pelagically at depths of 1500 feet or more. The head of the sperm whale is often marked with long stripes, which consist of a great number of circular scars made by the suckers of the squid. From this evidence we can imagine the battles that go on, in the darkness of the deep water, between these two huge creatures—the sperm whale with its 70-ton bulk, the squid with a body as long as 30 feet, and writhing, grasping arms extending the total length of the animal to perhaps 50 feet.

The greatest depth at which the giant squid lives is not definitely known, but there is one instructive piece of evidence about the depth to which sperm whales descend, presumably in search of the squids. In April 1932, the cable repair ship *All America* was investigating an apparent break in the submarine cable between Balboa in the Canal Zone and Esmeraldas, Ecuador. The cable was brought to the surface off the coast of Colombia. Entangled in it was a dead 45-foot male sperm whale. The submarine cable was twisted around the lower jaw and was wrapped around one flipper, the body, and the caudal flukes. The cable was raised from a depth of 540 fathoms, or 3240 feet.[4]

Some of the seals also appear to have discovered the hidden food reserves of the deep ocean. It has long been something of a mystery where, and on what, the northern fur seals of the eastern Pacific feed during the winter, which they spend off the coast of North America from California to Alaska. There is no evidence that they are feeding to any great extent on sardines, mackerel, or other commercially important fishes. Presumably four million seals could not compete with commercial fishermen for the same species without the fact being known. But there is some evidence on the diet of the fur seals, and it is highly significant. Their stomachs have yielded the bones of a species of fish that has never been seen alive. Indeed, not even its remains have been found anywhere except in the stomachs of seals. Ichthyologists say that this "seal fish" belongs to a group that typically inhabits very deep water, off the edge of the continental shelf.

How either whales or seals endure the tremendous pressure changes involved in dives of several hundred fathoms is not definitely known. They are warm-blooded mammals like ourselves. Caisson disease, which is caused by the rapid accumulation of nitrogen bubbles in the blood with sudden release of pressure, kills human divers if they are brought up rapidly from depths of 200 feet or so. Yet, according to the testimony of whalers, a baleen whale, when harpooned, can dive straight down to a depth of half a mile, as measured by the amount of line carried out. From these depths, where it has sustained a pressure of half a ton on every inch of body, it returns almost immediately to the surface. The most plausible explanation is that, unlike the diver, who has air pumped to him while he is under water, the whale has in its body only the limited supply it carries down, and does not have enough nitrogen in its blood to do serious harm. The plain truth is, however, that we really do not know, since it is obviously impossible to confine a living whale and experiment on it, and almost as difficult to dissect a dead one satisfactorily.

At first thought it seems a paradox that creatures of such great fragility as the glass sponge and the jellyfish can live under the conditions of immense pressure that prevail in deep water. For creatures at home in the deep sea, however, the saving fact is that the pressure inside their tissues is the same as that without, and, as long as this balance is preserved, they are no more inconvenienced by a pressure of a ton or so than we are by ordinary atmospheric pressure. And most abyssal creatures, it must be remembered, live out their whole lives in a comparatively restricted zone, and are never required to adjust themselves to extreme changes of pressure.

But of course there are exceptions, and the real miracle of sea life in relation to great pressure is not the animal that lives its whole life on the bottom, bearing a pressure of perhaps five or six tons, but those that regularly move up and down through hundreds or thousands of feet of vertical change. The small shrimps and other planktonic creatures that descend into deep water during the day are examples. Fish that possess air bladders, on the other hand, are vitally affected by abrupt changes of pressure, as anyone knows who has seen a trawler's net raised from a hundred fathoms. Apart from the accident of being captured in a net and hauled up through waters of rapidly diminishing pressures, fish may sometimes wander out of the zone to which they are adjusted and find themselves unable to return. Perhaps in their pursuit of food they roam upward to the ceiling of the zone that is theirs, and beyond whose invisible boundary they may not stray without meeting alien and inhospitable conditions. Moving from layer to layer of drifting plankton as they feed, they may pass beyond the boundary. In the lessened pressure of these upper waters the gas enclosed within the air bladder expands. The fish becomes lighter and more buoyant. Perhaps he tries to fight his way down again, opposing the upward lift with all the power of his muscles. If he does not succeed, he "falls" to the surface, injured and dying, for the abrupt release of pressure from without causes distension and rupture of the tissues.

The compression of the sea under its own weight is relatively slight, and there is no basis for the old and picturesque belief that, at the deeper levels, the water resists the downward passage of objects from the surface. According to this belief, sinking ships, the bodies of drowned men, and presumably the bodies of the larger sea animals not consumed above by hungry scavengers, never reach the bottom, but come to rest at some level determined by the relation of their own weight to the compression of the water, there to drift forever. The fact is that anything will continue to sink as long as its specific gravity is greater than that of the surrounding water, and all large bodies descend, in a matter of a few days, to the ocean floor. As mute testimony to this fact, we bring up from the deepest ocean basins the teeth of sharks and the hard ear bones of whales.

Nevertheless the weight of sea water—the pressing down of miles of water upon all the underlying layers—does have a certain effect upon the water itself. If this downward compression could suddenly be relaxed by some miraculous suspension of natural laws, the sea level would rise about 93 feet all over the world. This would shift the Atlantic coastline of the United States westward a hundred miles or more and alter other familiar geographic outlines all over the world.

Immense pressure, then, is one of the governing conditions of life in the deep sea; darkness is another. The unrelieved darkness of the deep waters has produced weird and incredible modifications of the abyssal fauna. It is a blackness so divorced from the world of the sunlight that probably only the few men who have seen it with their own eyes can visualize it. We know that light fades out rapidly with descent below the surface. The red rays are gone at the end of the first 200 or 300 feet, and with them all the orange and yellow warmth of the sun. Then the greens fade out, and at 1000 feet only a deep, dark, brilliant blue is left. In very clear waters the violet rays of the spectrum may penetrate another thousand feet. Beyond this is only the blackness of the deep sea.

In a curious way, the colors of marine animals tend to be related to the zone in which they live. Fishes of the surface waters, like the mackerel and herring, often are blue or green; so are the floats of the Portuguese men-of-war and the azure-tinted wings of the swimming snails. Down below the diatom meadows and the drifting sargassum weed, where the water becomes ever more deeply, brilliantly blue, many creatures are crystal clear. Their glassy, ghostly forms blend with their surroundings and make it easier for them to elude the ever-present, ever-hungry enemy. Such are the transparent hordes of the arrowworms or glassworms, the comb jellies, and the larvae of many fishes.

At a thousand feet, and on down to the very end of the sun's rays, silvery fishes are common, and many others are red, drab brown, or black. Pteropods are a dark violet. Arrowworms, whose relatives in the upper layers are colorless, are here a deep red. Jellyfish medusae, which above would be transparent, at a depth of 1000 feet are a deep brown.

At depths greater than 1500 feet, all the fishes are black, deep violet, or brown, but the prawns wear amazing hues of red, scarlet, and purple. Why, no one can say. Since all the red rays are strained out of the water far above this depth, the scarlet raiment of these creatures can only look black to their neighbors.

The deep sea has its stars, and perhaps here and there an eerie and transient equivalent of moonlight, for the mysterious phenomenon of luminescence is displayed by perhaps half of all the fishes that live in dimly lit or darkened waters, and by many of the lower forms as well. Many fishes carry luminous torches that can be turned on or off at will, presumably helping them find or pursue their prey. Others have rows of lights over their bodies, in patterns that vary from species to species and may be a sort of recognition mark or badge by which the bearer can be known as friend or enemy. The deep-sea squid ejects a spurt of fluid that becomes a luminous cloud, the counterpart of the "ink" of his shallow-water relative.

Down beyond the reach of even the longest and strongest of the sun's rays, the eyes of fishes become enlarged, as though to make the most of any chance illumination of whatever sort, or they may become telescopic, large of lens, and protruding. In deep-sea fishes, hunting always in dark waters, the eyes tend to lose the "cones" or color-perceiving cells of the retina, and to increase the "rods," which perceive dim light. Exactly the same modification is seen on land among the strictly nocturnal prowlers which, like abyssal fish, never see the sunlight.

In their world of darkness, it would seem likely that some of the animals might have become blind, as has happened to some cave fauna. So, indeed, many of them have, compensating for the lack of eyes with marvelously developed feelers and long, slender fins and processes with which they grope their way, like so many blind men with canes, their whole knowledge of friends, enemies, or food coming to them through the sense of touch.

The last traces of plant life are left behind in the thin upper layer of water, for no plant can live below about 600 feet even in very clear water, and few find enough sunlight for their food-manufacturing activities below 200 feet. Since no animal can make its own food, the creatures of the deeper waters live a strange, almost parasitic existence of utter dependence on the upper layers. These hungry carnivores prey fiercely and relentlessly upon each other, yet the whole community is ultimately dependent upon the slow rain of descending food particles from above. The components of this never-ending rain are the dead and dying plants and animals from the surface, or from one of the intermediate layers. For each of the horizontal zones or communities of the sea that lie, in tier after tier, between the surface and the sea bottom, the food supply is different and in general poorer than for the layer above. There is a hint of the fierce and uncompromising competition for food in the saber-toothed jaws of some of the small, dragonlike fishes of the deeper waters, in the immense mouths and in the elastic and distensible bodies that make it possible for a fish to swallow another several times its size, enjoying swift repletion after a long fast.

Pressure, darkness, and—we should have added only a few years ago—silence, are the conditions of life in the deep sea. But we know now that the conception of the sea as a silent place is wholly false. Wide experience with hydrophones and other listening devices for the detection of submarines has proved that, around the shore lines of much of the world, there is an extraordinary uproar produced by fishes, shrimps, porpoises, and probably other forms not yet identified. There has been little investigation as yet of sound in the deep, offshore areas, but when the crew of the *Atlantis* lowered a hydrophone into deep water off Bermuda, they recorded strange mewing sounds, shrieks, and ghostly moans, the sources of which have not been traced. But fish of shallower zones have been captured and confined in aquaria, where their voices have been recorded for comparison with sounds heard at sea, and in many cases satisfactory identification can be made.

During the Second World War the hydrophone network set up by the United States Navy to protect the entrance to Chesapeake Bay was temporarily made useless when, in the spring of 1942, the speakers at the surface began to give forth, every evening, a sound described as being like "a pneumatic drill tearing up pavement." The extraneous noises that came over the hydrophones completely masked the sounds of the passage of ships. Eventually it was discovered that the sounds were the voices of fish known as croakers, which in the spring move into Chesapeake Bay from their offshore wintering grounds. As soon as the noise had been identified and analyzed, it was possible to screen it out with an electric filter, so that once more only the sounds of ships came through the speakers.

Later in the same year, a chorus of croakers was discovered off the pier of the Scripps Institution at La Jolla. Every year from May until late September the evening chorus begins about sunset, and "increases gradually to a steady uproar of harsh froggy croaks, with a background of soft drumming. This continues unabated for two to three hours and finally tapers off to individual outbursts at rare intervals." Several species of croakers isolated in aquaria gave sounds similar to the "froggy croaks," but the authors of the soft background drumming—presumably another species of croaker—have not yet been discovered.

One of the most extraordinarily widespread sounds of the undersea is the crackling, sizzling sound, like dry twigs burning or fat frying, heard near beds of the snapping shrimp. This is a small, round shrimp, about half an inch in diameter, with one very large claw which it uses to stun its prey. The shrimp are forever clicking the two joints of this claw together, and it is the thousands of clicks that collectively produce the noise known as shrimp crackle. No one had any idea the little snapping shrimps were so abundant or so widely distributed until their signals began to be picked up on hydrophones. They have been heard all over a broad band that extends around the world, between latitudes 35° N and 35° S (for example, from Cape Hatteras to Buenos Aires), in ocean waters less than 30 fathoms deep.

Mammals as well as fishes and crustaceans contribute to the undersea chorus. Biologists listening through a hydrophone in an estuary of the St. Lawrence River heard "high-pitched resonant whistles and squeals, varied with the ticking and clucking sounds slightly reminiscent of a string orchestra tuning up, as well as mewing and occasional chirps." This remarkable medley of sounds was heard only while schools of the white porpoise were seen passing up or down the river, and so was assumed to be produced by them.[5]

The mysteriousness, the eerieness, the ancient unchangingness of the great depths have led many people to suppose that some very old forms of life—some "living fossils"—may be lurking undiscovered in the deep ocean. Some such hope may have been in the minds of the *Challenger* scientists. The forms they brought up in their nets were weird enough, and most of them had never before been seen by man. But basically they were modern types. There was nothing like the trilobites of Cambrian time or the sea scorpions of the Silurian, nothing reminiscent of the great marine reptiles that invaded the sea in the Mesozoic. Instead, there were modern fishes, squids, and shrimps, strangely and grotesquely modified, to be sure, for life in the difficult deep-sea world, but clearly types that have developed in rather recent geologic time.

Far from being the original home of life, the deep sea has probably been inhabited for a relatively short time. While life was developing and flourishing in the surface waters, along the shores, and perhaps in the rivers and swamps, two immense regions of the earth still forbade invasion by living things. These were the continents and the abyss. As we have seen, the immense difficulties of surviving on land were first overcome by colonists from the sea about 300 million years ago. The abyss, with its unending darkness, its crushing pressures, its glacial cold, presented even more formidable difficulties. Probably the successful invasion of this region—at least by higher forms of life—occurred somewhat later.

Yet in recent years there have been one or two significant happenings that have kept alive the hope that the deep sea may, after all, conceal strange links with the past. In December 1938, off the southeast tip of Africa, an amazing fish was caught alive in a trawl—a fish that was supposed to have been dead for at least 60 million years! This is to say, the last known fossil remains of its kind date from the Cretaceous, and no living example had been recognized in historic time until this lucky net-haul.

The fishermen who brought it up in their trawl from a depth of only 40 fathoms realized that this five-foot, bright blue fish, with its large head and strangely shaped scales, fins, and tail, was different from anything they had ever caught before, and on their return to port they took it to the nearest museum. This single specimen of Latimeria, as the fish was christened, is so far the only one that has been captured, and it seems a reasonable guess that it may inhabit depths below those ordinarily fished, and that the South African specimen was a stray from its usual habitat.[6]

Occasionally a very primitive type of shark, known from its puckered gills as a "frillshark," is taken in waters between a quarter of a mile and half a mile down. Most of these have been caught in Norwegian and Japanese waters—there are only about 50 preserved in the museums of Europe and America—but recently one was captured off Santa Barbara, California. The frillshark has many anatomical features similar to those of the ancient sharks that lived 25 to 30 million years ago. It has too many gills and too few dorsal fins for a modern shark, and its teeth, like those of fossil sharks, are three-pronged and briarlike. Some ichthyologists regard it as a relic derived from very ancient shark ancestors that have died out in the upper waters but, through this single species, are still carrying on their struggle for earthly survival, in the quiet of the deep sea.

Possibly there are other such anachronisms lurking down in these regions of which we know so little, but they are likely to be few and scattered. The terms of existence in these deep waters are far too uncompromising to support life unless that life is plastic, molding itself constantly to the harsh conditions, seizing every advantage that makes possible the survival of living protoplasm in a world only a little less hostile than the black reaches of interplanetary space.

Hidden Lands

Sand-strewn caverns, cool and deep, where the winds are all asleep.

—MATTHEW ARNOLD

THE FIRST EUROPEAN ever to sail across the wide Pacific was curious about the hidden worlds beneath his ship. Between the two coral islands of St. Paul and Los Tiburones in the Tuamotu Archipelago, Magellan ordered his sounding line to be lowered. It was the conventional line used by explorers of the day, no more than 200 fathoms long. It did not touch bottom, and Magellan declared that he was over the deepest part of the ocean. Of course he was completely mistaken, but the occasion was none the less historic. It was the first time in the history of the world that a navigator had attempted to sound the depths of the open ocean.

Three centuries later, in the year 1839, Sir James Clark Ross set out from England in command of two ships with names of dark foreboding, the *Erebus* and the *Terror*, bound for the "utmost navigable limits of the Antarctic Ocean." As he proceeded on his course he tried repeatedly to obtain soundings, but failed for lack of a proper line. Finally he had one constructed on board, of "three thousand six hundred fathoms, or rather more than four miles in length. . . . On the 3rd of January, in latitude 27° 26′ S., longitude 17° 29′ W., the weather and all other circumstances being propitious, we succeeded in obtaining soundings with two thousand four hundred and twenty-five fathoms of line, a depression of the bed of the ocean beneath its surface very little short of the elevation of Mount Blanc above it." This was the first successful abyssal sounding.

But taking soundings in the deep ocean was, and long remained, a laborious and time-consuming task, and knowledge of the undersea topography lagged considerably behind our acquaintance with the landscape of the near side of the moon. Over the years, methods were improved. For the heavy hemp line used by Ross, Maury of the United States Navy substituted a strong twine, and in 1870 Lord Kelvin used piano wire.

Even with improved gear a deep-water sounding required several hours or sometimes an entire day. By 1854, when Maury collected all available records, only 180 deep soundings were available from the Atlantic, and by the time that modern echo sounding was developed, the total that had been taken from all the ocean basins of the world was only about 15,000. This is roughly one sounding for an area of 6000 square miles.

Now hundreds of vessels are equipped with sonic sounding instruments that trace a continuous profile of the bottom beneath the moving ship (although only a few can obtain profiles at depths greater than 2000 fathoms[7]). Soundings are accumulating much faster than they can be plotted on the charts. Little by little, like the details of a huge map being filled in by an artist, the hidden contours of the ocean are emerging. But, even with this recent progress, it will be years before an accurate and detailed relief map of the ocean basins can be constructed.

The general bottom topography is, however, well established. Once we have passed the tide lines, the three great geographic provinces of ocean are the continental shelves, the continental slopes, and the floor of the deep sea. Each of these regions is as different from the others as an arctic tundra from a range of the Rocky Mountains.

The continental shelf is of the sea, yet of all regions of the ocean it is most like the land. Sunlight penetrates to all but its deepest parts. Plants drift in the waters above it; seaweeds cling to its rocks and sway to the passage of the waves. Familiar fishes—unlike the weird monsters of the abyss—move over its plains like herds of cattle. Much of its substance is derived from the land—the sand and the rock fragments and the rich topsoil carried by running water to the sea and gently deposited on the shelf. Its submerged valleys and hills, in appropriate parts of the world, have been carved by glaciers into a topography much like the northern landscapes we know and the terrain is strewn with rocks and gravel deposited by the moving ice sheets. Indeed many parts (or perhaps all) of the shelf have been dry land in the geologic past, for a comparatively slight fall of sea level has sufficed, time and again, to expose it to wind and sun and rain. The Grand Banks of Newfoundland rose above the ancient seas and were submerged again. The Dogger Bank of the North Sea shelf was once a forested land inhabited by prehistoric beasts; now its "forests" are seaweeds and its "beasts" are fishes.

Of all parts of the sea, the continental shelves are perhaps most directly important to man as a source of material things. The great fisheries of the world, with only a few exceptions, are confined to the relatively shallow waters over the continental shelves. Seaweeds are gathered from their submerged plains to make scores of substances used in foods, drugs, and articles of commerce. As the petroleum reserves left on continental areas by ancient seas become depleted, petroleum geologists look more and more to the oil that may lie, as yet unmapped and unexploited, under these bordering lands of the sea.

The shelves begin at the tidelines and extend seaward as gently sloping plains. The 100-fathom contour used to be taken as the boundary between the continental shelf and the slope; now it is customary to place the division wherever the gentle declivity of the shelf changes abruptly to a steeper descent toward abyssal depths. The world over, the average depth at which this change occurs is about 72 fathoms; the greatest depth of any shelf is probably 200 to 300 fathoms.

Nowhere off the Pacific coast of the United States is the continental shelf much more than 20 miles wide—a narrowness characteristic of coasts bordered by young mountains perhaps still in the process of formation. On the American east coast, however, north of Cape Hatteras the shelf is as much as 150 miles wide. But at Hatteras and off southern Florida it is merely the narrowest of thresholds to the sea. Here its scant development seems to be related to the press of that great and rapidly flowing river-in-the-sea, the Gulf Stream, which at these places swings close inshore.

The widest shelves in all the world are those bordering the Arctic. The Barents Sea shelf is 750 miles across. It is also relatively deep, lying for the most part 100 to 200 fathoms below the surface, as though its floor had sagged and been down-warped under the load of glacial ice. It is scored by deep troughs between which banks and islands rise—further evidence of the work of the ice. The deepest shelves surround the Antarctic continent, where soundings in many areas show depths of several hundred fathoms near the coast and continuing out across the shelf.

Once beyond the edge of the shelf, as we visualize the steeper declivities of the continental slope, we begin to feel the mystery and the alien quality of the deep sea—the gathering darkness, the growing pressure, the starkness of a seascape in which all plant life has been left behind and there are only the unrelieved contours of rock and clay, of mud and sand.

Biologically the world of the continental slope, like that of the abyss, is a world of animals—a world of carnivores where each creature preys upon another. For no plants live here, and the only ones that drift down from above are the dead husks of the flora of the sunlit waters. Most of the slopes are below the zone of surface wave action, yet the moving water masses of the ocean currents press against them in their coastwise passage; the pulse of the tide beats against them; they feel the surge of the deep, internal waves.

Geographically, the slopes are the most imposing features of all the surface of the earth. They are the walls of the deep-sea basins. They are the farthermost bounds of the continents, the true place of beginning of the sea. The slopes are the longest and highest escarpments found anywhere on the earth; their average height is 12,000 feet, but in some places they reach the immense height of 30,000 feet. No continental mountain range has so great a difference of elevation between its foothills and its peaks.

Nor is the grandeur of slope topography confined to steepness and height. The slopes are the site of one of the most mysterious features of the sea. These are the submarine canyons with their steep cliffs and winding valleys cutting back into the walls of the continents. The canyons have now been found in so many parts of the world that when soundings have been taken in presently unexplored areas we shall probably find that they are of worldwide occurrence. Geologists say that some of the canyons were formed well within the most recent division of geologic time, the Cenozoic, most of them probably within the Pleistocene, a million years ago, or less. But how and by what they were carved, no one can say. Their origin is one of the most hotly disputed problems of the ocean.

Only the fact that the canyons are deeply hidden in the darkness of the sea (many extending a mile or more below present sea level) prevents them from being classed with the world's most spectacular scenery. The comparison with the Grand Canyon of the Colorado is irresistible. Like river-cut land canyons, sea canyons are deep and winding valleys, V-shaped in cross section, their walls sloping down at a steep angle to a narrow floor. The location of many of the largest ones suggests a past connection with some of the great rivers of the earth of our time. Hudson Canyon, one of the largest on the Atlantic coast, is separated by only a shallow sill from a long valley that wanders for more than a hundred miles across the continental shelf, originating at the entrance of New York Harbor and the estuary of the Hudson River. There are large canyons off the Congo, the Indus, the Ganges, the Columbia, the São Francisco, and the Mississippi, according to Francis Shepard, one of the principal students of the canyon problem. Monterey Canyon in California, Professor Shepard points out, is located off an old mouth of the Salinas River; the Cap Breton Canyon in France appears to have no relation to an existing river but actually lies off an old fifteenth-century mouth of the Adour River.

Their shape and apparent relation to existing rivers have led Shepard to suggest that the submarine canyons were cut by rivers at some time when their gorges were above sea level. The relative youth of the canyons seems to relate them to some happenings in the world of the Ice Age. It is generally agreed that sea level was lowered during the existence of the great glaciers, for water was withdrawn from the sea and frozen in the ice sheet. But most geologists say that the sea was lowered only a few hundred feet—not the mile that would be necessary to account for the canyons. According to one theory, there were heavy submarine mud flows during the times when the glaciers were advancing and sea level fell the lowest; mud stirred up by waves poured down the continental slopes and scoured out the canyons. Since none of the present evidence is conclusive, however, we simply do not know how the canyons came into being, and their mystery remains.[8]

The floor of the deep ocean basins is probably as old as the sea itself. In all the hundreds of millions of years that have intervened since the formation of the abyss, these deeper depressions have never, as far as we can learn, been drained of their covering waters. While the bordering shelves of the continents have known, in alternating geologic ages, now the surge of waves and again the eroding tools of rain and wind and frost, always the abyss has lain under the all-enveloping cover of miles-deep water.

But this does not mean that the contours of the abyss have remained unchanged since the day of its creation. The floor of the sea, like the stuff of the continents, is a thin crust over the plastic mantle of the earth. It is here thrust up into folds and wrinkles as the interior cools by imperceptible degrees and shrinks away from its covering layer; there it falls away into deep trenches in answer to the stresses and strains of crustal adjustment; and again it pushes up into the conelike shapes of undersea mountains as volcanoes boil upward from fissures in the crust.

Until very recent years, it has been the fashion of geographers and oceanographers to speak of the floor of the deep sea as a vast and comparatively level plain. The existence of certain topographic features was recognized, as, for example, the Atlantic Ridge and a number of very deep depressions like the Mindanao Trench off the Philippines. But these were considered to be rather exceptional interruptions of a flat floor that otherwise showed little relief.

This legend of the flatness of the ocean floor was thoroughly destroyed by the Swedish Deep-Sea Expedition, which sailed from Göteborg in the summer of 1947 and spent the following 15 months exploring the bed of the ocean. While the Swedish *Albatross* was crossing the Atlantic in the direction of the Panama Canal, the scientists aboard were astonished by the extreme ruggedness of the ocean floor. Rarely did their fathometers reveal more than a few consecutive miles of level plain. Instead the bottom profile rose and fell in curious steps constructed on a Gargantuan scale, half a mile to several miles wide. In the Pacific, the uneven bottom contours made it difficult to use many of the oceanographic instruments. More than one coring tube was left behind, probably lodged in some undersea crevasse.

One of the exceptions to a hilly or mountainous floor was in the Indian Ocean, where, southeast of Ceylon, the *Albatross* ran for several hundred miles across a level plain. Attempts to take bottom samples from this plain had little success, for the corers were broken repeatedly, suggesting that the bottom was hardened lava and that the whole vast plateau might have been formed by the outpourings of submarine volcanoes on a stupendous scale. Perhaps this lava plain under the Indian Ocean is an undersea counterpart of the great basaltic plateau in the eastern part of the State of Washington, or of the Deccan plateau of India, built of basaltic rock 10,000 feet thick.

In parts of the Atlantic basin the Woods Hole Oceanographic Institution's vessel *Atlantis* has found a flat plain occupying much of the ocean basin from Bermuda to the Atlantic Ridge and also to the east of the Ridge. Only a series of knolls, probably of volcanic origin, interrupts the even contours of the plains. These particular regions are so flat that it seems they must have remained largely undisturbed, receiving deposits of sediments over an immense period of time.

The deepest depressions on the floor of the sea occur not in the centers of the oceanic basins as might be expected, but near the continents. One of the deepest trenches of all, the Mindanao, lies east of the Philippines and is an awesome pit in the sea, six and a half miles deep.[9] The Tuscarora Trench east of Japan, nearly as deep, is one of a series of long, narrow trenches that border the convex outer rim of a chain of islands including the Bonins, the Marianas, and the Palaus. On the seaward side of the Aleutian Islands is another group of trenches. The greatest deeps of the Atlantic lie adjacent to the islands of the West Indies, and also below Cape Horn, where other curving chains of islands go out like stepping stones into the Southern Ocean. And again in the Indian Ocean the curving island arcs of the East Indies have their accompanying deeps.

Always there is this association of island arcs and deep trenches, and always the two occur only in areas of volcanic unrest. The pattern, it is now agreed, is associated with mountain making and the sharp adjustments of the sea floor that accompany it. On the concave side of the island arcs are rows of volcanoes. On the convex side there is a sharp down-bending of the ocean floor, which results in the deep trenches with their broad V-shape. The two forces seem to be in a kind of uneasy balance: the upward folding of the earth's crust to form mountains, and the thrusting down of the crust of the sea floor into the basaltic substance of the underlying layer. Sometimes, it seems, the down-thrust mass of granite has shattered and risen again to form islands. Such is the supposed origin of Barbados in the West Indies and of Timor in the East Indies. Both have deep-sea deposits, as though they had once been part of the sea floor. Yet this must be exceptional. In the words of the great geologist Daly,

> Another property of the earth is its ability . . . to resist shearing pressures indefinitely . . . The continents, overlooking the sea bottom, stubbornly refuse to creep thither. The rock under the Pacific is strong enough to bear, with no known time limit, the huge stresses involved by the down-thrust of the crust at the Tonga Deep, and by the erection of the 10,000-meter dome of lavas and other volcanic products represented in the island of Hawaii.*

The least-known region of the ocean floor lies under the Arctic Sea. The physical difficulties of sounding here are enormous. A permanent sheet of ice, as much as fifteen feet thick, covers the whole central basin and is impenetrable to ships. Peary took several soundings in the course of his dash to the Pole by dog team in 1909. On one attempt a few miles from the Pole the wire broke with 1500 fathoms out. In 1927 Sir Hubert Wilkins landed his plane on the ice 550 miles north of Point Barrow and obtained a single echo sounding of 2975 fathoms, the deepest ever recorded from the Arctic Sea. Vessels deliberately frozen into the ice (such as the Norwegian *Fram* and the Russian *Sedov* and *Sadko*) in order to drift with it across the basin have obtained most of the depth records available for the central parts. In 1937 and 1938 Russian scientists were landed near the Pole and supplied by plane while they lived on the ice, drifting with it. These men took nearly a score of deep soundings.

The most daring plan for sounding the Arctic Sea was conceived by Wilkins, who actually set out in the submarine *Nautilus* in 1931 with the intention of traveling beneath the ice

---

*From *The Changing World of the Ice Age*, 1934 edition, Yale University Press, p. 116.

across the entire basin from Spitsbergen to Bering Strait. Mechanical failure of the diving equipment a few days after the *Nautilus* left Spitsbergen prevented the execution of the plan. By the middle 1940's, the total of soundings for deep arctic areas by all methods was only about 150, leaving most of the top of the world an unsounded sea whose contours can only be guessed. Soon after the close of the Second World War, the United States Navy began tests of a new method of obtaining soundings through the ice, which may provide the key to the arctic riddle. One interesting speculation to be tested by future soundings is that the mountain chain that bisects the Atlantic, and has been supposed to reach its northern terminus at Iceland, may actually continue across the arctic basin to the coast of Russia. The belt of earthquake epicenters that follows the Atlantic Ridge seems to extend across the Arctic Sea, and where there are submarine earthquakes it is at least reasonable to guess that there may be mountainous topography.[10]

A new feature on recent maps of undersea relief—something never included before the 1940's—is a group of about 160 curious, flat-topped sea mounts between Hawaii and the Marianas. It happened that a Princeton University geologist, H. H. Hess, was in command of the U.S.S. *Cape Johnson* during two years of the wartime cruising of this vessel in the Pacific. Hess was immediately struck by the number of these undersea mountains that appeared on the fathograms of the vessel. Time after time, as the moving pen of the fathometer traced the depth contours it would abruptly begin to rise in an outline of a steep-sided sea mount, standing solitarily on the bed of the sea. Unlike a typical volcanic cone, all of the mounts have broad, flat tops, as though the peaks had been cut off and planed down by waves. But the summits of the sea mounts are anywhere from half a mile to a mile or more below the surface of the sea. How they acquired their flat-topped contours is a mystery perhaps as great as that of the submarine canyons.

Unlike the scattered sea mounts, the long ranges of undersea mountains have been marked on the charts for a good many years. The Atlantic Ridge was discovered about a century ago. The early surveys for the route of the trans-Atlantic cable gave the first hint of its existence. The German oceanographic vessel *Meteor*, which crossed and recrossed the Atlantic during the

1920's, established the contours of much of the Ridge. The *Atlantis* of the Woods Hole Oceanographic Institution has spent several summers in an exhaustive study of the Ridge in the general vicinity of the Azores.

Now we can trace the outlines of this great mountain range, and dimly we begin to see the details of its hidden peaks and valleys. The Ridge rises in mid-Atlantic near Iceland. From this far-northern latitude it runs south midway between the continents, crosses the equator into the South Atlantic, and continues to about 50° south latitude, where it turns sharply eastward under the tip of Africa and runs toward the Indian Ocean. Its general course closely parallels the coastlines of the bordering continents, even to the definite flexure at the equator between the hump of Brazil and the eastward-curving coast of Africa. To some people this curvature has suggested that the Ridge was once part of a great continental mass, left behind in mid-ocean when, according to one theory, the continents of North and South America drifted away from Europe and Africa. However, recent work shows that on the floor of the Atlantic there are thick masses of sediments which must have required hundreds of millions of years for their accumulation.

Throughout much of its 10,000-mile length, the Atlantic Ridge is a place of disturbed and uneasy movements of the ocean floor, and the whole Ridge gives the impression of something formed by the interplay of great, opposing forces. From its western foothills across to where its slopes roll down into the eastern Atlantic basin, the range is about twice as wide as the Andes and several times the width of the Appalachians. Near the equator a deep gash cuts across it from east to west —the Romanche Trench. This is the only point of communication between the deep basins of the eastern and western Atlantic, although among its higher peaks there are other, lesser mountain passes.

The greater part of the Ridge is, of course, submerged. Its central backbone rises some 5000 to 10,000 feet above the sea floor, but another mile of water lies above most of its summits. Yet here and there a peak thrusts itself up out of the darkness of deep water and pushes above the surface of the ocean. These are the islands of the mid-Atlantic. The highest peak of the Ridge is Pico Island of the Azores. It rises 27,000 feet above the ocean floor, with only its upper 7000 to 8000 feet emergent. The sharpest peaks of the Ridge are the cluster of islets known as the Rocks of St. Paul, near the equator. The entire cluster of half a dozen islets is not more than a quarter of a mile across, and their rocky slopes drop off at so sheer an angle that water more than half a mile deep lies only a few feet off shore. The sultry volcanic bulk of Ascension is another peak of the Atlantic Ridge; so are Tristan da Cunha, Gough, and Bouvet.

But most of the Ridge lies forever hidden from human eyes. Its contours have been made out only indirectly by the marvelous probings of sound waves; bits of its substance have been brought up to us by corers and dredges; and some details of its landscape have been photographed with deep-sea cameras. With these aids our imaginations can picture the grandeur of the undersea mountains, with their sheer cliffs and rocky terraces, their deep valleys and towering peaks. If we are to compare the ocean's mountains with anything on the continents, we must think of terrestrial mountains far above the timber line, with their silent snow-filled valleys and their naked rocks swept by the winds. For the sea has an inverted "timber line" or plant line, below which no vegetation can grow. The slopes of the undersea mountains are far beyond the reach of the sun's rays, and there are only the bare rocks, and, in the valleys, the deep drifts of sediments that have been silently piling up through the millions upon millions of years.

Neither the Pacific Ocean nor the Indian Ocean has any submerged mountains that compare in length with the Atlantic Ridge, but they have their smaller ranges. The Hawaiian Islands are the peaks of a mountain range that runs across the central Pacific basin for a distance of nearly 2000 miles. The Gilbert and Marshall islands stand on the shoulders of another mid-Pacific mountain chain. In the eastern Pacific, a broad plateau connects the coast of South America and the Tuamotu Islands in the mid-Pacific, and in the Indian Ocean a long ridge runs from India to Antarctica, for most of its length broader and deeper than the Atlantic Ridge.

One of the most fascinating fields for speculation is the age of the submarine mountains compared with that of past and present mountains of the continents. Looking back over the past ages of geologic time (page 208), we realize that mountains have been thrust up on the continents, to the accompaniment of volcanic outpourings and violent tremblings of the earth, only to crumble and wear away under the attacks of rain and frost and flood. What of the sea's mountains? Were they formed in the same way and do they, too, begin to die as soon as they are born?

There are indications that the earth's crust is no more stable under sea than on land. Quite a fair proportion of the world's earthquakes are traced through seismographs to sources under the oceans, and, as we shall see later, there are probably as many active volcanoes under water as on land. Apparently the Atlantic Ridge arose along a line of crustal shifting and rearrangement; although its volcanic fires seem to be largely quiescent, it is at present the site of most of the earthquakes in the Atlantic area. Almost the whole continental rim of the Pacific basin is aquiver with earthquakes and fiery with volcanoes, some frequently active, some extinct, some merely sleeping a centuries-long sleep between periods of explosive violence. From the high mountains that form an almost continuous border around the shores of the Pacific, the contours of the land slope abruptly down to very deep water. The deep trenches that lie off the coast of South America, from Alaska along the Aleutian Islands and across to Japan, and southward off Japan and the Philippines give the impression of a landscape in process of formation, of a zone of earth subject to great strains.

Yet the submarine mountains are earth's nearest approach to the "eternal hills" of the poets. No sooner is a continental mountain thrust up than all the forces of nature conspire to level it. A mountain of the deep sea, in the years of its maturity, is beyond the reach of the ordinary erosive forces. It grows up on the ocean floor and may thrust volcanic peaks above the surface of the sea. These islands are attacked by the rains, and in time the young mountain is brought down within reach of the waves; in the tumult of the sea's attack it sinks again beneath the surface. Eventually the peak is worn down below the push and pull and drag of even the heaviest of storm waves. Here, in the twilight of the sea, in the calm of deep water, the mountain is secure from further attack. Here it is likely to remain almost unchanged, perhaps throughout the life of the earth.

Because of this virtual immortality, the oldest oceanic mountains must be infinitely older than any of the ranges left on land. Professor Hess, who discovered the sea mounts of the central Pacific, suggested that these "drowned ancient islands" may have been formed before the Cambrian period, or somewhere between 500 million and 1 billion years ago. This would make them perhaps of an age with the continental mountains of the Laurentian upheaval. But the sea mounts have changed little if at all, comparing in elevation with modern terrestrial peaks like the Jungfrau, Mt. Etna, or Mt. Hood; while of the mountains of the Laurentian period scarcely a trace remains. The Pacific sea mounts, according to this theory, must have been of substantial age when the Appalachians were thrust up, 200 million years ago; they stood almost unchanged while the Appalachians wore down to mere wrinkles on the earth's face. The sea mounts were old, 60 million years ago, when the Alps and the Himalayas, the Rockies and the Andes, rose to their majestic heights. Yet it is probable that they will be standing unchanged in the deep sea when these, too, shall have crumbled away to dust.

As the hidden lands beneath the sea become better known, there recurs again and again the query: can the submerged masses of the undersea mountains be linked with the famed "lost continents"? Shadowy and insubstantial as are the accounts of all such legendary lands—the fabled Lemuria of the Indian Ocean, St. Brendan's Island, the lost Atlantis they persistently recur like some deeply rooted racial memory in the folklore of many parts of the world.

Best known is Atlantis, which according to Plato's account was a large island or continent beyond the Pillars of Hercules. Atlantis was the home of a warlike people ruled by powerful kings who made frequent attacks upon the mainlands of Africa and Europe, brought much of Libya under their power, roamed the Mediterranean coast of Europe, and finally attacked Athens. However, "with great earthquakes and inundations, in a single day and one fatal night, all who had been warriors [against Greece] were swallowed up. The Island of Atlantis disappeared beneath the sea. Since that time the sea in these quarters has become unnavigable; vessels cannot pass there because of the sands which extend over the site of the buried isle."

The Atlantis legend has lived on through the centuries. As men became bold enough to sail out on the Atlantic, to cross it, and later to investigate its depths, they speculated about the location of the lost land. Various Atlantic islands have been said to be the remains of a land mass once more extensive. The lonely wave-washed Rocks of St. Paul, perhaps more often than any other, have been identified as the remains of Atlantis. During the past century, as the extent of the Atlantic Ridge became better known, speculations were often centered upon this great mass, far below the surface of the ocean.

Unfortunately for these picturesque imaginings, if the Ridge was ever exposed, it must have been at a time long before there were men to populate such an Atlantis. Some of the cores taken from the Ridge show a continuous series of sediments typical of open oceans, far from land, running back to a period some 60 million years ago. And man, even the most primitive type, has appeared only within the past million years or so.

Like other legends deeply rooted in folklore, the Atlantis story may have in it an element of truth. In the shadowy beginnings of human life on earth, primitive men here and there must have had knowledge of the sinking of an island or a peninsula, perhaps not with the dramatic suddenness attributed to Atlantis, but well within the time one man could observe. The witnesses of such a happening would have described it to their neighbors and children, and so the legend of a sinking continent might have been born.

Such a lost land lies today beneath the waters of the North Sea. Only a few scores of thousands of years ago, the Dogger Bank was dry land, but now the fishermen drag their nets over this famed fishing ground, catching cod and hake and flounders among its drowned tree trunks.

During the Pleistocene, when immense quantities of water were withdrawn from the ocean and locked up in the glaciers, the floor of the North Sea emerged and for a time became land. It was a low, wet land, covered with peat bogs; then little by little the forests from the neighboring high lands must have moved in, for there were willows and birches growing among the mosses and ferns. Animals moved down from the mainland

and became established on this land recently won from the sea. There were bears and wolves and hyenas, the wild ox, the bison, the woolly rhinoceros, and the mammoth. Primitive men moved through the forests, carrying crude stone instruments; they stalked deer and other game and with their flints grubbed up the roots of the damp forest.

Then as the glaciers began to retreat and floods from the melting ice poured into the sea and raised its level, this land became an island. Probably the men escaped to the mainland before the intervening channel had become too wide, leaving their stone implements behind. But most of the animals remained, perforce, and little by little their island shrank, and food became more and more scarce, but there was no escape. Finally the sea covered the island, claiming the land and all its life.

As for the men who escaped, perhaps in their primitive way they communicated this story to other men, who passed it down to others through the ages, until it became fixed in the memory of the race.

None of these facts were part of recorded history until, a generation ago, European fishermen moved out into the middle of the North Sea and began to trawl on the Dogger. They soon made out the contours of an irregular plateau nearly as large as Denmark, lying about 60 feet under water, but sloping off abruptly at its edges into much deeper water. Their trawls immediately began to bring up a great many things not found on any ordinary fishing bank. There were loose masses of peat, which the fishermen christened "moorlog." There were many bones, and, although the fishermen could not identify them, they seemed to belong to large land mammals. All of these objects damaged the nets and hindered fishing, so whenever possible the fishermen dragged them off the bank and sent them tumbling into deep water. But they brought back some of the bones, some of the moorlog and fragments of trees, and the crude stone implements; these specimens were turned over to scientists to identify. In this strange debris of the fishing nets the scientists recognized a whole Pleistocene fauna and flora, and the artifacts of Stone Age man. And remembering how once the North Sea had been dry land, they reconstructed the story of Dogger Bank, the lost island.

The Long Snowfall

A deep and tremulous earth-poetry.

—LLEWELYN POWYS

EVERY PART OF earth or air or sea has an atmosphere peculiarly its own, a quality or characteristic that sets it apart from all others. When I think of the floor of the deep sea, the single, overwhelming fact that possesses my imagination is the accumulation of sediments. I see always the steady, unremitting, downward drift of materials from above, flake upon flake, layer upon layer—a drift that has continued for hundreds of millions of years, that will go on as long as there are seas and continents.

For the sediments are the materials of the most stupendous "snowfall" the earth has ever seen. It began when the first rains fell on the barren rocks and set in motion the forces of erosion. It was accelerated when living creatures developed in the surface waters and the discarded little shells of lime or silica that had encased them in life began to drift downward to the bottom. Silently, endlessly, with the deliberation of earth processes that can afford to be slow because they have so much time for completion, the accumulation of the sediments has proceeded. So little in a year, or in a human lifetime, but so enormous an amount in the life of earth and sea.

The rains, the eroding away of the earth, the rush of sediment-laden waters have continued, with varying pulse and tempo, throughout all of geologic time. In addition to the silt load of every river that finds its way to the sea, there are other materials that compose the sediments. Volcanic dust, blown perhaps half way around the earth in the upper atmosphere, comes eventually to rest on the ocean, drifts in the currents, becomes waterlogged, and sinks. Sands from coastal deserts are carried seaward on offshore winds, fall to the sea, and sink. Gravel, pebbles, small boulders, and shells are carried by icebergs and drift ice, to be released to the water when the ice melts. Fragments of iron, nickel, and other meteoric debris that enter the earth's atmosphere over the sea—these, too, become flakes of the great snowfall. But most widely distributed of all are the billions upon billions of tiny shells and skeletons, the limy or silicious remains of all the minute creatures that once lived in the upper waters.

The sediments are a sort of epic poem of the earth. When we are wise enough, perhaps we can read in them all of past history. For all is written here. In the nature of the materials that compose them and in the arrangement of their successive layers the sediments reflect all that has happened in the waters above them and on the surrounding lands. The dramatic and the catastrophic in earth history have left their trace in the sediments—the outpourings of volcanoes, the advance and retreat of the ice, the searing aridity of desert lands, the sweeping destruction of floods.

The book of the sediments has been opened only within the lifetime of the present generation of scientists, with the most exciting progress in collecting and deciphering samples made since 1945. Early oceanographers could scrape up surface layers of sediment from the sea bottom with dredges. But what was needed was an instrument, operated on the principle of an apple corer, that could be driven vertically into the bottom to remove a long sample or "core" in which the order of the different layers was undisturbed. Such an instrument was invented by Dr. C. S. Piggot in 1935, and with the aid of this "gun" he obtained a series of cores across the deep Atlantic from Newfoundland to Ireland. These cores averaged about 10 feet long. A piston core sampler, developed by the Swedish oceanographer Kullenberg about 10 years later, now takes undisturbed cores 70 feet long. The rate of sedimentation in the different parts of the ocean is not definitely known, but it is very slow; certainly such a sample represents millions of years of geologic history.

Another ingenious method for studying the sediments has been used by Professor W. Maurice Ewing of Columbia University and the Woods Hole Oceanographic Institution. Professor Ewing found that he could measure the thickness of the carpeting layer of sediments that overlies the rock of the ocean floor by exploding depth charges and recording their echoes; one echo is received from the top of the sediment layer (the apparent bottom of the sea), another from the "bottom below the bottom" or the true rock floor. The carrying and use of explosives at sea is hazardous and cannot be attempted by all vessels, but this method was used by the Swedish *Albatross* as well as by the *Atlantis* in its exploration of the Atlantic Ridge. Ewing on the *Atlantis* also used a seismic refraction technique by which sound waves are made to travel horizontally through the rock layers of the ocean floor, providing information about the nature of the rock.

Before these techniques were developed, we could only guess at the thickness of the sediment blanket over the floor of the sea. We might have expected the amount to be vast, if we thought back through the ages of gentle, unending fall—one sand grain at a time, one fragile shell after another, here a shark's tooth, there a meteorite fragment—but the whole continuing persistently, relentlessly, endlessly. It is, of course, a process similar to that which has built up the layers of rock that help to make our mountains, for they, too, were once soft sediments under the shallow seas that have overflowed the continents from time to time. The sediments eventually became consolidated and cemented and, as the seas retreated again, gave the continents their thick, covering layers of sedimentary rocks—layers which we can see uplifted, tilted, compressed, and broken by the vast earth movements. And we know that in places the sedimentary rocks are many thousands of feet thick. Yet most people felt a shock of surprise and wonder when Hans Pettersson, leader of the Swedish Deep-Sea Expedition, announced that the *Albatross* measurements taken in the open Atlantic basin showed sediment layers as much as 12,000 feet thick.

If more than two miles of sediments have been deposited on the floor of the Atlantic, an interesting question arises: has the rocky floor sagged a corresponding distance under the terrific weight of the sediments? Geologists hold conflicting opinions. The recently discovered Pacific sea mounts may offer one piece of evidence that it has. If they are, as their discoverer called them, "drowned ancient islands," then they may have reached their present stand a mile or so below sea level through the sinking of the ocean floor. Hess believed the islands had been formed so long ago that coral animals had not yet evolved; otherwise the corals would presumably have settled on the flat, planed surfaces of the sea mounts and built them up as fast as their bases sank. In any event, it is hard to see how they could have been worn down so far below "wave base" unless the crust of the earth sagged under its load.

One thing seems probable—the sediments have been unevenly distributed both in place and time. In contrast to the 12,000-foot thickness found in parts of the Atlantic, the Swedish oceanographers never found sediments thicker than 1000 feet in the Pacific or in the Indian Ocean. Perhaps a deep layer of lava, from ancient submarine eruptions on a stupendous scale, underlies the upper layers of the sediments in these places and intercepts the sound waves.

Interesting variations in the thickness of the sediment layer of the Atlantic Ridge and the approaches to the Ridge from the American side were reported by Ewing. As the bottom contours became less even and began to slope up into the foothills of the Ridge, the sediments thickened, as though piling up into mammoth drifts 1000 to 2000 feet deep against the slopes of the hills. Farther up in the mountains of the Ridge, where there are many level terraces from a few to a score of miles wide, the sediments were even deeper, measuring up to 3000 feet. But along the backbone of the Ridge, on the steep slopes and peaks and pinnacles, the bare rock emerged, swept clean of sediments.[11]

Reflecting on these differences in thickness and distribution, our minds return inevitably to the simile of the long snowfall. We may think of the abyssal snowstorm in terms of a bleak and blizzard-ridden arctic tundra. Long days of storm visit this place, when driving snow fills the air; then a lull comes in the blizzard, and the snowfall is light. In the snowfall of the sediments, also, there is an alternation of light and heavy falls. The heavy falls correspond to the periods of mountain building on the continents, when the lands are lifted high and the rain rushes down their slopes, carrying mud and rock fragments to the sea; the light falls mark the lulls between the mountain-building periods, when the continents are flat and erosion is slowed. And again, on our imaginary tundra, the winds blow the snow into deep drifts, filling in all the valleys between the ridges, piling the snow up and up until the contours of the land are obliterated, but scouring the ridges clear. In the drifting sediments on the floor of the ocean we see the work of the "winds," which may be the deep ocean currents, distributing the sediments according to laws of their own, not as yet grasped by human minds.

We have known the general pattern of the sediment carpet, however, for a good many years. Around the foundations of the continents, in the deep waters off the borders of the continental slopes, are the muds of terrestrial origin. There are muds of many colors—blue, green, red, black, and white—apparently varying with climatic changes as well as with the dominant soils and rocks of the lands of their origin. Farther at sea are the oozes of predominantly marine origin—the remains of the trillions of tiny sea creatures. Over great areas of the temperate oceans the sea floor is largely covered with the remains of unicellular creatures known as foraminifera, of which the most abundant genus is Globigerina. The shells of Globigerina may be recognized in very ancient sediments as well as in modern ones, but over the ages the species have varied. Knowing this, we can date approximately the deposits in which they occur. But always they have been simple animals, living in an intricately sculptured shell of carbonate of lime, the whole so small you would need a microscope to see its details. After the fashion of unicellular beings, the individual Globigerina normally did not die, but by the division of its substance became two. At each division, the old shell was abandoned, and two new ones were formed. In warm, lime-rich seas these tiny creatures have always multiplied prodigiously, and so, although each is so minute, their innumerable shells blanket millions of square miles of ocean bottom, and to a depth of thousands of feet.

In the great depths of the ocean, however, the immense pressures and the high carbon-dioxide content of deep water dissolve much of the lime long before it reaches the bottom and return it to the great chemical reservoir of the sea. Silica is more resistant to solution. It is one of the curious paradoxes of the ocean that the bulk of the organic remains that reach the great depths intact belong to unicellular creatures seemingly of the most delicate construction. The radiolarians remind us irresistibly of snow flakes, as infinitely varied in pattern, as lacy, and as intricately made. Yet because their shells are fashioned of silica instead of carbonate of lime, they can descend unchanged into the abyssal depths. So there are broad bands of radiolarian ooze in the deep tropical waters of the North Pacific, underlying the surface zones where the living radiolarians occur most numerously.

Two other kinds of organic sediments are named for the creatures whose remains compose them. Diatoms, the microscopic plant life of the sea, flourish most abundantly in cold waters. There is a broad belt of diatom ooze on the floor of the Antarctic Ocean, outside the zone of glacial debris dropped by the ice pack. There is another across the North Pacific, along the chain of great deeps that run from Alaska to Japan. Both are zones where nutrient-laden water wells up from the depths, sustaining a rich growth of plants. The diatoms, like the radiolarians are encased in silicious coverings—small, boxlike cases of varied shape and meticulously etched design.

Then, in relatively shallow parts of the open Atlantic, there are patches of ooze composed of the remains of delicate swimming snails, called pteropods. These winged mollusks, possessing transparent shells of great beauty, are here and there incredibly abundant. Pteropod ooze is the characteristic bottom deposit in the vicinity of Bermuda, and a large patch occurs in the South Atlantic.

Mysterious and eerie are the immense areas, especially in the North Pacific, carpeted with a soft, red sediment in which there are no organic remains except sharks' teeth and the ear bones of whales. This red clay occurs at great depths. Perhaps all the materials of the other sediments are dissolved before they can reach this zone of immense pressures and glacial cold.

The reading of the story contained in the sediments has only begun. When more cores are collected and examined we shall certainly decipher many exciting chapters. Geologists have pointed out that a series of cores from the Mediterranean might settle several controversial problems concerning the history of the ocean and of the lands around the Mediterranean basin. For example, somewhere in the layers of sediment under this sea there must be evidence, in a sharply defined layer of sand, of the time when the deserts of the Sahara were formed and the hot, dry winds began to skim off the shifting surface layers and carry them seaward. Long cores recently obtained in the western Mediterranean off Algeria have given a record of volcanic activity extending back through thousands of years, and including great prehistoric eruptions of which we know nothing.

The Atlantic cores taken more than a decade ago by Piggot from the cable ship *Lord Kelvin* have been thoroughly studied by geologists. From their analysis it is possible to look back into the past 10,000 years or so and to sense the pulse of the earth's climatic rhythms; for the cores were composed of layers of cold-water Globigerina faunas (and hence glacial stage sediments), alternating with Globigerina ooze characteristic of warmer waters. From the clues furnished by these cores we can visualize interglacial stages when there were periods of mild climates, with warm water overlying the sea bottom and warmth-loving creatures living in the ocean. Between these periods the sea grew chill. Clouds gathered, the snows fell, and on the North American continent the great ice sheets grew and the ice mountains moved out to the coast. The glaciers reached the sea along a wide front; there they produced icebergs by the thousand. The slow-moving, majestic processions of the bergs passed out to sea, and because of the coldness of much of the earth they penetrated farther south than any but stray bergs do today. When finally they melted, they relinquished their loads of silt and sand and gravel and rock fragments that had become frozen into their under surfaces as they made their grinding way over the land. And so a layer of glacial sediment came to overlie the normal Globigerina ooze, and the record of an Ice Age was inscribed.

Then the sea grew warmer again, the glaciers melted and retreated, and once more the warmer-water species of Globigerina lived in the sea—lived and died and drifted down to build another layer of Globigerina ooze, this time over the clays and gravels from the glaciers. And the record of warmth and mildness was again written in the sediments. From the Piggot cores it has been possible to reconstruct four different periods of the advance of the ice, separated by periods of warm climate.

It is interesting to think that even now, in our own lifetime, the flakes of a new snow storm are falling, falling, one by one, out there on the ocean floor. The billions of Globigerina are drifting down, writing their unequivocal record that this, our present world, is on the whole a world of mild and temperate climate. Who will read their record, ten thousand years from now?

The Birth of an Island

Many a green isle needs must be in the deep, wide sea . . .

—SHELLEY

MILLIONS OF YEARS ago, a volcano built a mountain on the floor of the Atlantic. In eruption after eruption, it pushed up a great pile of volcanic rock, until it had accumulated a mass a hundred miles across at its base, reaching upward toward the surface of the sea. Finally its cone emerged as an island with an area of about 200 square miles. Thousands of years passed, and thousands of thousands. Eventually the waves of the Atlantic cut down the cone and reduced it to a shoal—all of it, that is, but a small fragment which remained above water. This fragment we know as Bermuda.

With variations, the life story of Bermuda has been repeated by almost every one of the islands that interrupt the watery expanses of the oceans far from land. For these isolated islands in the sea are fundamentally different from the continents. The major land masses and the ocean basins are today much as they have been throughout the greater part of geologic time. But islands are ephemeral, created today, destroyed tomorrow. With few exceptions, they are the result of the violent, explosive, earth-shaking eruptions of submarine volcanoes, working perhaps for millions of years to achieve their end. It is one of the paradoxes in the ways of earth and sea that a process seemingly so destructive, so catastrophic in nature, can result in an act of creation.

Islands have always fascinated the human mind. Perhaps it is the instinctive response of man, the land animal, welcoming a brief intrusion of earth in the vast, overwhelming expanse of sea. Here in a great ocean basin, a thousand miles from the nearest continent, with miles of water under our vessel, we come upon an island. Our imaginations can follow its slopes down through darkening waters to where it rests on the sea floor. We wonder why and how it arose here in the midst of the ocean.

The birth of a volcanic island is an event marked by prolonged and violent travail: the forces of the earth striving to create, and all the forces of the sea opposing. The sea floor, where an island begins, is probably nowhere more than about fifty miles thick—a thin covering over the vast bulk of the earth. In it are deep cracks and fissures, the results of unequal cooling and shrinkage in past ages. Along such lines of weakness the molten lava from the earth's interior presses up and finally bursts forth into the sea. But a submarine volcano is different from a terrestrial eruption, where the lava, molten rocks, gases, and other ejecta are hurled into the air through an open crater. Here on the bottom of the ocean the volcano has resisting it all the weight of the ocean water above it. Despite the immense pressure of, it may be, two or three miles of sea water, the new volcanic cone builds upward toward the surface, in flow after flow of lava. Once within reach of the waves, its soft ash and tuff are violently attacked, and for a long period the potential island may remain a shoal, unable to emerge. But, eventually, in new eruptions, the cone is pushed up into the air and a rampart against the attacks of the waves is built of hardened lava.

Navigators' charts are marked with numerous, recently discovered submarine mountains. Many of these are the submerged remnants of the islands of a geologic yesterday. The same charts show islands that emerged from the sea at least fifty million years ago, and others that arose within our own memory. Among the undersea mountains marked on the charts may be the islands of tomorrow, which at this moment are forming, unseen, on the floor of the ocean and are growing upward toward its surface.

For the sea is by no means done with submarine eruptions; they occur fairly commonly, sometimes detected only by instruments, sometimes obvious to the most casual observer. Ships in volcanic zones may suddenly find themselves in violently disturbed water. There are heavy discharges of steam. The sea appears to bubble or boil in a furious turbulence. Fountains spring from its surface. Floating up from the deep, hidden places of the actual eruption come the bodies of fishes and other deep-sea creatures, and quantities of volcanic ash and pumice.

One of the youngest of the large volcanic islands of the

world is Ascension in the South Atlantic. During the Second World War the American airmen sang

*If we don't find Ascension
Our wives will get a pension*

this island being the only piece of dry land between the hump of Brazil and the bulge of Africa. It is a forbidding mass of cinders, in which the vents of no less than forty extinct volcanoes can be counted. It has not always been so barren, for its slopes have yielded the fossil remains of trees. What happened to the forests no one knows; the first men to explore the island, about the year 1500, found it treeless, and today it has no natural greenness except on its highest peak, known as Green Mountain.

In modern times we have never seen the birth of an island as large as Ascension. But now and then there is a report of a small island appearing where none was before. Perhaps a month, a year, five years later, the island has disappeared into the sea again. These are the little, stillborn islands, doomed to only a brief emergence above the sea.

About 1830 such an island suddenly appeared in the Mediterranean between Sicily and the coast of Africa, rising from 100-fathom depths after there had been signs of volcanic activity in the area. It was little more than a black cinder pile, perhaps 200 feet high. Waves, wind, and rain attacked it. Its soft and porous materials were easily eroded; its substance was rapidly eaten away and it sank beneath the sea. Now it is a shoal, marked on the charts as Graham's Reef.

Falcon Island, the tip of a volcano projecting above the Pacific nearly two thousand miles east of Australia, suddenly disappeared in 1913. Thirteen years later, after violent eruptions in the vicinity, it as suddenly rose again above the surface and remained as a physical bit of the British Empire until 1949. Then it was reported by the Colonial Under Secretary to be missing again.

Almost from the moment of its creation, a volcanic island is foredoomed to destruction. It has in itself the seeds of its own dissolution, for new explosions, or landslides of the soft soil, may violently accelerate its disintegration. Whether the destruction of an island comes quickly or only after long ages of geologic time may also depend on external forces: the rains that wear away the loftiest of land mountains, the sea, and even man himself.

South Trinidad, or in the Portuguese spelling, "Ilha Trinidade," is an example of an island that has been sculptured into bizarre forms through centuries of weathering—an island in which the signs of dissolution are clearly apparent. This group of volcanic peaks lies in the open Atlantic, about a thousand miles northeast of Rio de Janeiro. E. F. Knight wrote in 1907 that Trinidad "is rotten throughout, its substance has been disintegrated by volcanic fires and by the action of water, so that it is everywhere tumbling to pieces." During an interval of nine years between Knight's visits, a whole mountainside had collapsed in a great landslide of broken rocks and volcanic debris.

Sometimes the disintegration takes abrupt and violent form. The greatest explosion of historic time was the literal evisceration of the island of Krakatoa. In 1680 there had been a premonitory eruption on this small island in Sunda Strait, between Java and Sumatra in the Netherlands Indies. Two hundred years later there had been a series of earthquakes. In the spring of 1883, smoke and steam began to ascend from fissures in the volcanic cone. The ground became noticeably warm, and warning rumblings and hissings came from the volcano. Then, on 27 August, Krakatoa literally exploded. In an appalling series of eruptions, that lasted two days, the whole northern half of the cone was carried away. The sudden inrush of ocean water added the fury of superheated steam to the cauldron. When the inferno of white-hot lava, molten rock, steam, and smoke had finally subsided, the island that had stood 1400 feet above the sea had become a cavity a thousand feet below sea level. Only along one edge of the former crater did a remnant of the island remain.

Krakatoa, in its destruction, became known to the entire world. The eruption gave rise to a hundred-foot wave that wiped out villages along the Strait and killed people by tens of thousands. The wave was felt on the shores of the Indian Ocean and at Cape Horn; rounding the Cape into the Atlantic, it sped northward and retained its identity even as far as the English Channel. The sound of the explosions was heard in the Philippine Islands, in Australia, and on the Island of Madagascar, nearly 3000 miles away. And clouds of volcanic dust, the pulverized rock that had been torn from the heart of Krakatoa, ascended into the stratosphere and were carried around the globe to give rise to a series of spectacular sunsets in every country of the world for nearly a year.

Although Krakatoa's dramatic passing was the most violent eruption that modern man has witnessed, Krakatoa itself seems to have been the product of an even greater one. There is evidence that an immense volcano once stood where the waters of Sunda Strait now lie. In some remote period a titanic explosion blew it away, leaving only its base represented by a broken ring of islands. The largest of these was Krakatoa, which, in its own demise, carried away what was left of the original crater ring. But in 1929 a new volcanic island arose in this place—Anak Krakatoa, Child of Krakatoa.

Subterranean fires and deep unrest disturb the whole area occupied by the Aleutians. The islands themselves are the peaks of a thousand-mile chain of undersea mountains, of which volcanic action was the chief architect. The geologic structure of the ridge is little known, but it rises abruptly from oceanic depths of about a mile on one side and two miles on the other. Apparently this long narrow ridge indicates a deep fracture of the earth's crust. On many of the islands volcanoes are now active, or only temporarily quiescent. In the short history of modern navigation in this region, it has often happened that a new island has been reported but perhaps only the following year could not be found.

The small island of Bogoslof, since it was first observed in 1796, has altered its shape and position several times and has even disappeared completely, only to emerge again. The original island was a mass of black rock, sculptured into fantastic, towerlike shapes. Explorers and sealers coming upon it in the fog were reminded of a castle and named it Castle Rock. At the present time there remain only one or two pinnacles of the castle, a long spit of black rocks where sea lions haul out, and a cluster of higher rocks resounding with the cries of thousands of sea birds. Each time the parent volcano erupts, as it has done at least half a dozen times since men have been observing it, new masses of steaming rocks emerge from the heated waters, some to reach heights of several hundred feet before they are destroyed in fresh explosions. Each new cone that appears is, as described by the volcanologist Jaggar, "the live crest, equivalent to a crater, of a great submarine heap of lava six thousand feet high, piled above the floor of Bering Sea where the Aleutian mountains fall off to the deep sea."

One of the few exceptions to the almost universal rule that oceanic islands have a volcanic origin seems to be the remarkable and fascinating group of islets known as the Rocks of St. Paul. Lying in the open Atlantic between Brazil and Africa, St. Paul's Rocks are an obstruction thrust up from the floor of the ocean into the midst of the racing Equatorial Current, a mass against which the seas, which have rolled a thousand miles unhindered, break in sudden violence. The entire cluster of rocks covers not more than a quarter of a mile, running in a curved line like a horseshoe. The highest rock is no more than sixty feet above the sea; spray wets it to the summit. Abruptly the rocks dip under water and slope steeply down into great depths. Geologists since the time of Darwin have puzzled over the origin of these black, wave-washed islets. Most of them agree that they are composed of material like that of the sea floor itself. In some remote period, inconceivable stresses in the earth's crust must have pushed a solid rock mass upward more than two miles.

So bare and desolate that not even a lichen grows on them, St. Paul's Rocks would seem one of the most unpromising places in the world to look for a spider, spinning its web in arachnidan hope of snaring passing insects. Yet Darwin found spiders when he visited the Rocks in 1833, and forty years later the naturalists of H.M.S. *Challenger* also reported them, busy at their web-spinning. A few insects are there, too, some as parasites on the sea birds, three species of which nest on the Rocks. One of the insects is a small brown moth that lives on feathers. This very nearly completes the inventory of the inhabitants of St. Paul's Rocks, except for the grotesque crabs that swarm over the islets, living chiefly on the flying fish brought by the birds to their young.

St. Paul's Rocks are not alone in having an extraordinary assortment of inhabitants, for the faunas and floras of oceanic islands are amazingly different from those of the continents. The pattern of island life is peculiar and significant. Aside from forms recently introduced by man, islands remote from the continents are never inhabited by any land mammals, except sometimes the one mammal that has learned to fly—the bat. There are never any frogs, salamanders, or other amphibians. Of reptiles, there may be a few snakes, lizards, and turtles, but the more remote the island from a major land mass, the fewer reptiles there are, and the really isolated islands have none. There are usually a few species of land birds, some insects, and some spiders. So remote an island as Tristan da Cunha in the South Atlantic, 1500 miles from the nearest continent, has no land animals but these: three species of land birds, a few insects, and several small snails.

With so selective a list, it is hard to see how, as some biologists believe, the islands could have been colonized by migration across land bridges, even if there were good evidence for the existence of the bridges. The very animals missing from the islands are the ones that would have had to come dry-shod, over the hypothetical bridges. The plants and animals that we find on oceanic islands, on the other hand, are the ones that could have come by wind or water. As an alternative, then, we must suppose that the stocking of the islands has been accomplished by the strangest migration in earth's history—a migration that began long before man appeared on earth and is still continuing, a migration that seems more like a series of cosmic accidents than an orderly process of nature.

We can only guess how long after its emergence from the sea an oceanic island may lie uninhabited. Certainly in its original state it is a land bare, harsh, and repelling beyond human experience. No living thing moves over the slopes of its volcanic hills; no plants cover its naked lava fields. But little by little, riding on the winds, drifting on the currents, or rafting in on logs, floating brush, or trees, the plants and animals that are to colonize it arrive from the distant continents.

So deliberate, so unhurried, so inexorable are the ways of nature that the stocking of an island may require thousands or millions of years. It may be that no more than half a dozen times in all these eons does a particular form, such as a tortoise, make a successful landing upon its shores. To wonder impatiently why man is not a constant witness of such arrivals is to fail to understand the majestic pace of the process.

Yet we have occasional glimpses of the method. Natural rafts of uprooted trees and matted vegetation have frequently been seen adrift at sea, more than a thousand miles off the mouths of such great tropical rivers as the Congo, the Ganges, the Amazon, and the Orinoco. Such rafts could easily carry an assortment of insect, reptile, or mollusk passengers. Some of the involuntary passengers might be able to withstand long weeks at sea; others would die during the first stages of the journey. Probably the ones best adapted for travel by raft are the wood-boring insects, which, of all the insect tribe, are most commonly found on oceanic islands. The poorest raft travelers must be the mammals. But even a mammal might cover short interisland distances. A few days after the explosion of Krakatoa, a small monkey was rescued from some drifting timber in Sunda Strait. She had been terribly burned, but survived the experience.

No less than the water, the winds and the air currents play their part in bringing inhabitants to the islands. The upper atmosphere, even during the ages before man entered it in his machines, was a place of congested traffic. Thousands of feet above the earth, the air is crowded with living creatures, drifting, flying, gliding, ballooning, or involuntarily swirling along on the high winds. Discovery of this rich aerial plankton had to wait until man himself had found means to make physical invasion of these regions. With special nets and traps, scientists have now collected from the upper atmosphere many of the forms that inhabit oceanic islands. Spiders, whose almost invariable presence on these islands is a fascinating problem, have been captured nearly three miles above the earth's surface. Airmen have passed through great numbers of the white, silken filaments of spiders' "parachutes" at heights of two to three miles. At altitudes of 6000 to 16,000 feet, and with wind velocities reaching 45 miles an hour, many living insects have been taken. At such heights and on such strong winds, they might well have been carried hundreds of miles. Seeds have been collected at altitudes up to 5000 feet. Among those commonly taken are members of the Composite family, especially the so-called "thistle-down" typical of oceanic islands.

An interesting point about transport of living plants and animals by wind is the fact that in the upper layers of the earth's atmosphere the winds do not necessarily blow in the same direction as at the earth's surface. The trade winds are notably shallow, so that a man standing on the cliffs of St. Helena, a thousand feet above the sea, is above the wind, which blows with great force below him. Once drawn into the upper air, insects, seeds, and the like can easily be carried in a direction contrary to that of the winds prevailing at island level.

The wide-ranging birds that visit islands of the ocean in migration may also have a good deal to do with the distribution of plants, and perhaps even of some insects and minute land shells. From a ball of mud taken from a bird's plumage, Charles Darwin raised eighty-two separate plants, belonging to five distinct species! Many plant seeds have hooks or prickles, ideal for attachment to feathers. Such birds as the Pacific golden plover, which annually flies from the mainland of Alaska to the Hawaiian Islands and even beyond, probably figure in many riddles of plant distribution.

The catastrophe of Krakatoa gave naturalists a perfect opportunity to observe the colonization of an island. With most of the island itself destroyed, and the remnant covered with a deep layer of lava and ash that remained hot for weeks, Krakatoa after the explosive eruptions of 1883 was, from a biological standpoint, a new volcanic island. As soon as it was possible to visit it, scientists searched for signs of life, although it was hard to imagine how any living thing could have survived. Not a single plant or animal could be found. It was not until nine months after the eruption that the naturalist Cotteau was able to report: "I only discovered one microscopic spider—only one. This strange pioneer of the renovation was busy spinning its web." Since there were no insects on the island, the webspinning of the bold little spider was presumably in vain, and except for a few blades of grass, practically nothing lived on Krakatoa for a quarter of a century. Then the colonists began to arrive—a few mammals in 1908; a number of birds, lizards, and snakes; various mollusks, insects, and earthworms. Ninety per cent of Krakatoa's new inhabitants, Dutch scientists found, were forms that could have arrived by air.

Isolated from the great mass of life on the continents, with no opportunity for the crossbreeding that tends to preserve the average and to eliminate the new and unusual, island life has developed in a remarkable manner. On these remote bits of earth, nature has excelled in the creation of strange and wonderful forms. As though to prove her incredible versatility, almost every island has developed species that are endemic—that is, they are peculiar to it alone and are duplicated nowhere else on earth.

It was from the pages of earth's history written on the lava fields of the Galapagos that young Charles Darwin got his first inkling of the great truths of the origin of species. Observing the strange plants and animals—giant tortoises, black, amazing lizards that hunted their food in the surf, sea lions, birds in extraordinary variety—Darwin was struck by their vague similarity to mainland species of South and Central America, yet was haunted by the differences, differences that distinguish them not only from the mainland species but from those on other islands of the archipelago. Years later he was to write in reminiscence: "Both in space and time, we seem to be brought somewhat near to that great fact—that mystery of mysteries—the first appearance of new beings on earth."

Of the "new beings" evolved on islands, some of the most striking examples have been birds. In some remote age before there were men, a small, pigeonlike bird found its way to the island of Mauritius, in the Indian Ocean. By processes of change at which we can only guess, this bird lost the power of flight, developed short, stout legs, and grew larger until it reached the size of a modern turkey. Such was the origin of the fabulous dodo, which did not long survive the advent of man on Mauritius. New Zealand was the sole home of the moas. One species of these ostrichlike birds stood twelve feet high. Moas had roamed New Zealand from the early part of the Tertiary; those that remained when the Maoris arrived soon died out.

Other island forms besides the dodo and the moas have tended to become large. Perhaps the Galapagos tortoise became a giant after its arrival on the islands, although fossil remains on the continents cast doubt on this. The loss of wing use and even of the wings themselves (the moas had none) are common results of insular life. Insects on small, wind-swept islands tend to lose the power of flight—those that retain it are in danger of being blown out to sea. The Galapagos Islands have a flightless cormorant. There have been at least fourteen species of flightless rails on the islands of the Pacific alone.

One of the most interesting and engaging characteristics of island species is their extraordinary tameness—a lack of sophistication in dealings with the human race, which even the bitter teachings of experience do not quickly alter. When Robert Cushman Murphy visited the island of South Trinidad in 1913 with a party from the brig *Daisy*, terns alighted on the heads of the men in the whaleboat and peered inquiringly into their faces. Albatrosses on Laysan, whose habits include wonderful ceremonial dances, allowed naturalists to walk among their colonies and responded with a grave bow to similar polite greetings from the visitors. When the British ornithologist David Lack visited the Galapagos Islands, a century after Darwin, he found that the hawks allowed themselves to be touched, and the flycatchers tried to remove hair from the heads of the men for nesting material. "It is a curious pleasure," he wrote, "to have the birds of the wilderness settling upon one's shoulders, and the pleasure could be much less rare were man less destructive."

But man, unhappily, has written one of his blackest records as a destroyer on the oceanic islands. He has seldom set foot on an island that he has not brought about disastrous changes. He has destroyed environments by cutting, clearing, and burning; he has brought with him as a chance associate the nefarious rat; and almost invariably he has turned loose upon the islands a whole Noah's Ark of goats, hogs, cattle, dogs, cats, and other non-native animals as well as plants. Upon species after species of island life, the black night of extinction has fallen.

In all the world of living things, it is doubtful whether there is a more delicately balanced relationship than that of island life to its environment. This environment is a remarkably uniform one. In the midst of a great ocean, ruled by currents and winds that rarely shift their course, climate changes little. There are few natural enemies, perhaps none at all. The harsh struggle for existence that is the normal lot of continental life is softened on the islands. When this gentle pattern of life is abruptly changed, the island creatures have little ability to make the adjustments necessary for survival.

Ernst Mayr tells of a steamer wrecked off Lord Howe Island east of Australia in 1918. Its rats swam ashore. In two years they had so nearly exterminated the native birds that an islander wrote, "This paradise of birds has become a wilderness, and the quietness of death reigns where all was melody."

On Tristan da Cunha almost all of the unique land birds that had evolved there in the course of the ages were exterminated by hogs and rats. The native fauna of the island of Tahiti is losing ground against the horde of alien species that man has introduced. The Hawaiian Islands, which have lost their native plants and animals faster than almost any other area in the world, are a classic example of the results of interfering with natural balances. Certain relations of animal to plant, and of plant to soil, had grown up through the centuries. When man came in and rudely disturbed this balance, he set off a whole series of chain reactions.

Vancouver brought cattle and goats to the Hawaiian Islands, and the resulting damage to forests and other vegetation was enormous. Many plant introductions were as bad. A plant known as the pamakani was brought in many years ago, according to report, by a Captain Makee for his beautiful gardens on the island of Maui. The pamakani, which has light, wind-borne seeds, quickly escaped from the captain's gardens, ruined the pasture lands on Maui, and proceeded to hop from island to island. The CCC boys were at one time put to work to clear it out of the Honouliuli Forest Reserve, but as fast as they destroyed it, the seeds of new plants arrived on the wind. Lantana was another plant brought in as an ornamental species. Now it covers thousands of acres with a thorny, scrambling growth—despite large sums of money spent to import parasitic insects to control it.

There was once a society in Hawaii for the special purpose of introducing exotic birds. Today when you go to the islands, you see, instead of the exquisite native birds that greeted Captain Cook, mynas from India, cardinals from the United States or Brazil, doves from Asia, weavers from Australia, skylarks from Europe, and titmice from Japan. Most of the original bird life has been wiped out, and to find its fugitive remnants you would have to search assiduously in the most remote hills.

Some of the island species have, at best, the most tenuous hold on life. The Laysan teal is found nowhere in the world but on the one small island of Laysan. Even on this island it occurs only on one end, where there is a seepage of fresh water. Probably the total population of this species does not exceed fifty individuals. Destruction of the small swampy bit of land that is its home, or the introduction of a hostile or competing species, could easily snap the slender thread of life.

Most of man's habitual tampering with nature's balance by introducing exotic species has been done in ignorance of the fatal chain of events that would follow. But in modern times, at least, we might profit by history. About the year 1513, the Portuguese introduced goats onto the recently discovered island of St. Helena, which had developed a magnificent forest of gumwood, ebony, and brazilwood. By 1560 or thereabouts, the goats had so multiplied that they wandered over the island by the thousand, in flocks a mile long. They trampled the young trees and ate the seedlings. By this time the colonists had begun to cut and burn the forests, so that it is hard to say whether men or goats were the more responsible for the destruction. But of the result there was no doubt. By the early 1800's the forests were gone, and the naturalist Alfred Wallace later described this once beautiful, forest-clad volcanic island as a "rocky desert," in which the remnants of the original flora persisted only in the most inaccessible peaks and crater ridges.

When the astronomer Halley visited the islands of the Atlantic about 1700, he put a few goats ashore on South Trinidad. This time, without the further aid of man, the work of deforestation proceeded so rapidly that it was nearly completed within the century. Today Trinidad's slopes are the place of a ghost forest, strewn with the fallen and decaying trunks of long-dead trees; its soft volcanic soils, no longer held by the interlacing roots, are sliding away into the sea.

One of the most interesting of the Pacific islands was Laysan, a tiny scrap of soil which is a far outrider of the Hawaiian chain. It once supported a forest of sandalwood and fanleaf palms and had five land birds, all peculiar to Laysan alone. One of them was the Laysan rail, a charming, gnomelike creature no more than six inches high, with wings that seemed too small (and were never used as wings), and feet that seemed too large, and a voice like distant, tinkling bells. About 1887, the captain of a visiting ship moved some of the rails to Midway, about 300 miles to the west, establishing a second colony. It seemed a fortunate move, for soon thereafter rabbits were introduced on Laysan. Within a quarter of a century, the rabbits had killed off the vegetation of the tiny island, reduced it to a sandy desert, and all but exterminated themselves. As for the rails, the devastation of their island was fatal, and the last rail died about 1924.

Perhaps the Laysan colony could later have been restored from the Midway group had not tragedy struck there also. During the war in the Pacific, rats went ashore to island after island from ships and landing craft. They invaded Midway in 1943. The adult rails were slaughtered. The eggs were eaten, and the young birds killed. The world's last Laysan rail was seen in 1944.

The tragedy of the oceanic islands lies in the uniqueness, the irreplaceability of the species they have developed by the slow processes of the ages. In a reasonable world men would have treated these islands as precious possessions, as natural museums filled with beautiful and curious works of creation, valuable beyond price because nowhere in the world are they duplicated. W. H. Hudson's lament for the birds of the Argentine pampas might even more truly have been spoken of the islands: "The beautiful has vanished and returns not."

The Shape of Ancient Seas

> Till the slow sea rise and the sheer cliff crumble, till terrace and meadow the deep gulfs drink.
>
> —SWINBURNE

WE LIVE IN an age of rising seas. Along all the coasts of the United States a continuing rise of sea level has been perceptible on the tide gauges of the Coast and Geodetic Survey since 1930. For the thousand-mile stretch from Massachusetts to Florida, and on the coast of the Gulf of Mexico, the rise amounted to about a third of a foot between 1930 and 1948. The water is also rising (but more slowly) along the Pacific shores. These records of the tide gauges do not include the transient advances and retreats of the water caused by winds and storms, but signify a steady, continuing advance of the sea upon the land.

This evidence of a rising sea is an interesting and even an exciting thing because it is rare that, in the short span of human life, we can actually observe and measure the progress of one of the great earth rhythms. What is happening is nothing new. Over the long span of geologic time, the ocean waters have come in over North America many times and have again retreated into their basins. For the boundary between sea and land is the most fleeting and transitory feature of the earth, and the sea is forever repeating its encroachments upon the continents. It rises and falls like a great tide, sometimes engulfing half a continent in its flood, reluctant in its ebb, moving in a rhythm mysterious and infinitely deliberate.

Now once again the ocean is overfull. It is spilling over the rims of its basins. It fills the shallow seas that border the continents, like the Barents, Bering, and China seas. Here and there it has advanced into the interior and lies in such inland seas as Hudson Bay, the St. Lawrence embayment, the Baltic, and the Sunda Sea. On the Atlantic coast of the United States the mouths of many rivers, like the Hudson and the Susquehanna, have been drowned by the advancing flood; the old, submerged channels are hidden under bays like the Chesapeake and the Delaware.

The advance noted so clearly on the tide gauges may be part of a long rise that began thousands of years ago—perhaps when the glaciers of the most recent Ice Age began to melt. But it is only within recent decades that there have been instruments to measure it in any part of the world. Even now the gauges are few and scattered, considering the world as a whole. Because of the scarcity of world records, it is not known whether the rise observed in the United States since 1930 is being duplicated on all other continents.

Where and when the ocean will halt its present advance and begin again its slow retreat into its basin, no one can say. If the rise over the continent of North America should amount to a hundred feet (and there is more than enough water now frozen in land ice to provide such a rise) most of the Atlantic seaboard, with its cities and towns, would be submerged. The surf would break against the foothills of the Appalachians. The coastal plain of the Gulf of Mexico would lie under water; the lower part of the Mississippi Valley would be submerged.

If, however, the rise should be as much as 600 feet, large areas in the eastern half of the continent would disappear under the waters. The Appalachians would become a chain of mountainous islands. The Gulf of Mexico would creep north, finally meeting in mid-continent with the flood that had entered from the Atlantic into the Great Lakes, through the valley of the St. Lawrence. Much of northern Canada would be covered by water from the Arctic Ocean and Hudson Bay.

All of this would seem to us extraordinary and catastrophic, but the truth is that North America and most other continents have known even more extensive invasions by the sea than the one we have just imagined. Probably the greatest submergence in the history of the earth took place in the Cretaceous period, about 100 million years ago. Then the ocean waters advanced upon North America from the north, south, and east, finally forming an inland sea about 1000 miles wide that extended from the Arctic to the Gulf of Mexico, and then spread eastward to cover the coastal plain from the Gulf to New Jersey. At the height of the Cretaceous flood about half of North America was submerged. All over the world the seas rose. They covered most of the British Isles, except for scattered outcroppings of ancient rocks. In southern Europe only the old, rocky highlands stood above the sea, which intruded in long bays and gulfs even into the central highlands of the continent. The ocean moved into Africa and laid down deposits of sandstones; later weathering of these rocks provided the desert sands of the Sahara. From a drowned Sweden, an inland sea flowed across Russia, covered the Caspian Sea, and extended to the Himalayas. Parts of India were submerged, and of Australia, Japan, and Siberia. On the South American continent, the area where later the Andes were to rise was covered by sea.

With variations of extent and detail, these events have been repeated again and again. The very ancient Ordovician seas, some 400 million years ago, submerged more than half of North America, leaving only a few large islands marking the borderlands of the continent, and a scattering of smaller ones rising out of the inland sea. The marine transgressions of Devonian and Silurian time were almost as extensive. But each time the pattern of invasion was a little different, and it is doubtful that there is any part of the continent that at some time has not lain at the bottom of one of these shallow seas.

You do not have to travel to find the sea, for the traces of its ancient stands are everywhere about. Though you may be a thousand miles inland, you can easily find reminders that will reconstruct for the eye and ear of the mind the processions of its ghostly waves and the roar of its surf, far back in time. So, on a mountain top in Pennsylvania, I have sat on rocks of whitened limestone, fashioned of the shells of billions upon billions of minute sea creatures. Once they had lived and died in an arm of the ocean that overlay this place, and their limy remains had settled to the bottom. There, after eons of time, they had become compacted into rock and the sea had receded; after yet more eons the rock had been uplifted by bucklings of the earth's crust and now it formed the backbone of a long mountain range.

Far in the interior of the Florida Everglades I have wondered at the feeling of the sea that came to me—wondered until I realized that here were the same flatness, the same immense spaces, the same dominance of the sky and its moving, changing clouds; wondered until I remembered that the hard rocky floor on which I stood, its flatness interrupted by upthrust masses of jagged coral rock, had been only recently constructed by the busy architects of the coral reefs under a warm sea. Now the rock is thinly covered with grass and water; but everywhere is the feeling that the land has formed only the thinnest veneer over the underlying platform of the sea, that at any moment the process might be reversed and the sea reclaim its own.

So in all lands we may sense the former presence of the sea. There are outcroppings of marine limestone in the Himalayas, now at an elevation of 20,000 feet. These rocks are reminders of a warm, clear sea that lay over southern Europe and northern Africa and extended into southwestern Asia. This was some 50 million years ago. Immense numbers of a large protozoan known as nummulites swarmed in this sea and each, in death, contributed to the building of a thick layer of nummulitic limestone. Eons later, the ancient Egyptians were to carve their Sphinx from a mass of this rock; other deposits of the same stone they quarried to obtain material to build their pyramids.

The famous white cliffs of Dover are composed of chalk deposited by the seas of the Cretaceous period, during that great inundation we have spoken of. The chalk extends from Ireland through Denmark and Germany, and forms its thickest beds in south Russia. It consists of shells of those minute sea creatures called foraminifera, the shells being cemented together with a fine-textured deposit of calcium carbonate. In contrast to the foraminiferal ooze that covers large areas of ocean bottom at moderate depths, the chalk seems to be a shallow-water deposit, but it is so pure in texture that the surrounding lands must have been low deserts, from which little material was carried seaward. Grains of wind-borne quartz sand, which frequently occur in the chalk, support this view. At certain levels the chalk contains nodules of flint. Stone Age men mined the flint for weapons and tools and also used this relic of the Cretaceous sea to light their fires.

Many of the natural wonders of the earth owe their existence to the fact that once the sea crept over the land, laid down its deposits of sediments, and then withdrew. There is Mammoth Cave in Kentucky, for example, where one may wander through miles of underground passages and enter rooms with ceilings 250 feet overhead. Caves and passageways have been dissolved by ground water out of an immense thickness of limestone, deposited by a Paleozoic sea. In the same way, the story of Niagara Falls goes back to Silurian time, when a vast embayment of the Arctic Sea crept southward over the continent. Its waters were clear, for the borderlands were low and little sediment or silt was carried into the inland sea. It deposited large beds of the hard rock called dolomite, and in time they formed a long escarpment near the present border between Canada and the United States. Millions of years later, floods of water released from melting glaciers poured over this cliff, cutting away the soft shales that underlay the dolomite, and causing mass after mass of the undercut rock to break away. In this fashion Niagara Falls and its gorge were created.

Some of these inland seas were immense and important features of their world, although all of them were shallow compared with the central basin where, since earliest time, the bulk of the ocean waters have resided. Some may have been as much as 600 feet deep, about the same as the depths over the outer edge of the continental shelf. No one knows the pattern of their currents, but often they must have carried the warmth of the tropics into far northern lands. During the Cretaceous period, for example, breadfruit, cinnamon, laurel, and fig trees grew in Greenland. When the continents were reduced to groups of islands there must have been few places that possessed a continental type of climate with its harsh extremes of heat and cold; mild oceanic climates must rather have been the rule.

Geologists say that each of the grander divisions of earth history consists of three phases: in the first the continents are high, erosion is active, and the seas are largely confined to their basins; in the second the continents are lowest and the seas have invaded them broadly; in the third the continents have begun once more to rise. According to the late Charles Schuchert, who devoted much of his distinguished career as a geologist to mapping the ancient seas and lands: "Today we are living in the beginning of a new cycle, when the continents are largest, highest, and scenically grandest. The oceans, however, have begun another invasion upon North America."

What brings the ocean out of its deep basins, where it has been contained for eons of time, to invade the lands? Probably there has always been not one alone, but a combination of causes.

The mobility of the earth's crust is inseparably linked with the changing relations of sea and land—the warping upward or downward of that surprisingly plastic substance which forms the outer covering of our earth. The crustal movements affect both land and sea bottom but are most marked near the continental margins. They may involve one or both shores of an ocean, one or all coasts of a continent. They proceed in a slow and mysterious cycle, one phase of which may require millions of years for its completion. Each downward movement of the continental crust is accompanied by a slow flooding of the land by the sea, each upward buckling by the retreat of the water.

But the movements of the earth's crust are not alone responsible for the invading seas. There are other important causes. Certainly one of them is the displacement of ocean water by land sediments. Every grain of sand or silt carried out by the rivers and deposited at sea displaces a corresponding amount of water. Disintegration of the land and the seaward freighting of its substance have gone on without interruption since the beginning of geologic time. It might be thought that the sea level would have been rising continuously, but the matter is not so simple. As they lose substance the continents tend to rise higher, like a ship relieved of part of its cargo. The ocean floor, to which the sediments are transferred, sags under its load. The exact combination of all these conditions that will result in a rising ocean level is a very complex matter, not easily recognized or predicted.

Then there is the growth of the great submarine volcanoes, which build up immense lava cones on the floor of the ocean. Some geologists believe these may have an important effect on the changing level of the sea. The bulk of some of these volcanoes is impressive. Bermuda is one of the smallest, but its volume beneath the surface is about 2500 cubic miles. The Hawaiian chain of volcanic islands extends for nearly 2000 miles across the Pacific and contains several islands of great size; its total displacement of water must be tremendous. Perhaps it is more than coincidence that this chain arose in Cretaceous time, when the greatest flood the world has ever seen advanced upon the continents.

For the past million years, all other causes of marine transgressions have been dwarfed by the dominating role of the glaciers. The Pleistocene period was marked by alternating advances and retreats of a great ice sheet. Four times the ice caps formed and grew deep over the land, pressing southward into the valleys and over the plains. And four times the ice melted and shrank and withdrew from the lands it had covered. We live now in the last stages of this fourth withdrawal. About half the ice formed in the last Pleistocene glaciation remains in the ice caps of Greenland and Antarctica and the scattered glaciers of certain mountains.

Each time the ice sheet thickened and expanded with the unmelted snows of winter after winter, its growth meant a corresponding lowering of the ocean level. For directly or indirectly, the moisture that falls on the earth's surface as rain or snow has been withdrawn from the reservoir of the sea. Ordinarily, the withdrawal is a temporary one, the water being returned via the normal runoff of rain and melting snow. But in the glacial period the summers were cool, and the snows of any winter did not melt entirely but were carried over to the succeeding winter, when the new snows found and covered them. So little by little the level of the sea dropped as the glaciers robbed it of its water, and at the climax of each of the major glaciations the ocean all over the world stood at a very low level.

Today, if you look in the right places, you will see the evidences of some of these old stands of the sea. Of course the strand marks left by the extreme low levels are now deeply covered by water and may be discovered only indirectly by sounding. But where, in past ages, the water level stood higher than it does today you can find its traces. In Samoa, at the foot of a cliff wall now 15 feet above the present level of the sea, you can find benches cut in the rocks by waves. You will find the same thing on other Pacific islands, and on St. Helena in the South Atlantic, on islands of the Indian Ocean, in the West Indies, and around the Cape of Good Hope.

Sea caves in cliffs now high above the battering assault and the flung spray of the waves that cut them are eloquent of the changed relation of sea and land. You will find such caves widely scattered over the world. On the west coast of Norway there is a remarkable, wave-cut tunnel. Out of the hard granite of the island of Torghattan, the pounding surf of a flooding interglacial sea cut a passageway through the island, a distance of about 530 feet, and in so doing removed nearly 5 million cubic feet of rock. The tunnel now stands 400 feet above the sea. Its elevation is due in part to the elastic, upward rebound of the crust after the melting of the ice.

During the other half of the cycle, when the seas sank lower and lower as the glaciers grew in thickness, the world's shorelines were undergoing changes even more far-reaching and dramatic. Every river felt the effect of the lowering sea; its waters were speeded in their course to the ocean and given new strength for the deepening and cutting of its channel. Following the downward-moving shorelines, the rivers extended their courses over the drying sands and muds of what only recently had been the sloping sea bottom. Here the rushing torrents—swollen with melting glacier water—picked up great quantities of loose mud and sand and rolled into the sea as a turgid flood.

During one or more of the Pleistocene lowerings of sea level, the floor of the North Sea was drained of its water and for a time became dry land. The rivers of northern Europe and of the British Isles followed the retreating waters seaward. Eventually the Rhine captured the whole drainage system of the Thames. The Elbe and the Weser became one river. The Seine rolled through what is now the English Channel and cut itself a trough out across the continental shelf—perhaps the same drowned channel now discernible by soundings beyond Lands End.

The greatest of all Pleistocene glaciations came rather late in the period—probably only about 200 thousand years ago, and well within the time of man. The tremendous lowering of sea level must have affected the life of Paleolithic man. Certainly he was able, at more than one period, to walk across a wide bridge at Bering Strait, which became dry land when the level of the ocean dropped below this shallow shelf. There were other land bridges, created in the same way. As the ocean receded from the coast of India, a long submarine bank became a shoal, then finally emerged, and primitive man walked across "Adam's Bridge" to the island of Ceylon.

Many of the settlements of ancient man must have been located on the seacoast or near the great deltas of the rivers, and relics of his civilization may lie in caves long since covered by the rising ocean. Our meager knowledge of Paleolithic man might be increased by searching along these old drowned shorelines. One archaeologist has recommended searching shallow portions of the Adriatic Sea, with "submarine boats casting strong electric lights" or even with glass-bottomed boats and artificial light in the hope of discovering the outlines of shell heaps—the kitchen middens of the early men who once lived here. Professor R. A. Daly has pointed out:

> The last Glacial stage was the Reindeer Age of French history. Men then lived in the famous caves overlooking the channels of the French rivers, and hunted the reindeer which throve on the cool plains of France south of the ice border. The Late-Glacial rise of general sea level was necessarily accompanied by a rise of the river waters downstream. Hence the lowest caves are likely to have been partly or wholly drowned . . . There the search for more relics of Paleolithic man should be pursued.*

Some of our Stone Age ancestors must have known the rigors of life near the glaciers. While men as well as plants and animals moved southward before the ice, some must have remained within sight and sound of the great frozen wall. To these the world was a place of storm and blizzard, with bitter winds roaring down out of the blue mountain of ice that dominated the horizon and reached upward into gray skies, all filled with the roaring tumult of the advancing glacier, and with the thunder of moving tons of ice breaking away and plunging into the sea.

But those who lived half the earth away, on some sunny coast of the Indian Ocean, walked and hunted on dry land over which the sea, only recently, had rolled deeply. These men knew nothing of the distant glaciers, nor did they understand that they walked and hunted where they did because quantities of ocean water were frozen as ice and snow in a distant land.

In any imaginative reconstruction of the world of the Ice Age, we are plagued by one tantalizing uncertainty: how low did the ocean level fall during the period of greatest spread of the glaciers, when unknown quantities of water were frozen in the ice? Was it only a moderate fall of 200 or 300 feet—

---

*From *The Changing World of the Ice Age*, 1934 edition, Yale University Press, p. 210.

a change paralleled many times in geologic history in the ebb and flow of the epicontinental seas? Or was it a dramatic drawing down of the ocean by 2000, even 3000 feet?

Each of these various levels has been suggested as an actual possibility by one or more geologists. Perhaps it is not surprising that there should be such radical disagreement. It has been only about a century since Louis Agassiz gave the world its first understanding of the moving mountains of ice and their dominating effect on the Pleistocene world. Since then, men in all parts of the earth have been patiently accumulating the facts and reconstructing the events of those four successive advances and retreats of the ice. Only the present generation of scientists, led by such daring thinkers as Daly, have understood that each thickening of the ice sheets meant a corresponding lowering of the ocean, and that with each retreat of the melting ice a returning flood of water raised the sea level.

Of this "alternate robbery and restitution" most geologists have taken a conservative view and said that the greatest lowering of the sea level could not have amounted to more than 400 feet, possibly only half as much. Most of those who argue that the drawing down was much greater base their reasoning upon the submarine canyons, those deep gorges cut in the continental slopes. The deeper canyons lie a mile or more below the present level of the sea. Geologists who maintain that at least the upper parts of the canyons were stream-cut say that the sea level must have fallen enough to permit this during the Pleistocene glaciation.

This question of the farthest retreat of the sea into its basins must await further searchings into the mysteries of the ocean. We seem on the verge of exciting new discoveries. Now oceanographers and geologists have better instruments than ever before to probe the depths of the sea, to sample its rocks and deeply layered sediments, and to read with greater clarity the dim pages of past history.

Meanwhile, the sea ebbs and flows in these grander tides of earth, whose stages are measurable not in hours but in millennia—tides so vast they are invisible and uncomprehended by the senses of man. Their ultimate cause, should it ever be discovered, may be found to be deep within the fiery center of the earth, or it may lie somewhere in the dark spaces of the universe.

II
THE RESTLESS SEA

Wind and Water

> The wind's feet shine along the sea.
>
> —SWINBURNE

AS THE WAVES roll in toward Lands End on the westernmost tip of England they bring the feel of the distant places of the Atlantic. Moving shoreward above the steeply rising floor of the deep sea, from dark blue water into troubled green, they pass the edge of "soundings" and roll up over the continental shelf in confused ripplings and turbulence. Over the shoaling bottom they sweep landward, breaking on the Seven Stones of the channel between the Scilly Isles and Lands End, coming in over the sunken ledges and the rocks that roll out their glistening backs at low water. As they approach the rocky tip of Lands End, they pass over a strange instrument lying on the sea bottom. By the fluctuating pressure of their rise and fall they tell this instrument many things of the distant Atlantic waters from which they have come, and their messages are translated by its mechanisms into symbols understandable to the human mind.

If you visited this place and talked to the meteorologist in charge, he could tell you the life histories of the waves that are rolling in, minute by minute and hour after hour, bringing their messages of far-off places. He could tell you where the waves were created by the action of wind on water, the strength of the winds that produced them, how fast the storm is moving, and how soon, if at all, it will become necessary to raise storm warnings along the coast of England. Most of the waves that roll over the recorder at Lands End, he would tell you, are born in the stormy North Atlantic eastward from Newfoundland and south of Greenland. Some can be traced to tropical storms on the opposite side of the Atlantic, moving through the West Indies and along the coast of Florida. A few have rolled up from the southernmost part of the world, taking a great-circle course all the way from Cape Horn to Lands End, a journey of 6000 miles.

On the coast of California wave recorders have detected swell from as great a distance, for some of the surf that breaks on that coast in summer is born in the west-wind belt of the Southern Hemisphere. The Cornwall recorders and those in California, as well as a few on the east coast of America, have been in use since the end of the Second World War. These experiments have several objects, among them the development of a new kind of weather forecasting. In the countries bordering the North Atlantic there is no practical need to turn to the waves for weather information because meteorological stations are numerous and strategically placed. The areas in which the wave recorders are presently used have served rather as a testing laboratory to develop the method. It will soon be ready for use in other parts of the world, for which there are no meteorological data except those the waves bring. Especially in the Southern Hemisphere, many coasts are washed by waves that have come from lonely, unvisited parts of the ocean, seldom crossed by vessels, off the normal routes of the air lines. Storms may develop in these remote places, unobserved, and sweep down suddenly on mid-ocean islands or exposed coasts. Over the millions of years the waves, running ahead of the storms, have been crying a warning, but only now are we learning to read their language. Or only now, at least, are we learning to do so scientifically. There is a basis in folklore for these modern achievements in wave research. To generations of Pacific Island natives, a certain kind of swell has signaled the approach of a typhoon. And centuries ago, when peasants on the lonely shores of Ireland saw the long swells that herald a storm rolling in upon their coasts, they shuddered and talked of death waves.

Now our study of waves has come of age, and on all sides we can find evidence that modern man is turning to the waves of the sea for practical purposes. Off the Fishing Pier at Long Branch, New Jersey, at the end of a quarter-mile pipeline on the bed of the ocean, a wave recording instrument silently and continuously takes note of the arrival of waves from the open Atlantic. By electric impulses transmitted through the pipeline, the height of each wave and the interval between succeeding crests are transmitted to a shore station and automatically recorded as a graph. These records are carefully studied by the Beach Erosion Board of the Army Corps of Engineers, which is concerned about the rate of erosion along the New Jersey coast.

Off the coast of Africa, high-flying planes recently took a series of overlapping photographs of the surf and the areas immediately offshore. From these photographs, trained men determined the speed of the waves moving in toward the shore. Then they applied a mathematical formula that relates the behavior of waves advancing into shallow water to the depths beneath them. All this information provided the British government with usable surveys of the depths off the coast of an almost inaccessible part of its empire, which could have been sounded in the ordinary way only at great expense and with endless difficulty. Like much of our new knowledge of waves, this practical method was born of wartime necessity.

Forecasts of the state of the sea and particularly the height of the surf became regular preliminaries to invasion in the Second World War, especially on the exposed beaches of Europe and Africa. But application of theory to practical conditions was at first difficult; so was the interpretation of the actual effect of any predicted height of surf or roughness of sea surface on the transfer of men and supplies between boats or from boats to beaches. This first attempt at practical military oceanography was, as one naval officer put it, a "most frightening lesson" concerning the "almost desperate lack of basic information on the fundamentals of the nature of the sea."

As long as there has been an earth, the moving masses of air that we call winds have swept back and forth across its surface. And as long as there has been an ocean, its waters have stirred to the passage of the winds. Most waves are the result of the action of wind on water. There are exceptions, such as the tidal waves sometimes produced by earthquakes under the sea. But the waves most of us know best are wind waves.

It is a confused pattern that the waves make in the open sea —a mixture of countless different wave trains, intermingling, overtaking, passing, or sometimes engulfing one another; each group differing from the others in the place and manner of its origin, in its speed, its direction of movement; some doomed never to reach any shore, others destined to roll across half an ocean before they dissolve in thunder on a distant beach.

Out of such seemingly hopeless confusion the patient study of many men over many years has brought a surprising amount of order. While there is still much to be learned about waves, and much to be done to apply what is known to man's advantage, there is a solid basis of fact on which to reconstruct the life history of a wave, predict its behavior under all the changing circumstances of its life, and foretell its effect on human affairs.

Before constructing an imaginary life history of a typical wave, we need to become familiar with some of its physical characteristics. A wave has height, from trough to crest. It has length, the distance from its crest to that of the following wave. The period of the wave refers to the time required for succeeding crests to pass a fixed point. None of these dimensions is static; all change, but bear definite relations to the wind, the depth of the water, and many other matters. Furthermore, the water that composes a wave does not advance with it across the sea; each water particle describes a circular or elliptical orbit with the passage of the wave form, but returns very nearly to its original position. And it is fortunate that this is so, for if the huge masses of water that comprise a wave actually moved across the sea, navigation would be impossible. Those who deal professionally in the lore of waves make frequent use of a picturesque expression—the "length of fetch." The "fetch" is the distance that the waves have run, under the drive of a wind blowing in a constant direction, without obstruction. The greater the fetch, the higher the waves. Really large waves cannot be generated within the confined space of a bay or a small area. A fetch of perhaps 600 to 800 miles, with winds of gale velocity, is required to get up the largest ocean waves.

Now let us suppose that, after a period of calm, a storm develops far out in the Atlantic, perhaps a thousand miles from the New Jersey coast where we are spending a summer holiday. Its winds blow irregularly, with sudden gusts, shifting direction but in general blowing shoreward. The sheet of water under the wind responds to the changing pressures. It is no longer a level surface; it becomes furrowed with alternating troughs and ridges. The waves move toward the coast, and the wind that created them controls their destiny. As the storm continues and the waves move shoreward, they receive energy from the wind and increase in height. Up to a point they will continue to take to themselves the fierce energy of the wind, growing in height as the strength of the gale is absorbed, but when a wave becomes about a seventh as high from trough to crest as the distance to the next crest it will begin to topple in foaming whitecaps. Winds of hurricane force often blow the tops off the waves by their sheer violence; in such a storm the highest waves may develop after the wind has begun to subside.

But to return to our typical wave, born of wind and water far out in the Atlantic, grown to its full height on the energy of the winds, with its fellow waves forming a confused, irregular pattern known as a "sea." As the waves gradually pass out of the storm area their height diminishes, the distance between successive crests increases, and the "sea" becomes a "swell," moving at an average speed of about 15 miles an hour. Near the coast a pattern of long, regular swells is substituted for the turbulence of open ocean. But as the swell enters shallow water a startling transformation takes place. For the first time in its existence, the wave feels the drag of shoaling bottom. Its speed slackens, crests of following waves crowd in toward it, abruptly its height increases and the wave form steepens. Then with a spilling, tumbling rush of water falling down into its trough, it dissolves in a seething confusion of foam.

An observer sitting on a beach can make at least an intelligent guess whether the surf spilling out onto the sand before him has been produced by a gale close offshore or by a distant storm. Young waves, only recently shaped by the wind, have a steep, peaked shape even well out at sea. From far out on the horizon you can see them forming whitecaps as they come in; bits of foam are spilling down their fronts and boiling and bubbling over the advancing face, and the final breaking of the wave is a prolonged and deliberate process. But if a wave, on coming into the surf zone, rears high as though gathering all its strength for the final act of its life, if the crest forms all along its advancing front and then begins to curl forward, if the whole mass of water plunges suddenly with a booming roar into its trough—then you may take it that these waves are visitors from some very distant part of the ocean, that they have traveled long and far before their final dissolution at your feet.

What is true of the Atlantic wave we have followed is true, in general, of wind waves the world over. The incidents in the life of a wave are many. How long it will live, how far it will travel, to what manner of end it will come are all determined, in large measure, by the conditions it meets in its progression across the face of the sea. For the one essential quality of a wave is that it moves; anything that retards or stops its motion dooms it to dissolution and death.

Forces within the sea itself may affect a wave most profoundly. Some of the most terrible furies of the ocean are unleashed when tidal currents cross the path of the waves or move in direct opposition to them. This is the cause of the famous "roosts" of Scotland, like the one off Sumburgh Head, at the southernmost tip of the Shetland Islands. During northeasterly winds the roost is quiescent, but when the wind-born waves roll in from any other quarter they encounter the tidal currents, either streaming shoreward in flood or seaward on the ebb. It is like the meeting of two wild beasts. The battle of the waves and tides is fought over an area of sea that may be three miles wide when the tides are running at full strength, first off Sumburgh Head, then gradually shifting seaward, subsiding only with the temporary slackening of the tide. "In this confused, tumbling, and bursting sea, vessels often become entirely unmanageable and sometimes founder," says the *British Islands Pilot*, "while others have been tossed about for days together." Such dangerous waters have been personified in many parts of the world by names that are handed down through generations of seafaring men. As in the time of our grandfathers and of their grandfathers, the Bore of Duncansby and the Merry Men of Mey rage at opposite ends of the Pentland Firth, which separates the Orkney Islands from the northern tip of Scotland. The sailing directions for the Firth in the *North Sea Pilot* for 1875 contained a warning to mariners, which is repeated verbatim in the modern *Pilot*:

> Before entering the Pentland Firth all vessels should be prepared to batten down, and the hatches of small vessels ought to be secured even in the finest weather, as it is difficult to see what may be going on in the distance, and the transition from smooth water to a broken sea is so sudden that no time is given for making arrangements.

Both roosts are caused by the meeting of swells from the open ocean and opposing tidal currents, so that at the east end of the Firth the Bore of Duncansby is to be feared with easterly swells and a flood tide, and at the west end the Merry Men of Mey stage their revelries with the ebb tides and a westerly swell. Then, according to the *Pilot*, "a sea is raised which cannot be imagined by those who have never experienced it."

Such a rip may offer protection to the near-by coast by the very fury and uncompromisingness of the struggle between waves and tide. Thomas Stevenson long ago observed that as long as the Sumburgh roost was breaking and cresting heavily off the Head there was little surf on shore; once the strength of the tide was spent and it could no longer run down the seas a heavy surf rolled in against the coast and rose to great heights on the cliffs. And in the western Atlantic, the confused and swiftly running tidal currents at the mouth of the Bay of Fundy offer such strong opposition to waves approaching from any quarter from southwest to southeast that such surf as develops within the Bay is almost entirely local in its origin.

Out in the open sea, a train of waves encountering a hostile wind may be rapidly destroyed, for the power that created a wave may also destroy it. So a fresh trade wind in the Atlantic has often flattened out the swells as they rolled down from Iceland toward Africa. Or a friendly wind, suddenly springing up to blow in the direction the waves are moving, may cause their height to increase at the rate of a foot or two per minute. Once a group of moving ridges has been created, the wind has only to fall into the troughs between them to push up their crests rapidly.

Rocky ledges, shoals of sand or clay or rock, and coastal islands in the mouths of bays all play their part in the fate of the waves that advance toward shore. The long swells that roll from the open ocean toward the shores of northern New England seldom reach it in full strength. Their energy is spent in passing over that great submerged highland known as Georges Bank, the crests of whose highest hills approach the surface over the Cultivator Shoals. The hindrance of these submarine hills, and of the tidal currents that swirl around and across them, robs the long ocean swells of their power. Or islands scattered within a bay or about its mouth may so absorb the strength of the waves that the head of the bay is free from surf. Even scattered reefs off a coast may offer it great protection, by causing the highest waves to break there, so that they never reach the shore.

Ice, snow, rain—all are enemies of the waves and under proper conditions may knock down a sea or cushion the force of surf on a beach. Within loose pack ice a vessel may count on smooth seas even if a gale is raging and surf is breaking heavily about the edges of the pack. Ice crystals forming in the sea will smooth the waves by increasing the friction between water particles; even the delicate, crystalline form of a snowflake has such an effect on a smaller scale. A hail storm will knock down a rough sea, and even a sudden downpour of rain may often turn the surface of the ocean to oiled-silk smoothness, rippling to the passage of the swells.

The divers of ancient times who carried oil in their mouths to release beneath the surface when rough water made their work difficult were applying what every seaman today knows —that oil appears to have a calming effect on the free waves of the open ocean. Instructions for the use of oil in emergencies at sea are carried by most official sailing directions of maritime nations. Oil has little effect on surf, however, once the dissolution of the wave form has begun.

In the Southern Ocean where the waves are not destroyed by breaking on any beach, the great swells produced by the westerly winds roll around and around the world. Here the longest waves, and those with the greatest sidewise expanse of crest, are formed. Here, it might be supposed, the highest waves would also be found. Yet there is no evidence that the waves of the Southern Ocean surpass the giants of any other ocean. A long series of reports culled from the publications of engineers and ships' officers show that waves higher than 25 feet from trough to crest are rare in all oceans. Storm waves may grow twice as high, and if a full gale blows long enough in one direction to have a fetch of 600 to 800 miles, the resulting waves may be even higher. The greatest possible height of storm waves at sea is a much debated question, with most textbooks citing a conservative 60 feet, and mariners stubbornly describing much higher waves. Throughout the century that has followed the report of Dumont d'Urville that he encountered a wave 100 feet high off the Cape of Good Hope, science generally has viewed such figures with skepticism. Yet there is one record of a giant wave which, because of the method of measurement, seems to be accepted as reliable.

In February 1933 the U.S.S. *Ramapo*, while proceeding from Manila to San Diego, encountered seven days of stormy weather. The storm was part of a weather disturbance that extended all the way from Kamchatka to New York and permitted the winds an unbroken fetch of thousands of miles. During the height of the storm the *Ramapo* maintained a course running down the wind and with the sea. On 6 February the gale reached its fiercest intensity. Winds of 68 knots came in gusts and squalls, and the seas reached mountainous height. While standing watch on the bridge during the early hours of that day, one of the officers of the *Ramapo* saw, in the moonlight, a great sea rising astern to a level above an iron strap on the crow's nest of the mainmast. The *Ramapo* was on even keel and her stern was in the trough of the sea. These circumstances made possible an exact line of sight from the bridge to the crest of the wave, and simple mathematical calculations based on the dimensions of the ship gave the height of the wave. It was 112 feet.

Waves have taken their toll of shipping and of human life on the open sea, but it is around the shorelines of the world that they are most destructive. Whatever the height of storm waves at sea, there is abundant evidence, as some of the case histories that follow will show, that breaking surf and the upward-leaping water masses from thundering breakers may engulf lighthouses, shatter buildings, and hurl stones through lighthouse windows anywhere from 100 to 300 feet above the sea. Before the power of such surf, piers and breakwaters and other shore installations are fragile as a child's toys.

Almost every coast of the world is visited periodically by violent storm surf, but there are some that have never known the sea in its milder moods. "There is not in the world a coast more terrible than this!" exclaimed Lord Bryce of Tierra del Fuego, where the breakers roar in upon the coast with a voice that, according to report, can be heard 20 miles inland on a still night. "The sight of such a coast," Darwin had written in his diary, "is enough to make a landsman dream for a week about death, peril, and shipwreck."

Others claim that the Pacific coast of the United States from northern California to the Straits of Juan de Fuca has a surf as heavy as any in the world. But it seems unlikely that any coast is visited more wrathfully by the sea's waves than the Shetlands and the Orkneys, in the path of the cyclonic storms that pass eastward between Iceland and the British Isles. All the feeling and the fury of such a storm, couched almost in Conradian prose, are contained in the usually prosaic *British Islands Pilot*:

> In the terrific gales which usually occur four or five times in every year all distinction between air and water is lost, the nearest objects are obscured by spray, and everything seems enveloped in a thick smoke; upon the open coast the sea rises at once, and striking upon the rocky shores rises in foam for several hundred feet and spreads over the whole country.
>
> The sea, however, is not so heavy in the violent gales of short continuance as when an ordinary gale has been blowing for many days; the whole force of the Atlantic is then beating against the shores of the Orkneys, rocks of many tons in weight are lifted from their beds, and the roar of the surge may be heard for twenty miles; the breakers rise to the height of 60 feet, and the broken sea on the North Shoal, which lies 12 miles northwestward of Costa Head, is visible at Skail and Birsay.

The first man who ever measured the force of an ocean wave was Thomas Stevenson, father of Robert Louis. Stevenson developed the instrument known as a wave dynamometer and with it studied the waves that battered the coast of his native Scotland. He found that in winter gales the force of a wave might be as great as 6000 pounds to the square foot. Perhaps it was waves of this strength that destroyed the breakwater at Wick on the coast of Scotland in a December storm in 1872. The seaward end of the Wick breakwater consisted of a block of concrete weighing more than 800 tons, bound solidly with iron rods to underlying blocks of stone. During the height of this winter gale the resident engineer watched the onslaught of the waves from a point on the cliff above the breakwater. Before his incredulous eyes, the block of concrete was lifted up and swept shoreward. After the storm had subsided divers investigated the wreckage. They found that not only the concrete monolith but the stones it was attached to had been carried away. The waves had torn loose, lifted, and bodily moved a mass weighing not less than 1350 tons, or 2,700,000 pounds. Five years later it became clear that this feat had been a mere dress rehearsal, for the new pier, weighing about 2600 tons, was then carried away in another storm.

A list of the perverse and freakish doings of the sea can easily be compiled from the records of the keepers of lights on lonely ledges at sea, or on rocky headlands exposed to the full strength of storm surf. At Unst, the most northern of the Shetland Islands, a door in the lighthouse was broken open 195 feet above the sea. At the Bishop Rock Light, on the English Channel, a bell was torn away from its attachment 100 feet above high water during a winter gale. About the Bell Rock Light on the coast of Scotland one November day a heavy ground swell was running, although there was no wind. Suddenly one of the swells rose about the tower, mounted to the gilded ball atop the lantern, 117 feet above the rock, and tore away a ladder that was attached to the tower 86 feet above the water. There have been happenings that, to some minds, are tinged with the supernatural, like that at the Eddystone Light in 1840. The entrance door of the tower had been made fast by strong bolts, as usual. During a night of heavy seas the door was broken open *from within*, and all its iron bolts and hinges were torn loose. Engineers say that such a thing happens as a result of pneumatic action—the sudden back draught created by the recession of a heavy wave combined with an abrupt release of pressure on the outside of the door.

On the Atlantic coast of the United States, the 97-foot tower on Minot's Ledge in Massachusetts is often completely enveloped by masses of water from breaking surf, and an earlier light on this ledge was swept away in 1851. Then there is the often quoted story of the December storm at Trinidad Head Light on the coast of northern California. As the keeper watched the storm from his lantern 196 feet above high water, he could see the near-by Pilot Rock engulfed again and again by waves that swept over its hundred-foot crest. Then a wave, larger than the rest, struck the cliffs at the base of the light. It seemed to rise in a solid wall of water to the level of the lantern, and it hurled its spray completely over the tower. The shock of the blow stopped the revolving of the light.

Along a rocky coast, the waves of a severe storm are likely to be armed with stones and rock fragments, which greatly increase their destructive power. Once a rock weighing 135 pounds was hurled high above the lightkeeper's house on Tillamook Rock on the coast of Oregon, 100 feet above sea level. In falling, it tore a 20-foot hole through the roof. The same day showers of smaller rocks broke many panes of glass in the lantern, 132 feet above the sea. The most amazing of such stories concerns the lighthouse at Dunnet Head, which stands on the summit of a 300-foot cliff at the southwestern entrance to Pentland Firth. The windows of this light have been broken repeatedly by stones swept from the cliff and tossed aloft by waves.

For millennia beyond computation, the sea's waves have battered the coastlines of the world with erosive effect, here cutting back a cliff, there stripping away tons of sand from a beach, and yet again, in a reversal of their destructiveness, building up a bar or a small island. Unlike the slow geologic changes that bring about the flooding of half a continent, the work of the waves is attuned to the brief span of human life, and so the sculpturing of the continent's edge is something each of us can see for ourselves.

The high clay cliff of Cape Cod, rising at Eastham and running north until it is lost in the sand dunes near Peaked Hill, is wearing back so fast that half of the ten acres which the Government acquired as a site for the Highland Light has disappeared, and the cliffs are said to be receding about three feet a year. Cape Cod is not old, in geologic terms, being the product of the glaciers of the most recent Ice Age, but apparently the waves have cut away, since its formation, a strip of land some two miles wide. At the present rate of erosion, the disappearance of the outer cape is foredoomed; it will presumably occur in another 4000 or 5000 years.

The sea's method on a rocky coast is to wear it down by grinding, to chisel out and wrench away fragments of rock, each of which becomes a tool to wear away the cliff. And as masses of rock are undercut, a whole huge mass will fall into the sea, there to be ground in the mill of the surf and to contribute more weapons for the attack. On a rocky shore this grinding and polishing of rocks and fragments of rocks goes on incessantly and audibly, for the breakers on such a coast have a different sound from those that have only sand to work with—a deep-toned mutter and rumble not easily forgotten, even by one who strolls casually along such a beach. Few people have heard the sounds of the surf mill practically from within the sea, as described by Henwood after his visit to a British mine extending out under the ocean:

> When standing beneath the base of the cliff, and in that part of the mine where but nine feet of rock stood between us and the ocean, the heavy roll of the larger boulders, the ceaseless grinding of the pebbles, the fierce thundering of the billows, with the crackling and boiling as they rebounded, placed a tempest in its most appalling form too vividly before me ever to be forgotten. More than once doubting the protection of our rocky shield we retreated in affright; and it was only after repeated trials that we had confidence to pursue our investigations.*

Great Britain, an island, has always been conscious of that "powerful marine gnawing" by which her coasts are eaten away. An old map dated 1786 and prepared by the county surveyor, John Tuke, gives a long list of lost towns and villages on the Holderness Coast. Among them are notations of Hornsea Burton, Hornsea Beck, and Hartburn—"washed away by the sea"; of Ancient Withernsea, Hyde, or Hythe—"lost by the sea." Many other old records allow comparison of present shorelines with former ones and show astonishing annual rates of cliff erosion on many parts of the coast—up to 15 feet at Holderness, 19 feet between Cromer and Mundesley, and 15 to 45 feet at Southwold. "The configuration of the coastline of Great Britain," one of her present engineers writes, "is not the same for two consecutive days."

And yet we owe some of the most beautiful and interesting shoreline scenery to the sculpturing effect of moving water. Sea caves are almost literally blasted out of the cliffs by waves, which pour into crevices in the rocks and force them apart

---

*From *Transactions*, Geol. Soc. Cornwall, vol. v, 1843.

by hydraulic pressure. Over the years the widening of fissures and the steady removal of fine rock particles in infinite number result in the excavation of a cave. Within such a cavern the weight of incoming water and the strange suctions and pressures caused by the movements of water in an enclosed space may continue the excavation upward. The roofs of such caves (and of overhanging cliffs) are subjected to blows like those from a battering ram as the water from a breaking wave is hurled upward, most of the energy of the wave passing into this smaller mass of water. Eventually a hole is torn through the roof of the cave, to form a spouting horn. Or, on a narrow promontory, what began as a cave may be cut through from side to side, so that a natural bridge is formed. Later, after years of erosion, the arch may fall, leaving the seaward mass of rock to stand alone—one of the strange, chimneylike formations known as a stack.

The sea waves that have fixed themselves most firmly in the human imagination are the so-called "tidal waves." The term is popularly applied to two very different kinds of waves, neither of which has any relation to the tide. One is a seismic sea wave produced by undersea earthquakes; the other is an exceptionally vast wind or storm wave—an immense mass of water driven by winds of hurricane force far above the normal high-water line.

Most of the seismic sea waves, now called "tsunamis," are born in the deepest trenches of the ocean floor. The Japanese, Aleutian, and Atacama trenches have each produced waves that claimed many human lives. Such a trench is, by its very nature, a breeder of earthquakes, being a place of disturbed and uneasy equilibrium, of buckling and warping downward of the sea floor to form the deepest pits of all the earth's surface. From the historic records of the ancients down to the modern newspaper, the writings of man contain frequent mention of the devastation of coastal settlements by these great waves that suddenly rise out of the sea. One of the earliest of record rose along the eastern shores of the Mediterranean in A.D. 358, passing completely over islands and low-lying shores, leaving boats on the housetops of Alexandria, and drowning thousands of people. After the Lisbon earthquake of 1755, the coast at Cadiz was visited by a wave said to have been 50 feet higher than the highest tide. This came about an hour after the earthquake. The waves from this same disturbance traveled across the Atlantic and reached the West Indies in 9½ hours. In 1868, a stretch of nearly 3000 miles of the western coast of South America was shaken by earthquakes. Shortly after the most violent shocks, the sea receded from the shore, leaving ships that had been anchored in 40 feet of water stranded in mud; then the water returned in a great wave, and boats were carried a quarter of a mile inland.

This ominous withdrawal of the sea from its normal stand is often the first warning of the approach of seismic sea waves. Natives on the beaches of Hawaii on the first of April 1946 were alarmed when the accustomed voice of the breakers was suddenly stilled, leaving a strange quiet. They could not know that this recession of the waves from the reefs and the shallow coastal waters was the sea's response to an earthquake on the steep slopes of a deep trench off the island of Unimak in the Aleutian chain, more than 2000 miles away; or that in a matter of moments the water would rise rapidly, as though the tide were coming in much too fast, but without surf. The rise carried the ocean waters 25 feet or more above the normal levels of the tide. According to an eyewitness account:

> The waves of the tsunami swept toward shore with steep fronts and great turbulence . . . Between crests the water withdrew from shore, exposing reefs, coastal mud-flats, and harbor bottoms for distances up to 500 feet or more from the normal strand-line. The outflow of the water was rapid and turbulent, making a loud hissing, roaring, and rattling noise. At several places houses were carried out to sea, and in some areas even large rocks and blocks of concrete were carried out onto the reefs . . . People and their belongings were swept to sea, some being rescued hours later by boats and life rafts dropped from planes.*

In the open ocean the waves produced by the Aleutian quake were only about a foot or two high and would not be noticed from vessels. Their length, however, was enormous, with a distance of about 90 miles between succeeding crests. It took the

*From *Annual Rept.*, Smithsonian Inst., 1947.

waves less than five hours to reach the Hawaiian chain, 2300 miles distant, so they must have moved at an average speed of about 470 miles per hour. Along eastern Pacific shores, they were recorded as far into the Southern Hemisphere as Valparaiso, Chile, the distance of 8066 miles from the epicenter being covered by the waves in about 18 hours.

This particular occurrence of seismic sea waves had one result that distinguished it from all its predecessors. It set people to thinking that perhaps we now know enough about such waves and how they behave that a warning system could be devised which would rob them of the terror of the unexpected. Seismologists and specialists on waves and tides co-operated, and now such a system has been established to protect the Hawaiian Islands. A network of stations equipped with special instruments is scattered over the Pacific from Kodiak to Pago Pago and from Balboa to Palau. There are two phases of the warning system. One is based on a new audible alarm at seismograph stations operated by the United States Coast and Geodetic Survey, which calls instant attention to the fact that an earthquake has occurred. If it is found that the epicenter of the quake is under the ocean and so might produce seismic sea waves, a warning is sent to observers at selected tide stations to watch their gauges for evidence of the passage of the racing tsunamis. (Even a very small seismic sea wave can be identified by its peculiar period, and though it may be small at one place, it may reach dangerous heights at another.) When seismologists in Honolulu are notified that an undersea earthquake has occurred and that its waves have actually been recorded at certain stations, they can calculate when the waves will arrive at any point between the epicenter of the quake and the Hawaiian Islands. They can then issue warnings for the evacuation of beaches and waterfront areas. And so, for the first time in history, there is an organized effort to prevent these ominous waves from racing undetected over the empty spaces of the Pacific, to roar up suddenly on some inhabited shore.[12]

The storm waves that sometimes rise over low-lying coast lands in hurricane zones belong in the class of wind waves, but unlike the waves of ordinary winds and storms, they are accompanied by a rise of the general water level, called a storm tide. The rise of water is often so sudden that it leaves no possibility of escape. Such storm waves claim about three-fourths of the lives lost by tropical hurricanes. The most notable disasters from storm waves in the United States have been those at Galveston, Texas, on 8 September, 1900, on the lower Florida Keys on 2 and 3 September, 1935, and the catastrophic rise of water accompanying the New England hurricane of 21 September, 1938. The most fearful destruction by hurricane waves within historic time occurred in the Bay of Bengal on 7 October, 1737, when 20,000 boats were destroyed and 300,000 people drowned.[13]

There are other great waves, usually called "rollers," that periodically rise on certain coasts and batter them for days with damaging surf. These, too, are wind waves, but they are related to changes in barometric pressure over the ocean, perhaps several thousand miles distant from the beaches on which the waves eventually arrive. Low-pressure areas—like the one south of Iceland—are notorious storm breeders, their winds lashing the sea into great waves. After the waves leave the storm area they tend to become lower and longer and after perhaps thousands of miles of travel across the sea they become transformed into the undulations known as a ground swell. These swells are so regular and so low that often they are unnoticed as they pass through the short, choppy, new-formed waves of other areas. But when a swell approaches a coast and feels beneath it the gradually shoaling bottom, it begins to "peak up" into a high, steep wave; within the surf zone the steepening becomes abruptly accentuated, a crest forms, breaks, and a great mass of water plunges downward.

Winter swell on the west coast of North America is the product of storms that travel south of the Aleutians into the Gulf of Alaska. Swell reaching this same coast during the summer has been traced back to its origin in the Southern Hemisphere belt of the "roaring forties," several thousand miles south of the equator. Because of the direction of the prevailing winds, the American east coast and the Gulf of Mexico do not receive the swell from far distant storms.

The coast of Morocco has always been particularly at the mercy of swell, for there is no protected harbor from the Strait of Gibraltar southward for some 500 miles. The rollers that visit the Atlantic islands of Ascension, St. Helena, South Trinidad, and Fernando de Noronha are historic. Apparently the same sort of waves occur on the South American coast near Rio de Janeiro, where they are known as *resacas*; others of kindred nature, having run their course from storms in the west-wind belt of the South Pacific, attack the shores of the Paumotos Islands; still others have been responsible for the well-known "surf days" that plague the Pacific coast of South America. According to Robert Cushman Murphy, it was formerly the custom of shipmasters in the guano trade to demand a special allowance for a certain number of days during which the loading of their vessels would be interrupted by the swell. On such surf days "mighty rollers come pouring over the sea wall, and have been known to carry away forty-ton freight cars, to uproot concrete piers, and to twist iron rails like wire."

The slow progression of swell from its place of origin made it possible for the Moroccan Protectorate to establish a service for the prediction of the state of the sea. This was done in 1921, after long and troublesome experience with wrecked vessels and wharves. Daily telegraphic reports of the condition of the sea give advance notice of troublesome surf days. Warned of the approach of swells, ships in port may seek safety in the open sea. Before this service was established, the port of Casablanca had once been paralyzed for seven months, and St. Helena had seen the wreckage of practically all the ships in her harbor on one or more occasions. Modern wave-recording instruments like those now being tested in England and the United States will soon provide even greater security for all such shores.

It is always the unseen that most deeply stirs our imagination, and so it is with waves. The largest and most awe-inspiring waves of the ocean are invisible; they move on their mysterious courses far down in the hidden depths of the sea, rolling ponderously and unceasingly. For many years it was known that the vessels of Arctic expeditions often became almost trapped and made headway only with difficulty in what was called "dead water"—now recognized as internal waves at the boundary between a thin surface layer of fresh water and the underlying salt water. In the early 1900's several Scandinavian hydrographers called attention to the existence of submarine waves, but another generation was to elapse before science had the instruments to study them thoroughly.

Now, even though mystery still surrounds the causes of these great waves that rise and fall, far below the surface, their ocean-wide occurrence is well established. Down in deep water they toss submarines about, just as their surface counterparts set ships to rolling. They seem to break against the Gulf Stream and other strong currents in a deep-sea version of the dramatic meeting of surface waves and opposing tidal currents. Probably internal waves occur wherever there is a boundary between layers of dissimilar water, just as the waves we see occur at the boundary between air and sea. But these are waves such as never moved at the surface of the ocean. The water masses involved are unthinkably great, some of the waves being as high as 300 feet.

Of their effect on fishes and other life of the deep sea we have only the faintest conception. Swedish scientists say that the herring are carried or drawn into some of the fiords of Sweden when the deep internal waves roll over the submerged sills and into the fiords. In the open ocean, we know that the boundary between water masses of different temperatures or salinities is often a barrier that may not be passed by living creatures, delicately adjusted to certain conditions. Do these creatures themselves then move up and down with the roll of the deep waves? And what happens to the bottom fauna of the continental slope, adjusted, it may be, to water of unchanging warmth? What is their fate when the waves move in from a region of arctic cold, rolling like a storm surf against those deep, dark slopes? At present we do not know. We can only sense that in the deep and turbulent recesses of the sea are hidden mysteries far greater than any we have solved.

Wind, Sun, and the Spinning of the Earth

> For thousands upon thousands of years the sunlight and the sea
> and the masterless winds have held tryst together.
>
> —LLEWELYN POWYS

As THE *Albatross III* groped through fog over Georges Bank all of one week in the midsummer of 1949, those of us aboard had a personal demonstration of the power of a great ocean current. There was never less than a hundred miles of cold Atlantic water between us and the Gulf Stream, but the winds blew persistently from the south and the warm breath of the Stream rolled over the Bank. The combination of warm air and cold water spelled unending fog. Day after day the *Albatross* moved in a small circular room, whose walls were soft gray curtains and whose floor had a glassy smoothness. Sometimes a petrel flew, with swallow-like flutterings, across this room, entering and leaving it by passing through its walls as if by sorcery. Evenings, the sun, before it set, was a pale silver disc hung in the ship's rigging, the drifting streamers of fog picking up a diffused radiance and creating a scene that set us to searching our memories for quotations from Coleridge. The sense of a powerful presence felt but not seen, its nearness made manifest but never revealed, was infinitely more dramatic than a direct encounter with the current.

The permanent currents of the ocean are, in a way, the most majestic of her phenomena. Reflecting upon them, our minds are at once taken out from the earth so that we can regard, as from another planet, the spinning of the globe, the winds that deeply trouble its surface or gently encompass it, and the influence of the sun and the moon. For all these cosmic forces are closely linked with the great currents of the ocean, earning for them the adjective I like best of all those applied to them—the planetary currents.

Since the world began, the ocean currents have undoubtedly changed their courses many times (we know, for example, that the Gulf Stream is no more than about 60 million years old); but it would be a bold writer who would try to describe their pattern in the Cambrian period, for example, or in the Devonian, or in the Jurassic. So far as the brief period of human history is concerned, however, it is most unlikely that there has been any important change in the major patterns of oceanic circulation, and the first thing that impresses us about the currents is their permanence. This is not surprising, for the forces that produce the currents show little disposition to change materially over the eons of earthly time. The primary driving power is supplied by the winds; the modifying influences are the sun, the revolving of the earth ever toward the east, and the obstructing masses of the continents.

The surface of the sea is unequally heated by the sun; as the water is warmed it expands and becomes lighter, while the cold water becomes heavier and more dense. Probably a slow exchange of polar and equatorial waters is brought about by these differences, the heated water of the tropics moving poleward in the upper layers, and polar water creeping toward the equator along the floor of the sea. But these movements are obscured and largely lost in the far greater sweep of the wind-driven currents. The steadiest winds are the trades, blowing diagonally toward the equator from the northeast and southeast. It is the trades that drive the equatorial currents around the globe. On wind and water alike, as on all that moves, be it a ship, a bullet, or a bird, the spinning earth exerts a deflecting force, turning all moving objects to the right in the Northern Hemisphere and to the left in the Southern. Through the combined action of these and other forces, the resulting current patterns are slowly circulating eddies, turning to the right, or clockwise, in the northern oceans, and to the left, or counterclockwise, in the southern.

There are exceptions, and the Indian Ocean, which seems never to be quite like the others, is an important one. Ruled by the capricious monsoons, its currents shift with the seasons. North of the equator, the direction of flow of immense masses of water may be either eastward or westward, depending on which of the monsoons is blowing. In the southern part of this ocean a fairly typical counterclockwise pattern exists: westward under the equator, south along the African coast, east to Australia on the westerly winds, northward by devious and seasonally shifting paths, here giving up water to the Pacific and there receiving contributions from it.

The Antarctic Ocean, being merely a continuous band of water encircling the globe, is another exception to the typical current pattern. Its waters are driven constantly into the east and the northeast by winds from the west and the southwest, and the currents are given speed by the quantities of fresh water pouring in from melting ice. It is not a closed circulation; water is given off, in surface currents and by deep paths, to the adjacent oceans, and in return other water is received from them.

It is in the Atlantic and Pacific that we see most clearly the interplay of cosmic forces producing the planetary currents.

Perhaps because of the long centuries over which the Atlantic has been crossed and recrossed by trade routes, its currents have been longest known to seafaring men and best studied by oceanographers. The strongly running Equatorial Currents were familiar to generations of seamen in the days of sail. So determined was their set to westward that vessels intending to pass down into the South Atlantic could make no headway unless they had gained the necessary easting in the region of the southeast trades. Ponce de Leon's three ships, sailing south from Cape Canaveral to Tortugas in 1513, sometimes were unable to stem the Gulf Stream, and "although they had great wind, they could not proceed forward, but backward." A few years later Spanish shipmasters learned to take advantage of the currents, sailing westward in the Equatorial Current, but returning home via the Gulf Stream as far as Cape Hatteras, whence they launched out into the open Atlantic.

The first chart of the Gulf Stream was prepared about 1769 under the direction of Benjamin Franklin while he was Deputy Postmaster General of the Colonies. The Board of Customs in Boston had complained that the mail packets coming from England took two weeks longer to make the westward crossing than did the Rhode Island merchant ships. Franklin, perplexed, took the problem to a Nantucket sea captain, Timothy Folger, who told him this might very well be true because the Rhode Island captains were well acquainted with the Gulf Stream and avoided it on the westward crossing, whereas the English captains were not. Folger and other Nantucket whalers were personally familiar with the Stream because, he explained,

> in our pursuit of whales, which keep to the sides of it but are not met within it, we run along the side and frequently cross it to change our side, and in crossing it have sometimes met and spoke with those packets who were in the middle of it and stemming it. We have informed them that they were stemming a current that was against them to the value of three miles an hour and advised them to cross it, but they were too wise to be counselled by simple American fishermen.*

Franklin, thinking "it was a pity no notice was taken of this current upon the charts," asked Folger to mark it out for him. The course of the Gulf Stream was then engraved on an old chart of the Atlantic and sent by Franklin to Falmouth, England, for the captains of the packets, "who slighted it, however." It was later printed in France and after the Revolution was published in the *Transactions of the American Philosophical Society*. The thriftiness of the Philosophical Society editors led them to combine in one plate Franklin's chart and a wholly separate figure intended to illustrate a paper by John Gilpin on the "Annual Migrations of the Herring." Some later historians have erroneously assumed a connection between Franklin's conception of the Gulf Stream and the insert in the upper left corner (see back end paper p. 408).

Were it not for the deflecting barrier of the Panamanian isthmus, the North Equatorial Current would cross into the Pacific, as indeed it must have done through the many geologic ages when the continents of North and South America were separated. After the Panama ridge was formed in the late Cretaceous period, the current was doubled back to the northeast to re-enter the Atlantic as the Gulf Stream. From the Yucatan Channel eastward through the Florida Straits the Stream attains impressive proportions. If thought of in the time-honored conception of a "river" in the sea, its width from bank to bank is 95 miles. It is a mile deep from surface to river bed. It flows with a velocity of nearly three knots and its volume is that of several hundred Mississippis.

*From Am. Phil. Soc. *Trans.*, vol. 2, 1786.

Even in these days of Diesel power, the coastwise shipping off southern Florida shows a wholesome respect for the Gulf Stream. Almost any day, if you are out in a small boat below Miami, you can see the big freighters and tankers moving south in a course that seems surprisingly close to the Keys. Landward is the almost unbroken wall of submerged reefs where the big niggerhead corals send their solid bulks up to within a fathom or two of the surface. To seaward is the Gulf Stream, and while the big boats could fight their way south against it, they would consume much time and fuel in doing so. Therefore they pick their way with care between the reefs and the Stream.

The energy of the Stream off southern Florida probably results from the fact that here it is actually flowing downhill. Strong easterly winds pile up so much surface water in the narrow Yucatan Channel and in the Gulf of Mexico that the sea level there is higher than in the open Atlantic. At Cedar Keys, on the Gulf coast of Florida, the level of the sea is 19 centimeters (about 7½ inches) higher than at St. Augustine. There is further unevenness of level within the current itself. The lighter water is deflected by the earth's rotation toward the right side of the current, so that within the Gulf Stream the sea surface actually slopes upward toward the right. Along the coast of Cuba, the ocean is about 18 inches higher than along the mainland, thus upsetting completely our notions that "sea level" is a literal expression.

Northward, the Stream follows the contours of the continental slope to the offing of Cape Hatteras, whence it turns more to seaward, deserting the sunken edge of the land. But it has left its impress on the continent. The four beautifully sculptured capes of the southern Atlantic coast—Canaveral, Fear, Lookout, Hatteras—apparently have been molded by powerful eddies set up by the passage of the Stream. Each is a cusp projecting seaward; between each pair of capes the beach runs in a long curving arc—the expression of the rhythmically swirling waters of the Gulf Stream eddies.

Beyond Hatteras, the Stream leaves the shelf, turning northeastward, as a narrow, meandering current, always sharply separated from the water on either side. Off the "tail" of the Grand Banks the line is most sharply drawn between the cold, bottle-green arctic water of the Labrador Current and the warm indigo blue of the Stream. In winter the temperature change across the current boundary is so abrupt that as a ship crosses into the Gulf Stream her bow may be momentarily in water 20° warmer than that at her stern, as though the "cold wall" were a solid barrier separating the two water masses. One of the densest fog banks in the world lies in this region over the cold water of the Labrador Current—a thick, blanketing whiteness that is the atmospheric response to the Gulf Stream's invasion of the cold northern seas.

Where the Stream feels the rise of the ocean floor known as the "tail" of the Grand Banks, it bends eastward and begins to spread out into many complexly curving tongues. Probably the force of the arctic water, the water that has come down from Baffin Bay and Greenland, freighting its icebergs, helps push the Stream to the east—that, and the deflecting force of the earth's rotation, always turning the currents to the right. The Labrador Current itself (being a southward-moving current) is turned in toward the mainland. The next time you wonder why the water is so cold at certain coastal resorts of the eastern United States, remember that the water of the Labrador Current is between you and the Gulf Stream.

Passing across the Atlantic, the Stream becomes less a current than a drift of water, fanning out in three main directions: southward into the Sargasso; northward into the Norwegian Sea, where it forms eddies and deep vortices; eastward to warm the coast of Europe (some of it even to pass into the Mediterranean) and thence as the Canary Current to rejoin the Equatorial Current and close the circuit.[14]

The Atlantic currents of the Southern Hemisphere are practically a mirror image of those of the Northern. The great spiral moves counterclockwise—west, south, east, north. Here the dominant current is in the eastern instead of the western part of the ocean. It is the Benguela Current, a river of cold water moving northward along the west coast of Africa. The South Equatorial Current, in mid-ocean a powerful stream (the *Challenger* scientists said it poured past St. Paul's Rocks like a millrace) loses a substantial part of its waters to the North Atlantic off the coast of South America—about 6 million cubic meters a second. The remainder becomes the Brazil Current, which circles south and then turns east as the South Atlantic

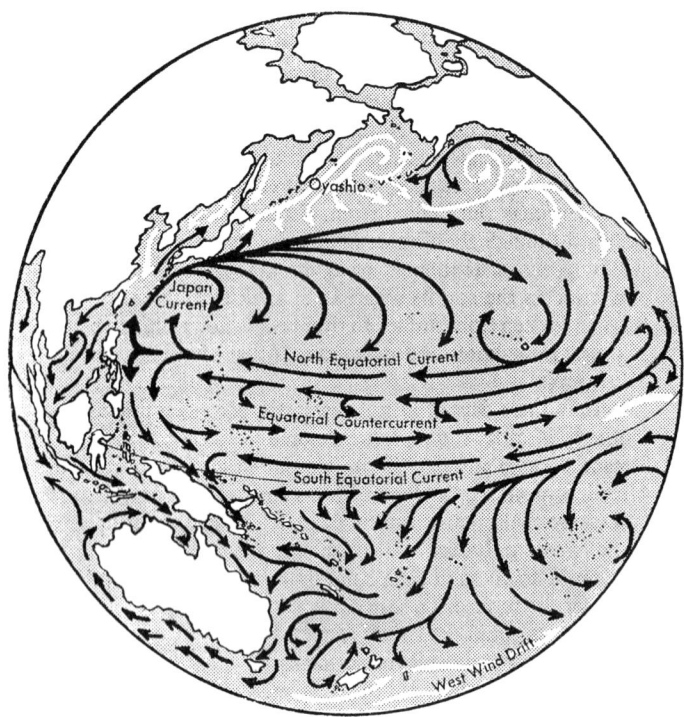

Course of the great, wind-driven current systems of the Atlantic and Pacific oceans. Cold currents appear in white; warm or intermediate ones in black.

or Antarctic Current. The whole is a system of shallow water movements, involving throughout much of its course not more than the upper hundred fathoms.

The North Equatorial Current of the Pacific is the longest westerly running current on earth, with nothing to deflect it in its 9000-mile course from Panama to the Philippines. There, meeting the barrier of the islands, most of it swings northward as the Japan Current—Asia's counterpart of the Gulf Stream. A small part persists on its westward course, feeling its way amid the labyrinth of Asiatic islands; part turns upon itself and streams back along the equator as the Equatorial Countercurrent. The Japan Current—called Kuroshio or Black Current because of the deep, indigo blue of its waters—rolls northward along the continental shelf off eastern Asia, until it is driven away from the continent by a mass of icy water—the Oyashio—that pours out of the Sea of Okhotsk and Bering Sea. The Japan Current and Oyashio meet in a region of fog and tempestuous winds, as, in the North Atlantic, the meeting of the Gulf Stream and the Labrador Current is marked with fog. Drifting toward America, the Japan Current forms the northern wall of the great North Pacific eddy. Its warm waters become chilled with infusions of cold polar water from Oyashio, the Aleutians, and Alaska. When it reaches the mainland of America it is a cool current, moving southward along the coast of California. There it is further cooled by updrafts of deep water and has much to do with the temperate summer climate of the American west coast. Off Lower California it rejoins the North Equatorial Current.

What with all the immensity of space in the South Pacific, we should expect to find here the most powerfully impressive of all ocean currents, but this does not seem to be true. The South Equatorial Current has its course so frequently interrupted by islands, which are forever deflecting streams of its water into the central basin, that by the time it approaches Asia it is, during most seasons, a comparatively feeble current, lost in a confused and ill-defined pattern around the East Indies and Australia.[15] The West Wind Drift or Antarctic Current—the poleward arc of the spiral—is born of the strongest winds in the world, roaring across stretches of ocean almost unbroken by land. The details of this, as of most of the currents of the

South Pacific, are but imperfectly known. Only one has been thoroughly studied—the Humboldt—and this has so direct an effect on human affairs that it overshadows all others.

The Humboldt Current, sometimes called the Peru, flows northward along the west coast of South America, carrying waters almost as cold as the Antarctic from which it comes. But its chill is actually that of the deep ocean, for the current is reinforced by almost continuous upwelling from lower oceanic layers. It is because of the Humboldt that penguins live almost under the equator, on the Galapagos Islands. In these cold waters, rich in minerals, there is an abundance of sea life perhaps unparalleled anywhere else in the world. The direct harvesters of this sea life are not men, but millions of sea birds. From the sun-baked accumulations of guano that whiten the coastal cliffs and islands, the South Americans obtain, at second hand, the wealth of the Humboldt Current.

Robert E. Coker, who studied the Peruvian guano industry at the request of that government, gives a vivid picture of the life of the Humboldt. He writes of

> . . . immense schools of small fishes, the anchobetas, which are followed by numbers of bonitos and other fishes and by sea lions, while at the same time they are preyed upon by the flocks of cormorants, pelicans, gannets, and other abundant sea birds . . . The long files of pelicans, the low-moving black clouds of cormorants, or the rainstorms of plunging gannets probably cannot be equaled in any other part of the world. The birds feed chiefly, almost exclusively, upon the anchobetas. The anchobeta, then, is not only . . . the food of the larger fishes, but, as the food of the birds, it is the source from which is derived each year probably a score of thousands of tons of high-grade bird guano.*

Dr. Coker estimated the annual consumption of fish by the guano-producing birds of Peru as equal to a fourth of the total production of all United States fisheries. Because of this diet, which links the birds with all the minerals of the sea, their excrement is the most valuable and efficient fertilizer in the world.

*From *Bulletin*, U. S. Bureau of Fisheries, vol. XXVIII, part 1, 1908, p. 338.

Leaving the coast of South America at about the latitude of Cape Blanco, the Humboldt Current turns westward into the Pacific, carrying its cool waters almost to the equator. About the Galapagos Islands it gives rise to a strange mixture of waters—the cool green of the Humboldt and the blue equatorial waters meeting in rips and foam lines, suggesting hidden movements and conflicts deep in the sea.

The conflict between opposing water masses may, in places, be one of the most dramatic of the ocean's phenomena. Superficial hissings and sighings, the striping of the surface waters with lines of froth, a confused turbulence and boiling, and even sounds like distant breakers accompany the displacement of the surface layers by deep water. As visible evidence of the upward movement of the water masses, some of the creatures that inhabit the deeper places of the sea may be carried up bodily into the surface, there to set off orgies of devouring and being devoured such as Robert Cushman Murphy witnessed one night off the coast of Colombia from the schooner *Askoy*. The night had been still and dark, but the behavior of the surface made it clear that deep water was rising and that some sort of conflict was in progress among opposing water masses far below the ship. All about the schooner small, steep waves leaped into being and dissolved in foaming whitecaps, pricked with the blue fire of luminescent organisms. Suddenly,

> On either side, and at a bafflingly uncertain distance from the ship, a dark line, like a wall of advancing water, seemed to be closing in upon us . . . We could hear the splash and murmur of a troubled surface close by . . . Presently we could see a gleam of foam sprinkled with points of luminescence on the slowly approaching swell or head to the left. Vague and unfounded thoughts of marine earthquake bores occurred to Fallon and me together, and we felt peculiarly helpless with a dismantled engine and no breeze to make the craft answer her helm. The dreamlike slowness of all that was going on, moreover, gave me a feeling that I had not yet fully shaken off the bonds of three hours' slumber.
>
> However, when the dark, white-outlined menace reached us, it proved to be nothing more than a field of the dancing water, tossing its little peaks a mere foot or so into the air and beating a tattoo on the steel flanks of "Askoy" . . .

Presently a sharp hissing sound, different in character from the bursting of small waves, came out of the darkness to starboard, and this was followed by strange sighings and puffings . . . The puffers were blackfish, many scores, or perhaps hundreds of them, rolling and lumbering along and diving to pass beneath "Askoy" shortly before they reached her bilge . . . We could hear the bacchanalian clamor of their rumblings and belchings. In the long beam of the searchlight, the hissing proved to come from the jumping of small fishes. In all directions as far as the light carried, they were shooting into the air and pouring down like hail . . .

The surface was seething, boiling with life, much of which was *de profundis.* Larvae of clawless lobsters, tinted jellyfish, nurse chains of salps, small herringlike fishes, a silvery hatchetfish with its face bitten off, rudder fishes, hanging head downward, luminous lantern-fishes with shining light pores, red and purple swimming crabs, other creatures which we could not name at sight and much that was too small even to see distinctly . . .

A general holocaust was in progress. The little fishes were eating invertebrates or straining out the plankton; the squids were pursuing and capturing fish of various sizes; and the blackfish were no doubt enjoying the squids . . .

As the night wore on, the amazing manifestations of abundance and devouring gradually, almost imperceptibly, died away. Eventually, "Askoy" lay once more in water that seemed as still and dead as oil, and the lap-lap of skipping waves drew off farther and farther into the distance until it was lost.*

Although such exciting displays of upwelling are seen and recognized by comparatively few people, the process takes place regularly off a number of coasts and at many places in the open ocean. Wherever it occurs, it is responsible for a profusion of life. Some of the world's largest fisheries are dependent on upwelling. The coast of Algeria is famous for its sardine fisheries; the sardines are abundant here because upward streams of deep, cold water provide the minerals to support astronomical numbers of diatoms. The west coast of Morocco, the area opposite the Canary and Cape Verde islands, and the southwest coast of Africa are other sites of

---

*From *Natural History*, vol. LIII, no. 8, 1944, p. 356.

extensive upwelling and consequent richness of marine life. There is an amazingly abundant fish fauna in the Arabian Sea near Oman and on the Somali Coast near Cape Hafun, both occurring in areas of cold water rising from the depths. In the South Equatorial Current north of Ascension Island is a "tongue of cold" produced by the rise of sea water from the bottom. It is extraordinarily rich in plankton. Upwelling around the island of South Georgia, east of Cape Horn, makes this one of the world's centers of whaling. On the west coast of the United States the catch of sardines is sometimes as much as a billion pounds in a year, supporting one of the largest fisheries in the world. The fishery could not exist except for upwelling, which sets off the old, familiar biological chain: salts, diatoms, copepods, herring. Down along the west coast of South America, the astonishing profusion of life in the Humboldt is maintained by upwelling, which not only keeps the waters of the current cold in all its 2500-mile course to the Galapagos Islands but brings up the nutrient salts from the deeper layers.

When upwelling takes place along coastlines, it is the result of the interplay of several forces—the winds, the surface currents, the rotation of the earth, and the shape of the hidden slopes of the continent's foundations. When the winds, combined with the deflecting effect of rotation, blow the surface waters offshore, deep water must rise to replace it.

Upwelling may occur in the open sea as well, but from entirely different causes. Wherever two strongly moving currents diverge, water must rise from below to fill the place where the streams separate. One such place lies at the westernmost bounds of the Equatorial Current in the Pacific, where the powerfully moving stream turns and pours part of its waters back into the countercurrent, and part northward toward Japan. These are confused and turbulent waters. There is the strong pull to the north by which the main stream, sensitive to the force of the rotating earth, turns to the right. There are the swirls and eddies by which the lesser stream turns again upon itself and flows back into the eastern Pacific. There is the rushing up from below to fill the otherwise deepening groove between the streams. In the resulting disquietude of the ocean waters, chilled and enriched from below, the smaller organisms of the plankton thrive. As they multiply, they provide food for the larger plankton creatures, which, in turn, provide food for squid and fish. These waters are prodigiously rich in life, and there is evidence that they may have been so for many thousands of years. Swedish oceanographers recently found that under these areas of divergence the sediment layer is exceptionally thick—the layer composed of all that remains of the billions upon billions of minute creatures that have lived and died in this place.

The downward movement of surface water into the depths is an occurrence as dramatic as upwelling, and perhaps it fills the human mind with an even greater sense of awe and mystery, because it cannot be seen but can only be imagined. At several known places the downward flow of enormous quantities of water takes place regularly. This water feeds the deep currents of whose courses we have only the dimmest knowledge. We do know that it is all part of the ocean's system of balances, by which she pays back to one part of her waters what she had latterly borrowed for distribution to another.

The North Atlantic, for example, receives quantities of surface water (some 6 million cubic meters a second) from the South Atlantic via the Equatorial Current. The return payment is made at deep levels, partly in very cold arctic water, and partly in some of the saltiest, warmest water in the world, that of the Mediterranean. There are two places for the down-flow of arctic water. One is in the Labrador Sea. Another is southeast of Greenland. At each the quantity of sinking water is prodigious —some 2 million cubic meters a second. The deep Mediterranean water flows out over the sill that separates the basin of the Mediterranean from the open Atlantic. This sill lies about 150 fathoms beneath the surface of the sea. The water that spills over its rocky edge does so because of the unusual conditions that prevail in the Mediterranean. The hot sun beating down on its nearly enclosed water creates an extraordinarily high rate of evaporation, drawing off into the atmosphere more water than is added by the inflow of rivers. The water becomes ever saltier and more dense; as evaporation continues the surface of the Mediterranean falls below that of the Atlantic. To correct the inequality, lighter water from the Atlantic pours past Gibraltar in surface streams of great strength.

Now we give the matter little thought, but in the days of sail, passage out into the Atlantic was a difficult problem because of this surface current. An old ship's log of the year 1855 has this to say of the current and its practical effect:

> Weather fine; made 1¼ pt. leeway. At noon, stood in to Almira Bay, and anchored off the village of Roguetas. Found a great number of vessels waiting for a chance to get to the westward, and learned from them that at least a thousand sail are weather-bound between this and Gibraltar. Some of them have been so for six weeks, and have even got so far as Malaga, only to be swept back by the current. Indeed, no vessel has been able to get out into the Atlantic for three months past.

Later measurements show that these surface currents flow into the Mediterranean with an average velocity of about three knots. The bottom current, moving out into the Atlantic, is even stronger. Its outward flow is so vigorous that it has been known to wreck oceanographic instruments sent down to measure it, apparently pounding them against stones on the bottom; and once the wire of the Falmouth cable near Gibraltar "was ground like the edge of a razor, so that it had to be abandoned and a new one laid well inshore."

The water that sinks in the arctic regions of the Atlantic, as well as that spilling over the Gibraltar sill, spreads out widely into the deeper parts of the ocean basins. Traversing the North Atlantic, it crosses the equator and continues to the south, there passing between two layers of water that are moving northward from the Antarctic Sea. Some of this antarctic water mingles with the Atlantic water—that from Greenland and Labrador and the Mediterranean—and with it returns south. But other antarctic water moves northward across the equator and has been traced as far as the latitude of Cape Hatteras.

The flow of these deep waters is hardly a "flow" at all; its pace is ponderously slow, the measured creep of icy, heavy water. But the volumes involved are prodigious, and the areas covered world-wide. It may even be that the deep ocean water, on such global wanderings, acts to distribute some of the marine fauna—not the surface forms but the dwellers in deep, dark layers. From our knowledge of the source of the currents, it seems significant that some of the same species of deep-water invertebrates and fishes have been collected off the coast of South Africa and off Greenland. And about Bermuda, where a greater variety of deep-water forms has been found than anywhere else, there is a mingling of deep water from the Antarctic, the Arctic, and the Mediterranean. Perhaps in these sunless streams the weird inhabitants of deep waters drift, generation after generation, surviving and multiplying because of the almost changeless character of these slowly moving currents.

There is, then, no water that is wholly of the Pacific, or wholly of the Atlantic, or of the Indian or the Antarctic. The surf that we find exhilarating at Virginia Beach or at La Jolla today may have lapped at the base of antarctic icebergs or sparkled in the Mediterranean sun, years ago, before it moved through dark and unseen waterways to the place we find it now. It is by the deep, hidden currents that the oceans are made one.

The Moving Tides

In every country the moon keeps ever the rule of alliance with
the sea which it once for all has agreed upon.

—THE VENERABLE BEDE

THERE IS NO drop of water in the ocean, not even in the deepest parts of the abyss, that does not know and respond to the mysterious forces that create the tide. No other force that affects the sea is so strong. Compared with the tide the wind-created waves are surface movements felt, at most, no more than a hundred fathoms below the surface. So, despite their impressive sweep, are the planetary currents, which seldom involve more than the upper several hundred fathoms. The masses of water affected by the tidal movement are enormous, as will be clear from one example. Into one small bay on the east coast of North America—Passamaquoddy—2 billion tons of water are carried by the tidal currents twice each day; into the whole Bay of Fundy, 100 billion tons.

Here and there we find dramatic illustration of the fact that the tides affect the whole ocean, from its surface to its floor. The meeting of opposing tidal currents in the Strait of Messina creates whirlpools (one of them is Charybdis of classical fame) which so deeply stir the waters of the strait that fish bearing all the marks of abyssal existence, their eyes atrophied or abnormally large, their bodies studded with phosphorescent organs, frequently are cast up on the lighthouse beach, and the whole area yields a rich collection of deep-sea fauna for the Institute of Marine Biology at Messina.

The tides are a response of the mobile waters of the ocean to the pull of the moon and the more distant sun. In theory, there is a gravitational attraction between every drop of sea water and even the outermost star of the universe. In practice, however, the pull of the remote stars is so slight as to be obliterated in the vaster movements by which the ocean yields to the moon and the sun. Anyone who has lived near tidewater knows that the moon, far more than the sun, controls the tides. He has noticed that, just as the moon rises later each day by fifty minutes, on the average, than the day before, so, in most places, the time of high tide is correspondingly later each day. And as the moon waxes and wanes in its monthly cycle, so the height of the tide varies. Twice each month, when the moon is a mere thread of silver in the sky, and again when it is full, we have the strongest tidal movements—the highest flood tides and the lowest ebb tides of the lunar month. These are called the spring tides. At these times sun, moon, and earth are directly in line and the pull of the two heavenly bodies is added together to bring the water high on the beaches, and send its surf leaping upward against the sea cliffs, and draw a brimming tide into the harbors so that the boats float high beside their wharfs. And twice each month, at the quarters of the moon, when sun, moon, and earth lie at the apexes of a triangle, and the pull of sun and moon are opposed, we have the moderate tidal movements called the neap tides. Then the difference between high and lower water is less than at any other time during the month.

That the sun, with a mass 27 million times that of the moon, should have less influence over the tides than a small satellite of the earth is at first surprising. But in the mechanics of the universe, nearness counts for more than distant mass, and when all the mathematical calculations have been made we find that the moon's power over the tides is more than twice that of the sun.

The tides are enormously more complicated than all this would suggest. The influence of sun and moon is constantly changing, varying with the phases of the moon, with the distance of moon and sun from the earth, and with the position of each to north or south of the equator. They are complicated further by the fact that every body of water, whether natural or artificial, has its own period of oscillation. Disturb its waters and they will move with a seesaw or rocking motion, with the most pronounced movement at the ends of the container, the least motion at the center. Tidal scientists now believe that the ocean contains a number of "basins," each with its own period of oscillation determined by its length and depth. The disturbance that sets the water in motion is the attracting force of the moon and sun. But the kind of motion, that is, the period of the swing of the water, depends upon the physical dimensions of the basin. What this means in terms of actual tides we shall presently see.

The tides present a striking paradox, and the essence of it is this: the force that sets them in motion is cosmic, lying wholly outside the earth and presumably acting impartially on all parts of the globe, but the nature of the tide at any particular place is a local matter, with astonishing differences occurring within a very short geographic distance. When we spend a long summer holiday at the seashore we may become aware that the tide in our cove behaves very differently from that at a friend's place twenty miles up the coast, and is strikingly different from what we may have known in some other locality. If we are summering on Nantucket Island our boating and swimming will be little disturbed by the tides, for the range between high water and low is only about a foot or two. But if we choose to vacation near the upper part of the Bay of Fundy, we must accommodate ourselves to a rise and fall of 40 to 50 feet, although both places are included within the same body of water—the Gulf of Maine. Or if we spend our holiday on Chesapeake Bay we may find that the time of high water each day varies by as much as 12 hours in different places on the shores of the same bay.

The truth of the matter is that local topography is all-important in determining the features that to our minds make "the tide." The attractive force of the heavenly bodies sets the water in motion, but how, and how far, and how strongly it will rise depend on such things as the slope of the bottom, the depth of a channel, or the width of a bay's entrance.

The United States Coast and Geodetic Survey has a remarkable, robotlike machine with which it can predict the time and height of the tide on any past or future date, for any part of the world, on one essential condition. This is that at some time local observations must have been made to show how the topographic features of the place modify and direct the tidal movements.

Perhaps the most striking differences are in the range of tide, which varies tremendously in different parts of the world, so that what the inhabitants of one place might consider disastrously high water might be regarded as no tide at all by coastal communities only a hundred miles distant. The highest tides in the world occur in the Bay of Fundy, with a rise of about 50 feet in Minas Basin near the head of the Bay at the spring tides.

At least half a dozen other places scattered around the world have a tidal range of more than 30 feet—Puerto Gallegos in Argentina and Cook Inlet in Alaska, Frobisher Bay in Davis Strait, the Koksoak River emptying into Hudson Strait, and the Bay of St. Malo in France come to mind. At many other places "high tide" may mean a rise of only a foot or so, perhaps only a few inches. The tides of Tahiti rise and fall in a gentle movement, with a difference of no more than a foot between high water and low. On most oceanic islands the range of the tide is slight. But it is never safe to generalize about the kinds of places that have high or low tides, because two areas that are not far apart may respond in very different ways to the tide-producing forces. At the Atlantic end of the Panama Canal the tidal range is not more than 1 or 2 feet, but at the Pacific end, only 40 miles away, the range is 12 to 16 feet. The Sea of Okhotsk is another example of the way the height of the tide varies. Throughout much of the Sea the tides are moderate —only about 2 feet—but in some parts of the Sea there is a 10-foot rise, and at the head of one of its arms—the Gulf of Penjinsk—the rise is 37 feet.

What is it about one place that will bring 40 or 50 feet of water rising about its shores, while at another place lying under the same moon and sun, the tide will rise only a few inches? What, for example, can be the explanation of the great tides on the Bay of Fundy, while only a few hundred miles away at Nantucket Island, on the shores of the same ocean, the tide range is little more than a foot?

The modern theory of tidal oscillation seems to offer the best explanation of such local differences—the rocking up and down of water in each natural basin about a central, virtually tideless node. Nantucket is located near the node of its basin, where there is little motion, hence a small tide range. Passing northeastward along the shores of this basin, we find the tides becoming progressively higher, with a 6-foot range at Nauset Harbor on Cape Cod, 8.9 feet at Gloucester, 15.7 feet at West Quoddy Head, 20.9 feet at St. John, and 39.4 feet at Folly Point. The Nova Scotia shore of the Bay of Fundy has somewhat higher tides than the corresponding points on the New Brunswick shore, and the highest tides of all are in Minas Basin at the head of the Bay. The immense movements of water in the Bay of Fundy result from a combination of circumstances. The bay lies at the end of an oscillating basin. Furthermore, the natural period of oscillation of the basin is approximately 12 hours. This very nearly coincides with the period of the ocean tide. Therefore the water movement within the bay is sustained and enormously increased by the ocean tide. The narrowing and shallowing of the bay in its upper reaches, compelling the huge masses of water to crowd into a constantly diminishing area, also contribute to the great heights of the Fundy tides.

The tidal rhythms, as well as the range of tide, vary from ocean to ocean. Flood tide and ebb succeed each other around the world, as night follows day, but as to whether there shall be two high tides and two low in each lunar day, or only one, there is no unvarying rule. To those who know best the Atlantic Ocean—either its eastern or western shores—the rhythm of two high tides and two low tides in each day seems "normal." Here, on each flood tide, the water advances about as far as the preceding high; and succeeding ebb tides fall about equally low. But in that great inland sea of the Atlantic, the Gulf of Mexico, a different rhythm prevails around most of its borders. At best the tidal rise here is but a slight movement, of no more than a foot or two. At certain places on the shores of the Gulf it is a long, deliberate undulation—one rise and one fall in the lunar day of 24 hours plus 50 minutes—resembling the untroubled breathing of that earth monster to whom the ancients attributed all tides. This "diurnal rhythm" is found in scattered places about the earth—such as at Saint Michael, Alaska, and at Do Son in French Indo-China—as well as in the Gulf of Mexico. By far the greater part of the world's coasts—most of the Pacific basin and the shores of the Indian Ocean—display a mixture of the diurnal and semidiurnal types of tide. There are two high and two low tides in a day, but the succeeding floods may be so unequal that the second scarcely rises to mean sea level; or it may be the ebb tides that are of extreme inequality.

There seems to be no simple explanation of why some parts of the ocean should respond to the pull of sun and moon with one rhythm and other parts with another, although the matter is perfectly clear to tidal scientists on the basis of mathematical calculations. To gain some inkling of the reasons, we must recall the many separate components of the tide-producing force, which in turn result from the changing relative positions of sun, moon, and earth. Depending on local geographic features, every part of earth and sea, while affected in some degree by each component, is more responsive to some than to others. Presumably the shape and depths of the Atlantic basin cause it to respond most strongly to the forces that produce a semidiurnal rhythm. The Pacific and Indian oceans, on the other hand, are affected by both the diurnal and semidiurnal forces, and a mixed tide results.

The island of Tahiti is a classic example of the way even a small area may react to one of the tide-producing forces to the virtual exclusion of the others. On Tahiti, it is sometimes said, you can tell the time of day by looking out at the beach and noticing the stage of the tide. This is not strictly true, but the legend has a certain basis. With slight variations, high tide occurs at noon and at midnight; low water, at six o'clock morning and evening. The tides thus ignore the effect of the moon, which is to advance the time of the tides by 50 minutes each day. Why should the tides of Tahiti follow the sun instead of the moon? The most favored explanation is that the island lies at the axis or node of one of the basins set in oscillation by the moon. There is very little motion in response to the moon at this point, and the waters are therefore free to move in the rhythm induced by the sun.

If the history of the earth's tides should one day be written by some observer of the universe, it would no doubt be said that they reached their greatest grandeur and power in the younger days of Earth, and that they slowly grew feebler and less imposing until one day they ceased to be. For the tides were not always as they are today, and as with all that is earthly, their days are numbered.

In the days when the earth was young, the coming in of the tide must have been a stupendous event. If the moon was, as we have supposed in an earlier chapter, formed by the tearing away of a part of the outer crust of the earth, it must have remained for a time very close to its parent. Its present position is the consequence of being pushed farther and farther away from the earth for some 2 billion years. When it was half its present distance from the earth, its power over the ocean tides was eight times as great as now, and the tidal range may even then have been several hundred feet on certain shores. But when the earth was only a few million years old, assuming that the deep ocean basins were then formed, the sweep of the tides must have been beyond all comprehension. Twice each day, the fury of the incoming waters would inundate all the margins of the continents. The range of the surf must have been enormously extended by the reach of the tides, so that the waves would batter the crests of high cliffs and sweep inland to erode the continents. The fury of such tides would contribute not a little to the general bleakness and grimness and uninhabitability of the young earth.

Under such conditions, no living thing could exist on the shores or pass beyond them, and, had conditions not changed, it is reasonable to suppose that life would have evolved no further than the fishes. But over the millions of years the moon has receded, driven away by the friction of the tides it creates. The very movement of the water over the bed of the ocean, over the shallow edges of the continents, and over the inland seas carries within itself the power that is slowly destroying the tides, for tidal friction is gradually slowing down the rotation of the earth. In those early days we have spoken of, it took the earth a much shorter time—perhaps only about 4 hours—to make a complete rotation on its axis. Since then, the spinning of the globe has been so greatly slowed that a rotation now requires, as everyone knows, about 24 hours. This retarding will continue, according to mathematicians, until the day is about 50 times as long as it is now.

And all the while the tidal friction will be exerting a second effect, pushing the moon farther away, just as it has already pushed it out more than 200,000 miles. (According to the laws of mechanics, as the rotation of the earth is retarded, that of the moon must be accelerated, and centrifugal force will carry it farther away.) As the moon recedes, it will, of course, have less power over the tides and they will grow weaker. It will also take the moon longer to complete its orbit around the earth. When finally the length of the day and of the month coincide, the moon will no longer rotate relatively to the earth, and there will be no lunar tides.

All this, of course, will require time on a scale the mind finds it difficult to conceive, and before it happens it is quite probable that the human race will have vanished from the earth. This may seem, then, like a Wellsian fantasy of a world so remote that we may dismiss it from our thoughts. But already, even in our allotted fraction of earthly time, we can see some of the effects of these cosmic processes. Our day is believed to be several seconds longer than that of Babylonian times. Britain's Astronomer Royal recently called the attention of the American Philosophical Society to the fact that the world will soon have to choose between two kinds of time. The tide-induced lengthening of the day has already complicated the problems of human systems of keeping time. Conventional clocks, geared to the earth's rotation, do not show the effect of the lengthening days. New atomic clocks now being constructed will show actual time and will differ from other clocks.

Although the tides have become tamer, and their range is now measured in tens instead of hundreds of feet, mariners are nevertheless greatly concerned not only with the stages of the tide and the set of the tidal currents, but with the many violent movements and disturbances of the sea that are indirectly related to the tides. Nothing the human mind has invented can tame a tide rip or control the rhythm of the water's ebb and flow, and the most modern instruments cannot carry a vessel over a shoal until the tide has brought a sufficient depth of water over it. Even the *Queen Mary* waits for slack water to come to her pier in New York; otherwise the set of the tidal current might swing her against the pier with enough force to crush it. On the Bay of Fundy, because of the great range of tide, harbor activities in some of the ports follow a pattern as rhythmic as the tides themselves, for vessels can come to the docks to take on or discharge cargo during only a few hours on each tide, leaving promptly to avoid being stranded in mud at low water.

In the confinement of narrow passages or when opposed by contrary winds and swells, the tidal currents often move with uncontrollable violence, creating some of the most dangerous waterways of the world. It is only necessary to read the Coast Pilots and Sailing Directions for various parts of the world to understand the menace of such tidal currents to navigation.

"Vessels around the Aleutians are in more danger from tidal currents than from any other cause, save the lack of surveys," says the postwar edition of the *Alaska Pilot*. Through Unalga and Akutan passes, which are among the most-used routes for vessels entering Bering Sea from the Pacific, strong tidal currents pour, making their force felt well offshore and setting vessels unexpectedly against the rocks. Through Akun Strait the flood tide has the velocity of a mountain torrent, with dangerous swirls and overfalls. In each of these passes the tide will raise heavy, choppy seas if opposed by wind or swells. "Vessels must be prepared to take seas aboard," warns the *Pilot*, for a 15-foot wave of a tide rip may suddenly rise and sweep across a vessel, and more than one man has been carried off to his death in this way.

On the opposite side of the world, the tide setting eastward from the open Atlantic presses between the islands of the Shetlands and Orkneys into the North Sea, and on the ebb returns through the same narrow passages. At certain stages of the tide these waters are dotted with dangerous eddies, with strange upward domings, or with sinister pits or depressions. Even in calm weather boats are warned to avoid the eddies of Pentland Firth, which are known as the Swilkie; and with an ebb tide and a northwest wind the heavy breaking seas of the Swilkie are a menace to vessels "which few, having once experienced, would be rash enough to encounter a second time."

Edgar Allan Poe, in his "Descent into the Maelstrom," converted one of the more evil manifestations of the tide into literature. Few who have read the story will forget its drama —how the old man led his companion to a mountain cliff high above the sea and let him watch the water far below in the narrow passageway between the islands, with its sinister foam and scum, its uneasy bubbling and boiling, until suddenly the whirlpool was formed before his eyes and rushed with an appalling sound through the narrow waterway. Then the old man told the story of his own descent into the whirlpool and of his miraculous escape. Most of us have wondered how much of the story was fact, how much the creation of Poe's fertile imagination. There actually is a Maelstrom and it exists where Poe placed it, between two of the islands of the Lofoten group off the west coast of Norway. It is, as he described it, a gigantic whirlpool or series of whirlpools, and men with their boats have actually been drawn down into these spinning funnels of water. Although Poe's account exaggerates certain details, the essential facts on which he based his narrative are verified in the *Sailing Directions for the Northwest and North Coasts of Norway*, a practical and circumstantial document:

> Though rumor has greatly exaggerated the importance of the Malström, or more properly Moskenstraumen, which runs between Mosken and Lofotodden, it is still the most dangerous tideway in Lofoten, its violence being due, in great measure, to the irregularity of the ground . . . As the strength of the tide increases the sea becomes heavier and the current more irregular, forming extensive eddies or whirlpools (Malström). During such periods no vessel should enter the Moskenstraumen.
>
> These whirlpools are cavities in the form of an inverted bell, wide and rounded at the mouth and narrower toward the bottom; they are largest when first formed and are carried along with the current, diminishing gradually until they disappear; before the extinction of one, two or three more will appear, following each other like so many pits in the sea . . . Fishermen affirm that if they are aware of their approach to a whirlpool and have time to throw an oar or any other bulky body into it they will get over it safely; the reason is that when the continuity is broken and the whirling motion of the sea interrupted by something thrown into it the water must rush suddenly in on all sides and fill up the cavity. For the same reason, in strong breezes, when the waves break, though there may be a whirling round, there can be no cavity. In the Saltström boats and men have been drawn down by these vortices, and much loss of life has resulted.

Among unusual creations of the tide, perhaps the best known are the bores. The world possesses half a dozen or more famous ones. A bore is created when a great part of the flood tide enters a river as a single wave, or at most two or three waves, with a steep and high front. The conditions that produce bores are several: there must be a considerable range of tide, combined with sand bars or other obstructions in the mouth of the river, so that the tide is hindered and held back, until it finally gathers itself together and rushes through. The Amazon is remarkable for the distance its bore travels upstream —some 200 miles—with the result that the bores of as many as 5 flood tides may actually be moving up the river at one time.

On the Tsientang River, which empties into the China Sea, all shipping is controlled by the bore—the largest, most dangerous, and best known in the world. The ancient Chinese used to throw offerings into the river to appease the angry spirit of this bore, whose size and fury appear to have varied from century to century, or perhaps even from decade to decade, as the silting of the estuary has shifted and changed. During most of the month the bore now advances up the river in a wave 8 to 11 feet high, moving at a speed of 12 to 13 knots, its front "a sloping cascade of bubbling foam, falling forward and pounding on itself and on the river." Its full ferocity is reserved for the spring tides of the full moon and the new moon, at which times the crest of the advancing wave is said to rise 25 feet above the surface of the river.

There are bores, though none so spectacular, in North America. There is one at Moncton, on New Brunswick's Petitcodiac River, but it is impressive only on the spring tides of the full or new moon. At Turnagain Arm in Cook Inlet, Alaska, where the tides are high and the currents strong, the flood tide under certain conditions comes in as a bore. Its advancing front may be four to six feet high and is recognized as being so dangerous to small craft that boats are beached well above the level of the flats when the bore is approaching. It can be heard about half an hour before its arrival at any point, traveling slowly with a sound as of breakers on a beach.

The influence of the tide over the affairs of sea creatures as well as men may be seen all over the world. The billions upon billions of sessile animals, like oysters, mussels, and barnacles, owe their very existence to the sweep of the tides, which brings them the food which they are unable to go in search of. By marvelous adaptations of form and structure, the inhabitants of the world between the tide lines are enabled to live in a zone where the danger of being dried up is matched against the danger of being washed away, where for every enemy that comes by sea there is another that comes by land, and where the most delicate of living tissues must somehow withstand the assault of storm waves that have the power to shift tons of rock or to crack the hardest granite.

The most curious and incredibly delicate adaptations, however, are the ones by which the breeding rhythm of certain marine animals is timed to coincide with the phases of the moon and the stages of the tide. In Europe it has been well established that the spawning activities of oysters reach their peak on the spring tides, which are about two days after the full or the new moon. In the waters of northern Africa there is a sea urchin that, on the nights when the moon is full and apparently only then, releases its reproductive cells into the sea. And in tropical waters in many parts of the world there are small marine worms whose spawning behavior is so precisely adjusted to the tidal calendar that, merely from observing them, one could tell the month, the day, and often the time of day as well.

Near Samoa in the Pacific, the palolo worm lives out its life on the bottom of the shallow sea, in holes in the rocks and among the masses of corals. Twice each year, during the neap tides of the moon's last quarter in October and November, the worms forsake their burrows and rise to the surface in swarms that cover the water. For this purpose, each worm has literally broken its body in two, half to remain in its rocky tunnel, half to carry the reproductive products to the surface and there to liberate the cells. This happens at dawn on the day before the moon reaches its last quarter, and again on the following day; on the second day of the spawning the quantity of eggs liberated is so great that the sea is discolored.

The Fijians, whose waters have a similar worm, call them "Mbalolo" and have designated the periods of their spawning "Mbalolo lailai" (little) for October and "Mbalolo levu" (large) for November. Similar forms near the Gilbert Islands respond to certain phases of the moon in June and July; in the Malay Archipelago a related worm swarms at the surface on the second and third nights after the full moon of March and April, when the tides are running highest. A Japanese palolo swarms after the new moon and again after the full moon in October and November.

Concerning each of these, the question recurs but remains unanswered: is it the state of the tides that in some unknown way supplies the impulse from which springs this behavior, or is it, even more mysteriously, some other influence of the moon? It is easier to imagine that it is the press and the rhythmic movement of the water that in some way brings about this response. But why is it only certain tides of the year, and why for some species is it the fullest tides of the month and for others the least movements of the waters that are related to the perpetuation of the race? At present, no one can answer.

No other creature displays so exquisite an adaptation to the tidal rhythm as the grunion—a small, shimmering fish about as long as a man's hand. Through no one can say what processes of adaptation, extending over no one knows how many millennia, the grunion has come to know not only the daily rhythm of the tides, but the monthly cycle by which certain tides sweep higher on the beaches than others. It has so adapted its spawning habits to the tidal cycle that the very existence of the race depends on the precision of this adjustment.

Shortly after the full moon of the months from March to August, the grunion appear in the surf on the beaches of California. The tide reaches flood stage, slackens, hesitates, and begins to ebb. Now on these waves of the ebbing tide the fish begin to come in. Their bodies shimmer in the light of the moon as they are borne up the beach on the crest of a wave, they lie glittering on the wet sand for a perceptible moment of time, then fling themselves into the wash of the next wave and are carried back to sea. For about an hour after the turn of the tide this continues, thousands upon thousands of grunion coming up onto the beach, leaving the water, returning to it. This is the spawning act of the species.

During the brief interval between successive waves, the male and female have come together in the wet sand, the one to shed her eggs, the other to fertilize them. When the parent fish return to the water, they have left behind a mass of eggs buried in the sand. Succeeding waves on that night do not wash out the eggs because the tide is already ebbing. The waves of the next high tide will not reach them, because for a time after the full of the moon each tide will halt its advance a little lower on the beach than the preceding one. The eggs, then, will be undisturbed for at least a fortnight. In the warm, damp, incubating sand they undergo their development. Within two weeks the magic change from fertilized egg to larval fishlet is completed, the perfectly formed little grunion still confined within the membranes of the egg, still buried in the sand, waiting for release. With the tides of the new moon it comes. Their waves wash over the places where the little masses of the grunion eggs were buried, the swirl and rush of the surf stirring the sand deeply. As the sand is washed away, and the eggs feel the touch of the cool sea water, the membranes rupture, the fishlets hatch, and the waves that released them bear them away to the sea.

But the link between tide and living creature I like best to remember is that of a very small worm, flat of body, with no distinction of appearance, but with one unforgettable quality. The name of this worm is *Convoluta roscoffensis*, and it lives on the sandy beaches of northern Brittany and the Channel Islands. Convoluta has entered into a remarkable partnership with a green alga, whose cells inhabit the body of the worm and lend to its tissues their own green color. The worm lives entirely on the starchy products manufactured by its plant guest, having become so completely dependent upon this means of nutrition that its digestive organs have degenerated. In order that the algal cells may carry on their function of photosynthesis (which is dependent upon sunlight) Convoluta rises from the damp sands of the intertidal zone as soon as the tide has ebbed, the sand becoming spotted with large green patches composed of thousands of the worms. For the several hours while the tide is out, the worms lie thus in the sun, and the plants manufacture their starches and sugars; but when the tide returns, the worms must again sink into the sand to avoid being washed away, out into deep water. So the whole lifetime of the worm is a succession of movements conditioned by the stages of the tide —upward into sunshine on the ebb, downward on the flood.

What I find most unforgettable about Convoluta is this: sometimes it happens that a marine biologist, wishing to study some related problem, will transfer a whole colony of the worms into the laboratory, there to establish them in an aquarium, where there are no tides. But twice each day Convoluta rises out of the sand on the bottom of the aquarium, into the light of the sun. And twice each day it sinks again into the sand. Without a brain, or what we would call a memory, or even any very clear perception, Convoluta continues to live out its life in this alien place, remembering, in every fiber of its small green body, the tidal rhythm of the distant sea.

III
MAN AND THE SEA ABOUT HIM

The Global Thermostat

> Out of the chamber of the south cometh the storm, and cold out of the north.
>
> —THE BOOK OF JOB

WHEN THE BUILDING of the Panama Canal was first suggested, the project was severely criticized in Europe. The French, especially, complained that such a canal would allow the waters of the Equatorial Current to escape into the Pacific, that there would then be no Gulf Stream, and that the winter climate of Europe would become unbearably frigid. The alarmed Frenchmen were completely wrong in their forecast of oceanographic events, but they were right in their recognition of a general principle—the close relation between climate and the pattern of ocean circulation.

There are recurrent schemes for deliberately changing—or attempting to change—the pattern of the currents and so modifying climate at will. We hear of projects for diverting the cold Oyashio from the Asiatic coast, and of others for controlling the Gulf Stream. About 1912 the Congress of the United States was asked to appropriate money to build a jetty from Cape Race eastward across the Grand Banks to obstruct the cold water flowing south from the Arctic. Advocates of the plan believed that the Gulf Stream would then swing in nearer the mainland of the northern United States and would presumably bring us warmer winters. The appropriation was not granted. Even if the money had been provided, there is little reason to suppose that engineers then—or later—could have succeeded in controlling the sweep of the ocean's currents. And fortunately so, for most of these plans would have effects different from those popularly expected. Bringing the Gulf Stream closer to the American east coast, for example, would make our winters worse instead of better. Along the Atlantic coast of North America, the prevailing winds blow eastward, across the land toward the sea. The air masses that have lain over the Gulf Stream seldom reach us. But the Stream, with its mass of warm water, does have something to do with bringing our weather to us. The cold winds of winter are pushed by gravity toward the low-pressure areas over the warm water. The winter of 1916, when Stream temperatures were above normal, was long remembered for its cold and snowy weather along the east coast. If we could move the Stream inshore, the result in winter would be colder, stronger winds from the interior of the continent—not milder weather.

But if the eastern North American climate is not dominated by the Gulf Stream, it is far otherwise for the lands lying "downstream." From the Newfoundland Banks, as we have seen, the warm water of the Stream drifts eastward, pushed along by the prevailing westerly winds. Almost immediately, however, it divides into several branches. One flows north to the western shore of Greenland; there the warm water attacks the ice brought around Cape Farewell by the East Greenland Current. Another passes to the southwest coast of Iceland and, before losing itself in arctic waters, brings a gentling influence to the southern shores of that island. But the main branch of the Gulf Stream or North Atlantic Drift flows eastward. Soon it divides again. The southernmost of these branches turns toward Spain and Africa and re-enters the Equatorial Current. The northernmost branch, hurried eastward by the winds blowing around the Icelandic "low," piles up against the coast of Europe the warmest water found at comparable latitudes anywhere in the world. From the Bay of Biscay north its influence is felt. And as the current rolls northeastward along the Scandinavian coast, it sends off many lateral branches that curve back westward to bring the breath of warm water to the arctic islands and to mingle with other currents in intricate whirls and eddies. The west coast of Spitsbergen, warmed by one of these lateral streams, is bright with flowers in the arctic summer; the east coast, with its polar current, remains barren and forbidding. Passing around the North Cape, the warm currents keep open such harbors as Hammerfest and Murmansk, although Riga, 800 miles farther south on the shores of the Baltic, is choked with ice. Somewhere in the Arctic Sea, near the island of Novaya Zemlya, the last traces of Atlantic water disappear, losing themselves at last in the overwhelming sweep of the icy northern sea.

It is always a warm-water current, but the temperature of the Gulf Stream nevertheless varies from year to year, and a seemingly slight change profoundly affects the air temperatures of Europe. The British meteorologist, C. E. P. Brooks, compares the North Atlantic to "a great bath, with a hot tap and two cold taps." The hot tap is the Gulf Stream; the cold taps are the East Greenland Current and the Labrador Current. Both the volume and the temperature of the hot-water tap vary. The cold taps are nearly constant in temperature but vary immensely in volume. The adjustment of the three taps determines surface temperatures in the eastern Atlantic and has a great deal to do with the weather of Europe and with happenings in arctic seas. A very slight winter warming of the eastern Atlantic temperatures means, for example, that the snow cover of northwestern Europe will melt earlier, that there will be an earlier thawing of the ground, that spring plowing may begin earlier, and that the harvest will be better. It means, too, that there will be relatively little ice near Iceland in the spring and that the amount of drift ice in the Barents Sea will diminish a year or two later. These relations have been clearly established by European scientists. Some day long-range weather forecasts for the continent of Europe will probably be based in part on ocean temperatures. But at present there are no means for collecting the temperatures over a large enough area, at frequent enough intervals.[16]

For the globe as a whole, the ocean is the great regulator, the great stabilizer of temperatures. It has been described as "a savings bank for solar energy, receiving deposits in seasons of excessive insolation and paying them back in seasons of want." Without the ocean, our world would be visited by unthinkably harsh extremes of temperature. For the water that covers three-fourths of the earth's surface with an enveloping mantle is a substance of remarkable qualities. It is an excellent absorber and radiator of heat. Because of its enormous heat capacity, the ocean can absorb a great deal of heat from the sun without becoming what we would consider "hot," or it can lose much of its heat without becoming "cold."

Through the agency of ocean currents, heat and cold may be distributed over thousands of miles. It is possible to follow the course of a mass of warm water that originates in the trade-wind belt of the Southern Hemisphere and remains recognizable for a year and a half, through a course of more than 7000 miles. This redistributing function of the ocean tends to make up for the uneven heating of the globe by the sun. As it is, ocean currents carry hot equatorial water toward the poles and return cold water equator-ward by such surface drifts as the Labrador Current and Oyashio, and even more importantly by deep currents. The redistribution of heat for the whole earth is accomplished about half by the ocean currents, and half by the winds.

At that thin interface between the ocean of water and the ocean of overlying air, lying as they do in direct contact over by far the greater part of the earth, there are continuous interactions of tremendous importance.

The atmosphere warms or cools the ocean. It receives vapors through evaporation, leaving most of the salts in the sea and so increasing the salinity of the water. With the changing weight of that whole mass of air that envelops the earth, the atmosphere brings variable pressure to bear on the surface of the sea, which is depressed under areas of high pressure and springs up in compensation under the atmospheric lows. With the moving force of the winds, the air grips the surface of the ocean and raises it into waves, drives the currents onward, lowers sea levels on windward shores, and raises it on lee shores.

But even more does the ocean dominate the air. Its effect on the temperature and humidity of the atmosphere is far greater than the small transfer of heat from air to sea. It takes 3000 times as much heat to warm a given volume of water 1° as to warm an equal volume of air by the same amount. The heat lost by a cubic meter of water on cooling 1° C. would raise the temperature of 3000 cubic meters of air by the same amount. Or to use another example, a layer of water a meter deep, on cooling .1° could warm a layer of air 33 meters thick by 10°. The temperature of the air is intimately related to atmospheric pressure. Where the air is cold, pressure tends to be high; warm air favors low pressures. The transfer of heat between ocean and air therefore alters the belts of high and low pressure; this profoundly affects the direction and strength of the winds and directs the storms on their paths.

There are six more or less permanent centers of high pressure over the oceans, three in each hemisphere. Not only do these areas play a controlling part in the climate of surrounding lands, but they affect the whole world because they are the birthplaces of most of the dominant winds of the globe. The trade winds originate in high-pressure belts of the Northern and Southern hemispheres. Over all the vast extent of ocean across which they blow, these great winds retain their identity; it is only over the continents that they become interrupted, confused, and modified.

In other ocean areas there are belts of low pressure, which develop, especially in winter, over waters that are then warmer than the surrounding lands. Traveling barometric depressions or cyclonic storms are attracted by these areas; they move rapidly across them or skirt around their edges. So winter storms take a path across the Icelandic "low" and over the Shetlands and Orkneys into the North Sea and the Norwegian Sea; other storms are directed by still other low-pressure areas over the Skagerrak and the Baltic into the interior of Europe. Perhaps more than any other condition, the low-pressure area over the warm water south of Iceland dominates the winter climate of Europe.

And most of the rains that fall on sea and land alike were raised from the sea. They are carried as vapor in the winds, and then with change of temperature the rains fall. Most of the European rain comes from evaporation of Atlantic water. In the United States, vapor and warm air from the Gulf of Mexico and the tropical waters of the western Atlantic ride the winds up the wide valley of the Mississippi and provide rains for much of the eastern part of North America.

Whether any place will know the harsh extremes of a continental climate or the moderating effect of the sea depends less on its nearness to the ocean than on the pattern of currents and winds and the relief of the continents. The east coast of North America receives little benefit from the sea, because the prevailing winds are from the west. The Pacific coast, on the other hand, lies in the path of the westerly winds that have blown across thousands of miles of ocean. The moist breath of the Pacific brings climatic mildness and creates the dense rain forests of British Columbia, Washington, and Oregon; but its full influence is largely restricted to a narrow strip by the coast ranges that follow a course parallel to the sea. Europe, in contrast, is wide open to the sea, and "Atlantic weather" carries hundreds of miles into the interior.

By a seeming paradox, there are parts of the world that owe their desert dryness to their nearness to the ocean. The aridity of the Atacama and Kalahari deserts is curiously related to the sea. Wherever such marine deserts occur, there is found this combination of circumstances: a western coast in the path of the prevailing winds, and a cold coastwise current. So on the west coast of South America the cold Humboldt streams northward off the shores of Chile and Peru—the great return flow of Pacific waters seeking the equator. The Humboldt, it will be remembered, is cold because it is continuously being reinforced by the upwelling of deeper water. The presence of this cold water offshore helps create the aridity of the region. The onshore breezes that push in toward the hot land in the afternoons are formed of cool air that has lain over a cool sea. As they reach the land they are forced to rise into the high coastal mountains—the ascent cooling them more than the land can warm them. So there is little condensation of water vapor, and although the cloud banks and the fogs forever seem to promise rain, the promise is not fulfilled so long as the Humboldt rolls on its accustomed course along these shores. On the stretch from Arica to Caldera there is normally less than an inch of rain in a year. It is a beautifully balanced system—as long as it remains in balance. What happens when the Humboldt is temporarily displaced is nothing short of catastrophic.

At irregular intervals the Humboldt is deflected away from the South American continent by a warm current of tropical water that comes down from the north. These are years of disaster. The whole economy of the area is adjusted to the normal aridity of climate. In the years of El Niño, as the warm current is called, torrential rains fall—the downpouring rains of the equatorial regions let loose upon the dust-dry hillsides of the Peruvian coast. The soil washes away, the mud huts literally dissolve and collapse, crops are destroyed. Even worse things happen at sea. The cold-water fauna of the Humboldt sickens and dies in the warm water, and the birds that fish the cold sea for a living must either migrate or starve.

Those parts of the coast of Africa that are bathed by the cool Benguela Current also lie between mountains and sea. The easterly winds are dry, descending winds, and the cool breezes from the sea have their moisture capacity increased by contact with the hot land. Mists form over the cold waters and roll in over the coast, but in a whole year the rainfall is the meagerest token. The mean rainfall at Swakopmund in Walvis Bay is 0.7 inches a year. But again this is true only as long as the Benguela holds sway along the coast, for there are times when the cold stream falters as does the Humboldt, and here also these are years of disaster.

The transforming influence of the sea is portrayed with beautiful clarity in the striking differences between the Arctic and Antarctic regions. As everyone knows, the Arctic is a nearly landlocked sea; the Antarctic, a continent surrounded by ocean. Whether this global balancing of a land pole against a water pole has a deep significance in the physics of the earth is uncertain; but the bearing of the fact on the climates of the two regions is plainly evident.

The ice-covered Antarctic continent, bathed by seas of uniform coldness, is in the grip of the polar anticyclone. High winds blow from the land and repel any warming influence that might seek to penetrate it. The mean temperature of this bitter world is never above the freezing point. On exposed rocks the lichens grow, covering the barrenness of cliffs with their gray or orange growths, and here and there over the snow is the red dust of the hardier algae. Mosses hide in the valleys and crevices less exposed to the winds, but of the higher plants only a few impoverished stands of grasses have managed to invade this land. There are no land mammals; the fauna of the Antarctic continent consists only of birds, wingless mosquitoes, a few flies, and microscopic mites.

In sharp contrast are the arctic summers, where the tundra is bright with many-colored flowers. Everywhere except on the Greenland icecap and some of the arctic islands, summer temperatures are high enough for the growth of plants, packing a year's development into the short, warm, arctic summer. The polar limit of plant growth is set not by latitude, but by the sea. For the influence of the warm Atlantic penetrates strongly within the Arctic Sea, entering, as we have seen, through the one large break in the land girdle, the Greenland Sea. But the streams of warm Atlantic water that enter the icy northern seas bring the gentling touch that makes the Arctic, in climate as well as in geography, a world apart from the Antarctic.

So, day by day and season by season, the ocean dominates the world's climate. Can it also be an agent in bringing about the long-period swings of climatic change that we know have occurred throughout the long history of the earth—the alternating periods of heat and cold, of drought and flood? There is a fascinating theory that it can. This theory links events in the deep, hidden places of the ocean with the cyclic changes of climate and their effects on human history. It was developed by the distinguished Swedish oceanographer, Otto Pettersson, whose almost century-long life closed in 1941. In many papers, Pettersson presented the different facets of his theory as he pieced it together, bit by bit. Many of his fellow scientists were impressed, others doubted. In those days few men could conceive of the dynamics of water movements in the deep sea. Now the theory is being re-examined in the light of modern oceanography and meteorology, and only recently C. E. P. Brooks said, "It seems that there is good support for Pettersson's theory as well as for that of solar activity, and that the actual variations of climate since about 3000 B.C. may have been to a large extent the result of these two agents."

To review the Pettersson theory is to review also a pageant of human history, of men and nations in the control of elemental forces whose nature they never understood and whose very existence they never recognized. Pettersson's work was perhaps a natural outcome of the circumstances of his life. He was born —as he died 93 years later—on the shores of the Baltic, a sea of complex and wonderful hydrography. In his laboratory atop a sheer cliff overlooking the deep waters of the Gulmarfiord, instruments recorded strange phenomena in the depths of this gateway to the Baltic. As the ocean water presses in toward that inland sea it dips down and lets the fresh surface water roll out above it; and at that deep level where salt and fresh water come into contact there is a sharp layer of discontinuity, like the surface film between water and air. Each day Pettersson's instruments revealed a strong, pulsing movement of that deep layer—the pressing inward of great submarine waves, of moving mountains of water. The movement was strongest every twelfth hour of the day, and between the 12-hour intervals it subsided. Pettersson soon established a link between these submarine waves and the daily tides. "Moon waves," he called them, and as he measured their height and timed their pulsing beat through the months and years, their relation to the ever-changing cycles of the tides became crystal clear.

Some of these deep waves of the Gulmarfiord were giants nearly 100 feet high. Pettersson believed they were formed by the impact of the oceanic tide wave on the submarine ridges of the North Atlantic, as though the waters moving to the pull of the sun and moon, far down in the lower levels of the sea, broke and spilled over in mountains of highly saline water to enter the fiords and sounds of the coast.

From the submarine tide waves, Pettersson's mind moved logically to another problem—the changing fortunes of the Swedish herring fishery. His native Bohuslan had been the site of the great Hanseatic herring fisheries of the Middle Ages. All through the thirteenth, fourteenth, and fifteenth centuries this great sea fishery was pursued in the Sund and the Belts, the narrow passageways into the Baltic. The towns of Skanor and Falsterbo knew unheard-of prosperity, for there seemed no end of the silvery, wealth-bringing fish. Then suddenly the fishery ceased, for the herring withdrew into the North Sea and came no more into the gateways of the Baltic—this to the enrichment of Holland and the impoverishment of Sweden. Why did the herring cease to come? Pettersson thought he knew, and the reason was intimately related to that moving pen in his laboratory, the pen that traced on a revolving drum the movements of the submarine waves far down in the depths of Gulmarfiord.

He had found that the submarine waves varied in height and power as the tide-producing power of the moon and sun varied. From astronomical calculations he learned that the tides must have been at their greatest strength during the closing centuries of the Middle Ages—those centuries when the Baltic herring fishery was flourishing. Then sun, moon, and earth came into such a position at the time of the winter solstice that they exerted the greatest possible attracting force upon the sea. Only about every eighteen centuries do the heavenly bodies assume this particular relation. But in that period of the Middle Ages, the great underwater waves pressed with unusual force into the narrow passages to the Baltic, and with the "water mountains" went the herring shoals. Later, when the tides became weaker, the herring remained outside the Baltic, in the North Sea.

Then Pettersson realized another fact of extreme significance —that those centuries of great tides had been a period of "startling and unusual occurrences" in the world of nature. Polar ice blocked much of the North Atlantic. The coasts of the North Sea and the Baltic were laid waste by violent storm floods. The winters were of "unexplained severity" and in consequence of the climatic rigors political and economic catastrophes occurred all over the populated regions of the earth. Could there be a connection between these events and those moving mountains of unseen water? Could the deep tides affect the lives of men as well as of herring?

From this germ of an idea, Pettersson's fertile mind evolved a theory of climatic variation, which he set forth in 1912 in an extraordinarily interesting document called *Climatic Variations in Historic and Prehistoric Time*.* Marshalling scientific, historic, and literary evidence, he showed that there are alternating periods of mild and severe climates which correspond to the long-period cycles of the oceanic tides. The world's most recent period of maximum tides, and most rigorous climate, occurred about 1433, its effect being felt, however, for several centuries before and after that year. The minimum tidal effect prevailed about A.D. 550, and it will occur again about the year 2400.

During the latest period of benevolent climate, snow and ice were little known on the coast of Europe and in the seas about Iceland and Greenland. Then the Vikings sailed freely over northern seas, monks went back and forth between Ireland and "Thyle" or Iceland, and there was easy intercourse between Great Britain and the Scandinavian countries. When Eric the Red voyaged to Greenland, according to the Sagas, he "came from the sea to land at the middle glacier—from thence he went south along the coast to see if the land was habitable.

* *Svenska Hydrog.-Biol. Komm. Skrifter*, No. 5, 1912.

The first year he wintered on Erik's Island . . ." This was probably in the year 984. There is no mention in the Sagas that Eric was hampered by drift ice in the several years of his exploration of the island; nor is there mention of drift ice anywhere about Greenland, or between Greenland and Wineland. Eric's route as described in the Sagas—proceeding directly west from Iceland and then down the east coast of Greenland—is one that would have been impossible during recent centuries. In the thirteenth century the Sagas contain for the first time a warning that those who sail for Greenland should not make the coast too directly west of Iceland on account of the ice in the sea, but no new route is then recommended. At the end of the fourteenth century, however, the old sailing route was abandoned and new sailing directions were given for a more southwesterly course that would avoid the ice.

The early Sagas spoke, too, of the abundant fruit of excellent quality growing in Greenland, and of the number of cattle that could be pastured there. The Norwegian settlements were located in places that are now at the foot of glaciers. There are Eskimo legends of old houses and churches buried under the ice. The Danish Archaeological Expedition sent out by the National Museum of Copenhagen was never able to find all of the villages mentioned in the old records. But its excavations indicated clearly that the colonists lived in a climate definitely milder than the present one.

But these bland climatic conditions began to deteriorate in the thirteenth century. The Eskimos began to make troublesome raids, perhaps because their northern sealing grounds were frozen over and they were hungry. They attacked the western settlement near the present Ameralik Fiord, and when an official mission went out from the eastern colony about 1342, not a single colonist could be found—only a few cattle remained. The eastern settlement was wiped out some time after 1418 and the houses and churches destroyed by fire. Perhaps the fate of the Greenland colonies was in part due to the fact that ships from Iceland and Europe were finding it increasingly difficult to reach Greenland, and the colonists had to be left to their own resources.

The climatic rigors experienced in Greenland in the thirteenth and fourteenth centuries were felt also in Europe in a series of unusual events and extraordinary catastrophes. The seacoast of Holland was devastated by storm floods. Old Icelandic records say that, in the winters of the early 1300's, packs of wolves crossed on the ice from Norway to Denmark. The entire Baltic froze over, forming a bridge of solid ice between Sweden and the Danish islands. Pedestrians and carriages crossed the frozen sea and hostelries were put up on the ice to accommodate them. The freezing of the Baltic seems to have shifted the course of storms originating in the low-pressure belt south of Iceland. In southern Europe, as a result, there were unusual storms, crop failures, famine, and distress. Icelandic literature abounds in tales of volcanic eruptions and other violent natural catastrophes that occurred during the fourteenth century.

What of the previous era of cold and storms, which should have occurred about the third or fourth century B.C., according to the tidal theory? There are shadowy hints in early literature and folklore. The dark and brooding poetry of the Edda deals with a great catastrophe, the Fimbul-winter or Götterdämmerung, when frost and snow ruled the world for generations. When Pytheas journeyed to the seas north of Iceland in 330 B.C., he spoke of the *mare pigrum*, a sluggish, congealed sea. Early history contains striking suggestions that the restless movements of the tribes of northern Europe—the southward migrations of the "barbarians" who shook the power of Rome —coincided with periods of storms, floods, and other climatic catastrophes that forced their migrations. Large-scale inundations of the sea destroyed the homelands of the Teutons and Cimbrians in Jutland and sent them southward into Gaul. Tradition among the Druids said that their ancestors had been expelled from their lands on the far side of the Rhine by enemy tribes and by "a great invasion of the ocean." And about the year 700 B.C. the trade routes for amber, found on the coasts of the North Sea, were suddenly shifted to the east. The old route came down along the Elbe, the Weser, and the Danube, through the Brenner Pass to Italy. The new route followed the Vistula, suggesting that the source of supply was then the Baltic. Perhaps storm floods had destroyed the earlier amber districts, as they invaded these same regions eighteen centuries later.

All these ancient records of climatic variations seemed to Pettersson an indication that cyclic changes in the oceanic circulation and in the conditions of the Atlantic had occurred. "No geologic alteration that could influence the climate has occurred for the past six or seven centuries," he wrote. The very nature of these phenomena—floods, inundations, ice blockades—suggested to him a dislocation of the oceanic circulation. Applying the discoveries in his laboratory on Gulmarfiord, he believed that the climatic changes were brought about as the tide-induced submarine waves disturbed the deep waters of polar seas. Although tidal movements are often weak at the surface of these seas, they set up strong pulsations at the submarine boundaries, where there is a layer of comparatively fresh, cold water lying upon a layer of salty, warmer water. In the years or the centuries of strong tidal forces, unusual quantities of warm Atlantic water press into the Arctic Sea at deep levels, moving in under the ice. Then thousands of square miles of ice that normally remain solidly frozen undergo partial thawing and break up. Drift ice, in extraordinary volume, enters the Labrador Current and is carried southward into the Atlantic. This changes the pattern of surface circulation, which is so intimately related to the winds, the rainfall, and the air temperatures. For the drift ice then attacks the Gulf Stream south of Newfoundland and sends it on a more easterly course, deflecting the streams of warm surface water that usually bring a softening effect to the climate of Greenland, Iceland, Spitsbergen, and northern Europe. The position of the low-pressure belt south of Iceland is also shifted, with further direct effect on European climate.

Although the really catastrophic disturbances of the polar regime come only every eighteen centuries, according to Pettersson, there are also rhythmically occurring periods that fall at varying intervals—for example, every 9, 18, or 36 years. These correspond to other tidal cycles. They produce climatic variations of shorter period and of less drastic nature.

The year 1903, for instance, was memorable for its outbursts of polar ice in the Arctic and for the repercussions on Scandinavian fisheries. There was "a general failure of cod, herring, and other fish along the coast from Finmarken and Lofoten to the Skagerrak and Kattegat. The greater part of the Barents

Sea was covered with pack ice up to May, the ice border approaching closer to the Murman and Finmarken coasts than ever before. Herds of arctic seals visited these coasts, and some species of the arctic whitefish extended their migrations to the Christiana Fiord and even entered into the Baltic." This outbreak of ice came in a year when earth, moon, and sun were in a relative position that gives a secondary maximum of the tide-producing forces. The similar constellation of 1912 was another great ice year in the Labrador Current—a year that brought the disaster of the *Titanic*.

Now in our own lifetime we are witnessing a startling alteration of climate, and it is intriguing to apply Otto Pettersson's ideas as a possible explanation. It is now established beyond question that a definite change in the arctic climate set in about 1900, that it became astonishingly marked about 1930, and that it is now spreading into sub-arctic and temperate regions. The frigid top of the world is very clearly warming up.

The trend toward a milder climate in the Arctic is perhaps most strikingly apparent in the greater ease of navigation in the North Atlantic and the Arctic Sea. In 1932, for example, the *Knipowitsch* sailed around Franz Josef Land for the first time in the history of arctic voyaging. And three years later the Russian ice-breaker *Sadko* went from the northern tip of Novaya Zemlya to a point north of Severnaya Zemlya (Northern Land) and thence to 82° 41' north latitude—the northernmost point ever reached by a ship under its own power.

In 1940 the whole northern coast of Europe and Asia was remarkably free from ice during the summer months, and more than 100 vessels engaged in trade via the arctic routes. In 1942 a vessel unloaded supplies at the west Greenland port of Upernivik (latitude 72° 43' N) during Christmas week "in almost complete winter darkness." During the 'forties the season for shipping coal from West Spitsbergen ports lengthened to seven months, compared with three at the beginning of the century. The season when pack ice lies about Iceland became shorter by about two months than it was a century ago. Drift ice in the Russian sector of the Arctic Sea decreased by a million square kilometers between 1924 and 1944, and in the Laptev Sea two islands of fossil ice melted away completely, their position being marked by submarine shoals.

Activities in the nonhuman world also reflect the warming of the Arctic—the changed habits and migrations of many fishes, birds, land mammals, and whales.

Many new birds are appearing in far northern lands for the first time in our records. The long list of southern visitors —birds never reported in Greenland before 1920—includes the American velvet scoter, the greater yellowlegs, American avocet, black-browed albatross, northern cliff swallow, oven-bird, common crossbill, Baltimore oriole, and Canada warbler. Some high-arctic forms, which thrive in cold climates, have shown their distaste for the warmer temperatures by visiting Greenland in sharply decreasing numbers. Such abstainers include the northern horned lark, the grey plover, and the pectoral sandpiper. Iceland, too, has had an extraordinary number of boreal and even subtropical avian visitors since 1935, coming from both America and Europe. Wood warblers, skylarks, and Siberian rubythroats, scarlet grosbeaks, pipits, and thrushes now provide exciting fare for Icelandic bird watchers.

When the cod first appeared at Angmagssalik in Greenland in 1912, it was a new and strange fish to the Eskimos and Danes. Within their memory it had never before appeared on the east coast of the island. But they began to catch it, and by the 1930's it supported so substantial a fishery in the area that the natives had become dependent upon it for food. They were also using its oil as fuel for their lamps and to heat their houses.

On the west coast of Greenland, too, the cod was a rarity at the turn of the century, although there was a small fishery, taking about 500 tons a year, at a few places on the southwest coast. About 1919 the cod began to move north along the west Greenland coast and to become more abundant. The center of the fishery has moved 300 miles farther north, and the catch is now about 15,000 tons a year.

Other fishes seldom or never before reported in Greenland have appeared there. The coalfish or green cod is a European fish so foreign to Greenland waters that when two of them were caught in 1831 they were promptly preserved in salt and sent to the Copenhagen Zoological Museum. But since 1924 this fish has often been found among the cod shoals. The haddock, cusk, and ling, unknown in Greenland waters until about 1930, are now taken regularly. Iceland, too, has strange visitors

—warmth-loving southern fishes, like the basking shark, the grotesque sunfish, the six-gilled shark, the swordfish, and the horse mackerel. Some of these same species have penetrated into the Barents and White seas and along the Murman coast.

As the chill of the northern waters has abated and the fish have moved poleward, the fisheries around Iceland have expanded enormously, and it has become profitable for trawlers to push on to Bear Island, Spitsbergen, and the Barents Sea. These waters now yield perhaps two billion pounds of cod a year—the largest catch of a single species by any fishery in the world. But its existence is tenuous. If the cycle turns, the waters begin to chill, and the ice floes creep southward again, there is nothing man can do that will preserve the arctic fisheries.

But for the present, the evidence that the top of the world is growing warmer is to be found on every hand. The recession of the northern glaciers is going on at such a rate that many smaller ones have already disappeared. If the present rate of melting continues others will soon follow them.

The melting away of the snowfields in the Opdal Mountains in Norway has exposed wooden-shafted arrows of a type used about A.D. 400 to 500. This suggests that the snow cover in this region must now be less than it has been at any time within the past 1400 to 1500 years.

The glaciologist Hans Ahlmann reports that most Norwegian glaciers "are living only on their own mass without receiving any annual fresh supply of snow"; that in the Alps there has been a general retreat and shrinkage of glaciers during the last decades, which became "catastrophic" in the summer of 1947; and that all glaciers around the Northern Atlantic coasts are shrinking. The most rapid recession of all is occurring in Alaska, where the Muir Glacier receded about 10½ kilometers in 12 years.

At present the vast antarctic glaciers are an enigma; no one can say whether they also are melting away, or at what rate. But reports from other parts of the world show that the northern glaciers are not the only ones that are receding. The glaciers of several East African high volcanoes have been diminishing since they were first studied in the 1800's—very rapidly since 1920—and there is glacial shrinkage in the Andes and also in the high mountains of central Asia.

The milder arctic and sub-arctic climate seems already to have resulted in longer growing seasons and better crops. The cultivation of oats has improved in Iceland. In Norway good seed years are now the rule rather than the exception, and even in northern Scandinavia the trees have spread rapidly above their former timber lines, and both pine and spruce are making a quicker annual growth than they have for some time.

The countries where the most striking changes are taking place are those whose climate is most directly under the control of the North Atlantic currents. Greenland, Iceland, Spitsbergen, and all of northern Europe, as we have seen, experience heat and cold, drought and flood in accordance with the varying strength and warmth of the eastward and northward-moving currents of the Atlantic. Oceanographers who have been studying the matter during the 1940's have discovered many significant changes in the temperature and distribution of great masses of ocean water. Apparently the branch of the Gulf Stream that flows past Spitsbergen has so increased in volume that it now brings in a great body of warm water. Surface waters of the North Atlantic show rising temperatures; so do the deeper layers around Iceland and Spitsbergen. Sea temperatures in the North Sea and along the coast of Norway have been growing warmer since the 1920's.

Unquestionably, there are other agents at work in bringing about the climatic changes in the Arctic and sub-Arctic regions. For one thing, it is almost certainly true that we are still in the warming-up stage following the last Pleistocene glaciation —that the world's climate, over the next thousands of years, will grow considerably warmer before beginning a downward swing into another Ice Age. But what we are experiencing now is perhaps a climatic change of shorter duration, measurable only in decades or centuries. Some scientists say that there must have been a small increase in solar activity, changing the pattern of air circulation and causing the southerly winds to blow more frequently in Scandinavia and Spitsbergen; changes in ocean currents, according to this view, are secondary effects of the shift of prevailing winds.

But if, as Professor Brooks thinks, the Pettersson tidal theory has as good a foundation as that of changing solar radiation, then it is interesting to calculate where our twentieth-century situation fits into the cosmic scheme of the shifting cycles of the tides. The great tides at the close of the Middle Ages, with their accompanying snow and ice, furious winds, and inundating floods, are more than five centuries behind us. The era of weakest tidal movements, with a climate as benign as that of the early Middle Ages, is about four centuries ahead. We have therefore begun to move strongly into a period of warmer, milder weather. There will be fluctuations, as earth and sun and moon move through space and the tidal power waxes and wanes. But the long trend is toward a warmer earth; the pendulum is swinging.

Wealth from the Salt Seas

A sea change into something rich and strange.

—SHAKESPEARE

THE OCEAN IS the earth's greatest storehouse of minerals. In a single cubic mile of sea water there are, on the average, 166 million tons of dissolved salts, and in all the ocean waters of the earth there are about 50 quadrillion tons. And it is in the nature of things for this quantity to be gradually increasing over the millennia, for although the earth is constantly shifting her component materials from place to place, the heaviest movements are forever seaward.

It has been assumed that the first seas were only faintly saline and that their saltiness has been growing over the eons of time. For the primary source of the ocean's salt is the rocky mantle of the continents. When those first rains came—the centuries-long rains that fell from the heavy clouds enveloping the young earth—they began the processes of wearing away the rocks and carrying their contained minerals to the sea. The annual flow of water seaward is believed to be about 6500 cubic miles, this inflow of river water adding to the ocean several billion tons of salts.

It is a curious fact that there is little similarity between the chemical composition of river water and that of sea water. The various elements are present in entirely different proportions. The rivers bring in four times as much calcium as chloride, for example, yet in the ocean the proportions are strongly reversed—46 times as much chloride as calcium. An important reason for the difference is that immense amounts of calcium salts are constantly being withdrawn from the sea water by marine animals and are used for building shells and skeletons—for the microscopic shells that house the foraminifera, for the massive structures of the coral reefs, and for the shells of oysters and clams and other mollusks. Another reason is the precipitation of calcium from sea water. There is a striking difference, too, in the silicon content of river and sea water—about 500 per cent greater in rivers than in the sea. The silica is required by diatoms to make their shells, and so the immense quantities brought in by rivers are largely utilized by these ubiquitous plants of the sea. Often there are exceptionally heavy growths of diatoms off the mouths of rivers. Because of the enormous total chemical requirements of all the fauna and flora of the sea, only a small part of the salts annually brought in by rivers goes to increasing the quantity of dissolved minerals in the water. The inequalities of chemical make-up are further reduced by reactions that are set in motion immediately the fresh water is discharged into the sea, and by the enormous disparities of volume between the incoming fresh water and the ocean.

There are other agencies by which minerals are added to the sea—from obscure sources buried deep within the earth. From every volcano chlorine and other gases escape into the atmosphere and are carried down in rain onto the surface of land and sea. Volcanic ash and rock bring up other materials. And all the submarine volcanoes, discharging through unseen craters directly into the sea, pour in boron, chlorine, sulphur, and iodine.

All this is a one-way flow of minerals to the sea. Only to a very limited extent is there any return of salts to the land. We attempt to recover some of them directly by chemical extraction and mining, and indirectly by harvesting the sea's plants and animals. There is another way, in the long, recurring cycles of the earth, by which the sea itself gives back to the land what it has received. This happens when the ocean waters rise over the lands, deposit their sediments, and at last withdraw, leaving over the continent another layer of sedimentary rocks. These contain some of the water and salts of the sea. But it is only a temporary loan of minerals to the land and the return payment begins at once by way of the old, familiar channels—rain, erosion, run-off to the rivers, transport to the sea.

There are other curious little exchanges of materials between sea and land. While the process of evaporation, which raises water vapor into the air, leaves most of the salts behind, a surprising amount of salt does intrude itself into the atmosphere and rides long distances on the wind. The so-called "cyclic salt" is picked up by the winds from the spray of a rough, cresting sea or breaking surf and is blown inland, then brought down in rain and returned by rivers to the ocean. These tiny, invisible particles of sea salt drifting in the atmosphere are, in fact, one of the many forms of atmospheric nuclei around which raindrops form. Areas nearest the sea, in general, receive the most salt. Published figures have listed 24 to 36 pounds per acre per year for England and more than 100 pounds for British Guiana. But the most astounding example of long-distance, large-scale transport of cyclic salts is furnished by Sambhar Salt Lake in northern India. It receives 3000 tons of salt a year, carried to it on the hot dry monsoons of summer from the sea, 400 miles away.

The plants and animals of the sea are very much better chemists than men, and so far our own efforts to extract the mineral wealth of the sea have been feeble compared with those of lower forms of life. They have been able to find and to utilize elements present in such minute traces that human chemists could not detect their presence until, very recently, highly refined methods of spectroscopic analysis were developed.

We did not know, for example, that vanadium occurred in the sea until it was discovered in the blood of certain sluggish and sedentary sea creatures, the holothurians (of which sea cucumbers are an example) and the ascidians. Relatively huge quantities of cobalt are extracted by lobsters and mussels, and nickel is utilized by various mollusks, yet it is only within recent years that we have been able to recover even traces of these elements. Copper is recoverable only as about a hundredth part in a million of sea water, yet it helps to constitute the life blood of lobsters, entering into their respiratory pigments as iron does into human blood.

In contrast to the accomplishments of invertebrate chemists, we have so far had only limited success in extracting sea salts in quantities we can use for commercial purposes, despite their prodigious quantity and considerable variety. We have recovered about fifty of the known elements by chemical analysis, and shall perhaps find that all the others are there, when we can develop proper methods to discover them. Five salts predominate and are present in fixed proportions. As we would expect, sodium chloride is by far the most abundant, making up 77.8 per cent of the total salts; magnesium chloride follows, with 10.9 per cent; then magnesium sulphate, 4.7 per cent; calcium sulphate, 3.6 per cent; and potassium sulphate, 2.5 per cent. All others combined make up the remaining .5 per cent.

Of all the elements present in the sea, probably none has stirred men's dreams more than gold. It is there—in all the waters covering the greater part of the earth's surface—enough in total quantity to make every person in the world a millionaire. But how can the sea be made to yield it? The most determined attempt to wrest a substantial quantity of gold from ocean waters—and also the most complete study of the gold in sea water—was made by the German chemist Fritz Haber after the First World War. Haber conceived the idea of extracting enough gold from the sea to pay the German war debt and his dream resulted in the German South Atlantic Expedition of the *Meteor*. The *Meteor* was equipped with a laboratory and filtration plant, and between the years 1924 and 1928 the vessel crossed and recrossed the Atlantic, sampling the water. But the quantity found was less than had been expected, and the cost of extraction far greater than the value of the gold recovered. The practical economics of the matter are about as follows: in a cubic mile of sea water there is about $93,000,000 in gold and $8,500,000 in silver. But to treat this volume of water in a year would require the twice-daily filling and emptying of 200 tanks of water, each 500 feet square and 5 feet deep. Probably this is no greater feat, relatively, than is accomplished regularly by corals, sponges, and oysters, but by human standards it is not economically feasible.

Most mysterious, perhaps, of all substances in the sea is iodine. In sea water it is one of the scarcest of the nonmetals, difficult to detect and resisting exact analysis. Yet it is found in almost every marine plant and animal. Sponges, corals, and certain seaweeds accumulate vast quantities of it. Apparently the iodine in the sea is in a constant state of chemical change, sometimes being oxidized, sometimes reduced, again entering into organic combinations. There seem to be constant interchanges between air and sea, the iodine in some form perhaps being carried into the air in spray, for the air at sea level contains detectable quantities, which decrease with altitude. From the time living things first made iodine a part of the chemistry of their tissues, they seem to have become increasingly dependent on it; now we ourselves could not exist without it as a regulator of the basal metabolism of our bodies, through the thyroid gland which accumulates it.

All commercial iodine was formerly obtained from seaweeds; then the deposits of crude nitrate of soda from the high deserts of North Chile were discovered. Probably the original source of this raw material—called "caliche"—was some prehistoric sea filled with marine vegetation, but that is a subject of controversy. Iodine is obtained also from brine deposits and from the subterranean waters of oil-bearing rocks—all indirectly of marine origin.

A monopoly on the world's bromine is held by the ocean, where 99 per cent of it is now concentrated. The tiny fraction present in rocks was originally deposited there by the sea. First we obtained it from the brines left in subterranean pools by prehistoric oceans; now there are large plants on the seacoasts —especially in the United States—which use ocean water as their raw material and extract the bromine directly. Thanks to modern methods of commercial production of bromine we have high-test gasoline for our cars. There is a long list of other uses, including the manufacture of sedatives, fire extinguishers, photographic chemicals, dyestuffs, and chemical warfare materials.

One of the oldest bromine derivatives known to man was Tyrian purple, which the Phoenicians made in their dyehouses from the purple snail, Murex. This snail may be linked in a curious and wonderful way with the prodigious and seemingly unreasonable quantities of bromine found today in the Dead Sea, which contains, it is estimated, some 850 million tons of the chemical. The concentration of bromine in Dead Sea water is 100 times that in the ocean. Apparently the supply is constantly renewed by underground hot springs, which discharge into the bottom of the Sea of Galilee, which in turn sends its waters to the Dead Sea by way of the River Jordan. Some authorities believe that the source of the bromine in the hot springs is a deposit of billions of ancient snails, laid down by the sea of a bygone age in a stratum long since buried.

Magnesium is another mineral we now obtain by collecting huge volumes of ocean water and treating it with chemicals, although originally it was derived only from brines or from the treatment of such magnesium-containing rocks as dolomite, of which whole mountain ranges are composed. In a cubic mile of sea water there are about 4 million tons of magnesium. Since the direct extraction method was developed about 1941, production has increased enormously. It was magnesium from the sea that made possible the wartime growth of the aviation industry, for every airplane made in the United States (and in most other countries as well) contains about half a ton of magnesium metal. And it has innumerable uses in other industries where a light-weight metal is desired, besides its long-standing utility as an insulating material, and its use in printing inks, medicines, and toothpastes, and in such war implements as incendiary bombs, star shells, and tracer ammunition.

Wherever climate has permitted it, men have evaporated salt from sea water for many centuries. Under the burning sun of the tropics the ancient Greeks, Romans, and Egyptians harvested the salt men and animals everywhere must have in order to live. Even today in parts of the world that are hot and dry and where drying winds blow, solar evaporation of salt is practiced—on the shores of the Persian Gulf, in China, India, and Japan, in the Philippines, and on the coast of California and the alkali flats of Utah.

Here and there are natural basins where the action of sun and wind and sea combine to carry on evaporation of salt on a scale far greater than human industry could accomplish. Such a natural basin is the Rann of Cutch on the west coast of India. The Rann is a flat plain, some 60 by 185 miles, separated from the sea by the island of Cutch. When the southwest monsoons blow, sea water is carried in by way of a channel to cover the plain. But in summer, in the season when the hot northeast monsoon blows from the desert, no more water enters, and that which is collected in pools over the plain evaporates into a salt crust, in some places several feet thick.

Where the sea has come in over the land, laid down its deposits, and then withdrawn, there have been created reservoirs of chemicals, upon which we can draw with comparatively little trouble. Hidden deep under the surface of our earth are pools of "fossil salt water," the brine of ancient seas; "fossil deserts," the salt of old seas that evaporated away under conditions of extreme heat and dryness; and layers of sedimentary rock in which are contained the organic sediments and the dissolved salts of the sea that deposited them.

1. Fossil remains of a trilobite, an ancient crustacean of Cambrian seas.

2. Sargassum fish in seaweed.

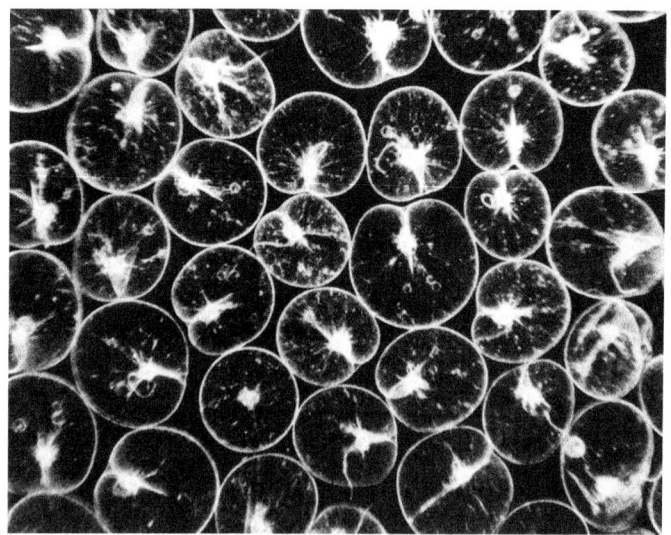

3. In summer seas, billions of tiny Noctiluca gleam like stars.

4. Camera reveals living creatures, tracks, and holes on sea floor.

5. and 6. In the bathyscaphe *Trieste* men first penetrated the greatest depths of the sea.

7. Coring tube being lowered for sample of bottom.

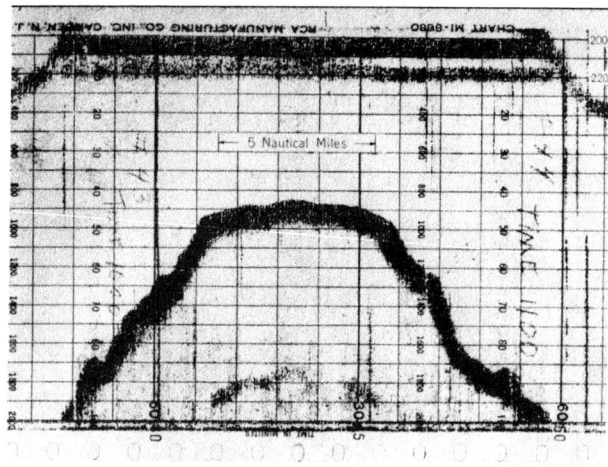

8. This sea mount was discovered by the U. S. Coast and Geodetic Survey's *Pathfinder* in the Gulf of Alaska; it rises 9600 feet from the ocean floor and is 857 fathoms below the surface.

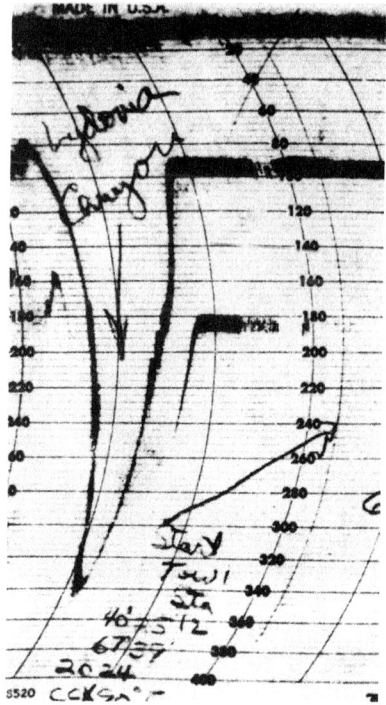

9. The U.S.S. *Albatross III* traced this profile of Lydia Canyon where it cuts across the outer edge of Georges Bank.

10. The birth of an island.

11. Countless billions of tiny shells compose the cliffs of Dover.

12. Surf pounds endlessly on the shores of the world.

13. Minot's Light withstands raging surf on the Massachusetts coast.

14. Waves have cut away softer rock, leaving chimney-like stack.

15. The face of the sea in a storm.

16. Coral rock, once formed beneath the sea, now is sculptured by waves.

17. Seismic sea waves of April 1, 1946, carried away a lighthouse at Scotch Cap, Alaska, 90 feet above the sea . . .

18. and also smashed shore structures on Hawaiian Islands.

19. Clouds draw heat energy from tropical seas to fuel the wind systems of the globe.

During the Permian period, which was a time of great heat and dryness and widespread deserts, a vast inland sea formed over much of Europe, covering parts of the present Britain, France, Germany, and Poland. Rains came seldom and the rate of evaporation was high. The sea became exceedingly salty, and it began to deposit layers of salts. For a period covering thousands of years, only gypsum was deposited, perhaps representing a time when water fresh from the ocean occasionally entered the inland sea to mix with its strong brine. Alternating with the gypsum were thicker beds of salt. Later, as its area shrank and the sea grew still more concentrated, deposits of potassium and magnesium sulphates were formed (this stage representing perhaps 500 years); still later, and perhaps for another 500 years, there were laid down mixed potassium and magnesium chlorides or carnallite. After the sea had completely evaporated, desert conditions prevailed, and soon the salt deposits were buried under sand. The richest beds form the famous deposits of Stassfurt and Alsace; toward the outskirts of the original area of the old sea (as, for example, in England) there are only beds of salt. The Stassfurt beds are about 2500 feet thick; their springs of brine have been known since the thirteenth century, and the salts have been mined since the seventeenth century.

At an even earlier geological period—the Silurian—a great salt basin was deposited in the northern part of the United States, extending from central New York State across Michigan, including northern Pennsylvania and Ohio and part of southern Ontario. Because of the hot, dry climate of that time, the inland sea lying over this place grew so salty that beds of salt and gypsum were deposited over a great area covering about 100,000 square miles. There are seven distinct beds of salt at Ithaca, New York, the uppermost lying at a depth of about half a mile. In southern Michigan some of the individual salt beds are more than 500 feet thick, and the aggregate thickness of salt in the center of the Michigan Basin is approximately 2000 feet. In some places rock salt is mined; in others wells are dug, water is forced down, and the resulting brine is pumped to the surface and evaporated to recover the salt.

One of the greatest stock piles of minerals in the world came from the evaporation of a great inland sea in the western United

States. This is Searles Lake in the Mohave Desert of California. An arm of the sea that overlay this region was cut off from the ocean by the thrusting up of a range of mountains; as the lake evaporated away, the water that remained became ever more salty through the inwash of minerals from all the surrounding land. Perhaps Searles Lake began its slow transformation from a landlocked sea to a "frozen" lake—a lake of solid minerals— only a few thousand years ago; now its surface is a hard crust of salts over which a car may be driven. The crystals of salts form a layer 50 to 70 feet deep. Below that is mud. Engineers have recently discovered a second layer of salts and brine, probably at least as thick as the upper layer, underlying the mud. Searles Lake was first worked in the 1870's for borax; then teams of 20 mules each carried the borax across desert and mountains to the railroads. In the 1930's the recovery of other substances from the lake began—bromine, lithium, and salts of potassium and sodium. Now Searles Lake yields 40 per cent of the production of potassium chloride in the United States and a large share of all the borax and lithium salts produced in the world.

In some future era the Dead Sea will probably repeat the history of Searles Lake, as the centuries pass and evaporation continues. The Dead Sea as we know it is all that remains of a much larger inland sea that once filled the entire Jordan Valley and was about 190 miles long; now it has shrunk to about a fourth of this length and a fourth of its former volume. And with the shrinkage and the evaporation in the hot dry climate has come the concentration of salts that makes the Dead Sea a great reservoir of minerals. No animal life can exist in its brine; such luckless fish as are brought down by the River Jordan die and provide food for the sea birds. It is 1300 feet below the Mediterranean, lying farther below sea level than any other body of water in the world. It occupies the lowest part of the rift valley of the Jordan, which was created by a down-slipping of a block of the earth's crust. The water of the Dead Sea is warmer than the air, a condition favoring evaporation, and clouds of its vapor float, nebulous and half formed, above it, while its brine grows more bitter and the salts accumulate.

Of all legacies of the ancient seas the most valuable is petroleum. Exactly what geologic processes have created the precious pools of liquid deep within the earth no one knows with enough certainty to describe the whole sequence of events. But this much seems to be true: Petroleum is a result of fundamental earth processes that have been operating ever since an abundant and varied life was developed in the sea—at least since the beginning of Paleozoic time, probably longer. Exceptional and catastrophic occurrences may now and then aid its formation but they are not essential; the mechanism that regularly generates petroleum consists of the normal processes of earth and sea—the living and dying of creatures, the deposit of sediments, the advance and retreat of the seas over the continents, the upward and downward foldings of the earth's crust.

The old inorganic theory that linked petroleum formation with volcanic action has been abandoned by most geologists. The origin of petroleum is most likely to be found in the bodies of plants and animals buried under the fine-grained sediments of former seas and there subjected to slow decomposition.

Perhaps the essence of conditions favoring petroleum production is represented by the stagnant waters of the Black Sea or of certain Norwegian fiords. The surprisingly abundant life of the Black Sea is confined to the upper layers; the deeper and especially the bottom waters are devoid of oxygen and are often permeated with hydrogen sulphide. In these poisoned waters there can be no bottom scavengers to devour the bodies of marine animals that drift down from above, so they are entombed in the fine sediments. In many Norwegian fiords the deep layers are foul and oxygenless because the mouth of the fiord is cut off from the circulation of the open sea by a shallow sill. The bottom layers of such fiords are poisoned by the hydrogen sulphide from decomposing organic matter. Sometimes storms drive in unusual quantities of oceanic water and through turbulence of waves stir deeply the waters of these lethal pools; the mixing of the water layers that follows brings death to hordes of fishes and invertebrates living near the surface. Such a catastrophe leads to the deposit of a rich layer of organic material on the bottom.

Wherever great oil fields are found, they are related to past or present seas. This is true of the inland fields as well as of those near the present seacoast. The great quantities of oil that have been obtained from the Oklahoma fields, for example, were trapped in spaces within sedimentary rocks laid down under seas that invaded this part of North America in Paleozoic time.

The search for petroleum has also led geologists repeatedly to those "unstable belts, covered much of the time by shallow seas, which lie around the margins of the main continental platforms, between them and the great oceanic deeps."

An example of such a depressed segment of crust lying between continental masses is the one between Europe and the Near East, occupied in part by the Persian Gulf, the Red, Black, and Caspian seas, and the Mediterranean Sea. The Gulf of Mexico and the Caribbean Sea lie in another basin or shallow sea between the Americas. A shallow, island-studded sea lies between the continents of Asia and Australia. Lastly, there is the nearly landlocked sea of the Arctic. In past ages all of these areas have been alternately raised and depressed, belonging at one time to the land, at another to the encroaching sea. During their periods of submersion they have received thick deposits of sediments, and in their waters a rich marine fauna has lived, died, and drifted down into the soft sediment carpet.

There are vast oil deposits in all these areas. In the Near East are the great fields of Saudi Arabia, Iran, and Iraq. The shallow depression between Asia and Australia yields the oil of Java, Sumatra, Borneo, and New Guinea. The American mediterranean is the center of oil production in the Western Hemisphere—half the proved resources of the United States come from the northern shore of the Gulf of Mexico, and Colombia, Venezuela, and Mexico have rich oil fields along the western and southern margins of the Gulf. The Arctic is one of the unproved frontiers of the petroleum industry, but oil seepages in northern Alaska, on islands north of the Canadian mainland, and along the Arctic coast of Siberia hint that this land recently raised from the sea may be one of the great oil fields of the future.

In recent years, the speculations of petroleum geologists have been focused in a new direction—under sea. By no means all of the land resources of petroleum have been discovered, but probably the richest and most easily worked fields are being tapped, and their possible production is known. The ancient seas gave us the oil that is now being drawn out of the earth. Can the ocean today be induced to give up some of the oil that must be trapped in sedimentary rocks under its floor, covered by water scores or hundreds of fathoms deep?

Oil is already being produced from offshore wells, on the continental shelf. Off California, Texas, and Louisiana, oil companies have drilled into the sediments of the shelf and are obtaining oil. In the United States the most active exploration has been centered in the Gulf of Mexico. Judging from its geologic history, this area has rich promise. For eons of time it was either dry land or a very shallow sea basin, receiving the sediments that washed into it from high lands to the north. Finally, about the middle of the Cretaceous period, the floor of the Gulf began to sink under the load of sediments and in time it acquired its present deep central basin.

By geophysical exploration, we can see that the layers of sedimentary rock underlying the coastal plain tilt steeply downward and pass under the broad continental shelf of the Gulf. Down in the layers deposited in the Jurassic period is a thick salt bed of enormous extent, probably formed when this part of the earth was hot and dry, a place of shrinking seas and encroaching deserts. In Louisiana and Texas, and also, it now appears, out in the Gulf itself, extraordinary features known as salt domes are associated with this deposit. These are fingerlike plugs of salt, usually less than a mile across, pushing up from the deep layer toward the earth's surface. They have been described by geologists as "driven up through 5000 to 15,000 feet of sediments by earth pressures, like nails through a board." In the states bordering the Gulf such structures have often been associated with oil. It seems probable that on the continental shelf, also, the salt domes may mark large oil deposits.

In exploring the Gulf for oil, therefore, geologists search for the salt domes where the larger oil fields are likely to lie. They use an instrument known as a magnetometer, which measures the variations in magnetic intensity brought about by the salt domes. Gravity meters also help locate the domes by measuring the variation in gravity near them, the specific gravity of salt being less than that of the surrounding sediments. The actual location and outline of the dome are discovered by seismographic exploration, which traces the inclination of the rock strata by recording the reflection of sound waves produced by dynamite explosions. These methods of exploration have been used on land for some years, but only since about 1945 have they been adapted to use in offshore Gulf waters. The magnetometer has been so improved that it will map continuously while being towed behind a boat or carried in or suspended from a plane. A gravity meter can now be lowered rapidly to the bottom and readings made by remote control. (Once an operator had to descend with it in a diving bell.) Seismic crews may shoot off their dynamite charges and make continuous recordings while their boats are under way.

Despite all these improvements which allow exploration to proceed rapidly, it is no simple matter to obtain oil from undersea fields. Prospecting must be followed by the leasing of potential oil-producing areas, and then by drilling to see whether oil is actually there. Offshore drilling platforms rest on piles that must be driven as far as 250 feet into the floor of the Gulf to withstand the force of waves, especially during the season for hurricanes. Winds, storm waves, fogs, the corrosive gnawing of sea water upon metal structures—all these are hazards that must be faced and overcome. Yet the technical difficulties of far more extensive offshore operations than any now attempted do not discourage specialists in petroleum engineering.

So our search for mineral wealth often leads us back to the seas of ancient times—to the oil pressed from the bodies of fishes, seaweeds, and other forms of plant and animal life and then stored away in ancient rocks; to the rich brines hidden in subterranean pools where the fossil water of old seas still remains; to the layers of salts that are the mineral substance of those old seas laid down as a covering mantle over the continents. Perhaps in time, as we learn the chemical secrets of the corals and sponges and diatoms, we shall depend less on the stored wealth of prehistoric seas and shall go more and more directly to the ocean and the rocks now forming under its shallow waters.

The Encircling Sea

A sea from which birds travel not within a year, so vast it is and fearful.

—HOMER

To the ancient Greeks the ocean was an endless stream that flowed forever around the border of the world, ceaselessly turning upon itself like a wheel, the end of earth, the beginning of heaven. This ocean was boundless; it was infinite. If a person were to venture far out upon it—were such a course thinkable—he would pass through gathering darkness and obscuring fog and would come at last to a dreadful and chaotic blending of sea and sky, a place where whirlpools and yawning abysses waited to draw the traveler down into a dark world from which there was no return.

These ideas are found, in varying form, in much of the literature of the ten centuries before the Christian era, and in later years they keep recurring even through the greater part of the Middle Ages. To the Greeks the familiar Mediterranean was The Sea. Outside, bathing the periphery of the land world, was Oceanus. Perhaps somewhere in its uttermost expanse was the home of the gods and of departed spirits, the Elysian fields. So we meet the ideas of unattainable continents or of beautiful islands in the distant ocean, confusedly mingled with references to a bottomless gulf at the edge of the world—but always around the disc of the habitable world was the vast ocean, encircling all.

Perhaps some word-of-mouth tales of the mysterious northern world, filtering down by way of the early trade routes for amber and tin, colored the conceptions of the early legends, so that the boundary of the land world came to be pictured as a place of fog and storms and darkness. Homer's *Odyssey* described the Cimmerians as dwelling in a distant realm of mist and darkness on the shores of Oceanus, and they told of the shepherds who lived in the land of the long day, where the paths of day and night were close. And again perhaps the early poets and historians derived some of their ideas of the ocean from the Phoenicians, whose craft roamed the shores of Europe, Asia, and Africa in search of gold, silver, gems, spices, and wood for their commerce with kings and emperors. It may well be that these sailor-merchants were the first ever to cross an ocean, but history does not record the fact. For at least 2000 years before Christ—probably longer—the flourishing trade of the Phoenicians was plied along the shores of the Red Sea to Syria, to Somaliland, to Arabia, even to India and perhaps to China. Herodotus wrote that they circumnavigated Africa from east to west about 600 B.C., reaching Egypt via the Straits of the Pillars and the Mediterranean. But the Phoenicians themselves said and wrote little or nothing of their voyagings, keeping their trade routes and the sources of their precious cargoes secret. So there are only the vaguest rumors, sketchily supported by archaeological findings, that the Phoenicians may have launched out into the open Pacific.

Nor are there anything but rumors and highly plausible suppositions that the Phoenicians, on their coastwise journeys along western Europe, may have sailed as far north as the Scandinavian peninsula and the Baltic, source of the precious amber. There are no definite traces of any such visits by them, and of course the Phoenicians have left no written record of any. Of one of their European voyages, however, there is a second-hand account. This was the expedition under Himlico of Carthage, which sailed northward along the European coast about the year 500 B.C. Himlico apparently wrote an account of this voyage, although his manuscript was not preserved. But his descriptions are quoted by the Roman Avienus, writing nearly a thousand years later. According to Avienus, Himlico painted a discouraging picture of the coastwise seas of Europe:

> These seas can scarcely be sailed through in four months . . . no breeze drives the ship forward, so dead is the sluggish wind of this idle sea . . . There is much seaweed among the waves . . . the surface of the earth is barely covered by a little water . . . The monsters of the sea move continually hither and thither, and the wild beasts swim among the sluggish and slowly creeping ships.

Perhaps the "wild beasts" are the whales of the Bay of Biscay, later to become a famous whaling ground; the shallow water areas that so impressed Himlico may have been the flats alternately exposed and covered by the ebb and flow of the great tides of the French coast—a strange phenomenon to one from the almost tideless Mediterranean. But Himlico also had ideas of the open ocean to the west, if the account of Avienus is to be trusted: "Farther to the west from these Pillars there is boundless sea . . . None has sailed ships over these waters, because propelling winds are lacking on these deeps . . . likewise because darkness screens the light of day with a sort of clothing, and because a fog always conceals the sea." Whether these descriptive details are touches of Phoenician canniness or merely the old ideas reasserting themselves it is hard to say, but much the same conceptions appear again and again in later accounts, echoing down the centuries to the very threshold of modern times.

So far as historical records are concerned, the first great voyage of marine exploration was by Pytheas of Massilia about 330 B.C. Unfortunately his writings, including one called *On the Ocean*, are lost and their substance is preserved for us only in fragmentary quotations passed on by later writers. We know very little of the controlling circumstances of the northward voyage of this astronomer and geographer, but probably Pytheas wished to see how far the *oecumene* or land world extended, to learn the position of the Arctic Circle, and to see the land of midnight sun. Some of these things he may have heard of through the merchants who brought down tin and amber from the Baltic lands by the overland trade routes.

Since Pytheas was the first to use astronomical measurements to determine the geographic location of a place and in other ways had proved his competence as an astronomer, he brought more than ordinary skill to an exploratory voyage. He seems to have sailed around Great Britain, to have reached the Shetland Islands, and then to have launched out into the open ocean to the north, coming at last to "Thule," the land of midnight sun. In this country, he is quoted as reporting, "the nights were very short, in some places two, in others three hours long, so that the sun rose again a short time after it had set." The country was inhabited by "barbarians" who showed Pytheas "the place where the sun goes to rest." The location of "Thule" is a point much disputed by later authorities, some believing it to have been Iceland, while others believe that Pytheas crossed the North Sea to Norway. Pytheas is also said to have described a "congealed sea" lying north of Thule, which accords better with Iceland.

But the Dark Ages were settling down over the civilized world, and little of the knowledge of distant places acquired by Pytheas on his voyagings seems to have impressed the learned men who followed him. The geographer Posidonius wrote of the ocean that "stretched to infinity" and from Rhodes he undertook a journey all the way to Gadir (Cadiz) to see the ocean, measure its tides, and determine the truth of the belief that the sun dropped with the hissing of a red-hot body into the great western sea.

Not for about 1200 years after Pytheas do we have another clear account of marine exploration—this time by the Norwegian Ottar. Ottar described his voyagings in northern seas to King Alfred, who recorded them in a straightforward narrative of geographic exploration strikingly free from sea monsters and other imaginary terrors. Ottar, on the basis of this account, was the first known explorer to round the North Cape, to enter the Polar or Barents Sea, and later to enter the White Sea. He found the coasts of these seas inhabited by people of whom he seems to have heard previously. According to the narrative, he went there "chiefly to explore the country, and for the sake of the walrus, for they have much valuable bone in their tusks." This voyage was probably made between A.D. 870 and 890.

Meanwhile the age of the Vikings had dawned. The beginning of their more important expeditions is usually considered to be the end of the eighth century. But long before that time they had visited other countries of northern Europe. "As early as the third century and until the close of the fifth century," wrote Fridtjof Nansen, "the roving Eruli sailed from Scandinavia, sometimes in company with Saxon pirates, over the seas of western Europe, ravaging the coasts of Gaul and Spain, and indeed penetrating in 455 into the Mediterranean as far as Lucca in Italy." As early as the sixth century the Vikings must have crossed the North Sea to the land of the Franks, and probably to southern Britain. They may have established themselves in Shetland by the beginning of the seventh century, and plundered the Hebrides and northwest Ireland about the same time. Later they sailed to the Faroes and to Iceland; in the last quarter of the tenth century they established two colonies in Greenland, and shortly thereafter they steered across the intervening Atlantic waters to North America. Of the place of these voyages in history Nansen writes:

> The shipbuilding and seamanship of the Norwegians mark a new epoch in the history both of navigation and discovery, and with their voyages the knowledge of northern lands and waters was at once completely changed . . . We find accounts of these voyages of discovery in the old writings and sagas, a large part of which was put into writing in Iceland. A somber undercurrent runs through these narratives of voyages in unknown seas—the silent struggle of hardy men with ice, storms, cold, and want.
> They had neither compass, nor astronomical instruments, nor any of the appliances of our time for finding their position at sea; they could only sail by the sun, moon, and stars, and it seems incomprehensible how for days and weeks, when these were invisible, they were able to find their course through fog and bad weather; but they found it, and in the open craft of the Norwegian Vikings, with their square sails, fared north and west over the whole ocean, from Novaya Zemlya and Spitsbergen to Greenland, Baffin Bay, Newfoundland, and North America. . . . It was not until five hundred years later that the ships of other nations were to make their way to the same regions.*

But only the vaguest rumors of any of these things had reached the "civilized world" of the Mediterranean. While the sagas of the Norsemen were giving clear and factual directions for the passage across oceans, from known to unknown worlds, the writings of the scholars of the medieval world dealt still with that outermost encircling ocean, the dread Sea of Darkness. About the year 1154 the noted Arab geographer Edrisi wrote for the Norman king of Sicily, Roger II, a description of the earth, accompanied by 70 maps, which portrayed on the outside of all the known earth the Dark Sea, forming the limit of the world. He wrote of the sea about the

*From *In Northern Mists*, 1912 edition, A. H. Clark, vol. I, pp. 234 and 247.

British Isles that it is "impossible to penetrate very far into this ocean." He hinted at the existence of far islands but thought the approach to them difficult because of the "fog and deep darkness that prevails on this sea." The scholarly Adam of Bremen, writing in the eleventh century, knew of the existence of Greenland and Wineland as distant islands in the great ocean, but could not separate the reality from the old ideas of that sea, "infinite and fearful to behold, which encompasses the whole world," that ocean flowing "endlessly around the circle of the earth." And even the Norsemen themselves, as they discovered lands across the Atlantic, seem merely to have pushed back the boundaries of the place where still there began that outermost ocean, for the idea of the outer ocean surrounding the disc of the earth appears in such Northern chronicles as the *Kings Mirror* and the *Heimskringla*. And so over that Western Ocean into which Columbus and his men set out there hung still the legend of a dead and stagnant sea, of monsters and entrapping weeds, of fog and gloom and ever present danger.

Yet centuries before Columbus—no one knows how many centuries—men on the opposite side of the world had laid aside whatever fears the ocean may have inspired and were boldly sailing their craft across the Pacific. We know little of the hardships, the difficulties, and the fears that may have beset the Polynesian colonists—we know only that somehow they came from the mainland to those islands, remote from any shore. Perhaps the aspect of these central Pacific waters was kindlier than that of the North Atlantic—it must have been—for in their open canoes they entrusted themselves to the stars and the signposts of the sea and found their way from island to island.

We do not know when the first Polynesian voyages took place. Concerning the later ones, there is some evidence that the last important colonizing voyage to the Hawaiian Islands was made in the thirteenth century, and that about the middle of the fourteenth century a fleet from Tahiti permanently colonized New Zealand. But again, all these things were unknown in Europe, and long after the Polynesians had mastered the art of navigating unknown seas, the European sailors still regarded the Pillars of Hercules as the gateway to a dreaded sea of darkness.

Once Columbus had shown the way to the West Indies and the Americas, once Balboa had seen the Pacific and Magellan had sailed around the globe, there arose, and long persisted, two new ideas. One concerned the existence of a northern passage by sea to Asia; the other had to do with a great southern continent generally believed to lie below the then-known lands.

Magellan, while sailing through the strait that now bears his name, had seen land to the south of him through all the thirty-seven days required for the passage through the strait. At night the lights of many fires glowed from the shores of this land, which Magellan named Tierra del Fuego—Land of Fires. He supposed that these were the near shores of that great land which the theoretical geographers had already decided should lie to the south.

Many voyagers after Magellan reported land they assumed to be outlying regions of the sought-for continent, but all proved to be islands. The locations of some, like Bouvet, were so indefinitely described that they were found and lost again many times before being definitely fixed on maps. Kerguelen believed firmly that the bleak, forbidding land he discovered in 1772 was the Southern Continent and so reported it to the French government. When, on a later voyage, he learned that he had found merely another island, Kerguelen unhappily named it "Isle of Desolation." Later geographers, however, gave his own name to it.

Discovery of the southern land was one of the objects of Captain Cook's voyages, but instead of a continent, he discovered an ocean. By making an almost complete circumnavigation of the globe in high southern latitudes, Cook revealed the existence of a stormy ocean running completely around the earth south of Africa, Australia, and South America. Perhaps he believed that the islands of the South Sandwich group were part of the Antarctic mainland, but it is by no means sure that he was the first to see these or other islands of the Antarctic Ocean. American sealers had quite possibly been there before him, yet this chapter of Antarctic exploration contains many blank pages. The Yankee sealers did not want their competitors to find the rich sealing grounds, and they kept the details of their voyages secret. Evidently they had operated in the vicinity of the outer Antarctic islands for many years before the beginning of the nineteenth century, because most of the fur seals in these waters had been exterminated by 1820. It was in this year that the Antarctic continent was first sighted, by Captain N. B. Palmer in command of the *Hero*, one of a fleet of eight sealers from Connecticut ports. A century later, explorers were still making fresh discoveries about the nature of that Southern Continent, dreamed of by the old geographers, so long searched for, then branded a myth, and finally established as one of the great continental masses of the earth.

At the opposite pole, meanwhile, the dream of a northern passage to the riches of Asia lured one expedition after another into the frozen seas of the north. Cabot, Frobisher, and Davis sought the passage to the northwest, failed, and turned back. Hudson was left by a mutinous crew to die in an open boat. Sir John Franklin set out with the *Erebus* and *Terror* in 1845, apparently entered the labyrinth of Arctic islands by what later proved a feasible route, but then lost his ships and perished with all his men. Later rescue ships coming from east and west met in Melville Sound and thus the Northwest Passage was established.

Meanwhile there had been repeated efforts to find a way to India by sailing eastward through the Arctic Sea. The Norwegians seem to have hunted walruses in the White Sea and had probably reached the coasts of Novaya Zemlya by the time of Ottar; they may have discovered Spitsbergen in 1194, although this is usually credited to Barents in 1596. The Russians had hunted seals in the polar seas as early as the sixteenth century, and whalers began to operate out of Spitsbergen soon after Hudson, in 1607, called attention to the great number of whales in the sea between Spitsbergen and Greenland. So at least the threshold of the ice-filled northern ocean was known when the British and Dutch traders began their desperate attempt to find a sea road north of Europe and Asia. There were many attempts, but few got beyond the coasts of Novaya Zemlya; the sixteenth and seventeenth centuries were marked by the wreckage of hopes as well as of vessels, and by the death of such brilliant navigators as William Barents under the hardships met by expeditions ill prepared for arctic winters. Finally the effort was abandoned. It was not until 1879, after the practical need for such a passage had largely disappeared, that Baron Nordenskiöld, in the Swedish *Vega*, passed from Gothenburg to Bering Strait.

So, little by little, through many voyages undertaken over many centuries, the fog and the frightening obscurity of the unknown were lifted from all the surface of the Sea of Darkness. How did they accomplish it—those first voyagers, who had not even the simplest instruments of navigation, who had never seen a nautical chart, to whom the modern miracles of loran, radar, and sonic sounding would have been fantasies beyond belief? Who was the first man to use a mariner's compass, and what were the embryonic beginnings of the charts and the sailing directions that are taken for granted today? None of these questions can be answered with finality; we know only enough to want to know more.

Of the methods of those secretive master mariners, the Phoenicians, we cannot even guess. We have more basis for conjecture about the Polynesians, for we can study their descendants today, and those who have done so find hints of the methods that led the ancient colonizers of the Pacific on their course from island to island. Certainly they seem to have followed the stars, which burned brightly in the heavens over those calm Pacific regions, which are so unlike the stormy and fog-bound northern seas. The Polynesians considered the stars as moving bands of light that passed across the inverted pit of the sky, and they sailed toward the stars which they knew passed over the islands of their destination. All the language of the sea was understood by them: the varying color of the water, the haze of surf breaking on rocks yet below the horizon, and the cloud patches that hang over every islet of the tropic seas and sometimes seem even to reflect the color of a lagoon within a coral atoll.

Students of primitive navigation believe that the migrations of birds had meaning for the Polynesians, and that they learned much from watching the flocks that gathered each year in the spring and fall, launched out over the ocean, and returned later out of the emptiness into which they had vanished. Harold Gatty believes the Hawaiians may have found their islands by following the spring migration of the golden plover from Tahiti to the Hawaiian chain, as the birds returned to the North American mainland. He has also suggested that the migratory path of the shining cuckoo may have guided other colonists from the Solomons to New Zealand.

Tradition and written records tell us that primitive navigators often carried with them birds which they would release and follow to land. The frigate bird or man-of-war bird was the shore-sighting bird of the Polynesians (even in recent times it has been used to carry messages between islands), and in the Norse Sagas we have an account of the use of "ravens" by Floki Vilgerdarson to show him the way to Iceland, "since seafaring men had no loadstone at that time in the north . . . Thence he sailed out to sea with the three ravens . . . And when he let loose the first it flew back astern. The second flew up into the air and back to the ship. The third flew forward over the prow, where they found land."

In thick and foggy weather, according to repeated statements in the Sagas, the Norsemen drifted for days without knowing where they were. Then they often had to rely on observing the flight of birds to judge the direction of land. The *Landnamabok* says that on the course from Norway to Greenland the voyager should keep far enough to the south of Iceland to have birds and whales from there. In shallow waters it appears that the Norsemen took some sort of soundings, for the *Historia Norwegiae* records that Ingolf and Hjorleif found Iceland "by probing the waves with the lead."

The first mention of the use of the magnetic needle as a guide to mariners occurs in the twelfth century after Christ, but as much as a century later scholars were expressing doubt that sailors would entrust their lives to an instrument so obviously invented by the devil. There is fair evidence, however, that the compass was in use in the Mediterranean about the end of the twelfth century, and in northern Europe within the next hundred years.

For navigating the known seas, there had been the equivalent of our modern Sailing Directions for a great many centuries before this. The *portolano* and the *peripli* guided the mariners of antiquity about the Mediterranean and Black seas. The *portolano* were harbor-finding charts, designed to accompany the coast pilots or *peripli*, and it is not known which of the two was developed first. The *Periplus of Scylax* is the oldest and most complete of these ancient Coast Pilots that have survived the hazards of the intervening centuries and are preserved for us. The chart which presumably accompanied it no longer exists, but the two were, in effect, a guide to navigation of the Mediterranean in the fourth or fifth century B.C.

The *periplus* called *Stadiasmus, or circumnavigation of the great sea* dates from about the fifth century after Christ but reads surprisingly like a modern Pilot, giving distances between points, the winds with which the various islands might be approached, and the facilities for anchorage or for obtaining fresh water. So for example, we read, "From Hermaea to Leuce Acte, 20 stadia hereby lies a low islet at a distance of two stadia from the land, there is anchorage for cargo boats, to be put into with west wind; but by the shore below the promontory is a wide anchoring-road for all kinds of vessels. Temple of Apollo, a famous oracle; by the temple there is water."

Lloyd Brown, in his *Story of Maps*, says that no true mariners' chart of the first thousand years after Christ has been preserved or is definitely known to have existed. This he ascribes to the fact that early mariners carefully guarded the secrets of how they made their passages from place to place; that sea charts were "keys to empire" and a "way to wealth" and as such were secret, hidden documents. Therefore, because the earliest specimen of such a chart now extant was made by Petrus Vesconte in 1311 does not mean that many had not existed before it.

It was a Dutchman who produced the first collection of navigational charts bound together in book form—Lucas Janssz Waghenaer. The *Mariner's Mirror* of Waghenaer, first published in 1584, covered the navigation of the western coast of Europe from the Zuyder Zee to Cadiz. Soon it was issued in several languages. For many years "Waggoners" guided Dutch, English, Scandinavian, and German navigators through eastern Atlantic waters, from the Canaries to Spitsbergen, for succeeding editions had extended the areas covered to include the Shetland and Faroe islands and even the northern coast of Russia as far as Novaya Zemlya.

In the sixteenth and seventeenth centuries, under the stimulus of fierce competition for the wealth of the East Indies, the finest charts were prepared not by governmental agencies, but by private enterprise. The East India companies employed their own hydrographers, prepared secret atlases, and generally guarded their knowledge of the sailing passages to the East as one of the most precious secrets of their trade. But in 1795 the East India Company's hydrographer, Alexander Dalrymple, became official hydrographer to the Admiralty, and under his direction the British Admiralty began its survey of the coasts of the world from which the modern Admiralty Pilots stem.

Shortly thereafter a young man joined the United States Navy—Matthew Fontaine Maury. In only a few years Lieutenant Maury was to make his influence felt on navigation all over the world, and was to write a book, *The Physical Geography of the Sea*, which is now considered the foundation of the science of oceanography. After a number of years at sea, Maury assumed charge of the Depot of Charts and Instruments—the forerunner of the present Hydrographic Office—and began a practical study of winds and currents from the standpoint of the navigator. Through his energy and initiative a worldwide co-operative system was organized. Ships' officers of all nations sent in the logs of their voyages, from which Maury assembled and organized information, which he incorporated in navigational charts. In return, the co-operating mariner received copies of the charts. Soon Maury's sailing directions were attracting world notice: he had shortened the passage for American east-coast vessels to Rio de Janeiro by 10 days, to Australia by 20 days, and around the Horn to California by 30 days. The co-operative exchange of information sponsored by Maury remains in effect today, and the Pilot Charts of the Hydrographic Office, the lineal descendants of Maury's charts, carry the inscription: "Founded on the researches of Matthew Fontaine Maury while serving as a Lieutenant in the United States Navy."

In the modern Sailing Directions and Coast Pilots now issued by every maritime nation of the world we find the most complete information that is available to guide the navigator over the ocean. Yet in these writings of the sea there is a pleasing blend of modernity and antiquity, with unmistakable touches by which we may trace their lineage back to the sailing directions of the sagas or the *peripli* of the ancient Mediterranean seamen.

It is surprising, but pleasant, that sailing directions of one and the same vintage should contain instructions for obtaining position by the use of loran, and should also counsel the navigator to be guided, like the Norsemen a millennium ago, by the flight of birds and the behavior of whales in making land in foggy weather. In the *Norway Pilot* we read as follows:

> [Of Jan Mayen Island] The presence of sea fowl in large numbers will give an indication of the approach to land and the noise of their rookeries may be useful in locating the shore.
>
> [Of Bear Island] The sea around the islands teems with guillemots. These flocks and the direction of their flight on approaching, together with the use of the lead, are of great value in making the island when it is foggy.

And the ultra-modern *United States Pilot* for Antarctica says:

> Navigators should observe the bird life, for deductions may often be drawn from the presence of certain species. Shags are . . . a sure sign of the close proximity of land . . . The snow petrel is invariably associated with ice and is of great interest to mariners as an augury of ice conditions in their course . . . Blowing whales usually travel in the direction of open water.

Sometimes the Pilots for remote areas of the sea can report only what the whalers or sealers or some old-time fisherman has said about the navigability of a channel or the set of the tidal currents; or they must include a chart prepared half a century ago by the last vessel to take soundings in the area. Often they must caution the navigator not to proceed without seeking information of those having "local knowledge." In phrases like these we get the feel of the unknown and the mysterious that never quite separates itself from the sea: "It is said that there was once an island there . . . such information as could be secured from reports of men with local knowledge . . . their position has been disputed . . . a bank reported by an old-time sealer."

So here and there, in a few out-of-the-way places, the darkness of antiquity still lingers over the surface of the waters. But it is rapidly being dispelled and most of the length and breadth of the ocean is known; it is only in thinking of its third dimension that we can still apply the concept of the Sea of Darkness. It took centuries to chart the surface of the sea; our progress in delineating the unseen world beneath it seems by comparison phenomenally rapid. But even with all our modern instruments for probing and sampling the deep ocean, no one now can say that we shall ever resolve the last, the ultimate mysteries of the sea.

In its broader meaning, that other concept of the ancients remains. For the sea lies all about us. The commerce of all lands must cross it. The very winds that move over the lands have been cradled on its broad expanse and seek ever to return to it. The continents themselves dissolve and pass to the sea, in grain after grain of eroded land. So the rains that rose from it return again in rivers. In its mysterious past it encompasses all the dim origins of life and receives in the end, after, it may be, many transmutations, the dead husks of that same life. For all at last return to the sea—to Oceanus, the ocean river, like the ever-flowing stream of time, the beginning and the end.

APPENDIX

1. *The Gray Beginnings, page 201*

Our concept of the age of the earth is constantly undergoing revision as older and older rocks are discovered and as methods of study are refined. The oldest rocks now known in North America are in the Canadian Shield area. Their precise age has not been determined, but some from Manitoba and Ontario are believed to have been formed about 3 billion years ago. Even older rocks have been discovered in the Karelia Peninsula in the U.S.S.R., and in South Africa. Geologists are generally of the opinion that present concepts of geologic time will be considerably lengthened in the future. Tentative adjustments of the length of the various periods have already been made (see chart, pages 208–11) and the age of the Cambrian has been pushed back 100 million years compared with the dating assigned to it a decade ago. It is in that immense and shadowy time that preceded the Cambrian, however, that the greatest uncertainty exists. This is the time of the pre-fossiliferous rocks. Whatever life may have inhabited the earth during that time has left few traces, although by indirect evidence we may infer that life existed in some abundance before its record was written in the rocks.

By studies of the rocks themselves geologists have established a few good benchmarks standing out in those vast stretches of time indicated on the chart as the Proterozoic and Archeozoic Eras. These indicate a billion-year age for the ancient Grenville Mountains of eastern North America. Where these rocks are exposed at the surface, as in Ontario, they contain large amounts of graphite, giving silent testimony to the abundance of plant life when these rocks were forming, for plants are a common source of carbon. An age-reading of 1,700,000,000 years has been obtained in the Penokean Mountains of Minnesota and Ontario, formerly known to geologists as the Killarney Mountains. The remains of these once lofty mountains are still to be seen as low, rolling hills. The discovery of even older rocks in Canada, Russia, and Africa, dating back more than 3 billion years, suggests that the earth itself may have been formed about 4½ billion years ago.

2. *The Sunless Sea, page 233*

Man's dream of personally exploring the deepest recesses of the sea has been realized during the past decade. Persistent effort, imaginative vision, and engineering skill have produced a type of underwater craft capable of withstanding the enormous stresses imposed by the greatest depths of the sea and of carrying human observers into these realms that only a few years ago would have seemed beyond the reach of man.

The pioneer in this area of deep ocean exploration was Professor Auguste Piccard, the Swiss physicist who had already attained fame through his ascent into the stratosphere in a balloon. Professor Piccard proposed a depth-exploring vehicle which, instead of being suspended at the end of a cable like the bathysphere, would move freely, independent of control from the surface. Three such bathyscaphes (depth boats) have now been constructed. Observers ride in a pressure-resisting ball suspended from a metal envelope containing high-octane gasoline, an extremely light, almost incompressible fluid. Silos loaded with iron pellets provide ballast; the pellets are held by electromagnets, to be released by the touch of a button when the divers are ready to return to the surface. The first bathyscaphe, provided by the Fonds National de la Recherche Scientifique, which is the Belgian scientific research fund, was known as the FNRS-2. (The FNRS-1 was the stratosphere balloon, which the Fund also provided for Piccard.) The FNRS-2, in experimental unmanned dives, revealed great promise but also had certain defects which were remedied in the craft built later. The second bathyscaphe, the FNRS-3, was built under a treaty between the Belgian and French governments, under the direction of Piccard and Jacques Cousteau. Before the completion of this bathyscaphe, Professor Piccard went to Italy to begin the building of a third bathyscaphe, to be christened *Trieste*.

The FNRS-3 and the *Trieste* made the history-making descents of the 1950's that carried man to the deepest parts of the abyss. In September 1953, Professor Piccard and his son Jacques descended in the *Trieste* to a depth of 10,395 feet in the Mediterranean. This was more than double the previous record. Then in 1954 two Frenchmen in the FNRS-3, Georges Houot and Pierre-Henri Willm, penetrated even deeper into the sea, to depths of 13,287 feet in the open ocean off Dakar on the coast of Africa. In 1958 the *Trieste* was purchased from the Piccards by the United States Office of Naval Research. The following year the *Trieste* was taken to Guam, in the vicinity of which lies the great Mariana Trench, in which echo soundings have revealed the deepest hole now known in any part of the ocean. On January 23, 1960, manned by Jacques Piccard and Don Walsh, the *Trieste* descended to the bottom of this trench, 35,800 feet (or nearly seven miles) beneath the surface.

3. *The Sunless Sea, page 239*

Even today the mystery of the scattering layer has not been completely resolved. Through an ingenious combination of new techniques, however, the picture is gradually becoming clearer. It now appears that at least in some areas—as over the continental shelf off New England—fishes may compose a substantial part of the layer. This has been determined by studying it with a sound source that embraces many frequencies (the ordinary echo sounder is a single-frequency device). This method not only reveals the vertical migration but brings out the fact that the very nature of the scattering changes with depth. Such changes are best interpreted as originating in the swim bladders of fishes, which are compressed under the increasing pressure of a descent into deeper levels of the sea but which expand with ascent toward the surface and consequent lessening of pressure. The formerly held objection that fishes could not possibly be abundant enough to account for the very widespread occurrence of the scattering layer has melted away in the light of information new techniques have given us. It was formerly supposed that a strong echo implied a very dense concentration of whatever creatures were returning the echo. Now it is realized that the tracings recorded by the echo sounder do not necessarily indicate the density of the animals in the scattering layer, so that actually a dark tracing on the record may be produced by only a few strong scatterers passing through the beam in any particular instant of time.

One of the study methods increasingly used during the 1950's was an underwater camera correlated with an echo sounder. All pictures of fishes so obtained have been accompanied by strong echoes. None of these findings rule out the possibility that other organisms may also help to compose the scattering layer. They do furnish rather convincing evidence that fishes compose an important part of a phenomenon that, in all probability, lends itself to no single explanation, but varies as to the species composing it over the vast areas of the ocean.

4. *The Sunless Sea, page 241*

In 1957 Bruce C. Heezen of the Lamont Geological Observatory published a fascinating compilation of fourteen instances of whales entangled in submarine cables between 1877 and 1955. Ten of these accidents occurred off the Pacific coast of Central and South America, two in the South Atlantic, one in the North Atlantic, and one in the Persian Gulf. All entanglements involved sperm whales and it is possible the concentration of reports off the coasts of Ecuador and Peru may be related to a seasonal migration of these whales. The greatest depth at which a whale was found entangled was 620 fathoms or nearly two-thirds of a mile. More whales were trapped by cables at about 500 fathoms than at any other depth, suggesting that the natural food of the sperm whale may be concentrated at about this level. Two significant details were observed in most of these cases: the entanglement occurred near the site of earlier repairs where slack cable lay on the bottom, and the cable was usually wrapped around the whale's jaw. Heezen suggests that as a whale skims along the ocean bottom in search of food its lower jaw may become entangled in a slack loop of cable lying on the bottom. The struggles of the whale to free itself could easily result in its complete entanglement in the cable.

5. *The Sunless Sea, page 247*

For years people have speculated as to the function served by sound production on the part of marine species. It has been known for at least 20 years that the bat finds its way about in lightless caves and on dark nights by means of a physiological equivalent of radar, emitting a stream of high-frequency sound, which returns to it as echoes from any obstructions in its path. Could the sounds produced by certain fishes and marine mammals serve a similar purpose, aiding inhabitants of deep waters to swim in darkness and to find prey? Among the early tape recordings of underwater sound obtained by the Woods Hole Oceanographic Institution was a recording of some mysterious calls that emanated from waters so deep as surely to be lightless. They were distinguished by the fact that each call was followed by a faint echo of itself, so that for want of a better name the unknown author of these eerie sounds was christened the "echo fish." Actual evidence of anything similar to the bat's echo location or echo ranging has come only recently in the form of ingenious experiments performed on captive porpoises by W. N. Kellogg of Florida State University. Dr. Kellogg finds that the porpoises emit streams of underwater sound pulses by which they are able to swim accurately through a field of obstructions without collision. They could do this in water too turbid for vision or in darkness. When the experimenters introduced any object into the tank the porpoises gave forth bursts of sound signals by which the animals appeared to be trying to locate the object. Splashing on the surface, as from a hose or a shower of rain, "produced great disturbance, loud sound signals, undulating porpoise 'alarm' whistles, and 'flight' swimming reactions." When food fish were introduced into the tank under such circumstances that they could not be located visually, the porpoises located them by streams of sound signals, turning their heads to right and left as the returning echoes allowed them to fix the exact location of their target.

6. *The Sunless Sea, page 248*

Latimeria was identified as a coelacanth, or one of an incredibly ancient group of fishes that first appeared in the seas some 300 million years ago. Rocks representing the next 200 million and more years of earth history yielded fossil coelacanths; then, in the Cretaceous, the record of these fishes came to an end. The reappearance of a coelacanth as a live fish off South Africa was at first considered a mysterious and extraordinary incident, not likely to be repeated. An ichthyologist in South Africa, Professor J. L. B. Smith, did not share this view. Believing there must be other coelacanths in the sea, he began a patient search that went on 14 years before it was successful. Then, in December 1952, a second fish of this group was captured near the island of Anjouan, off the northwestern tip of Madagascar. The search was then taken up by Professor J. Millot, Director of the Research Institute in Madagascar. By 1958 Professor Millot had obtained ten more specimens, consisting of seven males and three females.

A plausible explanation of the sixty-million-year gap in the occurrence of fossil coelacanths has been put forward by Dr. Bobb Schaeffer of the American Museum of Natural History. Dr. Schaeffer points out that the earliest coelacanths, from pre-Jurassic time, seem to have inhabited a variety of environments, including freshwater swamps as well as seas. From the Jurassic to the present time, on the other hand, they seem to have been exclusively marine. At the close of the Cretaceous, the great withdrawal of the sea from the continental areas it had overflowed may have confined the coelacanths to the permanent ocean basins. There, in the bottom sediments, their fossils would be so inaccessible that the chance of their discovery would be exceedingly remote.

7. *Hidden Lands, page 250*

The range of echo-sounding instruments has now been so greatly extended that under ideal conditions the most powerful of them are capable of sounding the maximum depths of the sea. Factors such as the nature of the underlying bottom and conditions in the intervening water layers influence the effectiveness with which the sounding devices operate under actual conditions at sea. Nevertheless, the potential range necessary for charting all parts of the sea is now at the command of oceanographers.

8. *Hidden Lands, page 253*

In the ten years that have elapsed since this account of the canyons was written much more has been learned about them, but it may still be said that there is no general agreement about their origin. Many of the resources of the modern oceanographer have been brought to bear on the problem. Divers have engaged in direct exploration of the shallow heads of some of the California canyons, collecting samples of their walls and photographing them. Other canyons have been studied by oceanographers using deep-sea corers or dredges to obtain samples of rocks and sediments. Precision depth recorders have given much new information about their shapes. As a result of these studies it is now known that there are at least five types of canyons, so different in their characteristics that almost certainly they have different origins. No single theory may be expected to explain all of them. Professor Francis S. Shepard, the marine geologist who originally put forward the theory that the canyons had been cut by rivers and later submerged, now feels this explanation is adequate for some canyons but not for others. For example, some marine valleys, trough-shaped and straight-walled and occurring in areas where the earth's crust is in a state of unrest, probably represent a fault or fracture of the rocky floor. The theory that some of the canyons have been cut by vast sediment flows called turbidity currents has gained support as a result of new concepts of dynamic activity on the floor of the sea. Further detailed study of all types of these extraordinarily fascinating features of the sea floor should not only clarify their own history but add greatly to our understanding of the history of the earth.

9. *Hidden Lands, page 255*

Somewhat greater depths have more recently been recorded in the Mariana Trench off the island of Guam, the trench into which the bathyscaphe *Trieste* made its record-breaking descent to the bottom. In this trench the *Challenger* in 1951 recorded a depth of 10,863 meters or about 6.7 miles. Since the exact location of the *Challenger* echo sounding was given, this depth is capable of verification and so is regarded as the maximum depth of which we have authentic record. In 1958, however, Russian scientists aboard the *Vitiaz* reported a finding of slightly greater depths (11,034 meters or 6.8 miles) also in the Mariana Trench, but at an unspecified location.

10. *Hidden Lands, page 257*

The supposition that the Atlantic Ridge may extend across the Arctic basin has been confirmed in exciting new developments in marine geology. Indeed, it is now suggested by some geologists that the whole mid-Atlantic ridge is part of a continuous range of mountains that runs for 40,000 miles across the bottom of the Atlantic, the Arctic, the Pacific, and the Indian Oceans (see Preface).

As for the exploration of the Arctic basin itself—the charting of details so long unknown and merely guessed at—the revolutionary development that made it possible to substitute fact for theory was the use of American nuclear-powered submarines to pass beneath the ice cover and directly explore the depths of this ocean. In 1957 the *Nautilus* (bearing the same name as Wilkins' conventional submarine) first penetrated beneath Arctic ice in a preliminary exploration designed to discover whether it was feasible to explore these regions by submarines. The *Nautilus* remained submerged for 74 hours and covered a distance of almost 1000 miles. A vast amount of data was collected, including depth soundings and measurements of the thickness of the overlying ice. Then in 1958 the *Nautilus* crossed the entire Arctic basin from Point Barrow in Alaska to the North Pole and thence to the Atlantic. In the course of this historic voyage it made the first continuously recorded echo-sounder profile across the center of the Arctic basin. Other nuclear submarines have subsequently contributed to our knowledge of the Arctic. It is now clear, from the work of the nuclear submarines and from other, more conventional explorations, that the bottom topography of the Arctic Ocean is for the most part that of a normal oceanic basin, with flat abyssal plains, scattered sea mounts, and rugged mountains. The greatest depth so far discovered is somewhat more than three miles. The shelf break (from which a steeper descent begins) falls at the unusually shallow depth of 35 fathoms off Alaska. From samplings by coring tubes and dredges and from deep-sea photography it was discovered during the International Geophysical Year that the bottom is widely covered with rocks, pebbles, and shells, the latter chiefly of shallow-water forms. The present ice cover seems to be carrying little or no material such as rock fragments and sand, so the material now found in bottom samples must have come from ice rafted in from surrounding continents during some past geologic time, when the Arctic was relatively open water.

Russian scientists, who have done rather extensive work in marine biology, obtained interesting data which seem to disprove Nansen's earlier belief that the waters of the central Arctic are extremely poor in both plant and animal life. Data collected from the drifting station "North Pole" indicate that both plant and animal plankton in great variety exist in the region of the Pole. Little-studied organisms develop on the surface of the ice; these contain much fat and tint the ice shades of yellow and red. Diatoms are not found on the surface of the ice but develop (along with other plankton) in the lakes that form on the surface of the ice as it melts. By absorbing a great amount of energy from the sun, the abundant diatom colonies contribute to further melting of the ice cover. The wealth of plankton during the Arctic summer attracts numbers of birds and various mammals.

11. *The Long Snowfall, page 267*

Now that the sediments have been measured over much greater areas of the ocean floor, the reaction of oceanographers is one of considerable amazement—but their surprise concerns the fact that on the whole the mantle of sediments is so much thinner than related facts would lead them to expect. Over vast areas of the Pacific the average thickness of the sediments (unconsolidated sediments plus sedimentary rock) is only about a quarter of a mile. It is little thicker over much of the Atlantic. (These are average figures; some much deeper deposits of course exist.) In some areas there has been almost no sedimentation. A few years ago several oceanographers obtained photographs of manganese nodules lying on the floor of the Atlantic at great depths and of others on the Easter Island Ridge of the southeast Pacific. Sharks' teeth dating from the Tertiary, hence possibly as much as 70 million years old, sometimes form the nuclei of these nodules. Certainly their growth, by deposit of successive layers around these nuclei, must be very slow. Hans Petterson has estimated a growth of about 1 mm. per thousand years. Yet during the period these nodules have lain on the ocean floor, sediments deep enough to cover them have not been accumulated.

Some idea of the rate of sedimentation during post-glacial time has been gained by observation of the rate of radioactive decay of some of the components of the sediments. If this sedimentation rate had prevailed during the supposed life of the oceans, the average thickness of the sediments would be enormously greater than it now appears to be. Did much of the deposited sediments dissolve? Were most of the present land masses submerged for far greater periods than we now assume, with consequently long periods of slight erosion? These and other explanations of the mystery of the sediments have been suggested, but none seems wholly satisfying. Possibly the dramatic project of boring holes in the floor of the ocean down to the Mohorovicic discontinuity (Project Mohole; see Preface) will provide the explanation that is now lacking.

12. *Wind and Water, page 312*

From the time of its establishment up to 1960, the warning system has issued eight alerts warning residents of the Hawaiian Islands of the approach of seismic waves. On three of these occasions, waves of major proportions have in fact struck the islands. None have been so large or so destructive, however, as those of May 23, 1960, which spread out across the Pacific from their place of origin in violent earthquakes on the coast of Chile. Without such warning the loss of life would almost certainly have been enormous. As soon as the seismograph at the Honolulu Observatory recorded the first of the Chilean quakes the system went into operation. Reports from the scattered tide stations gave ample notice that a seismic wave had formed and was spreading out across the Pacific. By early news bulletins and later by an official "sea wave warning" the Observatory alerted residents of the area and predicted the time the wave would arrive and the areas to be affected. These predictions proved to be accurate within reasonable limits, and although property damage was heavy, loss of life was limited to the few who disregarded the warnings. Sea wave activity was reported as far west as New Zealand and as far north as Alaska. The Japanese coasts were struck by heavy waves. Although the United States warning system does not now include other nations, officials at Honolulu sent to Japan warnings of the wave which, unfortunately, were disregarded.

The warning system now (in 1960) consists of eight seismograph stations at points on both eastern and western shores of the Pacific and on certain islands, and of twenty widely scattered wave stations, four of which are equipped with automatic wave detectors. The Coast and Geodetic Survey feels that additional wave-reporting tide stations would improve the effectiveness of the system. Its principal defect now, however, is the fact that it is not possible to predict the height of a wave as it reaches any particular shore, and therefore the same alert must be issued for all approaching seismic waves. Research on methods of forecasting wave height is therefore needed. Even with its present limitations, however, the system has filled so great a need that there is strong international interest in extending it to other parts of the world.

13. *Wind and Water, page 313*

The flood of ocean waters that overwhelmed the coast of the Netherlands on February 1, 1953, deserves a place in the history of great storm waves. A winter gale that formed west of Iceland swept across the Atlantic and into the North Sea. All its force was ultimately brought to bear on the first land mass to obstruct the course of its center—the southwestern corner of Holland. The storm-driven waves and tides battered against the dikes in such bitter violence that these ancient defenses were breached in a hundred places, through which the flood rushed in to inundate farms and villages. The storm struck on Saturday, January 31, and by midday of Sunday one-eighth of Holland was under water. The toll included about half a million acres of Holland's best agricultural land—ravaged by water and permeated with salt—thousands of buildings, hundreds of thousands of live stock, and an estimated 1400 people. In all the long history of Holland's struggle against the sea, there has been no comparable assault by ocean waters.

14. *Wind, Sun, and the Spinning of the Earth, page 321*

It is now the fashion among oceanographers to speak of the Gulf Stream System, reflecting the discovery that east of Cape Hatteras there is no longer a continuous river of warm water but a "series of overlapping currents arranged somewhat like the shingles on a roof." Not only do the streams "overlap" but they are narrow and swift. The main branches of the stream that have long been recognized east of the Grand Banks are now known to originate far to westward of the Banks, developing not as branches in the ordinary sense but as a series of new currents, each to the north of the next older one.

As oceanographers study more about the dynamics of circulation in the sea, they are more and more struck by parallels between the ocean of water and the ocean of air. One of the leading students of the Gulf Stream, Columbus Iselin, has commented on the branching of the Stream in terms of a fascinating analogy: "Much the same phenomena seem to be present in the jet streams found at high elevations in the great belts of prevailing westerly winds of mid-latitudes," he says, "although each atmospheric jet has greater dimensions than the overlapping subdivision of the Gulf Stream System."

15. *Wind, Sun, and the Spinning of the Earth, page 324*

One of the most exciting recent events in oceanography was the discovery of a powerful current running under the South Equatorial current but in the opposite direction. The core of the counter current lies about 300 feet below the surface (although shallower near its eastern terminal in the vicinity of the Galapagos Islands). This subsurface current is about 250 miles wide and it flows at least 3500 miles eastward along the equator at a speed of about 3 knots. (The speed of the surface current is only about one knot.) The existence of the current was discovered in 1952 by Townsend Cromwell in the course of a U. S. Fish and Wildlife Service investigation of methods of tuna fishing. Cromwell observed that long lines set for tuna at the equator did not move westward with the surface current, as would be expected, but drifted rapidly in the opposite direction. It was not until 1958, however, that an extensive survey of the current was made by the Scripps Institution of Oceanography and its impressive dimensions measured. This same survey gave further proof that the deep circulation of the ocean is far more complicated than has generally been realized, for beneath the swift-flowing eastward current was still another, flowing to the west. In only the uppermost half mile of Pacific equatorial waters, therefore, there are three great rivers of water, one above the other, each flowing on its own course independent of the other. When such surveys can be extended all the way to the floor of the ocean an even more complex picture will undoubtedly be revealed.

Only a year before the detailed charting of this Pacific current, British and American oceanographers discovered a south-flowing counter current running from the North to the South Atlantic under the Gulf Stream and the Brazil Current. The techniques that make such discoveries possible have only very recently become available to oceanographers. As their use becomes more widespread our almost complete ignorance of the deep circulation of the ocean will be dispelled.

16. *The Global Thermostat, page 351*

During the 1950's enormous advances were made in the development of instruments for the recording of water temperatures. A continuous recording of water temperatures to a depth of several hundred feet may be obtained by towing a thermistor chain behind a vessel. The electronic bathythermograph is potentially capable of obtaining temperatures at any depth, depending on the length of cable available. It is a vast improvement over the original bathythermograph because a recorder on deck traces a continuous graph of the temperatures being registered while the vessel is under way. An even more revolutionary development in the study of sea temperatures is the airborne radiation thermometer which, while flown above the sea, registers the surface temperature with an accuracy of a fraction of a degree. Oceanographers regard this instrument as still in the developmental stage, with further refinement of accuracy possible. However, in such work as tracing the edge of the Gulf Stream these airborne thermometers have already proven themselves enormously useful. During a 1960 survey of the Gulf Stream conducted by the Woods Hole Oceanographic Institution, a low-flying plane covered some 30,000 miles, obtaining surface temperatures in various areas of the Stream.

SUGGESTIONS FOR FURTHER READING*

General Information About the Ocean and Its Life.
- Bigelow, Henry B., and Edmonson, W. T. *Wind Waves at Sea, Breakers and Surf,* U.S. Navy, Hydrographic Office Pub. no. 602, Washington, U.S. Government Printing Office, 1947. 177 pp. *Extremely readable; full of interesting and practical information about waves at sea and along coasts.*
- Johnson, Douglas W. *Shore Processes and Shoreline Development.* New York, John Wiley and Sons, 1919. 584 pp. *Primarily for geologists and engineers concerned with shoreline changes, yet the chapter, The Work of Waves, is unmatched for sheer interest.* Out of print.
- Marmer, H. A. *The Tide.* New York, D. Appleton and Co., 1926. 282 pp. *In this book the late outstanding American authority on tidal phenomena explains the complex behavior of the tides.* Out of print.
- Maury, Matthew Fontaine. *Physical Geography of the Sea.* New York, Harper and Brothers, 1855. 287 pp. *Marks the foundation of the science of oceanography, as the first book to consider the sea as a dynamic whole.* Out of print.
- Murray, Sir John, and Hjort, Johan. *The Depths of the Ocean.* London, Macmillan, 1912. 822 pp. *Based chiefly on the work of the Norwegian research vessel* Michael Sars *in the North Atlantic, this work was for many years the bible of oceanography.* It is now out of print and copies are rare.
- Ommaney, F. D. *The Ocean.* London, Oxford University Press, 1949. 238 pp. *A thoughtful and pleasantly written account of the ocean and its life, for the general reader.*
- Russell, F. S., and Yonge, C. M. *The Seas.* London, Frederick Warne and Co., 1928. 379 pp. *Written chiefly from the biological point of view, this is one of the best general treatments of the subject.*
- Sverdrup, H. U., Fleming, Richard, and Johnson, Martin W. *The Oceans.* New York, Prentice-Hall, Inc., 1942. 1087 pp. *The standard modern textbook of oceanography.*

Some of the most rewarding sources of information about the sea are the Sailing Directions of the U. S. Hydrographic Office (for waters outside of the United States) and the Coast Pilots of the U. S. Coast and Geodetic Survey (for United States shores). Besides giving detailed accounts of the coastlines and coastal waters of the world, these books are repositories of fascinating information on icebergs and sea ice, storms, and fog at sea. Some approach the character of regional geographies. Those dealing with remote and inaccessible coasts are especially interesting. They may be purchased from the issuing agency. The British Admiralty publishes a similar series, as do the appropriate authorities of most maritime nations.

---

*Many of the old basic works on the sea are now out of print but they are well worth pursuing in libraries for the excellent background they provide.

Sea Life in Relation to Its Surroundings.
Hardy, Alister. *The Open Sea.* Part I, The World of Plankton. Boston, Houghton Mifflin Co., 1956. 335 pp. Part II, Fish and Fisheries, Boston, Houghton Mifflin Co., 1959. 322 pp. *A two-part study of marine biology, describing first the little-known creatures of the true sea world beyond the coastal areas, and then the fishes that depend on them.*

Hesse, Richard, Allee, W. C., and Schmidt, Karl P. *Ecological Animal Geography.* New York, John Wiley and Sons (2nd Ed., 1951). 597 pp. *This is an excellent source of information on the intricate relations of living things to their environment, with profuse references to source material. About a fourth of the book is concerned with marine animals.*

Murphy, Robert Cushman. *Oceanic Birds of South America.* New York, Macmillan, 1948. 1245 pp. 2 vols. (originally issued by American Museum of Natural History, 1936). *Highly recommended for an understanding of the relation of birds to the sea and of marine organisms to their environment. It describes little-known shores and islands in extremely readable prose, and contains an extensive bibliography.* Out of print.

Wallace, Alfred Russel. *Island Life.* London, Macmillan, 1880. 526 pp. *Deals in interesting fashion with the basic biology of island life.* Out of print.

Yonge, C. M. *The Sea Shore.* London, Collins, 1949. 311 pp. *For the general reader, a charming and authoritative account of the life of the shore; based chiefly on British localities.* Out of print.

Ricketts, E. F., and Calvin, Jack. *Between Pacific Tides.* Stanford, Stanford University Press, 1948. 365 pp. *An ideal companion for exploring American Pacific shores.*

Exploration and Discovery.
Babcock, William H. *Legendary Islands of the Atlantic; a study in medieval geography.* New York, American Geographical Society, 1922. 385 pp. *Deals with early exploration of the sea and the search for distant lands.* Out of print.

Beebe, William. *Half Mile Down.* New York, Harcourt Brace, 1934. 344 pp. *Stands alone as a vivid eyewitness account of the sea half a mile below the surface.*

Brown, Lloyd A. *The Story of Maps.* Boston, Little, Brown, 1940. 397 pp. *Contains, especially in the chapter, The Haven Finding Art, much of interest about early voyages.*

Challenger Staff. *Report on the Scientific Results of the Exploring Voyage of H. M. S. Challenger, 1873–76.* 40 vols. *See especially volume 1, parts 1 and 2—Narrative of the Cruise—which gives an interesting account of this historic expedition.* Consult in libraries.

Cousteau, Jacques-Yves, and Frederic Dumas. *The Silent World.* New York, Harper and Brothers, 1953. 288 pp. *A fascinating book in which the reader shares Cousteau's long and remarkable experience undersea.*

Darwin, Charles. *The Diary of the Voyage of* H. M. S. Beagle. Edited from the manuscript by Nora Barlow. Cambridge, Cambridge University Press,

1934. 451 pp. *A fresh and charming account, as Darwin actually set it down in the course of the* Beagle *voyage.*

Dugan, James. *Man Under the Sea.* New York, Harper and Brothers, 1956. 332 pp. *An interesting and useful account of man's explorations undersea during the past 5000 years.*

Heyerdahl, Thor. *Kon-Tiki.* Chicago, Rand McNally & Co., 1950. 304 pp. *The Odyssey of six modern Vikings who crossed the Pacific on a primitive raft —one of the great books of the sea.*

History of Earth and Sea.

Brooks, C. E. P. *Climate Through the Ages.* New York, McGraw-Hill, 1949. 395 pp. *Interprets clearly and readably the climatic changes of past ages.* Out of print.

Coleman, A. P. *Ice Ages, Recent and Ancient.* New York, Macmillan, 1926. 296 pp. *An account of Pleistocene glaciation, and also of earlier glacial epochs.* Out of print.

Daly, Reginald. *The Changing World of the Ice Age.* New Haven, Yale University Press, 1934. 271 pp. *A fresh, stimulating, and vigorous treatment of the subject, more easily read, however, against some background of geology.* Out of print.

Our Mobile Earth. New York, Charles Scribner's Sons, 1926. 342 pp. *For the general reader; an excellent picture of the earth's continuing development.* Out of print.

Hussey, Russell C. *Historical Geology: The Geological History of North America.* New York and London, McGraw-Hill, 1947. 465 pp. Out of print.

Miller, William J. *An Introduction to Historical Geology, with Special Reference to North America.* New York, D. Van Nostrand Co., 6th Ed. 1952. 499 pp.

Schuchert, Charles, and Dunbar, Carl O. *Outlines of Historical Geology.* New York, John Wiley and Sons, 1941. 291 pp. *Any one of these three books will give the general reader a good conception of this fascinating subject; the treatment by the various authors differs enough that all may be read with profit.*

Shepard, Francis P. *Submarine Geology.* New York, Harper and Brothers, 1948. 348 pp. *The first textbook in a field which is still in the pioneering stages.*

Outstanding Sea Prose.

These books are listed because each, in one way or another, captures the sea's varied and always changing moods; all are among my own favorite volumes.

Beston, Henry. *The Outermost House: A Year of Life on the Great Beach of Cape Cod.* New York, Rinehart and Company, 1949. 222 pp.

Conrad, Joseph. *The Mirror of the Sea.* New York, Doubleday, Anchor Books, 1960. 304 pp. (Combined with Conrad's *A Personal Record.*)

Hughes, Richard. *In Hazard.* New York, Harper and Brothers, 1938. 279 pp. (also published by Penguin Books, 1943).

Melville, Herman. *Moby-Dick*. Available in many editions, as Modern Library, New American Library, Pocket Books.

Nordhoff, Charles, and Hall, James Norman. *Men Against the Sea*. Boston, Little, Brown, 1934. 251 pp. (also published by Pocket Books, 1946).

Tomlinson, H. M. *The Sea and the Jungle*. New York, Modern Library, 1928. 332 pp. Paper: Dutton (Everyman).

Benjamin Franklin's Map of the Gulf Stream.

THE EDGE OF THE SEA

With illustrations by Bob Hines

ACKNOWLEDGMENTS

Our understanding of the nature of the shore and of the lives of sea animals has been acquired through the labor of many hundreds of people, some of whom have devoted a lifetime to the study of a single group of animals. In my researches for this book I have been deeply conscious of the debt of gratitude we owe these men and women, whose toil allows us to sense the wholeness of life as it is lived by many of the creatures of the shore. I am even more immediately aware of my debt to those I have consulted personally, comparing observations, seeking advice and information and always finding it freely and generously given. It is impossible to express my thanks to all these people by name, but a few must have special mention. Several members of the staff of the United States National Museum have not only settled many of my questions but have given invaluable advice and assistance to Bob Hines in his preparation of the drawings. For this help we are especially grateful to R. Tucker Abbott, Frederick M. Bayer, Fenner Chace, the late Austin H. Clark, Harald Rehder, and Leonard Schultz. Dr. W. N. Bradley of the United States Geological Survey has been my friendly advisor on geological matters, answering many questions and critically reading portions of the manuscript. Professor William Randolph Taylor of the University of Michigan has responded instantly and cheerfully to my calls for aid in identifying marine algae, and Professor and Mrs. T. A. Stephenson of the University College of Wales, whose work on the ecology of the shore has been especially stimulating, have advised and encouraged me in correspondence. To Professor Henry B. Bigelow of Harvard University I am everlastingly in debt for encouragement and friendly counsel over many years. The grant of a Guggenheim Fellowship helped finance the first year of study in which the foundations of this book were laid, and some of the field work that has taken me along the tide lines from Maine to Florida.

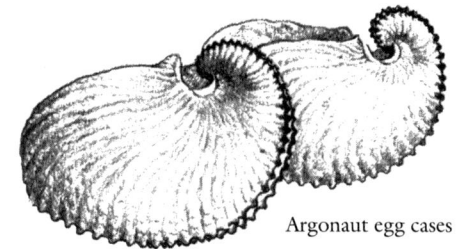
Argonaut egg cases

PREFACE

Like the sea itself, the shore fascinates us who return to it, the place of our dim ancestral beginnings. In the recurrent rhythms of tides and surf and in the varied life of the tide lines there is the obvious attraction of movement and change and beauty. There is also, I am convinced, a deeper fascination born of inner meaning and significance.

When we go down to the low-tide line, we enter a world that is as old as the earth itself—the primeval meeting place of the elements of earth and water, a place of compromise and conflict and eternal change. For us as living creatures it has special meaning as an area in or near which some entity that could be distinguished as Life first drifted in shallow waters—reproducing, evolving, yielding that endlessly varied stream of living things that has surged through time and space to occupy the earth.

To understand the shore, it is not enough to catalogue its life. Understanding comes only when, standing on a beach, we can sense the long rhythms of earth and sea that sculptured its land forms and produced the rock and sand of which it is composed; when we can sense with the eye and ear of the mind the surge of life beating always at its shores—blindly, inexorably pressing for a foothold. To understand the life of the shore, it is not enough to pick up an empty shell and say "This is a murex," or "That is an angel wing." True understanding demands intuitive comprehension of the whole life of the creature that once inhabited this empty shell: how it survived amid surf and storms, what were its enemies, how it found food and reproduced its kind, what were its relations to the particular sea world in which it lived.

The seashores of the world may be divided into three basic types: the rugged shores of rock, the sand beaches, and the coral reefs and all their associated features. Each has its typical community of plants and animals. The Atlantic coast of the United States is one of the few in the world that provide clear examples of each of these types. I have chosen it as the setting for my pictures of shore life, although—such is the universality of the sea world—the broad outlines of the pictures might apply on many shores of the earth.

I have tried to interpret the shore in terms of that essential unity that binds life to the earth. In Chapter I, in a series of recollections of places that have stirred me deeply, I have expressed some of the thoughts and feelings that make the sea's edge, for me, a place of exceeding beauty and fascination. Chapter II introduces as basic themes the sea forces that will recur again and again throughout the book as molding and determining the life of the shore: surf, currents, tides, the very waters of the sea. Chapters III, IV, and V are interpretations, respectively, of a rocky coast, the sand beaches, and the world of the coral reefs.

The drawings by Bob Hines have been provided in abundance so the reader may gain a sense of familiarity with the creatures that move through these pages, and may also be helped to recognize those he meets in his own explorations of the shore. For the convenience of those who like to pigeonhole their findings neatly in the classification schemes the human mind has devised, an appendix presents the conventional groups, or phyla, of plants and animals and describes typical examples. Each form mentioned in the book itself is listed under its Latin as well as its common name in the index.

CONTENTS

	Preface	415
I.	The Marginal World	421
II.	Patterns of Shore Life	429
III.	The Rocky Shores.........................	457
IV.	The Rim of Sand..........................	537
V.	The Coral Coast	599
VI.	The Enduring Sea.........................	653
	Appendix: Classification	655

To Dorothy and Stanley Freeman

*who have gone down with me into the low-tide world
and have felt its beauty and its mystery.*

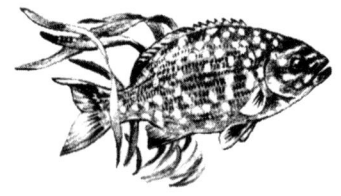

THE EDGE OF THE SEA

The Marginal World

THE EDGE OF the sea is a strange and beautiful place. All through the long history of Earth it has been an area of unrest where waves have broken heavily against the land, where the tides have pressed forward over the continents, receded, and then returned. For no two successive days is the shore line precisely the same. Not only do the tides advance and retreat in their eternal rhythms, but the level of the sea itself is never at rest. It rises or falls as the glaciers melt or grow, as the floor of the deep ocean basins shifts under its increasing load of sediments, or as the earth's crust along the continental margins warps up or down in adjustment to strain and tension. Today a little more land may belong to the sea, tomorrow a little less. Always the edge of the sea remains an elusive and indefinable boundary.

The shore has a dual nature, changing with the swing of the tides, belonging now to the land, now to the sea. On the ebb tide it knows the harsh extremes of the land world, being exposed to heat and cold, to wind, to rain and drying sun. On the flood tide it is a water world, returning briefly to the relative stability of the open sea.

Only the most hardy and adaptable can survive in a region so mutable, yet the area between the tide lines is crowded with plants and animals. In this difficult world of the shore, life displays its enormous toughness and vitality by occupying almost every conceivable niche. Visibly, it carpets the intertidal rocks; or half hidden, it descends into fissures and crevices, or hides under boulders, or lurks in the wet gloom of sea caves. Invisibly, where the casual observer would say there is no life, it lies deep in the sand, in burrows and tubes and passageways. It tunnels into solid rock and bores into peat and clay. It encrusts weeds or drifting spars or the hard, chitinous shell of a lobster. It exists minutely, as the film of bacteria that spreads over a rock surface or a wharf piling; as spheres of protozoa, small as pinpricks, sparkling at the surface of the sea; and as Lilliputian beings swimming through dark pools that lie between the grains of sand.

The shore is an ancient world, for as long as there has been an earth and sea there has been this place of the meeting of land and water. Yet it is a world that keeps alive the sense of continuing creation and of the relentless drive of life. Each time that I enter it, I gain some new awareness of its beauty and its deeper meanings, sensing that intricate fabric of life by which one creature is linked with another, and each with its surroundings.

In my thoughts of the shore, one place stands apart for its revelation of exquisite beauty. It is a pool hidden within a cave that one can visit only rarely and briefly when the lowest of the year's low tides fall below it, and perhaps from that very fact it acquires some of its special beauty. Choosing such a tide, I hoped for a glimpse of the pool. The ebb was to fall early in the morning. I knew that if the wind held from the northwest and no interfering swell ran in from a distant storm the level of the sea should drop below the entrance to the pool. There had been sudden ominous showers in the night, with rain like handfuls of gravel flung on the roof. When I looked out into the early morning the sky was full of a gray dawn light but the sun had not yet risen. Water and air were pallid. Across the bay the moon was a luminous disc in the western sky, suspended above the dim line of distant shore—the full August moon, drawing the tide to the low, low levels of the threshold of the alien sea world. As I watched, a gull flew by, above the spruces. Its breast was rosy with the light of the unrisen sun. The day was, after all, to be fair.

Later, as I stood above the tide near the entrance to the pool, the promise of that rosy light was sustained. From the base of the steep wall of rock on which I stood, a moss-covered ledge jutted seaward into deep water. In the surge at the rim of the ledge the dark fronds of oarweeds swayed, smooth and gleaming as leather. The projecting ledge was the path to the small hidden cave and its pool. Occasionally a swell, stronger than the rest, rolled smoothly over the rim and broke in foam against the cliff. But the intervals between such swells were long enough to admit me to the ledge and long enough for a glimpse of that fairy pool, so seldom and so briefly exposed.

And so I knelt on the wet carpet of sea moss and looked back into the dark cavern that held the pool in a shallow basin. The floor of the cave was only a few inches below the roof, and a mirror had been created in which all that grew on the ceiling was reflected in the still water below.

Under water that was clear as glass the pool was carpeted with green sponge. Gray patches of sea squirts glistened on the ceiling and colonies of soft coral were a pale apricot color. In the moment when I looked into the cave a little elfin starfish hung down, suspended by the merest thread, perhaps by only a single tube foot. It reached down to touch its own reflection, so perfectly delineated that there might have been, not one starfish, but two. The beauty of the reflected images and of the limpid pool itself was the poignant beauty of things that are ephemeral, existing only until the sea should return to fill the little cave.

Whenever I go down into this magical zone of the low water of the spring tides, I look for the most delicately beautiful of all the shore's inhabitants—flowers that are not plant but animal, blooming on the threshold of the deeper sea. In that fairy cave I was not disappointed. Hanging from its roof were the pendent flowers of the hydroid Tubularia, pale pink, fringed and delicate as the wind flower. Here were creatures so exquisitely fashioned that they seemed unreal, their beauty too fragile to exist in a world of crushing force. Yet every detail was functionally useful, every stalk and hydranth and petal-like tentacle fashioned for dealing with the realities of existence. I knew that they were merely waiting, in that moment of the tide's ebbing, for the return of the sea. Then in the rush of water, in the surge of surf and the pressure of the incoming tide, the delicate flower heads would stir with life. They would sway on their slender stalks, and their long tentacles would sweep the returning water, finding in it all that they needed for life.

And so in that enchanted place on the threshold of the sea the realities that possessed my mind were far from those of the land world I had left an hour before. In a different way the same sense of remoteness and of a world apart came to me in a twilight hour on a great beach on the coast of Georgia. I had come down after sunset and walked far out over sands that lay wet and gleaming, to the very edge of the retreating sea. Looking back across that immense flat, crossed by winding, water-filled gullies and here and there holding shallow pools left by the tide, I was filled with awareness that this intertidal area, although abandoned briefly and rhythmically by the sea, is always reclaimed by the rising tide. There at the edge of low water the beach with its reminders of the land seemed far away. The only sounds were those of the wind and the sea and the birds. There was one sound of wind moving over water, and another of water sliding over the sand and tumbling down the faces of its own wave forms. The flats were astir with birds, and the voice of the willet rang insistently. One of them stood at the edge of the water and gave its loud, urgent cry; an answer came from far up the beach and the two birds flew to join each other.

The flats took on a mysterious quality as dusk approached and the last evening light was reflected from the scattered pools and creeks. Then birds became only dark shadows, with no color discernible. Sanderlings scurried across the beach like little ghosts, and here and there the darker forms of the willets stood out. Often I could come very close to them before they would start up in alarm—the sanderlings running, the willets flying up, crying. Black skimmers flew along the ocean's edge silhouetted against the dull, metallic gleam, or they went flitting above the sand like large, dimly seen moths. Sometimes they "skimmed" the winding creeks of tidal water, where little spreading surface ripples marked the presence of small fish.

The shore at night is a different world, in which the very darkness that hides the distractions of daylight brings into sharper focus the elemental realities. Once, exploring the night beach, I surprised a small ghost crab in the searching beam of my torch. He was lying in a pit he had dug just above the surf, as though watching the sea and waiting. The blackness of the night possessed water, air, and beach. It was the darkness of an older world, before Man. There was no sound but the all-enveloping, primeval sounds of wind blowing over water and sand, and of waves crashing on the beach. There was no other visible life—just one small crab near the sea. I have seen hundreds of ghost crabs in other settings, but suddenly I was filled with the odd sensation that for the first time I knew the creature in its own world—that I understood, as never before, the essence of its being. In that moment time was suspended; the world to which I belonged did not exist and I might have been an onlooker from outer space. The little crab alone with the sea became a symbol that stood for life itself—for the delicate, destructible, yet incredibly vital force that somehow holds its place amid the harsh realities of the inorganic world.

The sense of creation comes with memories of a southern coast, where the sea and the mangroves, working together, are building a wilderness of thousands of small islands off the southwestern coast of Florida, separated from each other by a tortuous pattern of bays, lagoons, and narrow waterways. I remember a winter day when the sky was blue and drenched with sunlight; though there was no wind one was conscious of flowing air like cold clear crystal. I had landed on the surf-washed tip of one of those islands, and then worked my way around to the sheltered bay side. There I found the tide far out, exposing the broad mud flat of a cove bordered by the mangroves with their twisted branches, their glossy leaves, and their long prop roots reaching down, grasping and holding the mud, building the land out a little more, then again a little more.

The mud flats were strewn with the shells of that small, exquisitely colored mollusk, the rose tellin, looking like scattered petals of pink roses. There must have been a colony nearby, living buried just under the surface of the mud. At first the only creature visible was a small heron in gray and rusty plumage —a reddish egret that waded across the flat with the stealthy, hesitant movements of its kind. But other land creatures had been there, for a line of fresh tracks wound in and out among the mangrove roots, marking the path of a raccoon feeding on the oysters that gripped the supporting roots with projections from their shells. Soon I found the tracks of a shore bird, probably a sanderling, and followed them a little; then they turned toward the water and were lost, for the tide had erased them and made them as though they had never been.

Looking out over the cove I felt a strong sense of the interchangeability of land and sea in this marginal world of the shore, and of the links between the life of the two. There was also an awareness of the past and of the continuing flow of time, obliterating much that had gone before, as the sea had that morning washed away the tracks of the bird.

The sequence and meaning of the drift of time were quietly summarized in the existence of hundreds of small snails—the mangrove periwinkles—browsing on the branches and roots of the trees. Once their ancestors had been sea dwellers, bound to the salt waters by every tie of their life processes. Little by little over the thousands and millions of years the ties had been broken, the snails had adjusted themselves to life out of water, and now today they were living many feet above the tide to which they only occasionally returned. And perhaps, who could say how many ages hence, there would be in their descendants not even this gesture of remembrance for the sea.

The spiral shells of other snails—these quite minute—left winding tracks on the mud as they moved about in search of food. They were horn shells, and when I saw them I had a nostalgic moment when I wished I might see what Audubon saw, a century and more ago. For such little horn shells were the food of the flamingo, once so numerous on this coast, and when I half closed my eyes I could almost imagine a flock of these magnificent flame birds feeding in that cove, filling it with their color. It was a mere yesterday in the life of the earth that they were there; in nature, time and space are relative matters, perhaps most truly perceived subjectively in occasional flashes of insight, sparked by such a magical hour and place.

There is a common thread that links these scenes and memories—the spectacle of life in all its varied manifestations as it has appeared, evolved, and sometimes died out. Underlying the beauty of the spectacle there is meaning and significance. It is the elusiveness of that meaning that haunts us, that sends us again and again into the natural world where the key to the riddle is hidden. It sends us back to the edge of the sea, where the drama of life played its first scene on earth and perhaps even its prelude; where the forces of evolution are at work today, as they have been since the appearance of what we know as life; and where the spectacle of living creatures faced by the cosmic realities of their world is crystal clear.

Patterns of Shore Life

THE EARLY HISTORY of life as it is written in the rocks is exceedingly dim and fragmentary, and so it is not possible to say when living things first colonized the shore, nor even to indicate the exact time when life arose. The rocks that were laid down as sediments during the first half of the earth's history, in the Archeozoic era, have since been altered chemically and physically by the pressure of many thousands of feet of superimposed layers and by the intense heat of the deep regions to which they have been confined during much of their existence. Only in a few places, as in eastern Canada, are they exposed and accessible for study, but if these pages of the rock history ever contained any clear record of life, it has long since been obliterated.

The following pages—the rocks of the next several hundred million years, known as the Proterozoic era—are almost as disappointing. There are immense deposits of iron, which may possibly have been laid down with the help of certain algae and bacteria. Other deposits—strange globular masses of calcium carbonate—seem to have been formed by lime-secreting algae. Supposed fossils or faint impressions in these ancient rocks have been tentatively identified as sponges, jellyfish, or hard-shelled creatures with jointed legs called arthropods, but the more skeptical or conservative scientists regard these traces as having an inorganic origin.

Suddenly, following the early pages with their sketchy records, a whole section of the history seems to have been destroyed. Sedimentary rocks representing untold millions of years of pre-Cambrian history have disappeared, having been lost by erosion or possibly, through violent changes in the surface of the earth, brought into a location that now is at the bottom of the deep sea. Because of this loss a seemingly unbridgeable gap in the story of life exists.

The scarcity of fossil records in the early rocks and the loss of whole blocks of sediments may be linked with the chemical nature of the early sea and the atmosphere. Some specialists believe that the pre-Cambrian ocean was deficient in calcium or at least in the conditions that make easily possible the secretion of calcium shells and skeletons. If so, its inhabitants must have been for the most part soft-bodied and so not readily fossilized. A large amount of carbon dioxide in the atmosphere and its relative deficiency in the sea would also have affected the weathering of rock, according to geological theory, so that the sedimentary rocks of pre-Cambrian time must have been repeatedly eroded, washed away, and newly sedimented, with consequent destruction of fossils.

When the record is resumed in the rocks of the Cambrian period, which are about half a billion years old, all the major groups of invertebrate animals (including the principal inhabitants of the shore) suddenly appear, fully formed and flourishing. There are sponges and jellyfish, worms of all sorts, a few simple snail-like mollusks, and arthropods. Algae also are abundant, although no higher plants appear. But the basic plan of each of the large groups of animals and plants that now inhabit the shore had been at least projected in those Cambrian seas, and we may suppose, on good evidence, that the strip between the tide lines 500 million years ago bore at least a general resemblance to the intertidal area of the present stage of earth history.

We may suppose also that for at least the preceding half-billion years those invertebrate groups, so well developed in the Cambrian, had been evolving from simpler forms, although what they looked like we may never know. Possibly the larval stages of some of the species now living may resemble those ancestors whose remains the earth seems to have destroyed or failed to preserve.

During the hundreds of millions of years since the dawn of the Cambrian, sea life has continued to evolve. Subdivisions of the original basic groups have arisen, new species have been created, and many of the early forms have disappeared as evolution has developed others better fitted to meet the demands of their world. A few of the primitive creatures of Cambrian time have representatives today that are little changed from their early ancestors, but these are the exception. The shore, with its difficult and changing conditions, has been a testing ground in which the precise and perfect adaptation to environment is an indispensable condition of survival.

All the life of the shore—the past and the present—by the very fact of its existence there, gives evidence that it has dealt successfully with the realities of its world—the towering physical realities of the sea itself, and the subtle life relationships that bind each living thing to its own community. The patterns of life as created and shaped by these realities intermingle and overlap so that the major design is exceedingly complex.

Whether the bottom of the shallow waters and the intertidal area consists of rocky cliffs and boulders, of broad plains of sand, or of coral reefs and shallows determines the visible pattern of life. A rocky coast, even though it is swept by surf, allows life to exist openly through adaptations for clinging to the firm surfaces provided by the rocks and by other structural provisions for dissipating the force of the waves. The visible evidence of living things is everywhere about—a colorful tapestry of seaweeds, barnacles, mussels, and snails covering the rocks—while more delicate forms find refuge in cracks and crevices or by creeping under boulders. Sand, on the other hand, forms a yielding, shifting substratum of unstable nature, its particles incessantly stirred by the waves, so that few living things can establish or hold a place on its surface or even in its upper layers. All have gone below, and in burrows, tubes, and underground chambers the hidden life of the sands is lived. A

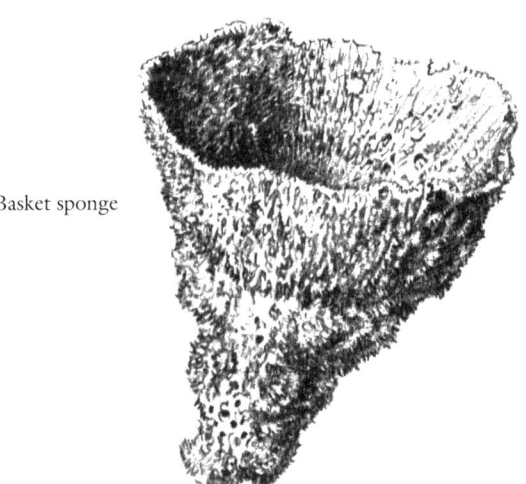

Basket sponge

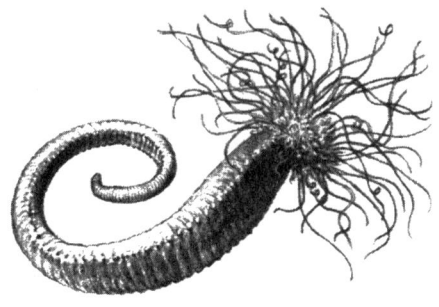

Amphitrite, a worm that inhabits muddy pockets among rocks.

coast dominated by coral reefs is necessarily a warm coast, its existence made possible by warm ocean currents establishing the climate in which the coral animals can thrive. The reefs, living or dead, provide a hard surface to which living things may cling. Such a coast is somewhat like one bordered by rocky cliffs, but with differences introduced by smothering layers of chalky sediments. The richly varied tropical fauna of coral coasts has therefore developed special adaptations that set it apart from the life of mineral rock or sand. Because the American Atlantic coast includes examples of all three types of shore, the various patterns of life related to the nature of the coast itself are displayed there with beautiful clarity.

Still other patterns are superimposed on the basic geologic ones. The surf dwellers are different from those who live in quiet waters, even if members of the same species. In a region of strong tides, life exists in successive bands or zones, from the high-water mark to the line of the lowest ebb tides; these zones are obscured where there is little tidal action or on sand beaches where life is driven underground. The currents, modifying temperature and distributing the larval stages of sea creatures, create still another world.

Again the physical facts of the American Atlantic coast are such that the observer of its life has spread before him, almost with the clarity of a well-conceived scientific experiment, a demonstration of the modifying effect of tides, surf, and currents. It happens that the northern rocks, where life is lived openly, lie in the region of some of the strongest tides of the world, those within the area of the Bay of Fundy. Here the zones of life created by the tides have the simple graphic force of a diagram. The tidal zones being obscured on sandy shores, one is free there to observe the effect of the surf. Neither strong tides nor heavy surf visits the southern tip of Florida. Here is a typical coral coast, built by the coral animals and the mangroves that multiply and spread in the calm, warm waters —a world whose inhabitants have drifted there on ocean currents from the West Indies, duplicating the strange tropical fauna of that region.

And over all these patterns there are others created by the sea water itself—bringing or withholding food, carrying substances of powerful chemical nature that, for good or ill, affect the lives of all they touch. Nowhere on the shore is the relation of a creature to its surroundings a matter of a single cause and effect; each living thing is bound to its world by many threads, weaving the intricate design of the fabric of life.

The problem of breaking waves need not be faced by inhabitants of the open ocean, for they can sink into deep water to avoid rough seas. An animal or plant of the shore has no such means of escape. The surf releases all its tremendous energy as it breaks against the shore, sometimes delivering blows of almost incredible violence. Exposed coasts of Great Britain and other eastern Atlantic islands receive some of the most violent surf in the world, created by winds that sweep across the whole expanse of ocean. It sometimes strikes with a force of two tons to the square foot. The American Atlantic coast, being a sheltered shore, receives no such surf, yet even here the waves of winter storms or of summer hurricanes have enormous size and destructive power. The island of Monhegan on the coast

Cake urchin,
a sand-dwelling animal

of Maine lies unprotected in the path of such storms and receives their waves on its steep seaward-facing cliffs. In a violent storm the spray from breaking waves is thrown over the crest of White Head, about 100 feet above the sea. In some storms the green water of actual waves sweeps over a lower cliff known as Gull Rock. It is about 60 feet high.

The effect of waves is felt on the bottom a considerable distance offshore. Lobster traps set in water nearly 200 feet deep often are shifted about or have stones carried into them. But the critical problem, of course, is the one that exists on or very close to the shore, where waves are breaking. Very few coasts have completely defeated the attempts of living things to gain a foothold. Beaches are apt to be barren if they are composed of loose coarse sand that shifts in the surf and then dries quickly when the tide falls. Others, of firm sand, though they may look barren, actually sustain a rich fauna in their deeper layers. A beach composed of many cobblestones that grind against each other in the surf is an impossible home for most creatures. But the shore formed of rocky cliffs and ledges, unless the surf be of extraordinary force, is host to a large and abundant fauna and flora.

Barnacles are perhaps the best example of successful inhabitants of the surf zone. Limpets do almost as well, and so do the small rock periwinkles. The coarse brown seaweeds called wracks or rockweeds possess species that thrive in moderately heavy surf, while others require a degree of protection. After a little experience one can learn to judge the exposure of any shore merely by identifying its fauna and flora. If, for example, there is a broad area covered by the knotted wrack—a long and slender weed that lies like a tangled mass of cordage when the tide is out—if this predominates, we know the shore is a moderately protected one, seldom visited by heavy surf. If, however, there is little or none of the knotted wrack but instead a zone covered by a rockweed of much shorter stature, branching repeatedly, its fronds flattened and tapering at the ends, then we sense more keenly the presence of the open sea and the crushing power of its surf. For the forked wrack and other members of a community of low-growing seaweeds with strong and elastic tissues are sure indicators of an exposed coast and can thrive in seas the knotted wrack cannot endure.

And if, on still another shore, there is little vegetation of any sort, but instead only a rock zone whitened by a living snow of barnacles—thousands upon thousands of them raising their sharp-pointed cones to the smother of the surf—we may be sure this coast is quite unprotected from the force of the sea.

The barnacle has two advantages that allow it to succeed where almost all other life fails to survive. Its low conical shape deflects the force of the waves and sends the water rolling off harmlessly. The whole base of the cone, moreover, is fixed to the rock with natural cement of extraordinary strength; to remove it one has to use a sharp-bladed knife. And so those twin dangers of the surf zone—the threat of being washed away and of being crushed—have little reality for the barnacle. Yet its existence in such a place takes on a touch of the miraculous when we remember this fact: it was not the adult creature, whose shape and firmly cemented base are precise adaptations to the surf, that gained a foothold here; it was the larva. In the turbulence of heavy seas, the delicate larva had to choose its spot on the wave-washed rocks, to settle there, and somehow not be washed away during those critical hours while its tissues were being reorganized in their transformation to the adult form, while the cement was extruded and hardened, and the shell plates grew up about the soft body. To accomplish all this in heavy surf seems to me a far more difficult thing than is required of the spore of a rockweed; yet the fact remains that the barnacles can colonize exposed rocks where the weeds are unable to gain a footing.

The streamlined form has been adopted and even improved upon by other creatures, some of whom have omitted the permanent attachment to the rocks. The limpet is one of these—a simple and primitive snail that wears above its tissues a shell like the hat of a Chinese coolie. From this smoothly sloping cone the surf rolls away harmlessly; indeed, the blows of falling water only press down more firmly the suction cup of fleshy tissue beneath the shell, strengthening its grip on the rock.

Still other creatures, while retaining a smoothly rounded contour, put out anchor lines to hold their places on the rocks. Such a device is used by the mussels, whose numbers in even a limited area may be almost astronomical. The shells of each animal are bound to the rock by a series of tough threads, each of shining silken appearance. The threads are a kind of natural silk, spun by a gland in the foot. These anchor lines extend out in all directions; if some are broken, the others hold while the damaged lines are being replaced. But most of the threads are directed forward and in the pounding of storm surf the mussel tends to swing around and head into the seas, taking them on the narrow "prow" and so minimizing their force.

Even the sea urchins can anchor themselves firmly in moderately strong surf. Their slender tube feet, each equipped with a suction disc at its tip, are thrust out in all directions. I have marveled at the green urchins on a Maine shore, clinging to the exposed rock at low water of spring tides, where the beautiful coralline algae spread a rose-colored crust beneath the shining green of their bodies. At that place the bottom slopes away steeply and when the waves at low tide break on the crest of the slope, they drain back to the sea with a strong rush of water. Yet as each wave recedes, the urchins remain on their accustomed stations, undisturbed.

For the long-stalked kelps that sway in dusky forests just below the level of the spring tides, survival in the surf zone is largely a matter of chemistry. Their tissues contain large amounts of alginic acid and its salts, which create a tensile strength and elasticity able to withstand the pulling and pounding of the waves.

Still others—animal and plant—have been able to invade the surf zone by reducing life to a thin creeping mat of cells. In such form many sponges, ascidians, bryozoans, and algae can endure the force of waves. Once removed from the shaping and conditioning effect of surf, however, the same species may take on entirely different forms. The pale green crumb-of-bread sponge lies flat and almost paper-thin on rocks facing toward the sea; back in one of the deep rock pools its tissues build up into thickened masses, sprinkled with the cone-and-crater structure that is one of the marks of the species. Or the golden-star tunicate may expose a simple sheet of jelly to the waves, though in quiet water it hangs down in pendulous lobes flecked with the starry forms of the creatures that comprise it.

As on the sands almost everything has learned to endure the surf by burrowing down to escape it, so on the rocks some have found safety by boring. Where ancient marl is exposed on the Carolina coast, it is riddled by date mussels. Masses of peat contain the delicately sculptured shells of mollusks called angel wings, seemingly fragile as china, but nevertheless able to bore into clay or rock; concrete piers are drilled by small boring clams; wooden timbers by other clams and isopods. All of these creatures have exchanged their freedom for a sanctuary from the waves, being imprisoned forever within the chambers they have carved.

The vast current systems, which flow through the oceans like rivers, lie for the most part offshore and one might suppose their influence in intertidal matters to be slight. Yet the currents have far-reaching effects, for they transport immense volumes of water over long distances—water that holds its original temperature through thousands of miles of its journey. In this way tropical warmth is carried northward and arctic cold brought far down toward the equator. The currents, probably more than any other single element, are the creators of the marine climate.

The importance of climate lies in the fact that life, even as broadly defined to include all living things of every sort, exists within a relatively narrow range of temperature, roughly between 32° F. and 210° F. The planet Earth is particularly favorable for life because it has a fairly stable temperature. Especially in the sea, temperature changes are moderate and gradual and many animals are so delicately adjusted to the accustomed water climate that an abrupt or drastic change is fatal. Animals

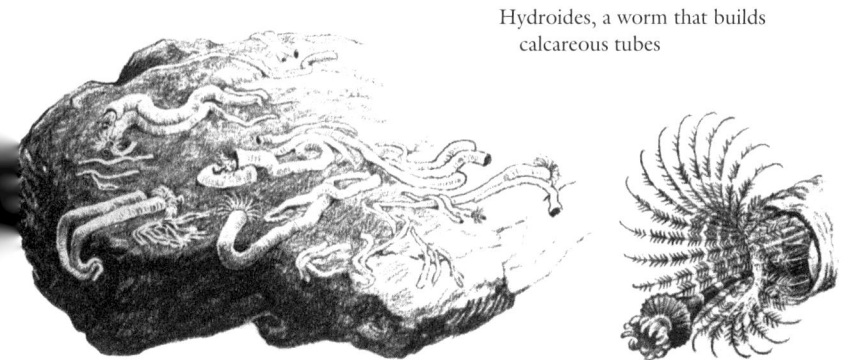

Hydroides, a worm that builds calcareous tubes

living on the shore and exposed to air temperatures at low tide are necessarily a little more hardy, but even these have their preferred range of heat and cold beyond which they seldom stray.

Most tropical animals are more sensitive to change—especially toward higher temperatures—than northern ones, and this is probably because the water in which they live normally varies by only a few degrees throughout the year. Some tropical sea urchins, keyhole limpets, and brittle stars die when the shallow waters heat to about 99° F. The arctic jellyfish Cyanea, on the other hand, is so hardy that it continues to pulsate when half its bell is imprisoned in ice, and may revive even after being solidly frozen for hours. The horseshoe crab is an example of an animal that is very tolerant of temperature change. It has a wide range as a species, and its northern forms can survive being frozen into ice in New England, while its southern representatives thrive in tropical waters of Florida and southward to Yucatán.

Shore animals for the most part endure the seasonal changes of temperate coasts, but some find it necessary to escape the extreme cold of winter. Ghost crabs and beach fleas are believed to dig very deep holes in the sand and go into hibernation. Mole crabs that feed in the surf much of the year retire to the bottom offshore in winter. Many of the hydroids, so like flowering plants in appearance, shrink down to the very core of their animal beings in winter, withdrawing all living tissues into the basal stalk. Other shore animals, like annuals in the plant kingdom, die at the end of summer. All of the white jellyfish, so common in coastal waters during the summer, are dead when the last autumn gale has blown itself out, but the next generation exists as little plant-like beings attached to the rocks below the tide.

For the great majority of shore inhabitants that continue to live in the accustomed places throughout the year, the most dangerous aspect of winter is not cold but ice. In years when much shore ice is formed, the rocks may be scraped clean of barnacles, mussels, and seaweeds simply by the mechanical action of ice grinding in the surf. After this happens, several growing seasons separated by moderate winters may be needed to restore the full community of living creatures.

Because most sea animals have definite preferences as to aquatic climate, it is possible to divide the coastal waters of eastern North America into zones of life. While variation in the temperature of the water within these zones is in part a matter of the advance from southern to northern latitudes, it is also strongly influenced by the pattern of the ocean currents—the sweep of warm tropical water carried northward in the Gulf Stream, and the chill Labrador Current creeping down from the north on the landward border of the Stream, with complex intermixing of warm and cold water between the boundaries of the currents.

From the point where it pours through the Florida straits up as far as Cape Hatteras, the Stream follows the outer edge of the continental shelf, which varies greatly in width. At Jupiter Inlet on the east coast of Florida this shelf is so narrow that one can stand on shore and look out across emerald-green shallows to the place where the water suddenly takes on the intense blue of the Stream. At about this point there seems to exist a temperature barrier, separating the tropical fauna of southern Florida and the Keys from the warm-temperate fauna of the area lying between Cape Canaveral and Cape Hatteras. Again at Hatteras the shelf becomes narrow, the Stream swings closer inshore, and the northward-moving water filters through a confused pattern of shoals and submerged sandy hills and valleys. Here again is a boundary between life zones, though it is a shifting and far from absolute one. During the winter, temperatures at Hatteras probably forbid the northward passage of migratory warm-water forms, but in summer the temperature barriers break down, the invisible gates open, and these same species may range far toward Cape Cod.

From Hatteras north the shelf broadens, the Stream moves far offshore, and there is a strong infiltration and mixing of colder water from the north, so that the progressive chilling is speeded. The difference in temperature between Hatteras and Cape Cod is as great as one would find on the opposite side of the Atlantic between the Canary Islands and southern Norway—a distance five times as long. For migratory sea fauna this is an intermediate zone, which cold-water forms enter in winter, and warm-water species in summer. Even the resident fauna has a mixed, indeterminate character, for this area seems

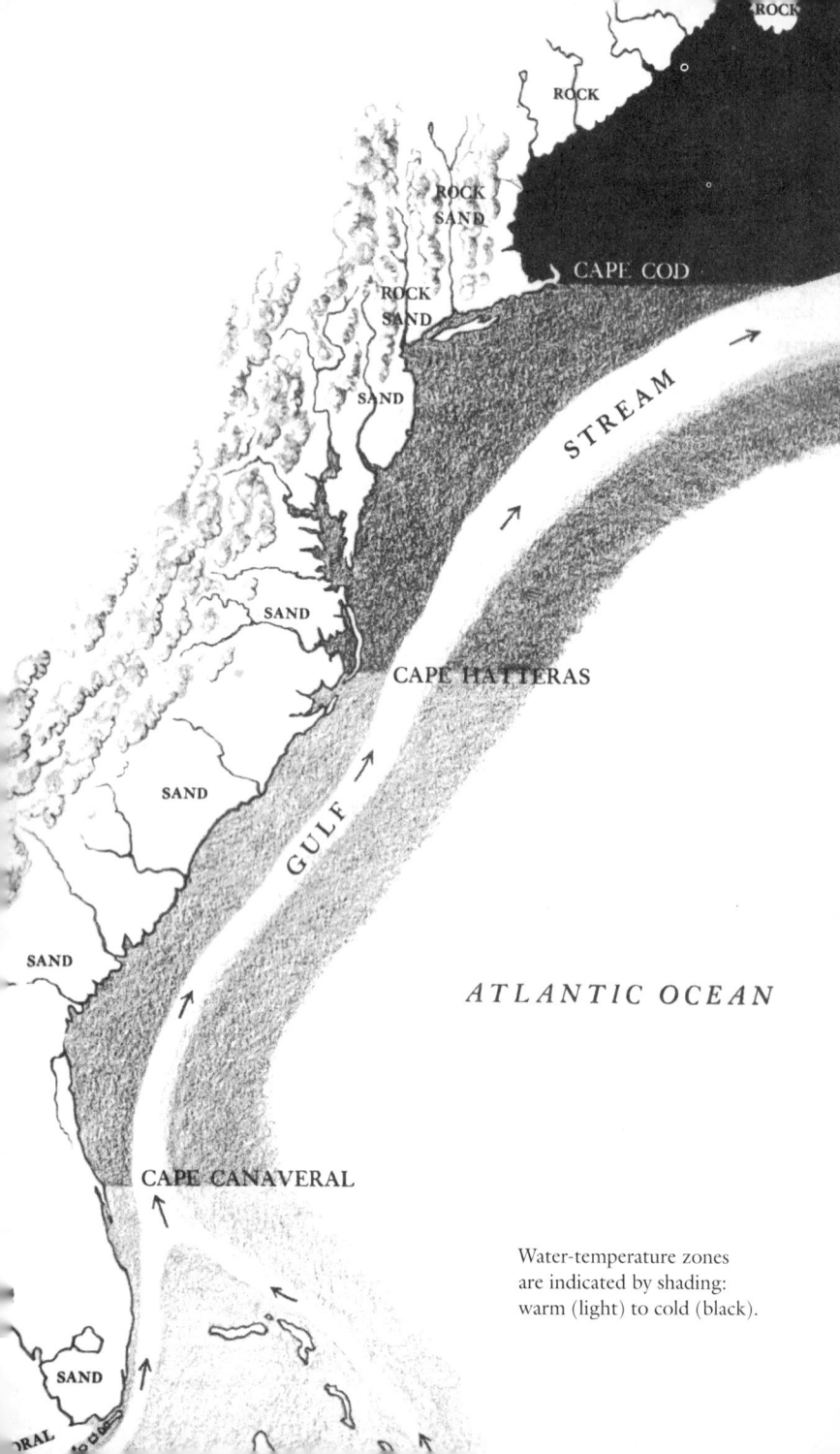

Water-temperature zones are indicated by shading: warm (light) to cold (black).

PATTERNS OF SHORE LIFE 441

to receive some of the more temperature-tolerant forms from both north and south, but to have few species that belong to it exclusively.

Cape Cod has long been recognized in zoology as marking the boundary of the range for thousands of creatures. Thrust far into the sea, it interferes with the passage of the warmer waters from the south and holds the cold waters of the north within the long curve of its shore. It is also a point of transition to a different kind of coast. The long sand strands of the south are replaced by rocks, which come more and more to dominate the coastal scene. They form the sea bottom as well as its shores; the same rugged contours that appear in the land forms of this region lie drowned and hidden from view offshore. Here zones of deep water, with accompanying low temperatures, lie generally closer to the shore than they do farther south, with interesting local effects on the populations of shore animals. Despite the deep inshore waters, the numerous islands and the jaggedly indented coast create a large intertidal area and so provide for a rich shore fauna. This is the cold-temperate region, inhabited by many species unable to tolerate the warm water south of the Cape. Partly because of the low temperatures and partly because of the rocky nature of the shore, heavy growths of seaweeds cover the ebb-tide rocks with a blanket of various hues, herds of periwinkles graze, and the shore is here whitened by millions of barnacles or there darkened by millions of mussels.

Beyond, in the waters bathing Labrador, southern Greenland, and parts of Newfoundland, the temperature of the sea and the nature of its flora and fauna are subarctic. Still farther to the north is the arctic province, with limits not yet precisely defined.

Although these basic zones are still convenient and well-founded divisions of the American coast, it became clear by about the third decade of the twentieth century that Cape Cod was not the absolute barrier it had once been for warm-water species attempting to round it from the south. Curious changes have been taking place, with many animals invading this cold-temperate zone from the south and pushing up through Maine and even into Canada. This new distribution is, of course, related to the widespread change of climate that seems to have set in about the beginning of the century and is now well recognized—a general warming-up noticed first in arctic regions, then in subarctic, and now in the temperate areas of northern states. With warmer ocean waters north of Cape Cod, not only the adults but the critically important young stages of various southern animals have been able to survive.

One of the most impressive examples of northward movement is provided by the green crab, once unknown north of the Cape, now familiar to every clam fisherman in Maine because of its habit of preying on the young stages of the clam. Around the turn of the century, zoological manuals gave its range as New Jersey to Cape Cod. In 1905 it was reported near Portland, and by 1930 specimens had been collected in Hancock County, about midway along the Maine coast. During the following decade it moved along to Winter Harbor, and in 1951 was found at Lubec. Then it spread up along the shores of Passamaquoddy Bay and crossed to Nova Scotia.

With higher water temperatures the sea herring is becoming scarce in Maine. The warmer waters may not be the only cause, but they are undoubtedly responsible in part. As the sea herring decline, other kinds of fish are coming in from the south. The menhaden is a larger member of the herring family, used in enormous quantities for manufacturing fertilizer, oils, and other industrial products. In the 1880's there was a fishery for menhaden in Maine, then they disappeared and for many years were confined almost entirely to areas south of New Jersey. About 1950, however, they began to return to Maine waters, followed by Virginia boats and fishermen. Another fish of the same tribe, called the round herring, is also ranging farther north. In the 1920's Professor Henry Bigelow of Harvard University reported it as occurring from the Gulf of Mexico to Cape Cod, and pointed out that it was rare anywhere on the Cape. (Two caught at Provincetown were preserved in the Museum of Comparative Zoölogy at Harvard.) In the 1950's, however, immense schools of this fish appeared in Maine waters, and the fishing industry began experiments with canning it.

Many other scattered reports follow the same trend. The mantis shrimp, formerly barred by the Cape, has now rounded it and spread into the southern part of the Gulf of Maine. Here and there the soft-shell clam shows signs of being adversely affected by warm summer temperatures and the hard-shell species is replacing it in New York waters. Whiting, once only summer fish north of the Cape, now are caught there throughout the year, and other fish once thought distinctively southern are able to spawn along the coast of New York, where their delicate juvenile stages formerly were killed by the cold winters.

Despite the present exceptions, the Cape Cod–Newfoundland coast is typically a zone of cool waters inhabited by a boreal flora and fauna. It displays strong and fascinating affinities with distant places of the northern world, linked by the unifying force of the sea with arctic waters and with the coasts of the British Isles and Scandinavia. So many of its species are duplicated in the eastern Atlantic that a handbook for the British Isles serves reasonably well for New England, covering probably 80 per cent of the seaweeds and 60 per cent of the marine animals. On the other hand, the American boreal zone has stronger ties with the arctic than does the British coast. One of the large Laminarian seaweeds, the arctic kelp, comes down to the Maine coast but is absent in the eastern Atlantic. An arctic sea anemone occurs in the western North Atlantic abundantly down to Nova Scotia and less numerously in Maine, but on the other side misses Great Britain and is confined to colder waters farther north. The occurrence of many species such as the green sea urchin, the blood-red starfish, the cod, and the herring are examples of a distribution that is circumboreal, extending right around the top of the earth and brought about through the agency of cold currents from melting glaciers and drifting pack ice that carry representatives of the northern faunas down into the North Pacific and North Atlantic.

The existence of so strong a common element between the faunas and floras of the two coasts of the North Atlantic suggests that the means of crossing must be relatively easy. The Gulf Stream carries many migrants away from American shores. The distance to the opposite side is great, however, and the situation is complicated by the short larval life of most species and the fact that shallow waters must be within reach when the time comes for assuming the life of the adult. In this northern part of the Atlantic intermediate way-stations are provided by submerged ridges, shallows, and islands, and the crossing may be broken into easy stages. In some earlier geologic times these shallows were even more extensive, so over long periods both active and involuntary migration across the Atlantic have been feasible.

In lower latitudes the deep basin of the Atlantic must be crossed, where few islands or shallows exist. Even here some transfer of larvae and adults takes place. The Bermuda Islands, after being raised above the sea by volcanic action, received their whole fauna as immigrants from the West Indies via the Gulf Stream. And on a smaller scale the long transatlantic crossings have been accomplished. Considering the difficulties, an impressive number of West Indian species are identical with, or closely related to African species, apparently having crossed in the Equatorial Current. They include species of starfish, shrimp, crayfish, and mollusks. Where such a long crossing has been made it is logical to assume that the migrants were adults, traveling on floating timber or drifting seaweed. In modern times, several African mollusks and starfish have been reported as arriving at the Island of St. Helena by these means.

The records of paleontology provide evidence of the changing shapes of continents and the changing flow of the ocean currents, for these earlier earth patterns account for the otherwise mysterious present distribution of many plants and animals. Once, for example, the West Indian region of the Atlantic was in direct communication, via sea currents, with the distant waters of the Pacific and Indian Oceans. Then a land bridge built up between the Americas, the Equatorial Current turned back on itself to the east, and a barrier to the dispersal of sea creatures was erected. But in species living today we find indications of how it was in the past. Once I discovered a curious little mollusk living in a meadow of turtle grass on the floor of a quiet bay among Florida's Ten Thousand Islands. It was the same bright green as the grass, and its little body was much too large for its thin shell, out of which it bulged. It was one of the scaphanders, and its nearest living relatives are inhabitants of the Indian Ocean. And on the beaches of the Carolinas I have found rocklike masses of calcareous tubes, secreted by colonies of a dark-bodied little worm. It is almost unknown in the Atlantic; again its relatives are Pacific and Indian Ocean forms.

Mud crabs

And so transport and wide dispersal are a continuing, universal process—an expression of the need of life to reach out and occupy all habitable parts of the earth. In any age the pattern is set by the shape of the continents and the flow of the currents; but it is never final, never completed.

On a shore where tidal action is strong and the range of the tide is great, one is aware of the ebb and flow of water with a daily, hourly awareness. Each recurrent high tide is a dramatic enactment of the advance of the sea against the continents, pressing up to the very threshold of the land, while the ebbs expose to view a strange and unfamiliar world. Perhaps it is a broad mud flat where curious holes, mounds, or tracks give evidence of a hidden life alien to the land; or perhaps it is a meadow of rockweeds lying prostrate and sodden now that the sea has left them, spreading a protective cloak over all the animal life beneath them. Even more directly the tides address the sense of hearing, speaking a language of their own distinct from the voice of the surf. The sound of a rising tide is heard most clearly on shores removed from the swell of the open ocean. In the stillness of night the strong waveless surge of a rising tide creates a confused tumult of water sounds—swashings and swirlings and a continuous slapping against the rocky rim of the land. Sometimes there are undertones of murmurings and whisperings; then suddenly all lesser sounds are obliterated by a torrential inpouring of water.

On such a shore the tides shape the nature and behavior of life. Their rise and fall give every creature that lives between the high- and low-water lines a twice-daily experience of land

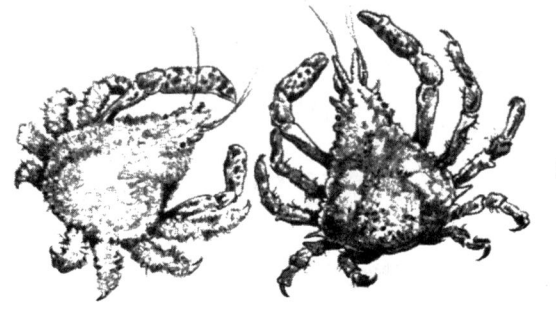

Decorator crabs

life. For those that live near the low-tide line the exposure to sun and air is brief; for those higher on the shore the interval in an alien environment is more prolonged and demands greater powers of endurance. But in all the intertidal area the pulse of life is adjusted to the rhythm of the tides. In a world that belongs alternately to sea and land, marine animals, breathing oxygen dissolved in sea water, must find ways of keeping moist; the few air breathers who have crossed the high-tide line from the land must protect themselves from drowning in the flood tide by bringing with them their own supply of oxygen. When the tide is low there is little or no food for most intertidal animals, and indeed the essential processes of life usually have to be carried on while water covers the shore. The tidal rhythm is therefore reflected in a biological rhythm of alternating activity and quiescence.

On a rising tide, animals that live deep in sand come to the surface, or thrust up the long breathing tubes or siphons, or begin to pump water through their burrows. Animals fixed to rocks open their shells or reach out tentacles to feed. Predators and grazers move about actively. When the water ebbs away the sand dwellers withdraw into the deep wet layers; the rock fauna brings into use all its varied means for avoiding desiccation. Worms that build calcareous tubes draw back into them, sealing the entrance with a modified gill filament that fits like a cork in a bottle. Barnacles close their shells, holding the moisture around their gills. Snails draw back into their shells, closing the doorlike operculum to shut out the air and keep some of the sea's wetness within. Scuds and beach fleas hide under rocks or weeds, waiting for the incoming tide to release them.

All through the lunar month, as the moon waxes and wanes, so the moon-drawn tides increase or decline in strength and the lines of high and low water shift from day to day. After the full moon, and again after the new moon, the forces acting on the sea to produce the tide are stronger than at any other time during the month. This is because the sun and moon then are directly in line with the earth and their attractive forces are added together. For complex astronomical reasons, the greatest tidal effect is exerted over a period of several days immediately after the full and the new moon, rather than at a time precisely coinciding with these lunar phases. During these periods the flood tides rise higher and the ebb tides fall lower than at any other time. These are called the "spring tides" from the Saxon "sprungen." The word refers not to a season, but to the brimming fullness of the water causing it to "spring" in the sense of a strong, active movement. No one who has watched a new-moon tide pressing against a rocky cliff will doubt the appropriateness of the term. In its quarter phases, the moon exerts its attraction at right angles to the pull of the sun so the two forces interfere with each other and the tidal movements are slack. Then the water neither rises as high nor falls as low as on the spring tides. These sluggish tides are called the "neaps"—a word that goes back to old Scandinavian roots meaning "barely touching" or "hardly enough."

On the Atlantic coast of North America the tides move in the so-called semidiurnal rhythm, with two high and two low waters in each tidal day of about 24 hours and 50 minutes.

Knobbed crabs

Each low tide follows the previous low by about 12 hours and 25 minutes, although slight local variations are possible. A like interval, of course, separates the high tides.

The range of tide shows enormous differences over the earth as a whole and even on the Atlantic coast of the United States there are important variations. There is a rise and fall of only a foot or two around the Florida Keys. On the long Atlantic coast of Florida the spring tides have a range of 3 to 4 feet, but a little to the north, among the Sea Islands of Georgia, these tides have an 8-foot rise. Then in the Carolinas and northward to New England they move less strongly, with spring tides of 6 feet at Charleston, South Carolina, 3 feet at Beaufort, North Carolina, and 5 feet at Cape May, New Jersey. Nantucket Island has little tide, but on the shores of Cape Cod Bay, less than 30 miles away, the spring tide range is 10 to 11 feet. Most of the rocky coast of New England falls within the zone of the great tides of the Bay of Fundy. From Cape Cod to Passamaquoddy Bay the amplitude of their range varies but is always considerable: 10 feet at Provincetown, 12 at Bar Harbor, 20 at Eastport, 22 at Calais. The conjunction of strong tides and a rocky shore, where much of the life is exposed, creates in this area a beautiful demonstration of the power of the tides over living things.

As day after day these great tides ebb and flow over the rocky rim of New England, their progress across the shore is visibly marked in stripes of color running parallel to the sea's edge. These bands, or zones, are composed of living things and reflect the stages of the tide, for the length of time that a particular level of shore is uncovered determines, in large measure, what can live there. The hardiest species live in the upper zones. Some of the earth's most ancient plants—the blue-green algae—though originating eons ago in the sea, have emerged from it to form dark tracings on the rocks above the high-tide line, a black zone visible on rocky shores in all parts of the world. Below the black zone, snails that are evolving toward a land existence browse on the film of vegetation or hide in seams and crevices in the rocks. But the most conspicuous zone begins at the upper line of the tides. On an open shore with moderately heavy surf, the rocks are whitened by the crowded millions of the barnacles just below the high-tide line. Here and there the white is interrupted by mussels growing in patches of darkest blue. Below them the seaweeds come in—the brown fields of the rockweeds. Toward the low-tide line the Irish moss spreads its low cushioning growth—a wide band of rich color that is not fully exposed by the sluggish movements of some of the neap tides, but appears on all of the greater tides. Sometimes the reddish brown of the moss is splashed with the bright green tangles of another seaweed, a hairlike growth of wiry texture. The lowest of the spring tides reveal still another zone during the last hour of their fall—that

1. Black zone   2. Periwinkle zone   3. Barnacle zone   4. Rockweed zone
5. Irish moss zone   6. Laminarian zone

sub-tide world where all the rock is painted a deep rose hue by the lime-secreting seaweeds that encrust it, and where the gleaming brown ribbons of the large kelps lie exposed on the rocks.

With only minor variations, this pattern of life exists in all parts of the world. The differences from place to place are related usually to the force of the surf, and one zone may be largely suppressed and another enormously developed. The barnacle zone, for example, spreads its white sheets over all the upper shore where waves are heavy, and the rockweed zone is greatly reduced. With protection from surf, the rockweeds not only occupy the middle shore in profusion but invade the upper rocks and make conditions difficult for the barnacles.

Perhaps in a sense the true intertidal zone is that band between high and low water of the neap tides, an area that is completely covered and uncovered during each tidal cycle, or twice during every day. Its inhabitants are the typical shore animals and plants, requiring some daily contact with the sea but able to endure limited exposure to land conditions.

Above high water of neaps is a band that seems more of earth than of sea. It is inhabited chiefly by pioneering species; already they have gone far along the road toward land life and can endure separation from the sea for many hours or days. One of the barnacles has colonized these higher high-tide rocks, where the sea comes only a few days and nights out of the month, on the spring tides. When the sea returns it brings food and oxygen, and in season carries away the young into the nursery of the surface waters; during these brief periods the barnacle is able to carry on all the processes necessary for life. But it is left again in an alien land world when the last of these highest tides of the fortnight ebbs away; then its only defense is the firm closing of the plates of its shell to hold some of the moisture of the sea about its body. In its life brief and intense activity alternates with long periods of a quiescent state resembling hibernation. Like the plants of the Arctic, which must crowd the making and storing of food, the putting forth of flowers, and the forming of seeds into a few brief weeks of summer, this barnacle has drastically adjusted its way of life so that it may survive in a region of harsh conditions.

Some few sea animals have pushed on even above high water of the spring tides into the splash zone, where the only salty moisture comes from the spray of breaking waves. Among such pioneers are snails of the periwinkle tribe. One of the West Indian species can endure months of separation from the sea. Another, the European rock periwinkle, waits for the waves of the spring tides to cast its eggs into the sea, in almost all activities except the vital one of reproduction being independent of the water.

Below the low water of neaps are the areas exposed only as the rhythmic swing of the tides falls lower and lower, approaching the level of the springs. Of all the intertidal zone this region is linked most closely with the sea. Many of its inhabitants are offshore forms, able to live here only because of the briefness and infrequency of exposure to the air.

The relation between the tides and the zones of life is clear, but in many less obvious ways animals have adjusted their activities to the tidal rhythm. Some seem to be a mechanical matter of utilizing the movement of water. The larval oyster, for example, uses the flow of the tides to carry it into areas favorable for its attachment. Adult oysters live in bays or sounds or river estuaries rather than in water of full oceanic salinity, and so it is to the advantage of the race for the dispersal of the young stages to take place in a direction away from the open sea. When first hatched the larvae drift passively, the tidal currents carrying them now toward the sea, now toward the headwaters of estuaries or bays. In many estuaries the ebb tide runs longer than the flood, having the added push and volume of stream discharge behind it, and the resulting seaward drift over the whole two-week period of larval life would carry the young oysters many miles to sea. A sharp change of behavior sets in, however, as the larvae grow older. They now drop to the bottom while the tide ebbs, avoiding the seaward drift of water, but with the return of the flood they rise into the currents that are pressing upstream, and so are carried into regions of lower salinity that are favorable for their adult life.

Others adjust the rhythm of spawning to protect their young from the danger of being carried into unsuitable waters. One of the tube-building worms living in or near the tidal zone follows a pattern that avoids the strong movements of the spring tides. It releases its larvae into the sea every fortnight on the neap tides, when the water movements are relatively sluggish; the young worms, which have a very brief swimming stage, then have a good chance of remaining within the most favorable zone of the shore.

There are other tidal effects, mysterious and intangible. Sometimes spawning is synchronized with the tides in a way that suggests response to change of pressure or to the difference between still and flowing water. A primitive mollusk called the chiton spawns in Bermuda when the low tide occurs early in the morning, with the return flow of water setting in just after sunrise. As soon as the chitons are covered with water they shed their spawn. One of the Japanese nereid worms spawns only on the strongest tides of the year, near the new- and full-moon tides of October and November, presumably stirred in some obscure way by the amplitude of the water movements.

Many other animals, belonging to quite unrelated groups throughout the whole range of sea life, spawn according to a definitely fixed rhythm that may coincide with the full moon or the new moon or its quarters, but whether the effect is

Oysters

produced by the altered pressure of the tides or the changing light of the moon is by no means clear. For example, there is a sea urchin in Tortugas that spawns on the night of the full moon, and apparently only then. Whatever the stimulus may be, all the individuals of the species respond to it, assuring the simultaneous release of immense numbers of reproductive cells. On the coast of England one of the hydroids, an animal of plantlike appearance that produces tiny medusae or jellyfish, releases these medusae during the moon's third quarter. At Woods Hole on the Massachusetts coast a clamlike mollusk spawns heavily between the full and the new moon but avoids the first quarter. And a nereid worm at Naples gathers in its nuptial swarms during the quarters of the moon but never when the moon is new or full; a related worm at Woods Hole shows no such correlation although exposed to the same moon and to stronger tides.

In none of these examples can we be sure whether the animal is responding to the tides or, as the tides themselves do, to the influence of the moon. With plants, however, the situation is different, and here and there we find scientific confirmation of the ancient and world-wide belief in the effect of moonlight on vegetation. Various bits of evidence suggest that the rapid multiplication of diatoms and other members of the plant plankton is related to the phases of the moon. Certain algae in river plankton reach the peak of their abundance at the full moon. One of the brown seaweeds on the coast of North Carolina releases its reproductive cells only on the full moon, and similar behavior has been reported for other seaweeds in Japan and other parts of the world. These responses are generally explained as the effect of varying intensities of polarized light on protoplasm.

Other observations suggest some connection between plants and the reproduction and growth of animals. Rapidly maturing herring collect around the edge of concentrations of plant plankton, although the fully adult herring may avoid them. Spawning adults, eggs, and young of various other marine creatures are reported to occur more often in dense phytoplankton than in sparse patches. In significant experiments, a Japanese scientist discovered he could induce oysters to spawn with an extract obtained from sea lettuce. The same seaweed produces a substance that influences growth and multiplication of diatoms, and is itself stimulated by water taken from the vicinity of a heavy growth of rockweeds.

The whole subject of the presence in sea water of the so-called "ectocrines" (external secretions or products of metabolism) has so recently become one of the frontiers of science that actual information is fragmentary and tantalizing. It appears, however, that we may be on the verge of solving some of the riddles that have plagued men's minds for centuries. Though the subject lies in the misty borderlands of advancing knowledge, almost everything that in the past has been taken for granted, as well as problems considered insoluble, bear renewed thought in the light of the discovery of these substances.

In the sea there are mysterious comings and goings, both in space and time: the movements of migratory species, the strange phenomenon of succession by which, in one and the same area, one species appears in profusion, flourishes for a time, and then dies out, only to have its place taken by another and then another, like actors in a pageant passing before our eyes. And there are other mysteries. The phenomenon of "red tides" has been known from early days, recurring again and again down to the present time—a phenomenon in which the sea becomes discolored because of the extraordinary multiplication of some minute form, often a dinoflagellate, and in which there are disastrous side effects in the shape of mass mortalities among fish and some of the invertebrates. Then there is the problem of curious and seemingly erratic movements of fish, into or away from certain areas, often with sharp economic consequences. When the so-called "Atlantic water" floods the south coast of England, herring become abundant within the range of the Plymouth fisheries, certain characteristic plankton animals occur in profusion, and certain species of invertebrates flourish in the intertidal zone. When, however, this water mass is replaced by Channel water, the cast of characters undergoes many changes.

In the discovery of the biological role played by the sea water and all it contains, we may be about to reach an understanding of these old mysteries. For it is now clear that in the sea nothing lives to itself. The very water is altered, in its chemical nature and in its capacity for influencing life processes, by the fact that certain forms have lived within it and have passed on to it new substances capable of inducing far-reaching effects. So the present is linked with past and future, and each living thing with all that surrounds it.

The Rocky Shores

WHEN THE TIDE is high on a rocky shore, when its brimming fullness creeps up almost to the bayberry and the junipers where they come down from the land, one might easily suppose that nothing at all lived in or on or under these waters of the sea's edge. For nothing is visible. Nothing except here and there a little group of herring gulls, for at high tide the gulls rest on ledges of rock, dry above the surf and the spray, and they tuck their yellow bills under their feathers and doze away the hours of the rising water. Then all the creatures of the tidal rocks are hidden from view, but the gulls know what is there, and they know that in time the water will fall away again and give them entrance to the strip between the tide lines.

When the tide is rising the shore is a place of unrest, with the surge leaping high over jutting rocks and running in lacy cascades of foam over the landward side of massive boulders. But on the ebb it is more peaceful, for then the waves do not have behind them the push of the inward pressing tides. There is no particular drama about the turn of the tide, but presently a zone of wetness shows on the gray rock slopes, and offshore the incoming swells begin to swirl and break over hidden ledges. Soon the rocks that the high tide had concealed rise into view and glisten with the wetness left on them by the receding water.

Small, dingy snails move about over rocks that are slippery with the growth of infinitesimal green plants; the snails scraping, scraping, scraping to find food before the surf returns.

Like drifts of old snow no longer white, the barnacles come into view; they blanket rocks and old spars wedged into rock crevices, and their sharp cones are sprinkled over empty mussel shells and lobster-pot buoys and the hard stipes of deep-water seaweeds, all mingled in the flotsam of the tide.

Meadows of brown rockweeds appear on the gently sloping rocks of the shore as the tide imperceptibly ebbs. Smaller patches of green weed, stringy as mermaids' hair, begin to turn white and crinkly where the sun has dried them.

Now the gulls, that lately rested on the higher ledges, pace with grave intentness along the walls of rock, and they probe under the hanging curtains of weed to find crabs and sea urchins.

In the low places little pools and gutters are left where the water trickles and gurgles and cascades in miniature waterfalls, and many of the dark caverns between and under the rocks are floored with still mirrors holding the reflections of delicate creatures that shun the light and avoid the shock of waves—the cream-colored flowers of the small anemones and the pink fingers of soft coral, pendent from the rocky ceiling.

In the calm world of the deeper rock pools, now undisturbed by the tumult of incoming waves, crabs sidle along the walls, their claws busily touching, feeling, exploring for bits of food. The pools are gardens of color composed of the delicate green and ocher-yellow of encrusting sponge, the pale pink of hydroids that stand like clusters of fragile spring flowers, the bronze and electric-blue gleams of the Irish moss, the old-rose beauty of the coralline algae.

And over it all there is the smell of low tide, compounded of the faint, pervasive smell of worms and snails and jellyfish and crabs—the sulphur smell of sponge, the iodine smell of rockweed, and the salt smell of the rime that glitters on the sun-dried rocks.

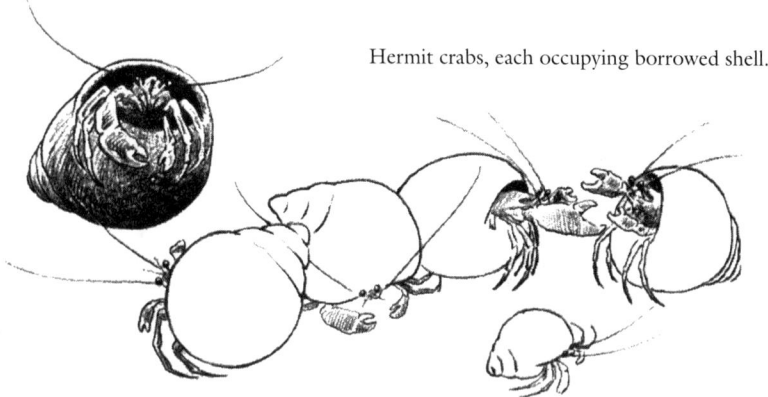

Hermit crabs, each occupying borrowed shell.

*

One of my own favorite approaches to a rocky seacoast is by a rough path through an evergreen forest that has its own peculiar enchantment. It is usually an early morning tide that takes me along that forest path, so that the light is still pale and fog drifts in from the sea beyond. It is almost a ghost forest, for among the living spruce and balsam are many dead trees—some still erect, some sagging earthward, some lying on the floor of the forest. All the trees, the living and the dead, are clothed with green and silver crusts of lichens. Tufts of the bearded lichen or old man's beard hang from the branches like bits of sea mist tangled there. Green woodland mosses and a yielding carpet of reindeer moss cover the ground. In the quiet of that place even the voice of the surf is reduced to a whispered echo and the sounds of the forest are but the ghosts of sound—the faint sighing of evergreen needles in the moving air; the creaks and heavier groans of half-fallen trees resting against their neighbors and rubbing bark against bark; the light rattling fall of a dead branch broken under the feet of a squirrel and sent bouncing and ricocheting earthward.

But finally the path emerges from the dimness of the deeper forest and comes to a place where the sound of surf rises above the forest sounds—the hollow boom of the sea, rhythmic and insistent, striking against the rocks, falling away, rising again.

Up and down the coast the line of the forest is drawn sharp and clean on the edge of a seascape of surf and sky and rocks. The softness of sea fog blurs the contours of the rocks; gray water and gray mists merge offshore in a dim and vaporous world that might be a world of creation, stirring with new life.

The sense of newness is more than illusion born of the early morning light and the fog, for this is in very fact a young coast. It was only yesterday in the life of the earth that the sea came in as the coast subsided, filling the valleys and rising about the slopes of the hills, creating these rugged shores where rocks rise out of the sea and evergreen forests come down to the coastal rocks. Once this shore was like the ancient land to the south, where the nature of the coast has changed little during the millions of years since the sea and the wind and the rain created its sands and shaped them into dune and beach and offshore bar and shoal. The northern coast, too, had its flat coastal plain bordered by wide beaches of sand. Behind these lay a landscape of rocky hills alternating with valleys that had been worn by streams and deepened and sculptured by glaciers. The hills were formed of gneiss and other crystalline rocks resistant to erosion; the lowlands had been created in beds of weaker rocks like sandstones, shale, and marl.

Then the scene changed. From a point somewhere in the vicinity of Long Island the flexible crust of the earth tilted downward under the burden of a vast glacier. The regions we know as eastern Maine and Nova Scotia were pressed down into the earth, some areas being carried as much as 1200 feet beneath the sea. All of the northern coastal plain was drowned. Some of its more elevated parts are now offshore shoals, the fishing banks off the New England and Canadian coasts—Georges, Browns, Quereau, the Grand Bank. None of it remains above the sea except here and there a high and isolated hill, like the present island of Monhegan, which in ancient times must have stood above the coastal plain as a bold monadnock.

Where the mountainous ridges and the valleys lay at an angle to the coast, the sea ran far up between the hills and occupied the valleys. This was the origin of the deeply indented and exceedingly irregular coast that is characteristic of much of Maine. The long narrow estuaries of the Kennebec, the Sheepscot, the Damariscotta and many other rivers run inland a score of miles. These salt-water rivers, now arms of the sea, are the drowned valleys in which grass and trees grew in a geologic yesterday. The rocky, forested ridges between them probably looked much as they do today. Offshore, chains of islands jut out obliquely into the sea, one beyond another—half-submerged ridges of the former land mass.

But where the shore line is parallel to the massive ridges of rock the coast line is smoother, with few indentations. The rains of earlier centuries cut only short valleys into the flanks of the granite hills, and so when the sea rose there were created only a few short, broad bays instead of long winding ones. Such a coast occurs typically in southern Nova Scotia, and also may be seen in the Cape Ann region of Massachusetts, where the belts of resistant rock curve eastward along the coast. On such a coast, islands, where they occur, lie parallel to the shore line instead of putting boldly out to sea.

As geologic events are reckoned, all this happened rather rapidly and suddenly, with no time for gradual adjustment of the landscape; also it happened quite recently, the present relation of land and sea being achieved perhaps no more than ten thousand years ago. In the chronology of Earth, a few thousand years are as nothing, and in so brief a time the waves have prevailed little against the hard rocks that the great ice sheet scraped clean of loose rock and ancient soil, and so have scarcely marked out the deep notches that in time they will cut in the cliffs.

For the most part, the ruggedness of this coast is the ruggedness of the hills themselves. There are none of the wave-cut stacks and arches that distinguish older coasts or coasts of softer rock. In a few, exceptional places the work of the waves may be seen. The south shore of Mount Desert Island is exposed to heavy pounding by surf; there the waves have cut out Anemone Cave and are working at Thunder Hole to batter through the roof of the small cave into which the surf roars at high tide.

In places the sea washes the foot of a steep cliff produced by the shearing effect of earth pressure along fault lines. Cliffs on Mount Desert—Schooner Head, Great Head, and Otter —tower a hundred feet or more above the sea. Such imposing structures might be taken for wave-cut cliffs if one did not know the geologic history of the region.

On the coasts of Cape Breton Island and New Brunswick the situation is very different and examples of advanced marine erosion occur on every hand. Here the sea is in contact with weak rock lowlands formed in the Carboniferous period. These shores have little resistance to the erosive power of the waves, and the soft sandstone and conglomerate rocks are being cut back at an annual rate averaging five or six inches, or in some places several feet. Marine stacks, caves, chimneys, and archways are common features of these shores.

Here and there on the predominantly rocky coast of northern New England there are small beaches of sand, pebbles, or cobblestones. These have a varied origin. Some came from glacial debris that covered the rocky surface when the land tilted and the sea came in. Boulders and pebbles often are carried in from deeper water offshore by seaweeds that have gripped them firmly with their "holdfasts." Storm waves then dislodge weed and stone and cast them on the shore. Even without the aid of weeds, waves carry in a considerable volume of sand, gravel, shell fragments, and even boulders. These occasional sandy or pebbly beaches are almost always in protected, incurving shores or dead-end coves, where the waves can deposit debris but from which they cannot easily remove it.

When, on those coastal rocks between the serrate line of spruces and the surf, the morning mists conceal the lighthouses and fishing boats and all other reminders of man, they also blur the sense of time and one might easily imagine that the sea came in only yesterday to create this particular line of coast. Yet the creatures that inhabit the intertidal rocks have had time to establish themselves here, replacing the fauna of the beaches of sand and mud that probably bordered the older coast. Out of the same sea that rose over the northern coast of New England, drowning the coastal plain and coming to rest against the hard uplands, the larvae of the rock dwellers came —the blindly searching larvae that drift in the ocean currents ready to colonize whatever suitable land may lie in their path or to die, if no such landfall is their lot.

Although no one recorded the first colonist or traced the succession of living forms, we may make a fairly confident guess as to the pioneers of the occupation of these rocks, and the forms that followed them. The invading sea must have brought the larvae and young of many kinds of shore animals, but only those able to find food could survive on the new shore. And in the beginning the only available food was the plankton that came in renewed clouds with every tide that washed the coastal rocks. The first permanent inhabitants must have been such plankton-strainers as the barnacles and mussels, who require little but a firm place to which they may attach themselves. Around and among the white cones of the barnacles and the dark shells of the mussels it is probable that the spores of algae settled, so that a living green film began to spread over the upper rocks. Then the grazers could come—the little herds of snails that laboriously scrape the rocks with their sharp tongues, licking off the nearly invisible covering of tiny plant cells. Only after the establishment of the plankton-strainers and the grazers could the carnivores settle and survive. The predatory dog whelks, the starfish, and many of the crabs and worms must, then, have been comparative latecomers to this rocky shore. But all of them are there now, living out their lives in the horizontal zones created by the tides, or in the little pockets or communities of life established by the need to take shelter from surf, or to find food, or to hide from enemies.

The pattern of life spread before me when I emerge from that forest path is one characteristic of exposed shores. From the edge of the spruce forests down to the dark groves of the kelps, the life of the land grades into the life of the sea, perhaps with less abruptness than one would expect, for by various little interlacing ties the ancient unity of the two is made clear.

Lichens live in the forest above the sea, in the silent intensity of their toil crumbling away the rocks as lichens have done for millions of years. Some leave the forest and advance over the bare rock toward the tide line; a few go even farther, enduring a periodic submersion by the sea so that they may work their strange magic on the rocks of the intertidal zone. In the dampness of foggy mornings the rock tripe on the seaward slopes is like sheets of thin, pliable green leather, but by midday under a drying sun it has become blackened and brittle; then the rocks look as though they were sloughing off a thin outer layer. Thriving in the salt spray, the wall lichen spreads its orange stain on the cliffs and even on the landward side of boulders that are visited by the highest tides of each moon. Scales of other lichens, sage-green, rolled and twisted into strange shapes, rise from the lower rocks; from their under surfaces black, hairy processes work down among the minute particles of rock substance, giving off an acid secretion to dissolve the rock. As the hairs absorb moisture and swell, fine grains of the rock are dislodged and so the work of creating soil from the rock is advanced.

Below the forest's edge the rock is white or gray or buff, according to its mineral nature. It is dry and belongs to the land; except for a few insects or other land creatures using it as pathways to the sea it is barren. But just above the area that clearly belongs to the sea, it shows a strange discoloration,

Rough periwinkle (top)

Common periwinkle

being strongly marked with streaks or patches or continuous bands of black. Nothing about this black zone suggests life; one would call it a dark stain, or at most a felty roughening of the rock surface. Yet it is actually a dense growth of minute plants. The species that compose it sometimes include a very small lichen, sometimes one or more of the green algae, but most numerously the simplest and most ancient of all plants, the blue-green algae. Some are enclosed in slimy sheaths that protect them from drying and fit them to endure long exposure to sun and air. All are so minute as to be invisible as individual plants. Their gelatinous sheaths and the fact that the whole area receives the spray of breaking waves make this entrance to the sea world slippery as the smoothest ice.

This black zone of the shore has a meaning above and beyond its drab and lifeless aspect—a meaning obscure, elusive, and infinitely tantalizing. Wherever rocks meet the sea, the microplants have written their dark inscription, a message only partially legible although it seems in some way to be concerned with the universality of tides and oceans. Though other elements of the intertidal world come and go, this darkening stain is omnipresent. The rockweeds, the barnacles, the snails, and the mussels appear and disappear in the intertidal zone according to the changing nature of their world, but the black inscriptions of the microplants are always there. Seeing them here on this Maine coast, I remember how they also blackened the coral rim of Key Largo, and streaked the smooth platform of coquina at St. Augustine, and left their tracings on the concrete jetties at Beaufort. It is the same all over the world—from South Africa to Norway and from the Aleutians to Australia. This is the sign of the meeting of land and sea.

Once below the dark film, I begin to look for the first of the sea creatures pressing up to the threshold of the land. In seams and crevices in the high rocks I find them—the smallest of the periwinkle tribe, the rock or rough periwinkle. Some—the infant snails—are so small that I need my hand lens to see them clearly, and among the hundreds that crowd into these cracks and depressions I can find a gradation of sizes up to the half-inch adults. If these were sea creatures of ordinary habits, I would think the small snails were young produced by some distant colony and drifted here as larvae after spending a period at sea. But the rough periwinkle sends no young into the sea; instead it is a viviparous species and the eggs, each encased within a cocoon, are held within the mother while they develop. The contents of the cocoon nourish the young snail until finally it breaks through the egg capsule and then emerges from the mother's body, a completely shelled little creature about the size of a grain of finely ground coffee. So small an animal might easily be washed out to sea; hence, no doubt, the habit of hiding in crevices and in empty barnacle shells, where often I have found them in numbers.

At the level where most of the rough periwinkles live, however, the sea comes only every fortnight on the spring tides, and in the long intervals the flying spray of breaking waves is their only contact with the water. While the rocks are thoroughly wet with spray the periwinkles can spend much time out on the rocks feeding, often working well up into the black zone. The microplants that create the slippery film on the rocks are their food; like all snails of their group, the periwinkles are vegetarians. They feed by scraping the rocks with a peculiar organ set with many rows of sharp, calcareous teeth. This organ, the radula, is a continuous belt or ribbon that lies on the floor of the pharynx. If unwound, it would be many times the length of the animal, but it is tightly coiled like a watch spring. The radula itself consists of chitin, the substance of insects' wings and lobsters' shells. The teeth that stud it are arranged in several hundred rows (in another species, the common periwinkle, the teeth total about 3500). A certain amount of wear is involved in scraping the rocks, and when the teeth in current use are worn down, an endless supply of new ones can be rolled up from behind.

And there is wear, also, on the rocks. Over the decades and the centuries, a large population of periwinkles scraping the rocks for food has a pronounced erosive effect, cutting away rock surfaces, grain by grain, deepening the tide pools. In a tide pool observed for sixteen years by a California biologist, periwinkles lowered the floor about three-eighths of an inch. Rain, frost, and floods—the earth's major forces of erosion—operate on approximately such a scale.

The periwinkles grazing on the intertidal rocks, waiting for the return of the tide, are poised also in time, waiting for the moment when they can complete their present phase of evolution and move forward onto the land. All snails that are now terrestrial came of marine ancestry, their forebears having at some time made the transitional crossing of the shore. The periwinkles now are in mid-passage. In the structure and habits of the three species found on the New England coast, one can see clearly the evolutionary stages by which a marine creature is transformed into a land dweller. The smooth periwinkle, still bound to the sea, can endure only brief exposure. At low tide it remains in wet seaweeds. The common periwinkle often lives where it is submerged only briefly at high tide. It still sheds eggs into the sea and so is not ready for land life. The rough periwinkle, however, has cut most of the ties that confine it to the sea; it is now almost a land animal. By becoming viviparous it has progressed beyond dependence on the sea for reproduction. It is able to thrive at the level of the high water of the spring tides because, unlike the related periwinkles of lower tidal levels, it possesses a gill cavity that is well supplied with blood vessels and functions almost as a lung to breathe oxygen from the air. Constant submersion is, in fact, fatal to it and at the present stage of its evolution it can endure up to thirty-one days of exposure to dry air.

Smooth periwinkle

The rough periwinkle has been found by a French experimenter to have the rhythm of the tides deeply impressed upon its behavior patterns, so that it "remembers" even when no longer exposed to the alternating rise and fall of the water. It is most active during the fortnightly visits of the spring tides to its rocks, but in the waterless intervals it becomes progressively more sluggish and its tissues undergo a certain desiccation. With the return of the spring tides the cycle is reversed. When taken into a laboratory the snails for many months reflect in their behavior the advance and retreat of the sea over their native shores.

On this exposed New England coast the most conspicuous animals of the high-tide zone are the rock or acorn barnacles, which are able to live in all but the most tumultuous surf. The rockweeds here are so stunted by wave action that they offer no competition, and so the barnacles have taken over the upper shore, except for such space as the mussels have been able to hold.

At low tide the barnacle-covered rocks seem a mineral landscape carved and sculptured into millions of little sharply pointed cones. There is no movement, no sign or suggestion of life. The stony shells, like those of mollusks, are calcareous and are secreted by the invisible animals within. Each cone-shaped shell consists of six neatly fitted plates forming an encircling ring. A covering door of four plates closes to protect the barnacle from drying when the tide has ebbed, or swings open to allow it to feed. The first ripples of incoming tide bring the petrified fields to life. Then, if one stands ankle-deep in water and observes closely, one sees tiny shadows flickering everywhere over the submerged rocks. Over each individual cone, a feathered plume is regularly thrust out and drawn back within the slightly opened portals of the central door—the rhythmic motions by which the barnacle sweeps in diatoms and other microscopic life of the returning sea.

The creature inside each shell is something like a small pinkish shrimp that lies head downward, firmly cemented to the base of this chamber it cannot leave. Only the appendages are ever exposed—six pairs of branched, slender wands, jointed and set with bristles. Acting together, they form a net of great efficiency.

Barnacles

The barnacle belongs to the group of arthropods known as the Crustacea, a varied horde including the lobsters, crabs, sand hoppers, brine shrimps, and water fleas. The barnacle is different from all related forms, however, in its fixed and sedentary existence. When and how it assumed such a way of life is one of the riddles of zoology, the transitional forms having been lost somewhere in the mists of the past. Some faint suggestions of a similar manner of life—the waiting in a fixed place for the sea to bring food—are found among the amphipods, another group of crustaceans. Some of these spin little webs or cocoons of natural silk and seaweed fibers; though remaining free to come and go they spend much of their time within them, taking their food from the currents. Another amphipod, a Pacific coast species, burrows into colonies of the tunicate called the sea pork, hollowing out for itself a chamber in the tough, translucent substance of its host. Lying in this excavation, it draws currents of sea water over its body and extracts the food.

However the barnacle became what it is, its larval stages clearly proclaim its crustacean ancestry, although early zoologists who looked at its hard shells labeled it a mollusk. The eggs develop inside the parent's shell and presently hatch into the sea in milky clouds of larvae. (The British zoologist Hilary Moore, after studying barnacles on the Isle of Man, estimated a yearly production of a million million larvae from a little over

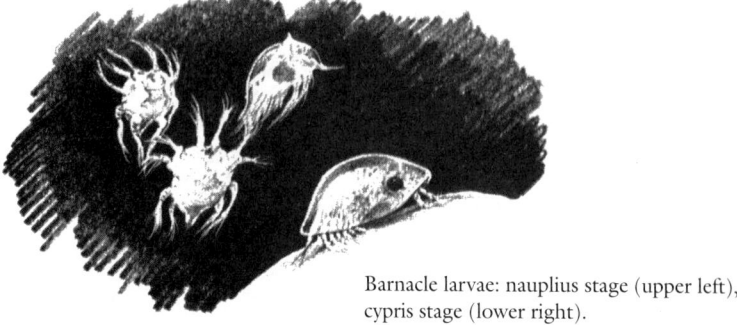

Barnacle larvae: nauplius stage (upper left), cypris stage (lower right).

half a mile of shore.) Larval life lasts about three months in the rock barnacle, with several molts and transformations of form. At first the larva, a little swimming creature called a nauplius, is indistinguishable from the larva of all other crustaceans. It is nourished by large globules of fat that not only feed it but keep it near the surface. As the fat globules dwindle, the larva begins to swim at lower water levels. Eventually it changes shape, acquires a pair of shells, six pairs of swimming legs, and a pair of antennae tipped with suckers. This "cypris" larva looks much like the adults of another group of crustaceans, the ostracods. Finally, guided by instinct to yield to gravity and to avoid light, it descends to the bottom ready to become an adult.

No one knows how many of the baby barnacles riding shoreward on the waves make a safe landing, how many fail in the quest for a clean, hard substratum. The settling down of a barnacle larva is not a haphazard process, but is performed only after a period of seeming deliberation. Biologists who have observed the act in the laboratory say the larvae "walk" about on the substratum for as long as an hour, pulling themselves along by the adhesive tips of the antennae, testing and rejecting many possible sites before they make a final choice. In nature they probably drift along in the currents for many days, coming down, examining the bottom at hand, then drifting on to another.

What are the conditions this infant creature requires? Probably it finds rock surfaces that are rough and pitted better than very smooth ones; probably it is repelled by a slimy film of microscopic plants, or even sometimes by the presence of hydroids or large algae. There is some reason to believe it may be drawn to existing colonies of barnacles perhaps through mysterious chemical attraction, detecting substances released by the adults and following these paths to the colony. Somehow, suddenly and irrevocably, the choice is made and the young barnacle cements itself to the chosen surface. Its tissues undergo a complete and drastic reorganization comparable to the metamorphosis of the larval butterfly. Then from an almost shapeless mass, the rudiments of the shell appear, the head and appendages are molded, and within twelve hours the complete cone of the shell, with all its plates delineated, has been formed.

Within its cup of lime the barnacle faces a dual growth problem. As a crustacean enclosed in a chitinous shell, the animal itself must periodically shed its unyielding skin so that its body may enlarge. Difficult as it seems, this feat is successfully accomplished, as I am reminded many times each summer. Almost every container of sea water that I bring up from the shore is flecked with white semitransparent objects, gossamer-fine, like the discarded garments of some very small fairy creature. Seen under the microscope, every detail of structure is perfectly represented. Evidently the barnacle accomplishes its withdrawal from the old skin with incredible neatness and thoroughness. In the little cellophane-like replicas I can count the joints of the appendages; even the bristles, growing at the bases of the joints, seem to have been slipped intact out of their casings.

The second problem is that of enlarging the hard cone to accommodate the growing body. Just how this is done no one seems to be sure, but probably there is some chemical secretion to dissolve the inner layers of the shell as new material is added on the outside.

Unless its life is prematurely ended by an enemy, a rock barnacle is likely to live about three years in the middle and lower tidal zones, or five years near the upper tidal levels. It can withstand high temperatures as rocks absorb the heat of the summer sun. Winter cold in itself is not harmful, but grinding ice may scrape the rocks clean. The pounding of the surf is part of the normal life of a barnacle; the sea is not its enemy.

When, through the attacks of fish, predatory worms, or snails, or through natural causes, the barnacle's life comes to an end, the shells remain attached to the rocks. These become shelter for many of the minute beings of the shore. Besides the baby periwinkles that regularly live there, the little tide-pool insects often hurry into these shelters if caught by the rising tide. And lower on the shore, or in tide pools, the empty shells are likely to house young anemones, tube worms, or even new generations of barnacles.

The chief enemy of the barnacle on these shores is a brightly colored carnivorous marine snail, the dog whelk. Although it preys also on mussels and even occasionally on periwinkles, it seems to prefer barnacles to all other food, probably because they are more easily eaten. Like all snails, the whelk possesses a radula. This is not used, periwinkle fashion, to scrape the rocks, but to drill a hole in any hard-shelled prey. It can then be pushed through the hole it has made, to reach and consume the soft parts within. To devour a barnacle, however, the whelk need only envelop the cone within its fleshy foot and force the valves open. It also produces a secretion that may have a narcotic effect. This is a substance called purpurin. In ancient times the secretion of a related snail in the Mediterranean was the source of the dye Tyrian purple. The pigment is an organic compound of bromine that changes in air to form a purple coloring matter.

Although violent surf excludes them, the dog whelks appear in numbers on most open shores, working up high into the

Dog whelk feeding on common blue mussels.

zone of the barnacles and mussels. By their voracious feeding they may actually alter the balance of life on the shore. There is a story, for example, about an area where the whelks had reduced the number of barnacles so drastically that mussels came in to fill the vacant niche. When the whelks could find no more barnacles they moved over to the mussels. At first they were clumsy, not knowing how to eat the new food. Some spent futile days boring holes in empty shells; others climbed into empty shells and bored from inside. In time, however, they adjusted to the new prey and ate so many mussels that the colony began to dwindle. Then the barnacles settled anew on the rocks and in the end the snails returned to them.

In the middle stretches of shore and even down toward the low-tide line the whelks live under the dripping curtains of weed hanging down from the rock walls, or within the turf of Irish moss or among the flat, slippery fronds of the red seaweed, dulse. They cling to the under sides of overhanging ledges or gather in deep crevices where salt water drips from weeds and mussels, and little streams of water trickle over the floor. In all such places the whelks collect in numbers to pair and lay their eggs in straw-colored containers, each about the size and shape of a grain of wheat and tough as parchment. Each capsule stands alone, attached by its own base to the substratum, but usually they are crowded so closely together that they form a pattern or mosaic.

A snail takes about an hour to make one capsule but seldom completes more than 10 in twenty-four hours. It may produce as many as 245 in a season. Although a single capsule may contain as many as a thousand eggs, most of these are unfertilized nurse eggs that serve as food for the developing embryos. On maturing, the capsules become purple, being colored by the same chemical purpurin that is secreted by the adult. In about four months embryonic life is completed, and from 15 to 20 young dog whelks emerge from the capsule. Newly hatched young seldom if ever are found in the zone where the adults live, although the capsules are deposited and development takes place there. Apparently the waves carry the young snails down to low-tide level or below. Probably many are washed out to sea and lost, but the survivors are to be found at low water. They are very small—about one-sixteenth of an inch high

Egg capsules of the dog whelk.
Right: young whelks emerging.

—and are feeding on the tube worm, Spirorbis. Apparently the tubes of these worms are easier to penetrate than the cones of even very small barnacles. Not until the dog whelk is about one-fourth or three-eighths of an inch high does it migrate higher on the shore and begin feeding on barnacles.

Down in the middle sections of the shore the limpets become abundant. They appear sprinkled over the open rock surfaces, but most live numerously in shallow tide pools. A limpet wears a simple cone of shell the size of a fingernail, unobtrusively mottled with soft browns and grays and blues. It is one of the most ancient and primitive types of snails, and yet the primitiveness and the simplicity are deceptive. The limpet is adapted with beautiful precision to the difficult world of the shore. One expects a snail to have a coiled shell; the limpet has instead a flattened cone. The periwinkles, which have coiled shells, are often rolled around by the surf unless they have hidden themselves securely in crevices or under weeds. The limpet merely presses its cone against the rocks and the water slides over the sloping contours without being able to get a grip; the heavier the waves, the more tightly they press it to the rocks. Most snails have an operculum to shut out enemies and keep moisture inside; the limpet has one in infancy and then discards it. The fit of the shell to the substratum is so close that an operculum is unnecessary; moisture is retained in a little groove that runs around just inside the shell, and the gills are bathed in a small sea of their own until the tide returns.

Ever since Aristotle reported that limpets leave their places on the rocks and go out to feed, people have been recording facts about their natural history. Their supposed possession of a sort of homing sense has been widely discussed. Each limpet is said to possess a "home" or spot to which it always returns. On some types of rock there may be a recognizable scar, either a discoloration or a depression, to which the contours of the shell have become precisely fitted. From this home the limpet wanders out on the high tides to feed, scraping the small algae off the rocks by licking motions of the radula. After an hour or two of feeding it returns by approximately the same path, and settles down to wait out the period of low water.

Many nineteenth-century naturalists tried unsuccessfully to discover by experiment the nature of the sense involved and the organ in which the homing sense resides, much as modern scientists try to find a physical basis for the homing abilities of birds. Most of these studies dealt with the common British limpet, Patella, and although no one could explain how the homing instinct worked, there seemed to be little doubt in anyone's mind that it did work, and with great precision.

Limpets

In recent years American scientists have investigated the matter with statistical methods, and some have concluded that Pacific coast limpets do not "home" very well at all. (No careful studies of homing have been made among New England limpets.) Other recent work in California, however, supports the homing theory. Dr. W. G. Hewatt marked a large number of limpets and their homes with identifying numbers. He found that on each high tide all the limpets left home, wandered about for some two and a half hours, then returned. The direction of their excursions changed from tide to tide, but they always returned to the home spot. Dr. Hewatt tried filing a deep groove across one animal's homeward path. The limpet halted on the edge of the groove and spent some time confronting this dilemma, but on the next tide it moved around the edge of the groove and returned home. Another limpet was taken about nine inches from its home and the edges of its shell were filed smooth. It was then released on the same spot. It returned to its home, but presumably the exact fit of shell to rock home had been destroyed by the filing and the next day the limpet moved about twenty-one inches away and did not return. On the fourth day it had taken up a new home and after eleven days it disappeared.

The limpet's relations with other inhabitants of the shore are simple. It lives entirely on the minute algae that coat the rocks with a slippery film, or on the cortical cells of larger algae. For either purpose, the radula is effective. The limpet scrapes the rocks so assiduously that fine particles of stone are found in its stomach; as the teeth of the radula wear away under hard use they are replaced by others, pushed up from behind. To the algal spores swarming in the water, ready to settle down and become sporelings and then adult plants, the limpets stand in the relation of enemy, since they keep the rocks scraped fairly clean where they are numerous. By this very act, however, they render a service to barnacles, making easier the attachment of their larvae. Indeed, the paths radiating out from a limpet's home are sometimes marked by a sprinkling of the starlike shells of young barnacles.

In its reproductive habits this deceptively simple little snail seems again to have defied exact observation. It seems certain, however, that the female limpet does not make protective capsules for her eggs in the fashion typical of many snails, but commits them directly to the sea. This is a primitive habit, followed by many of the simpler sea creatures. Whether the eggs are fertilized within the mother's body or while floating at sea is uncertain. The young larvae drift or swim for a time in the surface waters; the survivors then settle down on rocky surfaces and metamorphose from the larval to the adult form. Probably all young limpets are males, later transforming to females—a circumstance not at all uncommon among mollusks.

Like the animal life of this coast, the seaweeds tell a silent story of heavy surf. Back from the headlands and in bays and coves the rockweeds may grow seven feet tall; here on this open coast a seven-inch plant is a large one. In their sparse and stunted growth, the seaweed invaders of the upper rocks reveal the stringent conditions of life where waves beat heavily. In the middle and lower zones some hardy weeds have been able to establish themselves in greater abundance and profusion. These differ so greatly from the algae of quieter shores that they are almost a symbol of the wave-swept coast. Here and there the rocks sloping to the sea glisten with sheets composed of many individual plants of a curious seaweed, the purple laver. Its generic name, Porphyra, means "a purple dye." It belongs to the red algae, and although it has color variations, on the Maine coast it is most often a purplish brown. It resembles nothing so much as little pieces of brown transparent plastic cut out of someone's raincoat. In the thinness of its fronds it is like the sea lettuce, but there is a double layer of tissue, suggesting a child's rubber balloon that has collapsed so that the opposite walls are in contact. At the stem of the "balloon" Porphyra is attached strongly to the rocks by a cord of interwoven strands—hence its specific name, "umbilicalis." Occasionally it is attached to barnacles and very rarely it grows on other algae instead of directly on hard surfaces. When exposed at ebb tide under a hot sun, the laver may dry to brittle, papery layers, but the return of the sea restores the elastic nature of the plant, which, despite its seeming delicacy, allows it to yield unharmed to the push and pull of waves.

Down at the lower tidal levels is another curious weed—Leathesia, the sea potato. It grows in roughly globular form,

Purple laver (left), sea potato (right)

its surface seamed and drawn into lobes, forming fleshy, amber-colored tubers that are any size up to an inch or two in diameter. Usually it grows around the fronds of moss or another seaweed, seldom if ever attaching directly to the rocks.

The lower rocks and the walls of low tide pools are thickly matted with algae. Here the red weeds largely supplant the browns that grow higher up. Along with Irish moss, dulse lines the walls of the pools, its thin, dull red fronds deeply indented so that they bear a crude resemblance to the shape of a hand. Minute leaflets sometimes haphazardly attached along the margins create a strangely tattered appearance. With the water withdrawn, the dulse mats down against the rocks, paper-thin layers piled one upon another. Many small starfish, urchins, and mollusks live within the dulse, as well as in the deeper growth of Irish moss.

Dulse is one of the algae that have a long history of usefulness to man, as food for himself and his domestic animals. According to an old book on seaweeds, it used to be said in Scotland that "he who eats of the Dulse of Guerdie and drinks of the wells of Kildingie will escape all maladies except black death." In Great Britain, cattle are fond of it and sheep wander down into the tidal zone at low water in search of it. In Scotland, Ireland, and Iceland people eat dulse in various ways, or dry it and chew it like tobacco; even in the United States, where such foods are usually ignored, it is possible to buy dulse fresh or dried in some coastal cities.

In the very lowest pools the Laminarias begin to appear, called variously the oarweeds, devil's aprons, sea tangles, and kelps. The Laminarias belong to the brown algae, which flourish in the dimness of deep waters and polar seas. The horsetail kelp lives below the tidal zone with others of the group, but in deep pools also comes over the threshold, just above the line of the lowest tides. Its broad, flat, leathery frond is frayed into long ribbons, its surface is smooth and satiny, and its color richly, glowingly brown.

The water in these deep basins is icy cold, filled with dusky, swaying plants. To look into such a pool is to behold a dark forest, its foliage like the leaves of palm trees, the heavy stalks of the kelps also curiously like the trunks of palms. If one slides his fingers down along such a stalk and grips just above the holdfast, he can pull up the plant and find a whole microcosm held within its grasp.

One of these laminarian holdfasts is something like the roots of a forest tree, branching out, dividing, subdividing, in its very complexity a measure of the great seas that roar over this plant. Here, finding secure attachment, are plankton-strainers like mussels and sea squirts. Small starfish and urchins crowd in under the arching columns of plant tissue. Predacious worms

Dulse

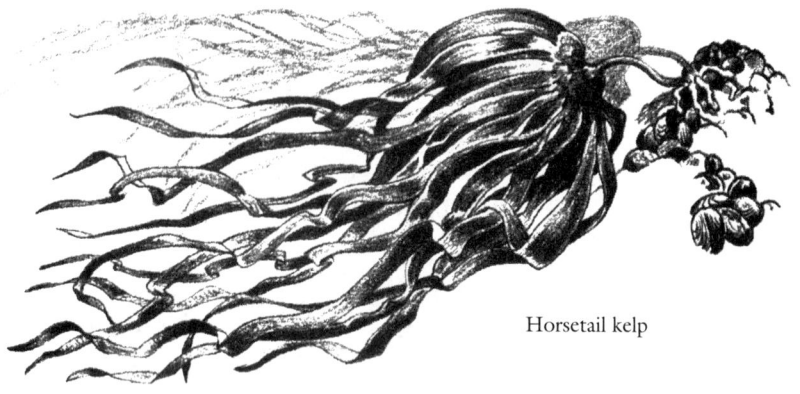

Horsetail kelp

that have foraged hungrily during the night return with the daylight and coil themselves into tangled knots in deep recesses and dark, wet caverns. Mats of sponge spread over the holdfasts, silently, endlessly at their work of straining the waters of the pool. One day a larval bryozoan settles here, builds its tiny shell, then builds another and another, until a film of frosty lace flows around one of the rootlets of the seaweed. And above all this busy community, and probably unaffected by it, the brown ribbons of the kelp roll out into the water, the plant living its own life, growing, replacing torn tissues as best it may, and in season sending clouds of reproductive cells streaming into the water. As for the fauna of the holdfasts, the survival of the kelp is their survival. While it stands firm their little world holds intact; if it is torn away in a surge of stormy seas, all will be scattered and many will perish with it.

The kelp's holdfast

Among the animals almost always inhabiting the holdfasts of the tide-pool kelps are the brittle stars. These fragile echinoderms are well named, for even gentle handling is likely to cause them to snap off one or more arms. This reaction may be useful to an animal living in a turbulent world, for if an arm is pinned down under a shifting rock, the owner can break it off and grow a new one. Brittle stars move about rapidly, using their flexible arms not only in locomotion, but also to capture small worms and other minute sea life and carry them to their mouths.

Sea squirt, Molgula

The scale worms also belong to the holdfast community. Their bodies are protected by a double row of plates forming armament over the back. Under these large plates is an ordinary segmented worm, bearing laterally projecting tufts of golden bristles on each segment. There is a suggestion of primitiveness in the armor plate that is reminiscent of the quite unrelated chitons. Some of the scale worms have developed interesting relations with their neighbors. One of the British species always lives with burrowing animals, although it may change associates from time to time. When young, it lives with a burrowing brittle star, probably stealing its food. When older and larger, it moves into the burrow of a sea cucumber or the tube of the much larger, plumed worm, Amphitrite.

Often the holdfast grips one of the large horse mussels, which have heavy shells and may be four or five inches long. The horse mussel lives only in the deep pools or farther offshore; it is never found in the upper zones with the smaller blue mussel, and it occurs only on or among rocks, where its attachment is relatively secure. Sometimes it constructs a small nest or den as a refuge, using tough byssal threads spun in typical mussel fashion, with pebbles and shell fragments matted among the strands.

A small clam common in laminarian holdfasts is the rockborer, which some English writers call the "red-nose" because of its red siphons. Ordinarily it is a boring form, living in cavities it excavates in limestone, clay, or concrete. Most of the New England rocks are too hard for boring, and so on this coast the clam lives in crusts of coralline algae or among the holdfasts of the kelp. On British coasts it is said to bore rocks that resist mechanical drills. And it does so without recourse to the chemical secretions some borers use, working entirely by repeated and endless mechanical abrasion with its sturdy shell.

The smooth and slippery fronds of the kelps support other populations, less abundant and less varied than those of the holdfasts. On the flat blades of the oarweeds, as well as on rock faces and under ledges, the golden-star tunicate, Botryllus, lays its spangled mats. Over a field of dark green gelatinous substance are sprinkled the little golden stars that mark the position of clusters of individual tunicates. Each starry cluster may consist of three to a dozen individual animals radiating around a central point; many clusters go to make up this continuous, encrusting mat, which may be six to eight inches long.

Beneath the surface beauty there is marvelous complexity of structure and function. Over each star there are infinitesimal disturbances in the water—little currents funneling down, one to each point of the star, and there being drawn in through a small opening. One heavier, outward-moving current emerges from the center of the cluster. The indrawn currents bring in food organisms and oxygen, and the outflowing current carries away the metabolic waste products of the group.

At first glance a colony of Botryllus may seem no more complex than a mat of encrusting sponge. In actual fact, however,

Golden-star tunicate

each of the individuals comprising the colony is a highly organized creature, in structure almost identical with such solitary ascidians as the sea grape and the sea vase, found so abundantly on wharves and sea walls. The individual Botryllus, however, is only one-sixteenth to one-eighth of an inch long.

One of these entire colonies, comprising perhaps hundreds of star clusters (and so perhaps a thousand or more individuals), may arise from a single fertilized ovum. In the parent colony, eggs are formed early in the summer, are fertilized, and begin their development while remaining within the parental tissues. (Each individual Botryllus produces both eggs and sperms, but since in any one animal they mature at different times, cross fertilization is insured, the spermatozoa being carried in the sea water and drawn in along with the water currents.) Presently the parent releases minute larvae shaped like tadpoles, with long, swimming tails. For perhaps an hour or two such a larva drifts and swims, then settles down on some ledge or weed and makes itself fast. Soon the tissues of the tail are absorbed and all suggestion of ability to swim is lost. Within two days the heart begins to beat in that curious tunicate rhythm—first driving the blood in one direction, pausing briefly, then reversing the direction of the flow. After nearly a fortnight, this small individual has completed the formation of its own body and begins to bud off other individuals. These, in turn, bud off others. Each new creature has its separate opening for the intake of water, but all retain connections with a central vent for the outflow of wastes. When the individuals

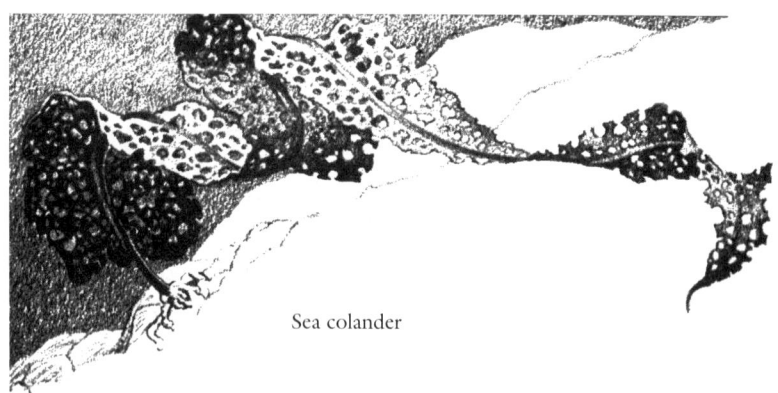

Sea colander

clustered around this common opening become too crowded, one or more newly formed buds are pushed out into the surrounding mat of gelatinous tissue, where they begin new star clusters. In this way the colony spreads.

The intertidal zone is sometimes invaded by a deep-water laminarian, the sea colander. It is a representative of those brown seaweeds that flourish in the cold waters of the Arctic, and has come down from Greenland as far as Cape Cod. Its appearance is strikingly different from that of the sea moss and horsetail kelp among which it sometimes appears. The wide frond is pierced by innumerable perforations; these are foreshadowed in the young plant by conical papillae, which later break through to form the perforations.

Beyond the rims of the lowest pools, growing on the rock walls that slope away steeply into deep water, is another laminarian seaweed, Alaria, the winged kelp, called the murlin in Great Britain. Its long, ruffled, streaming fronds rise with each surge and fall as the water pours away seaward. The fertile pinnae, in which the reproductive cells mature, are borne at the base of the frond, for in a plant so exposed to violent surf this location is safer than the tips of the main blade. (In the rockweeds, living higher on the shore and less subject to savage wave action, the reproductive cells are formed at the tips of the fronds.) Almost more than any of the other seaweeds, Alaria is a plant conditioned to constant pounding by the waves. Standing on the outermost point that gives safe footing, one can see its dark ribbons streaming out into the water, being tugged and tossed and pounded. The larger and older plants become much frayed and worn, the margins of the blade splitting or the tip of the midrib being worn off. By such concessions the plant saves some of the strain on its holdfasts. The stipe can withstand a relatively enormous pull, but severe storms tear away many plants.

Still farther down, one can sometimes and in some places get a glimpse of the dark, mysterious forests of the kelps, where they go down into deep water. Sometimes these giant kelps are cast ashore after a storm. They have a stiff, strong stipe from which the long ribbon of the frond extends. The sea tangle or sugar kelp, *Laminaria saccharina*, has a stipe up to 4 feet long, supporting a relatively narrow frond (6 to 18 inches wide) that may extend out and upward into the sea as much as 30 feet. The margin is greatly frilled and a powdery white substance (mannitol, a sugar) forms on the dried fronds. The long-stalked laminaria (*Laminaria longicruris*) has a stem comparable to the trunk of a small tree, being 6 to 12 feet long. The frond is up to 3 feet wide and 20 feet long, but may sometimes be shorter than the stipe.

The stands of sea tangles and long-stalked laminarias are, in their way, an Atlantic counterpart of the great submarine jungles of the Pacific, where the kelps rise like giant forest trees, 150 feet from the floor of the sea to the surface.

Winged kelp, Alaria

On all rocky coasts, this laminarian zone just below low water has been one of the least-known regions of the sea. We know little about what lives here throughout the year. We do not know whether some of the forms that disappear from the intertidal area in winter may merely move down into this zone. And perhaps some of the species we think have died out in a particular region, perhaps because of temperature changes, have gone down among the Laminarias. The area is obviously difficult to explore, with heavy seas breaking there most of the time. Such an area on the west coast of Scotland was, however, explored by helmet divers working with the British biologist, J. A. Kitching. Below the zone occupied by Alaria and the horsetail kelp, from about two fathoms below low water and beyond, the divers moved through a dense forest of the larger Laminarias. From the vertical stipes an immense canopy of fronds was spread above their heads. Although the sun shone brightly at the surface, the divers were almost in darkness as they pushed through this forest. Between three and six fathoms below low water of the spring tides the forest opened out, so that the men could walk between the plants without great difficulty. There the light was stronger, and through misty water they could see this more open "park" extending farther down the sloping floor of the sea. Among the holdfasts and stipes of the laminarias, as among the roots and trunks of a terrestrial forest, was a dense undergrowth, here formed of various red algae. And as small rodents and other creatures have their dens and runways under the forest trees, so a varied and abundant fauna lived on and among the holdfasts of the great seaweeds.

In quieter waters, protected from the heavy surf of coasts that face the open ocean, the seaweeds dominate the shore, occupying every inch of space that the conditions of tidal rise and fall allow them and by the sheer force of abundant and luxuriant growth forcing other shore inhabitants to accommodate to their pattern.

Although the same bands of life are spread between the tide lines whether the coast be open or sheltered, in their relative development the zones vary greatly on the two types of shore.

Above the high-tide line there is little change and on the shores of bays and estuaries, as elsewhere, the microplants blacken the rocks and the lichens come down and tentatively approach the sea. Below high water of spring tides, pioneering barnacles trace occasional white streaks in token occupation of the zone they dominate on open coasts. A few periwinkles graze on the upper rocks. But on sheltered coasts the whole band of shore marked out by the tides of the moon's quarters is occupied by a swaying submarine forest, sensitive to the movements of the waves and the tidal currents. The trees of the forest are the large seaweeds known as the rockweeds or sea wracks, stout of form and rubbery of texture. Here all other life exists within their shelter—a shelter so hospitable to small things needing protection from drying air, from rain, and from the surge of the running tides and the waves, that the life of these shores is incredibly abundant.

When covered at high tide, the rockweeds stand erect, rising and swaying with a life borrowed from the sea. Then, to one standing at the edge of a flooding tide, the only sign of their presence may be a scattering of dark patches on the water close inshore, where the tips of the weeds reach up to the surface. Down below those floating tips small fishes swim, passing between the weeds as birds fly through a forest, sea snails creep along the fronds, and crabs climb from branch to branch of the swaying plants. It is a fantastic jungle, mad in a Lewis Carroll sort of way. For what proper jungle, twice every twenty-four hours, begins to sag lower and lower and finally lies prostrate for several hours, only to rise again? Yet this is precisely what the rockweed jungles do. When the tide has retreated from the sloping rocks, when it has left the miniature seas of the tide pools, the rockweeds lie flat on the horizontal surfaces in layer above layer of sodden, rubbery fronds. From the sheer rock faces they hang down in a heavy curtain, holding the wetness of the sea, and nothing under their protective cover ever dries out.

By day the sunlight filters through the jungle of rockweeds to reach its floor only in shifting patches of shadow-flecked gold; by night the moonlight spreads a silver ceiling above the forest —a ceiling streaked and broken by the flowing tide streams; beneath it the dark fronds of the weeds sway in a world unquiet with moving shadows.

But the flow of time through this submarine forest is marked

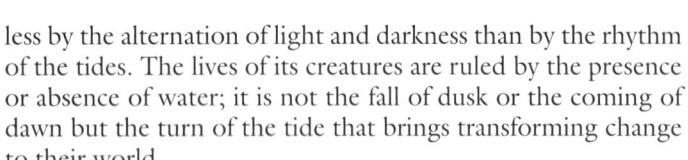

less by the alternation of light and darkness than by the rhythm of the tides. The lives of its creatures are ruled by the presence or absence of water; it is not the fall of dusk or the coming of dawn but the turn of the tide that brings transforming change to their world.

As the tide falls the tips of the weeds, lacking support, float out horizontally across the surface. Then the cloud shadows darken and a deepening gloom settles over the floor of the forest. As the overlying layer of water thins and gradually drains away, the weeds, still stirring, still responsive to each pulsation of the tide, drift closer to the rock floor and finally lie prostrate upon it, all their life and movement in abeyance.

By day an interval of quiet settles over the jungles of the land, when the hunters lie in their dens, and the weak and the slow hide from the daylight; so on the shore a waiting lull comes with every ebbing of the tide.

Rockweed forest of knotted wrack

The barnacles furl their nets and swing shut the twin doors that exclude the drying air and hold within the moisture of the sea. The mussels and the clams withdraw their feeding tubes or siphons and close their shells. Here and there a starfish, having invaded the forest from below on the previous high tide and incautiously lingered, still clasps a mussel within its sinuous arms, gripping the shells with the sucker-tipped ends of scores of slender tube feet. Pushing under and among the horizontal fronds of the weed, as a man would make his way with difficulty through trees blown down by a storm, a few crabs are active, digging their little slanting pits to expose the clams buried in the mud. Then they crack away pieces of shell with their heavy claws, while they hold the clam in the tips of the walking legs.

A few hunters and scavengers come down from the upper tidelands. The little gray-cloaked tide-pool insect, Anurida, wanders down from the upper shore and scurries over the rock floor, hunting out mussels with gaping shells, or dead fish, or fragments of crabs left by gulls. Crows walk about over the weeds; they sort them over strand by strand until they find a periwinkle hidden in the weed, or clinging to a rock that lies under the sodden cloak of the algae. Then the crow holds the shell in the strong toes of one foot, while with its beak it deftly extracts the snail.

The pulse of the returning tide at first beats gently. The advance during the beginning of the six-hour rise to high-water mark is slow, so that in two hours only a quarter of the intertidal zone has been covered. Then the pace of the water quickens. For the next two hours the tidal currents are stronger and the rising waters advance twice as far as in the first period; then again the tide slackens its pace for a leisurely advance over the upper shore. The rockweeds, covering the middle band of shore, receive the shock of heavier waves than the relatively bare shore above, yet their cushioning effect is so great that the animals that cling to them or live on the rock floor below them are far less affected by the surf than those of the upper rocks, or those of the zone below which experience all the heavy drag from the backwash of waves that break as the tide is advancing rapidly over the middle shore.

Darkness brings the jungles of the land to life, but the night of the rockweed jungles is the time of the rising tide, when water pours in under the masses of weed, stirring out of their low-tide quiescence all the inhabitants of this forest.

As the water from the open sea floods the floor of the weed jungles, shadows flicker again above the ivory cones of the barnacles as the almost invisible nets reach out to gather what the tide has brought. The shells of clams and mussels again open slightly and little vortices of water are drawn down, funneling into the complex straining mechanisms within the shellfish all the little spheres of marine vegetables that are their food.

Nereid worms emerge from the mud and swim off to other hunting grounds; if they are to reach them they must elude the fishes that have come in with the tide, for on the flood tide the rockweed forests become one with the sea and with its hungry predators.

Shrimp flicker in and out through the open spaces of the forest; they seek small crustaceans, baby fish, or minute bristle worms, but in their turn are pursued by following fish. Starfish move up from the great meadows of sea moss lower on the shore, hunting the mussels that grow on the floor of the forest.

The crows and the gulls are driven out of the tidelands. The little gray, velvet-cloaked insects move up the shore or, finding a secure crevice, wrap themselves in a glistening blanket of air to wait for the falling of the tide.

The rockweeds that create this intertidal forest are descendants of some of the earth's most ancient plants. Along with the great kelps lower on the shore, they belong to the group of brown seaweeds, in which the chlorophyll is masked by other pigments. The Greek name for the brown algae—the *Phaeophyceae*— means "the dusky or shadowy plants." According to some theories, they arose in that early period when the earth was still enveloped in heavy clouds and illuminated only by feeble rays of sunlight. Even today the brown seaweeds are plants of dim and shadowed places—the deep submarine slopes where giant kelps form dusky jungles and the dark rock ledges from which the oarweeds send their long ribbons streaming into the tides. And the rockweeds that grow between the tide lines do so on northern coasts, visited often by cloud and fog. Their rare invasions of the sunny tropics are accomplished under a protective cover of deep water.

The brown algae may have been the first of the sea plants to colonize the shore. They learned to adjust themselves to alternating periods of submersion and exposure on ancient coastlines swept by strong tides; they came as close to a land existence as they could without actually leaving the tidal zone.

One of the modern rockweeds, the channeled wrack of European shores, lives at the extreme upper edge of the tidelands. In some places its only contact with the sea is an occasional drenching with spray. In sun and air its fronds become blackened and crisp so that one would think it had surely been killed, but with the return of the sea its normal color and texture are restored.

The channeled wrack does not grow on the American Atlantic coast, but there a related plant, the spiral wrack, comes almost as far out of the sea. It is a weed of low growth, whose short sturdy fronds end in turgid, rough-textured swellings. Its heaviest growth is above the high-water mark of the neap tides, so of all the rockweeds it lives closest inshore or nearest the water line of exposed ledges. Although it spends nearly three-fourths of its life out of water, it is a true seaweed and its splashes of orange-brown color on the upper shore are a symbol of the threshold of the sea.

These plants, however, are but the outlying fringe of the intertidal forest, which is an almost pure stand of two other rockweeds—the knotted wrack and the bladder wrack. Both are sensitive indicators of the force of the surf. The knotted

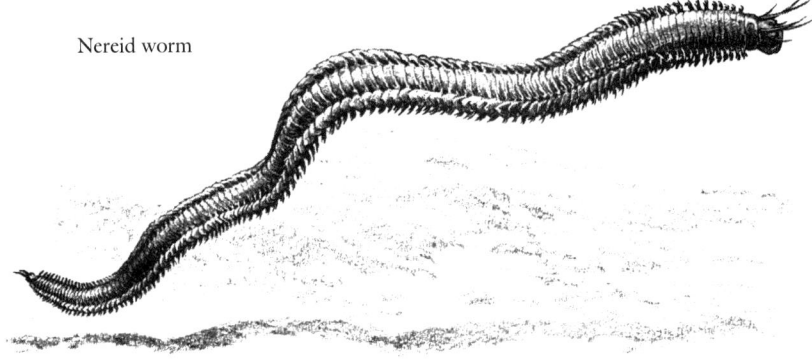

Nereid worm

wrack can live in profusion only on shores protected from heavy waves, and in such places is the dominant weed. Back from the headlands, on the shores of bays and tidal rivers where surf and tidal surge are subdued by remoteness from the open sea, the knotted wrack may grow taller than the tallest man, though its fronds are slender as straws. The long surge of the swell in sheltered water places no great strain on its elastic strands. Swellings or vesicles on the main stems or fronds contain oxygen and other gases secreted by the plant; these act as buoys when the weeds are covered by the tide. The bladder wrack has greater tensile strength and so can endure the sharp tugging and pulling of moderately heavy surf. Although it is much shorter than the knotted wrack it also needs the help of air bladders to rise in the water. In this species the bladders are paired, one of each pair on either side of the strong midrib; the bladders, however, may fail to develop where the plants are subjected to much pounding by surf, or when they grow at the lower levels of the tidal zone. At some seasons the ends of the branches of this wrack swell into bulbous, almost heart-shaped structures; from these the reproductive cells are liberated.

The sea wracks have no roots, but instead grip the rocks by means of a flattened, disc-like expansion of their tissues. It is almost as though the base of each weed melted a little, spreading over the rock and then congealing, thereby creating a union so firm that only the thundering seas of a very heavy storm, or the grinding of shore ice, can tear away the plants. The seaweeds do not have a land plant's need of roots to extract minerals from the soil, for they are bathed almost continuously by the sea and so live within a solution of all the minerals they need for life. Nor do they need the rigid supporting stem or trunk by which a land plant reaches upward into sunlight—they have only to yield themselves to the water. And so their structure is simple—merely a branching frond arising from the holdfast, with no division into roots and stems and leaves.

Looking at the prostrate, low-tide forests of the rockweeds that cover the shore with a many-layered blanket, one would suppose that the plants must spring from every available inch of rock surface. But actually the forest, when it rises and comes to life with the flooding tide, is fairly open and sprinkled with clearings. On my own shore in Maine, where the tides rise and fall over a wide expanse of intertidal rock, and the knotted wrack spreads its dark blanket between the high and low waters of the neap tides, the areas of open rock around the holdfast of each plant are sometimes as much as a foot in diameter. From the middle of such a clearing the plant rises, its fronds dividing repeatedly, until the upper branchings extend out over an area several feet across.

Far below, at the base of the fronds that swing with the undulation of the passing waves, the rocks are stained with vivid hues, painted in crimson and emerald by the activities of sea plants so minute that even in their thousands they seem but part of the rock, a surface revelation of jewel tones within. The green patches are growths of one of the green algae. The individual plants are so small that only a strong lens could reveal their identity—lost, as individual blades of grass are lost in the lush expanse of a meadow, in the spreading verdant stain created by the mass. Amid the green are other patches of a rich and intensely glowing red, and again the growth is not separable from the mineral floor. It is a creation of one of the red

Spiral wrack

seaweeds, a form that secretes lime in thin and closely adhering crusts over the rocks.

Against this background of glowing color the barnacles stand out with sharp distinctness, and in the clear water that pours through the forest like liquid glass, their cirri flicker in and out—extending, grasping, withdrawing, taking from the inpouring tides those minute atoms of life that our eyes cannot see. Around the bases of small wave-rounded boulders the mussels lie as though at anchor, held by gleaming lines spun by their own tissues. Their paired blue shells stand a little apart, the space between them revealing pale brown tissues with fluted edges.

Some parts of the forest are less open. In these the clumps of rockweeds rise from a short turf or undergrowth consisting chiefly of the flat fronds of Irish moss, with sometimes dark mats of another plant with the texture of Turkish toweling. And like a tropical jungle with its orchids, this sea forest has the counterpart of airplants in the epiphytic tufts of a red seaweed that grows on the fronds of the knotted wrack. Polysiphonia seems to have lost—or perhaps it never had—the ability to attach directly to the rocks and so its dark red balls of finely divided fronds cling to the wracks, and by them are lifted up into the water.

In the areas between the rocks and under loose boulders a substance that is neither sand nor mud has accumulated. It consists of minute and water-ground bits of the remains of sea creatures—the shells of mollusks, the spines of sea urchins, the opercula of snails. Clams live in pockets of this soft substance, digging down until they are buried to the tips of their siphons. Around the clams the mud is alive with ribbon worms, thin

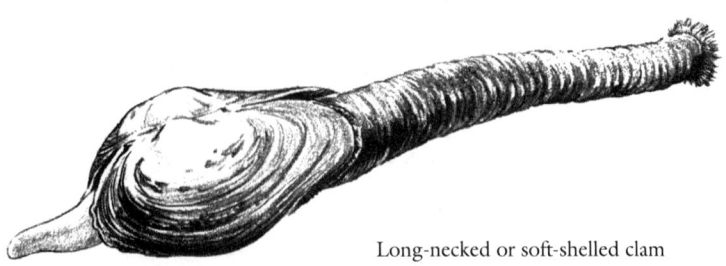

Long-necked or soft-shelled clam

Green crab eating clam

as threads, scarlet of color, each a small hunter searching out minute bristle worms and other prey. Here also are the nereids, given the Latin name for sea nymph because of their grace and iridescent beauty. The nereids are active predators that leave their burrows at night to search for small worms, crustaceans, and other prey. In the dark of the moon certain species gather at the surface in immense spawning swarms. Curious legends have become associated with them. In New England the so-called clam worm, *Nereis virens*, often takes shelter in empty clam shells. Fishermen, accustomed to finding it thus, believe it is the male clam.

Crabs of thumbnail size live in the weed and come down to hunt in these areas. They are the young of the green crab; the adults live below the tide lines on this shore except when they come into the shelter of the weeds to molt. The young crabs search the mud pockets, digging out pits and probing for clams that are about their own size.

Clams, crabs, and worms are part of a community of animals whose lives are closely interrelated. The crabs and the worms are the active predators, the beasts of prey. The clams, the mussels, and the barnacles are the plankton feeders, able to live sedentary lives because their food is brought to them by each tide. By an immutable law of nature, the plankton feeders as a group are more numerous than those that prey on them. Besides the clams and other large species, the rockweeds shelter thousands of small beings, all of them busy with filtering devices of varying design, straining out the plankton of each tide. There is, for example, a small, plumed worm called Spirorbis. Seeing it for the first time, one would certainly say that it is no worm, but a snail, for it is a tube-builder, having learned some feat of chemistry that allows it to secrete about itself a calcareous shell or tube. The tube is not much larger than the head of a pin and is wound in a flat, closely coiled spiral of chalky whiteness, its form strongly suggesting some of the land snails. The worm lives permanently within the tube, which is cemented to weed or rock, thrusting out its head from time to time to filter food animals through the fine filaments of its crown of tentacles. These exquisitely delicate and filmy tentacles serve not only as snares to entangle food but as gills for breathing. Among them is a structure like a long-stemmed goblet; when the worm draws back into its tube the goblet or operculum closes the opening like a neatly fitted trap door.

The fact that the tube worms have managed to live in the intertidal zone for perhaps millions of years is evidence of a sensitive adjustment of their way of life, on the one hand to conditions within the surrounding world of the rockweeds, on

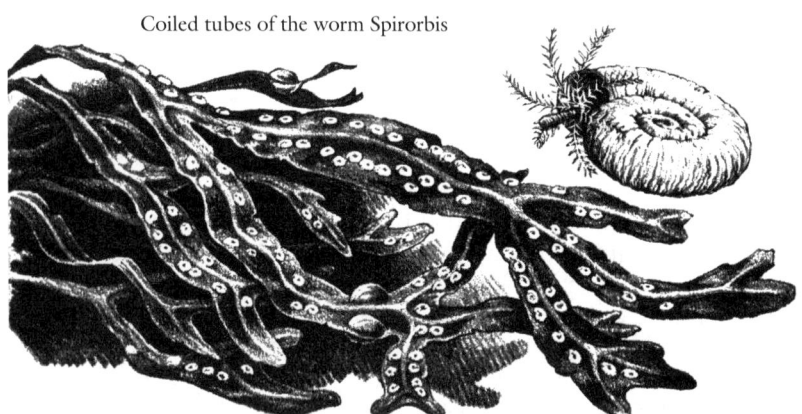

Coiled tubes of the worm Spirorbis

the other to vast tidal rhythms linked with the movements of earth, moon, and sun.

In the inmost coils of the tube are little chains of beads wrapped in cellophane—or so they appear. There are about twenty beads in a chain. The beads are developing eggs. When the embryos have developed into larvae, the cellophane membranes rupture and the young are sent forth into the sea. By keeping the embryonic stages within the parental tube Spirorbis protects its young from enemies and assures that the infant worms will be in the intertidal zone when they are ready to settle. Their period of active swimming is short—at most an hour or so, and well contained within a single rising or falling of the tide. They are stout little creatures with bright red eye spots; perhaps the larval eyes help in locating a place for attachment but in any event they degenerate soon after the larva settles.

In the laboratory, under my microscope, I have watched the larvae swimming about busily, all their little bristles whirring, then sometimes descending to the glass floor of their dish to bump it with their heads. Why and how do the infant tube worms settle in the same sort of place their ancestors chose? Apparently they make many trials, reacting more favorably to smooth surfaces than to rough, and displaying a strong instinct of gregariousness that leads them to settle by preference where others of their kind are already established. These tendencies help to keep the tube worms within their comparatively restricted world. There is also a response, not to familiar surroundings, but to cosmic forces. Every fortnight, on the moon's quarter, a batch of eggs is fertilized and taken into the brood chamber to begin its development. And at the same time the larvae that have been made ready during the previous fortnight are expelled into the sea. By this timing—this precise synchronizing with the phases of the moon—the release of the young always occurs on a neap tide, when neither the rise nor the fall of the water is of great extent, and even for so small a creature the chances of remaining within the rockweed zone are good.

Sea snails of the periwinkle tribe inhabit the upper branches of the weeds at high tide or take shelter under them when the tide is out. The orange and yellow and olive-green colors of their smoothly rounded, flat-topped shells suggest the fruiting bodies of the rockweeds, and perhaps the resemblance is protective. The smooth periwinkle, unlike the rough, is still an animal of the sea; the salty dampness it requires is provided by the wet and dripping fronds of the seaweeds when the tide is out. It lives by scraping off the cortical cells of the algae, seldom if ever descending to the rocks to feed on the surface film as related species do. Even in its spawning habits the smooth periwinkle is a creature of the rockweeds. There is no shedding of eggs into the sea, no period of juvenile drifting in the currents. All the stages of its life are lived in the rockweeds—it knows no other home.

Curious about the early stages of this abundant snail, I have gone down into my own rockweed forests on the summer low tides to search for them. Sorting over the prostrate wrack, examining its long strands for some signs of what I sought, I have occasionally been rewarded by discovering transparent masses of a substance like tough jelly, tightly adhering to the fronds. They averaged perhaps a quarter-inch long and half as wide. Within each mass I could see the eggs, round as bubbles, dozens of them embedded in the confining matrix. One such egg mass that I carried to the microscope contained a developing embryo within the membranes of each egg. They were clearly molluscan, but so undifferentiated that I could not have said what mollusk lay nascent within. In the cold waters of its home, about a month would intervene from the egg to the hatching stage, but in the warmer temperatures of the laboratory the remaining days of development were reduced to hours. The following day each sphere contained a tiny baby periwinkle, its shell completely formed, apparently ready to emerge and take up its life on the rocks. How do they hold their places there, I wondered, as the weeds sway in the tides and occasional storms send waves pounding in over the shore? Later in the summer there was at least a partial answer. I noticed that many of the air vesicles of the wracks bore little perforations, as though they had been chewed or punctured by some animal. I slit some of these vesicles carefully so that I might look inside. There, secure in a green-walled chamber, were the babies of the smooth periwinkle—from two to half a dozen of them sharing the refuge of a single vesicle, secure alike against storms and enemies.

The hydroid Clava

Down near the low water of the neap tides the hydroid Clava spreads its velvet patches on the fronds of the knotted wrack and the bladder wrack. Rising from its point of attachment like a plant from its root clump, each cluster of tubular animals looks like nothing so much as a spray of delicate flowers, shading from pink to rose and fringed with petal-like tentacles, all nodding in the water currents as woodland flowers nod in a gentle wind. But the swaying movements are purposive ones by which the hydroid reaches into the currents for food. In its way it is a voracious little jungle beast, all its tentacles studded with batteries of stinging cells that can be shot into its victims like poisoned arrows. When, in their ceaseless movements, the tentacles come into contact with a small crustacean or worm or the larva of some sea creature, a shower of darts is released; the prey animal becomes paralyzed and is seized and conveyed to the mouth by the tentacles.

Each of these colonies now established on the wracks came from a little swimming larva that once settled there, shed the hairy cilia by which it swam, attached itself, and began to elongate into a little plantlike being. A crown of tentacles formed at its free end. In time, from the base of the tubular creature, a seeming root, or stolon, began to creep over the rockweed, budding off new tubes, each complete with mouth and tentacles. So all the numerous individuals of the colony originated in a single fertilized ovum that yielded the wandering larva.

In season, the plantlike hydroid must reproduce, but by a strange circumstance it cannot itself yield the germ cells that would give rise to new larvae, for it can reproduce only nonsexually, by budding. So there is a curious alternation of generations, found again and again in many members of the large coelenterate group to which the hydroids belong, by which no individual produces offspring that resemble itself, but each is like the grandparental generation. Just below the tentacles of an individual Clava the buds of the new generation are produced—the alternate generation that intervenes between colonies of hydroids. They are pendent clusters shaped like berries. In some species the berries, or medusa buds, would drop from the parent and swim away—tiny, bell-shaped things like minute jellyfish. Clava, however, does not release its medusae but keeps them attached. Pink buds are male medusae; purple ones are female. When they are mature, each sheds its eggs or sperm into the sea. When fertilized, the eggs begin to divide and through their development yield the little protoplasmic threads of larvae, which swim off through unknown waters to found some distant colonies.

During many days of midsummer, the incoming tides bring the round opalescent forms of the moon jellies. Most of these are in the weakened condition that accompanies the fulfillment of their life cycle; their tissues are easily torn by the slightest turbulence of water, and when the tide carries them in over the rockweeds and then withdraws, leaving them there like crumpled cellophane, they seldom survive the tidal interval.

Each year they come, sometimes only a few at a time, sometimes in immense numbers. Drifting shoreward, their silent approach is unheralded even by the cries of sea birds, who have no interest in the jellyfish as food, for their tissues are largely water.

During much of the summer they have been drifting offshore, white gleams in the water, sometimes assembling in hundreds along the line of meeting of two currents, where they trace winding lines in the sea along these otherwise invisible

Winter stage of Aurelia, budding off young jellyfish

boundaries. But toward autumn, nearing the end of life, the moon jellies offer no resistance to the tidal currents, and almost every flood tide brings them in to the shore. At this season the adults are carrying the developing larvae, holding them in the flaps of tissue that hang from the under surface of the disc. The young are little pear-shaped creatures; when finally they are shaken loose from the parent (or freed by the stranding of the parent on the shore), they swim about in the shallow water, sometimes swarms of them together. Finally they seek bottom and each becomes attached by the end that was foremost when it swam. As a tiny plantlike growth, about an eighth of an inch high and bearing long tentacles, this strange child of the delicate moon jelly survives the winter storms. Then constrictions begin to encircle its body, so that it comes to resemble a pile of saucers. In the spring these "saucers" free themselves one after another and swim away, each a tiny jellyfish, fulfilling the alternation of the generations. North of Cape Cod these young grow to their full diameter of six to ten inches by July; they mature and produce eggs and sperm cells by late July or August; and in August and September they begin to yield the larvae that will become the attached generation. By the end of October all of the season's jellyfish have been destroyed by storms, but their offspring survive, attached to the rocks near the low-tide line or on nearby bottoms offshore.

Moon jelly, Aurelia

If the moon jellies are symbols of the coastal waters, seldom straying more than a few miles offshore, it is otherwise with the great red jellyfish, Cyanea, which in its periodic invasions of bays and harbors links the shallow green waters with the bright distances of the open sea. On fishing banks a hundred or more miles offshore one may see its immense bulk drifting at the surface as it swims lazily, its tentacles sometimes trailing for fifty feet or more. These tentacles spell danger for almost all sea creatures in their path and even for human beings, so powerful is the sting. Yet young cod, haddock, and sometimes other fishes adopt the great jellyfish as a "nurse," traveling through the shelterless sea under the protection of this large creature and somehow unharmed by the nettle-like stings of the tentacles.

Like Aurelia, the red jellyfish is an animal only of the summer seas, for whom the autumnal storms bring the end of life. Its offspring are the winter plantlike generation, duplicating in almost every detail the life history of the moon jelly. On bottoms no more than two hundred feet deep (and usually much less), little half-inch wisps of living tissue represent the heritage of the immense red jellyfish. They can survive the cold and the storms that the larger summer generation cannot endure; when the warmth of spring begins to dissipate the icy cold of the winter sea they will bud off the tiny discs that, by some inexplicable magic of development, grow in a single season into the adult jellyfish.

Great red or arctic jellyfish

As the tide falls below the rockweeds, the surf of the sea's edge washes over the cities of the mussels. Here, within these lower reaches of the intertidal zone, the blue-black shells form a living blanket over the rocks. The cover is so dense, so uniform in its texture and composition, that often one scarcely realizes that this is not rock, but living animals. In one place the shells, unimaginable in number, are no more than a quarter of an inch long; in another the mussels may be several times as large. But always they are packed so closely together, neighbor against neighbor, that it is hard to see how any one of them can open its shells enough to receive the currents of water that bring its food. Every inch, every hundredth of an inch of space, has been taken over by a living creature whose survival depends on gaining a foothold on this rocky shore.

The presence of each individual mussel in this crowded assemblage is evidence of the achievement of its unconscious, juvenile purpose, an expression of the will-to-live embodied in a minute transparent larva once set adrift in the sea to find its own solid bit of earth for attachment, or to die.

The setting adrift takes place on an astronomical scale. Along the American Atlantic coast the spawning season of the mussels is protracted, extending from April into September. What induces a wave of spawning at any particular time is unknown, but it seems clear that the spawning of a few mussels releases chemical substances into the water, and that these react on all mature individuals in the area and set them to pouring their eggs and milt into the sea. The female mussels discharge the eggs in a continuing, almost endless stream of short little rodlike masses—hundreds, thousands, millions of cells, each potentially an adult mussel. One large female may release up to twenty-five million at a single spawning. In quiet water the eggs drift gently to the bottom, but in the normal conditions of surf or swiftly moving currents they are at once possessed by the sea and carried away.

Simultaneously with the outflow of eggs, the water has become cloudy with the milt poured into the water by the male mussels, the number of individual sperm cells defying all attempts at calculation. Dozens of them cluster about a single egg, pressing against it, seeking entrance. But one male cell, and one only, is successful. With the entrance of this first sperm cell, an instantaneous physical change takes place in the outer membranes of the egg, and from this moment it cannot again be penetrated by a spermatozoan.

After the union of the male and female nuclei, the division of the fertilized cell proceeds rapidly. In less than the interval between a high and a low tide, the egg has been transformed into a little ball of cells, propelling itself through the water with glittering hairs, or cilia. In about twenty-four hours, it has assumed an odd, top-shaped form that is common to the larvae of all young mollusks and annelid worms. A few days more and it has become flattened and elongated and swims rapidly by vibrations of a membrane called the velum; it crawls over solid surfaces, and senses contact with foreign objects. Its journey through the sea is far from being a solitary one; in a square meter of surface over a bed of adult mussels there may be as many as 170,000 swimming larvae.

The thin larval shell takes form, but soon it is replaced by another, double-valved as in adult mussels. By this time the velum has disintegrated, and the mantle, foot, and other organs of the adult have begun their development.

From early summer these tiny shelled creatures live in prodigious numbers in the seaweeds of the shore. In almost every bit of weed I pick up for microscopic examination I find them creeping about, exploring their world with the long tubular organ called the foot, which bears an odd resemblance to the trunk of an elephant. The infant mussel uses it to test out objects in its path, to creep over level or steeply sloping rocks or through seaweeds, or even to walk on the under side of the surface film of quiet water. Soon, however, the foot assumes a new function: it aids in the work of spinning the tough silken threads that anchor a mussel to whatever offers a solid support and insurance against being washed away in the surf.

The very existence of the mussel fields of the low-tide zone is evidence that this chain of circumstances has proceeded unbroken to its consummation untold millions upon millions of times. Yet, for every mussel surviving upon the rocks, there must have been millions of larvae whose setting forth into the sea had a disastrous end. The system is in delicate balance; barring catastrophe, the forces that destroy neither outweigh nor are outweighed by those that create, and over the years of a man's life, as over the ages of recent geologic time, the total number of mussels on the shore probably has remained about the same.

In much of this low-water area the mussels live in intimate association with one of the red seaweeds, Gigartina, a plant of low-growing, bushy form and almost cartilaginous texture. Plants and mussels unite inseparably to form a tough mat. Very small mussels may grow about the plants so abundantly as to

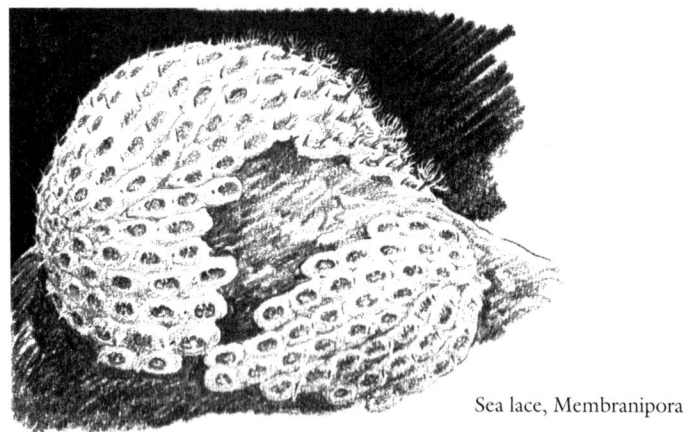

Sea lace, Membranipora

obscure their basal attachment to the rocks. Both the stems and the repeatedly subdivided branches of the seaweed are astir with life, but with life on so small a scale that the human eye can see its details only with the aid of a microscope.

Snails, some with brightly banded and deeply sculptured shells, crawl along the fronds, browsing on microscopic vegetable matter. Many of the basal stems of the weed are thickly encrusted with the bryozoan sea lace, Membranipora; from all its compartments the minute, be-tentacled heads of the resident creatures are thrust out. Another bryozoan of coarser growth, Flustrella, also forms mats investing the broken stems and stubble of the red weed, the substance of its own growth giving such a stem almost the thickness of a pencil. Rough hairs or bristles protrude from the mat, so that much foreign matter adheres to it. Like the sea laces, however, it is formed of hundreds of small, adjacent compartments. From one after another of these, as I watch through my microscope, a stout little creature cautiously emerges, then unfurls its crown of filmy tentacles as one would open an umbrella. Threadlike worms creep over the bryozoan, winding among the bristles like snakes through coarse stubble. A tiny, cyclopean crustacean, with one glittering ruby eye, runs ceaselessly and rather clumsily over the colony, apparently disturbing the inhabitants, for when one of them feels the touch of the blundering crustacean it quickly folds its tentacles and withdraws into its compartment.

In the upper branches of this jungle formed by the red weed, there are many nests or tubes occupied by amphipod crustaceans known as Amphithoë. These small creatures have the appearance of wearing cream-colored jerseys brightly splotched with brownish red; in each goatlike face are set two conspicuous eyes and two pairs of hornlike antennae. The nests are as firmly and skillfully constructed as a bird's but are subject to far more continuous use, for these amphipods are weak swimmers and ordinarily seem loath to leave their nests. They lie in their snug little sacs, often with the heads and upper parts of their bodies protruding. The water currents that pass through their seaweed home bring them small plant fragments and thus solve the problem of subsistence.

For most of the year Amphithoë lives singly, one to a nest. Early in the summer the males visit the females (who greatly outnumber them) and mating occurs within the nest. As the young develop the mother cares for them in a brood-pouch formed by the appendages of her abdomen. Often, while carrying her young, she emerges almost completely from her nest and vigorously fans currents of water through the pouch.

The eggs yield embryos, the embryos become larvae; but still the mother holds and cares for them until their small bodies have so developed that they are able to set forth into the seaweeds, to spin their own nests out of the fibers of plants and the silken threads mysteriously fashioned in their own bodies, and to feed and fend for themselves.

As her young become ready for independent life, the mother shows impatience to be rid of the swarm in her nest. Using claws and antennae, she pushes them to the rim and with shoves and nudges tries to expel them. The young cling with hooked and bristled claws to the walls and doorway of the familiar nursery. When finally thrust out they are likely to linger nearby; when the mother incautiously emerges, they leap to attach themselves to her body and so be drawn again into the security of their accustomed nest, until maternal impatience once more becomes strong.

Even the young just out of the brood-sac build their own nests and enlarge them as their growth requires. But the young seem to spend less time than the adults do inside their nests, and to creep about more freely over the weeds. It is common to see several tiny nests built close to the home of a large amphipod; perhaps the young like to stay close to the mother even after they have been ejected from her nest.

At low tide the water falls below the rockweeds and the mussels and enters a broad band clothed with the reddish-brown turf of the Irish moss. The time of its exposure to the atmosphere is so brief, the retreat of the sea so fleeting, that the moss retains a shining freshness, a wetness, and a sparkle that speak of its recent contact with the surf. Perhaps because we can visit this area only in that brief and magical hour of the tide's turning, perhaps because of the nearness of waves breaking on rocky rims, dissolving in foam and spray, and pouring seaward again to the accompaniment of many water sounds, we are reminded always that this low-tide area is of the sea and that we are trespassers.

Irish moss (right); sea lettuce (left)

Here, in this mossy turf, life exists in layers, one above another; life exists on other life, or within it, or under it, or above it. Because the moss is low-growing and branches profusely and intricately, it cushions the living things within it from the blows of the surf, and holds the wetness of the sea about them in these brief intervals of the low ebbing of the tide. After I have visited the shore and then at night have heard the surf trampling in over these moss-grown ledges with the heavy tread of the fall tides, I have wondered about the baby starfish, the urchins, the brittle stars, the tube-dwelling amphipods, the nudibranchs, and all the other small and delicate fauna of the moss; but I know that if there is security in their world it should be here, in this densest of intertidal jungles, over which the waves break harmlessly.

The moss forms so dense a covering that one cannot see what is beneath without intimate exploration. The abundance of life here, both in species and individuals, is on a scale that is hard to grasp. There is scarcely a stem of Irish moss that is not completely encased with one of the bryozoan sea mats—the white lacework of Membranipora or the glassy, brittle crust of Microporella. Such a crust consists of a mosaic of almost microscopic cells or compartments, arranged in regular rows and patterns, their surfaces finely sculptured. Each cell is the home of a minute, tentacled creature. By a conservative guess, several thousand such creatures live on a single stem of moss. On a square foot of rock surface there are probably several hundred such stems, providing living space for about a million of the bryozoans. On a stretch of Maine shore that the eye can take in at a glance, the population must run into the trillions for this single group of animals.

But there are further implications. If the population of the sea laces is so immense, that of the creatures they feed upon must be infinitely greater. A bryozoan colony acts as a highly efficient trap or filter to remove minute food animals from the sea water. One by one, the doors of the separate compartments open and from each a whorl of petal-like filaments is thrust out. In one moment the whole surface of the colony may be alive with crowns of tentacles swaying like flowers in a wind-swept field; the next instant, all may have snapped back into their protective cells and the colony is again a pavement of sculptured stone. But while the "flowers" sway over the stone field each spells death for many beings of the sea, as it draws in the minute spheres and ovals and crescents of the protozoans and the smallest algae, perhaps also some of the smallest of crustaceans and worms, or the larvae of mollusks and starfish, all of which are invisibly present in this mossy jungle, in numbers like the stars.

Larger animals are less numerous but still impressively abundant. Sea urchins, looking like large green cockleburs, often lie deep within the moss, their globular bodies anchored securely to the underlying rock by the adhesive discs of many tube feet. The ubiquitous common periwinkles, in some curious way unaffected by the conditions that confine most intertidal animals to certain zones, live above, within, and below the moss zone. Here their shells lie about over the surface of the weed at low tide; they hang heavily from its fronds, ready to drop at a touch.

And young starfish are here by the hundred, for these meadows of moss seem to be one of the chief nurseries for the starfish of northern shores. In the fall almost every other plant shelters quarter-inch and half-inch sizes. In these youthful starfish there are color patterns that become obliterated in maturity. The tube feet, the spines, and all the other curious epidermal outgrowths of these spiny-skinned creatures are large in proportion to the total size and have a clean perfection of form and structure.

On the rocky floor among the plant stems lie the infant stars. They are white insubstantial specks, in size and delicate beauty like snowflakes. There is an obvious newness about them, proclaiming that they have undergone their metamorphosis from the larval form to the adult shape only recently.

Perhaps it was on these very rocks that the swimming larvae, completing their period of life in the plankton, came to rest, attaching themselves firmly and becoming for a brief period sedentary animals. Then their bodies were like blown glass from which slender horns projected; the horns or lobes were covered with cilia for swimming and some of them bore suckers for use when the larvae should seek the firm underlying floor of the sea. During the short but critical period of attachment, the larval tissues were reorganized as completely as those of a pupal insect within a cocoon, the infant shape disappeared and in its place the five-rayed body of the adult was formed. Now as we find them, these new-made starfish use their tube feet competently, creeping over the rocks, righting their bodies if by mischance they are overturned, even, we may suppose, finding and devouring minute food animals in true starfish fashion.

The northern starfish lives in almost every low tide pool or waits out the tidal interval in wet moss or in the dripping coolness of a rock overhang. On a very low tide, when the departure of the sea is brief, these stars strew their variously hued forms over the moss like so many blossoms—pink, blue, purple, peach, or beige. Here and there is a gray or orange starfish on which the spines stand out conspicuously in a pattern of white dots. Its arms are rounder and firmer than those of the northern star and the round stony plate on its upper surface is usually a bright orange instead of pale yellow as in the northern species. This starfish is common south of Cape Cod and only a few individuals stray farther north. Still a third species inhabits these low-tide rocks—the blood-red starfish, Henricia, whose kind not only lives at these margins of the sea but goes down to lightless sea bottoms near the edge of the continental shelf. It is always an inhabitant of cool waters and south of Cape Cod must go offshore to find the temperatures it requires. But its dispersal is not, as one might suppose, by the larval stages, for unlike most other starfish it produces no swimming young; instead, the mother holds the eggs and the young that develop from them in a pouch

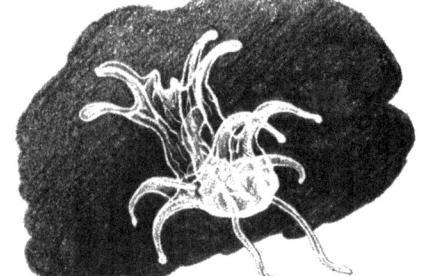

Swimming larva of starfish

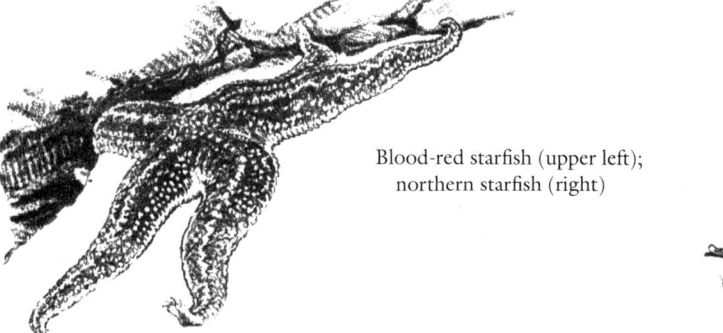

Blood-red starfish (upper left);
northern starfish (right)

formed by her arms as she assumes a humped position. Thus she broods them until they have become fully developed little starfish.

The Jonah crabs use the resilient cushion of moss as a hiding place to wait for the return of the tide or the coming of darkness. I remember a moss-carpeted ledge standing out from a rock wall, jutting out over sea depths where Laminaria rolled in the tide. The sea had only recently dropped below this ledge; its return was imminent and in fact was promised by every glassy swell that surged smoothly to its edge, then fell away. The moss was saturated, holding the water as faithfully as a sponge. Down within the deep pile of that carpet I caught a glimpse of a bright rosy color. At first I took it to be a growth of one of the encrusting corallines, but when I parted the fronds I was startled by abrupt movement as a large crab shifted its position and lapsed again into passive waiting. Only after search

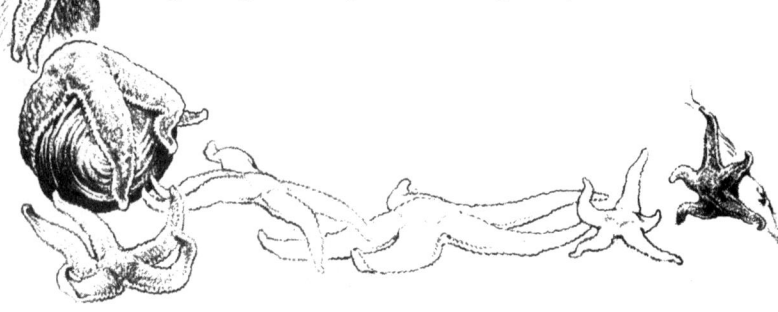

deep in the moss did I find several of the crabs, waiting out the brief interval of low tide and reasonably secure from detection by the gulls.

The seeming passivity of these northern crabs must be related to their need to escape the gulls—probably their most persistent enemies. By day one always has to search for the crabs. If not hidden deeply within the seaweeds, they may be wedged in the farthest recess afforded by an overhanging rock, secure there, in dim coolness, gently waving their antennae and waiting for the return of the sea. In darkness, however, the big crabs possess the shore. One night when the tide was ebbing I went down to the low-tide world to return a large starfish I had taken on the morning tide. The starfish was at home at the lowest level of these tides of the August moon, and to that level it must be returned. I took a flashlight and made my way down over the slippery rockweeds. It was an eerie world; ledges curtained with weed and boulders that by day were familiar landmarks seemed to loom larger than I remembered and to have assumed unfamiliar shapes, every projecting mass thrown into bold relief by the shadows. Everywhere I looked, directly in the beam of my flashlight or obliquely in the half-illuminated gloom, crabs were scuttling about. Boldly and possessively they inhabited the weed-shrouded rocks. All the grotesqueness of their form accentuated, they seemed to have transformed this once familiar place into a goblin world.

In some places, the moss is attached, not to the underlying rock, but to the next lower layer of life, a community of horse mussels. These large mollusks inhabit heavy, bulging shells, the smaller ends of which bristle with coarse yellow hairs that grow as excrescences from the epidermis. The horse mussels themselves are the basis of a whole community of animals that would find life on these wave-swept rocks impossible except for the presence and activities of the mollusks. The mussels have bound their shells to the underlying rock by an almost inextricable tangle of golden-hued byssus threads. These are the product of glands in the long slender foot, the threads being "spun" from a curious milky secretion that solidifies on contact with sea water. The threads possess a texture that is a remarkable combination of toughness, strength, softness, and elasticity; extending out in all directions they enable the mussels to hold their position not only against the thrust of incoming waves but also against the drag of the backwash, which in a heavy surf is tremendous.

Over the years that the mussels have been growing here, particles of muddy debris have settled under their shells and around the anchor lines of the byssus threads. This has created still another area for life, a sort of understory inhabited by a variety of animals including worms, crustaceans, echinoderms, and numerous mollusks, as well as the baby mussels of an oncoming generation—these as yet so small and transparent that the forms of their infant bodies show through newly formed shells.

Jonah crab (left); rock crab (right). Jonah crab has proportionally wider shell with deeper sculpturings.

Certain animals almost invariably live among the horse mussels. Brittle stars insinuate their thin bodies among the threads and under the shells of the mussels, gliding with serpentine motions of the long slender arms. The scale worms always live here, too, and down in the lower layers of this strange community of animals starfish may live below the scale worms and brittle stars, and sea urchins below the starfish, and sea cucumbers below the urchins.

Of the echinoderms that live here, few are the largest individuals of their species. The blanket of horse mussels seems to be a shelter for young, growing animals, and indeed the full-grown starfish and urchins could hardly be accommodated

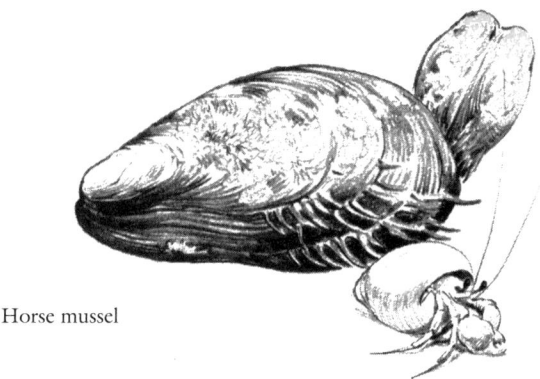

Horse mussel

there. In the waterless intervals of the low tide, the cucumbers draw themselves into little football-shaped ovals scarcely more than an inch long; returned to the water and fully relaxed, they extend their bodies to a length of five or six inches and unfurl a crown of tentacles. The cucumbers are detritus feeders, and explore the surrounding muddy debris with their soft tentacles, which periodically they pull back and draw across their mouths, as a child would lick his fingers.

In pockets deep in the moss under layers of mussels, a long, slender little fish of the blenny tribe, the rock eel, waits for the return of the tide, coiled in its water-filled refuge with several of its kind. Disturbed by an intruder, all thrash the water violently, squirming with eel-like undulations to escape.

Where the big mussels grow more sparsely, in the seaward suburbs of this mussel city, the moss carpet, too, becomes a little thinner; but still the underlying rock seldom is exposed. The green crumb-of-bread sponge, which at higher levels seeks the shelter of rock overhangs and tide pools, here seems able to face the direct force of the sea and forms soft, thick mats of pale green, dotted with the cones and craters typical of this species. And here and there patches of another color show amid the thinning moss—dull rose or a gleaming, reddish brown of satin finish—an intimation of what lies at lower levels.

During much of the year the spring tides drop down into the band of Irish moss but go no lower, returning then toward the land. But in certain months, depending on the changing

Crumb-of-bread sponge. Lower left, brittle star hunting food in sponge.

positions of sun and moon and earth, even the spring tides gain in amplitude, and their surge of water ebbs farther into the sea even as it rises higher against the land. Always, the autumn tides move strongly, and as the hunter's moon waxes and grows round, there come days and nights when the flood tides leap at the smooth rim of granite and send up their lace-edged wavelets to touch the roots of the bayberry; on their ebbs, with sun and moon combining to draw them back to the sea, they fall away from ledges not revealed since the April moon shone upon their dark shapes. Then they expose the sea's enameled floor—the rose of encrusting corallines, the green of sea urchins, the shining amber of the oarweeds.

At such a time of great tides I go down to that threshold of the sea world to which land creatures are admitted rarely in the cycle of the year. There I have known dark caves where tiny sea flowers bloom and masses of soft coral endure the transient withdrawal of the water. In these caves and in the wet gloom of deep crevices in the rocks I have found myself in the world of the sea anemones—creatures that spread a creamy-hued crown of tentacles above the shining brown columns of their bodies, like handsome chrysanthemums blooming in little pools held in depressions or on bottoms just below the tide line.

Where they are exposed by this extreme ebbing of the water, their appearance is so changed that they seem not meant for even this brief experience of land life. Wherever the contours of this uneven sea floor provide some shelter I have found their exposed colonies—dozens or scores of anemones crowded together, their translucent bodies touching, side against side. The anemones that cling to horizontal surfaces respond to the withdrawal of water by pulling all their tissues down into a flattened, conical mass of firm consistency. The crown of feather-soft tentacles is retracted and tucked within, with no suggestion of the beauty that resides in an expanded anemone. Those that grow on vertical rocks hang down limply, extended into curious, hourglass shapes, all their tissues flaccid in the unaccustomed withdrawal of water. They do not lack the ability to contract, for when they are touched they promptly begin to shorten the column, drawing it up into more normal proportions. These anemones, deserted by the sea, are bizarre objects rather than things of beauty, and indeed bear only the most remote resemblance to the anemones blooming under water just offshore, all their tentacles expanded in the search for food. As small water creatures come in contact with the tentacles of these expanded anemones, they receive a deadly discharge. Each of the thousand or more tentacles bears thousands of coiled darts embedded in its substance, each with a minute spine protruding. The spine may act as a trigger to set off the explosion, or perhaps the very nearness of prey acts as a sort of chemical trigger, causing the dart to explode with great violence, impaling or entangling its victim and injecting a poison.

Like the anemones, the soft coral hangs its thimble-sized colonies on the under side of ledges. Limp and dripping at low tide, they suggest nothing of the life and beauty to which the returning water restores them. Then from all the myriad pores of the surface of the colony, the tentacles of little tubular animals appear and the polyps thrust themselves out into the tide, seizing each for itself the minute shrimps and copepods and multiformed larvae brought by the water.

The soft coral, or sea finger, secretes no limy cups as the distantly related stony, or reef, corals do, but forms colonies in which many animals live embedded in a tough matrix strengthened with spicules of lime. Minute though the

Plumose anemones. Young anemone (lower right) produced from fragments of adult.

spicules are, they become geologically important where, in tropical reefs, the soft corals, or Alcyonaria, mingle with the true corals. With the death and dissolution of the soft tissues, the hard spicules become minute building stones, entering into the composition of the reef. Alcyonarians grow in lush profusion and variety on the coral reefs and flats of the Indian Ocean, for these soft corals are predominantly creatures of the tropics. A few, however, venture into polar waters. One very large species, tall as a tall man and branched like a tree, lives on the fishing banks off Nova Scotia and New England. Most of the group live in deep waters; for the most part the intertidal rocks are inhospitable to them and only an occasional low-lying ledge, rarely and briefly exposed on the low spring tides, bears their colonies on dark and hidden surfaces.

In seams and crevices of rock, in little water-filled pools, or on rock walls briefly exposed by the tide's low ebbing, colonies of the pink-hearted hydroid Tubularia form gardens of beauty. Where the water still covers them the flowerlike animals sway gracefully at the ends of long stalks, their tentacles reaching out to capture small animals of the plankton. Perhaps it is where they are permanently submerged, however, that they reach their fullest development. I have seen them coating wharf pilings, floats, and submerged ropes and cables so thickly that not a trace of the substratum could be seen, their growth giving the illusion of thousands of blossoms, each as large as the tip of my little finger.

Below the last clumps of Irish moss, a new kind of sea bottom is exposed. The transition is abrupt. As though a line had been drawn, suddenly there is no more moss, and one steps from the yielding brown cushion onto a surface that seemingly is of stone. Except that the color is wrong, the effect is almost that of a volcanic slope—there is the same barren nakedness. Yet this is not rock that we see. The underlying rock is coated on every surface, vertical or horizontal, exposed or hidden, with a crust of coralline algae, so that it wears a rich old-rose color. So intimate is the union that the plant seems part of the rock. Here the periwinkles wear little patches of pink on their shells, all the rock caverns and fissures are lined with the same color, and the rock bottom that slants away into green water carries down the rose hue as far as the eye can follow.

The coralline algae are plants of unusual fascination. They belong to the group of red seaweeds, most of which live in the deeper coastal waters, for the chemical nature of their pigments usually requires the protection of a screen of water between their tissues and the sun. The corallines, however, are extraordinary in their ability to withstand direct sunlight. They are able to incorporate carbonate of lime into their tissues so that they have become hardened. Most species form encrusting patches on rocks, shells, and other firm surfaces. The crust may be thin and smooth, suggesting a coat of enamel paint; or it may be thick and roughened by small nodules and protuberances. In the tropics the corallines often enter importantly

Stinging cell of a coelenterate

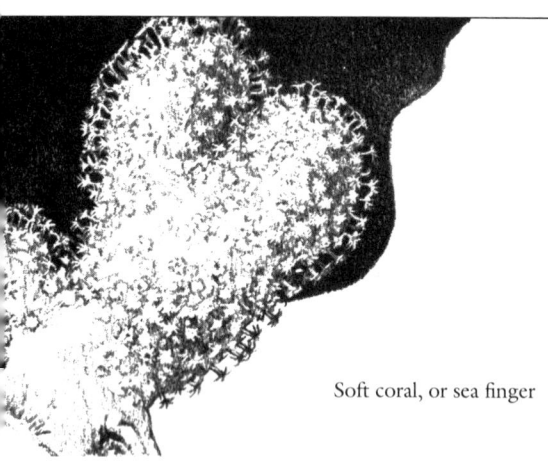

Soft coral, or sea finger

into the composition of the coral reefs, helping to cement the branching structures built by the coral animals into a solid reef. Here and there in the East Indies they cover the tidal flats as far as eye can see with their delicately hued crusts, and many of the "coral reefs" of the Indian Ocean contain no coral but are built largely of these plants. About the coasts of Spitsbergen, where under the dimly lit waters of the north the great forests of the brown algae grow, there are also vast calcareous banks, stretching mile after mile, formed by the coralline algae. Being able to live not only in tropical warmth but where water temperatures seldom rise above the freezing point, these plants flourish all the way from Arctic to Antarctic seas.

Where these same corallines paint a rose-colored band on the rocks of the Maine coast, as though to mark the low water line of the lowest spring tides, visible animal life is scarce. But although little else lives openly in this zone, thousands of sea urchins do. Instead of hiding in crevices or under rocks as they do at the higher levels, they live fully exposed on the flat or gently shelving rock faces. Groups of a score or half a hundred individuals lie together on the coralline-coated rocks, forming patches of pure green on the rose background. I have seen such herds of urchins lying on rocks that were being washed by a heavy surf, but apparently all the little anchors formed by their tube feet held securely. Though the waves broke heavily and poured back in a turbulent rush of waters, there the urchins remained undisturbed. Perhaps the strong tendency to hide and to wedge themselves into crevices and under boulders, as displayed by urchins in tide pools or up in the rockweed zone, is not so much an attempt to avoid the power of the surf as a means of escaping the eager eyes of the gulls, who hunt them relentlessly on every low tide. This coralline zone where the urchins live so openly is covered almost constantly with a protective layer of water; probably not more than a dozen daytime tides in the entire year fall to this level. At all other times, the depth of water over the urchins prevents the gulls from reaching them, for although a gull can make shallow plunges under water, it cannot dive as a tern does, and probably cannot reach a bottom deeper than the length of its own body.

The lives of many of these creatures of the low-tide rocks are bound together by interlacing ties, in the relation of predator to prey, or in the relation of species that compete for space or food. Over all these the sea itself exercises a directing and regulating force.

The urchins seek sanctuary from the gulls at this low level of the spring tides, but in themselves stand in the relation of dangerous predators to other animals. Where they advance into the Irish moss zone, hiding in deep crevices and sheltering

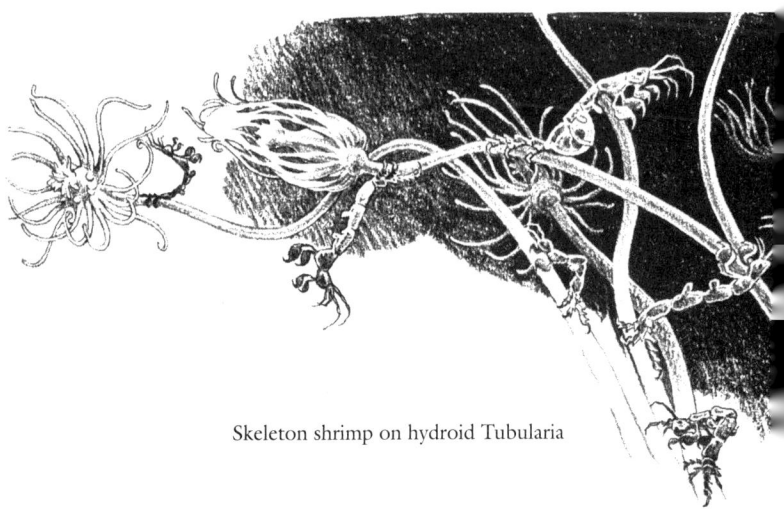

Skeleton shrimp on hydroid Tubularia

Green sea urchin on coralline algae

under rock overhangs, they devour numbers of periwinkles, and even attack barnacles and mussels. The number of urchins at any particular level of shore has a strong regulating effect on the populations of their prey. The starfish and a voracious snail, the common whelk, like the urchins, have their centers of population in deep water offshore and make predatory excursions of varying duration into the intertidal zone.

The position of the prey animals—the mussels, barnacles, and periwinkles—on sheltered shores has become difficult. They are hardy and adaptable, able to live at any level of the tide. Yet on such shores the rockweeds have crowded them out of the upper two-thirds of the shore, except for scattered individuals. At and just below the low-tide line are the hungry predators, so all that remains for these animals is the level near the low-water line of the neap tides. On protected coasts it is here that the barnacles and mussels assemble in their millions to spread their cover of white and blue over the rocks, and the legions of the common periwinkle gather.

But the sea, with its tempering and modifying effect, can alter the pattern. Whelks, starfish, and urchins are creatures of cold water. Where the offshore waters are cold and deep and the tidal flow is drawn from these icy reservoirs, the predators can range up into the intertidal zone, decimating the numbers of their prey. But when there is a layer of warm surface water the predators are confined to the cold deep levels. As they retreat seaward, the legions of their prey follow down in their wake, descending as far as they may into the world of the low spring tides.

Tide pools contain mysterious worlds within their depths, where all the beauty of the sea is subtly suggested and portrayed in miniature. Some of the pools occupy deep crevices or fissures; at their seaward ends these crevices disappear under water, but toward the land they run back slantingly into the cliffs and their walls rise higher, casting deep shadows over the water within them. Other pools are contained in rocky basins with a high rim on the seaward side to hold back the water when the last of the ebb drains away. Seaweeds line their walls. Sponges, hydroids, anemones, sea slugs, mussels, and starfish live in water that is calm for hours at a time, while just beyond the protecting rim the surf may be pounding.

The pools have many moods. At night they hold the stars and reflect the light of the Milky Way as it flows across the sky above them. Other, living stars come in from the sea: the shining emeralds of tiny phosphorescent diatoms—the glowing eyes of small fishes that swim at the surface of the dark water, their bodies slender as matchsticks, moving almost upright with little snouts uplifted—the elusive moonbeam flashes of comb jellies that have come in with a rising tide. Fishes and comb jellies hunt the black recesses of the rock basins, but like the tides they come and go, having no part in the permanent life of the pools.

By day there are other moods. Some of the most beautiful pools lie high on the shore. Their beauty is the beauty of simple elements—color and form and reflection. I know one that is only a few inches deep, yet it holds all the depth of the sky within it, capturing and confining the reflected blue of far distances. The pool is outlined by a band of bright green, a growth of one of the seaweeds called Enteromorpha. The fronds of the weed are shaped like simple tubes or straws. On the land side a wall of gray rock rises above the surface to the height of a man, and reflected, descends its own depth into the water. Beyond and below the reflected cliff are those far reaches of the sky. When the light and one's mood are right,

Comb jellies: sea gooseberry, Pleurobrachia (left);
sea walnut, Mnemiopsis, common south of Cape Cod (right)

one can look down into the blue so far that one would hesitate to set foot in so bottomless a pool. Clouds drift across it and wind ripples scud over its surface, but little else moves there, and the pool belongs to the rock and the plants and the sky.

In another high pool nearby, the green tube-weed rises from all of the floor. By some magic the pool transcends its realities of rock and water and plants, and out of these elements creates the illusion of another world. Looking into the pool, one sees no water but instead a pleasant landscape of hills and valleys with scattered forests. Yet the illusion is not so much that of an actual landscape as of a painting of one; like the strokes of a skillful artist's brush, the individual fronds of the algae do not literally portray trees, they merely suggest them. But the artistry of the pool, as of the painter, creates the image and the impression.

Little or no animal life is visible in any of these high pools —perhaps a few periwinkles and a scattering of little amber isopods. Conditions are difficult in all pools high on the shore because of the prolonged absence of the sea. The temperature of the water may rise many degrees, reflecting the heat of the day. The water freshens under heavy rains or becomes more salty under a hot sun. It varies between acid and alkaline in a short time through the chemical activity of the plants. Lower on the shore the pools provide far more stable conditions, and both plants and animals are able to live at higher levels than they could on open rock. The tide pools, then, have the effect of moving the life zones a little higher on the shore. Yet they, too, are affected by the duration of the sea's absence, and the inhabitants of a high pool are very different from those of a low-level pool that is separated from the sea only at long intervals and then briefly.

The highest of the pools scarcely belong to the sea at all; they hold the rains and receive only an occasional influx of sea water from storm surf or very high tides. But the gulls fly up from their hunting at the sea's edge, bringing a sea urchin or a crab or a mussel to drop on the rocks, in this way shattering the hard shelly covering and exposing the soft parts within. Bits of urchin tests or crab claws or mussel shells find their way into the pools, and as they disintegrate their limy substance enters into the chemistry of the water, which then becomes alkaline. A little one-celled plant called Sphaerella finds this a favorable climate for growth—a minute, globular bit of life almost invisible as an individual, but in its millions turning the waters of these high pools red as blood. Apparently the alkalinity is a necessary condition; other pools, outwardly similar except for the chance circumstance that they contain no shells, have none of the tiny crimson balls.

Even the smallest pools, filling depressions no larger than a teacup, have some life. Often it is a thin patch of scores of the little seashore insect, *Anurida maritima*—"the wingless one who goes to sea." These small insects run on the surface film when the water is undisturbed, crossing easily from one shore of a pool to another. Even the slightest rippling causes them to drift helplessly, however, so that scores or hundreds of them come together by chance, becoming conspicuous only as they form thin, leaflike patches on the water. A single Anurida is small as a gnat. Under a lens, it seems to be clothed in blue-gray velvet through which many bristles or hairs protrude. The bristles hold a film of air about the body of the insect when it enters the water, and so it need not return to the upper shore when the tide rises. Wrapped in its glistening air blanket, dry and provided with air for breathing, it waits in cracks and crevices until the tide ebbs again. Then it emerges to roam over the rocks, searching for the bodies of fish and crabs and the dead mollusks and barnacles that provide its food, for it is one of the

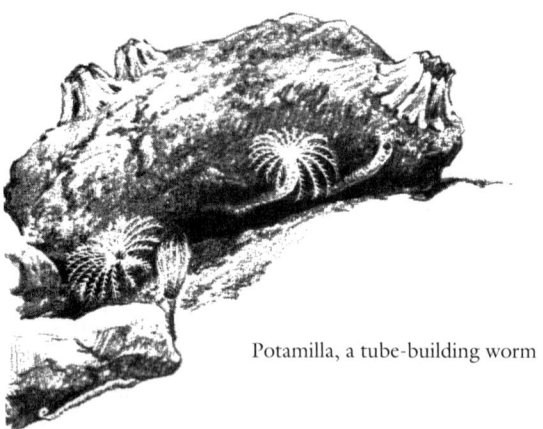
Potamilla, a tube-building worm

scavengers that play a part in the economy of the sea, keeping the organic materials in circulation.

And often I find the pools of the upper third of the shore lined with a brown velvety coating. My fingers, exploring, are able to peel it off the rocks in thin smooth-surfaced sheets like parchment. It is one of the brown seaweeds called Ralfsia; it appears on the rocks in small, lichen-like growths or, as here, spreading its thin crust over extensive areas. Wherever it grows its presence changes the nature of a pool, for it provides the shelter that many small creatures seek so urgently. Those small enough to creep in under it—to inhabit the dark pockets of space between the encrusting weed and the rock—have found security against being washed away by the surf. Looking at these pools with their velvet lining, one would say there is little life here—only a sprinkling of periwinkles browsing, their shells rocking gently as they scrape at the surface of the brown crust, or perhaps a few barnacles with their cones protruding through the sheet of plant tissue, opening their doors to sweep the water for food. But whenever I have brought a sample of this brown seaweed to my microscope, I have found it teeming with life. Always there have been many cylindrical tubes, needle-fine, built of a muddy substance. The architect of each is a small worm whose body is formed of a series of eleven infinitely small rings or segments, like eleven counters in a game of checkers, piled one above another. From its head arises a

structure that makes this otherwise drab worm beautiful—
a fanlike crown or plume composed of the finest feathery filaments. The filaments absorb oxygen and also serve to ensnare small food organisms when thrust out of the tube. And always, among this microfauna of the Ralfsia crust, there have been little fork-tailed crustaceans with glittering eyes the color of rubies. Other crustaceans called ostracods are enclosed in flattened, peach-colored shells fashioned of two parts, like a box with its lid; from the shell long appendages may be thrust out to row the creatures through the water. But most numerous of all are the minute worms hurrying across the crust—segmented bristle worms of many species and smooth-bodied, serpent-like ribbon worms or nemerteans, their appearance and rapid movements betraying their predatory errands.

A pool need not be large to hold beauty within pellucid depths. I remember one that occupied the shallowest of depressions; as I lay outstretched on the rocks beside it I could easily touch its far shore. This miniature pool was about midway between the tide lines, and for all I could see it was inhabited by only two kinds of life. Its floor was paved with mussels. Their shells were a soft color, the misty blue of distant mountain ranges, and their presence lent an illusion of depth. The water in which they lived was so clear as to be invisible to my eyes; I could detect the interface between air and water only by the sense of coldness on my fingertips. The crystal water was filled with sunshine—an infusion and distillation of light that reached down and surrounded each of these small but resplendent shellfish with its glowing radiance.

The mussels provided a place of attachment for the only other visible life of the pool. Fine as the finest threads, the basal stems of colonies of hydroids traced their almost invisible lines across the mussel shells. The hydroids belonged to the group called Sertularia, in which each individual of the colony and all the supporting and connecting branches are enclosed within transparent sheaths, like a tree in winter wearing a sheath of ice. From the basal stems erect branches arose, each branch the bearer of a double row of crystal cups within which the tiny beings of the colony dwelt. The whole was the very embodiment of beauty and fragility, and as I lay beside the pool and my lens brought the hydroids into clearer view they seemed to me to look like nothing so much as the finest cut glass—perhaps the individual segments of an intricately wrought chandelier. Each animal in its protective cup was something like a very small sea anemone—a little tubular being surmounted by a crown of tentacles. The central cavity of each communicated with a cavity that ran the length of the branch that bore it, and this in turn with the cavities of larger branches and with those of the main stem, so that the feeding activities of each animal contributed to the nourishment of the whole colony.

On what, I wondered, were these Sertularians feeding? From their very abundance I knew that whatever creatures served them as food must be infinitely more numerous than the carnivorous hydroids themselves. Yet I could see nothing. Obviously their food would be minute, for each of the feeders was of threadlike diameter and its tentacles were like the finest gossamer. Somewhere in the crystal clarity of the pool my eye —or so it seemed—could detect a fine mist of infinitely small particles, like dust motes in a ray of sunshine. Then as I looked more closely the motes had disappeared and there seemed to be once more only that perfect clarity, and the sense that there had been an optical illusion. Yet I knew it was only the human

Sertularian hydroid. The smaller cups contain feeding individuals; the larger ones the medusoid generation.

imperfection of my vision that prevented me from seeing those microscopic hordes that were the prey of the groping, searching tentacles I could barely see. Even more than the visible life, that which was unseen came to dominate my thoughts, and finally the invisible throng seemed to me the most powerful beings in the pool. Both the hydroids and the mussels were utterly dependent on this invisible flotsam of the tide streams, the mussels as passive strainers of the plant plankton, the hydroids as active predators seizing and ensnaring the minute water fleas and copepods and worms. But should the plankton become less abundant, should the incoming tide streams somehow become drained of this life, then the pool would become a pool of death, both for the mussels in their shells blue as mountains and for the crystal colonies of the hydroids.

Some of the most beautiful pools of the shore are not exposed to the view of the casual passer-by. They must be searched for —perhaps in low-lying basins hidden by great rocks that seem to be heaped in disorder and confusion, perhaps in darkened recesses under a projecting ledge, perhaps behind a thick curtain of concealing weeds.

I know such a hidden pool. It lies in a sea cave, at low tide filling perhaps the lower third of its chamber. As the flooding tide returns the pool grows, swelling in volume until all the cave is water-filled and the cave and the rocks that form and contain it are drowned beneath the fullness of the tide. When the tide is low, however, the cave may be approached from the landward side. Massive rocks form its floor and walls and roof. They are penetrated by only a few openings—two near the floor on the sea side and one high on the landward wall. Here one may lie on the rocky threshold and peer through the low entrance into the cave and down into its pool. The cave is not really dark; indeed on a bright day it glows with a cool green light. The source of this soft radiance is the sunlight that enters through the openings low on the floor of the pool, but only after its entrance into the pool does the light itself become transformed, invested with a living color of purest, palest green that is borrowed from the covering of sponge on the floor of the cave.

Through the same openings that admit the light, fish come in from the sea, explore the green hall, and depart again into the vaster waters beyond. Through those low portals the tides ebb and flow. Invisibly, they bring in minerals—the raw materials for the living chemistry of the plants and animals of the cave. They bring, invisibly again, the larvae of many sea creatures—drifting, drifting in their search for a resting place. Some may remain and settle here; others will go out on the next tide.

Looking down into the small world confined within the walls of the cave, one feels the rhythms of the greater sea world beyond. The waters of the pool are never still. Their level changes not only gradually with the rise and fall of the tide, but also abruptly with the pulse of the surf. As the backwash of a wave draws it seaward, the water falls away rapidly; then with a sudden reversal the inrushing water foams and surges upward almost to one's face.

On the outward movement one can look down and see the floor, its details revealed more clearly in the shallowing water. The green crumb-of-bread sponge covers much of the bottom of the pool, forming a thick-piled carpet built of tough little feltlike fibers laced together with glassy, double-pointed needles of silica—the spicules or skeletal supports of the sponge. The green color of the carpet is the pure color of chlorophyll, this plant pigment being confined within the cells of an alga that are scattered through the tissues of the animal host. The sponge clings closely to the rock, by the very smoothness and flatness of its growth testifying to the streamlining force of heavy surf. In quiet waters the same species sends up many projecting cones; here these would give the turbulent waters a surface to grip and tear.

Interrupting the green carpet are patches of other colors, one a deep, mustard yellow, probably a growth of the sulphur sponge. In the fleeting moment when most of the water has drained away, one has glimpses of a rich orchid color in the deepest part of the cave—the color of the encrusting coralline algae.

Sponges and corallines together form a background for the larger tide-pool animals. In the quiet of ebb tide there is little or no visible movement even among the predatory starfish that cling to the walls like ornamental fixtures painted orange or rose or purple. A group of large anemones lives on the wall

Sulphur or boring sponge on clam shell. Sponge larvae bore into shells and spread until shell is honeycombed.

of the cave, their apricot color vivid against the green sponge. Today all the anemones may be attached on the north wall of the pool, seemingly immobile and immovable; on the next spring tides when I visit the pool again some of them may have shifted over to the west wall and there taken up their station, again seemingly immovable.

There is abundant promise that the anemone colony is a thriving one and will be maintained. On the walls and ceiling of the cave are scores of baby anemones—little glistening mounds of soft tissue, a pale, translucent brown. But the real nursery of the colony seems to be in a sort of antechamber opening into the central cave. There a roughly cylindrical space no more than a foot across is enclosed by high perpendicular rock walls to which hundreds of baby anemones cling.

On the roof of the cave is written a starkly simple statement of the force of the surf. Waves entering a confined space always concentrate all their tremendous force for a driving, upward leap; in this manner the roofs of caves are gradually battered away. The open portal in which I lie saves the ceiling of this cave from receiving the full force of such upward-leaping waves; nevertheless, the creatures that live there are exclusively a heavy-surf fauna. It is a simple black and white mosaic—the black of mussel shells, on which the white cones of barnacles are growing. For some reason the barnacles, skilled colonizers of surf-swept rocks though they be, seem to have been unable to get a foothold directly on the roof of the cave. Yet the mussels have done so. I do not know how this happened but I can guess. I can imagine the young mussels creeping in over the damp rock while the tide is out, spinning their silk threads that bind them securely, anchoring them against the returning waters. And then in time, perhaps, the growing colony of mussels gave the infant barnacles a foothold more tenable than the smooth rock, so that they were able to cement themselves to the mussel shells. However it came about, that is the way we find them now.

As I lie and look into the pool there are moments of relative quiet, in the intervals when one wave has receded and the next has not yet entered. Then I can hear the small sounds: the sound of water dripping from the mussels on the ceiling or of water dripping from seaweeds that line the walls—small, silver splashes losing themselves in the vastness of the pool and in the

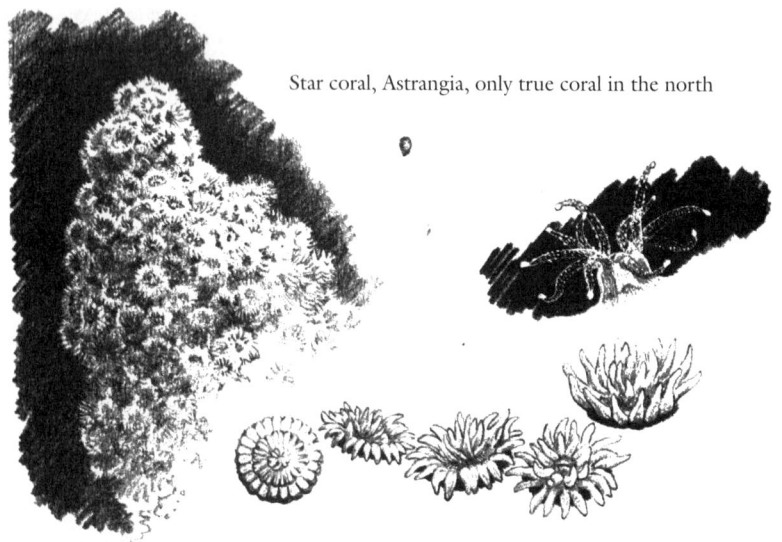

Star coral, Astrangia, only true coral in the north

confused, murmurous whisperings that emanate from the pool itself—the pool that is never quite still.

Then as my fingers explore among the dark red thongs of the dulse and push away the fronds of the Irish moss that cover the walls beneath me, I begin to find creatures of such extreme delicacy that I wonder how they can exist in this cave when the brute force of storm surf is unleashed within its confined space.

Adhering to the rock walls are thin crusts of one of the bryozoans, a form in which hundreds of minute, flask-shaped cells of a brittle structure, fragile as glass, lie one against another in regular rows to form a continuous crust. The color is a pale apricot; the whole seems an ephemeral creation that would crumble away at a touch, as hoarfrost before the sun.

A tiny spiderlike creature with long and slender legs runs about over the crust. For some reason that may have to do with its food, it is the same apricot color as the bryozoan carpet beneath it; the sea spider, too, seems the embodiment of fragility.

Another bryozoan of coarser, upright growth, Flustrella, sends up little club-shaped projections from a basal mat. Again, the lime-impregnated clubs seem brittle and glassy. Over and among them, innumerable little roundworms crawl with serpentine motion, slender as threads. Baby mussels creep in their tentative exploration of a world so new to them they have not yet found a place to anchor themselves by slender silken lines.

Exploring with my lens, I find many very small snails in the fronds of seaweed. One of them has obviously not been long in the world, for its pure white shell has formed only the first turn of the spiral that will turn many times upon itself in growth from infancy to maturity. Another, no larger, is nevertheless older. Its shining amber shell is coiled like a French horn and, as I watch, the tiny creature within thrusts out a bovine head and seems to be regarding its surroundings with two black eyes, small as the smallest pinpoints.

But seemingly most fragile of all are the little calcareous sponges that here and there exist among the seaweeds. They form masses of minute, upthrust tubes of vase-like form, none more than half an inch high. The wall of each is a mesh of fine threads—a web of starched lace made to fairy scale.

I could have crushed any of these fragile structures between my fingers—yet somehow they find it possible to exist here, amid the surging thunder of the surf that must fill this cave as the sea comes in. Perhaps the seaweeds are the key to the mystery, their resilient fronds a sufficient cushion for all the minute and delicate beings they contain.

But it is the sponges that give to the cave and its pool their special quality—the sense of a continuing flow of time. For each day that I visit the pool on the lowest tides of the summer they seem unchanged—the same in July, the same in August, the same in September. And they are the same this year as last, and presumably as they will be a hundred or a thousand summers hence.

Simple in structure, little different from the first sponges that spread their mats on ancient rocks and drew their food from a primordial sea, the sponges bridge the eons of time. The green sponge that carpets the floor of this cave grew in other pools before this shore was formed; it was old when the first creatures came out of the sea in those ancient eras of the Paleozoic,

Red-beard sponge, crimson spots of color on the walls of tide pools

300 million years ago; it existed even in the dim past before the first fossil record, for the hard little spicules—all that remains when the living tissue is gone—are found in the first fossil-bearing rocks, those of the Cambrian period.

So, in the hidden chamber of that pool, time echoes down the long ages to a present that is but a moment.

As I watched, a fish swam in, a shadow in the green light, entering the pool by one of the openings low on its seaward wall. Compared with the ancient sponges, the fish was almost a symbol of modernity, its fishlike ancestry traceable only half as far into the past. And I, in whose eyes the images of the two were beheld as though they were contemporaries, was a mere newcomer whose ancestors had inhabited the earth so briefly that my presence was almost anachronistic.

As I lay at the threshold of the cave thinking those thoughts, the surge of waters rose and flooded across the rock on which I rested. The tide was rising.

The Rim of Sand

On the sands of the sea's edge, especially where they are broad and bordered by unbroken lines of wind-built dunes, there is a sense of antiquity that is missing from the young rock coast of New England. It is in part a sense of the unhurried deliberation of earth processes that move with infinite leisure, with all eternity at their disposal. For unlike that sudden coming in of the sea to flood the valleys and surge against the mountain crests of the drowned lands of New England, the sea and the land lie here in a relation established gradually, over millions of years.

During those long ages of geologic time, the sea has ebbed and flowed over the great Atlantic coastal plain. It has crept toward the distant Appalachians, paused for a time, then slowly receded, sometimes far into its basin; and on each such advance it has rained down its sediments and left the fossils of its creatures over that vast and level plain. And so the particular place of its stand today is of little moment in the history of the earth or in the nature of the beach—a hundred feet higher, or a hundred feet lower, the seas would still rise and fall unhurried over shining flats of sand, as they do today.

And the materials of the beach are themselves steeped in antiquity. Sand is a substance that is beautiful, mysterious, and infinitely variable; each grain on a beach is the result of processes that go back into the shadowy beginnings of life, or of the earth itself.

The bulk of seashore sand is derived from the weathering and decay of rocks, transported from their place of origin to the sea by the rains and the rivers. In the unhurried processes of erosion, in the freighting seaward, in the interruptions and resumptions of that journey, the minerals have suffered various fates—some have been dropped, some have worn out and vanished. In the mountains the slow decay and disintegration of the rocks proceed, and the stream of sediments grows—suddenly and dramatically by rockslides—slowly, inexorably, by the wearing of rock by water. All begin their passage toward the sea. Some disappear through the solvent action of water or by grinding attrition in the rapids of a river's bed. Some are dropped on the riverbank by flood waters, there to lie for a hundred, a thousand years, to become locked in the sediments of the plain and wait another million years or so, during which, perhaps, the sea comes in and then returns to its basin. Then at last they are released by the persistent work of erosion's tools—wind, rain, and frost—to resume the journey to the sea. Once brought to salt water, a fresh rearranging, sorting, and transport begin. Light minerals, like flakes of mica, are carried away almost at once; heavy ones like the black sands of ilmenite and rutile are picked up by the violence of storm waves and thrown on the upper beach.

No individual sand grain remains long in any one place. The smaller it is, the more it is subject to long transport—the larger grains by water, the smaller by wind. An average grain of sand is only two and one half times the weight of an equal volume of water, but more than two thousand times as heavy as air, so only the smaller grains are available for transport by wind. But despite the constant working over of the sands by wind and water, a beach shows little visible change from day to day, for as one grain is carried away, another is usually brought to take its place.

The greater part of most beach sand consists of quartz, the most abundant of all minerals, found in almost every type of rock. But many other minerals occur among its crystal grains, and one small sample of sand might contain fragments of a dozen or more. Through the sorting action of wind, water, and gravity, fragments of darker, heavier minerals may form patches overlying the pale quartz. So there may be a curious purple shading over the sand, shifting with the wind, piling up in little ridges of deeper color like the ripple marks of waves—a concentration of almost pure garnet. Or there may be patches of dark green—sands formed of glauconite, a product of the sea's chemistry and the interaction of the living and the nonliving. Glauconite is a form of iron silicate that contains potassium; it has occurred in the deposits of all geologic ages. According to one theory, it is forming now in warm shallow areas of the sea's floor, where the shells of minute creatures called foraminifera are accumulating and disintegrating on muddy sea bottoms. On many Hawaiian beaches, the somber darkness of the earth's interior is reflected in sand grains of olivine derived from black basaltic lavas. And drifts of the "black sands" of rutile and ilmenite and other heavy minerals darken the beaches of Georgia's St. Simons and Sapelo Islands, clearly separated from the lighter quartz.

In some parts of the world the sands represent the remains of plants that in life had lime-hardened tissues, or fragments of the calcareous shells of sea creatures. Here and there on the coast of Scotland, for example, are beaches composed of glistening white "nullipore sands"—the shattered and sea-ground remains of coralline algae growing on the bottom offshore. On the coast of Galway in Ireland the dunes are built of sands composed of tiny perforated globes of calcium carbonate—the shells of foraminifera that once floated in the sea. The animals were mortal but the shells they built have endured. They drifted to the floor of the sea and became compacted into sediment. Later the sediments were uplifted to form cliffs, which were eroded and returned once more to the sea. The shells of foraminifera appear also in the sands of southern Florida and the Keys, along with coral debris and the shells of mollusks, shattered, ground, and polished by the waves.

From Eastport to Key West, the sands of the American Atlantic coast, by their changing nature, reveal a varied origin. Toward the northern part of the coast mineral sands predominate, for the waves are still sorting and rearranging and carrying from place to place the fragments of rock that the glaciers brought down from the north, thousands of years ago. Every grain of sand on a New England beach has a long and eventful history. Before it was sand, it was

Common cockle

rock—splintered by the chisels of the frost, crushed under advancing glaciers and carried forward with the ice in its slow advance, then ground and polished in the mill of the surf. And long ages before the advance of the ice, some of the rock had come up into the light of the sun from the black interior of the earth by ways unseen and for the most part unknown, made fluid by subterranean fires and rising along deep pipes and fissures. Now in this particular moment of its history, it belongs to the sea's edge—swept up and down the beaches with the tides or drifted alongshore with the currents, continuously sifted and sorted, packed down, washed out, or set adrift again, as always and endlessly the waves work over the sands.

On Long Island, where much glacial material has accumulated, the sands contain quantities of pink and red garnet and black tourmaline, along with many grains of magnetite. In New Jersey, where the coastal plain deposits of the south first appear, there is less magnetic material and less garnet. Smoky quartz predominates at Barnegat, glauconite at Monmouth Beach, and heavy minerals at Cape May. Here and there beryl occurs where molten magma has brought up deeply buried material of the ancient earth to crystallize near the surface.

North of Virginia, less than half of one per cent of the sands are of calcium carbonate; southward, about 5 per cent. In North Carolina the abundance of calcareous or shell sand suddenly increases, although quartz sand still forms the bulk of the beach materials. Between Capes Hatteras and Lookout as much as 10 per cent of the beach sand is calcareous. And in North Carolina also there are odd local accumulations of special materials such as silicified wood—the same substance that is contained in the famous "singing sands" of the Island of Eigg in the Hebrides.

The mineral sands of Florida are not of local origin but have been derived from the weathering of rocks in the Piedmont and Appalachian highlands of Georgia and South Carolina. The fragments are carried to the sea on southward-moving streams and rivers. Beaches of the northern part of Florida's Gulf Coast are almost pure quartz, composed of crystal grains that have descended from the mountains to sea level, accumulating there in plains of snowlike whiteness. About Venice there is a special sparkle and glitter over the sands, where crystals of the mineral zircon are dusted over its surface like diamonds; and here and there is a sprinkling of the blue, glasslike grains of cyanite. On the east coast of Florida, quartz sands predominate for much of the long coast line (it is the hard-packing quartz grains that compose the famous beaches of Daytona) but toward the south, the crystal sands are mingled more and more with fragments of shells. Near Miami the beach sands are less than half quartz; about Cape Sable and in the Keys the sand is almost entirely derived from coral and shell and the remains of foraminifera. And all along the east coast of Florida, the beaches receive small contributions of volcanic matter, as bits of floating pumice that have drifted for thousands of miles in ocean currents are stranded on the shore to become sand.

Infinitely small though it is, something of its history may be revealed in the shape and texture of a grain of sand. Wind-transported sands tend to be better rounded than water-borne; furthermore, their surface shows a frosted effect from the abrasion of other grains carried in the blast of air. The same effect is seen on panes of glass near the sea, or on old bottles in the beach flotsam. Ancient sand grains, by their surface etchings, may give a clue to the climate of past ages. In European deposits of Pleistocene sand, the grains have frosted surfaces etched by the great winds blowing off the glaciers of the Ice Age.

We think of rock as a symbol of durability, yet even the hardest rock shatters and wears away when attacked by rain, frost or surf. But a grain of sand is almost indestructible. It is the ultimate product of the work of the waves—the minute, hard core of mineral that remains after years of grinding and polishing.

Apple murex

The tiny grains of wet sand lie with little space between them, each holding a film of water about itself by capillary attraction. Because of this cushioning liquid film, there is little further wearing by attrition. Even the blows of heavy surf cannot cause one sand grain to rub against another.

In the intertidal zone, this minuscule world of the sand grains is also the world of inconceivably minute beings, which swim through the liquid film around a grain of sand as fish would swim through the ocean covering the sphere of the earth. Among this fauna and flora of the capillary water are single-celled animals and plants, water mites, shrimplike crustacea, insects, and the larvae of certain infinitely small worms—all living, dying, swimming, feeding, breathing, reproducing in a world so small that our human senses cannot grasp its scale, a world in which the micro-droplet of water separating one grain of sand from another is like a vast, dark sea.

Not all sands are inhabited by this "interstitial fauna." Those derived from the weathering of crystalline rocks are most abundantly populated. Shell or coral sand seldom if ever contains copepods and other microscopic life; perhaps this indicates that the grains of calcium carbonate create unfavorably alkaline conditions in the water around them.

On any beach the sum of all the little pools amid the sand grains represents the amount of water available to the animals of the sands during the low-tide interval. Sand of average fineness is able to contain almost its own volume of water, and so at low tide only the topmost layers dry out under a warm sun. Below it is damp and cool, for the contained water keeps the temperatures of the deeper sand practically constant. Even the salinity is fairly stable; only the most superficial layers are affected by rain falling on the beach or by streams of fresh water coursing across it.

Bearing on its surface only the wave-carved ripple marks, the fine traceries of sand grains dropped at last by the spent waves, and the scattered shells of long-dead mollusks, the beach has a lifeless look, as though not only uninhabited but indeed uninhabitable. In the sands almost all is hidden. The only clues to the inhabitants of most beaches are found in winding tracks, in slight movements disturbing the upper layers, or in barely protruding tubes and all but concealed openings leading down to hidden burrows.

The signs of living creatures are often visible, if not the animals themselves, in deep gullies that cut the beaches, parallel to the shore line, and hold at least a few inches of water from the fall of one tide until the return of the next. A little moving hill of sand may yield a moon snail intent on predatory errand. A V-shaped track may indicate the presence of a burrowing clam, a sea mouse, a heart urchin. A flat ribbonlike track may lead to a buried sand dollar or a starfish. And wherever protected flats of sand or sandy mud lie exposed between the tides, they are apt to be riddled with hundreds of holes, marked by the sign of the ghost shrimps within. Other flats may bristle with forests of protruding tubes, pencil thin and decorated weirdly with bits of shell or seaweed, an indication that legions of the plumed worm, Diopatra, live below. Or again there may be a wide area marked by the black conical mounds of the lugworm. Or here at the edge of the tide a chain of little parchment capsules, one end free and the other disappearing under the sand, shows that one of the large predatory whelks lies below, busy with the prolonged task of laying and protecting her eggs.

But almost always the essence of the lives—the finding of food, the hiding from enemies, the capturing of prey, the producing of young, all that makes up the living and dying and perpetuating of this sand-beach fauna—is concealed from the eyes of those who merely glance at the surface of the sands and declare them barren.

I remember a chill December morning on one of Florida's Ten Thousand Islands, with the sands wet from a recently fallen tide and the fresh, clean wind blowing handfuls of spindrift along the beach. For several hundred yards, where the shore ran in a long curve from the Gulf toward the shelter of the bay, there were peculiar markings on the dark wet sand just above the water's edge. The marks were arranged in groups, in each of which a series of thin spidery lines radiated out from a central spot, as though unsteadily traced there by a slender stick. At first no sign of any living animal was to be seen—nothing to tell what creature had made these seemingly careless scribblings. After kneeling on the wet sand and looking at one after another of these strange insignia, I found that under each of the central spots lay the flat pentagonal disc of a serpent starfish. The marks on the sand were made by its long and slender arms, inscribing the record of its forward progress.

And then I remember wading on a June day over Bird Shoal, which lies off the town of Beaufort in North Carolina, where at low tide acres of sand bottom are covered only by a few inches of water. Near the shore I found two sharply defined grooves in the sand; my index finger could have measured their span. Between the grooves was a faint, irregular line. Step by step, I was led out across the flat by the tracks; finally, at the temporary end of the trail, I came upon a young horseshoe crab, heading seaward.

For most of the fauna of the sand beaches, the key to survival is to burrow into the wet sand, and to possess means of feeding, breathing and reproducing while lying below reach of the surf. And so the story of the sand is in part the story of small lives lived deep within it, finding in its dark, damp coolness a retreat from fish that come hunting with the tide and from birds that forage at the water's edge when the tide has fallen. Once below the surface layers, the burrower has found not only stable conditions but also a refuge where few enemies threaten. Those few are likely to reach down from above—perhaps a bird thrusting a long bill into the hole of a fiddler crab—a sting ray flapping along the bottom, plowing up the sand for buried mollusks—an octopus sliding an exploring tentacle down into a hole. Only an occasional enemy comes through the sand. The

Sea mouse

Horseshoe crabs

moon snail is a predator that makes a successful living in this difficult way. It is a blind creature with no use for eyes because it is forever groping through dark sands, hunting mollusks that live as much as a foot below the surface. Its smoothly rounded shell eases its descent into the sand as it digs with the immense foot. On locating prey, it holds the animal with the foot and drills a round hole in the shell. The moon snails are voracious; young animals eat more than a third of their weight in clams each week. Some worms also are predatory burrowers; so are a few starfish. But for most predators, continuous burrowing consumes more energy than would be supplied by the prey thus found. Most of the burrowers in sand are passive feeders, digging only enough to establish a temporary or permanent home in which to lie while straining food from the water or sucking up detritus that accumulates on the sea bottom.

The rising tide sets in action a system of living filters through which prodigious quantities of water are strained. Buried mollusks push up their siphons through the sand to draw the incoming water through their bodies. Worms lying in U-shaped parchment tubes begin to pump, drawing the water in through one end of the tube, expelling it through the other. The incoming stream brings food and oxygen; the outgoing has been depleted of much of the food and bears away the organic wastes of the worm. Small crabs spread the feathery nets of their antennae like cast-nets to bring in food.

With the tide, predators come from offshore. A blue crab dashes out of the surf to seize a fat mole crab that is in the act of spreading its antennae to filter the backwash of a receding wave. Clouds of salt-water minnows move in with the tide, searching for the small amphipods of the upper beach. Launce, or sand eels, dart through the shallow water seeking copepods or fish fry; sometimes the launce are pursued by the shadowy forms of larger fish.

As the tide falls much of this extraordinary activity slackens. There is less eating and being eaten. In the wet sands, however, some animals can continue to eat even after the tide has receded. Lugworms can continue their work of passing sand through their bodies for the sake of the scraps of nutriment they contain. Heart urchins and sand dollars, lying in saturated sand, continue to sort out bits of food. But over most of the sands there is a lull of repletion—of waiting for the turn of the tide.

Although there are many places where, on quieter shores and protected shoals, such richness of life may be found, certain ones live most clearly in my memories. On one of the sea islands of Georgia is a great beach that is visited only by the most gentle surf, although it looks straight across to Africa. Storms usually pass it by, for it lies well inside the long, incurving arc of coast that swings between the Capes of Fear and Canaveral, and the prevailing winds are such that no heavy swells roll in upon it. The texture of the beach itself is unusually firm because of a mixture of mud and clay with the sand; permanent holes and burrows can be dug in it, and the streaming tidal currents carve little ripple marks that remain after the tide goes out, looking like a miniature model of the sea's waves. These sand ripples hold small food particles dropped by the currents, providing a store to be drawn on by detritus feeders.

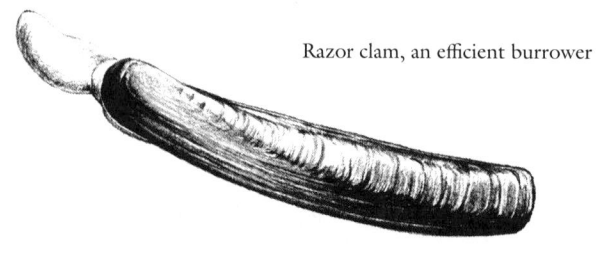

Razor clam, an efficient burrower

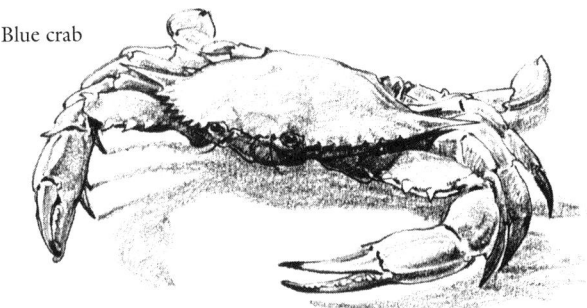
Blue crab

The slope of the beach is so gentle that, when the tide falls to its lowest ebb, a quarter of a mile of sand is exposed between the high-tide line and the low. But this broad sand flat is not a perfectly even plain, for winding gullies wander across it, like creeks across the land, holding a remnant of water from the last high tide and providing a living place for animals that cannot endure even a temporary withdrawal of the water.

It was in this place that I once found a large "bed" of sea pansies at the very edge of the tide. The day was heavily overcast, a fact that accounted for their being exposed. On sunny days I never saw them there, although undoubtedly they were just under the sand, protecting themselves from the drying rays of the sun.

But the day I saw them the pink and lavender flower faces were lifted so that they were exposed at the surface of the sand, though so slightly that one could easily pass them by unnoticed. Seeing them—even recognizing them for what they were—there was a sense of incongruity in finding what looked so definitely flowerlike here at the edge of the sea.

These flattened, heart-shaped sea pansies, raised on short stems above the sand, are not plants but animals. They belong to the same general group of simple beings as the jellyfish, sea anemones, and corals, but to find their nearest relatives one would have to desert the shore and go down to some deep-lying offshore bottom where, as fernlike growths in a strange animal forest, the sea pens thrust long stalks into the soft ooze.

Each sea pansy growing here at the edge of the tide is the product of a minute larva that once dropped from the currents to this shore. But through the extraordinary course of its development it has ceased to be that single being of its origin and has become instead a group or colony of many individuals, bound together into a whole of flowerlike form. The various individuals or polyps all have the shape of little tubes embedded in the fleshy substance of the colony. But some of the tubes bear tentacles and look like very small sea anemones; these capture food for the colony, and in the proper season form reproductive cells. Other tubes lack tentacles; these are the engineers of the colony, attending to the functions of water-intake and control. A hydraulic system of changing water pressure controls the movements of the colony; as the stem is made turgid it may be thrust down into the sand, drawing the main body after it.

As the rising tide streams over the flattened shapes of the sea pansies, all the tentacles of the feeding polyps are thrust up, reaching for the living motes that dance in the water—the copepods, the diatoms, the fish larvae small and tenuous as threads.

And at night the shallow water, rippling gently over these flats, must glow softly with hundreds of little lights marking out the zone where the sea pansies live, in a serpentine line of gleaming points, just as lights seen from an airplane at night wander across the dark landscape and show the path of settlement along a highway. For the sea pansies, like their deep-sea relatives, are beautifully luminescent.

In season, the tide sweeping over these flats carries many small, pear-shaped, swimming larvae from which new colonies of pansies will develop. In past ages, the currents that traversed the open water then separating North and South America carried such larvae, which established themselves on the Pacific coast, north to Mexico and south to Chile. Then a bridge of land rose between the American continents, closing the water highway. Today the presence of sea pansies on both Atlantic and Pacific coasts is one of the living reminders of that past geologic time when North and South America were separated, and sea creatures passed freely from one ocean to the other.

In that liquescent sand at the edge of the low tide, I often saw small bubblings and boilings under the surface as one or another of the sand dwellers slipped in or out of its hidden world.

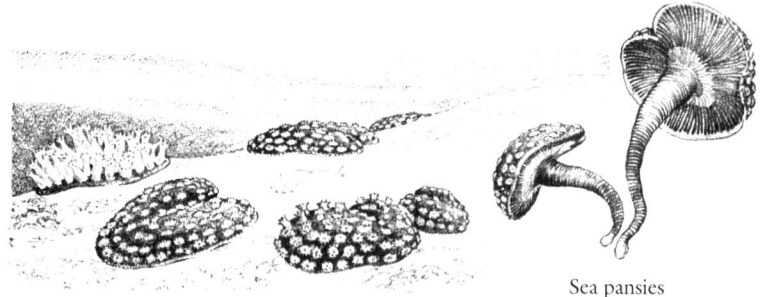

Sea pansies

There were sand dollars, or keyhole urchins, thin as wafers. As one of them buried itself the forward edge slipped obliquely into the sand, passing with effortless ease from the world of sunlight and water into those dim regions of which my senses knew nothing. Internally, the shells are strengthened for burrowing, and against the force of surf, by supporting pillars that occupy most of the region between upper and lower shells except in the center of the disc. The surface of the animal is covered with minute spines, soft as felt. The spines shimmered in the sunlight as their waving movements set up currents that kept the sand grains in motion and eased the passage of the creature from water into earth. On the back of the disc was dimly marked out a design like a five-petaled flower. Repeating the meaning and the symbolism of the number five—the sign of the echinoderms—were five holes perforating the flat disc. As the animal progressed just under the shifting film of surface sand, grains moved up from the under side through the holes, aiding its forward movement and spreading a concealing veil of sand over its body.

The sand dollars shared their dark world with other echinoderms. Down in the wet sand lived heart urchins, which one never sees at the surface until the thin little boxes that once contained them are found by the tide and carried in to the beach, to be blown about by the wind and left at last in the litter of the high-tide line. The oddly shaped heart urchins lay in chambers six inches or more below the surface of the sand, keeping open for themselves channels lined with sticky mucus; through these they reached up to the floor of

Sand dollars

the shallow sea, finding diatoms and other particles of food among the sand grains.

And sometimes a starlike pattern twinkled in that firmament of sand, proclaiming that one of the sand-dwelling starfishes lay below, marking out its image by the flow of water currents, as the animal drew sea water through its body for respiration, expelling it through many pores on its upper surface. If the sand was disturbed, the astral image trembled and faded, like a star disappearing in mist, as the animal glided away rapidly, paddling through the sand with flattened tube feet.

Walking back across the flats of that Georgia beach, I was always aware that I was treading on the thin rooftops of an underground city. Of the inhabitants themselves little or nothing was visible. There were the chimneys and stacks and ventilating pipes of underground dwellings, and various passages and runways leading down into darkness. There were little heaps of refuse that had been brought up to the surface as though in an attempt at some sort of civic sanitation. But the inhabitants remained hidden, dwelling silently in their dark, incomprehensible world.

The most numerous inhabitants of this city of burrowers were the ghost shrimps. Their holes were everywhere over the tidal flat, in diameter considerably smaller than a lead pencil, and surrounded by a little pile of fecal pellets. The pellets accumulate in great quantity because of the shrimp's way of life; it must eat an enormous amount of sand and mud to obtain the food that is mixed with this indigestible material. The holes are the visible entrances to burrows that extend down several feet

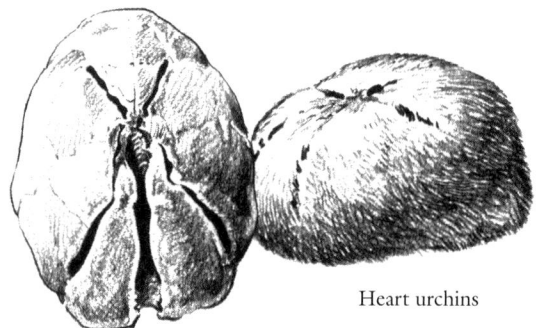
Heart urchins

into the sand—long, nearly vertical passageways from which other tunnels lead off, some continuing down into the dark, damp basement of this shrimp city, others leading up to the surface as though to provide emergency exit doors.

The owners of the burrows did not show themselves unless I tricked them into it by dropping sand grains, a few at a time, into their entrance halls. The ghost shrimp is a curiously formed creature with a long slender body. It seldom goes abroad and so has no need of a hard protective skeleton; it is covered, instead, with a flexible cuticle suited to the narrow tunnel in which it must be able to dig and turn about. On the under side of its body are several pairs of flattened appendages that beat continually to force a current of water through the burrow, for in the deep sand layers the oxygen supply is poor, and aerated water must be drawn down from above. When the tide comes in, the ghost shrimps go up to the mouths of their burrows and begin their work of sifting the sand grains for bacteria, diatoms, and perhaps larger particles of organic detritus. The food is brushed out of the sand by means of little hairs on several of the appendages, and is then transferred to the mouth.

Few of those who build permanent homes in this underground city of sand live by themselves. On the Atlantic coast, the ghost shrimp regularly gives lodging to a small rotund crab, related to the species often found in oysters. The pea crab, Pinnixa, finds in the well-aerated burrow of the shrimp both shelter and a steady supply of food. It strains food out

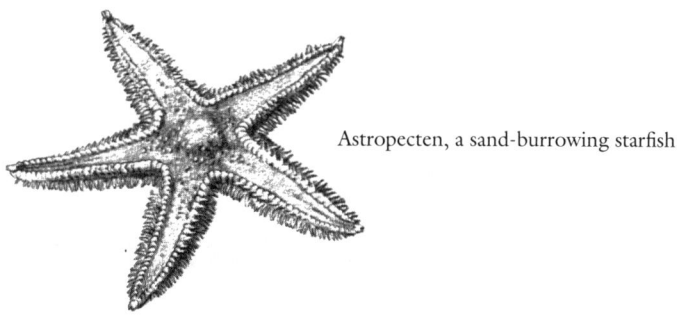

Astropecten, a sand-burrowing starfish

of the water currents that flow through the burrow, using little feathery outgrowths of its body as nets. On the California coast the ghost shrimp shelters as many as ten different species of animals. One is a fish—a small goby—that uses the burrow as a casual refuge while the tide is out, roaming through the passageways of the shrimp's home and pushing past the owner when necessary. Another is a clam that lives outside the burrow but thrusts its siphons through the walls and takes food from the water circulating through the tunnel. The clam has short siphons and in ordinary circumstances would have to live just under the surface of the sand to reach water and its food supply; by establishing connection with the shrimp's burrow it is able to enjoy the protective advantages of living at a deeper level.

On the muddier parts of these same Georgia flats the lugworm lives, its presence marked by round black domes, like

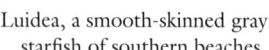

Luidea, a smooth-skinned gray starfish of southern beaches

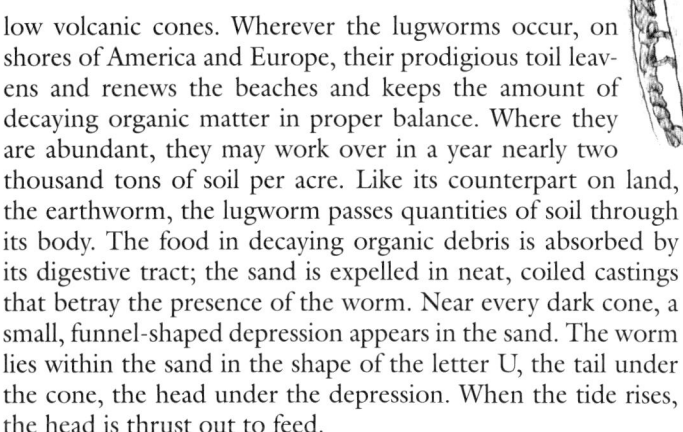

Ghost shrimp

low volcanic cones. Wherever the lugworms occur, on shores of America and Europe, their prodigious toil leavens and renews the beaches and keeps the amount of decaying organic matter in proper balance. Where they are abundant, they may work over in a year nearly two thousand tons of soil per acre. Like its counterpart on land, the earthworm, the lugworm passes quantities of soil through its body. The food in decaying organic debris is absorbed by its digestive tract; the sand is expelled in neat, coiled castings that betray the presence of the worm. Near every dark cone, a small, funnel-shaped depression appears in the sand. The worm lies within the sand in the shape of the letter U, the tail under the cone, the head under the depression. When the tide rises, the head is thrust out to feed.

Other signs of the lugworm appear in midsummer—large, translucent, pink sacs, each bobbing about in the water like a child's balloon, with one end drawn down into the sand. These compact masses of jelly are the egg masses of the worm, within each of which as many as 300,000 young are undergoing development.

Vast plains of sand are continually worked over by these and other marine worms. One—the trumpet worm—uses the very sand that contains its food to make a cone-shaped tube for the protection of its soft body in tunneling. One may sometimes see the living trumpet worm at work, for it allows its tube to project slightly above the surface. It is much more common, however, to find the empty tubes in the tidal debris. Despite their fragile appearance, they remain intact long after their architects are dead—natural mosaics of sand, one grain thick, the building stones fitted together with meticulous care.

A Scot named A. T. Watson once spent many years studying the habits of this worm. Because tube-building goes on under ground, he found it almost impossibly difficult to observe the fitting into place and cementing of sand grains until he hit upon the idea of collecting very young larvae, which could live and be observed in a thin layer of sand in the bottom of a laboratory dish. The building of the tube was begun soon after the larvae had ceased to swim about and had settled on the bottom of the dish. First each secreted a membranous tube about itself. This was to become the inner lining of the cone, and the foundation for the sand-grain mosaic. These young larvae had only two tentacles, which they used to collect grains of sand and pass them to the mouth. There the grains were rolled about experimentally, and if found suitable, were deposited on the chosen spot at the edge of the tube. Then a little fluid was expelled from the cement gland, after which the worm rubbed certain shield-like structures over the tube as though to smooth it.

"Each tube," wrote Watson, "is the life work of the tenant, and is most beautifully built with grains of sand, each grain placed in position with all the skill and accuracy of a human builder . . . The moment when an exact fit has been obtained is evidently ascertained by an exquisite sense of touch. On one occasion I saw the worm slightly alter (before cementing) the position of a sand grain which it had just deposited."

The tubes serve to house the owners during a lifetime of subterranean tunneling, for like the lugworm, this species finds its food in the subsurface sands. The digging organs, like the tubes, belie their fragile appearance. They are slender, sharp-pointed bristles arranged in two groups, or "combs," which look fantastically impractical. We could easily believe that someone, in whimsical mood, had cut them out of shining golden foil, fringing the margins with repeated snips of the scissors to fashion a Christmas tree ornament.

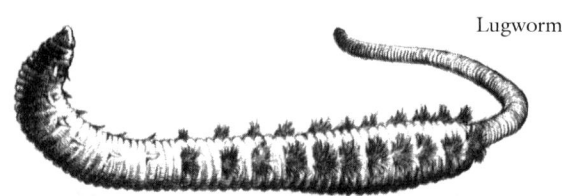

Lugworm

Trumpet worm and its tubes

I have watched the worms at work, in a miniature world of sand and sea created for them in my laboratory. Even in a thin layer of sand in a glass bowl, the combs are used with a sturdy efficiency that reminds one of a bulldozer. The worm emerges slightly from the tube, thrusts the combs into the sand, scoops up a load and throws it over its shoulder, as it were; then it seems to scrape the shovel blades clean by drawing them back over the edge of the tube. The whole thing is done with vigor and dispatch, with motions alternately to right and left. The golden shovels loosen the sand and allow the soft, food-gathering tentacles to explore among the grains, and bring to the mouth the food they discover.

Down along the line of barrier islands that stands between the mainland and the sea, the waves have cut inlets through which the tides pour into the bays and sounds behind the islands. The seaward shores of the islands are bathed by coastwise currents carrying their loads of sand and silt, mile after mile. In the confusion of meeting the tides that are racing to or from the inlets, the currents slacken and relax their hold on some of the sediments. So, off the mouths of many of the inlets, lines of shoals make out to sea—the wrecking sands of Diamond Shoal and Frying Pan Shoal and scores of others, named or nameless. But not all of the sediments are so deposited. Many are seized by the tides and swept through the

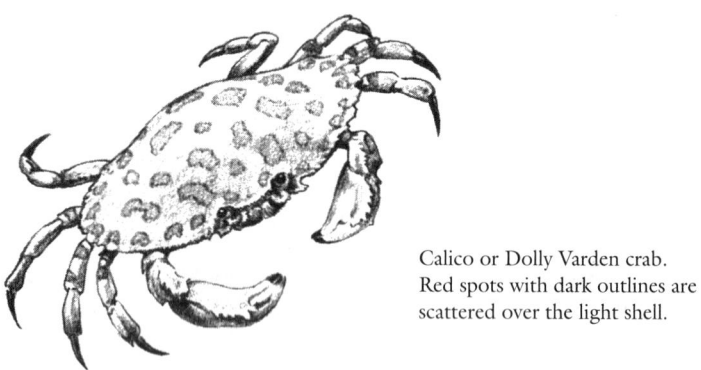

Calico or Dolly Varden crab.
Red spots with dark outlines are
scattered over the light shell.

inlets, only to be dropped in the quieter waters inside. Within the capes and the inlet mouths, in the bays and sounds, the shoals build up. Where they exist the searching larvae or young of sea creatures find them—creatures whose way of life requires quiet and shallow water.

Within the shelter of Cape Lookout there are such shoals reaching upward to the surface, emerging briefly into sun and air for the interval of the low tide, then sinking again into the sea. They are seldom crossed by heavy surf, and while the tidal currents that swirl over or around them may gradually alter their shape and extent—today borrowing some of their substance, tomorrow repaying it with sand or silt brought from other areas—they are on the whole a stable and peaceful world for the animals of the sands.

Some of the shoals bear the names of the creatures of air and water that visit them—Shark, Sheepshead, Bird. To visit Bird Shoal, one goes out by boat through channels winding through the Town Marsh of Beaufort and comes ashore on a rim of sand held firm by the deep roots of beach grasses—the landward border of the shoal. The burrows of thousands of fiddler crabs riddle the muddy beach on the side facing the marshes. The crabs shuffle across the flats at the approach of an intruder, and the sound of many small chitinous feet is like the crackling of paper. Crossing the ridge of sand, one looks out over the shoal. If the tide still has an hour or two to fall to its ebb, one sees only a sheet of water shimmering in the sun.

On the beach, as the tide falls, the border of wet sand

gradually retreats toward the sea. Offshore, a dull velvet patch takes form on the shining silk of the water, like the back of an immense fish slowly rolling out of the sea, as a long streak of sand begins to rise into view.

On spring tides the peak of this great sprawling shoal rises farther out of the water and is exposed longer; on the neaps, when the tidal pulse is feeble and the water movements sluggish, the shoal remains almost hidden, with a thin sheet of water rippling across it even at the low point of the ebb. But on any low tide of the month, in calm weather, one is able to wade out from the sand-dune rim over immense areas of the shoal, in water so shallow and so glassy clear that every detail of the bottom lies revealed.

Even on moderate tides I have gone so far out that the dry sand rim seemed far away. Then deep channels began to cut across the outlying parts of the shoal. Approaching them, I could see the bottom sloping down out of crystal clarity into a green that was dull and opaque. The steepness of the slope was accentuated when a little school of minnows flickered across the shallows and down into the darkness in a cascade of silver sparks. Larger fish wandered in from the sea along these narrow passages between the shoals. I knew there were beds of sun ray clams down there on the deeper bottoms, with whelks moving down to prey on them. Crabs swam about or buried themselves to the eyes in the sandy bottoms; then behind each crab two small vortices appeared in the sand, marking the respiratory currents drawn in through the gills.

Lady crab

Where water—even the shallowest of layers—covered the shoal, life came out of hiding. A young horseshoe crab hurried out into deeper water; a small toadfish huddled down in a clump of eelgrass and croaked an audible protest at the foot of a strange visitor in his world, where human beings seldom intrude. A snail with neat black spirals around its shell and a matching black foot and black, tubular siphons—a banded tulip shell—glided rapidly over the bottom, tracing a clear track across the sand.

Here and there the sea grasses had taken hold—those pioneers among the flowering plants that are venturing out into salt water. Their flat leaf blades pushed up through the sand and their interlacing roots lent firmness and stability to the bottom. In such glades I found colonies of a curious, sand-dwelling sea anemone. Because of their structure and habits, anemones require some firm support to grip while reaching into the water for food. In the north (or wherever there is firm bottom) they grasp the rocks; here they gain the same end by pushing down into the sand until only the crown of tentacles remains above the surface. The sand anemone burrows by contracting the downward-pointing end of its tube and thrusting downward, then as a slow wave of expansion travels up the body, the creature sinks into the sand. It was strange to see the soft tentacle-clusters of the anemones flowering here in the midst of the sands, for anemones seem always to belong to the rocks; yet buried in this firm bottom doubtless they were as secure as the great plumose anemone blooming on the wall of a Maine tide pool.

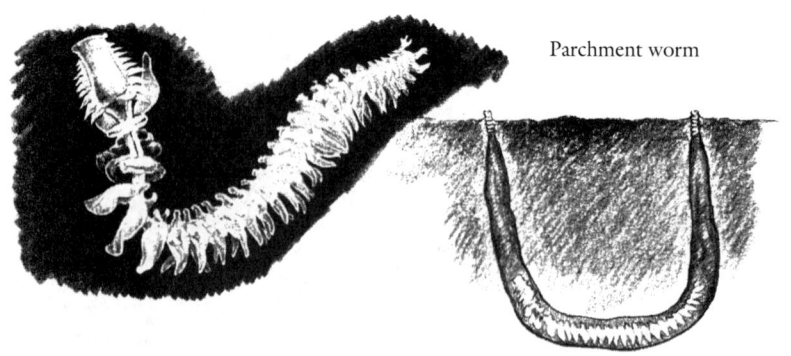

Parchment worm

Pea crabs

Here and there over the grassy parts of the shoal the twin chimneys of the parchment worm's tubes protruded slightly above the sand. The worm itself lives always underground, in a U-shaped tube whose narrowed tips are the animal's means of contact with the sea. Lying in its tube, it uses fanlike projections of the body to keep a current of water streaming through the dark tunnel of its home, bringing it the minute plant cells that are its principal food, carrying away its waste products and in season the seeds of a new generation.

The whole life of the worm is so spent except for the short period of larval life at sea. The larva soon ceases to swim and, becoming sluggish, settles to the bottom. It begins to creep about, perhaps finding food in the diatoms lying in the troughs of the sand ripples. As it creeps it leaves a trail of mucus. After perhaps a few days the young worm begins to make short, mucus-coated tunnels, burrowing into thick clumps of diatoms mixed with sand. From such a simple tunnel, extending perhaps several times the length of its body, the larva pushes up extensions to the surface of the sand, to create the U-shape. All later tunnels are the result of repeated remodelings and extensions of this one, to accommodate the growing body of the worm. After the worm dies the limp, empty tubes are washed out of the sand and are common in the flotsam of the beach.

At some time almost all parchment worms acquire lodgers —the small pea crabs whose relatives inhabit the burrows of the ghost shrimps. Often the association is for life. The crabs, lured by the continuous stream of food-laden water, enter the worm tube while young, but soon become too large to leave

Plumed worm, Diopatra

by the narrow exits. Nor does the worm itself actually leave its tube, although occasionally one sees a specimen with a regenerated head or tail—mute evidence that it may emerge enough to tempt a passing fish or crab. Against such attacks it has no defense, unless the weird blue-white light that illuminates its whole body when disturbed may sometimes alarm an enemy.

Other little protruding chimneys raised above the surface of the shoal belonged to the plumed or decorator worm, Diopatra. These occurred singly, instead of in pairs. They were curiously adorned with bits of shell or seaweed that effectively deceived the human eye, and were but the exposed ends of tubes that sometimes extended down into the sand as much as three feet. Perhaps the camouflage is effective also against natural enemies, yet to collect the materials that it glues to all exposed parts of its tube, the worm has to expose several inches of its body. Like the parchment worm, it is able to regenerate lost tissues as a defense against hungry fish.

Knobbed whelk

As the tide ebbed away, the great whelks could be seen here and there gliding about in search of their prey, the clams that lay buried in the sands, drawing through their bodies a stream of sea water and filtering from it microscopic plants. Yet the search of the whelks was not an aimless one, for their keen taste sense guided them to invisible streams of water pouring from the outlet siphons of the clams. Such a taste trail might lead to a stout razor clam, whose shells afford only the scantiest covering for its bulging flesh, or to a hard-shell clam, with tightly closed valves. Even these can be opened by a whelk, which grips the clam in its large foot and, by muscular contractions, delivers a series of hammer blows with its own massive shell.

Stone crab

Nor does the cycle of life—the intricate dependence of one species upon another—end there. Down in dark little dens of the sea floor live the enemies of the whelks, the stone crabs of massive purplish bodies and brightly colored crushing claws that are able to break away the whelk's shell, piece by piece. The crabs lurk in caves among the stones of jetties, in holes eroded out of shell rock, or in man-made homes such as old, discarded automobile tires. About their lairs, as about the abodes of legendary giants, lie the broken remains of their prey.

If the whelks escape this enemy, another comes by air. The gulls visit the shoal in numbers. They have no great claws to

Channeled whelk; its egg capsules are sharp-edged; those of knobbed whelk have a broad edge.

crush the shells of their victims, but some inherited wisdom has taught them another device. Finding an exposed whelk, a gull seizes it and carries it aloft. It seeks a paved road, a pier, or even the beach itself, soars high into the air and drops its prey, instantly following it earthward to recover the treasure from among the shattered bits of shell.

Coming back over the shoal, I saw spiraling up out of the sand, over the edge of a green undersea ravine, a looped and twisted strand—a tough string of parchment on which were threaded many scores of little purse-shaped capsules. This was the egg string of a female whelk, for it was June, and the spawning time of the species. In all the capsules, I knew, the mysterious forces of creation were at work, making ready thousands of baby whelks, of which perhaps hundreds would survive to emerge from the thin round door in the wall of each capsule, each a tiny being in a miniature shell like that of its parents.

Where the waves roll in from the open Atlantic, with no outlying islands or curving arm of land to break the force of their attack on the beach, the area between the tide lines is a difficult one for living things. It is a world of force and change and constant motion, where even the sand acquires some of the fluidity of water. These exposed beaches have few inhabitants, for only the most specialized creatures can live on sand amid heavy surf.

Animals of open beaches are typically small, always swift-moving. Theirs is a strange way of life. Each wave breaking on the beach is at once their friend and enemy; though it brings food, it threatens to carry them out to sea in its swirling backwash. Only by becoming amazingly proficient in rapid and constant digging can any animal exploit the turbulent surf and shifting sand for the plentiful food supplies brought in by the waves.

One of the successful exploiters is the mole crab, a surf-fisher who uses nets so efficient that they catch even microorganisms adrift in the water. Whole cities of mole crabs live where the waves are breaking, following the flood tide shoreward, retreating toward the sea on the ebb. Several times during the rising of a tide, a whole bed of them will shift its position, digging in again farther up the beach in what is probably a more favorable depth for feeding. In this spectacular mass movement, the sand area suddenly seems to bubble, for in a strangely concerted action, like the flocking of birds or the schooling of fish, the crabs all emerge from the sand as a wave sweeps over them. In the rush of turbulent water they are carried up the beach; then, as the wave's force slackens, they dig into the sand with magical ease, by means of a whirling motion of the tail appendages. With the ebbing of the tide, the crabs return toward the low-water mark, again making the journey in several stages. If by mischance a few linger until the tide has dropped below them, these crabs dig down several inches into the wet sand and wait for the return of the water.

As the name suggests, there is something mole-like in these small crustaceans, with their flattened, pawlike appendages. Their eyes are small and practically useless. Like all others who live within the sands the crabs depend less on sight than on the sense of touch, made wonderfully effective by the presence of many sensory bristles. But without the long, curling, feathery antennae, so efficiently constructed that even small bacteria become entangled in their strands, the mole crab could not survive as a fisher of the surf. In preparing to feed, the crab backs down into the wet sand until only the mouth parts and the antennae are exposed. Although it lies facing the ocean, it makes no attempt to take food from the incoming surf. Rather, it waits until a wave has spent its force on the beach and the backwash is draining seaward. When the spent wave has thinned to a depth of an inch or two, the mole crab extends

Mole crabs

its antennae into the streaming current. After "fishing" for a moment, it draws the antennae through the appendages surrounding its mouth, picking off the captured food. And again in this activity there is a curious display of group behavior, for when one crab thrusts up its antennae, all the others of the colony promptly follow its example.

It is an extraordinary thing to watch the sand come to life if one happens to be wading where there is a large colony of the crabs. One moment it may seem uninhabited. Then, in that fleeting instant when the water of a receding wave flows seaward like a thin stream of liquid glass, there are suddenly hundreds of little gnome-like faces peering through the sandy floor—beady-eyed, long-whiskered faces set in bodies so nearly the color of their background that they can barely be seen. And when, almost instantly, the faces fade back into invisibility, as though a host of strange little troglodytes had momentarily looked out through the curtains of their hidden world and as abruptly retired within it, the illusion is strong that one has seen nothing except in imagination—that there was merely an apparition induced by the magical quality of this world of shifting sand and foaming water.

Since their food-gathering activities keep them in the edge of the surf, mole crabs are exposed to enemies from both land and water—birds that probe in the wet sand, fish that swim in with the tide, feeding in the rising water, blue crabs darting out of the surf to seize them. So the mole crabs function in the sea's economy as an important link between the microscopic food of the waters and the large, carnivorous predators.

Even though the individual mole crab may escape the larger creatures that hunt the tide lines, the span of life is short, comprising a summer, a winter, and a summer. The crab begins life as a minute larva hatched from an orange-colored egg that has been carried for months by the mother crab, one of a mass firmly attached beneath her body. As the time for hatching nears, the mother foregoes the feeding movements up and down the beach with the other crabs and remains near the zone of the low tide, so avoiding the danger of stranding her offspring on the sands of the upper beach.

When it escapes from the protective capsule of the egg, the young larva is transparent, large-headed, and large-eyed as are all crustacean young, weirdly adorned with spines. It is a creature of the plankton, knowing nothing of life in the sands. As it grows it molts, shedding the vestments of its larval life. So it reaches a stage in which, although still swimming in larval fashion with waving motions of its bristled legs, it now seeks the bottom in the turbulent surf zone, where the waves stir and loosen the sand. Toward the summer's end there is another molt, this time bringing transformation to the adult stage, with the feeding behavior of the adult crabs.

During the protracted period of larval life, many of the young mole crabs have made long coastwise journeys in the currents, so that their final coming ashore (if they have survived the voyage) may be far from the parental sands. On the Pacific coast, where strong surface currents flow seaward, Martin Johnson found that great numbers of the crab larvae are carried out over oceanic depths, doomed to certain destruction unless they chance to find their way into a return current. Because of the long larval life, some of the young crabs are carried as far as 200 miles offshore. Perhaps in the prevailing coastwise current of Atlantic shores they travel even farther.

With the coming of winter the mole crabs remain active. In the northern part of their range, where frost bites deep into the sands and ice may form on the beaches, they go out beyond the low-tide zone to pass the cold months where a fathom or more of insulating water lies between them and the wintry air. Spring is the mating season and by July most or all of the males hatched the preceding summer have died. The females carry their egg masses for several months until the young hatch;

before winter all of these females have died and only a single generation of the species remains on the beach.

The only other creatures regularly at home between the tide lines of wave-swept Atlantic beaches are the tiny coquina clams. The life of the coquinas is one of extraordinary and almost ceaseless activity. When washed out by the waves, they must dig in again, using the stout, pointed foot as a spade to thrust down for a firm grip, after which the smooth shell is pulled rapidly into the sand. Once firmly entrenched, the clam pushes up its siphons. The intake siphon is about as long as the shell and flares widely at the mouth. Diatoms and other food materials brought in or stirred from the bottom by waves are drawn down into the siphon.

Like the mole crabs, the coquinas shift higher or lower on the beach in mass movements of scores or hundreds of individuals, perhaps to take advantage of the most favorable depth of water. Then the sand flashes with the brightly colored shells as the clams emerge from their holes and let the waves carry them. Sometimes other small burrowers move with the coquinas among the waves—companies of the little screw shell, Terebra, a carnivorous snail that preys on the coquina. Other enemies are sea birds. The ring-billed gulls hunt the clams persistently, treading them out of the sand in shallow water.

On any particular beach, the coquinas are transient inhabitants; they seem to work an area for the food it provides, and then move on. The presence on a beach of thousands of the beautifully variegated shells, shaped like butterflies and crossed by radiating bands of color, may mark only the site of a former colony.

Coquina clams

Being only briefly and sporadically possessed by the sea in those recurrent periods of the tides' farthest advance, the high-tide zone on any shore has in its own nature something of the land as well as of the sea. This intermediate, transitional quality pervades not only the physical world of the upper beach but also its life. Perhaps the ebb and flow of the tides has accustomed some of the intertidal animals, little by little, to living out of water; perhaps this is the reason there are among the inhabitants of this zone some who, at this moment of their history, belong neither to the land nor entirely to the sea.

The ghost crab, pale as the dry sand of the upper beaches it inhabits, seems almost a land animal. Often its deep holes are back where the dunes begin to rise from the beach. Yet it is not an air-breather; it carries with it a bit of the sea in the branchial chamber surrounding its gills, and at intervals must visit the sea to replenish the water. And there is another, almost symbolic return. Each of these crabs began its individual life as a tiny creature of the plankton; after maturity and in the spawning season, each female enters the sea again to liberate her young.

If it were not for these necessities, the lives of the adult crabs would be almost those of true land animals. But at intervals during each day they must go down to the water line to wet their gills, accomplishing their purpose with the least possible contact with the sea. Instead of wading directly into the water, they take up a position a little above the place where, at the moment, most of the waves are breaking on the beach. They stand sideways to the water, gripping the sand with the legs on the landward side. Human bathers know that in any surf an occasional wave will tower higher than the others and run farther up the beach. The crabs wait, as if they also know this, and after such a wave has washed over them, they return to the upper beach.

They are not always wary of contact with the sea. I have a mental picture of one sitting astride a sea-oats stem on a Virginia beach, one stormy October day, busily putting into its mouth food particles that it seemed to be picking off the stem. It munched away, intent on its pleasant occupation, ignoring the great, roaring ocean at its back. Suddenly the foam and froth of a breaking wave rolled over it, hurling the crab from the stem and sending both slithering up the wet beach. And almost any ghost crab, hard pressed by a person trying to catch it, will dash into the surf as though choosing a lesser evil. At such times they do not swim, but walk along on the bottom until their alarm has subsided and they venture out again.

Although on cloudy days and even occasionally in full sunshine the crabs may be abroad in small numbers, they are predominantly hunters of the night beaches. Drawing from the cloak of darkness a courage they lack by day, they swarm boldly over the sand. Sometimes they dig little temporary pits close to the water line, in which they lie watching for what the sea may bring them.

The individual crab in its brief life epitomizes the protracted racial drama, the evolutionary coming-to-land of a sea creature. The larva, like that of the mole crab, is oceanic, becoming a creature of the plankton once it has hatched from the egg that has been incubated and aerated by the mother. As the infant crab drifts in the currents it sheds its cuticle several times to accommodate the increasing size of its body; at each molt it undergoes slight changes of form. Finally the last larval stage, called the megalops, is reached. This is the form in which all the destiny of the race is symbolized, for it—a tiny creature alone in the sea—must obey whatever instinct drives it shoreward, and must make a successful landing on the beach. The long processes of evolution have fitted it to cope with its fate. Its structure is extraordinary when compared with like stages of closely related crabs. Jocelyn Crane, studying these larvae in various species of ghost crabs, found that the cuticle is always thick and heavy, the body rounded. The appendages are grooved and sculptured so that they may be folded down

Ghost crab

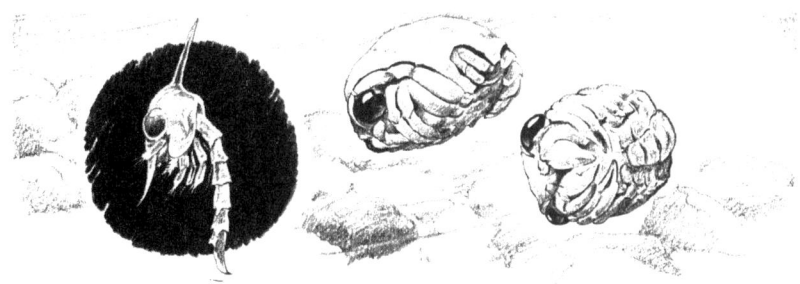

Ghost crab larva, early stage (left); Megalops (right).

tightly against the body, each fitting precisely against the adjacent ones. In the hazardous act of coming ashore, these structural adaptations protect the young crab against the battering of the surf and the scraping of sand.

Once on the beach, the larva digs a small hole, perhaps as protection from the waves, perhaps as a shelter in which to undergo the molt that will transform it into the shape of the adult. From then on, the life of the young crab is a gradual moving up the beach. When small it digs its burrows in wet sand that will be covered by the rising tide. When perhaps half grown, it digs above the high-tide line; when fully adult it goes well back into the upper beach or even among the dunes, attaining then the farthest point of the landward movement of the race.

On any beach inhabited by ghost crabs, their burrows appear and disappear in a daily and seasonal rhythm related to the habits of the owners. During the night the mouths of the burrows stand open while the crabs are out foraging on the beach. About dawn the crabs return. Whether each goes, as a rule, to the burrow it formerly occupied or merely to any convenient one is uncertain—the habit may vary with locality, the age of the crab, and other changing conditions.

Most of the tunnels are simple shafts running down into the sand at an angle of about forty-five degrees, ending in an enlarged den. Some few have an accessory shaft leading up from the chamber to the surface. This provides an emergency exit to be used if an enemy—perhaps a larger and hostile crab—comes down the main shaft. This second shaft usually runs to

Sand hopper or beach flea

the surface almost vertically. It is farther away from the water than the main tunnel, and may or may not break through the surface of the sand.

The early morning hours are spent repairing, enlarging, or improving the burrow selected for the day. A crab hauling up sand from its tunnel always emerges sideways, its load of sand carried like a package under the legs of the functional rear end of the body. Sometimes, immediately on reaching the burrow mouth, it will hurl the sand violently away and flash back into the hole; sometimes it will carry it a little distance away before depositing it. Often the crabs stock their burrows with food and then retire into them; nearly all crabs close the tunnel entrances about midday.

All through the summer the occurrence of holes on the beach follows this diurnal pattern. By autumn most of the crabs have moved up to the dry beach beyond the tide; their holes reach deeper into the sand as though their owners were feeling the chill of October. Then, apparently, the doors of sand are pulled shut, not to be opened again until spring. For the winter beaches show no sign either of the crabs or of their holes—from dime-sized youngsters to full-grown adults, all have disappeared, presumably into the long sleep of hibernation. But, walking the beach on a sunny day in April, one will see here and there an open burrow. And presently a ghost crab in an obviously new and shiny spring coat may appear at its door and very tentatively lean on its elbows in the spring sunshine. If there is a lingering chill in the air, it will soon retire and close its door. But the season has turned, and under all this expanse of upper beach, crabs are awakening from their sleep.

Like the ghost crab, the small amphipod known as the sand hopper or beach flea portrays one of those dramatic moments of evolution, in which a creature abandons an old way of life for a new. Its ancestors were completely marine; its remote descendants, if we read its future aright, will be terrestrial. Now it is midway in the transition from a sea life to a land life.

As in all such transitional existences, there are strange little contradictions and ironies in its way of life. The sand hopper has progressed as far as the upper beach; its predicament is that it is bound to the sea, yet menaced by the very element that gave it life. Apparently it never enters the water voluntarily. It is a poor swimmer and may drown if long submerged. Yet it requires dampness and probably needs the salt in the beach sand, and so it remains in bondage to the water world.

The movements of the sand hoppers follow the rhythm of the tides and the alternation of day and night. On the low tides that fall during the dark hours, they roam far into the intertidal zone in search of food. They gnaw at bits of sea lettuce or eelgrass or kelp, their small bodies swaying with the vigor of their chewing. In the litter of the tide lines they find morsels of dead fish or crab shells containing remnants of flesh; so the beach is cleaned and the phosphates, nitrates, and other mineral substances are recovered from the dead for use by the living.

If low water has fallen late in the night, the amphipods continue their foraging until shortly before daybreak. Before light has tinged the sky, however, all of the hoppers begin to move up the beach toward the high-water line. There each begins to dig the burrow into which it will retreat from daylight and rising water. As it works rapidly, it passes back the grains of sand from one pair of feet to the next until, with the third pair of thoracic legs, it piles the sand behind it. Now and then the small digger straightens out its body with a snap, so that the accumulated sand is thrown out of the hole. It works furiously at one wall of the tunnel, bracing itself with the fourth and fifth pairs of legs, then turns and begins work on the opposite wall. The creature is small and its legs are seemingly fragile, yet the tunnel may be completed within perhaps ten minutes, and a chamber hollowed out at the end of the shaft. At its maximum depth this shaft represents as prodigious a labor as though a man, working with no tools but his hands, had dug for himself a tunnel about 60 feet deep.

The work of excavation done, the sand flea often returns to the mouth of its burrow to test the security of the entrance door, formed by the accumulation of sand from the deeper parts of the shaft. It may thrust out its long antennae from the mouth of the burrow, feeling the sand, tugging at the grains to draw more of them into the hole. Then it curls up within the dark snug chamber.

As the tide rises overhead, the vibrations of breaking waves and shoreward-pressing tides may come down to the little creature in its burrow, bringing a warning that it must stay within to avoid water and the dangers brought by water. It is less easy to understand what arouses the protective instinct to avoid daylight, with all the dangers of foraging shore birds. There can be little difference between day and night in that deep burrow. Yet in some mysterious way the beach flea is held within the safety of the sandy chamber until the two essential conditions again prevail on the beach—darkness and a falling tide. Then it awakens from sleep, creeps up the long shaft, and pushes away the sand door. Once again the dark beach stretches before it, and a retreating line of white froth at the edge of the tide marks the boundary of its hunting grounds.

Each den that is dug with so much labor is merely a shelter for one night, or one tidal interval. After the low-tide feeding

Egg case of skate; sand dollar; sand collar of moon snail

period, each hopper will dig itself a new refuge. The holes that we see on the upper beach lead down to empty burrows from which the former occupants have gone. An occupied burrow has its "door" closed, and so its location cannot easily be detected. On the sandy edge of the sea there is, then, the abundant life of protected beaches and shoals, the sparse life of surf-swept sands, and the pioneering life that has reached the high-tide line and seems poised in space and time for invasion of the land.

But the sands contain also the record of other lives. A thin net of flotsam is spread over the beaches—the driftage of ocean brought to rest on the shore. It is a fabric of strange composition, woven with tireless energy by wind and wave and tide. The supply of materials is endless. Caught in the strands of dried beach grass and seaweeds there are crab claws and bits of sponge, scarred and broken mollusk shells, old spars crusted with sea growths, the bones of fishes, the feathers of birds. The weavers use the materials at hand, and the design of the net changes from north to south. It reflects the kind of bottom offshore—whether rolling sand hills or rocky reefs; it subtly hints of the nearness of a warm, tropical current, or tells of the intrusion of cold water from the north. In the litter and debris of the beach there may be few living creatures, but there is the suggestion, the intimation of a million, million lives, lived in the sands nearby or brought to this place from far sea distances.

Whelk egg string; Portuguese man-o'-war; moon snail; ghost crab

Ramshorn shell, Spirula

In the beach flotsam there are often strays from the surface waters of the open ocean, reminders of the fact that most sea creatures are the prisoners of the particular water masses they inhabit. When tongues of their native waters, driven by winds or drawn by varying temperature or salinity patterns, stray into unaccustomed territory, this drifting life is carried involuntarily with them.

In the several centuries that men of inquiring mind have been walking the world's shores many unknown sea animals have been discovered as strays from the open ocean in the flotsam of the tide lines. One such mysterious link between the open sea and the shore is the ramshorn shell, Spirula. For many years only the shell had been known—a small white spiral forming two or three loose coils. By holding such a shell to the light, one can see that it is divided into separate chambers, but seldom is there a trace of the animal that built and inhabited it. By 1912, about a dozen living specimens had been found, but still no one knew in what part of the sea the creature lived. Then Johannes Schmidt undertook his classic researches into the life history of the eel, crossing and recrossing the Atlantic and towing plankton nets at different levels from the surface down into depths perpetually black. Along with the glass-clear larvae of the eels that were the object of his search, he brought up other animals—among them many specimens of Spirula, which had been caught swimming at various depths down to a mile. In their zone of greatest abundance, which seems to lie between 900 and 1500 feet, they probably occur in dense schools. They are little squidlike animals with ten arms and a cylindrical body, bearing fins like propellers at one end. Placed in an aquarium, they are seen to swim with jerky, backward spurts of jet-propelled motion.

It may seem mysterious that the remains of such a deep-sea animal should come to rest in beach deposits, but the reason is, after all, not obscure. The shell is extremely light; when the animal dies and begins to decay, the gases of decomposition probably lift it toward the surface. There the fragile shell begins a slow drift in the currents, becoming a natural "drift bottle" whose eventual resting place is a clue not so much to the distribution of the species as to the course of the currents that bore it. The animals themselves live over deep oceans, perhaps most abundantly above the steep slopes that descend from the edges of the continents into the abyss. In such depths, they seem to occupy tropical and subtropical belts around the world. Now, in this little shell curved like the horn of a ram, we have one of the few persisting reminders of the days when great, spiral-shelled "cuttle fish" swarmed in the oceans of the Jurassic and earlier periods. All other cephalopods, except the pearly or chambered nautilus of the Pacific and Indian Oceans, have either abandoned their shells or converted them to internal remnants.

And sometimes, among the tidal debris, there appears a thin papery shell, bearing on its white surface a ribbed pattern like that which shore currents impress upon the sand. It is the shell of the paper nautilus or argonaut, an animal distantly related to

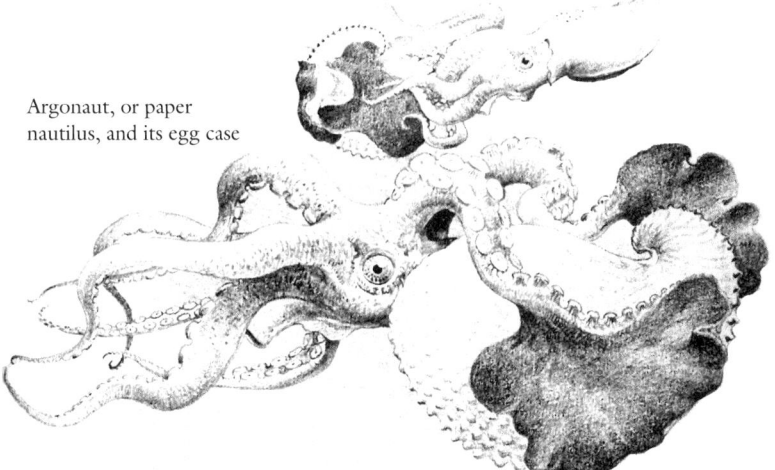

Argonaut, or paper nautilus, and its egg case

an octopus, and like it having eight arms. The argonaut lives on the high seas, in both Atlantic and Pacific Oceans. The "shell" is actually an elaborate egg case or cradle secreted by the female for the protection of her young. It is a separate structure that she can enter or leave at will. The much smaller male (about one tenth the size of his mate) secretes no shell. He inseminates the female in the strange manner of some other cephalopods: one of his arms breaks off and enters the mantle cavity of the female, carrying a load of spermatophores. For a long while the male of this creature went unrecognized. Cuvier, a French zoologist of the early nineteenth century, was familiar with the detached arm but supposed it to be an independent animal, probably a parasitic worm. The argonaut is not the chambered or pearly nautilus of Holmes's famous poem. Although also a cephalopod, the pearly nautilus belongs to a different group and bears a true shell secreted by the mantle. It inhabits tropical seas, and like Spirula is a descendant of the great spiral-shelled mollusks that dominated the seas of Mesozoic times.

Storms bring in many strays from tropical waters. In a shell shop at Nags Head, North Carolina, I once attempted to buy the beautiful violet snail, Janthina. The proprietor of the shop refused to sell this, her only specimen. I understood why when she told me of finding the living Janthina on the beach after a hurricane, its marvelous float still intact, and the surrounding sand stained purple as the little animal tried, in its extremity, to use its only defense against disaster. Later I found an empty

Purple snail, Janthina, suspended from its raft of bubbles

shell, light as thistledown, resting in a depression in the coral rock of Key Largo, where some gentle tide had laid it. I have never been so fortunate as my acquaintance at Nags Head, for I have never seen the living animal.

Janthina is a pelagic snail that drifts on the surface of the open ocean, hanging suspended from a raft of frothy bubbles. The raft is formed from mucus that the animal secretes; the mucus entraps bubbles of air, then hardens into a firm, clear substance like stiff cellophane. In the breeding season the snail fastens its egg capsules to the under side of the raft, which throughout the year serves to keep the little animal afloat.

Like most snails, Janthina is carnivorous; its prey is found among other plankton animals, including small jellyfishes, crustaceans, and even small goose barnacles. Now and then a swooping gull drops from the sky and takes a snail—but for the most part the bubble raft must be excellent camouflage, almost indistinguishable from a bit of drifting sea froth. There must be other enemies that come from below, for the blue-to-violet tints of the shell (which hangs below the raft) are the colors worn by many creatures that live at or near the surface film and need to conceal themselves from enemies looking up from below.

The strong northward flow of the Gulf Stream bears on its surface fleets of living sails—those strange coelenterates of the open sea, the siphonophores. Because of adverse winds and currents these small craft sometimes come into shallow water and are stranded on the beaches. This happens most often in the south, but the southern

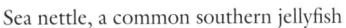

Sea nettle, a common southern jellyfish

coast of New England also receives strays from the Gulf Stream, for the shallows west of Nantucket act as a trap to collect them. Among such strays, the beautiful azure sail of the Portuguese man-of-war, Physalia, is known to almost everyone, for so conspicuous an object can hardly be missed by any beach walker. The little purple sail, or by-the-wind sailor, Velella, is known to fewer, perhaps because of its much smaller size and the fact that once left on the beach it dries quickly to an object that is hard to identify. Both are typically inhabitants of tropical waters, but in the warmth of the Gulf Stream they may sometimes go all the way across to the coast of Great Britain, where in certain years they appear in numbers.

In life the oval float of Velella is a beautiful blue color, with a little elevated crest or sail passing diagonally across it. The disc is about an inch and a half long and half as wide. This is not one animal but a composite one, or colony of inseparably associated individuals—the multiple offspring of a single fertilized egg. The various individuals carry on separate functions. A feeding individual hangs suspended from the center of the float. Small reproductive individuals cluster around it. Around the periphery of the float, feeding individuals in the form of long tentacles hang down to capture the small fry of the sea.

A whole fleet of Portuguese men-of-war is sometimes seen from vessels crossing the Gulf Stream when some peculiarity of the wind and current pattern has brought together a number of them. Then one can sail for hours or days with always some of the siphonophores in sight. With the float or sail set diagonally across its base, the creature sails before the wind; looking

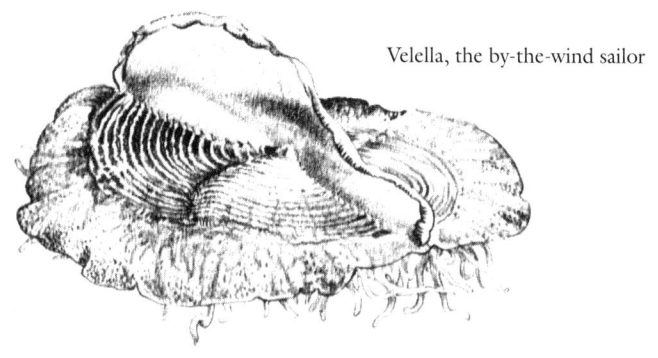

Velella, the by-the-wind sailor

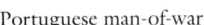

Portuguese man-of-war

down into the clear water one can see the tentacles trailing far below the float. The Portuguese man-of-war is like a small fishing boat trailing a drift net, but its "net" is more nearly like a group of high-voltage wires, so deadly is the sting of the tentacles to almost any fish or other small animal unlucky enough to encounter them.

The true nature of the man-of-war is difficult to grasp, and indeed many aspects of its biology are unknown. But, as with Velella, the central fact is that what appears to be one animal is really a colony of many different individuals, although no one of them could exist independently. The float and its base are thought to be one individual; each of the long trailing tentacles another. The food-capturing tentacles, which in a large specimen may extend down for 40 or 50 feet, are thickly studded with nematocysts or stinging cells. Because of the toxin injected by these cells, Physalia is the most dangerous of all the coelenterates.

For the human bather, even glancing contact with one of the tentacles produces a fiery welt; anyone heavily stung is fortunate to survive. The exact nature of the poison is unknown. Some people believe there are three toxins involved, one producing paralysis of the nervous system, another affecting respiration, the third resulting in extreme prostration and death, if a large dose is received. In areas where Physalia is abundant, bathers have learned to respect it. On some parts of the Florida coast the Gulf Stream passes so close inshore that many of these coelenterates are borne in toward the beaches by onshore winds. The Coast Guard at Lauderdale-by-the-Sea and other such places, when posting reports of tides and water temperatures, often includes forecasts of the relative number of Physalias to be expected inshore.

Because of the highly toxic nature of the nematocyst poisons, it is extraordinary to find a creature that apparently is unharmed by them. This is the small fish Nomeus, which lives always in the shallow of a Physalia. It has never been found in any other situation. It darts in and out among the tentacles with seeming impunity, presumably finding among them a refuge from enemies. In return, it probably lures other fish within range of the man-of-war. But what of its own safety? Is it actually immune to the poisons? Or does it live an incredibly hazardous life? A Japanese investigator reported years ago that Nomeus actually nibbles away bits of the stinging tentacles, perhaps in this way subjecting itself to minute doses of the poison throughout its life and so acquiring immunity. But some recent workers contend that the fish has no immunity whatever, and that every live Nomeus is simply a very lucky fish.

The sail, or float, of a Portuguese man-of-war is filled with gas secreted by the so-called gas gland. The gas is largely nitrogen (85 to 91 per cent) with a small amount of oxygen and a trace of argon. Although some siphonophores can deflate the air sac and sink into deep water if the surface is rough, Physalia apparently cannot. However, it does have some control over the position and degree of expansion of the sac. I once had a graphic demonstration of this when I found a medium-size man-of-war stranded on a South Carolina beach. After keeping it overnight in a bucket of salt water, I attempted to return it to the sea. The tide was ebbing; I waded out into the chilly March water, keeping the Physalia in its bucket out of respect for its stinging abilities, then hurled it as far into the sea as I could. Over and over, the incoming waves caught it and returned it to the shallows. Sometimes with my help, sometimes without, it would manage to take off again, visibly adjusting the shape and position of the sail as it scudded along before the wind, which was blowing out of the south, straight up the beach. Sometimes it could successfully ride over an incoming wave; sometimes it would be caught and hustled and bumped along through thinning waters. But whether in difficulty or enjoying momentary success, there was nothing passive in the attitude of the creature. There was, instead, a strong illusion of sentience. This was no helpless bit of flotsam, but a living creature exerting every means at its disposal to control its fate. When I last saw it, a small blue sail far up the beach, it was pointed out to sea, waiting for the moment it could take off again.

Although some of the derelicts of the beach reflect the pattern of the surface waters, others reveal with equal clarity the nature of the sea bottom offshore. For thousands of miles from southern New England to the tip of Florida the continent has a continuous rim of sand, extending in width from the dry sand hills above the beaches far out across the drowned lands of the continental shelf. Yet here and there within this world of sand there are hidden rocky areas. One of these is a scattered and broken chain of reefs and ledges, submerged beneath the green waters off the Carolinas, sometimes close inshore, sometimes far out on the western edge of the Gulf Stream. Fishermen call them "black rocks" because the blackfish congregate around them. The charts refer to "coral" although the closest reef-building corals are hundreds of miles away, in southern Florida.

In the 1940's, biologist divers from Duke University explored some of these reefs and found that they are not coral, but an outcropping of a soft claylike rock known as marl. It was formed during the Miocene many thousands of years ago, then buried under layers of sediment and drowned by a rising sea. As the divers described them, these submerged reefs are low-lying masses of rock sometimes rising a few feet above the sand, sometimes eroded away to level platforms from which swaying forests of brown sargassum grow. In deep fissures other algae find places of attachment. Much of the rock is smothered under curious sea growths, plant and animal. The stony coralline algae, whose relatives paint the low-tide rocks of New England a deep, old-rose hue, encrust the higher parts of the open reef and fill its interstices. Much of the reef is covered by a thick veneer of twisting, winding, limy tubes—the work of living snails

A bryozoan, Alcyonidium

and of tube-building worms, forming a calcareous layer over the old, fossil rock. Through the years the accumulation of algae and the growth of snail and worm tubes have added, little by little, to the structure of the reef.

Where the reef rock is free from crusts of algae and worm tubes, boring mollusks—date mussels, piddocks, and small boring clams—have drilled into it, scraping out holes in which they lodge, while feeding on the minute life of the water. Because of the firm support provided by the reef, gardens of color bloom in the midst of the drabness of shifting sand and silt. Sponges, orange or red or ocher, extend their branches into the currents that drift across the reef. Fragile, delicately branching hydroids rise from the rocks and from their pale "flowers," in season, tiny jellyfish swim away. Gorgonians are like tall wiry grasses, orange and yellow. And a curious shrubby form of moss animal or bryozoan lives here, the tough and gelatinous structure of its branches containing thousands of tiny polyps, which thrust out tentacled heads to feed. Often this bryozoan grows around a gorgonian, then appearing like gray insulation around a dark, wiry core.

Were it not for the reefs, none of these forms could exist on this sandy coast. But because, through the changing circumstances of geologic history, the old Miocene rocks are now cropping out on this shallow sea floor, there are places where the planktonic larvae of such animals, drifting in the currents, may end their eternal quest for solidity.

After almost any storm, at such places as South Carolina's Myrtle Beach, the creatures from the reefs begin to appear on the intertidal sands. Their presence is the visible result of a deep turbulence in the offshore waters, with waves reaching down to sweep violently over those old rocks that have not known the crash of surf since the sea drowned them, thousands of years ago. The storm waves dislodge many of the fixed and sessile animals and sweep off some of the free-living forms, carrying them away into an alien world of sandy bottoms, of waters shallowing ever more and more until there is no more water beneath them, only the sands of the beach.

I have walked these beaches in the biting wind that lingers after a northeast storm, with the waves jagged on the horizon and the ocean a cold leaden hue, and have been stirred by the sight of masses of the bright orange tree sponge lying on the beach, by smaller pieces of other sponges, green and red and yellow, by glistening chunks of "sea pork" of translucent orange or red or grayish white, by sea squirts like knobby old potatoes, and by living pearl oysters still gripping the thin

A colonial ascidian called "sea pork"

branches of gorgonians. Sometimes there have been living starfish—the dark red southern form of the rock-dwelling Asterias. Once there was an octopus in distress on the wet sands where the waves had thrown it. But life was still in it; when I helped it out beyond the breakers it darted away.

Pieces of the ancient reef itself are commonly found on the sand at Myrtle Beach and presumably at any place where such reefs lie offshore. The marl is a dull gray cement-like rock, full of the borings of mollusks and sometimes retaining their shells. The total number of borers is always so great that one thinks how intense must be the competition, down on that undersea rock platform, for every available inch of solid surface, and how many larvae must fail to find a footing.

Another kind of "rock" occurs on the beach in chunks of varied size and perhaps even more abundantly than the marl. It has almost the structure of honeycomb taffy, being completely riddled with little twisting passageways. The first time one sees this on the beach, especially if it is half buried in sand, one might almost take it for one of the sponges, until investigation proves it to be hard as rock. It is not of mineral origin, however —it is built by small sea worms, dark of body and tentacled of head. These worms, living in aggregations of many individuals, secrete about themselves a calcareous matrix, which hardens to the firmness of rock. Presumably it thickly encrusts the reefs or builds up solid masses from a rocky floor. This particular kind of "worm rock" had not been known from the Atlantic coast until Dr. Olga Hartman identified my specimens from Myrtle

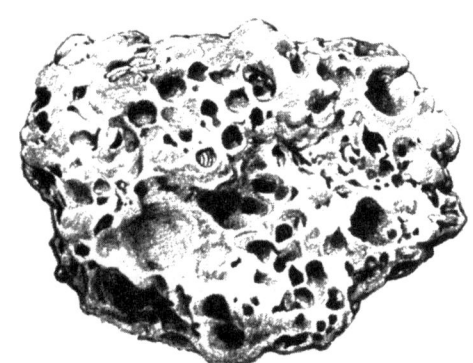

Marl from offshore reef

"Worm rock" of Carolina beaches

Beach as "a matrix-building species of Dodecaceria" whose closest relatives are Pacific and Indian Ocean inhabitants. How and when did this particular species reach the Atlantic? How extensive is its range there? These and many other questions remain to be answered; they are one small illustration of the fact that our knowledge is encompassed within restricted boundaries, whose windows look out upon the limitless spaces of the unknown.

On the upper beach, beyond the zone where the flood tide returns the sea water twice daily, the sands dry out. Then they are subjected to excesses of heat; their arid depths are barren, with little to attract life, or even to make life possible. The grains of dry sands rub one against another. The winds seize them and drive them in a thin mist above the beach, and the cutting edge of this wind-driven sand scours the driftwood to a silver sheen, polishes the trunks of old derelict trees, and scourges the birds that nest on the beach.

But if this area has little life within itself, it is full of the reminders of other lives. For here above the high-tide line, all the empty shells of the mollusks come to rest. Visiting the beach that borders Shackleford Shoals in North Carolina or Florida's Sanibel Island, one could almost believe that mollusks are the only inhabitants of the sea's edge, for their enduring remains dominate the beach debris long after the more fragile remnants of crabs and sea urchins and starfish have been returned to the elements. First the shells were dropped low on the beach by

Jingle shells

the waves; then, tide by tide, they were moved up across the sands to the line of the highest of the high tides. Here they will remain, till buried in drifting sand or carried away in a wild carnival of storm surf.

From north to south the composition of the shell windrows changes, reflecting the changing communities of the mollusks. Every little pocket of gravelly sand that accumulates in favorable spots amid the rocks of northern New England is strewn with mussels and periwinkles. And when I think of the sheltered beaches of Cape Cod I see in memory the windrows of jingle shells being shifted gently by the tide, their thin, scale-like valves (how can they house a living creature?) gleaming with a satin sheen. The arched upper valve occurs more often in beach flotsam than the flat lower one, which is perforated by a hole for the passage of the strong byssus cord that attaches the jingle to a rock or to another shell. Silver, gold, and apricot are the colors of the jingles, set against the deep blue of the mussels that dominate these northern shores. And scattered here and there are the ribbed fans of the scallops and the little white sloops of the boat shells stranded on the beach. The boat shell is a snail with a curiously modified shell, having a little "half deck" on the lower surface. It often becomes attached to its fellows in chains of half a dozen or more individuals. Each boat shell is in its lifetime first male then female. In the chains of attached shells those at the bottom of the chain are always females, the upper animals males.

On the Jersey beaches and the coastal islands of Maryland and Virginia the massive structure of the shells and the lack of ornamental spines have a meaning—that the offshore world of shifting sand is deeply stirred by the endless processions of the waves that roll in on this coast. The thick shell of the surf clam is its defense against the force of the waves. These shores are strewn, too, with the heavy armaments of the whelks, and with the smooth globes of the moon snails.

From the Carolinas south the beach world seems to belong to the several species of arks, whose shells outnumber all others. Though variously shaped, their shells are stout, with long straight hinges. The ponderous ark wears a black, beardlike growth, or periostracum, heavy in fresh specimens, scanty or absent in beach-worn shells. The turkey wing is a gaily colored ark, with reddish bands streaking its yellowish shell. It, too, wears a thick periostracum, and lives down in deep offshore crevices, where it attaches itself to rocks or any other support by a strong line or byssus. While a few kinds of arks extend the range of these mollusks throughout New England (for example, the small transverse ark and the so-called bloody clam —one of the few mollusks that has red blood) it is on southern beaches that the group becomes dominant. On famed Sanibel Island on the west coast of Florida, where the variety of shells

Boat shells

Ponderous ark

is probably greater than anywhere else on our Atlantic coast, the arks nevertheless make up about 95 per cent of the beach deposits.

The pen shells begin to appear in numbers on the beaches below Capes Hatteras and Lookout, but perhaps they, too, live in the most prodigious numbers on the Gulf coast of Florida. I have seen truckloads of them on the beach at Sanibel even in calm winter weather. In a violent tropical hurricane the destruction of this light-shelled mollusk is almost incredible. Sanibel Island presents about fifteen miles of beach to the Gulf of Mexico. On this strand, it has been estimated, about a million pen shells have been hurled by a single storm, having been torn loose by waves reaching down to bottoms lying as deep as 30 feet. The fragile shells of the pens are ground together in the buffeting of storm surf; many are broken, but even those not so destroyed have no way of returning to the sea, and so are doomed. As if knowing this, the commensal pea crabs that

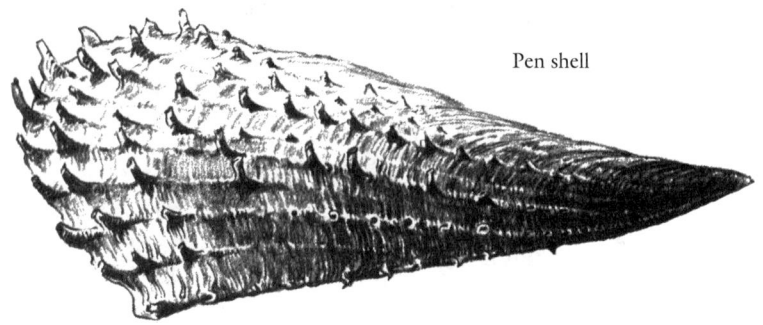

Pen shell

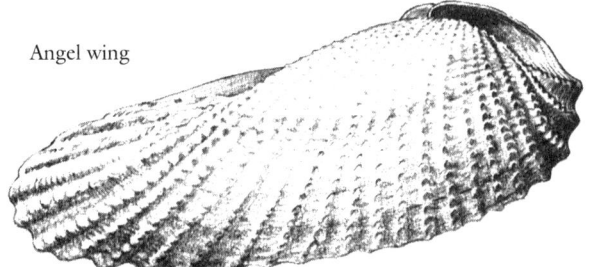

Angel wing

inhabit them creep out of the shells like the proverbial rats abandoning a sinking ship; they may be seen by the thousand swimming about in apparent bewilderment in the surf.

The pen shells spin anchoring byssus threads of golden sheen and remarkable texture; the ancients spun their cloth of gold from the byssus of the Mediterranean pens, producing a fabric so fine and soft it could be drawn through a finger ring. The industry persists at Italian Taranto, on the Ionian Sea, where gloves and other small garments are woven of this natural fabric as curios or tourists' souvenirs.

The survival of an undamaged angel wing in the debris of the upper beach seems extraordinary, so delicately fragile does it appear. Yet these valves of purest white, when worn by the living animals, are capable of penetrating peat or firm clay. The angel wing is one of the most powerful of the boring clams and, having very long siphons with which to maintain communication with the sea water, is able to burrow deeply. I have dug for them in peat beds in Buzzards Bay, and have found them on beach exposures of peat on the coast of New Jersey, but their occurrence north of Virginia is local and rare.

This purity of color, this delicacy of structure are buried throughout life in a bank of clay, for the angel wing's beauty seems destined to be hidden from view until, after the death of the animal, the shells are released by the waves and carried to the beach. In its dark prison the angel wing conceals an even more mysterious beauty. Secure from enemies, hidden from all other creatures, the animal itself glows with a strange green light. Why? For whose eyes? For what reason?

Besides the shells, there are other objects in the beach flotsam that are mysterious in shape and texture. Flat, horny or shell-like discs of various shapes and sizes are the opercula of sea snails—the protective doors that close over the opening when the animal has withdrawn into its shell. Some opercula are round, some leaf-shaped, some like slender, curving daggers. (The "cat's eye" of the South Pacific is the operculum of a snail, rounded on one surface and polished like a boy's marble.) The opercula of the various species are so characteristic in shape, material, and structure that they are a useful means of identifying otherwise difficult species.

The tidal flotsam abounds, too, in many little empty egg cases in which various sea creatures passed their first days of life. These are of various shapes and materials. The black "mermaid's purses" belong to one of the skates. They are flat, horny rectangles, with two long, curling prongs or tendrils extending from each end. With these the parent skate attaches the packet containing a fertilized egg to seaweeds on some offshore bottom. After the young skate matures and hatches, its discarded cradle is often washed up on the beach. Egg cases of the banded tulip shell remind one of the dried seed pods of a flower, a cluster of thin, parchment-like containers borne on a central stalk. Those of the channeled or the knobbed whelks are long, spiraling strings of little capsules, again parchment-like in texture. Each of the flat, ovoid capsules contains scores of baby whelks, incredible in the minute perfection of their shells. Sometimes a few remain in an egg string found on the beach; they rattle against the hard walls of the capsule like peas in a dried pod.

Perhaps the most baffling of all objects found on beaches are the egg cases of the sand collar snail or moon snail. If someone had cut a doll's shoulder cape out of a piece of fine sandpaper,

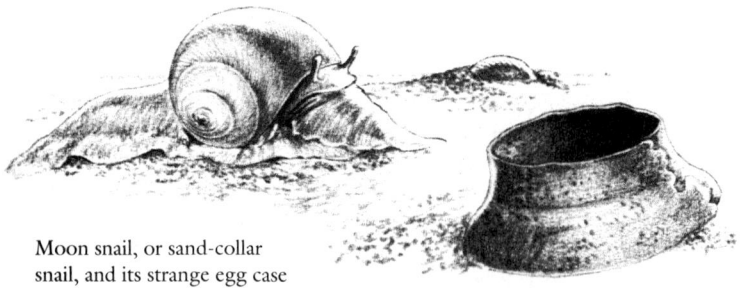

Moon snail, or sand-collar snail, and its strange egg case

the result would be about the same. The "collars" produced by the various species of the family of moon snails differ in size and, though slightly, in shape. In some the edges are smooth, in others scalloped. The arrangement of the eggs also follows slightly different patterns in the various species. This strange receptacle for the eggs of the snail is formed as a sheet of mucus pushed out from under the foot and molded on the outside of the shell. This results in the collar shape. The eggs are attached to the under side of the collar, which becomes completely impregnated with sand grains.

Mingled with the bits and fragments of sea creatures are the reminders of man's invasion of the sea—spars, pieces of rope, bottles, barrels, boxes of many shapes and sizes. If these have been long at sea, they bring their own collection of sea life, for in their period of drifting in the currents, they have served as a solid place of attachment for the searching larvae of the plankton.

On our Atlantic coast, the days following a northeast blow or a tropical storm are a time to look for the driftage of open ocean. I remember such a day on the beach at Nags Head, after a hurricane had passed by at sea during the night. The wind was still blowing a gale; there was a fine wild surf. That day the beach was strewn with many bits of driftwood, branches of trees, and heavy planks and spars, many of which bore growths of Lepas, the gooseneck barnacle of the open sea. One long plank was studded with tiny barnacles the size of a mouse's ear; on some of the other drifted timbers the barnacles had grown to a length of an inch or more, exclusive of the stalk. The size of the encrusting barnacles is a rough index of the time the spar has been at sea. In the profusion of their growth on almost every piece of timber one senses the incredible abundance of barnacle larvae drifting in the sea, ready to grasp any firm object adrift in their fluid world, for by strange irony none of them could complete their development in the sea water alone. Each of those weird-looking little beings, rowing through the water with feathered appendages, had to find a hard surface to which it could attach before assuming the adult form.

The life history of these stalked barnacles is very similar to that of the acorn barnacles of the rocks. Within the hard shells is a small crustacean body, bearing feathered appendages with

Gooseneck barnacles

which to sweep food into their mouths. The chief difference is that the shells are borne on a fleshy stalk instead of arising from a flat base firmly cemented to the substratum. When the animals are not feeding, the shells can be tightly closed, as in the rock barnacle; when they open to feed, there are the same sweeping, rhythmical motions of the appendages.

Seeing on the shore a branch from some tree that evidently has been long adrift and now is generously sprinkled with the fleshy brown stalks and the ivory-hued shells of the barnacle, with their marginal tints of blue and red, one can remember with tolerant understanding the old medieval misconception that conferred on these strange crustaceans the name "goose barnacle." The seventeenth-century English botanist John Gerard compiled a description of the "goose tree" or "Barnakle tree" on the basis of the following experience: "Traveling upon the shores of our English coast between Dover and Rummey, I founde the trunke of an olde rotten tree, which . . . we drewe out of the water upon dry lande; on this rotten tree I founde growing many thousands of long crimson bladders . . . at the neather end whereof did grow a shell fish, fashioned somewhat like a small Muskle . . . which after I had opened . . . I found living things that were very naked, in shape like a Birde; in others, the Birde covered with soft downe, the shell halfe open, and the Birde readie to fall out, which no doubt were the foules called Barnakles." Evidently Gerard's imaginative eye saw in the appendages of the barnacles the resemblance to a bird's feathers. On this slender basis he built the following pure fabrication: "They spawne as it were in March and April; the Geese are formed in Maie and June, and come to fulnesse of feathers in the moneth after." And so in many an old work of un-natural history from this time on, we see drawings of trees bearing fruit in the form of barnacles, and geese emerging from the shells to fly away.

Old spars and water-soaked timbers cast on the beach are full of the workings of the shipworm—long cylindrical tunnels penetrating all parts of the wood. Usually nothing remains of the creatures themselves except occasional fragments of their small calcareous shells; these proclaim that the shipworm is a true mollusk, despite its long, slender, and wormlike body.

There were shipworms long before there were men; yet within his own short tenancy of earth, man has greatly increased their numbers. The shipworm can live only in wood; if its young fail to discover some woody substance at a critical period of their existence, they die. This absolute dependence of a sea creature on something derived from the continents seems strange and incongruous. There could have been no shipworms until woody plants evolved on land. Their ancestors probably were clamlike forms burrowing in mud or clay, merely using their excavated holes as a base from which to extract the plankton of the sea. Then after trees evolved, these forerunners of the shipworms adapted themselves to a new habitat—the relatively few forest trees brought into the sea by rivers. But their numbers over all the earth must have been small until, scant thousands of years ago, men began to send wooden vessels across the sea and to build wharves at its edge; in all such wooden structures, the shipworm found a greatly extended range, to the cost of the human race.

The shipworm's place in history is secure. It was the scourge of the Romans with their galleys, of the seagoing Greeks and Phoenicians, of the explorers of the New World. In the 1700's it riddled the dikes that the Dutch had built to keep out the sea; by so doing it threatened the very life of Holland. (As an academic by-product, the first extensive studies of the shipworm were made by Dutch scientists, to whom knowledge of its biology had become a matter of life and death.

Snellius, in 1733, pointed out for the first time that this animal is a clamlike mollusk, not a worm.) About 1917 the shipworm invaded the harbor of San Francisco. Before its inroads were even suspected, ferry slips had begun to collapse, and wharves and loaded freight cars fell into the harbor. During the Second World War, especially in all tropical waters, the shipworm was an unseen but powerful enemy.

The female of the common shipworm retains the young in her burrow until they have attained the larval stage. Then they are launched into the sea—each a tiny being enclosed in two protective shells, looking like any other young bivalve. If it encounters wood when it has reached the threshold of adulthood, all goes well. It puts out a slender byssus thread as an anchor, a foot develops, and the shells become modified into efficient cutting tools, for rows of sharp ridges appear on their outer surfaces. The burrowing begins. With a powerful muscle, the animal scrapes the ridged shell against the wood, revolving meanwhile so that a smooth, cylindrical burrow is cut. As the burrow is extended, usually with the grain of the wood, the body of the shipworm grows. One end remains attached to the wall near the tiny point of entrance. This bears the siphons through which contact with the sea is maintained. The penetrating end carries the small shells. Between stretches a body that is thin as a lead pencil, but may reach a length of eighteen inches. Although a timber may be infested with hundreds of larvae, the burrows of the shipworms never interfere with each other. If an animal finds itself coming close to another burrow, it invariably turns aside. As it bores, it passes the loosened fragments of wood through its digestive tract. Some of the wood is digested and converted into glucose. This

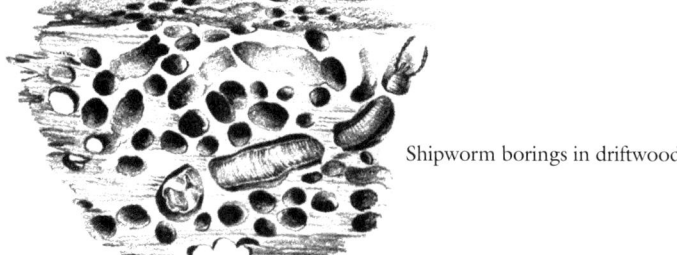

Shipworm borings in driftwood

ability to digest cellulose is rare in the animal world—only certain snails, certain insects, and a very few others possess it. But the shipworm makes little use of this difficult art, and feeds chiefly on the rich plankton streaming through its body.

Other timbers on the beach bear the marks of the wood piddock. These are shallow holes that penetrate only the outer portions just beneath the bark, but they are broad and cleanly cylindrical. The boring piddock is seeking only shelter and protection. Unlike the shipworm, it does not digest the wood, but lives only on the plankton that it draws into its body through a protruding siphon.

Empty piddock holes sometimes attract other lodgers, as abandoned birds' nests may become homes for insects. On the muddy banks of salt creeks at Bears Bluff in South Carolina, I have picked up timbers riddled with holes. Once stout little white-shelled piddocks dwelt in them. The piddocks were long since dead and even the shells were gone, but in each hole was a dark glistening body like a raisin embedded in a cake. They were the contracted tissues of small anemones, finding there, in this world of silt-laden water and yielding mud, that bit of firm foundation which anemones must have. Seeing anemones in such an improbable place, one wonders how the larvae happened to be there, ready to seize the chance opportunity presented by that timber with its neatly excavated apartments; and one is struck anew by the enormous waste of life, remembering that for each of these anemones that succeeded in finding a home, many thousands must have failed.

Always, then, in this flotsam and jetsam of the tide lines, we are reminded that a strange and different world lies offshore. Though what we see here may be but the husks and fragments of life, through it we are made aware of life and death, of movement and change, of the transport of living things by ocean currents, by tides, by wind-driven waves. Some of these involuntary migrants are adults. They may perish in midjourney; a few, being transported into a new home and finding there conditions that are favorable, may survive, may even produce surviving young to extend the range of the species. But many others are larvae, and whether or not they will make a successful landing depends on many things—on the length of their larval life (can they wait for a distant landfall before they

Bugula, a moss animal; or bryozoan. Its beach-worn remains are soft plantlike tufts.

reach the stage when they must take up an adult existence?)—on the temperature of the water they encounter—on the set of the currents that may carry them to favoring shoals, or off into deep water where they will be lost.

And so, walking the beach, we become aware of a most fascinating problem—the colonization of the shore, and especially of those "islands" of rock (or the semblance of rock) that occur in the midst of a sea of sand. For whenever a seawall is built, or a jetty, or pilings are sunk for a pier or a bridge, or rock, long hidden from sun and buried even beneath the sea, emerges again on the ocean floor, these hard surfaces immediately become peopled with typical animals of the rocks. But how did the colonizing rock fauna happen to be at hand—here in the midst of a sandy coast that stretches for hundreds of miles to north and south?

Pondering the answer, we become aware of that ceaseless migration, for the most part doomed to futility, yet ensuring that always, when opportunity arises, Life shall be waiting, ready to take advantage. For the ocean currents are not merely a movement of water; they are a stream of life, carrying always the eggs and young of countless sea creatures. They have carried the hardier ones across oceans, or step by step on long coastwise journeys. They have carried some along deep, hidden passageways where cold currents flow along the floor of the ocean. They have brought inhabitants to populate new islands pushing above the surface of the sea. These things they have done, we must suppose, since first there was life in the sea.

And as long as the currents move on their courses there is the possibility, the probability, even the certainty, that some particular form of life will extend its range, will come to occupy new territory.

As almost nothing else does, this to me expresses the pressure of the life force—the intense, blind, unconscious will to survive, to push on, to expand. It is one of life's mysteries that most of the participants in this cosmic migration are doomed to failure; it is no less mysterious that their failure turns into success when, for all the billions lost, a few succeed.

The Coral Coast

I DOUBT THAT ANYONE can travel the length of the Florida Keys without having communicated to his mind a sense of the uniqueness of this land of sky and water and scattered mangrove-covered islands. The atmosphere of the Keys is strongly and peculiarly their own. It may be that here, more than in most places, remembrance of the past and intimations of the future are linked with present reality. In bare and jaggedly corroded rock, sculptured with the patterns of the corals, there is the desolation of a dead past. In the multicolored sea gardens seen from a boat as one drifts above them, there is a tropical lushness and mystery, a throbbing sense of the pressure of life; in coral reef and mangrove swamp there are the dimly seen foreshadowings of the future.

This world of the Keys has no counterpart elsewhere in the United States, and indeed few coasts of the earth are like it. Offshore, living coral reefs fringe the island chain, while some of the Keys themselves are the dead remnants of an old reef whose builders lived and flourished in a warm sea perhaps a thousand years ago. This is a coast not formed of lifeless rock or sand, but created by the activities of living things which, though having bodies formed of protoplasm even as our own, are able to turn the substance of the sea into rock.

The living coral coasts of the world are confined to waters in which the temperature seldom falls below 70° F. (and never for prolonged periods), for the massive structures of the reefs can be built only where the coral animals are bathed by waters warm enough to favor the secretion of their calcareous skeletons. Reefs and all the associated structures of a coral coast are therefore restricted to the area bounded by the Tropics of Cancer and Capricorn. Moreover, they occur only on the eastern shores of continents, where currents of tropical water are carried toward the poles in a pattern determined by the earth's rotation and the direction of the winds. Western shores are inhospitable to corals because they are the site of upwellings of deep, cold water, with cold coastwise currents running toward the equator.

In North America, therefore, California and the Pacific coast of Mexico lack corals, while the West Indian region supports them in profusion. So do the coast of Brazil in South America, the tropical east African coast, and the northeastern shores of Australia, where the Great Barrier Reef creates a living wall for more than a thousand miles.

Within the United States the only coral coast is that of the Florida Keys. For nearly 200 miles these islands reach southwestward into tropical waters. They begin a little south of Miami where Sands, Elliott, and Old Rhodes Keys mark the entrance to Biscayne Bay; then other islands continue to the southwest, skirting the tip of the Florida mainland, from which they are separated by Florida Bay, and finally swinging out from the land to form a slender dividing line between the Gulf of Mexico and the Straits of Florida, through which the Gulf Stream pours its indigo flood.

To seaward of the Keys there is a shallow area three to seven miles wide where the sea bottom forms a gently sloping platform under depths generally less than five fathoms. An irregular channel (Hawk Channel) with depths to ten fathoms traverses these shallows and is navigable by small boats. A wall of living coral reefs forms the seaward boundary of the reef platform, standing on the edge of the deeper sea (see page 605).

The Keys are divided into two groups that have a dual nature and origin. The eastern islands, swinging in their smooth arc 110 miles from Sands to Loggerhead Key, are the exposed remnants of a Pleistocene coral reef. Its builders lived and flourished in a warm sea just before the last of the glacial periods, but today the corals, or all that remains of them, are dry land. These eastern Keys are long, narrow islands covered with low trees and shrubs, bordered with coral limestone where they are exposed to the open sea, passing into the shallow waters of Florida Bay through a maze of mangrove swamps on the sheltered side. The western group, known as the Pine Islands, are a different kind of land, formed of limestone rock that had its origin on the bottom of a shallow interglacial sea, and is now raised only slightly above the surface of the water. But in all the Keys, whether built by the coral animals or formed of solidifying sea drift, the shaping hand is the hand of the sea.

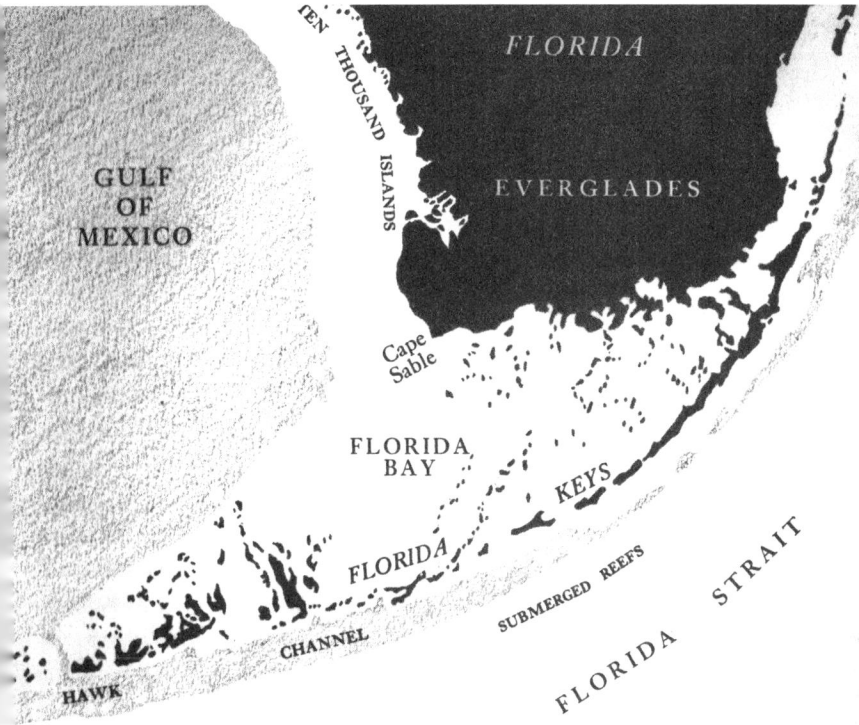

In its being and its meaning, this coast represents not merely an uneasy equilibrium of land and water masses; it is eloquent of a continuing change now actually in progress, a change being brought about by the life processes of living things. Perhaps the sense of this comes most clearly to one standing on a bridge between the Keys, looking out over miles of water, dotted with mangrove-covered islands to the horizon. This may seem a dreamy land, steeped in its past. But under the bridge a green mangrove seedling floats, long and slender, one end already beginning to show the development of roots, beginning to reach down through the water, ready to grasp and to root firmly in any muddy shoal that may lie across its path. Over the years the mangroves bridge the water gaps between the islands; they extend the mainland; they create new islands. And the currents that stream under the bridge, carrying the mangrove seedling, are one with the currents that carry plankton to the coral animals building the offshore reef, creating a wall of rocklike solidity, a wall that one day may be added to the mainland. So this coast is built.

To understand the living present, and the promise of the future, it is necessary to remember the past. During the Pleistocene, the earth experienced at least four glacial stages, when severe climates prevailed and immense sheets of ice crept southward. During each of these stages, large volumes of the earth's water were frozen into ice, and sea level dropped all over the world. The glacial intervals were separated by milder interglacial stages when, with water from melting glaciers returning to the sea, the level of the world ocean rose again. Since the most recent Ice Age, known as the Wisconsin, the general trend of the earth's climate has been toward a gradual, though not uniform warming up. The interglacial stage preceding the Wisconsin glaciation is known as the Sangamon, and with it the history of the Florida Keys is intimately linked.

The corals that now form the substance of the eastern Keys built their reef during that Sangamon interglacial period, probably only a few tens of thousands of years ago. Then the sea stood perhaps 100 feet higher than it does today, and covered all of the southern part of the Florida plateau. In the warm sea off the sloping southeastern edge of that plateau the corals began to grow, in water somewhat more than 100 feet deep. Later the sea level dropped about 30 feet (this was in the early stages of a new glaciation, when water drawn from the sea was falling as snow in the far north); then another 30 feet. In this shallower water the corals flourished even more luxuriantly and the reef grew upward, its structure mounting close to the sea surface. But the dropping sea level that at first favored the growth of the reef was to be its destruction, for as the ice increased in the north in the Wisconsin glacial stage, the ocean level fell so low that the reef was exposed and all its living coral animals were killed. Once again in its history the reef was submerged for a brief period, but this could not bring back the life that had created it. Later it emerged again and has remained above water, except for the lower portions, which now form the passes between the Keys. Where the old reef lies exposed, it is deeply corroded and dissected by the dissolving action of

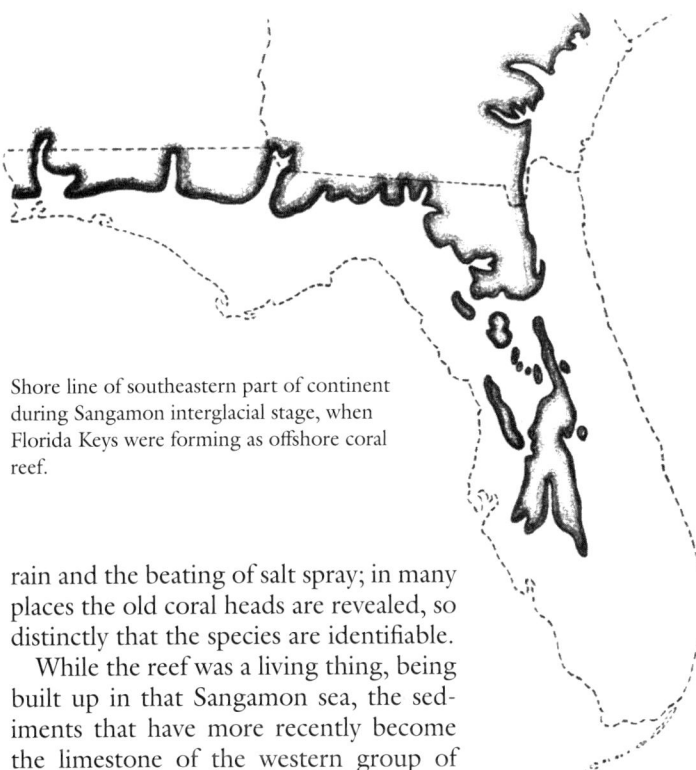

Shore line of southeastern part of continent during Sangamon interglacial stage, when Florida Keys were forming as offshore coral reef.

rain and the beating of salt spray; in many places the old coral heads are revealed, so distinctly that the species are identifiable.

While the reef was a living thing, being built up in that Sangamon sea, the sediments that have more recently become the limestone of the western group of Keys were accumulating on the landward side of the reef. Then the nearest land lay 150 miles to the north, for all the southern end of the present Florida peninsula was submerged. The remains of many sea creatures, the solution of limestone rocks, and chemical reactions in the sea water contributed to the soft ooze that covered the shallow bottoms. With the changing sea levels that followed, this ooze became compacted and solidified into a white, fine-textured limestone, containing many small spherules of calcium carbonate resembling the roe of fish; because of this characteristic it is sometimes known as "oölitic limestone," or "Miami oölite." This is the rock immediately underlying the southern part of the Florida mainland. It forms the bed of Florida Bay under the layer of recent sediments, and then rises above the surface in the Pine Islands, or western Keys, from Big Pine Key to Key

West. On the mainland, the cities of Palm Beach, Fort Lauderdale, and Miami stand on a ridge of this limestone formed when currents swept past an old shore line of the peninsula, molding the soft oozes into a curving bar. The Miami oölite is exposed on the floor of the Everglades as rock of strangely uneven surface, here rising in sharp peaks, there dropping away in solution holes. Builders of the Tamiami Trail and of the highway from Miami to Key Largo dredged up this limestone along the rights of way and with it built the foundations on which these highways are laid.

Knowing this past, we can see in the present a repetition of the pattern, a recurrence of earth processes of an earlier day. Now, as then, living reefs are building up offshore; sediments are accumulating in shallow waters; and the level of the sea, almost imperceptibly but certainly, is changing.

Off this coral coast the sea lies green in the shallows, blue in the far distances. After a storm, or even after a prolonged southeasterly blow, comes "white water." Then a thick, milk-white, richly calcareous sediment is washed out of the reefs and stirred from its deep beds over the floor of the reef flat. On such days the diving mask and the aqualung may as well be left behind, for the underwater visibility is little better than in a London fog.

"White water" is the indirect result of the very high rate of sedimentation that prevails in the shallows around the Keys. Anyone who wades out even a few steps from the shore notices the white, siltlike substance adrift in the water and accumulating on the bottom. It has visibly rained down on every surface. Its fine dust lies over sponge and gorgonian and anemone; it chokes and buries the low-growing algae and lies whitely over the dark bulks of the big loggerhead sponges. The wader stirs up clouds of it; winds and strong currents set it in motion. Its accumulation is going on at an astonishing rate; sometimes, after a storm, two or three inches of new sediment are deposited from one high tide to the next. It comes from various sources. Some is mechanically derived from the disintegration of dead plants and animals—mollusk shells, lime-depositing algae, coral skeletons, tubes of worms or snails, spicules of gorgonians and sponges, skeletal plates of holothurians. It is also derived in part from chemical precipitation of the calcium carbonate present in the water. This, in turn, has been leached out of the vast expanses of limestone rock that compose the surface of southern Florida, and has been carried to the sea by rivers and by the slow drainage of the Everglades.

A few miles outside the chain of the present Keys is the reef of living coral, forming the seaward rim of the shallows, and overlooking a steep descent into the trough of the Florida straits. The reefs extend from Fowey Rocks, south of Miami, to the Marquesas and Tortugas and in general they mark the 10-fathom depth contour. But often they rise to lesser depths and here and there they break the surface as tiny offshore islands, many of them marked by lighthouses.

Drifting over the reef in a small boat and peering down through a glass-bottomed bucket, one finds it hard to visualize the whole terrain, for so little of it can be seen at a time. Even a diver exploring more intimately finds it difficult to realize he is on the crest of a high hill, swept by currents instead of winds, where gorgonians are the shrubbery and stands of elkhorn coral are trees of stone. Toward the land, the sea floor slopes gently down from this hilltop into the wide water-filled valley of Hawk Channel; then it rises again and breaks water as a chain of low-lying islands—the Keys. But on the seaward side of the reef the bottom descends quickly into blue depths. Live corals grow down to a depth of about 10 fathoms. Below that it is too

Disk shell

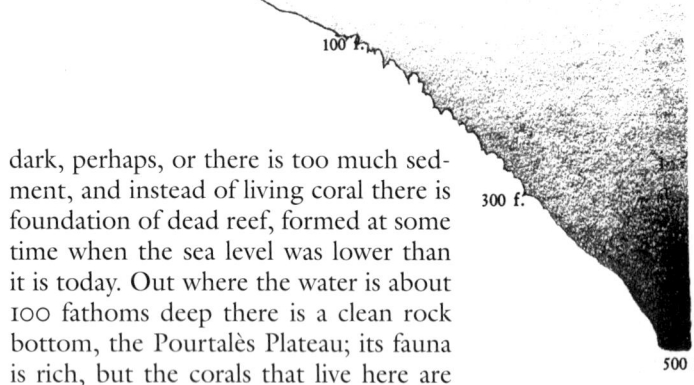

dark, perhaps, or there is too much sediment, and instead of living coral there is foundation of dead reef, formed at some time when the sea level was lower than it is today. Out where the water is about 100 fathoms deep there is a clean rock bottom, the Pourtalès Plateau; its fauna is rich, but the corals that live here are not reef builders. Between 300 and 500 fathoms sediments have again accumulated on a slope that descends to the trough of the Florida straits—the channel of the Gulf Stream.

As for the reef itself, many thousand thousand beings—plant and animal, living and dead—have entered into its composition. Corals of many species, building their little cups of lime and with them fashioning many strange and beautiful forms, are the foundation of the reef. But besides the corals there are other builders and all the interstices of the reef are filled with their shells or their limy tubes, or with coral rock cemented together with building stones of the most diverse origin. There are colonies of tube-building worms and there are mollusks of the snail tribe whose contorted, tubular shells may be intertwined into massive structures. Calcareous algae, which have the property of depositing lime in their living tissues, form part of the reef itself or, growing abundantly over the shallows on the landward side, add their substance at death to the coral sand of which limestone rock is later formed. The horny corals or gorgonians, known as sea fans and sea whips, all contain limestone spicules in their soft tissues. These, along with lime from starfish and sea urchins and sponges and an immense number of smaller creatures, will eventually, with the passage of time and through the chemistry of the sea, come to form part of the reef.

Along with those that build are others that destroy. The sulphur sponge dissolves away the calcareous rock. Boring mollusks riddle it with their tunnels, and worms with sharp, biting jaws eat into it, weakening its structure and so hastening the day when a mass of coral will yield to the force of the waves, will break away, and perhaps roll down the seaward face of the reef into deeper water.

The basis of this whole complex association is a minute creature of deceptively simple appearance, the coral polyp. The coral animal is formed on the same general lines as the sea anemone. It is a double-walled tube of cylindrical shape, closed at the base and open at the free end, where a crown of tentacles surrounds the mouth. The important difference—the fact on which the existence of coral reefs depends—is this: the coral polyp has the ability to secrete lime, forming a hard cup about itself. This is done by cells of the outer layer, much as the shell of a mollusk is secreted by an outer layer of soft tissue—the mantle. So the anemone-like coral polyp comes to sit in a compartment formed of a substance as hard as rock. Because the "skin" of the polyp is turned inward at intervals in a series of vertical folds, and because all of this skin is actively secreting lime, the cup does not have a smooth circumference, but is marked by partitions projecting inward, forming the starlike or flowerlike pattern familiar to anyone who has examined a coral skeleton.

Most corals build colonies of many individuals. All the individuals of any one colony, however, are derived from a single fertilized ovum that matured and then began to form new polyps by budding. The colony has a shape characteristic of the species—branched, boulderlike, flatly encrusting, or cup-shaped. Its core is solid, for only the surface is occupied by living polyps, which may be widely separated in some species or closely crowded in others. It is often true that the larger and more massive the colony, the smaller the individuals that compose it; the polyps of a branching coral taller than a man may themselves be only an eighth of an inch high.

The hard substance of the coral colony is usually white, but may take on the colors of minute plant cells that live within the soft tissues in a relation of mutual benefit. There is the exchange usual in such relations, the plants getting carbon dioxide and the animals making use of the oxygen given off by the plants. This particular association may have a deeper

Lima clams or file shells make nests of coral fragments and other debris. Sometimes the coral reef grows around these dens and imprisons the clams.

significance, however. The yellow, green, or brown pigments of the algae belong to the group of chemical substances known as carotinoids. Recent studies suggest that these pigments in the imprisoned algae may act on the corals, serving as "internal correlators" to influence the processes of reproduction. Under normal conditions, the presence of the algae seems to benefit the coral, but in dim light the coral animals rid themselves of the algae by excreting them. Perhaps this means that in weak light or in darkness the whole physiology of the plant is changed and the products of its metabolism are altered to something harmful, so that the animal must expel the plant guest.

Within the coral community there are other strange associations. In the Florida Keys and elsewhere in the West Indian region, a gall crab makes an oven-shaped cavity on the upper surface of a colony of living brain coral. As the coral grows the crab manages to keep open a semicircular entrance through which, while young, it enters and leaves its den. Once full grown, however, the crab is believed to be imprisoned within the coral. Few details of the existence of this Florida gall crab are known, but in a related species in corals of the Great Barrier

Reef only the females form galls. The males are minute, and apparently visit the females in the cavities where they are imprisoned. The female of this species depends on straining food organisms from indrawn currents of sea water and its digestive apparatus and appendages are much modified.

Everywhere, throughout the whole structure of the reef as well as inshore, the horny corals or gorgonians are abundant, sometimes outnumbering the corals. The violet-hued sea fan spreads its lace to the passing currents, and from all the structure of the fan innumerable mouths protrude through tiny pores, and tentacles reach out into the water to capture food. The little snail known as the flamingo tongue, wearing a solid and highly polished shell, often lives on the sea fans. The soft mantle, extended to cover the shell, is a pale flesh color with numerous black, roughly triangular markings. The gorgonians known as sea whips are more abundant, forming dense stands of undersea shrubbery, often waist-high, sometimes as tall as a man. Lilac, purple, yellow, orange, brown, and buff are the colors worn by these gorgonians of the coral reefs.

Encrusting sponges spread their mats of yellow, green, purple, and red over the walls of the reef; exotic mollusks like the jewel box and the spiny oyster cling to it; long-spined sea urchins make dark, bristling patches in the hollows and crevices; and schools of brightly colored fishes twinkle along the façade

Star coral (left); brain coral (center); starlet coral (right); massive species that help construct the outer reef.

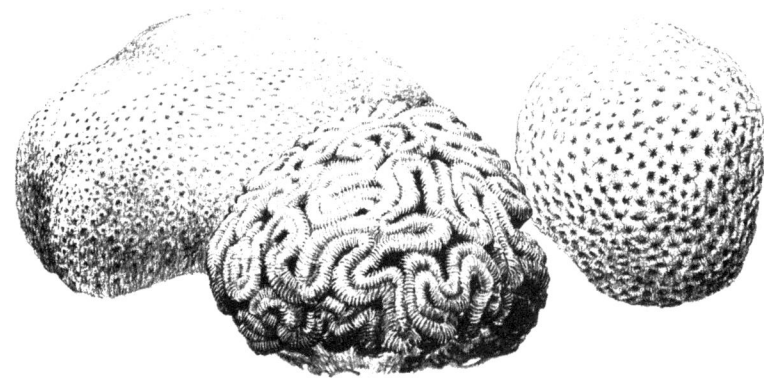

of the reef where the lone hunters, the gray snapper and the barracuda, wait to seize them.

At night the reef comes alive. From every stony branch and tower and domed façade, the little coral animals, who, avoiding daylight, had remained shrunken within their protective cups until darkness fell, now thrust out their tentacled heads and feed on the plankton that is rising toward the surface. Small crustacea and many other forms of microplankton, drifting or swimming against a branch of coral, are instant victims of the myriad stinging cells with which each tentacle is armed. Minute though the individual plankton animals be, the chances of passing unharmed through the interlacing branches of a stand of elkhorn coral seem slender indeed.

Other creatures of the reef respond to night and darkness and many of them emerge from the grottoes and crevices that served as daytime shelter. Even that strange hidden fauna of the massive sponges—the small shrimps and amphipods and other animals that live as unbidden guests deep within the canals of the sponge—at night creep up along those dark and narrow galleries and collect near their thresholds as though looking out upon the world of the reef.

On certain nights of the year, extraordinary events occur

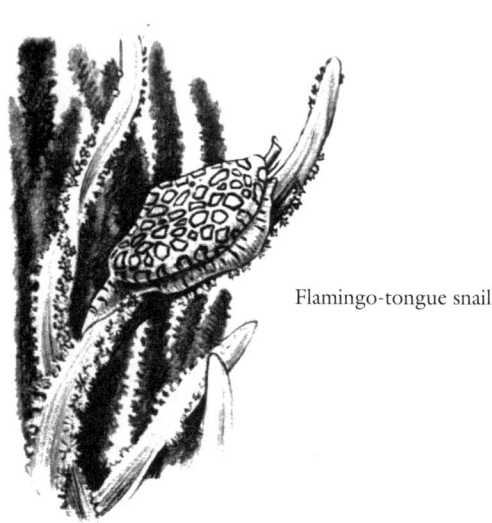

Flamingo-tongue snail

over the reefs. The famed palolo worm of the South Pacific, moved to gather in its prodigious spawning swarms on a certain moon of a certain month—and then only—has its less-known counterpart in a related worm that lives in the reefs of the West Indies and at least locally in the Florida Keys. The spawning of this Atlantic palolo has been observed repeatedly about the Dry Tortugas reefs, at Cape Florida, and in several West Indian localities. At Tortugas it takes place always in July, usually when the moon reaches its third quarter, though less often on the first quarter. The worms never spawn on the new moon.

Barracuda

The palolo inhabits burrows in dead coral rock, sometimes appropriating the tunnelings of other creatures, sometimes excavating its burrow by biting away fragments of rock. The life of this strange little creature seems to be ruled by light. In its immaturity the palolo is repelled by light—by sunlight, by the light of the full moon, even by paler moonlight. Only in the darkest hours of the night, when this strong inhibition of the light rays is removed, does it venture from its burrow, creeping out a few inches in order to nibble at the vegetation on the rocks. Then, as the season for spawning approaches, remarkable changes take place within the bodies of the worms. With the maturing of the sex cells, the segments of the posterior third of each animal take on a new color, deep pink in the males, greenish gray in the females. Moreover, this part of the body, distended with eggs or sperm, becomes exceedingly thin-walled and fragile, and a noticeable constriction develops between this and the anterior part of the worm.

At last there comes a night when these worms—so changed in their physical beings—respond in a new way to the light of the moon. No longer does the light repel and hold them prisoners within their burrows. Instead, it draws them out to the performance of a strange ritual. The worms back out of their burrows, thrusting out the swollen, thin-walled posterior ends, which immediately begin a series of twisting movements, writhing in spiral motions until suddenly the body breaks at the weak point and each worm becomes two. The two parts have different destinies—the one to remain behind in the burrow and resume the life of the timid forager of the dark hours, the other to swim up toward the surface of the sea, to become one of a vast swarm of thousands upon thousands of worms joining in the spawning activities of the species.

During the last hours of the night the number of swarming worms increases rapidly, and when dawn comes the sea over the reef is almost literally filled with them. When the first rays of the sun appear, the worms, strongly stimulated by the light, begin to twist and contract violently, their thin-walled bodies burst open, and the eggs from some and sperm from others are cast into the sea. The spent and empty worms may continue to swim weakly for a short time, preyed upon by fish that gather for a feast, but soon all that remain have sunk to the bottom and died. But floating at the surface of the sea are the fertilized eggs, drifting over areas many feet deep and acres in

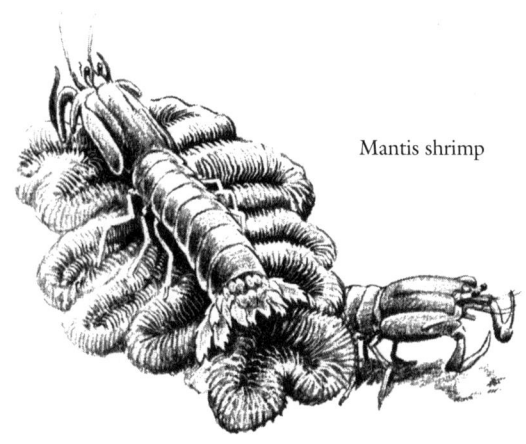

Mantis shrimp

extent. Within them swift changes have begun—the division of cells, the differentiation of structure. By evening of that same day the eggs have yielded up tiny larvae, swimming with spiral motions through the sea. For about three days the larvae live at the surface; then they become burrowers in the reefs below until, a year hence, they will repeat the spawning behavior of their kind.

Some related worms that swarm periodically about the Keys and the West Indies are luminous, creating beautiful pyrotechnic displays on dark nights. Some people believe that the mysterious light reported by Columbus as seen by him on the night of October 11, "about four hours before making the landfall and an hour before moonrise," may have been a display of some of these "fireworms."

The tides pouring in from the reefs and sweeping over the flats come to rest against the elevated coral rock of the shore. On some of the Keys the rock is smoothly weathered, with flattened surfaces and rounded contours, but on many others the erosive action of the sea has produced a rough and deeply pitted surface, reflecting the solvent action of centuries of waves and driven salt spray. It is almost like a stormy sea frozen into solidity, or as the surface of the moon might be. Little caves and solution holes extend above and below the line of the high tide. In such a place I am always strongly aware of the old, dead reef beneath my feet, and of the corals whose patterns, now crumbling and blurred, were once the delicately sculptured vessels that held the living creatures. All the builders now are dead—they have been dead for thousands of years—but that which they created remains, a part of the living present.

Crouching on the jagged rocks, I hear little murmurings and whisperings born of the movements of air and water over these surfaces—the audible voice of this nonhuman, intertidal world. There are few obvious signs of life to break the spell of brooding desolation. Perhaps a dark-bodied isopod—a sea roach—darts across the dry rock to disappear into one of the small sea caves, daring exposure to light and to sharp-eyed enemies only for the moment of its swift passage from one dark recess to another. There are thousands of its kind in the coral rock, but not until darkness covers the shore will they come

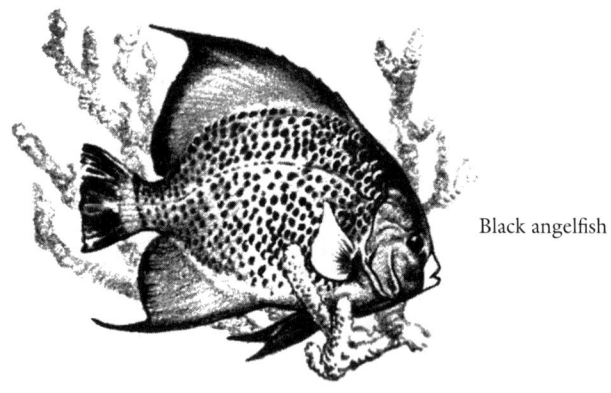

Black angelfish

out in numbers to search for the bits of animal and vegetable refuse that are their food.

At the high-tide line, growths of microscopic plants darken the coral rock, tracing that mysterious black line that marks the sea's edge on all rocky coasts of the world. Because of the irregular surface and deep dissection of the coral rock, the sea runs in under the high-tide rocks by way of crevices and depressions, and so the black zone darkens the jagged peaks and the rims of holes and little caves, while lighter rock of a yellowish-gray hue lines the depressions below that controlling tidal level.

Small snails whose shells are boldly striped or checked in black and white—the neritas—crowd down into cracks and cavities in the coral or rest on open rock surfaces waiting for the return of the tide when they can feed. Others, in rounded shells with roughly beaded surfaces, belong to the periwinkle tribe. Like many others of their kind, these beaded periwinkles are making a tentative invasion of the land, living under rocks or logs high on the shore or even entering the fringe of land vegetation. Black horn shells live in numbers just below the line of the high tides, feeding on the algal film over the rocks. The living snails are held by some intangible bonds to this tidal level, but the shells discarded after their death are found and taken as habitations by the smallest of the hermit crabs, who then carry them down onto the lower levels of the shore.

These deeply eroded rocks are the home of the chitons, whose primitive form harks back to some ancient group of mollusks of which they are the only living representatives. Their oval bodies, covered with a jointed shell of eight transverse plates, fit into depressions in the rocks when the tide is out. They grip the rocks so strongly that even heavy waves can get no hold on their sloping contours. When the high tide covers them, they begin to creep about, resuming their rasping of vegetation from the rocks, their bodies swaying to and fro in time to the scraping motions of the radula or file-like tongue. Month in and month out, a chiton moves only a few feet in any direction; because of this sedentary habit, the spores of algae and the larvae of barnacles and tube-building worms settle upon its shell and develop there. Sometimes, in dark wet caves, the chitons pile up, one on top of another, and each scrapes algae off the back of the one beneath it. In a small way these primitive mollusks may be an agent of geologic change as they feed on the rocks, each removing, along with the algae, minute scrapings of rock particles and so, over the centuries and the millennia in which this ancient race of beings has lived its simple life, contributing to the processes of erosion by which earth surfaces are worn away.

On some of these Keys a small intertidal mollusk called Onchidium lives deep in little rock caverns, the entrances of which are often overgrown by colonies of mussels. Although it is a mollusk and a snail, Onchidium has no shell. It belongs to a group that consists largely of land snails or slugs, in many of which the shell is lacking or concealed. Onchidium inhabits tropical seashores, living usually on beaches of roughly eroded rock. As the tide falls, processions of small black slugs emerge from their doorways, wriggling and pushing their way out through the impeding mussel threads, a dozen or more

Sea roaches

individuals coming out of a common cave to feed on the rocks, from which they scrape vegetation as the chitons do. As they emerge, each is invested with a tunic of slime that makes it look jet black, wet, and shining; in wind and sun the little slug dries to a deep blue-black, over which is a slight, milky bloom.

On these journeys the slugs seem to follow haphazard or irregular paths over the rocks. They continue feeding as the tide falls to its lowest ebb, and even as it turns and begins to rise. About half an hour before the returning sea has reached them, and before so much as a drop of water has splashed into their nests, all of the slugs cease their grazing and begin to return to the home nest. While the outgoing path was meandering, the return is by a direct route. The members of each community return to their own nest, even though the way may lie over greatly eroded rock surfaces and even though the path may cross the routes of other slugs returning to other nests. All of the individuals belonging to one nest-community, even though they may have been widely separated while feeding, begin the return journey at almost the same moment. What is the stimulus? It is not the returning water, for that has not touched them; when it laps again over their rocks they will be safe within their nests.

The whole pattern of behavior of this little creature is puzzling. Why should it be drawn to live again at the edge of the sea that its ancestors deserted thousands or millions of years ago? It comes forth only when the tide has fallen, then,

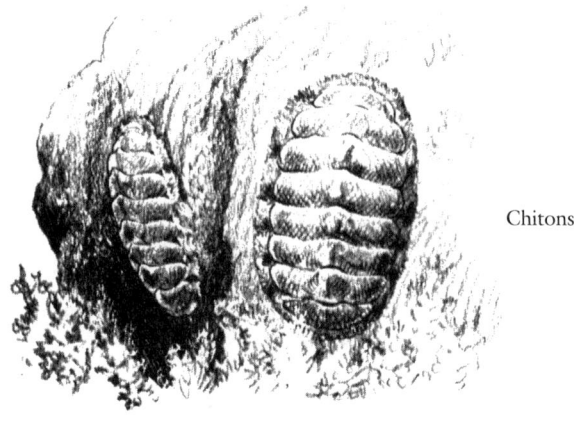

Chitons

somehow sensing the impending return of the sea and seeming to remember its recent affinities with the land, it hurries to safety before the tide can find it and carry it away. How has it acquired this behavior, attracted yet repelled by the sea? We can only ask these questions; we cannot answer them.

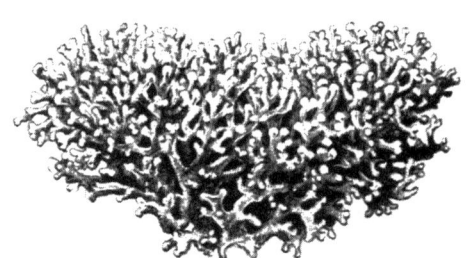

A lime-secreting alga, Goniolithon

For its protection during the feeding journeys, Onchidium is equipped with means of detecting and driving away its enemies. Minute papillae on its back are sensitive to light and passing shadows. Other, stouter papillae associated with the mantle are equipped with glands that secrete a milky, highly acid fluid. If the animal is suddenly disturbed, it expels spurting streams of this acid, the streams breaking up in the air to a fine spray that may be thrown five or six inches, or as much as a dozen times the length of the animal. The old German zoologist Semper, who studied a species of Onchidium in the Philippines, believed this dual equipment served to protect the slug from the beach-hopping blenny, a fish of many tropical mangrove coasts that leaps along above the tide, feeding on Onchidium and crabs. Semper thought the slugs could detect the shadow of an approaching fish and drive off the enemy by discharging the white acid spray. In Florida or elsewhere in the West Indian region there is no fish that comes out of water to pursue its prey. On the rocks where Onchidium must feed there are, however, scrambling crabs and isopods whose jostlings might well push the slugs into the water, for they have no means of gripping the rocks. For whatever reason, the slugs react to the crabs and to the isopods as to dangerous enemies, responding to their touch by discharging the repellant chemical.

In the strip between tropical tide lines, conditions are difficult for nearly all forms of life. The heat of the sun increases the hazards of exposure during the withdrawal of the tide. The shifting layers of choking sediment, accumulating on flat or gently sloping surfaces, discourage many plants and animals of types that inhabit rocky shores in the clearer, cooler waters of the north. Instead of the vast barnacle and mussel fields of New England there are only scattering patches of these creatures, varying from Key to Key but never really abundant. Instead of the great rockweed forests of the north, there are only scattered growths of small algae, including various brittle, lime-secreting forms, none of which offer shelter or security to any considerable number of animals.

If the area marked out by the advance and retreat of the neap tides is in general inhospitable, there are nevertheless two forms of life—one plant, one animal—that are thoroughly at home there, and live in profusion nowhere else. The plant is a peculiarly beautiful alga that resembles spheres of green glass clustered together in irregular masses. It is Valonia, the sea bottle, a green alga that forms large vesicles filled with a sap that bears a definite chemical relation to the water about it, varying the proportions of its contained ions of sodium and potassium according to variations in the intensity of sunlight, the exposure to surf, and other conditions of its world. Under overhanging rock and in other sheltered places it forms sheets and masses of its emerald globules, lying half buried in deep drifts of sediment.

Solitary vermetid snail
embedded in sponge

Intertwined shells of colonial vermetids

The animal symbol of this intertidal world of coral is a group of snails whose whole structure and being represent an extraordinary contrast to the way of life typical of this class of mollusks. They are called the vermetid or "wormlike" snails. The shell is no ordinary gastropod spire or cone, but a loose uncoiled tube very like the calcareous tubes built by many worms. The species that inhabit this intertidal zone have become colonial, and their tubes form closely packed and intertwined masses.

The very nature of these vermetid snails and their departure from the form and habits of related mollusks are eloquent of the circumstances of their world and of the readiness of life to adapt itself to a vacant niche. Here on this coral platform the tide ebbs and flows twice daily, and each flood brings renewed food supplies from offshore. There is but one perfect way to exploit such rich supplies: to remain in one place and fish the currents as they stream by. This is done on other shores by such animals as the barnacles, the mussels, and the tube-building worms. It is not ordinarily a snail's way of life, but in adaptation these extraordinary snails have become sedentary, abandoning the typical roaming habit. No longer solitary, they have become gregarious to an extreme degree, living in crowded colonies, with shells so intertwined that early geologists called their formations "worm rock." And they have given up the snail habits of scraping food from the rocks or of hunting and devouring other animals of large size; instead they draw the sea water into their bodies and strain out the minute planktonic food organisms. The tips of their gills are thrust out and drawn through the water like nets—an adaptation probably unique in all the group of snail-like mollusks. The vermetids give their own clear demonstration of the plasticity of the living organism

Flower anemone, Zoanthus. Anemones (upper left) exposed to show structure; in life often burrow to tentacles in silt, as at right.

and its responsiveness to the world about it. Again and again, in group after group of widely different and unrelated animals, the same problem has been met and solved by the evolution of diverse structures that function for a common purpose. So the legions of the barnacles sweep food from the tides on a New England shore, using a modification of what in their relatives would be a swimming appendage; mole crabs gather by the thousand where surf sweeps the southern beaches, straining out food with the bristles of their antennae; and here on this coral shore the crowded masses of this strange snail filter the waters of the incoming tide through their gills. By becoming the imperfect, the atypical snail, they have become the perfectly adapted exploiter of the opportunities of their world.

The edge of the low tide is a dark line traced by colonies of short-spined, rock-boring sea urchins. Every hole and every depression in the coral rock bristles with their small dark bodies. One spot in the Keys lives in my memory as an urchin paradise. This is the seaward shore of one of the eastern group of islands, where the rock drops in an abrupt terrace, somewhat undercut and deeply eroded into holes and small caves, many with their roofs open to the sky. I have stood on the dry rock above the tide and looked down into these little water-floored, rock-walled grottoes, finding twenty-five to thirty urchins in one of these caverns that was no larger than a bushel basket. The caves shine with a green water-light in the sun, and in this light the globular bodies of the urchins have a reddish color of glowing, luminous quality, in rich contrast to the black spines.

THE CORAL COAST

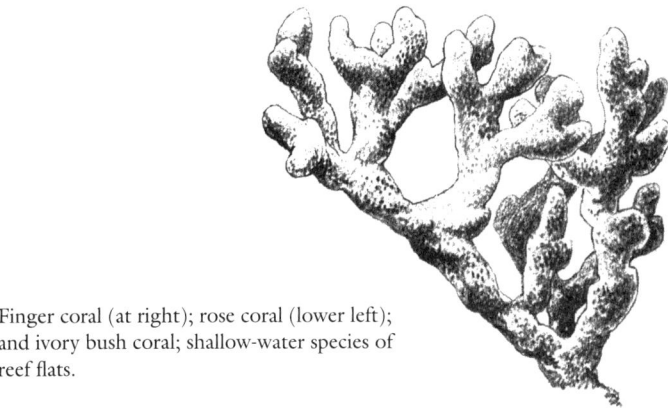

Finger coral (at right); rose coral (lower left); and ivory bush coral; shallow-water species of reef flats.

A little beyond this spot the sea bottom slopes under water more gradually, with no undercutting. Here the rock borers seem to have taken over every niche that can afford shelter; they give the illusion of shadows beside each small irregularity of bottom. It is not certain whether they use the five short stout teeth on their under surfaces to scrape out holes in the rock, or perhaps merely take advantage of natural depressions to find a safe anchorage against the occasional storms that sweep this coast. For some inscrutable reason, these rock-boring urchins

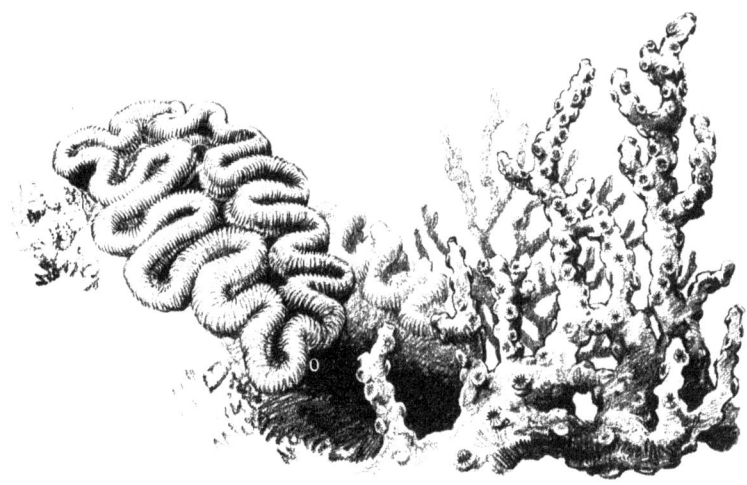

and related species in other parts of the world are bound to this particular tidal level, linked to it precisely and mysteriously by invisible ties that prevent their wandering farther out over the reef flat, although other species of urchins are abundant there.

Above and below the zone of the rock-boring urchins, closely crowded throngs of pale brown tubular creatures push up through the chalky sediment. When the tide leaves them their tissues retract and all that proclaims them to be animals is hidden; then one might pass them by as some strange marine fungi. With the return of the water their animal nature is revealed, and from each fawn-colored tube a crown of tentacles, of purest emerald green, is unfolded as each of these anemone-like creatures begins to search the tide for the food it has brought. Living where their very existence depends on keeping the delicate tissues of the tentacles above the choking dust of sediment, these zoanthids are able to stretch their bodies into slender threads where the sediments are deep, though normally their tubes are short and stout.

On the seaward side of many of the Keys the bottom slopes gently, with wading depths for perhaps a quarter of a mile or more. Once beyond the rock-boring sea urchins, the vermetid snails, and the green and brown jewel anemones, the bottom of coarse sand and coral fragments begins to be marked by dark patches of turtle grass, and larger animals begin to inhabit the reef flats. Sponges, dark and bulky, grow in water only deep enough to cover their massive forms. Small, shallow-water corals, somehow able to survive the rain of sediments that would be fatal to the larger reef-builders, erect their hard structures, stoutly branched or domed, on the floor of coral rock. The gorgonians, plantlike in their habit of growth, are a low shrubbery of delicate rose and brown and purple hues. And within and among and beneath them all is the infinitely varied fauna of a tropical coast, as many creatures that wander freely through the waters of this warm sea crawl or swim or glide over the flats.

Massive and inert, the loggerhead sponges by their appearance suggest nothing of the activity that goes on within their dark bulks. There is no sign of life for the casual passer-by to read, although if he waited and watched long enough he might sometimes see the deliberate closing of some of the round openings, large enough to admit an exploring finger, that penetrate the flat upper surface. These and other openings are the key to the nature of the giant sponge which, like even the smallest of its group, can exist only as long as it can keep the waters of the sea circulating through its body. Its vertical walls are pierced by intake canals of small diameter, groups of them covered by sieve plates with numerous perforations. From these the canals lead almost horizontally into the interior of the sponge, branching and rebranching into tubes of progressively smaller bore, to penetrate all the massive bulk of the sponge and finally to lead up to the large exit canals.

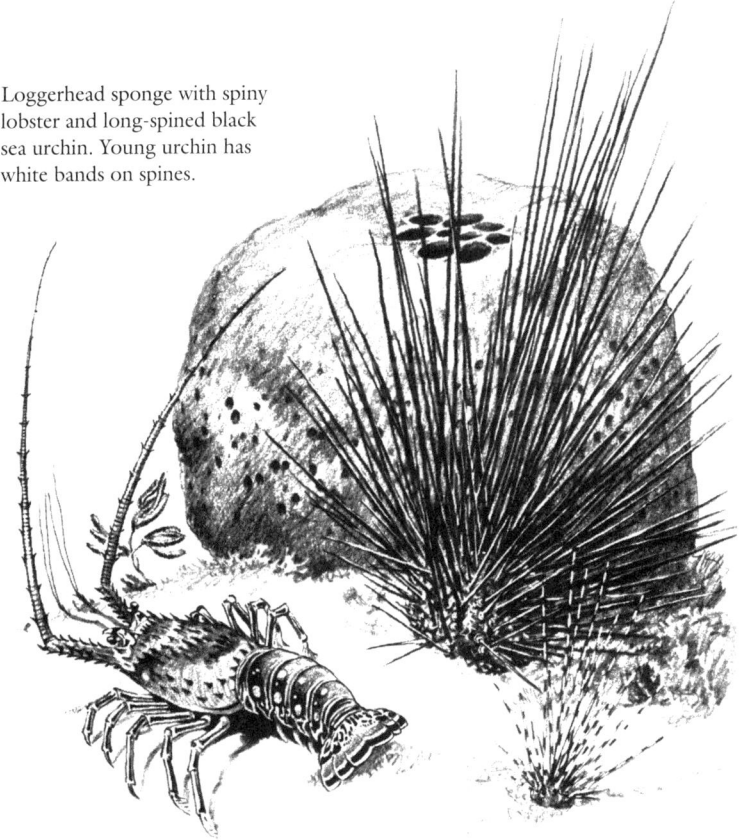

Loggerhead sponge with spiny lobster and long-spined black sea urchin. Young urchin has white bands on spines.

Snapping shrimp in passageways of loggerhead sponge. Detail of snapping claw at left; movable finger with suckers and peg fitting into socket.

Perhaps these exit holes are kept free of choking sediment by the strength of the outbound currents; at any rate they are the only part of the sponge that shows a pure black color, for the flour-like whiteness of the reef sediments has been sifted over all the sooty black surface of the body.

In its passage through the sponge, the water leaves a coating of minute food organisms and organic detritus on the walls of the canals; the cells of the sponge pick up the food, pass the digestible materials along from cell to cell, and return waste material to the flowing currents. Oxygen passes into the sponge cells; carbon dioxide is given off. And sometimes small sponge larvae, having undergone the early stages of their development within the parent sponge, detach themselves and enter the dark flowing river, to pass with it into the sea.

The intricate passageways, the shelter and available food they offer, have attracted many small creatures to live within the sponge. Some come and go; others never leave the sponge once they have taken up residence within it. One such permanent lodger is a small shrimp—one of the group known as snapping shrimp because of the sound made by snapping the large claw. Although the adults are imprisoned, the young shrimp, hatched from eggs adhering to the appendages of their mothers, pass out with the water currents into the sea and live for a time in the currents and tides, drifting, swimming, perhaps carried far afield. By mischance they may occasionally find their way into deep water where no sponges grow. But many of the young shrimp will in time find and approach the dark bulk of some loggerhead sponge and, entering it, will take up the strange life of their parents. Wandering through its dark halls, they scrape food from the walls of the sponge. As they creep along these cylindrical passageways, they carry their antennae and their large claws extended before them, as though to sense the approach of a larger and possibly dangerous creature, for the sponge has many lodgers of many species—other shrimps, amphipods, worms, isopods—and their numbers may reach into the thousands if the sponge is large.

There, on the flats off some of the Keys, I have opened small loggerheads and heard the warning snapping of claws as the resident shrimps, small, amber-colored beings, hurried into the deeper cavities. I had heard the same sound filling the air about me, as, on an evening low tide, I waded in to the shore. From all the exposed reef rock there were strange little knockings and hammerings, yet the sounds, to a maddening degree, were impossible to locate. Surely this nearby hammering came from this particular bit of rock; yet when I knelt to examine it closely there was silence; then from all around, from everywhere but this bit of rock at hand, all the elfin hammering was resumed. I could never find the little shrimps in the rocks, yet I knew they were related to those I had seen in the loggerhead sponges. Each has one immense hammer claw almost as long as the rest of its body. The movable finger of the claw bears a peg that fits into a socket in the rigid finger. Apparently the movable finger, when raised, is held in position by suction. To lower it, extra muscular force must be applied, and when the suction is overcome, it snaps into place with audible sound, at the same time ejecting a spurt of water from its socket. Perhaps the water jet repels enemies and aids in capturing prey, which may also be stunned by a blow from the forcibly retracted claw. Whatever the value of the mechanism, the snapping shrimps are so abundant in the shallows of tropical and subtropical regions, and snap their claws so incessantly, that they are responsible for much of the extraneous noise picked up on underwater listening devices, filling the water world with a continuous sizzling, crackling sound.

It was on the reef flats off Ohio Key, on a day early in May, that I had my first, startled encounter with tropical sea hares. I was wading over a part of the flat that had an unusually heavy growth of rather tall seaweeds when sudden movement drew my eyes to several heavy-bodied, foot-long animals moving among the weeds. They were a pale tan color, marked with black rings, and when I touched one cautiously with my foot, it responded instantly by expelling a concealing cloud of fluid the color of cranberry juice.

I had met my first sea hare years before on the North Carolina coast. It was a small creature about as long as my little finger, browsing peacefully among some seaweeds near a stone jetty. I slipped my hand under it and gently brought it toward me, then, its identity confirmed, I returned the little creature carefully to the algae, where it resumed its grazing. Only by drastic revision of my mental image could I accept these tropical creatures, which seemed to belong in some book of mythology, as relatives of that first little elfin being.

The large West Indian sea hares inhabit the Florida Keys as well as the Bahamas, Bermuda, and the Cape Verde Islands. Within their range they usually live offshore, but at the spawning season they move in to the shallows, where I had found them, to attach their eggs, in tangled threads, to the weeds near the low-tide mark. They are marine snails of a sort, but have lost their external shells and possess only an internal remnant, hidden by the soft mantle tissue. Two prominent tentacles suggestive of ears, and the rabbit-like body shape, are responsible for the common name (see page 639).

Whether because of its strange appearance, or because of its defensive fluids, often thought to be poisonous, the Old World sea hare has long had a secure place in folk lore, superstition, and witchcraft. Pliny declared it was poisonous to the touch, and recommended as an antidote asses' milk and ground asses' bones, boiled together. Apuleius, known chiefly as the author of *The Golden Ass*, became curious about the internal anatomy of the sea hare and persuaded two fishermen to bring him a specimen; whereupon he was accused of witchcraft and poisoning. Some fifteen centuries were to pass before anyone else ventured to publish a description of the internal anatomy of the creature—then Redi in 1684 described it, and although popular belief called it sometimes a worm, sometimes a holothurian, sometimes a fish, he placed it correctly, at least as to general relationships, as a marine slug. For the past century or more the harmless nature of the sea hares has been recognized for the most part, but although they are fairly well known in Europe and Great Britain, the American sea hares, largely confined to tropical waters, are less familiar animals.

Perhaps this anonymity is due in part to the infrequency of their spawning migrations into tidal waters. An individual animal is both male and female; it may function as either sex, or as both. In laying its eggs, the sea hare extrudes a long thread in little spurts, about an inch at a time, continuing the slow process until the string has reached a length sometimes as great as 65 feet, and contains about 100,000 eggs. As the pink or orange-colored thread is expelled it curls about the surrounding vegetation, forming a tangled mass of spawn. The eggs and the resulting young meet the common fate of marine creatures; many eggs are destroyed, being eaten by crustacea or other predators (even by their own kind), and many of the hatching larvae fail to survive the dangers of life in the plankton. In the drift of the currents the larvae are carried offshore, and when they undergo metamorphosis to the adult form and seek the bottom they are in deep water. Their color changes with changing food as they migrate shoreward: first they are a deep rose color, then they are brown, then olive-green like the adults. For one of the European species, at least, the known life history suggests a curious parallel with that of the Pacific salmon. With maturity, the sea hares turn shoreward to spawn. It is a journey from which there is no return; they do not reappear on the offshore feeding grounds, but apparently die after this single spawning.

The world of the reef flats is inhabited by echinoderms of every sort: starfishes, brittle stars, sea urchins, sand dollars, and holothurians all are at home on the coral rock, in the shifting coral sands, among the gorgonian sea gardens and the grass-carpeted bottoms. All are important in the economy of the marine world—as links in the living chains by which materials are taken from the sea, passed from one to another, returned to the sea, borrowed again. Some are important also in the geologic processes of earth building and earth destruction—the processes by which rock is worn away and ground to sand, by which the sediments that carpet the sea floor are accumulated, shifted, sorted, and distributed. And at death their hard skeletons contribute calcium for the needs of other animals or for the building of the reefs.

Out on the reefs the long-spined black sea urchin excavates cavities along the base of the coral wall; each sinks into its depression and turns its spines outward, so that a swimmer moving along the reef sees forests of black quills. This urchin also wanders in over the reef flats, where it nestles close to the base of a loggerhead sponge, or sometimes, apparently finding no need of concealment, rests in open, sand-floored areas.

A full-grown black urchin may have a body or test nearly 4 inches in diameter, with spines 12 to 15 inches long. This is one of the comparatively few shore animals that are poisonous to the touch, and the effect of contact with one of the slender, hollow spines is said to be like that of a hornet sting, or may even be more serious for a child or an especially susceptible adult. Apparently the mucous coating of the spines bears the irritant or poison.

This urchin is extraordinary in the degree of its awareness of the surroundings. A hand extended over it will cause all the spines to swivel about on their mountings, pointing menacingly at the intruding object. If the hand is moved from side to side the spines swing about, following it. According to Professor Norman Millott of the University College of the West Indies, nerve receptors scattered widely over the body receive the message conveyed by a change in the intensity of light, responding most sharply to suddenly decreased light as a shadowy portent of danger. To this extent, then, the urchin may actually "see" moving objects passing nearby.

Linked in some mysterious way with one of the great rhythms of nature, this sea urchin spawns at the time of the full moon. The eggs and sperm are shed into the water once in each lunar month during the summer season, on the nights of strongest moonlight. Whatever the stimulus to which all the individuals of the species respond, it assures that prodigal and simultaneous release of reproductive cells that nature often demands for the perpetuation of a species.

Off some of the Keys, in shallow water, lives the so-called slate-pencil urchin, named for its short stout spines. This is an urchin of solitary habit, single individuals sheltering under or among the reef rocks near the low-tide level. It seems a sluggish creature of dull perceptions, unaware of the presence of an intruder, and making no effort to cling by means of its tube feet when it is picked up. It belongs to the only family of modern echinoderms that also existed in Paleozoic time; the recent members of the group show little change from the form of ancestors that lived hundreds of millions of years ago.

Another urchin with short and slender spines and color variations ranging from deep violet to green, rose, or white, sometimes occurs abundantly on sandy bottoms carpeted with turtle grass, camouflaging itself with bits of grass and shell and coral fragments held in its tube feet. Like many other urchins, it performs a geologic function. Nibbling away at shells and coral rock with its white teeth, it chips off fragments that are then passed through the grinding mill of its digestive tract; these organic fragments, trimmed, ground, and polished within the urchins, contribute to the sands of tropical beaches.

And the tribes of the starfish and the brittle stars are everywhere represented on these coral flats. The great sea star, Oreaster, stout and powerful of body, perhaps lives more abundantly a little offshore, where whole constellations of them gather on the white sand. But solitary specimens wander inshore, seeking especially the grassy areas.

A small reddish-brown starfish, Linkia, has the strange habit of breaking off an arm, which then grows a cluster of four new arms that are temporarily in a "comet" form. Sometimes the animal breaks across the central disc; regeneration may result

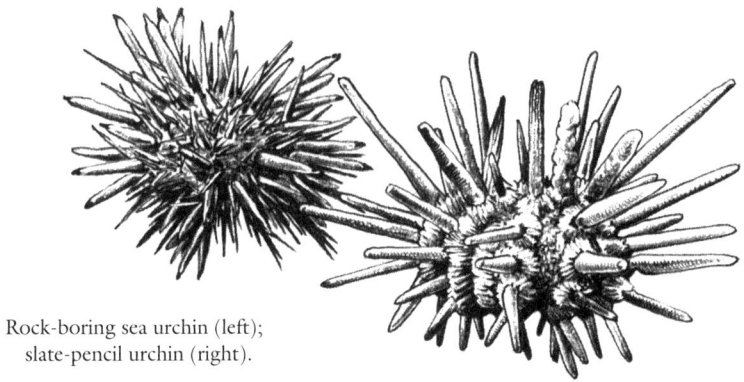

Rock-boring sea urchin (left); slate-pencil urchin (right).

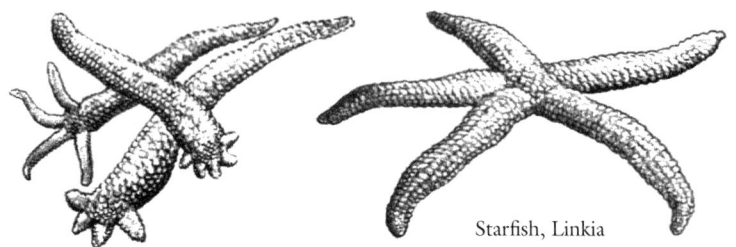

Starfish, Linkia

in six- or seven-rayed animals. These divisions seem to be a method of reproduction practiced by the young, for adult animals cease to fragment and produce eggs.

About the bases of gorgonians, under and inside of sponges, under movable rocks and down in little, eroded caverns in the coral rock live the brittle stars. With their long and flexible arms, each composed of a series of "vertebrae" shaped like hourglasses, they are capable of sinuous and graceful motion. Sometimes they stand on the tips of two arms and sway in the motion of the water currents, bending the other arms in movements as graceful as those of a ballet dancer. They creep over the substratum by throwing two of their arms forward and pulling up the body or disc and the remaining arms. The brittle stars feed on minute mollusks and worms and other small animals. In turn, they are eaten by many fish and other predators, and sometimes fall victims to certain parasites. A small green alga may live in the skin of the brittle star; there it dissolves the calcareous plates, so that the arms may break apart. Or a curious little degenerate copepod may live as a parasite within the gonads, destroying them and rendering the animal sterile.

My first meeting with a live West Indian basket star was something I shall never forget. I was wading off Ohio Key in water little more than knee deep when I found it among some seaweeds, gently drifting on the tide. Its upper surface was the color of a young fawn, with lighter shades beneath. The searching, exploring, testing branchlets at the tips of the arms reminded me of the delicate tendrils by which a growing vine seeks out places to which it may attach itself. For many minutes I stood beside it, lost to all but its extraordinary and somehow fragile beauty. I had no wish to "collect" it; to disturb such a being would have seemed a desecration. Finally the rising tide and the need to visit other parts of the flat before they became too deeply flooded drove me on, and when I returned the basket star had disappeared.

The basket starfish or basket fish is related to the brittle stars and serpent stars but displays remarkable differences of structure: each of the five arms diverges into branching V's, which branch again, and then again and again until a maze of curling tendrils forms the periphery of the animal. Indulging their taste for the dramatic, early naturalists named the basket stars for those monsters of Greek mythology, the Gorgons, who wore snakes in place of hair and whose hideous aspect was supposed to turn men to stone; so the family comprising these bizarre echinoderms is known as the Gorgonocephalidae. To some imaginations their appearance may be "snaky-locked," but the effect is one of beauty, grace, and elegance.

All the way from the Arctic to the West Indies basket stars of one species or another live in coastal waters, and many go down to lightless sea bottoms nearly a mile beneath the surface. They may walk about over the ocean floor, moving delicately on the tips of their arms. As Alexander Agassiz long ago described it, the animal stands "as it were on tiptoe, so that the ramifications of the arms form a kind of trellis-work all around it, reaching to the ground, while the disk forms a roof." Or

Spiny brittle star, dark with creamy markings, common on tropical shores. Disc may be an inch across with six-inch arms.

again they may cling to gorgonians or other fixed sea growths and reach out into the water. The branching arms serve as a fine-meshed net to ensnare small sea creatures. On some grounds the basket stars are not only abundant but associate in herds of many individuals as though for a common purpose. Then the arms of neighboring animals become entwined in a continuous living net to capture all the small fry of the sea who venture, or are helplessly carried, within reach of the millions of grasping tendrils.

To see a basket starfish close inshore is one of those rare happenings that lives always in memory, but it is far otherwise with certain other members of the spiny-skinned tribe of echinoderms—the holothurians, or sea cucumbers. I have never waded far out onto the flats without meeting them. Their large dark forms, shaped much like the vegetable whose

Gorgonian sea whip, basket starfish, sea fan, young black angelfish, and gorgonian sea whip.

name they have been given, stand out clearly against the white sand where they lie sluggishly, sometimes partly buried. The holothurians perform a function in the sea that is roughly comparable to that of earthworms on land, ingesting quantities of sand and mud and passing it through their bodies. Most of them use a crown of blunt tentacles operated by strong muscles to shovel the bottom sediments into their mouths, then extract food particles from this detritus as it passes through their bodies. Perhaps some calcareous materials are dissolved out by the chemistry of the holothurian body.

Because of their abundance and the nature of their activities, the sea cucumbers profoundly influence the distribution of the

West Indian sea cucumber

bottom deposits around the coral reefs and islands. In a single year, it has been estimated, the holothurians in an area less than two miles square may redistribute 1000 tons of bottom substance. And there is evidence also concerning their work on sea bottoms lying at abyssal depths. The carpeting sediments, which accumulate slowly but unceasingly, lie in orderly layers from which geologists can read many chapters of the past history of the earth. But sometimes the layers are curiously disturbed. Bits of volcanic ash shard originating, for example, from some ancient eruptions of Vesuvius, may in some places lie, not in a thin layer representing and dating the eruption, but widely scattered through the overlying layers of other sediments. Geologists regard this as the work of deep-sea holothurians. And other evidence from deep dredgings and bottom samplings suggests the existence of herds of holothurians on the sea floor at great depths, working over a bottom area, then moving on in a vast migration directed, not by seasonal change, but by the scarcity of food in those deep and lightless regions.

Except in those parts of the world where they are sought as human food (they are the "trepang," or *bêche-de-mer*, of Oriental markets) the sea cucumbers have few known enemies, yet they possess a strange defense mechanism that they employ when strongly disturbed. Then the holothurian may contract strongly and hurl out the greater part of its internal organs through a rupture in the body wall. Sometimes this action is suicidal, but often the creature continues to live and grows a new set of organs.

Dr. Ross Nigrelli and his associates of the New York Zoological Society have recently discovered that the large West Indian sea cucumber (also found about the Florida Keys) produces one of the most powerful of all known animal poisons, presumably as a chemical means of defense. Laboratory experiments showed that even small doses of the poison affect all kinds of animals, from protozoa to mammals. Fish confined in a tank with the cucumber always die when the act of evisceration occurs. The study of this natural toxin reveals the hazardous existence of many small creatures that live in association with another. The sea cucumber attracts a number of such animal associates or commensals. This particular species very often has a small pearl fish, Fierasfer, living within the shelter of the cloacal cavity, which the respiratory activities of the cucumber keep supplied with well-oxygenated water. But the well-being, and indeed the very life of the small Fierasfer seem to be constantly endangered, for the commensal fish is actually living beside a vat of deadly poison that may at any moment be ruptured. Apparently the fish has not developed an immunity to the poison of the holothurian, for Dr. Nigrelli found that if the cucumber was disturbed, its tenant Fierasfer would drift out in a moribund condition, even if actual evisceration did not take place.

Dark patches like the shadows of clouds are scattered over the inshore shallows of the reef flats. Each is a dense growth of sea grass pushing up flat blades through the sand, forming a drowned island of shelter and security for many animals. About the Keys these grass patches consist largely of stands of turtle grass, with which manatee grass and shoal grass may be intermingled. All belong to the highest group of plants—the seed plants—and so are different from the algae or seaweeds. The algae are the earth's oldest plants, and they have always belonged to the sea or the fresh waters. But the seed plants originated on land only within the past 60 million years or so and those now living in the sea are descended from ancestors who returned to it from the land—how or why it is hard to say. Now they live where the salt sea covers them and rises above them. They open their flowers under the water; their pollen is water-borne; their seeds mature and fall and are carried away

Lightning or left-handed whelk

by the tide. Thrusting down their roots into the sand and the shifting coral debris, the sea grasses achieve a firmer attachment than the rootless algae do; where they grow thickly they help to secure the offshore sands against the currents, as on land the dune grasses hold the dry sands against the winds.

In the islands of turtle grass many animals find food and shelter. The giant starfish, Oreaster, lives here. So do the large pink or queen conch, the fighting conch, the tulip band shell, the helmet shells and the cask shells. A strange, armor-encased fish, the cowfish, swims just above the bottom, parting grass blades to which pipefish and sea horses cling. Baby octopuses hide among the roots and when pursued dive down deep into the yielding sand and disappear from view. Down in that grass-root under-turf many other small beings, of diverse kinds, live deep within the shadowed coolness, to come out only when night and darkness hide them.

But by day many of the bolder inhabitants may be seen by one who wades to the grassy patches and peers down through the clarifying glass of a water telescope, or, swimming above the deeper patches, looks down through a face mask. Here one is most apt to find, in life, the large mollusks that are familiar because their dead and empty shells are common on the beach or in shell collections.

Here in the grass is the queen conch, which in earlier days had a place on almost every Victorian mantel or hearth, and even today is displayed by the hundred at every Florida roadside stand selling tourist souvenirs. Through excessive fishing, however, it is becoming rare in the Florida Keys and is now exported from the Bahamas for use in cutting cameos. The weight and massiveness of its shell, the sharp spire and the heavily armored whorls are eloquent of the defenses raised, through the slow interaction of biology and environment, by myriad ancestral generations. Despite the cumbrous shell and the massive body that thrusts itself out to move over the bottom by grotesque leaps and tumblings, the queen conch seems an alert and sentient creature. Perhaps this effect is heightened by the eyes borne on the tips of two long tubular tentacles. The way the eyes are moved and directed leaves little doubt that they receive impressions of the animal's surroundings and transmit them to the nerve centers that serve in place of a brain.

Although its strength and awareness seem to fit the queen conch for a predatory life, it is probably a scavenger that only occasionally turns to live prey. Its enemies must be comparatively few and ineffectual, but the conch has formed one very curious association. A small fish habitually lives within its mantle cavity. There can be little free space when all of the body and foot are drawn into the shell, but somehow there is room for the cardinal fish, an inch-long creature. Whenever danger threatens, it darts into the fleshy cavern deep within the shell

Tulip shell

of the conch. There it is temporarily imprisoned when the snail pulls back into its shell and closes the sickle-shaped operculum.

To other, smaller beings that find their way into the interior of the shell, the conch reacts less tolerantly. Current-borne eggs of many sea creatures, larvae of marine worms, minute shrimp or even fish, or non-living particles like grains of sand, may swim or drift inside and, lodging on shell or mantle, set up an irritation. To this the conch responds with ancient defenses, acting to wall off the particle so that it can no longer irritate delicate tissues. The glands of the mantle secrete about this nucleus of foreign matter layer after layer of mother-of-pearl —the same lustrous substance that lines the inside of the shell. In this way the conch creates the pink pearls sometimes found within it.

The human swimmer drifting idly above the turtle grass—if he is patient enough and observant enough—may see something of other lives being lived above the coral sand, from which the thin flat blades of grass reach upward and sway to the motion of the water, leaning shoreward on a flooding tide and seaward on the ebb. If, for example, he looks very carefully he may see what he had thought to be a blade of grass (so perfectly did it simulate one by form and color and movement)

Queen or pink conch

detach itself from the sand and go swimming through the water. The pipefish—an incredibly long, slender, and bony-ringed creature that seems quite unfishlike—swims between the grasses slowly and with deliberate movement, now with its body held vertically, now leaning horizontally into the water. The slim head with its long, bony snout is thrust with probing motions into clusters of turtle grass leaves or down among the roots, as the fish searches for small food animals. Suddenly there is a quick, inflating motion of the cheek, and a tiny crustacean is sucked in through the tube-like beak, as one would suck a soda through a straw.

The pipefish begins life in a strange manner, being developed, nurtured, and reared beyond the stage of helpless infancy by the male parent, who keeps his young within a protective pouch. During the mating act of the pair, the ova are fertilized and are placed in this pouch by the female; there they develop and hatch, and to this marsupium the young may return again and again in moments of danger, even long after they are able to swim out into the sea at will.

So effective is the camouflage of another inhabitant of the grass—the sea horse—that only the sharpest eye can detect one at rest, its flexible tail gripping a blade of grass and its bony little body leaning out into the currents like a piece of vegetation. The sea horse is completely encased in an armor composed of interlocking bony plates; these take the place of ordinary scales and seem to be a sort of evolutionary harking back to the time when fish depended on heavy armor to protect them from their enemies. The edges of the plates, where they join and interlock, are produced into ridges, knobs, and spines to form the characteristic surface pattern.

Sea horses often live in vegetation that is floating rather than rooted; such individuals may then become part of that steady northward drift bearing plants, associated animals, and the larvae of countless sea forms into the open Atlantic and eastward toward Europe, or into the Sargasso Sea. Such sea-horse voyagers in the Gulf Stream sometimes are carried ashore on the southern Atlantic coast along with bits of wind- and current-borne sargassum weed to which they cling.

In some of the turtle-grass jungles all of the smaller inhabitants seem to borrow a protective color from their surroundings.

I have dragged a small dredge in such a place and found, entangled in the handfuls of grass that came up, dozens of small animals of different species, all an amazing, bright green hue. There were green spider crabs with extremely long, jointed legs. There were small shrimp, also grass-green. Perhaps the most fantastic touch was contributed by several baby cowfish. Like their elders, whose remains one often finds in the debris of the high-tide line, these little cowfish were encased in bony boxes that held head and body in an inflexible case, from which fins and tail protruded as the only movable parts. From tip of tail to the little forward-projecting, bovine horns, these small cowfish were the green of the grass in which they lived.

Especially where they border the channels between the Keys, the shoals carpeted with marine grasses are visited from time to time by sea turtles, which live in some numbers about the outer reef. The hawksbill wanders far out to sea, and seldom turns landward; but the green and loggerhead turtles often swim into the shallow waters of Hawk Channel or seek the passages between the Keys, where the tides race swiftly. When

Horse conch, octopus, pipefish, sea horses, sea hare, giant starfish, and cowfish

these turtles visit the grassy shoals they are usually seeking those inflated sand dollars, the sea biscuits, whose home is among the grass, or they may seize some of the conchs. Apart from others of their own kind, the conchs probably have no more dangerous enemies than the big turtles.

However far they may wander, loggerhead, green, or hawksbill all must return to land for the spawning season. There are no spawning places on the Keys of coral rock or limestone, but on some of the sand keys of the Tortugas group the loggerhead and the green turtles emerge from the ocean and lumber over the sand like prehistoric beasts to dig their nests and bury their eggs. The chief spawning places of the turtles, however, are on the beaches of Cape Sable and other sand strands of Florida, and farther north in Georgia and the Carolinas.

If the predatory visits of the big turtles to the sea-grass meadows are sporadic, it is far otherwise with the ceaseless, day-by-day preying of the various conchs, one upon another, and all upon mussels or oysters, sea urchins and sand dollars. The chief predator of all the conchs is the dusky-red spindle-shaped

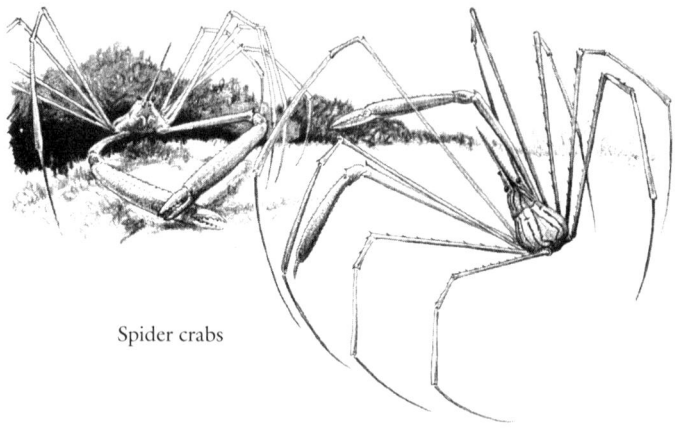

Spider crabs

one called the horse conch. One has only to see it feeding to realize how powerful it is; when the massive body, brick-red like the shell, is extended to enfold and overwhelm its prey, it seems impossible to believe that so much flesh can ever be drawn back into the shell again. Even the king crown conch, itself a predator on many other conchs, is no match for it. No other American gastropods approach its size. (One-foot individuals are fairly common and the giants of its kind are two feet long.) The big cask shells also are victims of the horse conch, while they themselves feed usually on urchins. Yet I have felt little awareness of this relentless predation on making a casual visit to the habitat of the conchs. There are long periods of somnolence and repletion, and the grassy world by day seems a peaceful place. A conch gliding over the coral sand, a sea cucumber burrowing sluggishly among the roots of the grasses, or the dark and swiftly fleeting forms of sea hares in sudden passage may be the only visible signs of life and motion. For by day life is in retreat; life is buried and hidden in crevices and corners of ledge and rock; life has crept under or within the shelter of sponge or gorgonian or coral or empty shell. In the shallow waters of the shore, many creatures must avoid the penetrating sunlight that irritates sensitive tissues and reveals prey to predator.

But that which seems quiescent—a dream world inhabited by creatures that move sluggishly or not at all—comes swiftly to life when the day ends. When I have lingered on the reef flat until dusk fell, a strange new world, full of tensions and alarms, has replaced the peaceful languor of the day. For then hunter and hunted are abroad. The spiny lobster steals out from under the sheltering bulk of a big sponge and flashes away across the open water. The gray snapper and the barracuda patrol the channels between the Keys and dart into the shallows in swift pursuit. Crabs emerge from hidden caverns; sea snails of varied shape and size creep out from under rocks. In sudden movements, swirling waters, and half-seen shadows that dart across my path as I wade shoreward, I sense the ancient drama of the strong against the weak.

Or if I have listened from the deck of a boat anchored at night among the Keys, I have heard splashings of large bodies moving in the shallows nearby, or the slap of a broad form striking water as a sting ray leaps into the air and falls, leaps and falls again. One of those whom the night stirs to activity is the needle-fish, long, slender, and powerful of body, armed with a sharp beak that would seem more appropriate in a bird. By day the small needle-fish may be seen from wharves and sea walls as they come close inshore, floating at the surface like straws adrift in the water. At night the large fish, that have ranged far to sea, come in to feed in the shallows, sometimes singly, sometimes in large schools. They leap out of the water or go skipping along the surface, making a disturbance that

Loggerhead turtle; hawksbill turtle

can be heard for a long distance on a calm night. Fishermen say that the needle-fish jump toward a light—that if one is out in a small boat at night where the needle-fish are hunting, it is dangerous, if not suicidal, to show a light, for the fish will leap across the boat. Probably there is an element of truth in the belief, for in some places in the Keys the beam of a searchlight thrown out across the water on a calm night—even if no fish have been heard about—will often be greeted by a series of splashes as a dozen or more large fish leap out of the water. The leaps, however, are usually at right angles to the beam, and the fish seem to be trying to escape the light.

This coral coast is the drowned world of the offshore reef and the world of the shallow reef flats with their fringing, rocky rim; it is also the green world of the mangrove, silent, mysterious, always changing—eloquent of a life force strong enough to alter the visible face of its world. As the corals dominate the seaward margin of the keys, the mangroves possess the sheltered or bay shores, completely covering many of the smaller keys, pushing out into the water to lessen the spaces between the islands, building an island where once there was only a shoal, creating land where once there was sea.

Mangroves are among the far migrants of the plant kingdom, forever sending their young stages off to establish pioneer colonies a score, a hundred, or a thousand miles from the parent stock. The same species live on the tropical coasts of America and the west coast of Africa. Probably the American

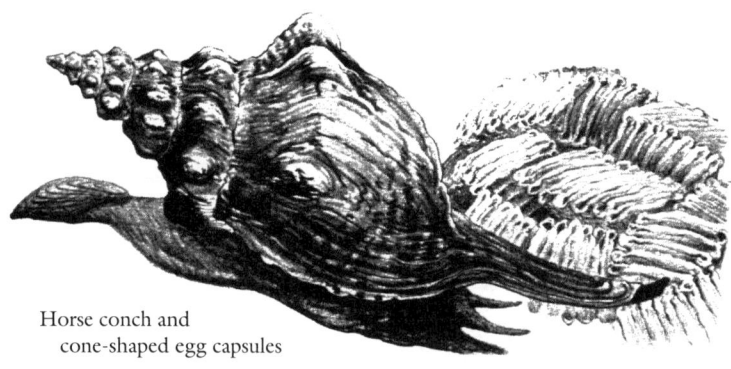

Horse conch and
  cone-shaped egg capsules

Common crown conch

mangroves crossed from Africa eons ago, via the Equatorial Current—and probably such migrants continue to arrive unnoticed from time to time. How the mangroves got to the Pacific coast of tropical America is an interesting problem. There is no continuous system of currents that would have carried them around the Horn, and besides the cold water to the south would be a barrier. It is not certain how early the mangroves arose, but definite fossil records seem to go back only to the Cenozoic, whereas the Panama Ridge, separating Atlantic from Pacific waters, probably arose much earlier, toward the end of the Mesozoic. By some means, however, the mangroves made the journey to Pacific shores, where they became established. Their further migrations also are mysterious. They must have dispatched their migrant seedlings into the great currents of the Pacific, for at least one American species grows on the islands of Fiji and Tonga and seems to have drifted as well to Cocos-Keeling and Christmas Islands. And some appeared as

Mangrove snapper

new colonists on the devastated island of Krakatoa, after it was virtually destroyed by volcanic eruption in 1883.

The mangroves belong to the highest group of plants, the spermatophytes or seed-bearers, whose earliest forms developed on land, and as such they are a botanical example of that return toward the sea that is always fascinating to observe. Among mammals, the seals and whales made such a return to the habitat of their ancestors. The marine grasses have gone even farther than the mangrove, for they live permanently submerged. But why this return to salt water? Perhaps the mangroves or their ancestral stock were forced out of more crowded habitats by the competition of other species. Whatever the reason, they have invaded and established themselves in the difficult world of the shore with such success that no plant now threatens their dominance there.

The saga of an individual mangrove begins when the long pendent green seedling, produced on the parent tree, drops to the floor of the swamp. Perhaps this happens at low tide when all the water has drained away; then the seedling lies amid the tangled roots, waiting till the salt flood comes in to lift it and later float it seaward on the turn of the tide. Of all the hundreds of thousands of red mangrove seedlings produced annually on the southern Florida coast, probably less than half remain to develop near the parent trees. The rest put out to sea, their buoyant structure keeping them in the surface waters, moving with the flow of the currents. They may drift for many months, being able to survive the normal vicissitudes of such a journey —sun, rain, the battering of a rough sea. At first they float horizontally, but with increasing age and the development of their tissues for a new phase of life they gradually come to lie almost vertically with the future root end downward, ready for that contact with earth upon which their future existence depends.

Perhaps in the path of such a pelagic seedling there may lie a small shoal, a little ridge off an island shore, deposited, grain by grain, by the waves. As the tide floats the young mangrove into the shallows, the downward-pressing tip touches the shoal; the sharp point, pressing earthward, becomes embedded. The water movements of later tides rising and falling press the young plant firmly into the receptive soil. Later, perhaps, they bring other seedlings to lodge beside it.

No sooner have the young mangroves anchored themselves than they begin to grow, sending out tiers of roots that arch out and downward to form a circle of supporting props. Among this rapidly increasing tangle of roots, debris of all sorts comes to rest—decaying vegetation, driftwood, shells, coral fragments, uprooted sponges and other sea growths. From such simple beginnings, an island is born.

In twenty to thirty years the young mangroves have acquired the stature of trees. These mature mangroves can resist the battering of a considerable surf, and probably are destroyed only by violent hurricanes. Once in many years such a hurricane comes. Because of the efficiency of their buttressing roots, few mangroves are uprooted even by a violent blow. But the high storm tides press far inland through the swamp, carrying the salt of the open sea into the forested interior. Leaves and small branches are stripped off and carried away, and if the wind is truly violent the trunks and limbs of the great trees are shaken and battered until the bark separates and blows away in sheets, exposing the naked trunk to the burning salt breath of the storm. This may be the history of some of the mangrove ghost forests bordering the Florida coast. But such catastrophes are rare, and in southwestern Florida whole islands of mangroves come to maturity without any serious interruption of their growth.

Coon oysters growing on mangroves. Mangrove periwinkle (upper right) lives on mangroves above high tide or on pilings and sea walls.

Fiddler crabs

A mangrove forest, its fringing trees literally standing in salt water, extending back into darkening swamps of its own creation, is full of the mysterious beauty of massive and contorted trunks, of tangled roots, and of dark green foliage spreading an almost unbroken canopy. The forest with its associated swamp forms a curious world. On their flood the tides rise over the roots of the outermost trees and penetrate into the swamplands, carrying many small migrants—the pelagic larvae of sea creatures. Over the ages many of these have found a suitable climate for their survival and have become established, some on the roots or trunks of the mangroves, some in the soft mud of the intertidal zone, some on the bottom of the bay offshore. The mangrove may be the only kind of tree, or the only seed plant growing there; all the associated plants and animals are bound to it by biological ties.

Within the range of the tides the prop roots of the mangroves are thickly overgrown with an oyster whose shell has fingerlike projections to grasp these firm supports and so to remain above the mud. On the night ebb tides, raccoons follow the water down, leaving meandering tracks across the mud as they move from root to root, finding food within the shells of the oysters. The crown conch also preys heavily on these oysters of the mangroves. Fiddler crabs dig tunnels in

the mud, sheltering deep within them when the salt tide rises. These crabs are remarkable for the possession, by the males, of one immense claw—the "fiddle"—that is incessantly waved about, apparently serving for communication as well as for defense. Fiddlers eat plant debris picked from the surface of sand or mud. For this the female has two spoon claws; the male, because of his fiddle, only one. By their activities the crabs help to aerate the heavy mud, which is saturated with organic debris and so deficient in oxygen that the mangroves must breathe through their aerial roots to supplement what their buried roots can obtain. Brittle stars and strange burrowing crustaceans live among the roots, while overhead in the upper branches great colonies of pelicans and herons find roosting and nesting places.

Here on these mangrove-fringed shores some of the pioneering mollusks and crustaceans are learning to live out of the sea from which they recently came. Among the mangroves and in marshy areas where the tides rise over the roots of sea grasses there is a small snail whose race is moving landward. This is the coffee-bean shell, a small creature within a short, widely ovate shell tinted with the greens and browns of its environment. When the tide rises the snails clamber up on the mangrove roots or climb the stems of the grasses, deferring as long as

Purple-clawed or land hermit crab

possible the moment of contact with the sea. Among the crabs, too, land forms are evolving. The purple-clawed hermit inhabits the strip above the highest tidal flotsam, where land vegetation fringes the shore, but in the breeding season it moves down toward the sea. Then hundreds of them lurk under logs and bits of driftwood, waiting for the moment when the eggs, carried by the female under her body, shall be ready to hatch. At that time the crabs dash into the sea, liberating the young into the ancestral waters. Nearing the end of its evolutionary journey is the large white crab of the Bahamas and southern Florida. It is a land dweller and an air-breather, and it seems to have cut its ties with the sea—all its ties, that is, but one. For in the spring the white crabs engage in a lemming-like march to the sea, entering it to release their young. In time the crabs of a new generation, having completed their embryonic life in the sea, emerge from the water and seek the land home of their parents.

For hundreds of miles this world of swamp and forest created by the mangroves extends northward, sweeping from the Keys around the southern tip of the Florida mainland, reaching from Cape Sable north along the coast of the Gulf of Mexico through all the Ten Thousand Islands. This is one of the great mangrove swamps of the world, a wilderness untamed and almost unvisited by man. Flying above it, one can see the mangroves at work. From the air the Ten Thousand Islands show a significant shape and structure. Geologists describe them as looking like a school of fish swimming in a southeasterly direction—each fish-shaped island having an "eye" of water in its enlarged end, the heads of all the little "fish" pointing to the southeast. Before these islands came to be, one may suppose, the wavelets of a shallow sea heaped the sand of its floor into little ridges. Then came the colonizing mangroves, converting the ripple marks to islands, perpetuating in living green forest the shape and trend of the sand ripples.

Today we can see, from one generation of man to another, where several small islands have coalesced to form one, or where the land has grown out and an island has merged with it—sea becoming land almost before our eyes.

What is the future of this mangrove coast? If it is written in its recent past we can foretell it: the building of a vast land area where today there is water with scattered islands. But we who live today can only wonder; a rising sea could write a different history.

Meanwhile the mangroves press on, spreading their silent forests mile upon mile under tropical skies, sending down their grasping roots, dropping their migrant seedlings one by one, launching them into the drifting tides on far voyages.

And offshore, under the surface waters where the moonlight falls in broken, argent beams, under the tidal currents streaming shoreward in the still night, the pulse of life surges on the reef. As all the billions of the coral animals draw from the sea the necessities of their existence, by swift metabolism converting the tissues of copepods and snail larvae and minuscule worms into the substance of their own bodies, so the corals grow and reproduce and bud, each of the tiny creatures adding its own limy chamber to the structure of the reef.

And as the years pass, and the centuries merge into the unbroken stream of time, these architects of coral reef and mangrove swamp build toward a shadowy future. But neither the corals nor the mangroves, but the sea itself will determine when that which they build will belong to the land, or when it will be reclaimed for the sea.

Tube sponge

The Enduring Sea

Now I hear the sea sounds about me; the night high tide is rising, swirling with a confused rush of waters against the rocks below my study window. Fog has come into the bay from the open sea, and it lies over water and over the land's edge, seeping back into the spruces and stealing softly among the juniper and the bayberry. The restive waters, the cold wet breath of the fog, are of a world in which man is an uneasy trespasser; he punctuates the night with the complaining groan and grunt of a foghorn, sensing the power and menace of the sea.

Hearing the rising tide, I think how it is pressing also against other shores I know—rising on a southern beach where there is no fog, but a moon edging all the waves with silver and touching the wet sands with lambent sheen, and on a still more distant shore sending its streaming currents against the moonlit pinnacles and the dark caves of the coral rock.

Then in my thoughts these shores, so different in their nature and in the inhabitants they support, are made one by the unifying touch of the sea. For the differences I sense in this particular instant of time that is mine are but the differences of a moment, determined by our place in the stream of time and in the long rhythms of the sea. Once this rocky coast beneath me was a plain of sand; then the sea rose and found a new shore line. And again in some shadowy future the surf will have ground these rocks to sand and will have returned the coast to its earlier state. And so in my mind's eye these coastal forms merge and blend in a shifting, kaleidoscopic pattern in which there is no finality, no ultimate and fixed reality—earth becoming fluid as the sea itself.

On all these shores there are echoes of past and future: of the flow of time, obliterating yet containing all that has gone before; of the sea's eternal rhythms—the tides, the beat of surf, the pressing rivers of the currents—shaping, changing, dominating; of the stream of life, flowing as inexorably as any ocean current, from past to unknown future. For as the shore configuration changes in the flow of time, the pattern of life changes, never static, never quite the same from year to year. Whenever the sea builds a new coast, waves of living creatures surge against it, seeking a foothold, establishing their colonies. And so we come to perceive life as a force as tangible as any of the physical realities of the sea, a force strong and purposeful, as incapable of being crushed or diverted from its ends as the rising tide.

Contemplating the teeming life of the shore, we have an uneasy sense of the communication of some universal truth that lies just beyond our grasp. What is the message signaled by the hordes of diatoms, flashing their microscopic lights in the night sea? What truth is expressed by the legions of the barnacles, whitening the rocks with their habitations, each small creature within finding the necessities of its existence in the sweep of the surf? And what is the meaning of so tiny a being as the transparent wisp of protoplasm that is a sea lace, existing for some reason inscrutable to us—a reason that demands its presence by the trillion amid the rocks and weeds of the shore? The meaning haunts and ever eludes us, and in its very pursuit we approach the ultimate mystery of Life itself.

Appendix: Classification

Protophyta, Protozoa: One-celled Plants and Animals

The simplest forms of cellular life are the one-celled plants (Protophyta) and one-celled animals (Protozoa). In both groups, however, there are many forms that defy attempts to place them definitely in one category or another because they display characteristics usually considered animal-like along with others usually thought definitive of plants. The *Dinoflagellata* form such an indeterminate group, and are claimed both by zoologists and by botanists. Although a few are large enough to be seen without magnification, most are smaller. Some wear shells with spines and elaborate markings. Some have a remarkable, eye-like sense organ. All dinoflagellates are immensely important in the economy of the sea as food for certain fishes and other animals. Noctiluca is a relatively large dinoflagellate of coastal waters, where it produces brilliant displays of phosphorescence, or by day reddens the water by the abundance of its pigmented cells. Other species are the cause of the phenomenon known as "red tide," in which the sea is discolored and fishes and other animals die from poisons given off by the minute cells. The red or green scum of high tide pools, "red rain," and "red snow" are growths of these forms, or of green algae (e.g., Sphaerella). Much phosphorescence or "burning" of the sea is caused by dinoflagellates, which create a uniformly diffused light, lacking large spots of illumination. Examined closely, in a vessel of water, the light is seen to consist of tiny sparks.

Sphaerella

The *Radiolaria* are one-celled animals whose protoplasm is contained in siliceous shells of extraordinary beauty. These minute shells, sinking to the bottom, accumulate there to form one of the characteristic oozes or sediments of the sea floor. The *Foraminifera* are another

Dinoflagellates

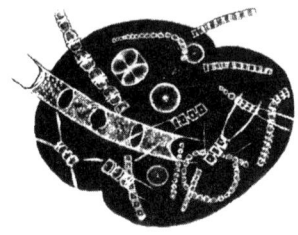

Diatoms

unicellular group. Most have calcareous shells, though some build their protective structures with sand grains or sponge spicules. The shells, eventually drifting to the floor of the ocean, cover vast areas with calcareous sediments that, through geologic change, may become compacted into limestone or chalk, and raised to form such features of the present landscape as the chalk cliffs of England. Most Foraminifera are so minute that one gram of sand might contain up to 50,000 shells. On the other hand, a fossil species, Nummulites, was sometimes 6 or 7 inches across and formed limestone beds in Northern Africa, Europe, and Asia. This limestone was used in the building of the Sphinx and the great pyramids. Fossil Foraminifera are much used by geologists in the oil industry in correlating rock strata.

Diatoms (Greek, *diatomos*—cut in two) are minute plants usually classified among the yellow-green algae because they contain granules of yellow pigment. They exist as single cells or in chains of cells. The living tissue of a diatom is encased within a shell of silica, of which one half fits over the other, as a lid over a box. Fine etchings on the surface of the shell create beautiful patterns and are characteristic for the various species. Most diatoms live in the open sea, and because they exist in inconceivable abundance are the most important single food stuff in the ocean, being eaten not only by many small animals of the plankton, but by many larger creatures, as mussels and oysters. The hard shells sink to the bottom after the death of the tissues, and accumulate there to form diatom oozes that cover vast areas of ocean floor.

Blue-green alga

The *blue-green algae*, or *Cyanophyceae*, are among the simplest and oldest forms of life and are the most ancient plants that still exist. They are widely distributed and occur even in hot springs and other places where conditions are so difficult that no other plant life can exist. They often multiply in phenomenal numbers, giving the surface of ponds and other still waters a colored film known as water bloom. Most are encased in gelatinous sheaths that protect them from extreme heat or cold. They are well represented in the "black zone" above high-tide line on rocky shores.

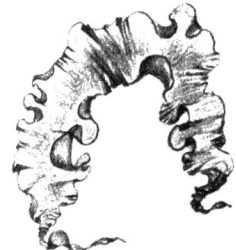
Sea lettuce

Thallophyta: Higher Algae

The green algae, or *Chlorophyceae*, are able to endure strong light and thrive high in the intertidal zone. They include such familiar forms as the leafy sea lettuce and a stringy, tube-like alga of high rocks and tide pools called Enteromorpha ("intestine-shaped"). In the tropics some of the most common green algae are the brush-shaped Penicillus that forms minute groves over the coral reef flats, and the beautiful little cup alga, Acetabularia, like tiny, inverted mushrooms of purest green. Some of the green algae of the tropics are important in the economy of the sea as concentrators of calcium. Although the group is most typical of warm, tropical seas, the green algae are found on the shore wherever there is strong sunlight, and others of the group live in fresh water.

The *brown algae*, or *Phaeophyceae*, possess various pigments that conceal their chlorophyll, so their prevailing colors are brown, yellowish, or olive-green. They are largely absent from warmer latitudes except in deep water, being unable to endure heat and strong sun. An exception is the Sargassum weed of tropical shores, which drifts northward in the Gulf Stream. On northern coasts the brown rockweeds live between tide lines, and the kelps or oarweeds from the low-tide line down to depths of 40 to 50 feet. Although all of the algae select and concentrate in their tissues many different chemicals present in sea water, the brown seaweeds and especially the kelps are extraordinary in the quantity of iodine stored.

Sargassum weed

Dulse

Formerly they were utilized widely in the industrial production of iodine. The same seaweeds now are important in the production of the carbohydrate algin for use in fire-resistant textiles, jellies, ice cream, cosmetics, and various industrial processes. The presence of alginic acid gives these seaweeds their great resilience in heavy surf.

The *red algae*, or *Rhodophyceae*, most sensitive to light of all the seaweeds, send only a few hardy species (including Irish moss and dulse) into the intertidal zone; most are delicate and graceful seaweeds living for the most part below low water. Some live deeper than any other seaweeds, going down into the dim regions 200 fathoms or more below the surface. Some (the corallines) form hard crusts on rocks or shells. Containing magnesium carbonate as well as calcium carbonate, these algae seem to have played an important geochemical role in earth history, perhaps having aided the formation of the magnesium-rich marble dolomite.

Porifera: Sponges

The sponges (Porifera, or pore-bearers) are among the simplest of animals, being little more than an aggregation of cells. Yet they have gone a step beyond the Protozoa, for there are inner and outer layers of cells, with some hint of specialization of function—some for drawing in water, some for taking in food, some for reproduction. All these cells cohere and work together to carry out the single purpose of the sponge—to pass the waters of the sea through the sieves of its own being. A sponge is an elaborate system of canals contained in a matrix of fibrous or mineral substance, the whole pierced by numerous small entrance pores and larger exit holes. The inmost or central cavities are lined with flagellated cells that remind

Sponge

one of protozoan flagellates. The lashing of the whiplike flagella creates currents to draw in water. In passage through the sponge, the water gives up food, minerals, and oxygen, and carries away waste products.

Sponge spicules

To a certain extent, each of the smaller groups within the sponge phylum has a physical appearance and habit of life that is characteristic, yet the sponges are probably more plastic in relation to their environment than any other animals. In surf they take the form of a flattened crust, almost without regard to species; in deep, quiet water they may assume an upright tubular form, or branch in a way suggestive of shrubbery. Their shape, therefore, is little or no aid in identification, and the classification of sponges is based chiefly on the nature of their skeleton, which is a loose network of minute hard structures called spicules. In some the spicules are calcareous. In others they are siliceous, although sea water contains only a trace of silica and the sponge must have to filter prodigious quantities to obtain enough for its spicules. The function of extracting silica from sea water is confined to primitive forms of life, and among animals does not occur above the sponges. Commercial sponges fall into a third group, having a skeleton of horny fibers. They are confined to tropical waters.

From such a beginning toward specialization, nature seems to have gone back and made a fresh start with other materials. All evidence points toward a separate origin for the coelenterates and all other more complex animals, leaving the sponges in an evolutionary blind alley.

Coelenterata: Anemones, Corals, Jellyfish, Hydroids

The coelenterates, despite their simplicity, foreshadow the basic plan on which, with elaborations, all the more highly developed animals are formed. They possess two distinct layers of cells, the outer ectoderm and the inner endoderm, sometimes with an undifferentiated

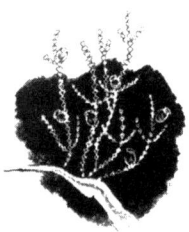

Hydroid

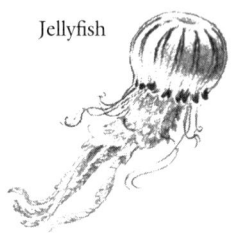
Jellyfish

middle layer that is not cellular but is the forerunner of the third cell layer, the mesoderm, of the higher groups. Each coelenterate is basically a hollow double-walled tube, closed at one end and open at the other. Variations of this plan have resulted in such diverse forms as the sea anemones, corals, jellyfish, and hydroids.

All coelenterates possess stinging cells called nematocysts, each of which is a coiled, pointed thread contained in a sac of turgid fluid, ready to be expelled to impale or entangle passing prey. Stinging cells are not developed in higher animals; although they have been reported in flatworms and sea slugs, they have been secondarily acquired by eating coelenterates.

The Hydrozoa display most clearly another peculiarity of this group, known as alternation of generations. An attached, plantlike generation produces a medusoid generation, shaped like small jellyfish. These, in turn, produce another plantlike generation. In the hydroids the more conspicuous generation is an attached, branching colony bearing tentacled individuals, or hydranths, on its "stems." Most of these are shaped like small sea anemones and capture food. Other individuals bud off the new generation—tiny medusae that (in many forms) swim away, mature, and shed eggs or sperm cells into the sea. An egg produced by such a medusa, when fertilized, develops into another plantlike stage.

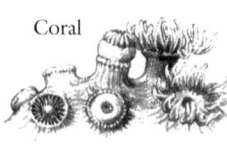
Coral

In another group, the Scyphozoa, or true jellyfish, the plantlike generation is the inconspicuous one, and the medusae are highly developed. The jellyfish range from very small creatures to the immense arctic jelly, Cyanea, which reaches an extreme diameter of 8 feet (1 to 3 feet is more common) with tentacles up to 75 feet long.

In the Anthozoa (flower animals) the medusoid generation has been completely lost. This group includes the anemones, corals, sea fans, and sea whips. The anemone represents the basic plan; all the rest of this group are colonial forms in which the individual,

Anemone

anemone-like polyps are embedded in some sort of matrix, which may be stony, as in the reef-building corals, or, in the sea fans and sea whips, may consist of a horny substance of protein nature, similar to the keratin of vertebrate hair, nails, and scales.

Ctenophora: Comb Jellies

The English writer Barbellion once said that a comb jelly in sunlight is the most beautiful thing in the world. Its tissues are almost crystal clear, and as this little ovoid creature twirls in the water it flashes iridescent lights. The ctenophores, or comb jellies, are sometimes mistaken for jellyfish because of their transparency, but there are various structural differences, with the "comb-plates" being characteristic of the phylum. These occur in eight rows on the outer surface. Each plate has a hinged attachment and bears hairlike cilia along its free edge; as the plates flash in succession to propel the animal through the water, the cilia break up the rays of sunlight and produce the characteristic flashing.

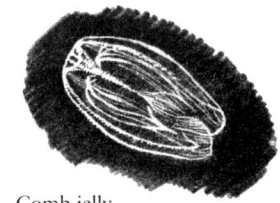

Comb jelly

Like some of the jellyfish, most ctenophores possess long tentacles. These are equipped not with stinging cells, but with sticky pads that capture prey by entanglement. Ctenophores eat enormous numbers of fish fry and other small animals. They live chiefly in the surface waters.

The ctenophores comprise a small phylum, with less than 100 species. Members of one of their groups have flattened bodies and do not swim, but creep on the ocean floor. Some specialists believe these creeping ctenophores have given rise to the flatworms.

Platyhelminthes: Flatworms

The flatworms include many parasitic as well as many free-living forms. Leafy thin, the free-living flatworms flow like a living film over rocks or sometimes swim by flapping undulations in a way reminiscent of skates. They have made significant

Flatworm

advances in an evolutionary sense. They are the first to possess three primary layers of cells, a characteristic of all higher animals. They also have a bilateral type of symmetry (one side being a mirror image of the other), with a head end that always goes first. They have the simple beginnings of a nervous system and eyes that may be only simple pigment spots or, in some species, well-developed organs with lenses. There is no circulatory system, and perhaps it is because of this that all flatworms have such thin bodies, in which all parts are in easy communication with the exterior, and oxygen and carbon dioxide are easily passed through surface membranes to underlying tissues.

Flatworms are found among seaweeds, on rocks, in tide pools, and lurking in dead mollusk shells. They are usually carnivorous, devouring worms, crustaceans, and mollusks of minute size.

Nemertea: Ribbon Worms

The ribbon worms have extraordinarily elastic bodies, sometimes round, sometimes flat. One of them, the bootlace worm (*Lineus longissimus*) of British waters, may attain a length of 90 feet and is the longest of all the invertebrates. The American Cerebratulus of shallow coastal waters often is 20 feet long and about an inch wide. Most, however, are only a few inches long and many are considerably less than an inch. They habitually contract into coils or knots when disturbed.

All ribbon worms are highly muscular but lack the coordination of nerve and muscle that higher worms have. There is a brain consisting of simple nerve ganglia. Some have primitive hearing organs, and the characteristic slits along the sides of the head (suggestive of a mouth) seem to contain important organs of sensation. Although there are a few hermaphroditic species, in most ribbon worms the sexes are separate. There is, however, a strong tendency toward asexual reproduction, and associated with this is a habit of breaking

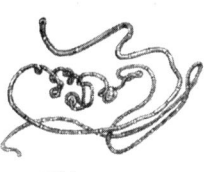
Ribbon worm

up into many pieces when handled. The fragments then regenerate complete worms. Professor Wesley Coe of Yale University found that a certain species of ribbon worm could be cut repeatedly until eventually miniature worms less than one one-hundred thousandth the volume of the original were obtained. An adult can live a year without food, according to Professor Coe, compensating for lack of nourishment by diminishing in size.

The ribbon worms are unique in the possession of an extensible weapon called a proboscis, enclosed in a sheath and capable of being suddenly everted, hurled out, and coiled around the prey, which is then drawn back toward the mouth. In many species the proboscis is armed with a sharp lance, or stylet, which if lost is quickly replaced by another held in reserve. All ribbon worms are carnivorous, and many prey on the bristle worms.

Annelida: Bristle Worms

The annelid (ringed, or segmented) worms include several classes, one of which, the Polychaeta (many bristles) includes most marine annelids. Many of the polychaetes, or bristle worms, are active swimmers that make their living as predators; others are more or less sedentary, building tubes of various sorts in which they live, either feeding on detritus in sand or mud or on plankton which they strain from the water. Some of these worms are among the most beautiful creatures of the sea, their bodies shining with iridescent splendor, or adorned with feathery crowns of tentacles in soft and beautiful colors.

In their structure they represent a great advance over lower forms. Most of them possess a circulatory system (although the blood worm, Glycera, much used as bait, has no blood vessels but a blood-filled cavity between the skin and the alimentary canal) and so are able to dispense with the thinness of body of the flatworms, for the blood flowing through vessels transports food and oxygen to all parts of the body. The blood is red in some, green in others. The body consists of a series of

Bristle worm

segments, several of the anterior ones being fused to form the head. Each segment bears a pair of unbranched, unsegmented paddle-like appendages for crawling or swimming.

Bristle worms include many diverse forms. The familiar nereids, or clam worms, often used for bait, spend most of their lives in crude burrows among stones on the sea bottom but emerge to hunt or, in swarms, to spawn. The sluggish scale worms live under rocks, in muddy burrows, or among the holdfasts of seaweeds. The serpulid worms build variously shaped limy tubes from which only their heads emerge; other worms, like the beautifully plumed Amphitrite, form mucous tubes under rocks or crusts of coralline algae or on muddy bottoms, and a worm of colonial habit, Sabellaria, uses coarse sand grains to build elaborate structures that may be several feet across. Though honeycombed with the burrows of the worms, these massive dwelling places are strong enough to bear the weight of a man.

Arthropoda: Lobsters, Barnacles, Amphipods

The arthropod (jointed foot) phylum is an enormous group, comprising five times as many species as are included in all the rest of the animal phyla combined. The arthropods include the crustacea (e.g., crabs, shrimps, lobsters), the insects, the myriopods (centipedes and millipedes), the arachnids (spiders, mites, and king crabs) and the tropical, wormlike Onychophora. All marine arthropods belong to the class Crustacea except for a scant handful of insects, a few mites and sea spiders, and the king crabs.

Whereas the paired appendages of the annelids are simple flaps, those of the arthropods possess multiple joints and are specialized to perform such varied functions as swimming, walking, handling food, and gaining sensory impressions of the environment. Whereas the annelids interpose only a simple cuticle between their internal organs and the environment, the arthropods protect themselves by a rigid skeleton of chitin impregnated with lime salts. This, in addition to being protective, has the advantage of giving a firm support for the insertion of muscles. On the other hand there is the disadvantage that, as the animal grows, the rigid outer covering must be shed from time to time.

The crustaceans include such familiar animals as crabs, lobsters, shrimps, and barnacles, as well as less-known creatures like the ostracods, isopods, amphipods, and copepods, all of which are important or interesting for one reason or another.

The *ostracods* are unusual arthropods in that they are not segmented but are enclosed in a two-part carapace, or shell, flattened from side to side, and opened and closed by muscles like a mollusk's shell. The antennae act as oars and are extended through the opened carapace to row the little animal through the water. Ostracods often live in seaweeds or in sand on the ocean floor, usually being quiet by day and coming out to feed at night. Many marine ostracods are luminous and as they swim about emit little puffs of bluish light. They are one of the chief sources of phosphorescence at sea. Even when dead and dried they retain the phosphorescent quality to an astonishing degree. Professor E. Newton Harvey of Princeton University says in his authoritative volume *Bioluminescence* that during the Second World War Japanese army officers used dried ostracod powder in advanced positions where use of flashlights was prohibited—by adding a few drops of water to a little powder in the palm of the hand, they could obtain enough light to read dispatches.

Copepods (oar-footed) are very small crustaceans with rounded bodies, jointed tails, and oarlike legs with which to propel themselves jerkily. In spite of their minute size (from microscopic to half-inch) the copepods form one of the basic populations of the sea, and are food for an immense variety of other animals. They are an indispensable link in the food chain by which the nutrient salts of the sea are eventually made available (via plant plankton, animal plankton, carnivores) to larger animals such as fishes and whales. Copepods of the genus Calanus, known as "red feed," redden large areas of ocean surface and are eaten in prodigious numbers by herring and mackerel and also by certain whales. Birds of the open sea such as petrels and

Copepod

albatrosses are plankton feeders and sometimes subsist largely on copepods. In their turn, the copepods graze on diatoms, eating sometimes as much as their own weight in a day.

Amphipods are small crustaceans that are flattened from side to side, while *isopods* are flattened from upper to lower surface. The names are a scientific reference to the kinds of appendages possessed by these small creatures. The amphipods have feet that can be used both for swimming and walking or crawling. The isopods, or "equal-footed" animals, have appendages that show little difference in size and shape from one end of the body to the other.

Amphipod

On the shore the amphipods include the beach hoppers, or sand fleas, that rise in clouds (leaping, not flying) from masses of seaweed when they are disturbed, and others that live offshore in seaweed and under rocks. They eat fragments and bits of organic debris and are themselves eaten in great number by fish, birds, and other larger creatures. Many amphipods wriggle along on their sides when out of water. Sand hoppers use their tails and posterior legs as a spring and progress by leaps; other species swim.

Isopods of the shore (closely related to the familiar sow bugs of the garden) include the slaters (sea roaches, wharf rats, quay lice) often seen running over rocks and wharf pilings. These have left the water and seldom return to it; they drown if long submerged. Others live offshore, often in seaweeds whose color and form they mimic. Still others swarm in tide pools, sometimes nipping the skin of human waders to produce a tingling or itching sensation. Most are scavengers; some are parasites; and some form habitual associations (commensalism) with an animal of unrelated species.

Isopod

Both amphipods and isopods carry their young in brood chambers instead of liberating eggs into the sea. This habit has helped some in each group to live high on the shore and is a necessary preliminary to land existence.

The barnacles belong to the order Cirripedia (Latin, *cirrus*—a ringlet or curl), presumably named because of their gracefully curving feathery appendages. The larval stages are free-living and resemble the larvae of many other crustaceans, but the adults are attached, living in a shell of calcareous material, fixed to rocks or other hard objects. The gooseneck barnacles are attached by a leathery stalk; the rock or acorn barnacles are attached directly. The gooseneck barnacles are often oceanic, attaching themselves to ships and floating objects of all sorts. Some of the acorn barnacles grow on the hide of whales or the shells of sea turtles.

Barnacles

The large crustaceans—shrimps, crabs, and lobsters—not only are most familiar but display the typical arthropod plan of body most clearly. The head and thoracic regions usually are fused and covered with a hard shell, or carapace; only the appendages indicate the division into segments. The flexible abdomen or "tail," on the other hand, is divided into segments and usually is an important aid to swimming. Crabs, however, keep the tail segments folded under the body.

Crab

The hard shell of an arthropod must be shed periodically as the animal grows. The creature gets out of the old shell through a slit that opens up usually across the back. Underneath is the new shell, much folded and wrinkled, soft and tender. The crustacean, after shedding, may spend days in seclusion, hiding from enemies until its armor has hardened.

The class Arachnoidea includes in one group the horseshoe crabs, and in another diverse one the spiders and mites, only a few of which are marine. The horseshoe, or king, crab has a peculiar distribution, being very abundant on the Atlantic coast of America, absent from Europe, and represented by three species on the Asiatic coast from India to Japan. Its larval stages closely resemble the ancient trilobites of Cambrian times and as a reminder of those past ages it is often called a living fossil. Horseshoe crabs are abundant along the shores of bays and other relatively

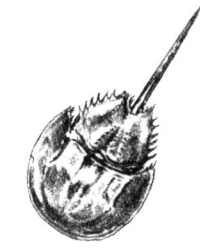
Horseshoe crab

quiet waters, where they eat clams, worms, and other small animals. They come out on beaches early in the summer to lay eggs in depressions scooped out in the sand.

Bryozoa: Moss Animals, Sea Laces

The Bryozoa are a group of uncertain position and relationships, including rather diverse forms. They may appear as fluffy plantlike growths often mistaken for seaweeds, especially when found dried on the shore. Another form grows as flat hard patches encrusting seaweeds or rocks and having a lacy appearance. Still another type is a branched and upright growth of gelatinous texture. All of these are colonial forms or associations of many individual polyps, all living in adjoining cells or embedded in a unifying matrix.

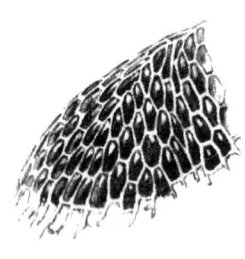

Bryozoan

The encrusting Bryozoa, or sea laces, are beautiful mosaics of closely set compartments, each inhabited by a small tentacled creature that superficially resembles the hydroid polyp, but possesses a complete digestive system, a body cavity, simple nervous system, and many other features of higher animals. The individuals of a bryozoan colony are largely independent of each other, instead of being connected as the hydroids are.

The Bryozoa are an ancient group dating from the Cambrian. They were considered seaweeds by early zoologists, and later were classified as hydroids. There are about 3000 marine species, compared with only about 35 in fresh waters.

Echinodermata: Starfish, Sea Urchins, Brittle Stars, Sea Cucumbers

Of all the invertebrates, the echinoderms are most truly marine, for among their nearly 5000 species not one lives in fresh water or on land. They are an ancient group, dating from the Cambrian, but in all the hundreds of millions of years since then none has even attempted to make the transition to a land existence.

The earliest echinoderms were the crinoids, or sea lilies, stalked forms that lived attached to the floor of Paleozoic seas. Some 2100 fossil species of crinoids are known, in contrast to about 800 living species. Today most crinoids live in East Indian waters; a few occur in the West Indian region and come as far north as Cape Hatteras, but there are none in the shallow waters of New England.

The common echinoderms of the shore represent the four remaining classes of the phylum: the sea stars, the brittle and serpent stars, the sea urchins and sand dollars, and the holothurians, or sea cucumbers. In all members of the group there is a recurrent insistence on the number five, many of the structures occurring in fives or multiples of five, so that the figure is almost a symbol of the group.

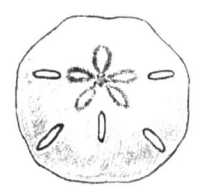

Sand dollar

The sea stars, or starfish, have flattened bodies, many in the conventional five-pointed shape, though the number of arms varies. The skin is roughened by hard limy plates from which short spines grow. In most species the skin also bears structures like minute forceps on flexible stalks (called pedicellaria); with these the animal keeps the skin clear of sand grains and also picks off larvae of sedentary forms that try to settle there. This is necessary because the delicate breathing organs—soft rosettes of tissue—also project through the skin.

Like all other echinoderms, the starfish possess a so-called water-vascular system that functions in locomotion and secondarily in other ways, and consists of a series of water-filled tubes running to all parts of the body. Intake of sea water is accomplished, in starfish, through a conspicuous perforated plate on the upper surface—the madreporite (mother of pores). The fluid passes along the water canals and eventually into the many short flexible tubes (tube feet) that occupy the long grooves on the under surface of the arms. Each tube bears a sucker at its tip. The tube feet can be lengthened or contracted by changes of hydrostatic pressure —when extended, the suckers grip the underlying rock or other hard surface and the animal pulls itself along. The tube feet are used also to grip the shells of mussels or other bivalve

Starfish

mollusks on which the starfish preys. As the starfish moves, any of its various arms may go first and thus serve as temporary "head."

In the slender, graceful brittle stars and serpent stars the arms are not grooved and the tube feet are reduced. However, these animals progress rapidly by writhing motions of the arms. They are active predators and feed on a variety of small animals. Sometimes they lie in "beds" of many hundreds of animals on the sea bottom offshore—a living net through which scarcely any small creature can safely reach bottom.

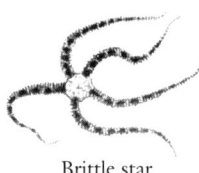
Brittle star

In the sea urchins the tube feet are arranged in five avenues or rows running from upper to lower apexes of the body, just as the meridians on a globe run from pole to pole. The skeletal plates of the urchins are articulated rigidly to form a globular shell, or test. The only movable structures are the tube feet, which are thrust out through perforations in the test, the pedicellaria, and the spines, which are mounted on protuberances on the plates. The tube feet are retracted when the animal is out of water, but when submerged they may be extended beyond the spines to grasp the substratum or to capture prey. They may also perform some sensory functions. In the various species the spines differ greatly in length and thickness.

Sea urchin

The mouth is on the under surface, surrounded by five white, shining teeth used to scrape vegetation off the rocks and also to assist in locomotion. (Although other invertebrates —e.g., the annelids—have biting jaws, the urchins are the first to have grinding or chewing organs.) The teeth are operated by an internally projecting apparatus of calcareous rods and muscles known to zoologists as Aristotle's lantern. On the upper surface the digestive tract opens to the exterior through a centrally placed anal pore. Around this are five petal-shaped plates, each bearing a pore that serves to discharge eggs or sperm. The

Aristotle's lantern

reproductive organs are arranged in five clusters just under the upper or dorsal surface. They are practically the only soft parts the animal possesses and it is for these that the sea urchins are sought as human food, especially in Mediterranean countries. Gulls hunt the urchins for a similar purpose, often dropping them on the rocks to break the tests so that they can eat out the soft parts.

The eggs of the sea urchins have been used extensively in biological studies of the nature of the cell, and Jacques Loeb in 1899 used them in a historic demonstration of artificial parthenogenesis, causing an unfertilized egg to develop merely by treating it with chemicals or by mechanical stimulus.

The holothurians, or sea cucumbers, are curious echinoderms with soft, elongated bodies. They crawl on one surface with the mouth end foremost and so have secondarily substituted a functional bilateral symmetry for the radial symmetry characteristic of the phylum. Tube feet, where present, are confined to three rows on the functional under surface of the body. Some holothurians are burrowing forms, using small spicules embedded in the body surface to grasp the surrounding mud

Sea cucumber

or sand and aid their progress. The shapes of these spicules vary with the species and often must be studied microscopically before correct identification can be made. The holothurians are large and abundant in tropical seas (they are the trepang, or *bêche-de-mer*, of commerce) and in northern waters are represented by smaller species living on offshore bottoms or among intertidal rocks and seaweeds.

Mollusca: Clams, Snails, Squids, Chitons

Because of their endlessly varied shells, often intricately made and beautifully adorned, some of the mollusks probably are better known than any other animals of the shore. As a group they possess qualities different from those of any other invertebrates, although their more primitive members and the nature of their larvae suggest that their remote ancestors may have resembled those of the flatworms. They have soft, unsegmented bodies typically protected by a hard shell. One of the most remarkable and characteristic molluscan structures is the mantle, a cloaklike tissue that encloses the body, secretes the shell, and is responsible for its complex structure and adornment.

The most familiar mollusks are the snail-like gastropods and the clamlike bivalves. The most primitive mollusks are the creeping, sluggish coat-of-mail shells, or chitons, the least known are the tusk shells, or scaphopods, and the most highly developed class the cephalopods, represented by the squids.

The shells of the gastropods are univalve or in one piece, and coiled in more or less spiral fashion. Nearly all snails are "right-handed," that is, the opening is to the right as it faces the observer. One of the exceptions is the "left-handed conch," one of the most common gastropods of Florida beaches. Occasionally a left-handed individual occurs in a normally right-handed species. Some gastropods have reduced the shell to an internal remnant, as in the sea hares, or have lost it entirely, as in the sea slugs or nudibranchs (in which, however, a coiled shell is present in the embryo).

The snails are for the most part active animals, both the vegetarians that move about scraping plant food from the rocks and the carnivores that capture and devour animal prey. The sedentary boat shells, or slipper shells, are exceptions; they attach themselves to shells or to the sea bottom and live on diatoms strained from the water, in the manner of oysters, clams, and other bivalves. Most snails glide about on a flattened muscular "foot," or they may use this same organ to burrow into the sand. When disturbed, or at low tide, they draw back into their shells, the opening being closed by a calcareous or horny plate called the operculum. The shape and structure of the operculum vary greatly in the different species and sometimes it is useful in identification. In common with other mollusks (except the bivalves) the gastropods have a remarkable, tooth-studded band, the radula, on the floor of the pharynx, or, in some species, on the end of a long proboscis. The radula is used to scrape off vegetation or to drill holes in shelled prey.

Snail

The bivalves, with few exceptions, are sedentary. Some (e.g., the oyster) fix themselves permanently to a hard surface. Mussels and some others anchor themselves by secreting silklike byssus threads. The scallops and the lima clams are examples of the few bivalves that possess the ability to swim. The razor clams have a slender pointed foot by means of which they dig deeply and with incredible speed into the sand or mud.

Clams

Bivalves that bury deeply in the substratum are able to do so because they possess a long breathing tube, or siphon, through which they draw in water and so receive oxygen and food. Although most are suspension feeders, filtering minute food organisms from the water, some, including the tellins and coquina clams, live on detritus that accumulates on the sea floor. There are no carnivorous bivalves.

The shells of gastropods and bivalves are secreted by the mantle. The basic chemical material of molluscan shells is calcium carbonate, which forms the outer layer of calcite, and the inner layer of aragonite, which is a heavier and harder substance although it has the same chemical composition. Calcium phosphate and magnesium carbonate also are contained in mollusk shells. The limy materials are laid down on an organic matrix of conchiolin, a substance chemically allied to chitin. The mantle contains pigment-forming cells as well as shell-secreting cells. The rhythm of activity of these two kinds of cells results in the marvelous sculpturing and color patterns of molluscan shells. Although shell formation is affected by many factors in the environment and in the physiology of the animal itself, the basic hereditary pattern is so strongly determined that each species of mollusk has its characteristic shell by which it may be identified.

A third class of the mollusk phylum consists of the cephalopods, so unlike the snails and clams that superficially it is hard to reconcile the relationship. Although ancient seas were dominated by shelled cephalopods, all but one (the chambered nautilus) have now lost the external shell, retaining only an inconspicuous internal remnant. One large group, the decapods, have cylindrical bodies with ten arms; they are represented by the squids, the ramshorn shell, and the cuttlefish. Another group, the octopods, have baglike bodies with eight arms; examples are the octopus and the argonaut.

The squids are strong and agile; over short distances they are probably the swiftest animals of the sea. They swim by expelling a jet of water through the siphon, controlling the direction of motion by pointing the siphon forward or backward. Some of the smaller species swim in schools. All squids are carnivorous, preying on fish, crustaceans, and various small invertebrates. They are sought by cod, mackerel, and other large fish, and are a favorite bait. The giant squid is the largest of all invertebrates. The record specimen, taken on the Grand Banks of Newfoundland, measured about 55 feet including the arms.

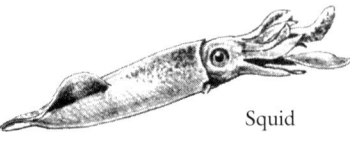
Squid

Octopuses are nocturnal animals and, according to those most familiar with their habits, are timid and retiring. They live in holes or among rocks, feeding on crabs, mollusks, and small fish. Sometimes the location of an octopus den may be discovered by the pile of empty mollusk shells near the entrance.

The chitons belong to a primitive order of mollusks, the Amphineura. Most of them wear a shell consisting of eight transverse plates bounded by a tough band, or girdle. They creep sluggishly over rocks, scraping off vegetation. At rest, they settle into a depression, blending so well with their surroundings that they are easily overlooked. They are sought as food (sea beef) by West Indian natives.

Chiton

The fifth class of mollusks consists of the little-known scaphopods (tooth shells or tusk shells), which form shells resembling an elephant's tusk, from one to several inches long and open at both ends. They dig into sandy bottoms, using a small, pointed foot. Some specialists think their structure may be similar to that of the ancestors of all mollusks. However, this is a field for speculation, since the principal classes of mollusks were all defined early in the Cambrian, and clues to the nature of the ancestral forms are exceedingly vague. The tooth shells number about 200 species, and are widely distributed in all seas. None, however, are intertidal.

Chordata: Subphylum Tunicata

The ascidians, or sea squirts, are the most common representatives on the shore of that interesting group of early chordates, the Tunicata. As forerunners of the vertebrates, or backboned animals, all of the chordates have at some time a stiffening rod of cartilaginous material, an evolutionary forecast of the vertebral column which all the higher animals were to possess.

Sea squirt

The adult ascidian paradoxically suggests a creature of low and simple organization, with a physiology somewhat like that of oysters or clams. It is only in the larva that the chordate characteristics are clear. Though minute, the larva strongly resembles the tadpole of a frog, possessing a notochord and a tail and swimming actively. At the end of the larval period it settles down, becomes attached, and undergoes metamorphosis to the much simpler adult form, in which the chordate characters are lost. This is a curious phenomenon of evolution, which seems to be degenerative rather than progressive, with the larva displaying more advanced characteristics than the adult.

The adult sea squirt is shaped like a bag with two tubular openings or siphons for water intake and outgo, and a pharynx perforated with many slits through which water is strained. The common name refers to the fact that when the animal is disturbed it contracts sharply, forcing jets of water out through the siphons. In the so-called simple ascidians the animals live as separate individuals, each enclosed in a tough covering or test of material chemically akin to cellulose. Sand and debris often adhere to this test, forming a mat in which the actual shape of the animal is seldom apparent. In this form they often grow profusely on wharf pilings, floats, and rocky ledges. In the compound, or colonial, type of ascidian many individuals live together, embedded in a tough gelatinous substance.

Unlike a group of simple ascidians, the various individuals of a colony are derived by asexual budding from one individual, the founder of the colony. One of the commonest compound sea squirts is the sea pork, Amaroucium, named from the usually gray, gristly appearance of its colonies. These may form a thin mat on the under side of a rock or, offshore, grow erect, forming thick slabs that may break off and be carried in to shore. The individuals composing the colony are not easily seen, but under a lens pits in the surface appear, each the opening through which a single sea squirt communicates with the outside world. In the beautiful compound sea squirt Botryllus, however, the individuals form flowerlike clusters, easily visible.

OTHER WRITINGS

Shad Going Way of the Buffalo, Atlantic Conservation Group Told

Fish Washington Relished Dwindles in Last Century

Catch One Fifth of Former Abundance, Group
Representing Ten States Hears. Restoration Is Planned

REPRESENTATIVES OF TEN states from Maine to South Carolina met at Atlantic City February 6 to confer on the alarming condition of the shad fishery. Action followed a century of indifference to the dwindling of a great natural resource as the first Atlantic States Shad conference convened at the call of U.S. Commissioner of Fisheries Frank T. Bell.

The convention brought commissioners and other representatives of the States of Maine, Rhode Island, Connecticut, New York, New Jersey, Delaware, Maryland, Virginia, North Carolina and South Carolina into round table discussions with congressmen and officials of the Federal Bureau of Fisheries. By vigorous and concerted action, the conference hopes to halt the depletion of the shad fishery before it is too late.

Backers of the save-the-shad movement are not voicing a sentimental plea when they intercede for another bit of wildlife that is going the way of the buffalo. Shad conservationists are fighting to preserve an important food fish which occupies a unique place on the nation's bill of fare.

Esteemed as a delicacy in the days when the spring runs up the Potomac brought it to the tables of George Washington and John Marshall, the shad is no less a favorite today. Springtime is shad time throughout the length of the Atlantic seaboard, where planked shad, garnished with its own roe and bacon, is considered an epicurean dish. There is no substitute for the shad, yet by a century of exploitation we have reduced this fishery to the point where commercial extinction is threatened.

Within the memory of fishermen now living the shad nets from Maine to Florida reaped a harvest of more than 64,000,000 pounds, but this prize delicacy of the Eastern states is now reduced to one-fifth of the former abundance.

As late as 1900 the shad ranked among the three most abundant food fishes of the Atlantic coast, and afforded income to some 21,000 people in small communities along virtually all the coastal rivers. The industry has now declined to the rank of twenty-fourth in volume of production.

Nevertheless it claims twelfth place from the standpoint of value, because fish that once brought a few cents a pound apiece now sell for $1 to $2 each. From 1900 to 1927 shad fishermen received from 2,000,000 to 2,750,000 dollars annually for their catch; in 1934 it was worth only $884,000.

By an unlucky trick of fate, the shad, so eagerly sought by man, is an easy prey to his greed. Although it spends most of its life in the ocean, it returns each spring to fresh waters to spawn. Converging from the broad ocean upon the narrow rivers, such anadromous fishes tempt the fisherman to take more than a fair toll. Like the alewives and the Pacific salmon, the shad must run a gauntlet of nets and traps lining the shores or extending well across the streams to reach its spawning grounds.

The seasonal run begins in November in the southernmost river of the range, the St. John's. The rivers of Georgia and South Carolina are entered in January, and the streams to the northward in more or less regular sequence. By late May shad are running in the rivers of New Brunswick.

Although the run of any particular stream lasts for several months the main body of fish ascends from the rivers when the temperature is from 54 to 64 degrees F. After spawning in fresh water the adult shad return to the ocean, unlike the Pacific salmon which die after spawning. Although an individual shad is thought to spawn more than once, it is not known how often nor how many times it undertakes the long migration.

Thirty thousand eggs is average production for the female shad, while large fish may yield as many as 100,000. The eggs are deposited loosely, without a nest, and quickly sink to the bottom. Many fail to be fertilized, some are buried under mud washed down by spring rains, and others are subject to the development of a cottony fungus that blots out the fragile life within.

Human gourmets are not alone in their fondness for shad roe. Eels and other predators of the waters dine well when the shad spawning season is on. Fishermen complain that these river brigands actually attack fish caught in the nets and may mutilate half the catch for the sake of the roe.

The greatly reduced numbers that escape these dangers hatch in from six to ten days. When the young shad first views the world he is an extremely active, transparent being less than half an inch long. He grows rapidly, and by fall has attained a length of from three to seven inches, depending largely upon the food supply of his native waters. During these months a considerable number have furnished provender for the predacious fishes infesting the rivers, and it is probable that comparatively few of the original 20,000 remain to follow their parents to the sea. The seaward journey of young shad begins with the approach of cold weather, and the last of the stragglers are usually gone by November or December.

The destination of the young shad as they drop downstream toward the sea is a secret known only to themselves. How far do they wander from the parent stream? What food does the sea provide for them and what enemies to harass them? How many years do they roam the ocean before physical maturity and some little understood instinct draw them back to fresh waters to spawn? Do they, like some of the Pacific salmons, return to the very stream that gave them birth? These and other questions must be answered by the fishery biologists, the men behind any conservation program that gets results. The little that is known about this mystery fish of the Atlantic coast is the result of scattered observations made during its brief and disastrous visits to fresh waters.

Because the vast concentration of shad in the rivers comes only once a year, the whole intensity of the fishery centers upon the spawning period. In Colonial times it may well have seemed that the teeming abundance of life in the waters could never be exhausted. A writer of the day describes the common runs of shad on the Delaware and Susquehanna rivers as coming in "such vast multitudes that the still waters seemed filled with eddies, and the shallows were beaten into foam by them in their struggles to reach the spawning grounds."

In the early 1800s shad ascended the rivers for long distances. On the St. Johns, the Edisto, and the Neuse these fish were originally taken at the headwaters, distances varying from

300 to 375 miles from the sea. They ran up the Savannah to Tallulah Falls, a distance of 334 miles, and ascended the James for 350 miles. Great Falls, 130 miles from the mouth of the Potomac, marked the end of the run of that river, while on the Susquehanna the shad traveled 313 miles from the sea to Binghamton, New York.

The colonists made the most of this important food that the rivers brought to their very doors. Fishing gear was imported, and devices were adapted from the primitive traps and weirs of the Indians. In some places stakes were driven into the stream bed to form pens, and fishermen in canoes swept the river with ropes of grape vine and bushes, driving the shad into the enclosures. It is said that over 1,000 shad were driven into one such pound at a time.

On the Schuylkill river racks were built from shore to shore, and a basin cleared out below. The bars were so close together that the shad could not pass and the fishermen took as many as they wished.

When the spring runs were on, people traveled long distances in wagons to lay in a supply. All but the poorest families had their barrels of shad salted away for the winter, and some smoked shad hanging in their kitchen chimneys. We read that the low prices tempted many master mechanics to keep their apprentices almost entirely on a fish diet, and that striking apprentices in Philadelphia went back to work on condition that they should be given shad not oftener than twice a week.

The largest seine in the world was one operated for a century on the shores of the Potomac at Stony Point, Virginia. In it as many as 3,000 shad were taken at one haul and 120,000 in a season. By 1900 the yield had dropped to 1,000 and in 1901 the fishery was discontinued.

Soon the supply was so generally diminished that some of the best rivers scarcely yielded profitable returns. Many of the major rivers of New England, where shad once furnished a commercial catch of 2,000,000 pounds, are no longer considered shad streams. From New York to Delaware the catch has dropped from nearly 22,000,000 pounds in 1901 to less than a million in 1934. Shad fishermen of the Chesapeake, center of the industry, took 17,000,000 pounds annually in the late 1890s. In 1934 the catch failed to total 5,000,000 pounds. On the South Atlantic coast the yield has dropped from 11,000,000 to 2,500,000 pounds.

This amazing picture of depletion is the product of the triple menace of overfishing, obstructing dams, and polluted waterways. In narrow-mouthed bays and river estuaries the maze of nets and traps obstructing the passage upstream takes a heavy toll of fish before they have spawned. Dams for industry and navigation have spelled the destruction of the shad runs in the upper and middle reaches of the rivers. Fishways providing a graded ascent have been built into certain of the dams, but the shad, in contrast to the aggressive salmon, is a shy and retiring fish and will not use the ladders.

In other areas lumber mills have dumped sawdust into the streams, choking their channels, silt washed from eroded hillsides covers the spawning beds, smothering the eggs and fry. Industrial and municipal pollution has poisoned other waters so that shad will not enter or spawn in them.

Fish culturists came to the rescue of the shad fishery as early as the 1870s for even at that date evidence of depletion in scattered instances was unmistakable. A successful hatching device was not perfected until 1867, and in 1873 the United States Fish Commission first began hatching shad on the Connecticut river. The following year saw 93,000 young shad brought into the world in hatching jars on the Potomac. Hatching has been continued from year to year by the federal government, and more or less intermittently by Maryland, Connecticut, New York, and other coastal states.

The government fish culturist, at considerable expense, obtains eggs taken from market fish at the time of capture. The eggs thus salvaged represent the recovery of an important by-product, which otherwise would be marketed with the fish. It is usually the commercial fishermen who strip the eggs of the roe shad into a pan, to which they add milt from the buck shad and a little water. Each day's collection is promptly delivered to the hatchery. After delivery, the good eggs are carefully segregated, and the fishermen receive payment at the rate of approximately $22 per million eggs, the measurement being reckoned at 20,000 eggs to a fluid quart.

One of the triumphs of fish culture was the successful introduction of shad on the Pacific Coast. There had evidently been no place in Nature's original scheme for Pacific shad, but today through the activities of fish culturists this area ranks second only to the Chesapeake in the production of shad.

In 1871, the first band of 12,000 shad emigrants from the persecution of the Atlantic seaboard was sent out from the Hudson river to find a haven in the waters of the Sacramento. Two years later the federal government made a second plant of 31,000 young and other colonies followed. In spite of the extreme difficulties of transplanting the delicate fry across the continent, in 1877, six years after the original young were liberated, the first run of spawning shad entered California waters. A decade later a million marketable shad are estimated to have been taken from the waters of the state and marketed locally.

From the small original colonies the shad have multiplied and distributed themselves along nearly 2,000 miles of the Pacific Coast from Southern California to Alaska. The region of commercial abundance extends from Monterey to the Columbia river.

Transplanting shad to the Pacific was not only an important conservation measure, it was a remarkable financial success. The initial cost of the project was less than $4,000, but the aggregate catch during the next forty years was worth nearly a hundred times that figure. Large shipments of Pacific shad are sent annually to eastern cities to augment the declining catch of the Atlantic seaboard.

On the eastern coast shad culturists have struggled against greater odds. In 1915, forty-six million fry were hatched and distributed from Delaware to Georgia, fifty-six and one half million in 1920, and nearly five million in 1930. In most cases these figures represent the maximum amount of eggs that were obtainable on the major fishing grounds. Although artificial propagation of shad has been practiced at some time on nearly every stream from Massachusetts southward, in most cases the scarcity of eggs has compelled the abandonment of operations.

Where hatcheries have continued to function, it has been necessary to return the entire product to local spawning grounds. It is obvious that a continuation of the present system of artificial propagation is ineffective in stemming the decline.

At the Atlantic City conference, the first step toward restoration of the shad fishery was taken by the establishment of a continuing organization known as the Atlantic Coast Shad Conservation Council. This body will be composed of one official representative from each of the states in which the shad fishery is or has been important. The goal of the organization is coordinated action in the interest of restoring the shad supplies, regulating the commercial fishery, and conducting artificial propagation. As Chairman, Commissioner Richard Armstrong of Virginia is expected to give vigorous and energetic direction to the program.

The Federal Bureau of Fisheries has been called upon to detail scientific investigators to solve the biological mysteries of the shad. If conservation is not to be haphazard and ineffectual, knowledge must be had of their years at sea, their migrations, their enemies, and the factors that bring them back to the fishermen's nets at spawning time. The growth and food requirements of the young in fresh water must be studied, the effects of stream pollution upon their development observed, and the toll of the commercial fishery upon the supply measured. One of the most important riddles demanding solution is the question of whether each river system has its own stock of shad that return year after year. If the answer is in the affirmative, conservation measures in any particular locality would tend to improve greatly the runs of that area. Such information is the essential basis of a program of conservation in which all states concerned can unite for tangible results.

Artificial propagation will also get a helping hand under the new program. Virtually no improvements of method have been introduced since the first development of shad culture. Streams in the Carolinas will probably be the open-air laboratories where shad hatching operations will be conducted by the U.S. Bureau of Fisheries. Attempts will be made to rear the fry to a larger size than is now possible before liberating them in the rivers.

By such a program, with the cooperation of all the states that have an interest in the fishery, it is hoped to reestablish the shad as a staple food fish, rather than a luxury.

Undersea

WHO HAS KNOWN the ocean? Neither you nor I, with our earth-bound senses, know the foam and surge of the tide that beats over the crab hiding under the seaweed of his tidepool home; or the lilt of the long, slow swells of mid-ocean, where shoals of wandering fish prey and are preyed upon, and the dolphin breaks the waves to breathe the upper atmosphere. Nor can we know the vicissitudes of life on the ocean floor, where the sunlight, filtering through a hundred feet of water, makes but a fleeting, bluish twilight, in which dwell sponge and mollusk and starfish and coral, where swarms of diminutive fish twinkle through the dusk like a silver rain of meteors, and eels lie in wait among the rocks. Even less is it given to man to descend those six incomprehensible miles into the recesses of the abyss, where reign utter silence and unvarying cold and eternal night.

To sense this world of waters known to the creatures of the sea we must shed our human perceptions of length and breadth and time and place, and enter vicariously into a universe of all-pervading water. For to the sea's children nothing is so important as the fluidity of their world. It is water that they breathe; water that brings them food; water through which they see, by filtered sunshine from which first the red rays, then the greens, and finally the purples have been strained; water through which they sense vibrations equivalent to sound. And indeed it is nothing more or less than sea water, in all its varying conditions of temperature, saltiness, and pressure, that forms the invisible barriers that confine each marine type within a special zone of life—one to the shore line, another to some submarine chasm on the far slopes of the continental shelf, and yet another, perhaps, to an imperceptibly defined stratum at mid-depths of ocean.

There are comparatively few living things whose shifting pattern of life embraces both land and sea. Such are the creatures of the tide pools among the rocks and of the mud flats sloping away from dune and beach grass to the water's edge.

Between low water and the flotsam and jetsam of the high-tide mark, land and sea wage a never-ending conflict for possession.

As on land the coming of night brings a change over the face of field and forest, sending some wild things into the safe retreat of their burrows and bringing others forth to prowl and forage, so at ebb tide the creatures of the waters largely disappear from sight, and in their place come marauders from the land to search the tide pools and to probe the sands for the silent, waiting fauna of the shore.

Twice between succeeding dawns, as the waters abandon pursuit of the beckoning moon and fall back, foot by foot, periwinkle and starfish and crab are cast upon the mercy of the sands. Every heap of brine-drenched seaweed, every pool forgotten by the retreating sea in recess of sand or rock, offers sanctuary from sun and biting sand.

In the tide pools, seas in miniature, sponges of the simpler kinds encrust the rocks, each hungrily drawing in through its myriad mouths the nutriment-laden water. Starfishes and sea anemones are common dwellers in such rock-girt pools. Shell-less cousins of the snail, the naked sea slugs are spots of brilliant rose and bronze, spreading arborescent gills to the waters, while the tube worms, architects of the tide pools, fashion their conical dwellings of sand grains, cemented one against another in glistening mosaic.

On the sands the clams burrow down in search of coolness and moisture, and oysters close their all-excluding shells and wait for the return of the water. Crabs crowd into damp rock caverns, where periwinkles cling to the walls. Colonies of gnome-like shrimps find refuge under dripping strands of brown, leathery weed heaped on the beach.

Hard upon the retreating sea press invaders from the land. Shore birds patter along the beach by day, and legions of the ghost crab shuffle across the damp sands by night. Chief, perhaps, among the plunderers is man, probing the soft mud flats and dipping his nets into the shallow waters.

At last comes a tentative ripple, then another, and finally the full, surging sweep of the incoming tide. The folk of the pools awake—clams stir in the mud. Barnacles open their shells and begin a rhythmic sifting of the waters. One by one, brilliant-hued flowers blossom in the shallow water as tube worms extend cautious tentacles.

The ocean is a place of paradoxes. It is the home of the great white shark, two-thousand-pound killer of the seas, and of the hundred-foot blue whale, the largest animal that ever lived. It is also the home of living things so small that your two hands might scoop up as many of them as there are stars in the Milky Way. And it is because of the flowering of astronomical numbers of these diminutive plants, known as diatoms, that the surface waters of the ocean are in reality boundless pastures. Every marine animal, from the smallest to the sharks and whales, is ultimately dependent for its food upon these microscopic entities of the vegetable life of the ocean. Within their fragile walls, the sea performs a vital alchemy that utilizes the sterile chemical elements dissolved in the water and welds them with the torch of sunlight into the stuff of life. Only through this little-understood synthesis of proteins, fats, and carbohydrates by myriad plant "producers" is the mineral wealth of the sea made available to the animal "consumers" that browse as they float with the currents. Drifting endlessly, midway between the sea of air above and the depths of the abyss below, these strange creatures and the marine inflorescence that sustains them are called "plankton" —the wanderers.

Many of the fishes, as well as the bottom-dwelling mollusks and worms and starfish, begin life as temporary members of this roving company, for the ocean cradles their young in its surface waters. The sea is not a solicitous foster mother. The delicate eggs and fragile larvæ are buffeted by storms raging across the open ocean and preyed upon by diminutive monsters, the hungry glassworms and comb jellies of the plankton.

These ocean pastures are also the domain of vast shoals of adult fishes: herring, anchovy, menhaden, and mackerel, feeding upon the animals of the plankton and in their turn preyed upon; for here the dogfish hunt in packs, and the ravenous bluefish, like roving buccaneers, take their booty where they find it.

Dropping downward a scant hundred feet to the white sand beneath, an undersea traveler would discover a land where the noonday sun is swathed in twilight blues and purples, and where the blackness of midnight is eerily aglow with the cold phosphorescence of living things. Dwelling among the crepuscular shadows of the ocean floor are creatures whose terrestrial counterparts are drab and commonplace, but which are themselves invested with delicate beauty by the sea. Crystal cones form the shells of pteropods or winged snails that drift downward from the surface to these dim regions by day; and the translucent spires of lovely *Ianthina* are tinged with Tyrian purple.

Other creatures of the sea's bottom may be fantastic rather than beautiful. Spine-studded urchins, like rotund hedgehogs of the sea, tumble over the sands, where mollusks lie with slightly opened shells, busily straining the water for débris. Life flows on monotonously for these passive sifters of the currents, who move little or not at all from year to year. Among the rock ledges, eels and cunners forage greedily, while the lobster feels his way with nimble wariness through the perpetual twilight.

Farther out on the continental shelf, the ocean floor is scarred with deep ravines, perhaps the valleys of drowned rivers, and dotted with undersea plateaus. Hosts of fish graze on these submerged islands, which are richly carpeted with sluggish or sessile forms of life. Chief among the ground fish are haddock, cods, flounders and their mightier relative, the halibut. From these and shallower waters man, the predator, exacts a yearly tribute of nearly thirty billion pounds of fish.

If the underwater traveler might continue to explore the ocean floor, he would traverse miles of level prairie lands; he would ascend the sloping sides of hills; and he would skirt deep and ragged crevasses yawning suddenly at his feet. Through the gathering darkness, he would come at last to the edge of the continental shelf. The ceiling of the ocean would lie a hundred fathoms above him, and his feet would rest upon the brink of a slope that drops precipitously another mile, and then descends more gently into an inky void that is the abyss.

What human mind can visualize conditions in the uttermost depths of the ocean? Increasing with every foot of depth, enormous pressures reach, three thousand fathoms down, the inconceivable magnitude of three tons to every square inch of surface. In these silent deeps a glacial cold prevails, a bleak iciness which never varies, summer or winter, years melting into centuries, and centuries into ages of geologic time. There, too, darkness reigns—the blackness of primeval night in which the ocean came into being, unbroken, through æons of succeeding time, by the gray light of dawn.

It is easy to understand why early students of the ocean believed these regions were devoid of life, but strange creatures have now been dredged from the depths to bear mute and fragmentary testimony concerning life in the abyss.

The "monsters" of the deep sea are small, voracious fishes with gaping, tooth-studded jaws, some with sensitive feelers serving the function of eyes, others bearing luminous torches or lures to search out or entice their living prey. Through the night of the abyss, the flickering lights of these foragers move to and fro. Many of the sessile bottom dwellers glow with a strange radiance suffusing the entire body, while other swimming creatures may have tiny, glittering lights picked out in rows and patterns. The deep-sea prawn and the abyssal cuttlefish eject a luminous cloud, and under cover of this pillar of fire escape from their enemies.

Monotones of red and brown and lustreless black are the prevailing colors in the deep sea, allowing the wearers to reflect the minimum of the phosphorescent gleams, and to blend into the safe obscurity of the surrounding gloom.

On the muddy bottom of the abyss, treacherous oozes threaten to engulf small scavengers as they busily sift the débris for food. Crabs and prawns pick their way over the yielding mud on stilt-like legs; sea spiders creep over sponges raised on delicate stalks above the slime.

Because the last vestige of plant life was left behind in the shallow zone penetrated by the rays of the sun, the inhabitants of these depths contrast strangely with the self-supporting assemblage of the surface waters. Preying one upon another, the abyssal creatures are ultimately dependent upon the slow rain of dead plants and animals from above. Every living thing of the ocean, plant and animal alike, returns to the water at the end of its own life span the materials that had been temporarily assembled to form its body. So there descends into the depths a gentle, never-ending rain of the disintegrating particles of what once were living creatures of the sunlit surface waters, or of those twilight regions beneath.

Here in the sea mingle elements which, in their long and amazing history, have lent life and strength and beauty to a bewildering variety of living creatures. Ions of calcium, now free in the water, were borrowed years ago from the sea to form part of the protective armor of a mollusk, returned to the main reservoir when their temporary owner had ceased to have need of them, and later incorporated into the delicate statuary of a coral reef. Here are atoms of silica, once imprisoned in a layer of flint in subterranean darkness; later, within the fragile shell of a diatom, tossed by waves and warmed by the sun; and again entering into the exquisite structure of a radiolarian shell, that miracle of ephemeral beauty that might be the work of a fairy glass-blower with a snowflake as his pattern.

Except for precipitous slopes and regions swept bare by submarine currents, the ocean floor is covered with primeval oozes in which there have been accumulating for æons deposits of varied origin; earth-born materials freighted seaward by rivers or worn from the shores of continents by the ceaseless grinding of waves; volcanic dust transported long distances by wind, floating lightly on the surface and eventually sinking into the depths to mingle with the products of no less mighty eruptions of submarine volcanoes; spherules of iron and nickel from interstellar space; and substances of organic origin—the silicious skeletons of Radiolaria and the frustules of diatoms, the limey remains of algæ and corals, and the shells of minute Foraminifera and delicate pelagic snails.

While the bottoms near the shore are covered with detritus from the land, the remains of the floating and swimming creatures of the sea prevail in the deep waters of the open ocean. Beneath tropical seas, in depths of 1000 to 1500 fathoms, calcareous oozes cover nearly a third of the ocean floor; while the colder waters of the temperate and polar regions release to the underlying bottom the silicious remains of diatoms and Radiolaria. In the red clay that carpets the great deeps at 3000 fathoms or more, such delicate skeletons are extremely rare. Among the few organic remains not dissolved before they reach these cold and silent depths are the ear bones of whales and the teeth of sharks.

Thus we see the parts of the plan fall into place: the water receiving from earth and air the simple materials, storing them up until the gathering energy of the spring sun wakens the sleeping plants to a burst of dynamic activity, hungry swarms of planktonic animals growing and multiplying upon the abundant plants, and themselves falling prey to the shoals of fish; all, in the end, to be redissolved into their component substances when the inexorable laws of the sea demand it. Individual elements are lost to view, only to reappear again and again in different incarnations in a kind of material immortality. Kindred forces to those which, in some period inconceivably remote, gave birth to that primeval bit of protoplasm tossing on the ancient seas continue their mighty and incomprehensible work. Against this cosmic background the life span of a particular plant or animal appears, not as a drama complete in itself, but only as a brief interlude in a panorama of endless change.

Memo to Mrs. Eales on Under the Sea-Wind

BACKGROUND OF THE BOOK

IT ISN'T AT ALL surprising that I should have written a book about the sea, because as long as I can remember it has fascinated me. Even as a child—long before I had ever seen it— I used to imagine what it would look like, and what the surf sounded like. Since I grew up in an inland community, where we hadn't even a migrating seagull, I had to wait a long time to have my curiosity satisfied. As a matter of fact, it wasn't until I had graduated from college and gone to the famous Marine Biological Laboratory at Woods Hole, Massachusetts, that I saw the ocean. There, too, I began to get my first real understanding of the real sea world—that is, the world as it is known by shore birds and fishes and beach crabs and all the other creatures that live in the sea or along its edge. At Woods Hole we used to go out in a little dredging boat and steam up and down Vineyard Sound or Buzzards Bay. After a time, with much violent rocking of the little boat, the dredge would be pulled up and its load of sea animals, rocks, shells, and seaweeds spilled out on the deck. Most of these animals I had never seen before; some I had never heard of. But there they were before me, dripping with sea water and perhaps clinging to a piece of rock or shell or weed that they had brought up from their home down there on the bottom of the sound. Probably that was when I first began to let my imagination go down through the water and piece together bits of scientific fact until I could see the whole life of those creatures as they lived them in that strange sea world.

In a way, *Under the Sea-Wind* had its beginning about six years ago, when I happened to write a short essay on life in the sea. A friend who read it suggested that I send it to the *Atlantic*. At first I didn't take the suggestion very seriously, for I let the essay lie in my desk for about a year; but finally I polished it up a little and sent it to the *Atlantic*. In due time a letter of acceptance came. A few weeks after the essay—which was called "Undersea"—had been published, I received a letter from Mr. Quincy Howe, who is editor-in-chief of the firm of Simon and

Schuster. Mr. Howe said he had enjoyed the undersea article, and wondered if I was planning a book on the same general subject; if so, would I care to talk it over with him? As a matter of fact, I had never seriously considered writing a book, but naturally that letter put ideas in my head. I went to New York and we talked over a general plan for a book which would give the non-biologist a true picture of life in the sea. It was left that when I got around to writing such a book, the firm would like to consider it for publication. Actually, it was nearly two years later that the definite plan of the present book took form in my mind and I began to write, doing it all during my evenings and Saturday afternoons and Sundays. After I had written the first section the publishers signed a contract for publication of the book, and from that time on the writing went a lot faster, because a deadline had been set and I was writing under pressure, which sometimes isn't a bad thing.

GENERAL PLAN AND VIEWPOINT OF BOOK

I believe that most popular books about the ocean are written from the viewpoint of a human observer—usually a deep-sea diver or sometimes a fisherman—and record his impressions and interpretations of what he saw. I was determined to avoid this human bias as much as possible. The ocean is too big and vast and its forces are too mighty to be much affected by human activity. So I decided that the author as a person or a human observer should never enter the story, but that it should be told as a simple narrative of the lives of certain animals of the sea. As far as possible, I wanted my readers to feel that they were, for a time, actually living the lives of sea creatures. To bring this about I had first, of course, to think myself into the role of an animal that lives in the sea. I had to forget a lot of human conceptions. For example, time measured by the clock means nothing to a shorebird. His measure of time is not an hour, but the rise and fall of the tides—exposing his food supply or covering it again. Again, light and dark may mean merely the difference between the time when you are relatively safe and the time when an enemy can find you easily. All these adjustments in my thinking had to be made; and in writing the book I was successively a sandpiper, a crab, a mackerel, an eel, and half a dozen other animals. Hardest of all, I had to get the feel of a world that was entirely water.

I very soon realized that the central character of the book was the ocean itself. The smell of the sea's edge, the feeling of vast movements of water, the sound of waves, crept into every page, and over all was the ocean as the force dominating all its creatures.

In order to give a fairly complete picture of sea life, I divided the book into three parts, one to picture the life of the shore, one for the open sea, and one for the deep abyss. In each of these parts, or books, I told the life story of one particular animal.

BOOK I—EDGE OF THE SEA

Almost everyone knows the sea beach in a general way. Unfortunately, though, most people stay within sight of the piers and boardwalks of a resort beach, and never become acquainted with the animals of the beach, except for the few whose remains may be found in the litter along the high-tide mark. I always seek out the wild sections of beach that are usually to be found a few miles above or below a resort. One particularly lovely stretch of wild ocean beach in North Carolina forms the setting for most of the chapters about the shore. It is a beach that is separated from the mainland towns by a wide sound, fringing one of those narrow strips of outer land which the Carolinians call "banks." I have visited that beach in spring and fall to watch the comings and goings of the shorebirds. I have spent hours on end among the dunes or on the beach, saturating myself with the sounds of water and the feel of hot sun and blowing sand. I have watched the fiddler crabs and ghost crabs, and, in autumn, seen the mullet fishermen draw their seines on the beach. This was the background for the story of a bird that almost everyone who has visited the beach has seen as it runs along at the edge of the waves—a special kind of sandpiper called a sanderling. I chose the sanderling as the main character of the shore section because of its fascinating life story. The sanderling is one of the bird tribe's long-range migrants. I believe that few of the people who like to watch the sanderling on the beach have any idea of the hardships these birds endure, or the long and hard flights they make. Some of them actually travel more than eight thousand miles every spring and return the same distance every fall. These little birds winter as far south as Patagonia, at the extreme southern end of South America, and in the spring they migrate northward, most of them beyond the Arctic Circle, and some to within a few miles of the North Pole. This seems a strange place to choose to rear their young, but many of the shore and ocean birds nest in the Arctic. Probably they are obeying some instinct inherited from forgotten generations of ancestors. We see the sanderlings in the spring as they are migrating up along our coastline, then, about May and June in Maryland and Virginia, all but a few immature birds disappear. This is during the period when the adult birds are nesting on the Arctic tundras. When they first arrive in the Arctic the snow and ice have not melted, food is scarce, and late-season blizzards may take a heavy toll of life. Eventually, spring comes even to these frozen tundras, the birds prepare their nests and lay their eggs, and the young are hatched. There are many enemies abroad on the tundra. Some of these are the large snowy owls, the foxes, and hawk-like birds of the gull tribe known as jaegers. After the chicks have hatched, the mother sanderling takes great precautions to hide the egg shells, so that enemies will not be led to the nest by them. Usually she leads the young away from the nest when they are only a few days or even hours old, if she has been frightened by marauders. Very quickly, however, the young become able to take care of themselves. As soon as they are no longer needed, the old birds leave for the south. The young remain behind until their wing feathers have grown strong enough for the long journey down across the two Americas. By late July the older sanderlings are seen on our beaches again, and a few weeks later we begin to see young birds.

This is the story that I have told in the first section, against a background of Carolina beach and Arctic tundra.

BOOK II—THE GULL'S WAY

The central character of the second section is another long-distance migrant, but this time a fish. In this section, which pictures the strange world of the open sea, I have written the biography of a mackerel, beginning, as biographies usually do, with the birth of my central character. There could scarcely be any stranger place in which to begin life than the surface waters of the open sea. Yet these waters are a sort of nursery where literally hundreds of kinds of sea creatures deposit their eggs, and where the young get their start in life. Parenthood in the sea is a relatively simple matter, for as a usual thing the parents do not care for their young and probably never even see them.

The open sea *is* a strange place for anything so fragile as a mackerel egg to be set adrift: just sky and water, and great silences, but teeming, incredibly abundant life. In the first place there are the eggs of all sorts of animals—fishes, crabs, shrimps, clams, worms, starfish, and the like. From all these eggs larvae or young animals are hatching. Almost immediately, each larva is on its own resources. It begins to swim about and seek food, eating almost anything that is small enough to take into its mouth, or to overpower and swallow. All sorts of enemies of young fishes prowl through these surface waters: small jellyfish with enormous appetites, little, transparent worms with sharp, biting jaws, schools of small fishes that eat smaller fishes, and larger fishes that eat them. Just to give an idea of some of the hazards of sea life: a full-grown mackerel may produce half a million eggs in a season, or a large cod may shed three or four million. But the destruction of the young is so enormous that, on the average, only two young mackerel or cod will survive out of all the potential offspring produced by the mother fish during her whole life. This ceaseless ebb and flow of life—the constant destruction of individuals contrasted with the survival of whole species—is one of the most impressive spectacles which the sea presents.

As the young mackerel grows rapidly during the first months of life, sea animals that were once deadly enemies become his prey as he, too, joins the ranks of sea hunters. After spending the summer in a sheltered New England harbor, he and other young mackerel wander out into the open sea again. There new and larger enemies await them: fish-eating birds, swordfish, tunas, and fishermen. In the concluding chapter of this series, I described the setting of a mackerel seine from the viewpoint of a fish—something that I do not believe has been done before.

In many ways, I found this section the hardest to write, and so I get a good deal of satisfaction out of the fact that most reviewers and readers seem to like it best. I believe it was hard because of the endless waste of waters—no fixed points around which to orient one's characters. I said a few minutes ago that I really lived the things I wrote about, and I don't mind admitting that I was very thankful to climb out on dry land in beginning the concluding section.

BOOK III—RIVER AND SEA

For the last section of the book, I had left the gently sloping sea bottom from the tidelines out to the edge of the continental shelf, and the deep Atlantic abyss. There was one fish whose migrations include all that varied undersea terrain—the eel. I know many people shudder at the sight of an eel. To me (and I believe to anyone who knows its story) to see an eel is something like meeting a person who has travelled to the most remote and wonderful places of the earth; in a flash I see a vivid picture of the strange places that eel has been—places which I, being merely human, can never visit.

Every eel that lives along our Atlantic coast began life in the distant Sargasso Sea. It lived, at first, so far below the surface that only the faintest blue haze ever penetrates there. For the most part, the water in which the baby eels are born is eternally dark and still and cold. The pressure is so great that it would instantly crush our unaccustomed bodies to nothing. All about the baby eels are the strange animals that live permanently in the abyss. Many of them carry their own lights, perhaps to help them see their way about in the darkness and find food.

As the young eels grow they work up toward the surface, and as they move up the light becomes stronger. By this time they look like tiny willow leaves, flat, oval, and transparent. In a few months' time, they begin their thousand-mile journey toward the American coast. At first, probably, they are carried along by the ocean currents; later, they must swim independently. But here is the really remarkable part of the story. In the Sargasso, the young of eels from America mingle with the young of European eels, for the eels from all the European Atlantic coast make the long westward crossing to spawn in the Sargasso. But although many of the two species of young are intermingled during their first weeks or months of life, soon after the migration begins the travelers separate. They form two great bands, one company proceeding westward toward America, the other eastward to Europe. The two kinds of eels are so similar that a scientist can distinguish them only by counting the number of vertebrae in the backbone, but the little eels themselves never make a mistake. They always return to the continent from which their parents came.

In the spring the young eels begin to arrive in our coastal waters. They are, by this time, a little more than a year old, but they are no longer than a man's finger and so transparent that one could read print through their bodies. They move into the bays and river estuaries, and some begin to ascend the rivers and streams. It is thought that the young males remain in salt or brackish water, and that it is only the females that ascend the fresh-water streams. There they live for 8, 10, or 12 years before they reach physical maturity. Then the awakening of some race instinct causes them to begin a downstream migration. This happens in the fall of the year. Usually the eels migrate at night, and apparently dark, stormy nights are times of large movements of eels. In the estuaries of the rivers the migrating females are joined by the males and together they enter the sea and pass out through the coastal waters. Fishing boats take a few; then the eels completely disappear from sight and never are seen again. We know, though, that they returned to their birthplace a thousand miles out in the Atlantic, because, very early in the spring, the eggs of the new generation of young can be found there. Evidently the old eels die after they spawn, for they never return to the coast. They begin and end their lives in the deep abyss.

GENERAL

Each of these stories seems to me not only to challenge the imagination, but also to give us a little better perspective on human problems. They are stories of things that have been going on for countless thousands of years. They are as ageless as sun and rain, or as the sea itself. The relentless struggle for survival in the sea epitomizes the struggle of all earthly life, human and nonhuman. As one reviewer said: "Our own battles for existence seem less a matter for dismay and more a simple reason for fortitude when compared in the mind with the ceaseless ebb and flow of life and death that are under all the sea winds."

CHRONOLOGY

NOTE ON THE TEXTS

NOTES

INDEX

Chronology

1907–12 Born Rachel Louise Carson on May 27, 1907, in Springdale, Pennsylvania, the third child of Robert Warden Carson, forty-three, and Maria Frazier (McLean) Carson, thirty-eight. Father, eldest of six children of Irish immigrants, works as travelling insurance salesman; mother, a graduate of Washington Female Seminary and former schoolteacher, keeps house and gives piano lessons. Married in 1894, they had daughter Marian Frazier in 1897 and son Robert McLean in 1898, moving to Springdale in 1900. In 1910, father subdivides their wooded, sixty-four-acre property, advertising lots for sale to supplement his irregular earnings.

1913–17 Attends School Street School in Springdale; mother encourages outdoor nature study. Reads Beatrix Potter, Kenneth Grahame, and Gene Stratton-Porter; later describes herself as a "solitary child" who was "happiest with wild birds and creatures as companions." Sister Marian marries in 1915; the next year, her husband is arrested for desertion. In 1917 is confirmed in Sunday school classes at Cheswick Presbyterian Church. Brother Robert enlists in Army Air Service.

1918–19 Writes story "A Battle in the Clouds," based on one of brother's letters; it is published in children's magazine *St. Nicholas* in September 1918. Contributes additional stories in January, February, and August of next year. Brother, returning from France, works at electrical repair company. Sister Marian's divorce finalized.

1920–22 Takes high school classes at School Street School. Continues to write and publish in children's magazines, beginning a ledger of literary submissions, acceptances, and rejections. Sister Marian remarries.

1923–24 Transfers to high school in Parnassus, Pennsylvania, in class of 1925. Plays basketball and field hockey. Sister Marian has daughter, Virginia; brother Robert marries.

1925 Graduates from high school in May, first in her small class, and is accepted at Pennsylvania College for Women in

Pittsburgh. Wins state tuition scholarship; family borrows money, sells land and china to help pay for room and board. Arriving at school in September, hopes to major in English and fulfill literary aspirations. Writes in composition class: "I love all the beautiful things of nature, and the wild creatures are my friends." Mother frequently visits campus on weekends. Sister Marian has second daughter, Marjorie Louise; brother Robert's wife has daughter Frances.

1926 Becomes goalkeeper on field hockey team and plays basketball as substitute. Publishes "The Master of the Ship's Light," a sea story, in *The Englicode*, literary supplement of student newspaper *The Arrow*. In June is selected for freshman honors list. Returns to crowded family home over summer, brother and sister-in-law, now-separated sister, and young nieces having moved in. Joins staff of *The Arrow* in September. Finds mentor in biology teacher Mary Scott Skinker.

1927 Story "Broken Lamps" wins college literary prize. Decides to add a science minor to her English major. Writes more for *The Englicode*.

1928 Changes major to biology, hoping to work toward master's degree. In May, is accepted to Johns Hopkins University graduate program in zoology but is unable to afford graduate tuition; completes senior year at Pennsylvania College for Women instead. Tutors high school students in Springdale over summer. Corresponds frequently with Mary Scott Skinker, now at Marine Biological Laboratory in Woods Hole, Massachusetts. Cofounds a science club; takes histology, genetics, organic chemistry, and physics. Reapplies to Johns Hopkins in December.

1929 Graduates magna cum laude in June. After a month in Springdale and a hiking trip in the Shenandoah Valley with Skinker, spends six weeks as beginning investigator at Marine Biological Laboratory in Woods Hole. In October begins graduate study at Johns Hopkins with a one-year full-tuition scholarship.

1930 Rents a house in Stemmers Run, Maryland, within commuting distance of Baltimore; parents, sister, and nieces move in. Works over summer as teaching assistant for an undergraduate biology class at Hopkins, taught by Grace Lippy; continues as Lippy's assistant for the next four summers. Unable to afford increased second-year tuition, becomes a part-time student, taking part-time job as laboratory technician at the Institute for Biological Research in Hopkins' School of Hygiene and Public Health.

1931 Abandons preliminary work on African *Anomalurus* squirrels, a potential thesis subject, after specimens prove too difficult to obtain. Brother Robert, working as a radio technician, moves in with family. Begins dissertation research on catfish. In September, obtains a teaching assistantship at University of Maryland Dental and Pharmacy School in College Park, Maryland.

1932 Completes thesis, "The Development of the Pronephros During the Embryonic and Early Larval Life of the Catfish (*Ictalurus punctatus*)" and in June receives master's degree from Johns Hopkins. After summer teaching assistantship, returns to Marine Biological Laboratory at Woods Hole for six weeks. Back in Baltimore, begins experiments at Hopkins on salt tolerance in eels, intending to pursue doctorate. In lieu of long-overdue student loan payments, gives Pennsylvania College for Women title to mortgaged family property in Springdale.

1933 Continues teaching biology at University of Maryland. Sister Marian, now diabetic, increasingly unable to support herself and her children; father's health declines.

1934 Formally withdraws from doctoral program at Hopkins and seeks full-time employment as biology instructor. Unsuccessfully submits poems and short fiction to literary magazines.

1935 Passes federal civil service exams for various positions including junior parasitologist, junior wildlife biologist, and junior aquatic biologist, but finds none available. Father dies on July 6. In October, takes part-time job writing radio scripts for Bureau of Fisheries educational series "Romance Under the Waters." Elmer Higgins, head of Division of Scientific Inquiry, attempts to find permanent job for her.

1936 Publishes articles based on Bureau of Fisheries research ("It'll Be Shad-Time Soon" and "Numbering the Fish of the Sea") in the Baltimore *Sun*. In April, completes introductory pamphlet on marine life for Bureau; Higgins recommends she submit her work, "The World of Waters," to *The Atlantic*. Hired in July as junior aquatic biologist, works with assistant bureau chief Robert Nesbit in Baltimore field office on study of Chesapeake Bay fishes.

1937 Sister Marian Williams dies of pneumonia in January. With mother, takes responsibility for care of nieces Virginia, twelve, and Marjorie, eleven; they move to a larger house in Silver Spring, Maryland, in July. Writes articles on Chesapeake fisheries for the Baltimore *Sun*, the Charleston *News and Courier*, and the *Richmond Times Dispatch*. "Undersea," a revision of "The World of Waters," is published in *The Atlantic* in September; after reading the essay, Simon & Schuster editor Quincy Howe and historian Hendrik Willem van Loon encourage her to write a book about marine life.

1938 Meets with Howe and Van Loon in January at the latter's home in Greenwich, Connecticut, and with Howe at Simon & Schuster the next day to discuss further book plans. Hoping to make an undersea dive, asks Van Loon for an introduction to naturalist and ocean explorer William Beebe. Attends North American Wildlife Conference in Baltimore. Reviews books for *The Atlantic*, and continues to write on wildlife and marine subjects for Baltimore *Sun*. In July, takes vacation with family in Beaufort, North Carolina, visiting U.S. Fisheries Station and exploring Outer Banks.

1939 In June, is transferred to Bureau's field office in College Park, Maryland, continuing work as Nesbit's research assistant. Writes brochures for series "Our Aquatic Food Animals." Publishes articles in Baltimore *Sun* on trout hatcheries, starlings, and shad. In August, spends ten days at Fisheries Biological Station in Woods Hole; visits nearby wetlands, birdwatching with friend and fellow researcher Dorothy Hamilton. Moves into a larger house in Silver Spring. Writes mornings, evenings, and weekends; reads passages aloud with mother, who helps with typing.

1940 Sends preliminary book chapters to Quincy Howe, who offers contract in June. Commissions Baltimore *Sun* artist Howard Frech to work on illustrations. Returns to Woods Hole in July, visiting naturalist Henry Beston's "outermost house" at Eastham, Massachusetts, with Hamilton. Completes *Under the Sea-Wind*, sending manuscript to Simon & Schuster on December 31, her deadline.

1941	*Under the Sea-Wind* is published on November 1. William Beebe, Howard Zahniser, and others review the book favorably, and it is offered as a main selection of the Scientific Book Club, but in the wake of the December 7 attack on Pearl Harbor, it attracts little further attention and sales fail to meet expectations.
1942	Promoted to assistant aquatic biologist in May, begins working in the Bureau of Fisheries' offices at the Department of the Interior in D.C. Edits *Progressive Fish-Culturist*; writes press releases and pamphlets for the Fish and Wildlife Service. In August is transferred to Chicago, the Bureau of Fisheries forced to give up office space to other wartime agencies. Moves with mother to Evanston, Illinois. Begins work on "Food from the Sea" series.
1943	Returns to the D.C. area in May, newly promoted to associate aquatic biologist in Office of the Coordinator of Fisheries; rents house in Takoma Park, Maryland. *Food from the Sea: Fish and Shellfish of New England* and *Food from Home Waters: Fishes of the Middle West* published.
1944	Publishes "The Bat Knew It First," on bat sonar, in *Collier's* magazine, and a feature article on milkweed. *Fish and Shellfish of the South Atlantic and Gulf Coasts* appears; chapters from *Under the Sea-Wind* are selected for William Beebe's anthology *The Book of Naturalists*. Unsuccessfully seeks position as science editor at *Reader's Digest*.
1945	Has appendix removed. Moves back to Silver Spring. Article about oceanarium in Marineland, Florida, appears in April *Transatlantic Review*. Proposes article on DDT research at Patuxent, Maryland, for *Reader's Digest*. Visits Maryland coast with artist Shirley Briggs, a new colleague; they later join others on a trip to Hawk Mountain Sanctuary in Pennsylvania. Asks William Beebe about possible employment in public education at the New York Zoological Society, and inquires about editorial positions at *Audubon* magazine. "Sky Dwellers," condensed from a longer article about chimney swift migration patterns, appears in *Coronet*. Begins friendly correspondence with ornithologist Ada Govan, author of *Wings at My Window*.
1946	Plans series of Fish and Wildlife Service booklets on national wildlife refuge system, "Conservation in Action." In April, with Shirley Briggs, visits recently established refuge near

Chincoteague, Virginia, researching first booklet. Takes monthlong summer vacation with mother in Boothbay Harbor, Maine. Writes Briggs: "My greatest ambition is to be able to buy a place here and manage to spend a great deal of time in it—summers at least!" *Under the Sea-Wind* goes out of print, having sold only about 2,000 copies. In September, for second "Conservation in Action" booklet, travels to Parker River in northern Massachusetts with colleague Kay Howe, a designer and illustrator. Researches refuge history at Massachusetts Audubon Society library in Lincoln, Massachusetts. Contemplating a new book of her own, meets with Harvard marine biologist and oceanographer Henry Bigelow. Receives $1,000 prize from *Outdoor Life* magazine for "Conservation Pledge": "I pledge myself to preserve and protect America's fertile soils, her mighty forests and rivers, her wildlife and minerals, for on these her greatness was established and her strength depends."

1947 Makes additional trips with Howe for "Conservation in Action": in February to Mattamuskeet National Wildlife Refuge in eastern North Carolina, and in September to refuges in Montana and Utah and fish hatcheries in Oregon. Also joins in several local Audubon Society outings. In May, while birding near Seneca, Maryland, meets Louis Halle, author of *Spring in Washington*; later has lunch with Halle and nature writer Edwin Way Teale.

1948 Publishes "The Great Red Tide Mystery" in February *Field and Stream*. Meets with literary agents recommended by friend Charles Alldredge; decides to work with Marie Rodell, a mystery novelist and editor then setting up her own New York firm. *Guarding Our Wildlife Resources*, part of the "Conservation in Action" series, appears in October. Flies to Chicago to visit Mary Scott Skinker, who dies of cancer in December. Drafts chapters for new sea book. Is elected to board of Washington, D.C., Audubon Society.

1949 Travels to New York in April, birding on Long Island with Edwin and Nellie Teale and visiting William Beebe at the New York Zoological Society. Receives writing fellowship to work on book tentatively titled "Return to the Sea." Oxford University Press editor Philip Vaudrin asks to see manuscript; after meeting him in Washington, she signs a contract. Makes two summer research trips: with Shirley Briggs, tours the Florida Everglades and briefly attempts an undersea dive; with Marie Rodell, sails from Woods Hole to Georges Bank on an Atlantic fisheries survey aboard *Albatross III*. Plans another book, for which she would write the introduction, collecting Louis Agassiz Fuertes' illustrations of Mexican birds; Oxford declines the project. Discussing it with Houghton Mifflin editor Paul Brooks, agrees instead to write an Atlantic coast guidebook. Takes leave of absence from Fish and Wildlife Service beginning in October.

1950 Decides on *The Sea Around Us* as title for Oxford book (rejecting others, including "Out of My Depth" and "Carson at Sea"). Meets with climatologists and oceanographers at Harvard and Yale; sends a draft chapter to wave expert Walter Munk at Scripps Institution of Oceanography in San Diego, and another to *Kon-Tiki* author Thor Heyerdahl. Enlists Kay Howe as illustrator. Submits manuscript to Oxford at end of June; in August, William Shawn proposes that a three-part condensation appear in *The New Yorker*. Has surgery in September to remove a breast tumor, biopsied as nonmalignant. Recuperates for a week at Nags Head, North Carolina. Applies for Guggenheim Fellowship to support research on Atlantic coast guidebook. Plans for Fuertes volume frustrated by artist's daughter. Travels to Cleveland in December to accept American Academy of Arts and Sciences–Westinghouse science writing prize for essay "The Birth of an Island," published earlier in *The Yale Review*. Proofs of *The Sea Around Us* arrive.

1951 Awarded Guggenheim Fellowship in March, obtains further leave of absence from Fish and Wildlife Service. Meets with Shawn to discuss *New Yorker* serialization of *The Sea Around Us*; it appears in the magazine on June 2, 9, and 16. Oxford hosts book party at National Press Club in Washington, D.C. Published July 12, the book is a surprise runaway best seller; it is later offered as alternate Book-of-the-Month Club selection. Spends time in Maine with Marie Rodell and Fish and Wildlife colleague Bob Hines, who agrees to illustrate guidebook, now titled "Guide to Seashore Life on the Atlantic Coast." Writes liner notes for new recording of Debussy's *La Mer*. Speaks at *New York Herald Tribune* luncheon in October, presenting hydrophone recordings of shrimp, fish, and whale sounds, and later at benefit for National Symphony Orchestra. In December sells film rights to *The Sea Around Us*. Oxford publishes new edition of first book, *Under the Sea-Wind*.

1952   Receives Henry Grier Bryant medal from Geographical Society of Philadelphia and, in New York, National Book Award for nonfiction, giving acceptance speeches. Niece Marjorie has son, Roger Allen Christie, on February 18. Accepts John Burroughs Medal in New York in April. Researching new book, now tentatively titled "Rock, Sand, and Coral: A Beachcomber's Guide to the Atlantic Coast," visits Myrtle Beach, South Carolina; Simons Island, Georgia; and Florida Keys. Receives honorary doctorates from Oberlin, Drexel Institute of Technology, and her alma mater. Formally resigns from Fish and Wildlife Service. In June, new edition of *Under the Sea-Wind* is made available as an alternate selection of Book-of-the-Month Club and is serialized in *Life*; it joins *The Sea Around Us* on best-seller lists. Spends July at Marine Biological Laboratory in Woods Hole; is elected to MBL Corporation. Visits Nantucket with Edwin and Nellie Teale. Purchases property on Southport Island, Maine, and hires contractor to build cottage. Declines invitation to join four-month South Pacific research expedition, citing family and publishing obligations. Reads script for RKO documentary *The Sea Around Us*, finding it "really dreadful." Visits Sanibel and Marco Islands, Florida, with Rodell.

1953   In January, accepting New York Zoological Society gold medal, praises society's Coney Island Aquarium project. Takes long March vacation in Myrtle Beach, South Carolina. Receives honorary doctorate from Smith College. Moves into new cottage on Southport Island, naming it "Silverledges"; niece Marjorie and grandnephew Roger follow later. In July meets Southport neighbors Dorothy and Stanley Freeman. Presents paper "The Edge of the Sea" at American Academy of Arts and Sciences symposium in Boston. RKO film *The Sea Around Us* wins Academy Award for Best Documentary Feature. Signs contract with Harper & Brothers for book on evolution, to be titled "Origin of Life." Writes and calls Dorothy Freeman frequently, sometimes enclosing intimate letters ("apples") within letters to Freeman and family. ("Our brand of 'craziness' would be a little hard for anyone but us to understand," she later explains.)

1954   Writes letter to *The Washington Post*, published on April 22, arguing that dismissal of Fish and Wildlife Service director Albert M. Day constitutes "an ominous threat to the cause of conservation." Presents material from book-in-progress, now titled *The Edge of the Sea*, as a lecture at Cranbrook Institute of Science in Bloomfield Hills, Michigan; later addresses Theta Sigma Phi Matrix Table Dinner in Columbus, Ohio. With Dorothy Freeman, visits Henry Beston and wife Elizabeth Coatsworth at home in Nobleboro, Maine; they exchange visits in subsequent years. *The New Yorker* asks to publish chapters from *The Edge of the Sea*. Over summer in Maine, takes photographs of shore creatures with Stanley Freeman; uses their slides to illustrate December lecture at Audubon Society dinner in D.C.

1955   Sends nearly completed manuscript of *The Edge of the Sea* to Paul Brooks at Houghton Mifflin, who suggests minor revisions. Hires friend Dorothy Algire to help complete taxonomic appendix for the book. Dorothy Freeman arrives in Maryland in March for a weeklong visit; *The Edge of the Sea* is dedicated to Freeman and her husband. Speaks at publisher's sales conference in Boston. Spends summer in Southport. After first serial publication in *The New Yorker* on August 20 and 27, *The Edge of the Sea* appears on October 26. Attends book party at New York's 21 Club. Elected honorary fellow of Boston Museum of Science. Asked to write television script about clouds, meets in New York with meteorologist and producer.

1956   *The Edge of the Sea* nominated for National Book Award. Program "Something About the Sky" is broadcast in March. "Help Your Child to Wonder," article for *Woman's Home Companion*, is published in July; Marie Rodell and Paul Brooks suggest she expand it as a book. In April visits correspondent Curtis Bok and wife Nellie Lee Bok in Radnor, Pennsylvania; later, conceiving plan to purchase forest land near her Southport cottage, turns to Bok for counsel. Receives Achievement Award of the American Association of University Women in Washington. Allows juvenile adaptation of *The Sea Around Us* to proceed, assigning royalties to niece Marjorie. Is invited by Maria Leiper at Simon & Schuster to edit nature anthology. Organizes a Maine chapter of The Nature Conservancy, becoming honorary chairman.

1957   Marjorie dies of pneumonia on January 30. Takes responsibility for care of grandnephew Roger, now five. Builds larger home in Silver Spring, occupying it in July, and adds extensions to Southport cottage. Abandons plan to purchase "Lost Woods" in Southport, finding the property too costly. Postpones editing of nature anthology. Writes "Our Ever-Changing Shore" for *Holiday* magazine.

1958 In February, studying dangers of insecticide use, decides to write a magazine article; drafts memorandum on "the horrifying facts about what is happening." Writes to E. B. White, encouraging him to report for *The New Yorker* on a Long Island lawsuit against Department of Agriculture gypsy moth spraying program. Contacts Marjorie Spock and Polly Richards, plaintiffs in the suit, who share trial transcript and extensive research. Working with Paul Brooks, initially envisions a "small, quick" book on insecticide problem, "How to Balance Nature"; Rodell enlists *Newsweek* science editor Edwin Diamond as project collaborator. After discussions with William Shawn at *The New Yorker*, decides longer treatment of subject is called for. Withdraws from collaboration with Diamond and hires research assistant, Bette Haney. Over summer, befriends Beverly Knecht, a young blind woman hospitalized with diabetic complications; they call and write each other often. Meets Spock and Richards in Southport, and has productive visit with Robert Rudd, University of California professor at work on *Pesticides and the Living Landscape*. Corresponds with physicians, geneticists, agronomists, ornithologists, entomologists, and others on aspects of new subject. Mother dies on December 2, after a stroke.

1959 Studies health effects of insecticides in libraries of National Cancer Institute and National Institutes of Health. Writes introduction for new edition of *The Sea Around Us*. Attends February meetings of National Wildlife Federation in New York; declines invitation to present preliminary findings. With other members of D.C. Audubon Society, sends letter to Agriculture Secretary Ezra Taft Benson, protesting film *The Fire Ant on Trial* and ant-eradication efforts; finds her access to USDA entomologists blocked. Throws party for Lois Crisler, author of 1956 memoir *Arctic Wild* and new friend. Tentatively titles book "Man Against the Earth," hoping for publication in spring 1960; hires another research assistant, Jeanne Davis. Addresses outdoor meeting of Quaint Acres Community Association in Silver Spring, convincing residents to reject a proposed spraying program. In October, presents research-in-progress at meeting of Audubon and allied societies at The Brookings Institution in Washington, D.C. Attends November Food and Drug Administration hearings on the "Great Cranberry Scare," the carcinogenic herbicide aminotriazole having been detected in the year's cranberry crop.

1960 Is diagnosed with duodenal ulcer in January. In April, discovering lumps in breast, has radical mastectomy; is told falsely that no malignancy has been found. Serves on Natural Resources Committee of Democratic Advisory Council, making recommendations about environmental priorities in a future Democratic administration. After summer in Maine, also serves on Women's Committee for New Frontiers, meeting at Georgetown home of Senator John F. Kennedy and Jacqueline Kennedy. Makes several visits to USDA laboratory of Edward F. Knipling, investigating biological alternatives to chemical insecticides. Rodell suggests *Silent Spring* as book title. In November finds swelling on rib near operation site. After initial radiation treatments seeks additional medical opinion, writing to George Crile at Cleveland Clinic: "I want to do what must be done, but no more. I still have several books to write, and can't spend the rest of my life in hospitals." Travels to Cleveland, where metastasized cancer is confirmed.

1961 Attends Reception for Distinguished Ladies at National Gallery of Art during Kennedy Inauguration. Undergoes radiation treatments later in January and continuing into March; suffers staphylococcus infection and septic arthritis as complications. In April, recovering, writes Marjorie Spock: "I have been working quite steadily on The Book again." Meets with Brooks in June, in Washington, to discuss chapter revisions, and again in New York in September; he hires Louis and Lois Darling as illustrators. Spends summer in Maine, photographers Charles Pratt and Alfred Eisenstaedt among few visitors. Learns that Beverly Knecht has died. Steady writing progress interrupted in November by painful iritis and loss of vision.

1962 Sends fifteen of seventeen chapters of *Silent Spring* to Rodell in January. William Shawn calls to offer praise ("you have made it literature"). Confides to Freeman: "suddenly the tensions of four years were broken and I got down and put my arms around [cat] Jeffie and let the tears come." Travels to Cleveland in March for further radiation treatments. Finishes another chapter and works on bibliography; is fitted for wig. In May, meets Supreme Court Justice William O. Douglas at dinner of National Parks Association Trustees and Conservation Forum; he later praises *Silent Spring* as "the most revolutionary book since *Uncle Tom's Cabin*." Flies to Los Angeles in June to deliver commencement address at Scripps College, stopping in Denver to see Lois Crisler. A condensed *Silent Spring* appears in *The New Yorker* on June 16, 23, and 30, prompting unprecedented reader response. *The New York Times* publishes article "'Silent Spring' Is Now Noisy Summer"; President Kennedy refers to "Miss Carson's book" at a press conference. Published by Houghton Mifflin on September 27, *Silent Spring* is chosen as October main selection of the Book-of-the-Month Club and reaches top of best-seller lists; Carson is subject of *Life* magazine profile, "The Gentle Storm Center." Speaks at annual meeting of National Parks Association in Washington, D.C., at meetings of National Council of Women and before Women's National Press Club. Attends informal "Kennedy Seminar" at home of Interior Secretary Stewart Udall; is interviewed by Eric Sevareid for *CBS Reports*. Returns to hospital for additional radiation at end of December; collapses in a Chevy Chase department store while shopping for Roger's Christmas gifts.

1963   Begins letter to be read after her death, to Dorothy Freeman. Receives Albert Schweitzer medal from Animal Welfare Institute. Meets with President's Science Advisory Committee; its subsequent report, *Use of Pesticides*, confirms findings and recommendations of *Silent Spring*. Has "difficult days" in March, suffering through pain and nausea after radiation; bone metastasis evident. Investigates now-discredited Krebiozen as alternative therapy. Hour-long special "The Silent Spring of Rachel Carson" airs on *CBS Reports* on April 3, with an estimated audience of 10–15 million. Appears on *Today* show late in May, and before Congress, twice, in June. Receives "Woman of Conscience" award from National Council of Women. After summer in Maine, travels to San Francisco with Marie Rodell to speak at symposium "Man Against Himself." Visits Muir Woods, in a wheelchair, with Sierra Club director David Brower. Works with Marie Rodell to organize her papers. Attends dinner of American Geographical Society and is inducted into American Academy of Arts and Letters.

1964   Attends Connecticut funeral of Stanley Freeman, who dies of a heart attack on January 14. Signs new will in February, establishing trust for Roger; leaves papers to Yale University and bequests to many, including The Nature Conservancy and the Sierra Club. Undergoes final radiation treatments at Cleveland Clinic in March and April. Dorothy Freeman visits. Dies of a heart attack on April 14. After a large public funeral at the Washington National Cathedral and smaller memorial service at All Souls Unitarian Church in Washington, D.C., her ashes are divided, half buried by brother Robert near mother's grave, half scattered by Dorothy off Southport Island.

Note on the Texts

This volume contains Rachel Carson's first three books, sometimes described as her "sea trilogy"—*Under the Sea-Wind* (1941), *The Sea Around Us* (1951), and *The Edge of the Sea* (1955)—along with a brief section of other writings. A companion volume in the Library of America series, *Silent Spring & Other Environmental Writings*, presents her final book, *Silent Spring* (1962), and a selection of letters, essays, and other short items. The texts of her sea books have been taken from the last printings to which she contributed: in the case of *Under the Sea-Wind* and *The Sea Around Us* from revised and corrected printings, published in 1952 and 1961 respectively, and in the case of *The Edge of the Sea* from the first edition of 1955. The texts of items in the *Other Writings* have been taken from original printings and a typescript, as described below.

Under the Sea-Wind: A Naturalist's Picture of Ocean Life. In April 1936, while employed at the U.S. Bureau of Fisheries, Carson wrote a short essay, "The World of Waters," as an introduction to a fisheries brochure. Her supervisor at the Bureau, Elmer Higgins, felt the piece was inappropriately lyrical for a government publication but recommended she send it to *The Atlantic*, where it appeared in September 1937, after some revision, as "Undersea." This *Atlantic* essay attracted the attention of Quincy Howe, an editor at Simon & Schuster, who wrote to ask if Carson was at work on a book. Hendrik van Loon, a Simon & Schuster author, also wrote her in praise of the piece, and both he and Howe met with her on several occasions to encourage her to continue, and to discuss her initial book ideas. Working in the evenings, her mother typing and reading her drafts back to her aloud, Carson finished the first five chapters of *Under the Sea-Wind* in the spring of 1940. Howe sent a contract in June, and on December 31, 1940, the date of her deadline, she mailed her completed manuscript. Editorial responsibility for the new book at Simon & Schuster fell to Maria Leiper, with whom Carson developed a friendly relationship.

Simon & Schuster published *Under the Sea-Wind* on November 1, 1941. Although it was named a selection of the Scientific Book Club and received some favorable reviews, the book was quickly overshadowed by news of America's entry into the Second World War, and only about 2,000 copies were sold before it went out of print. Carson herself purchased the remainder of the first printing, giving copies as gifts to friends and new acquaintances. The appearance of a second edition, a decade after the first, had everything to do with the runaway success of her second book, *The Sea Around Us*. In December 1951—the latter title having topped best-seller lists for several months, and Carson's new publisher, Oxford University Press, eager for a sequel—Carson's agent Marie Rodell arranged for Oxford to republish *Under the Sea-Wind*. Carson took advantage of this new printing, which appeared on April 13, 1952, and which ultimately joined *The Sea Around Us* on best-seller lists, to make revisions and corrections. She is not known to have sought further changes for the first British printing, published in London by Staples Press on October 3, 1952, or for a New American Library edition, published in paperback in 1955. The text of *Under the Sea-Wind* in the present volume is that of the revised and corrected Oxford first printing of April 1952. Two entries in the book's glossary—"Avens, Mountain" and "Aurelia," on page 154 of the present volume—are out of alphabetical order in all previous editions, an error that has been corrected here.

The Sea Around Us. Among the projects Carson discussed with her new literary agent, Marie Rodell, when they met for the first time in New York in the spring of 1948, was a book tentatively titled *Return to the Sea*, for which she had at that point only sketched an outline. By September, she had finished a first chapter, "The Birth of an Island." Rodell promptly submitted both chapter and outline to William Sloane Associates for possible publication, and they promptly declined. Carson resolved to draft four additional chapters by the following spring, and applied for a writing fellowship, in the end successfully, from the Eugene F. Saxton Memorial Trust.

In April 1949, Rodell received an unsolicited letter about the book-in-progress from Philip Vaudrin, an editor at Oxford University Press, who had heard about it from one of Oxford's sales representatives, who in turn had heard about it from a Georgetown bookseller. On the basis of her outline and initial chapters, he asked to meet with Carson during an upcoming trip to Washington, D.C. On June 28, she signed a contract with Oxford for *Return to the Sea*, her completed manuscript to be due on March 1, 1950. Sharing chapter-drafts with friends and experts along the way—and rejecting a string of titles for the book, including *Empire of the Sea*, *Sea Without End*, and *The Story of the Ocean*, before she chose *The Sea Around Us*—she finished writing at the end of June, only narrowly missing her original deadline.

On August 15, William Shawn at *The New Yorker* called Rodell with the news that the magazine hoped to feature large sections of the book. Adapting and condensing nine of its fourteen chapters, and conferring closely with Carson by phone over the course of ten days in May 1951, Shawn published her work in three installments—"The Sea: Unforgotten World," "The Sea: The Abyss," and "The Sea: Wind, Sun, and Moon"—on June 2, 9, and 16, 1951. Rodell placed other chapters in magazines as well: "The Birth of an Island" appeared in *The Yale Review* in September 1950; "Wealth from the Salt Seas" in *Science Digest* and "The Global Thermostat" in *Vogue*, both in October 1950; and "The Shape of Ancient Seas" in *Nature Magazine* in May 1951.

Carson began revising and correcting her Oxford galley proofs in December 1950, and Oxford published the book on July 2, 1951. Staples Press in London followed with a British printing in October. Even before *The Sea Around Us* appeared in print, however, Carson began keeping a file of new information, hoping she might be able to update the book at some point in the future. In September and October 1960 she had the opportunity to do so, writing a new preface and a section of endnotes describing current research, for a second Oxford edition, published on February 23, 1961. The text of *The Sea Around Us* in the present volume is that of the first printing of the revised Oxford edition. At two points in the text, on pages 196 and 319 of the present volume, Carson refers to the Oxford edition's endpaper maps, which are reproduced here on pages 184–85 and 408–9; these references have been emended to enable the reader to locate the maps.

The Edge of the Sea. In December 1949, while finishing *The Sea Around Us*, Carson met with Paul Brooks, editor-in-chief at Houghton Mifflin in Boston, to discuss another book she hoped to see published: a collection of Louis Agassiz Fuertes's illustrations of Mexican birds, for which she would write an introduction. Brooks later declined her Fuertes proposal, but during their conversation he encouraged her to consider Houghton Mifflin as a publisher for her future work. He wondered in particular if she might be interested in writing a kind of "shore guide" or handbook to the fauna and flora of the U.S. Atlantic coast—a project for which he had unsuccessfully been seeking the right author.

Carson liked this idea, and gradually figured out how she wanted to approach the book, envisioning it as "chiefly a creative work" about ecosystems, though it would include a handbook-like identificatory appendix. In October 1950, during a trip to the shore at Nags Head, North Carolina, she applied for a Guggenheim fellowship to support field and library research and visits to laboratories, and in March 1951—having been awarded the fellowship—she signed a contract with Houghton Mifflin for a "Guide to Seashore Life on the Atlantic Coast," which was due two years later.

The Edge of the Sea ultimately took her longer to write than expected. She sent Brooks an initial chapter, about the Florida Keys, in June 1953, and a completed manuscript, excluding the book's appendix, in March 1955. In the interim, she delivered lectures from her work-in-progress at the Cranbrook Institute of Science in Bloomfield Hills, Michigan, and before the Audubon Society of Washington, D.C., and shared individual chapters with a number of expert readers. *The New Yorker* purchased first serial rights and published two sections of the book ("The Edge of the Sea: The Rocky Shores" and "The Edge of the Sea: The Rim of Sand") on August 20 and 27, 1955.

The Edge of the Sea was published by Houghton Mifflin on October 26, 1955. A British printing followed in December, from Staples Press in London. Carson is not known to have revised or corrected her work after its initial appearance. The text of *The Edge of the Sea* in the present volume is that of the first Houghton Mifflin printing.

Other Writings. This volume concludes with a selection of three short items related to Carson's sea books: one of her early newspaper articles on Atlantic fisheries, her first maritime magazine piece, and an author questionnaire she completed to help publicize *Under the Sea-Wind*. The texts of these items have been taken from the following sources:

> Shad Going Way of the Buffalo, Atlantic Conservation Group Told. *News and Courier* (Charleston, South Carolina), February 14, 1937.
> Undersea. *The Atlantic Monthly*, September 1937.
> Memo to Mrs. Eales on *Under the Sea-Wind*. c. 1942. Typescript, Rachel Carson Papers (YCAL MSS 46), Beinecke Rare Book & Manuscript Library, Yale University.

The title and dating of the last item, "Memo to Mrs. Eales on *Under the Sea-Wind*," have been supplied from the first version of Carson's text to appear in print: *Lost Woods: The Discovered Writing of Rachel Carson*, edited by Linda Lear and published by Beacon Press in 1998.

This volume presents the texts of the original printings and single typescript chosen for inclusion here, but it does not attempt to reproduce features of their typographic design, such as the display capitalization of chapter openings. The texts are reprinted without change, except for the correction of typographical errors and the few emendations described above. Spelling, punctuation, and capitalization are often expressive features, and they are not altered, even when inconsistent or irregular. The following is a list of errors corrected, cited by page and line number: 12.29, chiton; 134.4, fish hold; 168.13, it eggs; 196.18, have; 209.35, appeared; 210.5, seem; 224.1, other; 266.24, Deep Sea; 394.27, FRNS-3; 398.15, sate; 399.6, Wilkin's; 402.5, *Hidden Lands*; 519.28 (caption), Stringing; 555.6, than; 679.5, is.

CREDITS FOR PHOTO INSERT FOLLOWING PAGE 372

1. Photograph by Andreas Feininger/The LIFE Picture Collection courtesy of Getty Images.
2. Photograph by Fritz Goro/The LIFE Picture Collection courtesy of Getty Images.
3. Douglas Wilson.
4. Lamont-Doherty Earth Observatory (Columbia University).
5. Official U.S. Navy Photograph.
6. Official U.S. Navy Photograph.
7. Lamont-Doherty Earth Observatory (Columbia University).
8. U.S. Fish and Wildlife Service.
9. U.S. Coast and Geodetic Survey.
10. Wide World Photos.
11. Paul Popper, Ltd.
12. Ludwig Schuster.
13. A. Devaney, Inc., N.Y.
14. Paul Popper, Ltd.
15. Philip Gendreau.
16. Paul Popper, Ltd.
17. Official U.S. Coast Guard Photograph.
18. Photograph © CORBIS courtesy of Getty Images.
19. Dr. Wolff & Tritschler.

Notes

In the notes below, the reference numbers denote page and line of this volume (the line count includes chapter headings but not blank lines). Quotations from Shakespeare are keyed to *The Riverside Shakespeare*, ed. G. Blakemore Evans (Boston: Houghton Mifflin, 1974). Biblical references are keyed to the King James Version. For further information about Carson's life and works, and references to other studies, see Paul Brooks, *The House of Life: Rachel Carson at Work* (Boston: Houghton Mifflin, 1972); Martha Freeman, ed., *Always, Rachel: The Letters of Rachel Carson and Dorothy Freeman, 1952–1964* (Boston: Beacon Press, 1995); Linda Lear, *Rachel Carson: Witness for Nature* (New York: Henry Holt, 1997); Linda Lear, ed., *Lost Woods: The Discovered Writing of Rachel Carson* (Boston: Beacon Press, 1998); Peter Matthiessen, ed., *Courage for the Earth: Writers, Scientists, and Activists Celebrate the Life and Writing of Rachel Carson* (New York: Houghton Mifflin, 2007); William Souder, *On a Farther Shore: The Life and Legacy of Rachel Carson* (New York: Crown, 2012); Philip Sterling, *Sea and Earth: The Life of Rachel Carson* (New York: Thomas Y. Crowell, 1970); and the website www.rachelcarson.org.

UNDER THE SEA-WIND

1.3–6 *While the sun* . . . SWINBURNE] From "A Forsaken Garden" by Algernon Charles Swinburne (1837–1909), first collected in *Poems and Ballads, Second Series* (1878).

7.15 yaupons.] *Ilex vomitoria*, a kind of holly found in the southeastern United States.

12.29 chitin fiddles] Crickets and grasshoppers, like other arthropods, have chitin exoskeletons.

66.13–15 as the earth was once dimmed . . . passenger pigeons.] Declared extinct in 1914, the passenger pigeon (*Ectopistes migratorius*) was once known to migrate across eastern North America in massive flocks, famously described by John James Audubon in his *Ornithological Biography* (1831).

122.17 the chara] A type of algae, commonly known as stonewort.

122.30–31 the insect's name . . . "a marsh treader,"] Also known as water measurers, insects in the family Hydrometridae.

129.5 spar buoys] Tall, thin buoys.

129.6–7 whistle and bell buoys] Large buoys with wave-activated whistles and bells at the top.

132.23 nun buoy] Conically shaped buoys, used to indicate the right or starboard side of a channel.

145.19 frustules] The cell walls of diatoms, made of silica.

166.16 Grinnell Land] A region on Ellesmere Island in northern Nunavut, Canada.

166.17 Victoria Land] A region in eastern Antarctica, to the east of the Ross Ice Shelf.

166.33 *shoaler*] Shallower.

167.21 "long straggling flocks, all singing together."] See *The Birds of Manitoba* (1891) by Ernest Thompson Seton.

THE SEA AROUND US

186.1 HENRY BRYANT BIGELOW] Carson met Bigelow (1879–1967), a curator of oceanography at the Museum of Comparative Zoology at Harvard and founding former director of the Woods Hole Oceanographic Institution, in 1946. He encouraged her plans for *The Sea Around Us*, and they became friends.

189.37–39 Bruce Heezen . . . lower slopes."] See Bruce C. Heezen, "Dynamic Processes of Abyssal Sedimentation: Erosion, Transportation, and Redeposition on the Deep-sea Floor," *Geophysical Journal International*, June 1959.

193.3 the Bikini bomb test] From 1946 to 1958, the United States exploded twenty-three nuclear weapons over Bikini Atoll in the Marshall Islands.

214.2–4 There is . . . MELVILLE] See Melville's *Moby-Dick; or, The Whale* (1851), chapter CXI ("The Pacific").

225.2–3 Thus with the year . . . MILTON] See *Paradise Lost* (1667), book 3.

233.2–4 Where great whales . . . ARNOLD] See Arnold's "The Forsaken Merman," first collected in *The Strayed Reveller, and Other Poems* (1849).

234.14–19 Edward Forbes . . . lingering presence."] See Forbes's *The Natural History of the European Seas* (1859).

234.22–28 Sir John Ross . . . superincumbent water."] The significance of Ross's findings is described in the first volume of the *Report of the Scientific Results of the Voyage of H.M.S. Challenger During the Years 1873–76* (1885), by C. Wyville Thomson and John Murray.

234.34–35 the ship's naturalist . . . message."] See G. C. Wallich, *The North-Atlantic Sea-Bed: Comprising a Diary of the Voyage on Board H.M.S. Bulldog, in 1860* (1862).

239.25–33 William Beebe's . . . the beam."] See Beebe's *Half Mile Down* (1934).

247.2–6 Biologists listening . . . chirps."] See William E. Schevill and Barbara Lawrence, "Underwater Listening to the White Porpoise (*Delphinapterus leucas*)," *Science*, February 11, 1949.

249.2–4 Sand-strewn caverns . . . ARNOLD] See note 233.2–4.

249.16–29 Sir James Clark Ross . . . above it."] See Ross's *A Voyage of Discovery and Research in the Southern and Antarctic Regions, During the Years 1839–43* (1847).

261.29–262.2 Plato's account . . . buried isle."] See Plato's *Timaeus* (c. 360 B.C.E.), as quoted in Pierre Termier, "Atlantis," *Smithsonian Report for 1915* (1916).

261.30 the Pillars of Hercules.] Promontories on either side of the Strait of Gibraltar.

264.1–2 A deep . . . POWYS] See Powys's essay "Bats Head," first collected in *Dorset Essays* (1935).

271.2–3 Many a green . . . SHELLEY] From the opening of "Lines Written among the Euganean Hills" by Percy Bysshe Shelley, first collected in *Rosalind and Helen, A Modern Eclogue* (1819).

274.11–14 E. F. Knight . . . tumbling to pieces."] See Knight's book *The Cruise of the "Alerte": The Narrative of a Search for Treasure on the Desert Island of Trinidad* (1890).

276.4–7 Jaggar . . . the deep sea."] See T. A. Jaggar, "The Evolution of Bogoslof Volcano," *Bulletin of the American Geographical Society of New York*, vol. 40, 1908.

279.30–33 Cotteau . . . spinning its web."] See Edmond Cotteau's "Notes on a Trip to Borneo in May, 1884," presented at a meeting of the Geographical Society of Australia on September 9, 1884, and published in the *Sydney Morning Herald* on September 11.

280.19–22 Years later . . . beings on earth."] See *The Voyage of the Beagle* (1839), chapter XVII.

281.20–23 "It is a curious . . . destructive."] See David Lack, *Darwin's Finches: An Essay on the General Biological Theory of Evolution* (1947).

282.4–8 Ernst Mayr . . . melody."] See Allan R. McCulloch, "Lord Howe Island—A Naturalist's Paradise," *Australian Museum Magazine*, August 1921. McCulloch is quoted in Mayr's "Bird Conservation Problems in the Southwest Pacific," *Audubon Magazine*, September–October 1945.

284.24–26 W. H. Hudson's lament . . . returns not."] See Hudson's *A Hind in Richmond Park* (1922).

285.2–4 Till the slow sea . . . SWINBURNE] From "A Forsaken Garden" by Algernon Charles Swinburne (1837–1909), first collected in *Poems and Ballads, Second Series* (1878).

294.13 Daly] Reginald A. Daly (1871–1957), a Canadian geologist.

297.2–3 The wind's . . . SWINBURNE] From Swinburne's "Laus Veneris," first collected in *Poems and Ballads* (1866).

299.23–25 as one naval officer . . . the sea."] See Harold E. Saunders, "The Advantages of Collaboration Between Engineering and Scientific Fields," *Proceedings of the Third Hydraulics Conference, June 10–12, 1946* (1947).

305.1–2 the report . . . Good Hope] See Dumont D'Urville's *Voyage de la corvette Astrolabe pendant les années 1826–29* (1830).

305.36–37 "There is not . . . Lord Bryce] See James Bryce, *South America: Observations and Impressions* (1912).

314.8–14 Robert Cushman Murphy . . . like wire."] See the first volume of Murphy's *Oceanic Birds of South America* (1936).

316.2–4 For thousands . . . POWYS] See note 264.1–2.

316.20 quotations from Coleridge.] The scene Carson describes recalls Coleridge's "Rime of the Ancient Mariner," first collected in *Lyrical Ballads* (1798).

318.22–26 Ponce de Leon's . . . backward."] Ponce de Leon's original reports of his voyage are not known to survive, but are paraphrased and summarized in the *Historia General de los hechos de los Castellanos en las Islas, y Tierra firme del mar Océano* (1601–5) by Antonio Herrera y Tordesillas (1549–c. 1625).

330.3–12 An old ship's log . . . months past.] From the log of Lt. William Grenville Temple of the U.S.S. *Levant*, quoted in Matthew Fontaine Maury's *Physical Geography of the Sea* (1855).

330.20–22 the Falmouth cable . . . inshore."] See Douglas Wilson Johnson, *Shore Processes and Shoreline Development* (1919).

332.2–4 In every country . . . BEDE] See "De Concordia Maris et Lunae," section 29 of *Bedae Opera de Temporibus*, as quoted in H. A. Marmer's *The Tide* (1926).

342.9–11 "a sloping cascade . . . the river."] See Charles Keyser Edmunds, "A Visit to the Hangchow Bore," *Popular Science Monthly*, March 1908.

349.2–4 Out of the chamber . . . JOB] See Job 37:9.

351.2–4 C.E.P. Brooks . . . cold taps."] See Brooks's "The Rôle of the Oceans in the Weather of Western Europe," *Quarterly Journal of the Royal Meteorological Society*, April 1930.

351.25–27 It has been described . . . seasons of want."] See Hans Pettersson, "Meteorological Aspects of Oceanography," *Monthly Weather Review*, June 1916.

356.21–24 C.E.P. Brooks . . . two agents."] See Brooks's *Climate Through the Ages* (revised edition, 1949).

364.24–26 Hans Ahlmann . . . snow"] See Ahlmann's paper "The Present Climatic Fluctuation," *The Geographical Journal*, October–December 1948.

367.2–3 A sea change . . . SHAKESPEARE] See *The Tempest*, I.i.401–2.

376.4–7 geologists . . . oceanic deeps."] See Wallace E. Pratt, "Our Petroleum Resources," *American Scientist*, April 1944.

379.2–4 A sea . . . HOMER] See *The Odyssey*, Book 3, in George Herbert Palmer's translation of 1884.

387.14 loran] Short for long-range navigation, a radio-based navigational system used by ships and planes beginning in World War II.

402.18–23 Columbus Iselin . . . Gulf Stream System."] See "The Gulf Stream System," *Proceedings of the American Philosophical Society*, December 20, 1952.

THE EDGE OF THE SEA

476.6–9 Dr. W. G. Hewatt . . . then returned.] See "Observations of the Homing Limpet *Acmaea scabra* Gould," *American Midland Naturalist*, July 1940.

478.18–21 an old book . . . black death."] See the Rev. David Landsborough's *Popular History of British Sea-Weeds* (1849).

554.17–23 "Each tube . . . deposited."] See Arnold T. Watson, "On the Habits of *Amphictenidae*," *The Annals and Magazine of Natural History*, July 1894.

568.26–569.4 Jocelyn Crane . . . scraping of sand.] See Crane's paper "On the Growth and Ecology of Brachyuran Crabs of the Genus *Ocypode*," *Zoologica* (1941).

576.14 Holmes's famous poem.] See "The Chambered Nautilus" by Oliver Wendell Holmes, Sr. (1809–1894), first collected in *The Autocrat of the Breakfast-Table* (1858).

592.13–25 The seventeenth-century . . . Barnakles."] See Gerard's *Herball, or Generall Historie of Plantes* (1597).

631.20–23 As Alexander Agassiz . . . a roof."] See Elizabeth C. Agassiz and Alexander Agassiz, *Seaside Studies in Natural History* (1865).

661.7–8 The English writer Barbellion . . . world.] See "The Brightest Thing in the World," a June 1, 1919, entry in *A Last Diary* (1920) by W.N.P. Barbellion (Bruce Frederick Cummings, pseud., 1889–1919): "Rupert Brooke said the brightest thing in the world was a leaf with the sun shining on it. God pity his ignorance! The brightest thing in the world is a Ctenophor in a glass jar standing in the sun. This is a bit of a secret, for no one knows about it save only the naturalist."

OTHER WRITINGS

681.33–37 A writer of the day . . . grounds."] See William E. Meehan, *Fish, Fishing, and Fisheries of Pennsylvania* (1893), which paraphrases "an old author."

Index

Abyss, 63–65, 142–46, 148, 153, 189–90, 222, 233–61, 264–69, 276, 332, 394, 575, 634, 686, 690
Acetabularia, 657
Acorn barnacles, 468–74, 591, 667
Adam of Bremen, 384
Agassiz, Alexander, 631
Agassiz, Louis, 294
Ahlmann, Hans, 364
Alaria, 484–86
Albatross and *Albatross III* (research vessels), 254–55, 266–67, 316
Albatrosses, 219, 666; white-browed, 363
Alcids, 219, 227
Alcyonaria, 518–19
Alcyonidium, 582
Aleutian Islands, 229, 255, 260, 275–76, 311–13, 324, 339–40
Aleutian Trench, 310
Alewife, 227, 680
Alfred the Great, 382
Algae, 24, 54, 88, 96, 98, 102, 122, 127, 145–46, 153, 155, 157, 160, 169, 205, 216–17, 222, 227, 230, 345, 355, 429–30, 436, 448, 453, 458, 462, 465, 471, 475–80, 486, 489–90, 494, 498, 506–7, 510, 520–22, 524, 530, 539, 581–82, 604, 606, 608–9, 615–18, 626, 630, 635, 655–58, 664, 691
All America (cable repair ship), 240–41
Alps, 261, 364
Amaroucium, 676
Amazon River, 278, 341
American golden plovers, 42–43
American robins, 125
Amphibians, earliest, 211–12. *See also* Frogs
Amphineura. *See* Chitons
Amphipods, 13, 54, 82–83, 101, 105, 153, 175, 438, 446, 469, 507–9, 546, 570–73, 611, 625, 665–66
Amphithoë, 507–8
Amphitrites, 432, 481, 664

Anchovy, 66, 75–76, 153, 325, 688
Andes Mountains, 261, 287, 364
Angelfish, 614, 632–33
Angel wing clams, 437, 589
Anglerfish, 136–39, 154
Annelida, 219, 490, 495, 505, 527, 663–64, 670
Antarctica, 291, 355, 364, 385–86, 391
Antarctic Current, 318, 324
Antarctic Ocean, 26, 74, 170, 253, 255, 269, 304, 318, 325, 330–31, 385–86
Anthozoa. *See* Corals; Sea anemones
Anurida, 489–90, 525–26
Appalachian Mountains, 123, 261, 286, 537
Apple murexes, 541
Apuleius, 626
Arachnoidea. *See* Horseshoe crabs
Archeozoic era, 210–11, 393, 429
Architeuthis, 240, 674
Arctic, 28–43, 45, 99, 149, 267, 314, 355–56, 362, 365, 376, 381, 387, 399, 450
Arctic Current, 221
Arctic foxes, 28–29, 31–32, 34–35, 38–40
Arctic hares, 31
Arctic Ocean, 256–57, 286, 289, 331, 350, 355, 362, 376, 386, 398–99, 484
Arctic terns, 34–35, 180
Argonauts, 414, 575–76, 674
Aristotle, 475
Arks: ponderous, 587–88; transverse, 587; turkey wing, 587
Armstrong, Richard, 685
Army Corps of Engineers, U.S., 298
Arnold, Matthew, 233, 249
Arrowworms, 216, 244
Arthropoda, 205, 207, 429–30, 469–71, 664–68. *See also* Amphipods; Barnacles; Copepods; Crabs; Crayfish; Isopods; Lobsters; Shrimps
Ascension Island, 273, 313, 328
Ascidians. *See* Sea squirts
Ashes, mountain, 119

728 INDEX

Askoy (research vessel), 326–27
Asteria, 584
Astrangia, 532
Astropecten, 552
Atacama Desert, 354
Atacama Trench, 310
Atlantic Ocean, 218, 221–24, 228, 250, 253–55, 257–62, 266, 269–71, 276, 285–86, 291, 297–98, 300–303, 306–8, 311, 318–21, 329–31, 336–37, 349–51, 355–58, 361, 364–65, 384, 395, 398, 400–401, 403, 432–33, 439, 443–44, 447–48, 491, 504, 537, 539, 565–66, 576, 584–85, 591, 667, 679–85
Atlantic Ridge, 190, 254–55, 257–60, 262, 266–67, 398
Atlantis (research vessel), 245, 255, 258, 266
Atlantis legend, 261–62
Atomic energy waste, 191–93
Audubon, John James, 426
Aurelia, 88–89, 154, 228, 500–502
Avens, mountain, 35–39, 154
Avienus, 380–81
Avocets, 363

Bacteria, 204–5, 421, 429, 551, 563
Bahamas, 626, 637
Baird's sandpipers, 34
Balboa, Vasco Núñez de, 385
Bald eagles, 49, 51–52
Baleen whales, 241
Balsams, 459
Baltic Sea, 285, 353, 356–58, 360, 362, 381
Baltimore orioles, 363
Barbados, 256
Barbellion, W. N. P., 661
Barents, William, 387
Barents Sea, 219–20, 251, 285, 361–62, 364, 382
Barnacles, 53–54, 66–67, 74, 82, 100, 127, 135, 154, 212, 216, 342, 431, 434–35, 438, 441, 446, 448–51, 457, 462, 465–66, 476, 478, 487, 489–90, 494–95, 522, 525–26, 532, 615, 618–20, 654, 665–67, 687; acorn, 468–74, 592, 667; gooseneck, 577, 591–93, 667; rock, 468–74, 592, 667
Barometric pressure, 313, 352–53

Barracuda, 610–11, 643
Barrier islands, 12, 18–27, 45, 47–49, 55–56, 555
Barton, Otis, 233
Basalt, 202–3, 255–56
Basket sea stars, 98, 100, 155, 630–32
Basket sponges, 431
Basking sharks, 364
Bass, 23, 58, 90, 131, 140, 150
Bats, 277, 290, 396
Bayberry, 91, 457, 516, 653
Bay of Fundy tides, 303, 332, 334–36, 339, 432, 448
Beach plums, 91
Beaded periwinkles, 614
Beagle, H.M.S., 217, 230
Bearded lichens, 459
Bêche-de-mer. See Sea cucumbers
Bede, Venerable, 332
Beebe, William, 233, 239
Beeches, 120–21, 124
Bees, 36, 40
Beetles, 43, 120, 123
Bell, Frank T., 679
Belted kingfishers, 150
Benguela Current, 220, 321, 355
Bering land bridge, 292
Bering Sea, 228–29, 236, 276, 285, 324, 340, 387
Bermuda, 142, 145, 147, 221, 233, 255, 269, 271, 290, 331, 444, 452, 626
Beroë, 78–79, 155
Betony, 35–39, 154
Bible, 201, 349
Bigelow, Henry B., 186, 195, 404, 413, 442
Birches, 262, 442
Birds, earliest, 211–12
Bitterns, 119
Bivalves. *See* Clams; Mussels; Oysters; Scallops
Black angelfish, 614, 632–33
Black-bellied plovers, 22, 363
Blackfish, 327
Black horn shells, 614
Black-legged kittiwakes, 64, 99, 114, 166
Black Sea, 375–76, 389
Black skimmers, 7–10, 17, 20, 25, 50, 174, 424
Bladder wrack, 491–92, 499

INDEX

Blenny, 8, 97, 155, 515, 617
Blood-red sea stars, 443, 511–12
Bloodworms, 663–64
Bloody clams, 587
Blue crabs, 132, 545, 547, 564
Bluefish, 75–76, 216, 688
Blue mussels, 482, 494, 503–6, 508, 522, 527, 529, 532–33, 586
Blue whales, 688
Blue-winged teal, 21, 180
Boat shells, 586–87, 672
Bogoslof Island, 275–76
Bonito, 325
Boobies, 325
Borax, 374
Bores, tidal, 341–42
Boron, 368
Botryllus, 482–83, 676
Bottlenose whales, 238
Bouvet de Lozier, Jean-Baptiste, 385
Brain corals, 608–9
Brant, 21, 155
Brazil Current, 321, 403
Brazilwood, 283
Bristle worms, 490, 527, 663–64
Brittle stars, 438, 481, 509, 514, 627, 629–31, 649, 668–70
Broad-winged hawks, 123
Bromine, 371, 374
Brooks, C. E. P., 351, 356, 365
Brooks, S. C., 220–21
Brown, Lloyd, 389
Bryozoa, 54, 156, 436, 480, 505–6, 509–10, 533, 582, 595, 654, 668
Bugula, 596
Bulldog (research vessel), 234
Buntings, snow, 28, 31, 36, 179
Buttercups, 36
Butterflies, 36, 471
Byce, James, 305
By-the-word sailors, 578–79

Cabot, John, 386
Cake urchins, 433
Calanus, 66, 93–94, 100, 156, 665
Calcium, 367, 369
Calico crabs, 556
Cambrian period, 155, 207, 210–12, 247, 261, 317, 393, 430, 535, 667–68, 674
Canada warblers, 363

Canadian Shield, 393
Canary Current, 321
Canvasbacks, 21
Canyons, submarine, 252–53, 257, 294, 397–98
Cape Cod, 308, 335, 441–43, 586
Cape Johnson, U.S.S., 257
Capelin, 227
Cape Verde Islands, 626
Caprella, 153
Carboniferous period, 208–9, 461
Cardinal fish, 637
Cardinals, 282
Caribbean Sea, 376
Caribou, 28, 32–33, 41
Carolina wrens, 50
Carroll, Lewis, 487
Carson, Mary Frazier, 4
Cask shells, 636, 642
Caspian Sea, 287, 376
Catfish, 51–52
Cedars, 7, 12, 23, 81
Cenozoic era, 208–9, 252, 645
Cephalopods. *See* Nautiluses; Octopuses; Squids
Ceratium, 100, 156
Cerebratulus, 662
Cero, 58, 156
Challenger, H.M.S., 235, 247, 276, 321, 398
Chambered nautiluses, 575–76, 673
Channeled whelks, 562, 590
Channeled wrack, 491
Chara, 122, 157
Chesapeake Bay, 285, 334, 682, 684
Chestnuts, 119
China Sea, 285, 342
Chinook salmon, 227
Chitons, 12, 452, 615–16, 672, 674
Chlorine, 367–68, 373–74
Chlorophyceae, 657
Chlorophyll, 205
Chordata, 675
Christensen, R. J., 236
Chukchi Sea, 236
Cirripedia. *See* Barnacles
Clams, 64, 98, 136, 367, 442, 489–90, 495–96, 543, 545, 552, 582, 668, 672–73, 675, 687; angel wing, 437, 589; bloody, 587; coquina, 566, 673; hard-shelled, 561; lima, 608, 673;

long-necked, 443, 494; razor, 546, 561, 673; red-nose, 482; sea, 97; sunray, 54, 557; surf, 587
Clamworms, 83–84, 144, 495, 664
Clava, 499–500
Cliff swallows, 363
Climate change, 270, 285–86, 356, 361–66, 441–42, 602, 651
Coalfish, 363
Coast and Geodetic Survey, 285, 312, 334, 401
Cobalt, 369
Cobblestones, 461–62
Cockles, 64, 98, 132, 157, 539
Cod, 80, 83, 94, 96–98, 106, 126, 139–40, 216, 227–28, 232, 239, 262, 361, 363–64, 443, 502, 674, 689
Coe, Wesley, 662–63
Coelacanths, 247–48, 397
Coelenterates, 519, 577, 659–61. *See also* Corals; Hydroids; Jellyfish; Sea anemones
Coffee-bean shells, 649–50
Coker, Robert E., 325
Coleridge, Samuel Taylor, 316
Colors, oceanic, 217–18
Columbia River, 227, 253, 684
Columbus, Christopher, 224, 384–85, 613
Comb jellies, 216, 230, 244, 523–24, 661, 688
Common crown conchs, 645
Common periwinkles, 466, 510, 522
Common whelks, 522
Conchs, 50, 641; common crown, 643; fighting, 636; horse, 638, 642–43; king crown, 642; left-handed, 672; queen, 636–39
Congo River, 253, 278
Conrad, Joseph, 231, 306
Continental shelf, 63–67, 84, 94, 99, 104, 116, 139–40, 142, 148, 157–58, 225, 231, 233, 237, 241, 250–54, 289, 292, 297, 320, 324, 377, 395, 439, 512, 575, 581
Continental slope, 250–53, 268, 294, 315, 320, 328
Convoluta, 345
Cook, James, 282, 385
Cook Inlet, 335, 342
Coon oysters, 647–48

Copepods, 66, 69, 71, 81, 85, 93–94, 100, 106, 109, 143, 146, 156, 158, 216, 219, 226, 230, 232, 240, 328, 517, 529, 542, 546, 548, 630, 651, 665–66
Copper, 369
Coquina clams, 566, 673
Corallines, 512, 516, 519–20, 522, 530, 539, 581, 658, 664
Coral reefs, 218–19, 222, 288, 320, 343, 367, 387, 415–16, 431–33, 465, 517–18, 519–20, 581, 599–644, 651, 653–54
Corals, 66, 145, 205, 235, 266, 320, 370, 378, 423, 432–33, 458, 516, 521, 539, 541–42, 547, 576, 581, 599–600, 602–3, 607, 613–14, 651, 660–61, 686, 691; brain, 608–9; elkhorn, 605, 610; finger, 622; horny, 582, 584, 605–6, 609; rose, 622; soft, 518–19; star, 532, 609; starlet, 609; stony, 518, 520
Core, earth's, 202–3, 294
Cormorants, 325, 391; flightless, 281
Cotteau, Gustave, 279
Cousteau, Jacques, 394
Cowfish, 636, 640
Crabs, 64, 67, 71–72, 86, 94, 97–98, 100, 128, 134–36, 139, 158, 216, 222, 227, 276, 327, 458, 463, 469, 487, 489, 525, 571, 585, 617, 643, 664–65, 667–68, 674, 690, 694; blue, 132, 545, 547, 564; calico, 556; decorator, 446; fiddler, 23–25, 161, 544, 556, 648–49, 695; gall, 608; ghost, 10, 21–23, 58–59, 163, 207, 424–25, 567–70, 573, 687, 695; green, 442, 495; hermit, 12, 66, 164–65, 458, 614, 650; Hippa, 18–19, 33, 45, 174; horseshoe, 438, 544–45, 558, 667–68; Jonah, 512, 514; knobbed, 447; lady, 557; mole, 438, 545, 563–66, 568, 620; mud, 445; pea, 552–53, 559–60, 588–89; purple-clawed, 650; rock, 513; spider, 640, 642; stone, 561; white, 650
Crane, Jocelyn, 568
Crane flies, 34, 123, 158
Crayfish, 120, 124, 444
Crested terns, 220
Cretaceous period, 208–9, 248, 286, 288–90, 319, 377, 397

INDEX

Crinoids, 669
Croaker, 131–32, 140, 150, 158–59, 246
Cromwell, Townsend, 402
Crossbills, 363
Crowberry, 36, 43, 159
Crown conchs, 642–43, 645, 648
Crows, 9, 150, 489–90; fish, 58, 86
Crumb-of-bread sponges, 436, 515–16, 529–30, 534
Crust, earth's, 189, 203–4, 206, 254, 256, 260, 266, 276, 287, 290, 292, 337, 374–76, 398
Crustaceans, 247, 429–30, 469–71, 610, 627, 640, 649, 662, 664–68, 674. *See also* Amphipods; Barnacles; Copepods; Crabs; Crayfish; Isopods; Lobsters; Shrimps
Ctenophora, 68–69, 71, 84, 159, 661; Beroë, 78–79, 155; Mnemiopsis, 72, 78, 168; Pleurobrachia, 76–79, 171
Cuckoos, shining, 388
Cunner, 80, 82, 96–97, 105, 135, 137, 689
Curlews, Eskimo, 159
Currents, oceanic, 316–31, 349–52, 354–55, 361, 402–3
Cusk, 94–96, 363
Cuttlefish, 674
Cuvier, Georges, 576
Cyanea, 72, 160, 228, 438, 502–3, 660
Cyanophyceae, 656–57
Cyclic salts, 368–69
Cypress swamps, 14, 45

Dace, 119
Daisy (research vessel), 281
Dalrymple, Alexander, 390
Daly, Reginald A., 256, 293–94
Darwin, Charles, 217, 230, 276, 279–81, 306
Date mussels, 437, 582
Davis, John, 386
Dead Sea, 371, 374
Decapods. *See* Squids
Decorator crabs, 446
Deer, 263
Deforestation, 283
Delaware Bay, 285
Delaware River, 681
Desmids, 122, 160
Devil's aprons, 479

Devonian period, 208–9, 211, 287, 317
Diatoms, 63, 68, 122, 145, 147, 160, 162, 214, 216, 225–28, 232, 243, 269, 328, 367–68, 378, 399, 453–54, 468, 523, 548, 550–51, 559, 566, 654, 656, 666, 672, 688, 691
Dinoflagellata, 101, 169, 229–30, 454, 655
Diopatra, 543, 560
Disk shells, 605
Dodecaceria, 584–85
Dodo, 280
Dogfish, 102, 105–6, 115–16, 688
Dogger Bank, 251, 262–63, 292
Dog whelks, 463, 472–74
Dogwoods, 125
Dolomite, 289, 371
Dolphins, 50, 228; orcas, 107–8, 169, 221
Dovekies, 99, 160
Dover white cliffs, 288
Doves, 282; mourning, 9
Dowitchers, 22, 160
Dragonfish, 143, 160–61
Dry Tortugas, 605, 611
Ducks, 34; blue-winged teal, 21, 180; canvasbacks, 21; eiders, 137–39, 161; Laysan teal, 283; long-tailed, 130, 149, 169; mergansers, 21, 168
Dulse, 473, 478–79, 533, 658
Dumont d'Urville, Jules, 305
Dunlins, 34

E. W. Scripps (research vessel), 236
Eagles, bald, 49, 51–52
Eales, Mrs., 693–700
Earthworms, 279, 553, 633
Easter Island Ridge, 400
Ebb tides, 333, 335–36, 421–24, 432, 445–52
Ebony, 283
Echinodermata, 668–71. *See also* Brittle stars; Sand dollars; Sea anemones; Sea cucumbers; Sea stars; Sea urchins
Eddies, 332, 340–41, 350
Edrisi, 383–84
Eel grass, 21, 46–47, 84, 155, 558, 571
Eels, 15–17, 45, 96, 574, 689; conger, 53–54, 104–6, 157; lamprey, 125–26; rock, 515–16; sand, 66, 83, 85–86, 91–

92, 166, 546; silver, 119–29, 139, 142–51, 154, 178, 694, 698–99
Egrets: reddish, 425; snowy, 22–23, 161
Eiders, 137–39, 161
Elephant seals, 212
Elkhorn corals, 605, 610
El Niño Current, 354
Enteromorpha, 523, 657
Equatorial Countercurrent, 324, 328
Equatorial Current, 215, 220–21, 276, 317–19, 321, 324, 326, 328–29, 349–50, 402, 444, 645
Erebus, H.M.S., 249, 386
Eric the Red, 358–59
Eskimo curlews, 159
Estuaries, 13–17, 21, 45, 47–48, 50–51, 53, 119, 127, 131, 149–50, 451, 460
Euphausiid shrimps, 216, 239
Everglades, 287–88, 604–5
Ewing, W. Maurice, 265–67
Eyring, C. F., 236

Falcon Island, 273
Fanleaf palms, 283
Ferns, 145, 211, 262
Fiddler crabs, 23–25, 161, 544, 556, 648–49, 695
Fierasfer, 635
Fighting conchs, 636
Fiji, 343, 645
File shells, 608
Finger corals, 622
Fish, earliest, 207, 212
Flamingos, 426
Flamingo-tongue snails, 609–10
Flatworms, 660–62, 672
Fleming, Richard, 238
Flies: crane, 34, 123, 158; may-, 34, 168; soldier, 123, 179
Flightless cormorants, 281
Flint, 288
Flood tides, 333, 335–36, 421, 424, 445–52
Florida Keys, 320, 438–39, 444, 541, 543, 599–651
Flounder, 11, 94, 97–98, 131, 138, 140, 161–62, 262, 689
Flower anemones, 620–21
Flustrella, 506, 533
Flycatchers, 281

Flying fish, 147, 215, 220–23, 276
Folger, Timothy, 318–19
Foraminifera, 145, 162, 268, 270, 288, 367, 538–39, 541, 655–56
Forbes, Edward, 234
Forked wrack, 434
Fossils, 206–7, 239, 247–48, 273, 280, 362, 372, 378, 397, 429–30, 535, 537, 582, 645, 656, 667, 669
Foxes, arctic, 28–29, 31–32, 34–35, 38–40
Fram (research vessel), 256
Franklin, Benjamin, 318–19, 408–9
Franklin, John, 386
Freeman, Dorothy and Stanley, 418
Frigatebirds, 388
Frilled sharks, 248
Frobisher, Martin, 386
Frogs, 120, 124–25, 225, 277, 675
Fulmars, 99, 110, 162, 219, 221, 227
Fur seals, 229, 241, 386

Galapagos Islands, 215, 280–81, 321, 326, 328, 402
Galathea (research vessel), 191
Gall crabs, 608
Ganges River, 253, 278
Gannets, 74, 88, 99, 162–63, 325
Gastropods. *See* Snails
Gatty, Harold, 388
Geese, 593; brant, 21, 155; snow, 21
Geologic time periods, 208–11
Georges Bank, 140, 162, 303, 316, 460, 518
Gerard, John, 592–93
Ghost crabs, 10, 21–23, 58–59, 163, 207, 424–25, 567–70, 573, 687, 695
Ghost shrimps, 543, 550–53, 559
Giant sea stars, 629, 636, 638
Giant squids, 240, 674
Giant tortoises, 280
Gibraltar, 329–30
Gigartina, 505, 507
Gilbert Islands, 259, 343
Gilpin, John, 319
Glaciers, 209, 253, 262–63, 270, 286, 289, 291–94, 308, 364–65, 460–62, 539–41, 600, 602–3
Glass sponges, 242
Glassworms, 69–71, 163, 226, 230, 239, 244, 688

Globigerina, 268, 270
Glycera, 663–64
Gneiss, 460
Goby, 552
Godwits, Hudsonian, 25, 159
Gold, 370
Golden-star tunicates, 436, 482–84
Goniolithon, 618
Gonyaulax, 229–30
Gooseneck barnacles, 577, 591–93, 667
Gorgonians, 582, 584, 604–6, 609, 622, 627, 630, 632, 642
Graham's Reef, 273
Grand Banks, 140, 162, 220–21, 250–51, 320–21, 349–50, 402, 460, 518, 674
Granite, 202–3, 206, 256, 291, 342, 460, 516
Grasses, 231, 355; beach, 21, 26, 55, 133, 556, 558, 573, 636; eel, 21, 46–47, 84, 155, 558, 571; gorgonian, 582, 584; manatee, 635; marsh, 7, 10–12, 16, 22, 25–26, 46–48, 54, 128; sea, 636–43, 646, 649; shoal, 635; tundra, 37–38; turtle, 444, 622, 629, 635, 638–39, 641; widgeon, 17, 47, 181
Grasshoppers, 231
Gray snapper, 610, 643
Great Barrier Reef, 600
Great blue herons, 10–12
Greater shearwaters, 177–78
Great white sharks, 688
Grebes, 15, 150, 163
Green crabs, 442, 495
Green herons, 50
Greenland, 99, 155, 289, 291, 321, 329–30, 355–56, 358–59, 361–63, 363, 365, 383–84, 388, 484
Greenland Currents, 350–51
Green sea urchins, 436, 443, 516, 521–22
Green turtles, 640–41
Grenville Mountains, 393
Grunion, 344–45
Guano, 325
Guillemots, 391
Gulf of Maine, 334, 443
Gulf of Mexico, 149, 162, 285–86, 320, 336, 353, 376–77, 442, 540, 543, 600, 650
Gulf of Penjinsk, 335

Gulf of St. Lawrence, 74, 100, 155, 162
Gulf Stream, 88, 140, 184–85, 190, 218–19, 221–24, 251, 315–16, 318–21, 324, 349–51, 361, 368, 402–3, 439–40, 443–44, 577–78, 580–81, 600, 606, 639, 657
Gulls, 7, 17, 20, 34–36, 52, 54, 56, 58, 67, 76, 81, 87–88, 92–93, 102, 107, 127, 150, 214, 422, 489–90, 512, 521, 525, 561, 577, 671; black-legged kittiwakes, 64, 99, 114, 166; herring, 25–26, 84, 86, 91, 457–58; laughing, 26, 86; ring-billed, 566
Gumwood, 283
Gypsum, 373
Gyrfalcons, 38, 40, 163–64

Haber, Fritz, 370
Haddock, 94–95, 97–98, 106, 126, 140, 164, 228, 363, 502, 689
Hake, 94, 164, 262
Halibut, 98
Halley, Edmond, 283
Hammerhead sharks, 220
Hard-shelled clams, 561
Hares, arctic, 31
Hartman, Olga, 584–85
Harvey, E. Newton, 665
Hatchet fish, 144, 164, 327
Hawaiian Islands, 257, 259, 279, 282–83, 290, 311–12, 384, 388, 400–401, 538–39
Hawks, 46, 281; broad-winged, 123
Hawksbill turtles, 640–41, 643
Heart urchins, 543, 546, 549, 551
Heezen, Bruce C., 189, 395–96
Helmet shells, 636
Hemlocks, 119
Henderson, U.S.S., 236
Henricia, 443, 511–12
Henwood, William J., 309
Hermit crabs, 12, 66, 164–65, 458, 615, 650
Hero (sealer), 386
Herodotus, 380
Herons, 46, 87, 150, 649; great blue, 10–12; green, 50
Herring, 74, 77–78, 80, 82–83, 91–93, 95, 106, 138, 216, 219, 227, 235, 243, 315, 319, 328, 357–58, 361, 442–43, 453–54, 665, 688

Herring gulls, 25–26, 84, 86, 91, 457–58
Hess, H. H., 257, 261, 266
Hewatt, W. G., 476
Heyerdahl, Thor, 215–16, 238
Hickories, 119–21
Himalaya Mountains, 261, 287
Himlico, 380–81
Hines, Bob, 411, 413, 416
Hippa crabs, 18–19, 33, 45, 174
Hjorleif, 388
Hjort, Johan, 238
Holmes, Oliver Wendell, 576
Holothurians. *See* Sea cucumbers
Homer, 379
Horned larks, 37
Horny corals, 582, 584, 605–6, 609
Horse conchs, 640, 642, 644
Horse mackerel, 364
Horse mussels, 482, 513–15
Horseshoe crabs, 438, 544–45, 558, 667–68
Horsetail kelp, 479, 484, 486
Houot, Georges, 394
Howe, Quincy, 693–94
Hudson, Henry, 386
Hudson, W. H., 284
Hudson Bay, 33, 43, 45, 155, 206, 285–86
Hudson Canyon, 253
Hudsonian godwits, 25, 159
Hudson River, 227, 253, 684
Humboldt Current, 220, 325–28, 354–55
Hurricanes, 301, 310, 312–13, 378
Hydroids, 64, 135, 165, 437, 453, 458, 471, 523, 582, 659–60, 668; Clava, 499–500; Sertularia, 527–29; Tubularia, 423, 519–20
Hydrozoa. *See* Hydroids

Ianthina, 689
Ice Age, 209, 253, 262–63, 270, 286, 289, 291–94, 308, 365, 461, 539–41, 600, 602–3
Icebergs, 264, 270, 321, 361–62
Iceland, 227, 257–58, 350, 353, 358–65, 383, 388
Indian Ocean, 255, 258–59, 291, 293, 317, 331, 336–37, 398, 444, 518, 520, 585

Indus River, 253
Ingolf, 388
International Geophysical Year, 188, 399
Iodine, 368, 370–71
Ionian Sea, 589
Irish moss, 97, 449, 458, 473, 478–79, 484, 490, 494, 508–15, 519, 521, 533, 658
Iron, 202–3, 294, 691
Iselin, Columbus, 402
Islands, formation of, 271–84
Isopods, 437, 524, 613, 617, 625, 665–66

Jaegers, 26, 35–36, 38, 40, 99, 103–4, 165, 221
Jaggar, Thomas, 276
James Bay, 45
Janthina, 576–77
Japan Current, 324
Japan Trench, 310
Jasper, U.S.S., 236
Jellyfish, 66, 68, 143–44, 147, 205, 214, 232, 242, 327, 429–30, 547, 660–61; Aurelia, 88–89, 154, 228, 500–502; Cyanea, 72, 160, 228, 438, 502–3, 660; medusa, 71, 168, 244, 453; Portuguese men-of-war, 147, 171–72, 221, 243, 573, 578–81; sea nettles, 577; Vellela, 578–79
Jet Stream, 402
Jewel sea anemones, 622
Jingle shells, 166, 586
Johan Hjort (research vessel), 239
Johnson, Martin W., 236, 565
Jonah crabs, 512, 514
Junipers, 457, 653
Jurassic period, 208–9, 317, 377, 397, 575

Kalahari Desert, 354–55
Kellogg, W. N., 396
Kelps, 436, 443, 450, 463, 479–94, 571, 657; horsetail, 479, 484, 486; winged, 484–86
Kelvin, Baron (William Thomson), 249–50
Kerguelen, Yves-Joseph de, 385
Keyhole limpets, 438
Keyhole urchins, 139, 174–75, 543, 549–50

Killdeer, 171
Killer whales, 107–8, 169
Killifish, 8–10, 22, 24, 47, 166
King crabs. *See* Horseshoe crabs
King crown conchs, 642
Kingfishers, belted, 150
Kitching, J. A., 486
Kittiwakes, black-legged, 64, 99, 114, 166
Knight, E. F., 274
Knipowitsch (research vessel), 362
Knobbed crabs, 447
Knobbed whelks, 560, 562, 590
Knots, red, 27, 34–35, 37, 41, 166
Knotted wrack, 434, 488, 491–94, 499
"Kon-Tiki" expedition, 215–16
Krakatoa, 274–75, 278–79, 646
Krill, 228
Kullenberg, Börje, 265
Kuroshio Current, 324

Labrador Current, 320–21, 324, 349, 351–52, 361–62, 439
Labrador Sea, 329–30
Lack, David, 281
Lady crabs, 557
Laminarian seaweeds, 443, 449, 479–86, 512
Lampreys, 125–26
Land bridges, 277, 292
Lantana, 282
Lantern fish, 327
Lapland longspurs, 31, 37–38, 167
Laptev Sea, 362
Larks: horned, 37; sky-, 282, 363
Latimeria, 247–48, 397
Laughing gulls, 26, 86
Launce, 66, 83, 85–86, 91–92, 166, 546
Laurentian Mountains, 206, 261
Laver, purple, 477–78
Laysan Island, 281, 283–84
Laysan rails, 283–84
Laysan teal, 283
Least sandpipers, 27
Leathesia, 477–78
Left-handed conchs, 672
Lemmings, 29–32, 34, 36, 38–39, 166–67
Lepas, 577, 591–93
Lichens, 35–36, 40, 120, 276, 355, 463, 465, 487; bearded, 459

Lima clams, 608, 673
Limestone, 287–89, 603–6, 656
Limpets, 434–35, 474–77; keyhole, 438
Lineus, 662
Ling, 363
Linkia, 629–30
Lisbon earthquake, 310–11
Lithium, 374
Lizards, 277, 279–80
Lobsters, 96, 135–36, 157, 327, 369, 434, 466, 469, 664–65, 667, 689; spiny, 623, 643
Loeb, Jacques, 671
Lofoten Islands, 227, 361
Loggerhead sponges, 604, 622–25, 628
Loggerhead turtles, 640–41, 643
Long-necked clams, 443, 494
Long-spined sea urchins, 609, 623, 628
Longspurs, Lapland, 31, 37–38, 167
Long-stalked laminaria, 485
Long-tailed ducks, 130, 149, 169
Lookdown fish, 134, 137, 167–68
Loons, 40, 150
Lord Howe Island, 282
Lord Kelvin (cable repair ship), 270
Lugworms, 543, 546, 553–54
Luidea, 552

Mackerel, 63–116, 126, 176, 216, 219, 241, 243, 665, 674, 688, 694, 697; horse, 364; snake, 215–16
Maelstrom, 340–41
Magellan, Ferdinand, 249, 385
Magnesium, 369, 371–73
Malay Archipelago, 343
Mammals, earliest, 211–13
Mammoth Cave, 288
Mammoths, 263
Manatee grass, 636
Manganese, 400
Mangrove periwinkles, 647
Mangroves/mangrove swamps, 425–26, 433, 599–602, 617, 644–51
Mangrove snapper, 645
Mantis shrimps, 442–43, 612
Mantle, earth's, 189, 254, 367
Mariana Islands, 255, 257
Mariana Trench, 394, 398
Marl, 581–84, 596
Marshall Islands, 259

Marsh samphire, 46–47, 168
Marsh treaders, 122, 168
Mauritius, 280
Maury, Matthew Fontaine, 249–50, 390
Mayflies, 34, 168
Mayr, Ernst, 282
Meadow voles, 46
Mediterranean Sea, 234–35, 261, 269, 273, 310, 327, 329–31, 376, 380–83, 388–89, 472, 589
Medusa jellyfish, 71, 168, 244, 453
Meganyctiphanes, 228
Melville, Herman, 214
Membranipora, 505–6, 509–10
Menhaden, 74, 106, 168, 216, 442, 688
Mergansers, 21, 168
Mesozoic era, 208–9, 247, 576, 645
Meteor (research vessel), 257–58, 370
Meteorites, 264, 266
Mice, 123
Microporella, 509–10
Midges, 123
Midway Island, 284
Millot, J., 397
Millott, Norman, 628
Milton, John, 225, 230
Mindanao Trench, 254–55
Minnow, 9, 22, 56, 119, 546, 557
Miocene epoch, 581–82
Mississippi River, 253, 286, 353
Mnemiopsis, 72, 78, 168, 523
Moas, 280
Mockingbirds, 12, 27
Mohorovicic discontinuity, 189, 400
Mojave Desert, 374
Mole crabs, 438, 545–46, 563–66, 568, 620
Moles, 123
Molgula, 480–81
Mollusks, 278–79, 444, 469, 477, 478, 480, 539, 542, 573, 585, 607, 630, 636, 662, 671–75, 686, 691. *See also* Chitons; Clams; Mussels; Nautiluses; Octopuses; Oysters; Scallops; Shipworms; Snails; Squids
Monhegan Island, 460
Monkeys, 278
Monsoons, 317, 369, 372

Moon: birth of, 202–3; effect on tides, 332–33, 336–38, 343
Moon jellyfish. *See* Aurelia
Moon snails, 543, 545, 572–73, 587, 590–91
Moore, Hilary, 469
Mosquitoes, 34, 122, 355
Mosses, 35–36, 54, 82, 97, 120, 135, 150, 211, 262, 355, 422–23; Irish, 97, 448, 458, 473, 478–79, 484, 490, 494, 508–15, 519, 521, 533, 658; reindeer, 28, 459; sphagnum, 122–23
Moths, 276
Mountain ashes, 119
Mountain avens, 35–39, 154
Mount Desert Island, 461
Mourning doves, 9
Mud crabs, 445
Muir Glacier, 364
Mullet, 10, 22, 46–50, 53–59, 695
Murexes, 371; apple, 541
Murphy, Robert Cushman, 281, 314, 326–27
Mussels, 54, 67, 81, 100, 130, 227, 229–30, 342, 369, 378, 431, 435–38, 441, 457, 462, 465, 468, 472–73, 489–90, 495, 523, 525, 615–18, 620, 641, 656, 670, 673; blue, 482, 494, 503–5, 508, 522, 527, 529, 532–33, 586; date, 437, 582; horse, 482, 514–16
Mynas, 282

Nansen, Fridtjof, 382, 399
Nantucket, 334–35, 578
Nautilus (research vessel), 256–57
Nautilus, U.S.S., 399
Nautiluses: chambered, 575–76, 673; paper, 414, 575–76
Neap tides, 333, 447, 449–52
Needlefish, 643–44
Nemertea, 494–95, 527, 662–63
Nereids, 83–84, 144, 168–69, 452, 491, 495, 664
Nereus, U.S.S., 236
Neritas, 614
New Zealand, 280, 384, 388
Niagara Falls, 289
Nickel, 369, 691
Nigrelli, Ross, 635
Noctiluca, 101, 169, 228, 655

INDEX

Nomeus, 580
Nordenskiöld, Adolf, 387
North Atlantic Current, 221–22
Northern passage, 385–87
Northern sea stars, 511–12
North Sea, 251, 262–63, 292, 340, 353, 357–58, 360, 382, 401
Norwegian Sea, 321, 340, 353, 375
Novaya Zemlya, 350, 362, 383, 386, 389
Nudibranchs, 509, 523, 616–17, 625–27, 660, 672
Nummulites, 288, 656

Oaks, 119–21, 125, 231; scrub, 81
Oarweed, 96, 98, 169, 422, 479, 482, 490, 516, 657
Oceans: ancient, 285–94; creation of, 204
Octopods. *See* Octopuses
Octopuses, 134–35, 545, 575, 584, 636, 640, 674
Onchidium, 615–17
Onychophora, 664
Orcas, 107–8, 169, 221
Orchids, 494
Ordovician period, 210–11, 287
Oreaster, 629, 636
Orinoco River, 278
Orioles, Baltimore, 363
Orkney Islands, 306, 340, 353
Oscillation, tidal, 335–37
Ospreys, 49–52
Ostracods, 470, 527, 665
Ottar, 382, 386
Ovenbirds, 363
Owls, 50, 123; snowy, 28, 30–32, 34, 40
Oyashio Current, 324, 349, 352
Oysters, 27, 49, 53–54, 66, 127, 129, 342–43, 367, 370, 425, 451–53, 641, 656, 672–73, 675, 687; coon, 647–48; pearl, 583–84; spiny, 609

Pacific golden plovers, 279, 388
Pacific Ocean, 203, 229, 236, 254–55, 259, 261, 266, 269, 273, 285, 291, 306, 311–12, 314, 318, 324–28, 331, 336–37, 343, 349, 353, 384, 387–88, 395, 398, 400–401, 403, 443, 576, 585, 590, 600, 627, 645, 680–81, 683–84

Paleolithic Age, 263, 288, 291–93
Paleozoic era, 208–11, 289, 375–76, 534–35, 629, 669
Palmer, N. B., 386
Palms, 480; fanleaf, 283
Palolo worms, 343, 611–13
Pamakani, 282
Pampas, 29
Panama Canal, 254, 335, 349
Panama Ridge, 319, 645
Paper nautiluses, 414, 575–76
Parchment worms, 558–60
Parr, A. E., 223–24
Passenger pigeons, 66
Patagonia, 29, 33
Patella, 475
Pea crabs, 552–53, 559–60, 588–89
Pearl fish, 635
Pearl oysters, 583–84
Pearly nautiluses, 575–76
Peary, Robert, 256
Pectoral sandpipers, 363
Pelicans, 325, 649
Penguins, 217, 325
Penicillus, 657
Penokean Mountains, 393
Pen shells, 588–89
Periwinkles, 426, 434, 441, 449, 451, 472, 474, 487, 489, 497, 520, 524, 526, 586, 687; beaded, 614–15; common, 467, 510, 522; mangrove, 647; rough, 464–68, 498; smooth, 466–67, 498
Permian period, 208–9, 373
Persian Gulf, 218, 372, 376
Petitcodiac River, 342
Petrels, 219–21, 391, 665
Petroleum, 374–78
Pettersson, Hans, 266, 400
Pettersson, Otto, 356–58, 361–62, 365
Phacophyceae, 491, 657–58
Phaeocystis, 227
Phalaropes, 36–39, 41, 99, 170, 228
Phoenecians, 371, 379–81, 387, 593
Physalia, 147, 171–72, 573, 578–81
Piccard, Auguste, 394
Piccard, Jacques, 394
Pickerel, 150
Pickerelweed, 119
Piddocks, 582, 595

Pigeons, passenger, 66
Piggot, C. S., 265, 270
Pines, 42, 120, 365; loblolly, 49–52
Pink conchs, 636–37
Pinnixa, 552–53
Pipefish, 636, 639–40
Pipits, 363
Plankton, 65, 67, 69–80, 83, 92–94, 97, 99–102, 109, 112, 146–47, 171, 216–17, 219, 221, 226–29, 237, 239–40, 242, 327–29, 399, 453–54, 462–63, 479, 495–96, 510, 518, 529, 565, 567–68, 574, 577, 583, 591, 593, 595, 602, 610, 619, 627, 656, 663, 666, 688, 692
Plato, 261
Platyhelminthes, 660–62
Pleistocene epoch, 208–9, 252, 262–63, 291–92, 294, 365, 541, 600, 602
Pleurobrachia, 76–79, 171, 523
Pliny the Elder, 626
Plovers, 20–21, 34–36, 130; American golden, 42–43; black-bellied, 22, 363; killdeer, 171; Pacific golden, 279, 388; semipalmated, 27, 171
Plumed worms, 543, 560
Plumose sea anemones, 518, 558
Poe, Edgar Allan, 340–41
Pollock, 80, 82–84, 91, 106
Polychaeta, 663
Polynesians, 215, 384, 387–88
Polysiphonia, 494
Pompano, 47, 58
Ponce de León, Juan, 318
Ponderous arks, 587–88
Porifera. *See* Sponges
Porphyra, 477
Porpoises, 74, 91–92, 105, 221, 245, 396; white, 247
Portuguese men-of-war, 147, 171–72, 221, 243, 573, 578–81
Posidonius, 382
Potamilla, 526–27
Potassium, 369, 373–74
Potomac River, 679, 682–83
Powys, Llewelyn, 264, 316
Prawns. *See* Shrimps
Precambian period, 429–30
Proterozoic era, 210–11, 393, 429
Protophyta, 204–5, 655–57

Protozoa, 100–101, 204–5, 216, 228, 288, 421, 510, 635, 655–58
Ptarmigans, willow, 28–32, 172–73
Pterophryne, 223
Pteropods, 71, 106–8, 143, 173, 225, 244, 269, 689
Purple-clawed crabs, 650
Purple laver, 477–78
Purple snails, 576–77
Pytheas of Massilia, 360, 381–82

Qiantang River, 342
Quartz sands, 288, 538–40
Quaternary period, 208–9
Queen conchs, 636–39

Raccoons, 124–25, 425, 648
Radioactivity, in oceans, 191–93
Radiolaria, 145, 173, 225, 268–69, 655, 691
Rails, 281; Laysan, 283–84
Raitt, R. W., 236
Ralfsia, 526–27
Ramapo, U.S.S., 305
Ramshorn shells, 574–76, 674
Rann of Cutch, 372
Rats, 281–82, 284; water, 11–12, 120, 150
Ravens, 33, 38, 388
Razor clams, 546, 561, 673
Red-beard sponges, 533–34
Reddish egrets, 425
Redfish, 140
Redi, Francesco, 626
Red knots, 27, 34–35, 37, 41, 166
Red-nose clams, 482
Red Sea, 218, 376, 380
"Red tide," 214, 217–18, 454, 655
Reindeer moss, 28, 459
Reptiles, earliest, 211–12
Rhine River, 292
Rhodophyceae, 658
Ribbon worms, 494–95, 527, 662–63
Ring-billed gulls, 566
Rips, tidal, 339–40
Rivers, 13–14, 16–17, 45, 50, 119, 126–28, 131, 133, 149–50
Robins, American, 125
Rock barnacles, 468–74, 592, 667
Rock-boring sea urchins, 621–22, 629
Rock corals, 621–22
Rock crabs, 514

Rock eels, 515–16
Rockweeds. *See* Seaweeds; Wracks
Rocky Mountains, 160, 261
Rocky shores, 415–16, 431–32, 434, 436, 457–535, 653–54
Roger II of Sicily, 383
Rollefson, Gunnar, 239
Rollers, 313–14, 324
Romanche Trench, 258
Rose corals, 622
Rose tellins, 425
Ross, James Clark, 249
Ross, John, 234
Rotation of earth, 338–39
Rough periwinkles, 464–68, 498
Round herring, 442
Round-mouthed fish, 174
Roundworms, 533
Rubythroats, Siberian, 363
Rudder fish, 327
Ruddy turnstones, 27, 34–35, 37, 86–87, 180–81

Sabellaria, 664
Sadko (research vessel), 256, 362
St. Helena, 279, 283, 291, 313–14, 444
St. Lawrence River, 247, 285–86
St. Paul's Rocks, 259, 262, 276, 321
Salamanders, 277
Salinity, oceanic, 204, 218, 222, 329, 352, 367
Salmon, 126, 627, 680–81, 683; chinook, 227
Salps, 72, 174, 327–28
Salt domes, 377
Salt marshes, 7–13, 16–17, 21, 23–25, 45–48, 128–31, 142
Salts, 367–74, 377–78
Sambhar Lake, 369
Samoa, 291, 343
Sand, 431, 537–42
Sandalwood, 283
Sand anemones, 558
Sand beaches, 415–16, 431–34, 436, 537–97, 653–54
Sand bugs, 18–19, 33, 45, 174
Sand collar snails. *See* Moon snails
Sand dollars, 139, 174–75, 543, 546, 549–50, 572, 627, 641–42, 669
Sand eels. *See* Launce

Sanderlings, 18–42, 45, 175, 424, 426, 694–96
Sand fleas, 9–10, 21–23, 33, 59, 86, 153, 175, 438, 446, 469, 570–73, 666
Sandhoppers. *See* Sand fleas
Sandpipers, 130; Baird's, 34; dowitchers, 22, 160; dunlins, 34; least, 27; pectoral, 363; sanderlings, 18–42, 45, 175, 424, 426, 694–96; stilt, 34; white-rumped, 27
Sandstone, 287, 460–61
Sandworms, 90
Sangamon interglacial stage, 602–3
Sardine, 241, 327–28
Sargasso Sea, 218, 221–24, 321, 639, 698–99
Sargassum weed, 88, 144, 146–47, 221–24, 243, 581, 639, 657
Saxifrage, 28, 36
Scale worms, 481, 514, 664
Scallops, 8–9, 175–76, 586, 673
Scaphanders, 444
Scaphopods, 672, 674–75
Schaeffer, Bobb, 397
Schmidt, Johannes, 574
Schuchert, Charles, 289
Scoters, velvet, 363
Screw snails, 566
Scripps Institution of Oceanography, 236, 246, 402
Scuds, 446
Sculpin, 95, 97, 165, 176
Scup, 74, 139–40, 176
Scyphozoa. *See* Jellyfish
Sea anemones, 54–55, 66, 176, 443, 458, 472, 516–18, 523, 528, 530–31, 547, 595, 604, 606, 660–61, 687; flower, 620, 622; jewel, 622; plumose, 518, 558; Zoanthus, 620–21
Sea bass, 23, 58, 90, 131, 140, 150
"Sea beef," 674
Sea bottles, 618
Sea caves, 309–10, 529–35
Sea clams, 97
Sea colanders, 484
Sea cucumbers, 98, 176, 369, 481, 515, 605, 626–27, 632–35, 668–69, 671
Sea elephants, 212
Sea fans, 605–6, 609, 632, 660–61
Sea fingers, 517, 520
Sea gooseberries, 76–79, 171, 524

Sea grapes, 483
Sea hares, 625–27, 640, 642, 672
Sea hay, 9
Seahorses, 636, 639–40
Sea laces, 506, 509–10, 654, 668
Sea lettuce, 9, 21, 176, 453, 477, 508, 571, 657
Sea level, 320
Sea lilies, 669
Sea lions, 212, 275, 280, 325
Seals, 193, 212–13, 217, 219, 238–39, 359, 362, 385, 391, 646; fur, 229, 241, 386
Sea mice, 543–44
Sea mounts, 257, 260, 266
Sea nettles, 577
Sea oats, 7, 21, 23, 46, 58, 133, 567
Sea of Okhotsk, 324, 335
Sea pansies, 547–49
Sea pens, 548
Sea pork, 469, 583
Sea potatoes, 477–78
Sea ravens, 97, 176–77
Searles Lake, 374
Sea roaches, 613, 615, 666
Sea robins, 97, 177
Sea salts, 367–74, 377–78
Sea scorpions, 247
Sea slugs, 223, 509, 523, 615–17, 625–27, 660, 672, 687
Seasons, oceanic, 225–32
Sea spiders, 144, 533, 664
Sea squirts, 54, 177, 423, 436, 469, 479, 481–84, 583, 675–76
Sea stars, 54, 66, 135–36, 423, 444, 463, 479–80, 489–90, 510, 513–14, 522–23, 530, 543, 545, 585, 606, 668–70; Asteria, 584; Astropecten, 552; basket, 98, 100, 155, 630–32; blood-red, 443, 511–12; giant, 629, 636, 638; Linkia, 629–30; Luidea, 552; northern, 511–12
Sea tangles, 479, 485
Sea trout, 58, 78, 131–34, 136–40, 150
Sea urchins, 205, 234, 343, 438, 453, 458, 479–80, 494, 509–10, 514, 525, 585, 606, 627, 641, 668–71, 686–89; cake, 433; green, 436, 443, 516, 522; heart, 543, 546, 550; keyhole, 139, 174–75, 543, 549–50; long-spined, 609, 623, 628; rock-boring, 621–22, 629; slate-pencil, 628–29

Sea vases, 483
Sea walnuts, 72, 78, 168, 523
Seaweeds, 50, 53, 78, 81–83, 85–86, 96, 100, 132–37, 139, 153, 169, 205, 207, 250–51, 370–71, 378, 431, 434–35, 438, 441, 443–45, 449–50, 453–54, 457–58, 465, 467–69, 473, 477–99, 505–8, 512–13, 516, 520–27, 532–34, 543, 560, 573, 590, 618, 626, 630, 635, 657–58, 662, 664–66, 668, 671
Sea whips, 605–6, 609, 632, 660–61
Sea wracks, 434, 487–94
Sedges, 37–38
Sediments, oceanic, 264–70, 400
Sedov (research vessel), 256
Semipalmated plovers, 27, 171
Semper, Carl, 617
Serpent stars, 544, 631, 669–70
Serpulids, 664
Shad, 13–17, 45–46, 74, 132, 150, 227, 679–85
Shakespeare, William, 367
Shale, 289, 460
Sharks, 23, 74, 127, 138, 145, 216, 221, 243, 266, 269, 400, 691; basking, 364; blue, 104; dogfish, 102, 105–6, 115–16, 688; frilled, 248; great white, 688; hammerhead, 220; six-gilled, 364
Shearwaters, 36, 103–4, 110, 219, 221; greater, 177–78
Sheepshead, 58, 178
Shelley, Percy Bysshe, 271
Shepard, Francis S., 253, 398
Shetland Islands, 302–3, 306–7, 353, 381–82
Shiner, 119
Shining cuckoos, 388
Shipworms, 593–95
Shoal grass, 636
Shoals, 555–62
Shrimps, 8, 12–13, 46, 58, 64, 66–71, 81, 84, 98, 106, 109, 127, 132, 136, 143–44, 146–47, 178, 215, 217, 222, 226, 230, 237–38, 240, 242, 244–45, 247, 468, 490, 517, 542, 640, 664–65, 667, 687, 690; big-eyed, 67, 92–94; euphausiid, 216, 239; ghost, 543, 551–53, 559; mantis, 442–44, 612; Meganyctiphanes, 228; skeleton, 520; snapping, 246, 624–25

INDEX

Siberian rubythroats, 363
Silicon, 367
Silurian period, 207–10, 247, 287, 289, 373
Silver, 370
Silver eels, 119–29, 139, 142–51, 154, 178, 694, 698–99
Silverside, 20, 46–47, 54, 80, 178
Six-gilled sharks, 364
Skates, 97, 572, 590, 661
Skeleton shrimps, 520
Skimmers, black, 7–10, 17, 20, 25, 27, 50, 174, 424
Skuas, 99, 178–79, 221
Skylarks, 282, 363
Slate-pencil sea urchins, 628–29
Slaters, 614, 666
Slipper shells, 672
Smith, J. L. B., 397
Smooth periwinkles, 466–67, 498
Snails, 10, 87, 127, 219, 277, 430–31, 446, 448, 457–58, 462, 471, 487, 494, 496, 506, 533, 558, 581–82, 595, 605–6, 643, 651, 672, 687; boat shells, 586–87, 672; coffee-bean shells, 649–50; conchs, 50, 636–39, 641–43, 672; flamingo-tongue, 609–10; limpets, 434–35, 437, 474–77; moon, 543, 545, 572–73, 587, 590–91; Murex, 371, 541; Nerita, 614; Onchidium, 616–17; periwinkles, 426, 434, 441, 449, 451, 464–68, 472, 474, 487, 489, 497–98, 510, 520, 522, 524, 526, 586, 614–15, 647; pteropods, 71, 106–8, 143, 173, 225, 244, 269, 689; purple, 576–77; screw, 566; sea hares, 625–27, 638, 643, 672; vermetid, 618–21; whelks, 463, 472–74, 522, 543, 557, 560–62, 587; winged, 71, 106–8, 143, 173, 226, 243, 689
Snake mackerel, 215–16
Snakes, 277, 279
Snapper: gray, 610, 643; mangrove, 645
Snapping shrimps, 246, 624–25
Snellius, Gotfren, 594
Snow buntings, 28, 31, 36, 179
Snow geese, 21
Snowy egrets, 22–23, 161
Snowy owls, 28, 30–32, 34, 40

Sodium, 369, 374
Soft corals, 517, 520
Soldier flies, 123, 179
Solomon Islands, 388
Sooty terns, 220
South Trinidad Island, 274, 281, 283, 313
Spadefish, 134, 136–37, 179
Sparrows, 50
Spatterdock, 120
Sperling, 91
Sperm whales, 238, 240–41, 395–96
Sphaerella, 525, 655
Sphagnum moss, 122–23
Spider crabs, 640, 642
Spiders, 276–79. *See also* Sea spiders
Spiny brittle stars, 631
Spiny lobsters, 623, 643
Spiny oysters, 609
Spiral wrack, 491, 493
Spirorbis, 472, 474, 496–97
Spirula, 574–76
Spitsbergen (Svalbard), 350, 361–62, 364–65, 383, 386, 389, 520
Sponges, 205, 219, 370, 423, 429–30, 458, 480, 482, 523, 535, 573, 582, 584, 609, 611, 618, 622, 630, 642–43, 647, 658–59, 686; basket, 431; crumb-of-bread, 436, 515–16, 529–30, 534; glass, 242; loggerhead, 605, 622–25, 628; red-beard, 533–34; sulphur, 530–31, 606; tree, 583; tube, 652
Spot, 131, 150, 179
Spring peepers, 120
Spring tides, 333, 447, 450–52
Spruces, 365, 459, 462–63, 653
Squids, 25, 84–86, 91, 99, 102–4, 147, 179–80, 215–17, 228, 237–38, 244, 247, 327, 329, 574, 672–74, 690; giant, 240, 674
Squirrels, 459
Star corals, 532, 609
Starfish. *See* Sea stars
Starlet corals, 609
Starlings, 50, 125
Stevenson, Thomas, 303, 306–7
Stilt sandpipers, 34
Stingrays, 95, 97–98, 180, 544, 643
Stone Age, 263, 288, 292–93
Stone crabs, 561

Stoneworts, 122
Stony corals, 517, 520
Storm-petrels, 26, 74, 103, 170, 220, 316
Storm tides, 312–13, 401–2
Strait of Messina, 332
Submarine canyons, 252–53, 257, 294, 397–98
Submarine currents, 326–31
Submarine trenches, 254–56, 260, 310, 394, 398
Submarine volcanoes, 271–79, 290, 368, 691
Submarine waves, 314–15, 356–58, 361
Sulphur, 368
Sulphur sponges, 530–31, 606
Sun, effect on tides, 332–33, 336–37
Sunda Sea, 285
Sunda Strait, 274–75
Sunfish, 364
Sunray clams, 54, 557
Surf clams, 587
Susquehanna River, 681–82
Swallows, cliff, 363
Swans, tundra, 21, 149
Sweet gums, 46
Swells, 313–14, 324
Swinburne, Algernon Charles, 1, 285, 297
Swordfish, 92–93, 364
Sycamores, 125

Tahiti, 282, 335, 337, 384, 388
Teal: blue-winged, 21, 180; Laysan, 283
Tellins, 673; rose, 425
Temperatures, oceanic, 218–19, 403, 437
Terebra, 566
Terns, 19–20, 22–23, 46, 48, 50, 81, 87–88, 91, 102–3, 281, 521; arctic, 34–35, 180; crested, 220; sooty, 223
Terrapins, diamondback, 10–12
Terror, H.M.S., 249, 386
Tertiary period, 208–9, 280, 400
Thallophyta, 657–58
Thrushes, 363
"Thule," 381–82
Tide lines, 415, 421–22, 430, 445–50
Tides, 332–45, 421–24, 432, 445–52

Tierra del Fuego, 305–6, 385
Timor, 256
Titmice, 282
Toadfish, 558
Tonga, 645
Tooth shells, 672, 674–75
Torghattan Island, 291–92
Tortoises. *See* Turtles
Trade winds, 215, 317–18, 353
Transverse arks, 587
Tree sponges, 583
Trenches, submarine, 254–56, 260, 310, 394, 398
Triassic period, 208–9, 212
Trieste (bathyscaphe), 394, 398
Triggerfish, 134
Trilobites, 247, 667
Tristan da Cunha, 177, 259, 277, 282
Tropicbirds, 220–21
Trout, 58, 78, 131–34, 136–40, 150
Trumpet worms, 553–55
Tsunamis, 299, 310–12, 400–401
Tuamotu Archipelago, 249, 259
Tube sponges, 652
Tubeweed, 524
Tubeworms, 223, 227, 472, 474, 496–97, 526, 582, 605–6, 615, 618–19, 663–64, 688
Tubularia, 423, 518, 521
Tuke, John, 309
Tulip shells, 590, 636–37
Tuna, 107–8, 193, 216, 402
Tundra, 28–43, 45, 99, 149, 267, 355–56, 450
Tundra swans, 21, 149
Tunicates, 675–76; golden-star, 436, 482–84; salps, 72, 174, 327–28; sea squirts, 54, 177, 423, 436, 469, 480–84, 583, 675–76
Turkey wing arks, 587
Turnstones, ruddy, 27, 34–35, 37, 86–87, 180–81
Turtle grass, 444, 622, 629, 636, 638–39, 641
Turtles, 74, 212, 217, 277, 667; diamondback terrapins, 10–12; giant tortoises, 280; green, 640–41; hawksbill, 640–41, 643; loggerhead, 640–41, 643
Tuscarora Trench, 255
Tusk shells, 672, 674–75

Upwelling, 326–29

Valonia, 618
Vanadium, 369
Vancouver, George, 282
Vega (research vessel), 387
Vellela, 578–79
Velvet scoters, 363
Vermetids, 618–21
Vesconte, Petrus, 389
Vesuvius eruptions, 634
Vikings, 382–84, 388, 391
Vilgerdarson, Floki, 388
Vitiaz (research vessel), 398
Voles, meadow, 46

Waghenaer, Lucas Janssz, 389
Wallace, Alfred Russel, 283
Walruses, 382
Walsh, Don, 394
Warblers: Canada, 363; ovenbirds, 363
Water boatmen, 122, 181
Water fleas, 101, 469, 529
Watson, A. T., 553–54
Weasels, 28–29, 41
Weavers, 282
Wells, H. G., 339
Whales, 33, 37, 67, 106, 111, 127, 145, 193, 212–13, 217, 219–21, 227–28, 233, 235, 239–43, 269, 319, 328, 363, 380, 386, 388, 391, 646, 665, 667, 691; baleen, 241; blue, 688; bottlenose, 238; sperm, 238, 240–41, 395–96
Whelks, 543, 557, 561, 587, 636; channeled, 562, 590; common, 522; dog, 463, 472–74; knobbed, 560, 562, 590
Whimbrels, 21, 23–25, 27, 34, 45, 159
Whirlpools, 332, 340–41, 350
White-browed albatrosses, 363
White crabs, 650
Whitefish, 362
White porpoises, 247
White-rumped sandpipers, 27
White Sea, 364, 382, 386
"White water," 604–5
Whiting, 85–86, 181, 443
Widgeon grass, 17, 47, 181
Wild celery, 21
Wilkins, Hubert, 256, 399
Willets, 424

Willm, Pierre-Henri, 394
Willow ptarmigans, 28–32, 172–73
Willows, 28–32, 35–37, 39, 119–20, 126, 262
Wind: effect on currents, 317–18, 320, 328; effect on waves, 297–310, 312–13, 332
Winged kelp, 484–86
Winged snails, 71, 106–8, 143, 173, 226, 243, 689
Wisconsin glacial stage, 602
Wolves, 33, 108, 360
Wood-boring insects, 278
Woods Hole Oceanographic Institution, 239, 255, 258, 265, 396, 403, 693
"Worm rock," 584–85, 619
Worms, 66–68, 95, 98, 100, 127, 136, 139, 147, 205, 219, 234, 430, 444, 446, 463, 479, 499, 506, 510, 514, 529, 542, 545–46, 607, 625, 630, 639, 651, 668; amphitrite, 432, 481, 664; arrow-, 216, 244; blood-, 663–64; bristle, 490, 495, 527, 505, 663–64; clam-, 83–84, 144, 495, 664; Convoluta, 345; Dodecaceria, 584–85; earth-, 279, 553, 633; flat-, 660–62, 672; glass-, 69–71, 163, 226, 230, 239, 244, 688; lug-, 543, 546, 553–54; nereid, 83–84, 144, 168–69, 452, 490, 495, 664; palolo, 343, 611–13; parchment, 558–60; plumed, 543, 560; Potamilla, 526–27; ribbon, 494–95, 527, 662–63; round-, 533; Sabellaria, 664; sand-, 90; scale, 481, 515, 664; serpulid, 664; Spirorbis, 472, 474, 496–97; trumpet, 553–55; tube-, 223, 227, 472, 474, 496–97, 526, 582, 605–6, 615, 618–19, 663–64, 688
Wracks, 488–90, 498; bladder, 491–92, 499; channeled, 491; forked, 434; knobbed, 434, 487, 491–94, 499; spiral, 491, 493
Wrens, Carolina, 50

Yaupons, 7
Yellowlegs, 27, 181, 363
Yucatán, 7, 319, 438

Zoanthus, 620, 622

*This book is set in 10 point ITC Galliard Pro, a face
designed for digital composition by Matthew Carter and based
on the sixteenth-century face Granjon. The paper is acid-free
lightweight opaque that will not turn yellow or brittle with age.
The binding is sewn, which allows the book to open easily and lie flat.
The binding board is covered in Brillianta, a woven rayon cloth
made by Van Heek–Scholco Textielfabrieken, Holland.
Composition by Publishers' Design and Production Services, Inc.
Printing and binding by LSC Communications, Crawfordsville, IN.
Designed by Bruce Campbell.*

THE LIBRARY OF AMERICA SERIES

Library of America fosters appreciation of America's literary heritage by publishing, and keeping permanently in print, authoritative editions of America's best and most significant writing. An independent nonprofit organization, it was founded in 1979 with seed funding from the National Endowment for the Humanities and the Ford Foundation.

1. Herman Melville: Typee, Omoo, Mardi
2. Nathaniel Hawthorne: Tales & Sketches
3. Walt Whitman: Poetry & Prose
4. Harriet Beecher Stowe: Three Novels
5. Mark Twain: Mississippi Writings
6. Jack London: Novels & Stories
7. Jack London: Novels & Social Writings
8. William Dean Howells: Novels 1875–1886
9. Herman Melville: Redburn, White-Jacket, Moby-Dick
10. Nathaniel Hawthorne: Collected Novels
11 & 12. Francis Parkman: France and England in North America
13. Henry James: Novels 1871–1880
14. Henry Adams: Novels, Mont Saint Michel, The Education
15. Ralph Waldo Emerson: Essays & Lectures
16. Washington Irving: History, Tales & Sketches
17. Thomas Jefferson: Writings
18. Stephen Crane: Prose & Poetry
19. Edgar Allan Poe: Poetry & Tales
20. Edgar Allan Poe: Essays & Reviews
21. Mark Twain: The Innocents Abroad, Roughing It
22 & 23. Henry James: Literary Criticism
24. Herman Melville: Pierre, Israel Potter, The Confidence-Man, Tales & Billy Budd
25. William Faulkner: Novels 1930–1935
26 & 27. James Fenimore Cooper: The Leatherstocking Tales
28. Henry David Thoreau: A Week, Walden, The Maine Woods, Cape Cod
29. Henry James: Novels 1881–1886
30. Edith Wharton: Novels
31 & 32. Henry Adams: History of the U.S. during the Administrations of Jefferson & Madison
33. Frank Norris: Novels & Essays
34. W.E.B. Du Bois: Writings
35. Willa Cather: Early Novels & Stories
36. Theodore Dreiser: Sister Carrie, Jennie Gerhardt, Twelve Men
37. Benjamin Franklin: Writings (2 vols.)
38. William James: Writings 1902–1910
39. Flannery O'Connor: Collected Works
40, 41, & 42. Eugene O'Neill: Complete Plays
43. Henry James: Novels 1886–1890
44. William Dean Howells: Novels 1886–1888
45 & 46. Abraham Lincoln: Speeches & Writings
47. Edith Wharton: Novellas & Other Writings
48. William Faulkner: Novels 1936–1940
49. Willa Cather: Later Novels
50. Ulysses S. Grant: Memoirs & Selected Letters
51. William Tecumseh Sherman: Memoirs
52. Washington Irving: Bracebridge Hall, Tales of a Traveller, The Alhambra
53. Francis Parkman: The Oregon Trail, The Conspiracy of Pontiac
54. James Fenimore Cooper: Sea Tales
55 & 56. Richard Wright: Works
57. Willa Cather: Stories, Poems, & Other Writings
58. William James: Writings 1878–1899
59. Sinclair Lewis: Main Street & Babbitt
60 & 61. Mark Twain: Collected Tales, Sketches, Speeches, & Essays
62 & 63. The Debate on the Constitution
64 & 65. Henry James: Collected Travel Writings
66 & 67. American Poetry: The Nineteenth Century
68. Frederick Douglass: Autobiographies
69. Sarah Orne Jewett: Novels & Stories
70. Ralph Waldo Emerson: Collected Poems & Translations
71. Mark Twain: Historical Romances
72. John Steinbeck: Novels & Stories 1932–1937
73. William Faulkner: Novels 1942–1954
74 & 75. Zora Neale Hurston: Novels, Stories, & Other Writings
76. Thomas Paine: Collected Writings
77 & 78. Reporting World War II: American Journalism
79 & 80. Raymond Chandler: Novels, Stories, & Other Writings

81. Robert Frost: Collected Poems, Prose, & Plays
82 & 83. Henry James: Complete Stories 1892–1910
84. William Bartram: Travels & Other Writings
85. John Dos Passos: U.S.A.
86. John Steinbeck: The Grapes of Wrath & Other Writings 1936–1941
87, 88, & 89. Vladimir Nabokov: Novels & Other Writings
90. James Thurber: Writings & Drawings
91. George Washington: Writings
92. John Muir: Nature Writings
93. Nathanael West: Novels & Other Writings
94 & 95. Crime Novels: American Noir of the 1930s, 40s, & 50s
96. Wallace Stevens: Collected Poetry & Prose
97. James Baldwin: Early Novels & Stories
98. James Baldwin: Collected Essays
99 & 100. Gertrude Stein: Writings
101 & 102. Eudora Welty: Novels, Stories, & Other Writings
103. Charles Brockden Brown: Three Gothic Novels
104 & 105. Reporting Vietnam: American Journalism
106 & 107. Henry James: Complete Stories 1874–1891
108. American Sermons
109. James Madison: Writings
110. Dashiell Hammett: Complete Novels
111. Henry James: Complete Stories 1864–1874
112. William Faulkner: Novels 1957–1962
113. John James Audubon: Writings & Drawings
114. Slave Narratives
115 & 116. American Poetry: The Twentieth Century
117. F. Scott Fitzgerald: Novels & Stories 1920–1922
118. Henry Wadsworth Longfellow: Poems & Other Writings
119 & 120. Tennessee Williams: Collected Plays
121 & 122. Edith Wharton: Collected Stories
123. The American Revolution: Writings from the War of Independence
124. Henry David Thoreau: Collected Essays & Poems
125. Dashiell Hammett: Crime Stories & Other Writings
126 & 127. Dawn Powell: Novels
128. Carson McCullers: Complete Novels
129. Alexander Hamilton: Writings
130. Mark Twain: The Gilded Age & Later Novels
131. Charles W. Chesnutt: Stories, Novels, & Essays
132. John Steinbeck: Novels 1942–1952
133. Sinclair Lewis: Arrowsmith, Elmer Gantry, Dodsworth
134 & 135. Paul Bowles: Novels, Stories, & Other Writings
136. Kate Chopin: Complete Novels & Stories
137 & 138. Reporting Civil Rights: American Journalism
139. Henry James: Novels 1896–1899
140. Theodore Dreiser: An American Tragedy
141. Saul Bellow: Novels 1944–1953
142. John Dos Passos: Novels 1920–1925
143. John Dos Passos: Travel Books & Other Writings
144. Ezra Pound: Poems & Translations
145. James Weldon Johnson: Writings
146. Washington Irving: Three Western Narratives
147. Alexis de Tocqueville: Democracy in America
148. James T. Farrell: Studs Lonigan Trilogy
149, 150, & 151. Isaac Bashevis Singer: Collected Stories
152. Kaufman & Co.: Broadway Comedies
153. Theodore Roosevelt: Rough Riders, An Autobiography
154. Theodore Roosevelt: Letters & Speeches
155. H. P. Lovecraft: Tales
156. Louisa May Alcott: Little Women, Little Men, Jo's Boys
157. Philip Roth: Novels & Stories 1959–1962
158. Philip Roth: Novels 1967–1972
159. James Agee: Let Us Now Praise Famous Men, A Death in the Family, Shorter Fiction
160. James Agee: Film Writing & Selected Journalism
161. Richard Henry Dana Jr.: Two Years Before the Mast & Other Voyages
162. Henry James: Novels 1901–1902
163. Arthur Miller: Plays 1944–1961
164. William Faulkner: Novels 1926–1929
165. Philip Roth: Novels 1973–1977
166 & 167. American Speeches: Political Oratory
168. Hart Crane: Complete Poems & Selected Letters

169. Saul Bellow: Novels 1956–1964
170. John Steinbeck: Travels with Charley & Later Novels
171. Capt. John Smith: Writings with Other Narratives
172. Thornton Wilder: Collected Plays & Writings on Theater
173. Philip K. Dick: Four Novels of the 1960s
174. Jack Kerouac: Road Novels 1957–1960
175. Philip Roth: Zuckerman Bound
176 & 177. Edmund Wilson: Literary Essays & Reviews
178. American Poetry: The 17th & 18th Centuries
179. William Maxwell: Early Novels & Stories
180. Elizabeth Bishop: Poems, Prose, & Letters
181. A. J. Liebling: World War II Writings
182. American Earth: Environmental Writing Since Thoreau
183. Philip K. Dick: Five Novels of the 1960s & 70s
184. William Maxwell: Later Novels & Stories
185. Philip Roth: Novels & Other Narratives 1986–1991
186. Katherine Anne Porter: Collected Stories & Other Writings
187. John Ashbery: Collected Poems 1956–1987
188 & 189. John Cheever: Complete Novels & Collected Stories
190. Lafcadio Hearn: American Writings
191. A. J. Liebling: The Sweet Science & Other Writings
192. The Lincoln Anthology
193. Philip K. Dick: VALIS & Later Novels
194. Thornton Wilder: The Bridge of San Luis Rey & Other Novels 1926–1948
195. Raymond Carver: Collected Stories
196 & 197. American Fantastic Tales
198. John Marshall: Writings
199. The Mark Twain Anthology
200. Mark Twain: A Tramp Abroad, Following the Equator, Other Travels
201 & 202. Ralph Waldo Emerson: Selected Journals
203. The American Stage: Writing on Theater
204. Shirley Jackson: Novels & Stories
205. Philip Roth: Novels 1993–1995
206 & 207. H. L. Mencken: Prejudices
208. John Kenneth Galbraith: The Affluent Society & Other Writings 1952–1967
209. Saul Bellow: Novels 1970–1982
210 & 211. Lynd Ward: Six Novels in Woodcuts
212. The Civil War: The First Year
213 & 214. John Adams: Revolutionary Writings
215. Henry James: Novels 1903–1911
216. Kurt Vonnegut: Novels & Stories 1963–1973
217 & 218. Harlem Renaissance Novels
219. Ambrose Bierce: The Devil's Dictionary, Tales, & Memoirs
220. Philip Roth: The American Trilogy 1997–2000
221. The Civil War: The Second Year
222. Barbara W. Tuchman: The Guns of August, The Proud Tower
223. Arthur Miller: Plays 1964–1982
224. Thornton Wilder: The Eighth Day, Theophilus North, Autobiographical Writings
225. David Goodis: Five Noir Novels of the 1940s & 50s
226. Kurt Vonnegut: Novels & Stories 1950–1962
227 & 228. American Science Fiction: Nine Novels of the 1950s
229 & 230. Laura Ingalls Wilder: The Little House Books
231. Jack Kerouac: Collected Poems
232. The War of 1812
233. American Antislavery Writings
234. The Civil War: The Third Year
235. Sherwood Anderson: Collected Stories
236. Philip Roth: Novels 2001–2007
237. Philip Roth: Nemeses
238. Aldo Leopold: A Sand County Almanac & Other Writings
239. May Swenson: Collected Poems
240 & 241. W. S. Merwin: Collected Poems
242 & 243. John Updike: Collected Stories
244. Ring Lardner: Stories & Other Writings
245. Jonathan Edwards: Writings from the Great Awakening
246. Susan Sontag: Essays of the 1960s & 70s
247. William Wells Brown: Clotel & Other Writings
248 & 249. Bernard Malamud: Novels & Stories of the 1940s, 50s, & 60s
250. The Civil War: The Final Year
251. Shakespeare in America

252. Kurt Vonnegut: Novels 1976–1985
253 & 254. American Musicals 1927–1969
255. Elmore Leonard: Four Novels of the 1970s
256. Louisa May Alcott: Work, Eight Cousins, Rose in Bloom, Stories & Other Writings
257. H. L. Mencken: The Days Trilogy
258. Virgil Thomson: Music Chronicles 1940–1954
259. Art in America 1945–1970
260. Saul Bellow: Novels 1984–2000
261. Arthur Miller: Plays 1987–2004
262. Jack Kerouac: Visions of Cody, Visions of Gerard, Big Sur
263. Reinhold Niebuhr: Major Works on Religion & Politics
264. Ross Macdonald: Four Novels of the 1950s
265 & 266. The American Revolution: Writings from the Pamphlet Debate
267. Elmore Leonard: Four Novels of the 1980s
268 & 269. Women Crime Writers: Suspense Novels of the 1940s & 50s
270. Frederick Law Olmsted: Writings on Landscape, Culture, & Society
271. Edith Wharton: Four Novels of the 1920s
272. James Baldwin: Later Novels
273. Kurt Vonnegut: Novels 1987–1997
274. Henry James: Autobiographies
275. Abigail Adams: Letters
276. John Adams: Writings from the New Nation 1784–1826
277. Virgil Thomson: The State of Music & Other Writings
278. War No More: American Antiwar & Peace Writing
279. Ross Macdonald: Three Novels of the Early 1960s
280. Elmore Leonard: Four Later Novels
281. Ursula K. Le Guin: The Complete Orsinia
282. John O'Hara: Stories
283. The Unknown Kerouac: Rare, Unpublished & Newly Translated Writings
284. Albert Murray: Collected Essays & Memoirs
285 & 286. Loren Eiseley: Collected Essays on Evolution, Nature, & the Cosmos
287. Carson McCullers: Stories, Plays & Other Writings
288. Jane Bowles: Collected Writings
289. World War I and America: Told by the Americans Who Lived It
290 & 291. Mary McCarthy: The Complete Fiction
292. Susan Sontag: Later Essays
293 & 294. John Quincy Adams: Diaries
295. Ross Macdonald: Four Later Novels
296 & 297. Ursula K. Le Guin: The Hainish Novels & Stories
298 & 299. Peter Taylor: The Complete Stories
300. Philip Roth: Why Write? Collected Nonfiction 1960–2014
301. John Ashbery: Collected Poems 1991–2000
302. Wendell Berry: Port William Novels & Stories: The Civil War to World War II
303. Reconstruction: Voices from America's First Great Struggle for Racial Equality
304. Albert Murray: Collected Novels & Poems
305 & 306. Norman Mailer: The Sixties
307. Rachel Carson: Silent Spring & Other Writings on the Environment
308. Elmore Leonard: Westerns
309 & 310. Madeleine L'Engle: The Kairos Novels
311. John Updike: Novels 1959–1965
312. James Fenimore Cooper: Two Novels of the American Revolution
313. John O'Hara: Four Novels of the 1930s
314. Ann Petry: The Street, The Narrows
315. Ursula K. Le Guin: Always Coming Home
316 & 317. Wendell Berry: Collected Essays
318. Cornelius Ryan: The Longest Day, A Bridge Too Far
319. Booth Tarkington: Novels & Stories
320. Herman Melville: Complete Poems
321 & 322. American Science Fiction: Eight Classic Novels of the 1960s
323. Frances Hodgson Burnett: The Secret Garden, A Little Princess, Little Lord Fauntleroy
324. Jean Stafford: Complete Novels
325. Joan Didion: The 1960s & 70s
326. John Updike: Novels 1968–1975
327. Constance Fenimore Woolson: Collected Stories
328. Robert Stone: Dog Soldiers, Flag for Sunrise, Outerbridge Reach
329. Jonathan Schell: The Fate of the Earth, The Abolition, The Unconquerable World
330. Richard Hofstadter: Anti-Intellectualism in American Life, The Paranoid Style in American Politics, Uncollected Essays 1956–1965

WITHDRAWN